SETON HALL UNIVERSITY

SETON HALL UNIVERSITY

A HISTORY, 1856-2006

DERMOT QUINN

RUTGERS UNIVERSITY PRESS

New Brunswick, Camden, and Newark, New Jersey
London and Oxford, UK

Rutgers University Press is a department of Rutgers, The State University
of New Jersey, one of the leading public research universities in the nation.
By publishing worldwide, it furthers the University's mission of dedication
to excellence in teaching, scholarship, research, and clinical care.

Library of Congress Cataloging-in-Publication Data
Names: Quinn, Dermot, author.
Title: Seton Hall University : a history, 1856-2006 / Dermot Quinn.
Description: New Brunswick : Rutgers University Press, [2023] |
Includes bibliographical references and index.
Identifiers: LCCN 2022009792 | ISBN 9781978806948 (hardback) |
ISBN 9781978806955 (epub) | ISBN 9781978806979 (pdf)
Subjects: LCSH: Seton Hall University—History. | BISAC: HISTORY /
United States / State & Local / Middle Atlantic (DC, DE, MD, NJ, NY, PA) |
RELIGION / History
Classification: LCC LD4931.S32 Q56 2023 | DDC 378.749/33—dc23/eng/20220525
LC record available at https://lccn.loc.gov/2022009792

A British Cataloging-in-Publication record for this book is available from the British Library.

References to internet websites (URLs) were accurate at the time of writing.
Neither the editors nor Rutgers University Press is responsible for URLs that
may have expired or changed since the manuscript was prepared.

∞ The paper used in this publication meets the requirements of the
American National Standard for Information Sciences—Permanence of Paper
for Printed Library Materials, ANSI Z39.48-1992.

rutgersuniversitypress.org

Manufactured in the United States of America

For Paul, Katharine, Brian, Philip, and Vincent—
among my earliest teachers

Contents

CHAPTER 1

Foundations

The Making of a School

In 1856 James Roosevelt Bayley, Roman Catholic Bishop of Newark, founded a school in Madison, New Jersey, calling it Seton Hall College in honor of his aunt, Elizabeth Ann Bayley Seton. The name was a gesture of piety and a statement of intent. By honoring the greatest promoter of Catholic schools in early nineteenth century America, Bayley wished to continue her work of building American Catholicism through education, charity, and moral instruction. The new school was thus, in various senses, an act of faith. In the first place, it kept faith with a remarkable woman. In the second place, it promoted a particular faith, Roman Catholicism, and a particular people, the Catholics of New Jersey. Seton Hall was to cater for a new flock spiritually and socially, giving it a place in the world and, perhaps, in the world to come. "The school-house has become second in importance to the House of God itself," he wrote shortly before he became bishop in 1853. "We must . . . imbue the minds of the rising generation with sound religious principles."[1] As Catholicism took root in America, it needed such practical theologies of bricks and mortar. Bayley's diocese, only three years old in 1856, was mission territory. His people were poor, unsophisticated, and unlettered, mainly immigrants and laborers with a handful of businessmen and professional people thrown into the mix. Immigrants held to their Catholicism as a living faith or as a diminishing memory of the world they had left behind. Not much higher up the social scale, business people were also condescended to by Protestants. It took imagination and courage to see in this unpromising terrain a future harvest. Bayley had both. Seton Hall was the seed and fruit of his vision. In the thin soil of mid-Victorian New Jersey Catholicism, he built more than a school. He built a people.

Bayley's faith in the progressive value of education, in the pious purposes of Catholic schools, in the powerful generosity of poor people, had to do with the future. In another sense, though, Seton Hall had to do with the past. By naming the college in memory of his aunt, he committed his enterprise in a particular way to the spiritual custodianship of an extraordinary human being. To understand her is to understand him, and to understand both is to understand their school. Bayley was always her spiritual heir, a child of her light. Visiting her religious foundation in Emmitsburg in 1845, he was "most interested in those portions which had been occupied by Aunt Seton." One of the nuns showed him "the room in the wooden house in which she died, her grave in the cemetery . . . [and every interesting spot]." These remnants became for him a silent sermon. "[She has] left an impression upon their hearts never to be effaced . . . The memory of the good is as a sweet odour."[2] Bayley hoped to preserve something of her sanctity in the college he established in Madison in 1856.

A nephew's piety accounts for some of this devotion but another impulse was a sense of unseen presences. Bayley never met John Henry Newman (although he once corresponded with him)[3] but like Newman he believed that human attachments hint at a divine economy, an invisible communion of saints. "I am a link in a chain," Newman wrote, "a bond of connection between persons. [God] has not created me for naught." Bayley was also a link in a chain. Being touched by one human being and touching another, he became part of many stories and those stories became part of his own, so that, piece by piece and year by year, a spiritual family came into being. Seton Hall was to be part of that widening circle. Its name was not an accident.

The Making of a Family

Who were these people? Where did they come from? Why do they matter? If Bayley was unusually conscious of family bonds that was because his own were distinguished. The first significant sighting of a Bayley in America may be traced to 1726, when William Bayley of Hertfordshire sailed from Lynn Regis in Norfolk to New York. Bayley's purpose was to visit America and return home, a common journey in the eighteenth century when not every traveler was an immigrant. But in New Rochelle, he found a bride, Susanne LeConte, and together they had two sons, Richard, born in Fairfield, Connecticut around 1744, and William, born in New Rochelle in 1745.[4] The Bayleys were sufficiently well off to send Richard to New York in 1764 to work with Dr. John Charlton, a Broadway physician, and to fund his further studies in England with Dr. William Hunter. In 1767, Richard Bayley married Charlton's sister Catherine. He then embarked on a medical career that was to see him as surgeon to General Sir Guy Carleton, professor of anatomy and surgery at Columbia College, surgeon at New York Hospital, and health officer of the port of New York. He died of ship-fever in August 1801, "a martyr to his profession."[5]

The marriage of Richard Bayley and Catherine Charlton lasted ten years and produced three daughters—Mary Magdalen in 1768, Elizabeth Ann in 1774, and Catherine in 1776. Wife Catherine died in 1777 and daughter Catherine in 1778. Bayley then remarried, taking as his second wife Charlotte Barclay, daughter of Andrew Barclay and Helena Roosevelt. Seven children came of this union, the youngest child, Guy

Carleton Bayley, born in 1786. He, like his father, eventually became a doctor and married Grace, daughter of James Roosevelt and Maria Walton in 1813. Of this marriage a son was born, James Roosevelt Bayley, the following year. James Roosevelt Bayley—"Rosey" to his family—was thus the nephew of Elizabeth Ann Bayley, second of Dr. Richard Bayley's ten children by his two marriages. He was to be the founder of Seton Hall in 1856.

Meanwhile, in 1794, Elizabeth Ann Bayley, now 20, married William Magee Seton, son of a well-known Scottish American merchant family. Like the Bayleys, the Setons were socially and economically ambitious. William Seton's father, also William, was born in Scotland in 1746, raised in Yorkshire, farmed out to relatives in Spain, and by the age of 17 found himself in New Jersey, then New York, where he acquired an interest in the "Mohawk Lands." He married one Rebecca Curson in 1767, the year Richard Bayley married Catherine Charlton. Rebecca Seton produced five children but died within nine years. William Seton remarried in 1776, looking no farther than his sister-in-law, Anna-Maria, who gave him at least eight more children. William Magee Seton, born in April 1768, was the eldest child of the first marriage.

This second marriage kept intact the family business of Seton and Curson, an import company which flourished in the War of Independence thanks in part to Seton's Toryism.[6] After the war he diversified into banking, becoming cashier of the Bank of New York in 1784, a position through which he secured for his son William the post of clerk of discount. But shipping remained the family's first calling. A new firm of Seton, Maitland and Company was established in 1793, with father and son both closely involved in it. The younger Seton was by then the product of a thoroughly Atlanticized education, having studied in England for six years before being sent to Barcelona, Madrid, Genoa, Leghorn, and Rome to learn the ways of shipping. As with his father and father-in-law, he would rise or fall by the vagaries of commerce.

This, then, was Elizabeth Ann Bayley Seton's world: one in which dynastic and family ties consolidated social ascendancy or staved off social decline. She fitted it perfectly. Elizabeth enjoyed the role Manhattan society allotted to her and for most of its duration the marriage was entirely ordinary. Five children were born of it—Anna Maria (1795), William (1796), Richard (1798), Catherine (1800), and Rebecca (1802). Yet there were worries and sadness. The death of her father-in-law William Seton left the business in a precarious state. Her father Richard Bayley, to whom she was close, died in 1801. Worst of all, her husband's health declined alarmingly and to hasten his recovery they sailed for Italy in October 1803, bringing their eldest child, Anna Maria, with them.

It was a fateful voyage. Quarantined in Leghorn because the journey had begun in fever-ridden New York, they were able to travel to Pisa only through some string-pulling by two brothers, Filippo and Antonio Filicchi, with whom William was in business. The delay seemed to crush William's remaining strength. He died two days after Christmas 1803 and was buried in Leghorn, leaving his widow to raise of five children and manage a business that had seen better days.[7] Like her father, Elizabeth Seton was fated to contract a marriage only to see it end shortly afterwards in death. Unlike her father, she never married again.

The calamity was eased by the friendship of the Filicchi brothers. In the months between William Seton's death and Elizabeth's and Anna Maria's return to America these men were her only support. Elizabeth noted that they were Catholics, followers of a faith despised in her own social circle. A seed was planted.

Elizabeth Ann and Anna Maria Seton left Italy for New York in April 1804, arriving home in June. Recently widowed, of uncertain prospects, soon after returning to America she also lost her sister-in-law Rebecca, who had looked after her remaining children during the Italian sojourn. Her soul was also troubled. More and more she felt attracted to Roman Catholicism. Writing to her friend and former pastor Reverend Henry Hobart, she intimated a breach with Episcopalianism: "The tears fall fast through my fingers at the insupportable thought of being separated from you. And yet . . . you will not be severe. You will respect sincerity, and though you will think me in error, I know that heavenly Christian charity will plead for me in your affections. You have certainly . . . been dearer to me than God, for whom my reason, my judgment, and my conviction used their combined force against the value of your esteem. The combat was in vain, until I considered that yourself would no longer oppose, or desire, so severe a struggle which was destroying my mortal life, and, more than that, my peace with God."[8] On March 14, 1805, she was received into the Roman Catholic Church by Reverend Matthew O'Brien at Saint Peter's Church, Barclay Street, New York. At once the doubts melted away.

Conversion brought social isolation, loss of friendship, an entirely new way of life. New York had few Catholics and none who frequented the drawing rooms where once she moved. The failing business meant a move to a smaller house. She survived by teaching for three years until her pupils dried up, with only a loan from Antonio Filicchi keeping the family going. For a time she thought of going to Canada but instead, thanks again to Filicchi, she came to the attention of Bishop John Carroll and Father William DuBourg, a Sulpician, who persuaded her to move to Baltimore to teach Catholic girls in that city. She did not move until June 1808, her concern not the call to some kind of religious life—that had been clear "from the time I was in Leghorn"—but the education of her own children. "You are destined, I think, for some great good in the United States," one of DuBourg's confreres wrote to her. "A prudent delay only brings to maturity the good desires which [God] awakens in us."[9] When her sons transferred from Georgetown College to St. Mary's College in Baltimore, her daughters remaining with her, she traveled to Maryland.

The school was a success. At first Elizabeth Ann Seton was the only teacher. In time, Cecilia O'Conway, a young Philadelphian, joined her in December 1809. As other women joined, John Carroll, now Archbishop of Baltimore, recognized the band as a religious community, conferring vows on Elizabeth Ann Seton—"Mother Seton"—and enjoining her companions to bring to fulfillment the work that God had begun in them.

The school outgrew its original accommodation and moved in June 1809 to a site in Emmitsburg given by a wealthy convert, Samuel Cooper, which became the motherhouse of the community. Despite financial difficulties, Mother Seton and her companions persevered. Among early members were her sisters-in-law Harriet and Cecelia Seton, converts to the Church. Harriet remained in the lay state; Cecelia became a nun. But a rapid succession of deaths stunned the group. Harriet Seton died in December 1809. Sister Cecelia Seton died in April 1810. Most crushing of all, Anna Maria Seton, eldest daughter of Mother Seton and herself a nun, died in March 1812, not yet eighteen years old.

Elizabeth Ann Seton never recovered from the death of her daughter. Work provided solace but was increasingly burdensome as she attended to the spiritual and practical duties of leading a religious community, the financial and legal obligations of directing an incorporated body, and the day-to-day task of teaching children. The death of her daughter Rebecca in November 1816 was another blow. Yet outwardly her mission prospered, as did the lives of her remaining children: William became a midshipman, Richard joined the Filicchi firm in Leghorn, Catherine came to live with the community at Emmitsburg. "All our affairs at Saint Joseph's go on with the blessing of God," she wrote to Antonio Filicchi in 1817. "Sisters are just now established in New York, as in Philadelphia, for the care of orphans." Less than a decade after arriving in Baltimore, Mother Seton saw her venture spread to New York.

"Theirs was a life freely chosen," writes Judith Metz of these first Sisters of Charity. "Fervor and religious enthusiasm inspired each to . . . sacrifice for a larger vision." Elizabeth Ann Seton was "a charismatic leader" who evinced devotion in her followers—devotion to herself and devotion to Christ. She, in turn, "loved and respected the uniqueness of each of them. She challenged these women to become strong and dedicated Sisters of Charity through her example, her instructions, and the deep personal relationships she developed with many of them."[10]

By the beginning of the 1820s Elizabeth Ann Seton was exhausted, her work almost done: "Even when her rapidly declining weakness gave way to acute suffering, she uttered no word of complaint and assured those about her that she was happy in her pain . . . Admonishing the Sisters to devote themselves to the carrying on of their work, and asking their pardon for the inconveniences her confinement . . . had caused, Mother Seton, courageous yet humble to the end, died with the murmur of a prayer on her lips."[11] The room where she died became a shrine dedicated to recollection of a singular life. The tasks she set herself—founding schools, teaching orphans, and promoting the religious life—were embraced by her surviving sisters. In Canada, Pennsylvania, Missouri, Maryland, New York, Ohio, New Jersey, nuns devoted to the care of the poor built on the legacy of Mother Seton. It was, and continues to be, a remarkable legacy.

The Making of a Bishop

In the generation after Mother Seton's death, few showed more devotion to her memory than James Roosevelt Bayley. His life, like hers, was eventful and impressive, a Victorian tale of loss and gain, in its own way a sermon. There were similarities—both of them were well-born converts excluded from the company of their peers—but also dissimilarities—Bayley's social rejection (although real) was nothing compared to his aunt's. For her, the journey to Rome meant penury and loneliness. For him, it meant a chance to transfer a commanding personality from one sphere of influence to another.

Bayley was born in Rye, New York on August 23, 1814, the eldest son, as we have seen, of Dr. Guy Carleton Bayley and Grace Roosevelt Bayley. He attended Amherst College (for which he retained life-long affection) but left without taking a degree to study classics and scripture at Trinity College in Hartford, Connecticut. Completing studies under Reverend Samuel Jarvis of Middletown, Connecticut, he was ordained an Episcopalian priest and appointed rector of Saint Peter's Church in New York. But despite this training and ordination, maybe because of it, Bayley started to question the validity of Anglican orders, even the apostolicity of Anglicanism itself. It was a frightening realization. At Saint Peter's he became friendly with a Roman Catholic priest, Father Michael Curran, who mentored him through these difficulties but, his doubts persisting, he resigned his parish in 1841 and left for a European tour that was to end in with his reception into the Roman Catholic Church in April 1842. He was ordained a Roman Catholic priest in 1844. The conversion was reported in the Catholic world as a coup. "Mr. Bayley of New York, a nephew, I believe of Madam Seton, an Anglican clergyman, visited Rome more from curiosity than otherwise but was so struck by what he saw as to determine to embrace our Holy Faith. I have had the pleasure of meeting him twice. He is a man of some twenty-eight years, and I was delighted with his affable, frank and pleasing manners." [12]

When Elizabeth Ann Seton became a Catholic she was almost alone in her "perversion." Not so her nephew. If anything, Bayley was part of a transatlantic trend, at one with the likes of John Henry Newman, Henry Edward Manning, Frederick Faber, Orestes Brownson, and many others who were all drawn one way or another to Catholicism's unbroken duration, its philosophic completeness, its magnificent ritual, its claim to universal sovereignty. Bayley's moment of nonconformity, in that sense, was hardly nonconformist at all. His story of high society, of personal doubt, of disinheritance, of new life, seems drawn from the pages of a novel, a pious confection, a series of clichés. But Bayley was more than a type. He was a real human being. An 1842 journal of his trip to Europe shows him a funny, sharp, ironic chronicler of human foible, tolerant of weakness in others because aware of it in himself—a man, more or less, in full. Nine days in Paris confirmed the French as a "vain, selfish, impolite . . . rascally" people.[13] An encounter in Geneva revealed that "one might as well hope to extract blood from a beet as to get paid money back from a Swiss."[14] A sacristan in Rome was "either sick or a philosopher for he presented the remarkable specimen of a custodian insensible to the jingling of silver."[15] Only the Irish were indifferent to money: they preferred violence and whiskey. Bayley, a character from a novel, could have passed for a novelist himself. Everything was noticed and recorded. Nothing was wasted. Roman practices grated on him (he was "not pleased" with services at Saint Peter's and he found Saint Mark's Basilica in Venice "grotesque") but these irritations had to be endured for the sake of the truth. And that truth? Shortly after Easter 1842, following "much consideration," he "finally determined to act" in accordance with his convictions.[16] "This morning," he wrote on April 28, "I recieved [sic] confirmation, and made my first communion from the hands of Cardinal Franzoni."[17] He was twenty-eight years old.

Received into the church, Bayley studied for the priesthood at St. Sulpice in Paris, a friend, Daniel Robinson, warning him of what lay ahead: "Do you not almost shrink from the responsibilities you have assumed? I can easily apprehend the sacrifices you have made, and the strong torrent of opposition and prejudice you will have to encounter when you return to this pope-hating country. If you are right you will carry with you a consciousness that the ridicule or opposition of the world cannot reach. But what is *truth?*"[18] But others, such as the editor of the *Freeman's Journal and Catholic Register*, saw his conversion as a boon: "We have had the pleasure of a personal acquaintance with the Reverend Mr. Bayley, and we have never known a person of greater amiability, higher religious feeling, more extensive and profound acquirements in every branch of literature, but especially Ecclesiastical history; the whole enhanced by the most engaging and winning manners. We have always regarded him as a model of a Christian gentleman. He will, we are confident, prove an ornament to the Church."[19]

Ordained a priest by Bishop John Hughes in New York in March 1844, Bayley then made rapid progress. He was appointed professor of rhetoric and Holy Scripture at Saint John's College, Fordham, where he developed an interest in the history of Catholicity in New York City. Leaving Fordham following its transfer to the Society of Jesus, he became pastor at the Quarantine Station on Staten Island. Finally, he was appointed secretary to Bishop Hughes, a post that showed him that the New York diocese was too large geographically for one man to govern. Covering most of New Jersey as well as New York, it was divided in two in 1853. With some territory in south Jersey taken from the diocese of Philadelphia, the diocese of Newark was created, the territory covering the whole of the state of New Jersey. Bayley was appointed bishop of this creation in 1853, his consecration taking place in Saint Patrick's Cathedral, Newark, on October 30.

Bayley became a bishop when the American church was at last beginning to take seriously the huge task of organizing dioceses for a rapidly expanding flock. [20] He also took office at the height of the fretful Protestantism of the mid-nineteenth century.[21] For the rest of his life, he was conscious that, of all American prejudices, anti-Catholicism was deepest.[22]

"I cannot understand now how I was prevailed upon to accept my nomination—of which I am in every way so unworthy," he wrote before his consecration. "I am overcome with fear and trembling at the thought of being a bishop."[23] Yet Bayley turned out to be a fine bishop precisely because he worried that he would not be. "There was nothing spectacular or brilliantly arresting about [him] or his career," one historian has written.

> His conversion to the Catholic faith was the culmination of an orderly process of study and prayer, with nothing of the road to Damascus about it. His life as a priest was like that of thousands of other priests of his day and since; his episcopate was fruitful but not brilliant. He was a talented administrator and a gifted student, but he had no flashing oratorical power nor any conspicuous mental gifts. But he was thoroughly rounded out—a good student, a forceful preacher, a capable administrator and above all a thoroughly religious and devout churchman . . . He exemplifies above all . . . the great importance of unflagging intellectual discipline even in the midst of an exceptionally busy life—the importance of being before doing.[24]

Seton Hall's founder was no genius but being down-to-earth turned out to be his most important gift.

And so all sorts of stories came together in 1856 when Bayley opened his school for business. It was a family story—in fact, the story of several colonial and early national families connected to each other by ties of intimacy and interest. It was personal story—in fact, several personal stories, each made intricate by the complex interplay of character: Elizabeth Ann Seton with her restless desire for rest; James Roosevelt Bayley with his bluff practicality. It was a social story—in fact, thousands of stories of people whose lives, patched together, made up the early days of the diocese of Newark. It was an American story of need and opportunity, of supply and demand. Above all, it was a Catholic story, the story of a faith that Seton Hall came into being in order to promote and sustain. To Bayley, that was the only reason that all these other patterned stories made any sense at all.

CHAPTER 2

A College Begins

Bayley's Challenge

Bayley's diocese covered all of New Jersey. He was its first bishop but by no means its first Catholic. A long, checkered, and difficult history preceded him[1] and, ahead, a challenging future emerged before his very eyes. "We traveled to Newark," wrote an Irish visitor in 1802, "[a town] much larger than Elizabeth-town and very beautiful; [it] is much resorted by fugitives from New York during the continuation of the Yellow Fever; it is inhabited by a considerable number of shoe-makers."[2] Fifty years later, the shoemakers were still there, but other people too—Irish, Germans, young, old, rich, poor—all constituting social challenges to stagger the imagination.[3] Surveying the diocese in 1854, Bayley saw few priests (twenty-five of them), fewer schools, no religious orders, no charitable institutions except a small orphanage under the care of five nuns, a negligible parochial structure, and a scarcely literate population.[4] "The field was large and inviting," said Michael Corrigan, who was to succeed him as bishop in 1872, "but not only was the harvest not ripe, the seeds were hardly yet planted."[5] Bayley's task, and Seton Hall's, was to plant and bring them to fruition.

Education, for Bayley, was answer to most if not all of these problems. Without decent schools, his flock would remain little use to themselves or anyone else. It was "most regrettable," he said, that a state with fifty to sixty thousand Catholics (in August 1855 he lowered the number to forty thousand) did not possess "a single institution of learning or religion, so necessary to the establishment and progress of religion."[6] Bayley's priests did their best but in some cases their best was not very good. For every Patrick Moran, a remarkable figure in early nineteenth century Newark, there were the likes of John McDermott of Salem, who was lazy and insolent,[7] and others who did a lot more harm than good.[8] Bayley needed more priests and better ones, and he needed them fast.

Where to get help? At first, he sought support from the Society for the Propagation of the Faith based in Lyons, France, which obliged with a donation enabling him to keep open two churches that would otherwise have been "lost to religion." Recession and shuttered factories were the problems. His "poor diocesans," he told the Society, were quite unable "to build [for themselves] houses of education and charity."[9] But "helped in the beginning, the Diocese of Newark will soon be able to take care of itself."[10] This shortage of "holy, well instructed priests"[11] was repeated like a mantra. In 1860, Bayley wrote to the Rector of All Hallows College in Dublin asking for as many clerics as the latter could send him. "The emigration is again flowing in on us," he explained. "I was never more in want of good zealous priests." "Nothing is dearer to my heart than the establishment of good parochial schools," he wrote in July 1855. "In them is our only hope of making Catholicity take root here."[12] "The only way . . . in which we can hope to make an impression on the proud and worldly spirit of the Protestants who surround us," he wrote in 1856, "is to elevate [our own] social condition." Schools, and only schools, would do that.

Seton Hall was thus uniquely of its own time and place. But it was not uniquely Bayley's creation. He would never have succeeded had it not been for the "indomitable energy and zeal of Father [Bernard] McQuaid,"[13] who was as much a Newark pioneer as the bishop and as great a figure in American Catholic history. In old age, when most of the battles were over, McQuaid remembered coming to Madison as a pastor in 1848 and seeing the virgin earth of New Jersey Catholicism. It brought out his inner Willa Cather. "I crossed yonder mountain above South Orange . . . and when I reached the summit of that mountain I stood for a few moments to raise my heart to God in prayer and praise . . . Signs of the Catholic Church there were none. No chapel, no church, no schoolhouse. But then the people were few and the need had not yet come upon them."[14] Together, McQuaid and Bayley would be partners in building those places of prayer and pious instruction. But, although partners, they were also worlds apart. Born in New York City in 1823 (perhaps 1825) of Irish emigrants, Bernard McQuaid was orphaned young—his father was beaten to death by a fellow immigrant—and sent for adoption to the Prince Street Orphan Asylum, in New York City, before enrolling at Saint Joseph's Seminary, Fordham, probably around 1843. Bayley was president of Fordham at the time (and on one occasion seems to have saved McQuaid's life during a hemorrhage of the lungs). During this training the nearest McQuaid had to a family were the Sisters of Charity, to whom he remained attached for the rest of his days.

Bayley and McQuaid were therefore well acquainted with each other before they worked on Seton Hall. It was not the easiest relationship. McQuaid's later years were spent privately claiming what he was reluctant to claim in public, namely that he, not Bayley, was the true founder of the college: a plausible but ultimately unconvincing notion. McQuaid's competence and strength of personality were undeniably crucial. It was he who kept it going: raising money, entertaining parents, commissioning buildings, attracting (and occasionally repelling) faculty, teaching students. Here is an extraordinary achievement for which respect is due. Yet Bayley is rightly credited as Seton Hall's founder. Without him, there would have been no college. McQuaid was to have his difficulties with Bayley—McQuaid was to have his difficulties with many people—but it was as partners, not rivals, that they made the school.

This is to get ahead of the story. When Bayley was appointed to Newark, the intelligent, courageous, unflappable McQuaid was the obvious man to execute his plans for a college.[15] McQuaid thought so, too. "I had one natural gift in high degree [and] not a saintly one," he boasted. "The more the opposition, the stronger the determination to succeed."[16] That determination was necessary from the beginning. Seton Hall's first intimations could not have been more understated or obscure. "Coll[ege] at Madison," wrote Bayley in his diary for April 10, 1854. "Purchased the Chegaray Farm at Madison for $8000." Formerly a "Seminary for Young Ladies" under the supervision of one Madame Chegaray, this property offered size, location, and respectability, three important considerations in the establishment of any school. But it did not come cheap and Bayley's first effort to drum up funds was a flop. "I today sent the Reverend Mr. Madden of Madison to make a commencement in favor of the new college," he recorded a month later. "Amounted to nothing."[17] "The Reverend Father McQuaid went yesterday to Burlington and Mount Holly to collect for the College," he noted on June 11, 1855, half expecting him to fail and knowing that the most likely source of funds was outside the diocese—either France (the Society for the Propagation of the Faith)[18] or New York (his former diocese). Even the latter had to be handled carefully: "The most Reverend Archbishop [John Hughes] has given permission to Bishop Bayley to collect for a few weeks to help defray the expenses attending the purchase and opening of this institution [reported the Irish *Freeman's Journal* of June 2, 1855]. This is the only object for which the Diocese of Newark has asked, or is likely to ask, for aid from New York and the affection due to this young Diocese . . . will plead successfully in favor of the appeal.[19]

This second New York collection (after Madden's effort the year before) was disappointing, raising only $600, of which $150 came from one man, Edward Tiers. "Two thirds of the diocese were against Seton Hall for years," McQuaid later wrote, "and three fourths were sneering at Saint Elizabeth's."[20] Still, the scheme was under way, applications for admission had already been received, and so Bayley and McQuaid had no option but to continue.[21] A diocesan fund was opened in 1855, subscribers assured that money devoted to "the cause of religion" was guaranteed "an equal if not better return" than other investments. Within five years it held deposits of $26,000 from 347 people, the sums recorded in Bayley's neat script until Father George Doane took over the task in 1860. The money was not exclusively for Seton Hall but was vital to it nonetheless. Help also came in kind. The Sisters of Charity in New York promised to take charge of the domestic life of the college, running the kitchen, mending and laundering linen, caring for the sick. "The Sisters would be the making of me," Bayley wrote to Archbishop John Hughes in April 1856, "and I really need some extra lift."[22]

Students had to be secured and a faculty found. Bayley thought that one source of pupils would be parents reluctant to send their children to Fordham, preferring "a school under the charge of secular priests."[23] Colleges such as Mount Saint Mary's in Emmitsburg being "too far away," Seton Hall would also have local appeal.[24] As for faculty, McQuaid was the obvious president and other teachers could be drawn from the diocese, from other dioceses, by advertisement, or by word of mouth. News of the college spread through the academic grapevine, encouraging many would-be professors to apply. "[Wrote] to W.J. Brownson informing him that I was unwilling to make any further engagement for the College at present," Bayley recorded on May 30, 1856. "To Mr. J.G. Moylan to the same effect."[25] On the other hand, he was not unafraid to poach. Three months before opening day Bayley "wrote to Mr. Young, Paris, asking him to steal a good young French deacon or sub-deacon for the College if possible."[26]

Two years of begging and borrowing brought Seton Hall to opening day. A staff had been assembled: McQuaid as president, Reverend Alfred Young as vice-president and professor of Latin and Greek, Reverend Lawrence Hoey as professor of mathematics, Reverend Daniel Fisher as professor of English literature, Peter Tolin as professor of French, Achille Magni as assistant professor of Latin, James Fagan as teacher of natural philosophy, and Messrs. James and Philip O'Ryan as tutors.[27] A few weeks later came James Monroe, grand-nephew of the late President Monroe who (the *State Gazette* of Trenton reported) "has just been appointed to a Professorship in Seton Hall, the new Roman Catholic College just established at Madison, N.J."[28] Monroe had had correspondence with McQuaid the previous year about becoming a Catholic but he does not seem to have stayed long, if indeed he showed up at all.[29] All that was needed were pupils. "Father McQuaid and the rest have been very busy getting ready to open the College tomorrow," Bayley told his diary on August 31, 1856. "Will probably have Twenty to Thirty boys to start with." He was ready for them: McQuaid bought twenty wooden desks in Boston two weeks before classes began, $140 the lot. He bought another ten a year later.[30] Bayley's estimates were off the mark but the numbers bulked up to twenty-five before the month was out. The success was achieved, he noted, despite the fact that "some of our *friends* in New York are doing all they can to help us *downwards*," shadowy adversaries who failed to stop the school but were never forgotten or forgiven by bishop or president thereafter. And so, on September 1, 1856, Seton Hall College welcomed for its first day of classes Leo Thebaud, Louis and Alfred Boisaubin of Madison, Peter Meehan of Hoboken, and John Moore of New York City.

The college was clearly a joint enterprise, McQuaid sowing the seeds in Bayley's mind, encouraging him to persevere when others doubted. Although Bayley was happy to recognize the debt, McQuaid for his part always insisted on his own priority, writing to Father Joseph Flynn in 1883 that he cared "very little when they stole the credit of Seton Hall from me" (thus revealing that he cared very much). Building parochial schools in Madison and Morristown meant more to him, he said, than "having established Seton Hall College and Seminary for the education of the rich or of Levites for the sanctuary of God." Such class resentment did him little credit. He refused to preach at the Month's Mind Mass for Bayley in 1877 because that would require acknowledging Bayley, not himself, as true founder of the college. He protested too much. His role was vital but without Bayley there would have been no Seton Hall.

Early Days

And so, with the suddenness of a curtain rising on a play, Seton Hall presented itself to the public. Readers of the Dublin *Freeman's Journal* soon heard of its success: "The new Catholic College in New Jersey, Seton Hall, has opened and is progressing fairly . . . [It] is in one of the loveliest situations in the vicinity of New York, and its success is now past all doubt. It shows strikingly the increase of the Faith, that a few years go one such establishment near the city would have been deemed a hazardous undertaking, and now the opening of this new college has not detracted from the others."[31]

Naturally, promotional literature betrayed no hint of its precariousness. The *Catholic Almanac* of 1857 announced that

> The College buildings are large and commodious; the location is upon high ground, overlooking a beautiful country, and is unsurpassed for healthfulness by any portion of the United States. The object of the institution is to impart a good education in the proper and highest sense of the word. The course of instruction embraces a complete classical and commercial education. Particular attention will be paid to instruction in the French and English languages. Board and tuition $200 per annum . . . The Morris and Essex R.R., which runs through the village of Madison, renders the College accessible from New York in about an hour and a half.[32]

The college had one building, not several, a substantial three-story colonial farmhouse, five windows wide and pleasantly surrounded by trees and shrubbery. For five students it was grand; for thirty adequate; for more than that, small. With lots of fresh air (a national obsession)[33] it had everything a college could want. The curriculum catered to mercantile families of New Jersey, New York, and Connecticut who wanted their sons to gain practical training enabling them to thrive in business or in the professions. It was not exclusively a seminary: indeed, it was not a seminary at all. Seton Hall was for boys who might wish to become seminarians but that was not its sole or even primary function. With its own commercial imperatives—the need for fee-paying students—it could not afford to cater exclusively for future priests, even had it wished to.

Little is known of the first nine months of the college except that, at the end of them, Seton Hall treated itself to a public academic exercise. "Yesterday (Wedn. 24th Feast of St. Joann. Bap.) we held the first commencement of Seton Hall College, if it may be called by so dignified a name," Bayley recorded on June 25, 1857. "The weather was beautiful, the first really fine day almost this season. Everything went off well." A graduation without graduates, this bestowal of awards and prizes was also in a sense a prize to the school itself for having survived its first year. (The first graduation proper dates to 1862.) The year also ended with a change at the top. McQuaid stepped down to resume work as pastor of the cathedral and was replaced by Reverend Daniel Fisher, professor of English literature.

A New Yorker, Fisher was educated at Saint John's Seminary and after ordination went in 1852 to work in the diocese of Saint Paul, Minnesota, "a faithful and laborious missionary amongst the Indians and the Scattered Catholics of that distant Country."[34] But Minnesota ruined his health and in 1855 he returned east, intending to spend one year in Newark, in the end spending four. As well as teaching at Seton Hall, he did parish work in Plainfield and Trenton before being appointed McQuaid's successor on July 1, 1857, serving two years until, his health restored, he returned to the Midwest. After five years, he came back east again. Eighteen sixty-four saw him as a curate in Hoboken, still very sickly, where he died in April 1869. To Bayley he was a "beautiful English scholar" who preached well and "read the Gospel better than almost anyone I ever listened to."[35]

Competence and crisis marked Fisher's time in charge. The competence may be inferred from Bayley's confidence in him and from good reports of the school's doings. A second commencement in 1858 went off "admirably—fine weather, pleasant people, happy boys—a great many priests from N.Y."[36] and a third the next year, a day of intense heat, was capped by an address from Orestes Brownson, convert, man of letters, and polemicist.[37] The crisis came in the Easter recess of 1859 when a pupil, Francis Bonier, died of scarlet fever. "It has created quite a panic," Bayley admitted, "and the most exaggerated stories have been put into circulation."[38] Seton Hall's doctor, William O'Gorman, ("an Irish gentleman and a Catholic in religion")[39] calmed nerves but the episode was a reminder that publicity could break as well as make a school. The obsession with fresh air was not foolish.

Seton Hall quickly gained a reputation as an attractive and up-and-coming establishment, taken seriously even by New Yorkers who, then as now, loved to laugh at their neighbors across the Hudson. ("We, too, were of the opinion that New Jersey, if not a perfect Sahara, was only a few removes therefrom in point of dreary and monotonous barrenness, but our visit to Seton Hall most effectually relieved us from this mistaken notion. [It is] is a very handsome structure, and the grounds about which are laid out with much taste.") The third commencement showed a school finding its feet. One student, John Lynch, gave a Greek oration and another, Emile Vatable, an oration in Latin "which was really one of the best we have ever heard." Other speeches followed in French, Spanish, and German and an essay was given on "Old and New Ireland" (by the well-named Moses Green) which "as a retrospect of the last thirty or forty years of Irish history possessed a good deal of merit." Once prizes were handed out—on the Alice in Wonderland principle that everyone should have one—Bayley offered an interim assessment:

> We never made any great pretensions, or, rather, I never made any. Some of our friends did, but the only object we had in view was simply to establish here a quiet, good old-fashioned school. . . . We did not pretend to point out any royal road to learning. We merely promised those who sent their children here, that we would instruct them well—I think I used the expression feed them well (laughter)—and discipline them well, if we were able to do so. All this, I think we may say, we have done.
>
> We did not profess to have found out any particular way in which a boy without brains in his head could be made a genius; and I have never heard of anyone having invented a method by which a lazy boy could be made, without exertion, a learned one.
>
> There is a want of discipline at home, and when a boy comes to college it is difficult to discipline him properly . . . The majority of our institutions have no discipline whatsoever. The only institutions that pretend to any are those under the charge of Catholics; in nearly all others the pupils are allowed to have pretty much their own way . . . Boys after all are not angels, as many mothers and fathers imagine they are.[40]

Seton Hall was homely and down-to-earth. With luck, it might last.

A New Home

Success depended on leadership and here the story took a turn for the better. Fisher relinquished the presidency in 1859, forcing Bayley to turn again to McQuaid. "Have been obliged to re-appoint the Rev. Father McQuaid to the Presidency of the College," he wrote in his diary on July 16, 1859. "He is still retaining the pastorship of the Cathedral. It is more difficult to find a good College Pres. Than to find a good anything else in this world. All that the College needs to ensure its permanent prosperity is a President. Everything else is there."[41] If there is a hint of reluctance here, a sense of anticipated difficulty with a deputy now assured of his indispensability, McQuaid's return nonetheless brought nothing but benefit to Seton Hall. Bayley deserves credit for it.

Coinciding with this second act and perhaps prompting it was a recognition that Seton Hall had outgrown its original premises. As early as 1857, Bayley was complaining of "the smallness of the College for Ecc[lesiastical] Students."[42] In 1859 he declined admission to Samuel Seaman from Philadelphia: "cannot receive him, have 30 Ecc. Students at present: would give him a situation at the College but have no place for him."[43] Students wishing to study for the priesthood needed to be closer to Newark to take part in diocesan liturgies, and proximity to New York would also encourage wealthier parents to send their boys to the college. "The object I have in view," he told priests in May 1860, "is to enlarge the present institution—to unite to it as soon as possible a Theological School similar to that connected with Mount S. Mary's near Emmitsburg—and by bringing it nearer to the Episcopal City to increase its usefulness and to render it more readily accessible to the Clergy of the diocese for retreats, Conferences, and other Ecclesiastical purposes."[44] With numbers stuck at about sixty, Bayley and McQuaid had to find another place at a reasonable price, bearing in mind that other institutions (such as the recently established North American College in Rome) were also seeking support.[45] Nonetheless, a site was secured, almost by accident:

> One bright day in the early spring of 1860, Bishop Bayley and Father McQuaid were returning from a long drive over the Orange Hills from what had proved a fruitless search for a location for the new college; rather discouraged, they were driving slowly homeward over the South Orange and Newark turnpike, when Bishop Bayley's attention was attracted to a large white marble villa surrounded by superb grounds and stately trees. He turned to Father McQuaid and said "do you think that property can be purchased." "I don't know, but we'll try," answered the young priest with assurance and ready promptness. For Father McQuaid to will, was to accomplish, when he once set to work with a purpose, and despite several obstacles it was not long before the property was bought and the deed transferred to Bishop Bayley . . . on April 2, 1860.[46]

Bayley recorded the transaction laconically: "New College. Purchased the House and Farm known as the Marble House near South Orange for $35,000: the house was built by a person named Elphinstone, who spent some $40,000 on it and failed before it was completed. Intend to give the property at Madison to the Sisters of Charity & remove the College to this new place."[47]

The Elphinstone house and over sixty acres of land in South Orange were a bargain. Moreover, conveying the Madison property to the Sisters of Charity was not a gift. They paid $25,000 for it, which included the forty-eight acres purchased in 1854 and an additional thirteen acres bought in 1859. (The building and land formed the nucleus of a convent and, later, the College of Saint Elizabeth.) Bayley asked a real estate agent, Michael MacEntee of Vailsburg in Newark, to handle the sale, knowing that there would be local opposition had the purchaser been known as a Roman Catholic bishop.

Bayley's reference to the Elphinstone failure is obscure. It may have been financial, personal, or domestic, the inability of two brothers of that name to live under the same roof. (The brothers, it should be added, were not the vendors; the property belonged to a Mr. Charles Osborne of Exchange Place, New York.) At any rate, the farm alone was worth more than the price Bayley and McQuaid paid for house and land together. McQuaid noted in 1886 that "the value of the land has greatly appreciated since I bought it in 1860 . . . the buying price was about $500 per acre, with the Marble Building thrown in [for nothing]. The land today, about sixty-eight acres, should be worth from two to three thousand dollars per acre."[48] The village of South Orange added to the appeal, an hour by train from New York. With the Orange Mountains adding a touch of grandeur to the estate, the Elphinstone property overlooked "a beautiful country," the College Catalogue of 1862 boasted, "noted for healthfulness" with "villas and mansions on every available site for miles around."[49] It was perfectly chosen.

The removal of Seton Hall from Madison to South Orange was a diocesan event and Bayley made the most of it. Clergy and laity contributed $8,100 to an appeal launched in May 1860, enabling work to begin immediately on modifying the villa but insufficient to offset the purchase price. Almost as soon as the ink was dry, the Marble House was customized to serve the needs of seminarians with the addition of dormitories and a study hall. On May 15, 1860 Bayley laid and blessed a cornerstone— a "large number of people present—made an address"[50]—for a new building to house the college proper as opposed to the seminary (whose independent life may be said to begin with the move to South Orange). On September 10, 1860, Bayley recorded that "the new college building at South Orange is finished and has opened,"[51] which does scant justice to its extraordinarily rapid construction. This "College Building"— the first of several—housed fifty students taught by seventeen faculty members. A three-story building in brick with dormer rooms, two chimney stacks, and a pointed tower, it was to the left of the Marble Villa. The household was again under the Sisters of Charity.

The Marble Villa and College Building were set in pleasant surroundings of parkland, some well-tended lawns, and a couple of playing fields. The rest of the property consisted of a farm providing vegetables and milk for the college kitchen. In October 1864 a further purchase of farmland was made, adding to the supplies of fresh produce for the seminary. Long after Bayley and McQuaid were dead, this farm and its modest set of outbuildings would form the basis of a legal case that ended before the United States Supreme Court. But that is a story for a later chapter. In 1864, it produced fodder, not lawyers' fees.

Academic Life

In South Orange as in Madison, Seton Hall's curriculum was classical, linguistic, and mathematical with an emphasis on commercially useful subjects such as book-keeping. The purpose was to cover subjects from rudimentary to advanced level (some of the students were hardly even teenagers) with a view to future employment. There were four courses: Classical, English, French, and Mathematical. Students could not take logic, metaphysics, and ethics without first mastering the sixth and seventh years of the classical course. French was compulsory, Spanish and German optional. Pupils could do music, drawing, and painting, for which an extra fee was charged. Sport did not feature but games played a large if informal part in college life.

The classical course was textual. The first year was spent doing basic Latin grammar, the second year proceeded to Caesar's *Gallic Wars*, elementary Greek, and Aesop's Fables. By the third year students did Latin prose composition and were translating Sallust, Ovid, and Virgil's Ecologues. In Greek, they studied the Anabasis of Xenophon. In the fourth year, the curriculum consisted of Virgil, Cicero, Xenophon, and Homer; in the fifth, Livy, Horace, Cicero, Demosthenes, and Aeschylus; in the sixth, Tacitus, Horace, Cicero, Euripides, and Longinus; in the seventh, Juvenal, Perseus, Herodotus, and Thucydides.

The mathematical course was a combination of theoretical and practical work taking in some hard science. After the gentle slopes of mental arithmetic and algebra, students climbed through plane, solid, and spherical geometry; trigonometry; surveying and navigation; analytical geometry; differential and integral calculus; mechanics and civil engineering; natural philosophy (that is to say, physics); chemistry; and astronomy. Anyone who mastered it could hope for a career in engineering, building, the maritime industries, accounting, or commerce. The hard sciences proper consisted of physics, chemistry, and astronomy but not biology.

English covered a range of materials. Rudiments came first—reading, spelling, prose composition, the taking of dictation. Harder material followed—elocution, precepts of rhetoric and poetry, criticism of ancient authors, finally "English Classical Reading." English covered more than the word suggested, taking in historical material (Hale's *History of the United States*, Lingard's *History of England*, Fredet's *Ancient and Modern Histories*) and also (oddly) Geography.

French was the foreign language *non pareil*. A number of students knew Spanish already and German was the first language of others. The course was linguistic than literary. Grammar, conversation, dictation, and composition came first, poetry and prose second. The catalogue announced that student would undertake "the Study of French Literature" but without specifying what: probably whatever took the professor's fancy on a given day.

Every class assumed the truth of the Catholic worldview. Astronomy, for example, was taught as a subset of natural theology, English history as branch of counter-reformation apologetics, and so on. Catholic teaching itself also had to be imparted. Student were expected to master "in regular succession" the *Small Catechism*, Butler's *Catechism*, Collot's *Doctrinal and Scriptural Catechism*, and *Lectures on the Doctrines and Evidences of the Catholic Church*. These exercises were reinforced in the sixth and seventh years by logic, metaphysics, and ethics.

Not every student undertook every course. The early curriculum was high school standard, the later stages more advanced. One option was to attend Seton Hall for a few years, then leave to find work. Getting a degree was not necessarily a goal. Those intent on ordination stayed longer. To receive a diploma, a student had to persevere for seven years. "Candidates for the degree of A.B.," said the catalogue of 1861–62, "must undergo a public examination in the full course of studies pursued in the College." Their scrolls were hard won.

Life outside the classroom was equally tough. Discipline and moral wariness were the watchwords:

> No student ever leaves the College grounds without a teacher. Leaving the College grounds after night-fall subjects the student to expulsion.
> The use of tobacco is forbidden . . .
> No books of any kind can be held by the Students, unless by permission of the President.
> Students are not allowed to receive newspapers, except for their Reading Room, which is under the direction of the President.
> No correspondence is permitted, except under cover, to and from parents and guardians; and the President will exercise his right to examine all letters, as, in his judgment, it may be necessary.
> No student of low and vicious habits will be retained in this College . . .

The number of letters scrutinized cannot be known; few enough, in all likelihood. The interdiction of "books of any kind" was designed to perfect reading, not prevent it. Cheap novels were disdained and anything worse, the surreptitious currency of dormitories, was ground for expulsion. Every school banned tobacco, less for reasons of health than safety. The rules were no better or worse than those of comparable institutions. Indeed, they were directed as much at parents as at pupils: "Parents have the right to withdraw their children at any time; they have not the right to interfere with the established discipline of the College; they have not the right to keep us and our punctual students waiting for laggards who want *one more day of idleness*."[52] McQuaid sought and achieved mastery over adults as well as children. He could be a torture at times.

The academic year lasted two terms of five months each, beginning on the last Wednesday in August and ending on the last Wednesday in June. Except for a ten-day vacation at Christmas and a brief *exeat* in May, students remained in college throughout the academic session. (Exceptionally, a student might also stay during summer.) Board and tuition, $225 per annum payable half-yearly the beginning of each term, included linen, laundry, the mending of clothes, but not the doctor's fee ($5) or the cost of medicine. Other extras included music lessons ($50), drawing ($40), and tuition in German, Italian, and Spanish ($25 each). Students were allowed pocket money, lodged with the college treasurer, who disbursed or withheld it as he saw fit. Rich or poor, the typical student had an *equipage* fit for a prince: "On entering [he] must be supplied with four Summer suits, if he enters in the Spring; or three Winter suits if he enters in the Fall. He must also have at least twelve shirts, twelve pair of stockings, twelve pocket handkerchiefs, six towels, six napkins, three pairs of shoes or boots, and a napkin ring marked with his name."[53]

Thus dressed, he faced an unknown but rule-bound world.

School Begins

To read a catalogue and think that it describes a school is to open a recipe-book and mistake it for a cake. Rhetoric and reality are different things. Strong-minded men and energetic boys cooped up together for ten months of the year had to make the best of a life that few of them would have chosen otherwise. The compensations of camaraderie could not conceal the fact that the existence was more to be endured than enjoyed.

For all that, McQuaid assembled teachers of high caliber. Apart from himself, other instructors in 1860 included Father Januarius de Concilio, professor of logic and metaphysics, Leo Thebaud, "Professor of French" but in reality a prefect, and Winand Wigger, A.B., assistant professor of mathematics and English. De Concilio did not stay long. "Father De C. has got the kink in his head that his health is suffering, and it will not be possible to retain him," McQuaid reported to Bayley in 1862. "Try, therefore, to pick some suitable person, if you possibly can."[54] His replacement was Reverend Henry Brann, D.D., ordained in Rome in June 1862 and appointed to the vice-presidency of Seton Hall the following September. Intellectually distinguished, he was to prove a difficult colleague, but at first he was quiet. Of greater durability was the oddly named Winand Michael Wigger whose parents had come to America from Westphalia in the 1830s. (He succeeded to the see of Newark in 1881 but lived at Seton Hall until his death in 1901.) "The Bishop always thought of his experience in the seminary at South Orange with much pleasure," wrote his obituarist, "and especially recalled with delight the ease with which he had mastered the unruly spirits in the study hall."[55] This was a sad little boast for a grown man. Quiet, shy, frail, Wigger was a Seton Hall fixture for decades.

The best account of the college's early days comes from Henry Brann:

Bishop Bayley appointed me Vice-President of Seton Hall and director of the Seminary in August 1862. I had just come from the American College in Rome. I went from Jersey City to the College, met Father McQuaid, the president, and presented my credential. I shall never forget that first meeting . . . Father McQuaid wore a high hat, rather worse for wear, and clothes that were dusty for he had been rambling over the College farm. I met him outside near the front of the College. "Good morning, Father," said I. He paused a little before returning my greeting and then said: "Oh! I suppose you are Dr Brann?" I told him I was. He then gave me a sharp patronizing look that took me in from head to foot and rather roused in me a little bit of combativeness. "Well," said he more civilly, "Come In! You will not find here all the luxuries you have been accustomed to in St. Sulpice at Paris or in the American College at Rome. And I hope you will be happy in your new home." "Oh I am sure of that," I replied, "for I love theology and study and this is a beautiful place." "Well," said he, "come out and I'll show you my farm." Out we walked together. Pointing to a couple of gentlemen: "there," said he, "are a couple of *my* Seminarians." A few paces further on: "there are some of *my* college boys;" and he continued: "that's my man Simon you see yonder; here are some of my potatoes; there are my horses, over there my barn," and pointing at it, "there is my manure heap." He is evidently a farmer, I thought to myself, and is very emphatic and prolific with his "I's". . . ."Seton Hall under my care," said he, "must above all things turn out young gentlemen." I . . . took possession of my room where I was perfectly happy for two years.[56]

There was every reason for happiness. Brann loved Seton Hall's quirkiness, its social comedy, its *esprit de corps*. In the first flush of a new job, everything appealed: the fact, for instance, that Bayley loved music but was hopeless at it—"when he came to a high note rose on his toes, and when the note was low he leaned back on his heels"; the fact that McQuaid could not tell the difference between a *basso profundo* and a bad cold; the fact that Seton Hall had oddballs and *prima donnas* (himself included) but also spiritual heroes. Endearing weakness abounded: "Kain was the oldest of the Seminarians, pious, studious and popular. But . . . he was not sharp enough for practical jokers like Reilly, Dalton and McCarthy . . . In fact, Reilly, Dalton, Connolly, Darcy, Daly and Smith [seminarians] all died young. Hospitable Newark was a dangerous place for young men in those days. The laity killed many of the clergy by over-kindness."[57] Alcohol was a problem for a number of Newark priests and some of them were sent to Seton Hall to dry out. (The cure did not always work. It may have made the condition worse.)

"I see your College mentioned in high terms by the *Freeman*," his cousin Robert Seton wrote to Bayley in September 1862. "My goodness! How quickly the time passes."[58] Despite the new college building there was still insufficient room for the liturgical life Bayley had in mind when he moved from Madison. The Marble House oratory seated only twenty-five people, quite inadequate for training seminarians and too poky for local Catholics who were beginning to regard Seton Hall as their parish. "The Sanctuary of the present Chapel will barely hold the Celebrant, and the boy to serve his Mass," Bayley wrote to clergy in May 1862 looking for support for a new chapel. "The Catholics residing in the neighborhood of the College are poor and few in number, and can do no more than assist in the building of the Church; whilst the College, struggling through its years of infancy, can do but little for the same purpose."[59] A year later, he repeated the argument. The lack of a chapel was a disgrace, the current oratory being "confined and inconvenient." If a proper chapel was important for the College, he said, "it is absolutely necessary for the Seminary"[60] and allow diocesan priests to pray together when in synod or on retreat. A "neat gothic chapel of stone" would be "a finish to the present group of College buildings" and give "a proper religious character to the whole place."

No project was closer to Bayley's heart. With the chapel completed, he said, seminarians could carry out the Roman Ritual "to their own great improvement and the edification of the Students."[61] (Collegians were supposed to be inspired by the piety of their ecclesiastical counterparts.) Priests who failed to raise money for it could expect a scorching. "The collection for the Seminary Chapel is, as you must have felt and probably intended by your utter neglect of my instructions [is] an insult to me," he rebuked Father John Kelly of Jersey City. "The next time anything of the sort occurs, I will feel it my duty to appoint [a pastor] who will co-operate with me in building up the College, Seminary, Sisterhood and whatever good works I may think best to undertake."[62] These rockets reached their target. The cornerstone was laid on May 21, 1863, McQuaid preaching and the future Cardinal McCloskey in attendance. Designed by the lively and largely self-taught Dublin-born architect Jeremiah O'Rourke, the building was a handsomely proportioned Gothic brownstone structure one hundred feet long with a belltower although, as yet, no sacristy. Dedicated in 1870, it was in use much earlier. (When Seton Hall had money, or the prospect of it, a building could go up quickly. Bayley and McQuaid spent as if there might be no tomorrow because, had they not done so, there might not have been.) Built on the western side of the seminary, the chapel was started less than a month after the circular letter requesting funds. There was enough of a building by December 19, 1863 to allow an ordination ceremony to take place. (The ordinands were James D'Arcy and Patrick Cody.) The first funeral, held on November 2, 1866, was of Henry Howard Burgess, the college registrar. (His memorial plaque is still there.) There were two side entrances, one on the east for collegians and seminarians, one on the west for the general public. (Today's main entrance came fifty years later.) It cost about $8,000 but when furnishing and an organ were added the total was nearer $25,000.

The chapel was the highpoint of 1863. A row between Bayley and McQuaid was the low point. The argument was trivial—whether seminarians should attend Holy Week ceremonies at the Cathedral or in the Seminary—but because it concerned the authority of the bishop, who wanted the men at the Cathedral, and because it touched on the *amour propre* of McQuaid, who found it difficult to obey orders, the matter developed into a full-scale fight that did neither much credit. As a result of it, McQuaid packed his bags, handed over the account books to Brann, left South Orange for New York, and arrived, still furious, at Saint Michael's Church, Ninth Avenue where an old friend was pastor. Asking for a post as assistant priest, he proposed to remove himself altogether from Newark and the authority of Bayley. He eventually calmed down and, in the words of Henry Brann, "changed his mind, [ate] humble pie and remained in the College until his promotion to the See of Rochester [in 1868]." Bayley and McQuaid were so different in character, temper, and social origins that collaboration was always likely to be fraught. Brann, much preferring Bayley, thought that McQuaid was "a strong character and a stubborn one when . . . young"[63] although he mellowed with age. Some part of Bayley may have wished him to stay in New York. It would have made for a quieter life.

Boring normality, not rows, was what everyone wanted. Happily, McQuaid achieved it. "I might have obtained a hundred scholars this year, if I had room for them," he told Bayley in September 1862. "I have now seventy in the house and places engaged for ten more. Five have been refused." "Could you not find in your journeying $20,000 or a little more with which to build the other wing of the College?" he asked as Bayley prepared to travel to Europe on ecclesiastical business. In 1863, as the chapel was going up, the cornerstone was laid for an infirmary, an unsophisticated building which would also serve as a residence for the Sisters of Charity. Some of the tension between Bayley and McQuaid arose from these seemingly endless demands for money.

Who taught the students? Henry Brann captures the small faculty of laymen: "The old professors? Blume, professor of Greek, was very quiet and a first-class Greek scholar. Fagan, professor of Mathematics, was out West when last heard from; Brown, professor of literature, has disappeared, as has the Frenchman La Ferriere; Fritsch, professor of music. Fritsch was . . . a Jew. No-one ever suspected it."[64]

Theodore Blume, an 1838 graduate of the University of Bonn in Germany, taught languages for twenty-three years and at his death in 1883, aged sixty-five, was the longest serving member of the early faculty.[65] Edward Fritsch (who came to Seton Hall later than Brann remembered) was the first Jew employed at the College but not the first musician. His predecessor, Ambrose Rieff, was dismissed for signing a petition complaining about the food.[66] Fritsch's appointment reflected not so much tolerance as oversight. Had his faith been known, he would not have been hired. Seton Hall was in the business of employing Catholics to teach Catholics. That was an axiom.

Academic regimentation was total. Each pupil had his own page in a ledger, a detailed record of triumph or disaster. A test took place in every subject every week, the marks calibrated to the decimal point. A student could do 1st Geography, Writing, and Rhetoric at the same time as 2nd English, History, Catechism, and Arithmetic, 3rd French, and 6th Latin and Greek. It was also possible to change to a different class during term, say from 3rd to 4th French. With nightly homework (even away from home), students had no time to rest on laurels.

Seton Hall had moral as well as physical boundaries. Minor offenses meant detention. Major offenses meant expulsion. All offenses meant a place in the punishment book, a chronicle of human frailty as vivid as a monastic penitential. On September 22, 1867, John Kerr and a companion were caught "smoking in the study hall." Joseph Coyle misbehaved at table. The following day Joseph Hayes was found smoking. A student by the name of Ashman (not, alas, a smoker) was caught "throwing an apple . . . after first bell." Three students were "talkative in study," two misbehaved in French class, and one, a frequent offender called James McNeely, was caught using "unbecoming language." The next day three boys were discovered "causing disorder in dormitory," an offence, detected or otherwise, which probably occurred most nights in most dormitories across the world. On the 29th, Kukuck was "amusing himself with story book during spiritual reading and impertinent and insolent when reprimanded."

Names recur—O'Gorman, Hayes, McNeely, Randolph—and offenses—"whistling in dormitory, "generally too giddy during silence," "continuing to look around in the chapel after being prohibited," "talking and laughing after Angelus," "humming in Mr. Glennon's studies." On October 5, 1867, Joseph Hayes was guilty of "not returning to Mass until sent [and] playing billiards at the wrong time." Hunter and Horsfal were punished for "handling service at table before grace after repeated prohibitions." "Hayes et al." were recorded on November 6, 1867 as being "extremely disorderly in bible history class last Tuesday night"—the "et al." being Latin for "the usual suspects."[67] On the whole, the sins were venial. No-one was in the same league as James Fennimore Cooper at Yale, put on probation for using gunpowder to open a door and finally expelled for tying a donkey to a professor's chair.[68]

More decorous recreation came in the form of the Roosevelt Debating Club (1860). With Bayley as patron and Father Edward Hickey as first president, the club took itself seriously, four seminarians designated in advance to prepare arguments on either side of a motion, the president deciding the winner. Only once was there disagreement between audience and president when in 1865 the Irish Fenian Brotherhood was defended against the charge of being a secret society (it was) and commended instead for its "laudable" aim of ridding Ireland of English rule. The case was "loudly applauded" until the president signaled disapproval.[69] "That the South is Justified in Seceding" was to have been debated on January 6, 1861 but no meeting took place. "The Negro's Complaint" was the subject of an oration in in September 1864. "Is it expedient that the Sovereign Pontiff should retain his temporal dominion?" was debated in October 1864 and unsurprisingly decided in the affirmative. "Was the French Revolution in its effects beneficial to France?" (yes); "Do the learned professions afford a better field for wealth than mercantile pursuits?"; "Is a man in the civilized state happier than a man in the savage state?"; "Can Pope Adrian be justified in his negotiations with Henry II of England with regard to the conquest of Ireland?" (a split decision). Mostly the views were conventional but, when it came to Ireland, real debate could happen when invariably students proved more radical than masters.

The Roosevelt Debating Society was dissolved in 1866 because of a dispute about money. Some seminarians wanted to end the academic year by buying "books, pamphlets, or something of that kind." Others wanted to buy "ice cream, strawberries, cake etc." Perhaps in so arguing they revealed the priests they would turn out to be.[70]

Their short-lived little club was part of a success story. As Seton Hall approached its first decade, there much to celebrate. The move from Madison to South Orange allowed enrollments continued to grow. The new academic building was up and running. A charter was granted on March 8, 1861 by which the New Jersey Legislature constituted "Seton Hall College" as a corporate body with the right "to sue and be sued, implead and be impleaded, purchase and hold property" and with all other rights pertaining to such bodies. In 1865, funds were found to double the size of the College building. A second decade of progress awaited.

The Paying Public

McQuaid's duties were mundane but miscellaneous. Dealing with parents was a reminder that every student had a story. The bright, the dim, the sickly, the strong, the pampered, the neglected: they all seemed to end up in South Orange. McQuaid exercised his authority under constraint, knowing that unhappy students or parents could spell doom. "You are perfectly powerless against the combined influences of many," one father wrote to him, imagining a hundred angry mothers invading his realm.[71] He was not far off the mark.

The chief duty, of course, was to educate. Most parents insisted on a curriculum to meet the individual needs, as if Seton Hall's bill of fare were *a la carte*, not *table d'hôte*. "I wish him to have a good education—the usual branches of Latin and Greek and a good English education, with composition in English and . . . public speaking."[72] The customer always knew best. "Particular attention [should] be paid to the tuition of arithmetic and book keeping . . . If there are no professors of those branches in your establishment . . . special teachers may be employed with every facility given them as to time and compensation."[73] Anything fancy was frowned upon. "I intend him for commercial pursuits. I have no objection to his studying Latin but I don't consider it important."[74] "You can mould him as you please but my view is to fit him for business and [I] desire him to study those things which are most useful and profitable. I prefer him to know fewer things and know them well."[75] For some, even that could be a challenge. "He will be sixteen years old tomorrow . . . His self-esteem is so great that he cannot realize how ignorant he is."[76] To the extent that any student may be said to be typical, it was Jim Fullerton, who was "unaffected by any extraordinary outbreaks of suppressed genius."[77] Such emanations were frowned upon.

Satisfied customers expressed satisfaction by renewing custom, dissatisfied ones by mounting a high horse and refusing to come down. "We have pleasant letters from the boys every week," wrote a parent who had "never received a slight complaining letter from them while they have been at the College. It shows that they have been wonderfully well cared for in every respect."[78] "I must thank you . . . for the kindness which you extended to my son when he was one of your pupils," wrote a mother from Missouri. "He has never uttered a word of complaint."[79] Others were less happy. "One of your assistants, Father Cody, frequently indulges his temper . . . If he be a priest, cannot he be made to feel the impropriety of petulance? I observe I think a growing inclination on the part of my boy to quit your College."[80] McQuaid was himself an occasional object of complaint. "Inasmuch as your course has been intemperate and discourteous since the time Francis was compelled to leave Seton Hall on account of the unusual and cruel treatment he received, I am advised that I should avail myself of all my legal rights."[81] (This was a row about money.) The demanded apology was unforthcoming.

Arguments about money were arguments about value for money. Here the story was mixed. "With respect to the food," wrote one father, "I have been informed that the children have Roast Beef every day and what is left they have it hashed the next morning. There is nothing better and no more expensive dinner than a good roast beef, but no stomach can bear every day the same thing."[82] (This parent rubbed salt in the wound by unfavorably comparing Seton Hall's food with Tufts College in Boston.)

Parents could be generous. Alfonse Bossier from Cuba offered $500 to endow an annual prize, hoping for a place at Seton Hall for his son Herman who was "unfortunately very backward in learning considering his age [nearly 18]."[83] The Bossier prize was duly established and Herman Bossier admitted to Seton Hall. The first winner of it was . . . Herman Bossier.

House-training was McQuaid's *forte*. "He is <u>very</u> wild and needs <u>strict</u> disciple," he was told of Joseph Tiers. "It would be wisest and safest to place him under you."[84] (The Tiers family sent several sons to Seton Hall over the years.) "The volatility of <u>Boy</u> nature is remarkable," wrote a mother from Cincinnati who was "surprised and mortified" at her son's delinquency. "I devoutly trust he will eventually be broken into the proper temperament."[85] Such requests arrived with calendrical regularity, receiving from McQuaid hearty agreement. "You say to me that my boys need a great deal of discipline. I know it and I beg of you . . . not to spare them."[86]

A country that had lost its own discipline, collapsing into civil war within half a decade of Seton Hall's start, made it harder for parents to exert discipline of their own. "The war came on—schools were broken up—and boys of all classes became wild— and my boy amongst others," Eugenia Bertinatti wrote from Georgetown, DC. "[My eldest nephew] is about 17 years of age but rather backward as his studies have been interrupted by the war. The younger one is more advanced and is about 13 years of age . . . I am anxious to have them at Seton Hall."[87] The college could only do so much. Children who wanted to go to war and parents who wanted to stop them were hardly what Bayley had in mind in 1856.

Disaster and Recovery

These trivialities were as nothing to the disaster that befell Seton Hall on January 27, 1866, a date that could have finished it off. Fire broke out late that night and by the time it was over the Marble Villa, and Bayley's hopes, were in ashes. This was not the college's first fire—the gymnasium burned in 1863—but it was the worst. Bayley took the news stoically: "28 January 1866. In the afternoon after my return to the [Passionist] Monastery [in Union City], Father George [Doane] came in a sleigh to tell me that the Marble House at the College was burnt last night—cost 24,000 without furniture, insured for 19,000—probable cause a lighted match being carelessly thrown down the aperture by the steam pipe. Returned home with him."[88]

Newspaper accounts were more dramatic:

The principal building of Seton Hall College was almost entirely destroyed by fire on Saturday night last . . . The whole house was heated by steam, and baked almost to a tinder, and the conflagration, therefore, once fairly started, spread with fearful rapidity to all parts of the building. The alarm created a terrible sensation among the inmates of the college, and the students, whose dormitories were in the side buildings, immediately left their beds and got to work like men, endeavoring to stay the flames and carrying out the movable property. The neighboring villagers also came to their assistance, and in a short time all the books of the college library . . .

were deposited at a safe distance from the burning building. The north wing of the college, which is within a few feet of the main building, to the north, was saved from destruction by the heroic exertions of three men, Father Cody, Mr. Durning, and Mr. Reilly, who mounted to its roof and actually standing in the flames, fought the fierce element with indomitable energy and entire success . . .

Mr. Durning, one of the instructors in the college, was a principal sufferer from the fire, receiving a number of blows from falling timbers and having one of his hands severely crushed . . . A student from Turkey named Ballidore, whose room was in the marble building, lost $200 in money and two gold watches.[89]

McQuaid's concern was to break the news to Bayley but Doane took care of that. "Father McQuaid, did they save my grandmother's blue armchair?" he asked when he arrived. Apparently they did. "That's good: we can build another college but could not replace my grandmother's armchair."[90] Things could have been worse.

Chair saved or not, McQuaid now had the troubles of the world on his shoulders: "You may imagine how shocked and distressed I was yesterday on receiving a dispatch from John saying the College had been burned down, and the boys were going home. . . . There is a College in Wilmington but I heard it was a kind of place of exile for the troublesome boys of Philadelphia. Would you advise my putting them there for the present?"[91] Even as his college lay in ruins, McQuaid had to deal with anxious parents and academically orphaned children. He could have been forgiven irritation.

Yet this was also the kind of crisis for which he was made, an opportunity to channel his massive energy to renewed purpose. Within days classes resumed with other buildings requisitioned for service. Within a week he was receiving unsolicited advice from architects.[92] Within a fortnight he was thinking about contracts for quarrymen and stone cutters.[93] Almost within hours of the disaster, an appeal was launched:

> The general cry is, "Give us something larger, grander, more suitable for College purposes." It is my intention, with God's blessing and your kind help, to do so . . .
>
> The new building will cost $50,000. My insurances amount to $19,000; there are $4,000 worth of materials on hand; Bishop Bayley will order a general collection in all the churches of the Diocese, which will amount to $10,000. The balance I must find elsewhere. I can only look to those parents who appreciate the work SETON HALL is doing for their children: to the personal friends of Bishop Bayley . . . ; and to those friends I have found in my labors in behalf of education . . . [94]

This *cri de coeur*, honest and specific, not concealing but making a virtue of the crisis, almost did the trick. Seventy-four donations of fifty dollars or more were raised.

Daniel Coghlan (on the Board of Trustees) contributed $2,000, Joseph Butler $500, Edward Robins (a banker from Philadelphia) $300.[95] Other amounts ranged from $250 to $50, $100 the most popular sum. Most donations came from parents (which spoke well of the school) or local parishes and some gifts—Joseph Butler's, for example—came from the heart.[96] Money came from California—$250 from Robert Hamilton of Sacramento—but most originated closer to home. A concert held in Delmonico's, New York in April 1866 raised $2,000, among the patrons some of "the most distinguished and aristocratic Catholics in New York."[97] "I got nearly $600 in Madison yesterday," a pastor wrote to McQuaid. "If every parish would do as well, you would have no trouble in getting fifteen thousand in the diocese."[98]

There were begrudgers. "Hudson County will do little for you," Henry Brann told McQuaid. "[Reverend John] Kelly will do next to nothing and will allow me to do nothing. So he has told me." (This was the same Father Kelly who received a rocket for poor fund-raising for the chapel.) Friendliness toward Seton Hall was thin on the ground in Jersey City, with its own schools to build and limited sympathy for subsidizing the education of the well-to-do at the expense of the poor. Brann himself gave $100: "more than personally I can afford but I give it cheerfully."[99]

These handsome sums still required the Board of Trustees in March 1867 to borrow $20,000 "to meet the demands occasioned by the erection and completion of the new building."[100] By that point, the new building was complete: twice the size of the structure it replaced and grander by far in ambition. This "Seminary Building"—now called Presidents Hall—remains the architectural centerpiece of the campus. Bayley hoped for something "plain and substantial" (to keep costs down) [101] but he got a lot more. Designed by Jeremiah O'Rourke, the building was stamped with McQuaid's taste rather than Bayley's. At first the bishop baulked at plans he claimed were poorly proportioned and McQuaid, half conceding the point, cleverly used it to his own purpose, bit by bit conspiring with O'Rourke to restore grandeur to the design. Together they pulled the wool over Bayley's eyes. O'Rourke came up with a handsome brownstone Gothic hall three stories high, 134 feet long, 50 feet deep, its finest features the hallway and central staircase, wide and airy and with rooms to right and left, sweeping the eye to the mezzanine beyond. (The cheap and rickety wooden steps leading to this entrance hall were rebuilt in stone in the 1890s.) At the top of the first flight of stairs were three stained glass windows showing the Immaculate Conception, Saint Joseph to the left, Mother Seton to the right. (The seminary was dedicated to the Immaculate Conception. Saint Joseph was an important saint in the life of the College. Mother Seton spoke for herself.) The building had fifty-four rooms in which to house and teach seminarians, to accommodate visitors, and to provide a home for successive bishops of Newark who were to live there for many years. The first floor had apartments for the bishop and the president. Priests had rooms on the second floor (where there was also a small oratory). Seminarians lived on the third floor (where there was also a classroom). The refectory was in the basement.

The new building, set aside for seminarians, freed up classroom space to be used for an enlarged enrollment of lay students in the adjacent College building. McQuaid made a point of meeting parents who visited the college, assuring them of his personal interest in their sons. In his last five or six years he had more applications than places, meaning between fifteen and thirty refusals every September. "The College is very prosperous," he told Bayley in May 1867, "having 123 at the present time . . . All is moving along very nicely." "We shall open in September with a full school."[102] The fire was the making of him, and the college.

But his presidency was coming to its close. In 1867, McQuaid took temporary charge of the diocese of Newark when Bayley went on pilgrimage to the Holy Land and Rome, this turning out to be an apprenticeship for running a diocese of his own. When the diocese of Rochester was carved out of the older diocese of Buffalo, McQuaid was appointed its first bishop. He was consecrated in New York on July 12, 1868. Bayley was reluctant to see him go but there was nothing he could do about it.[103]

McQuaid's day-to-day link with the college was thus severed, although he continued to sit on the Board of Trustees, returning frequently. In twelve years, with one interval, he had created not one Seton Hall but, in a sense, three: the first college and proto-seminary in Madison; the second foundation in South Orange in 1860–65 with new buildings to add to the property he acquired and customized; and the college's third iteration in 1867 with a new seminary building to replace the Marble Villa burned to the ground the year before. In later life he thought his services insufficiently recognized. Bishop Bayley had had them for free "and they were as much as are ordinarily done by three priests."[104] There was truth to that. A difficult man, not always easy to like, he had compensating qualities of vision, intelligence, and authority. Seton Hall was the finest achievement of the first years of his priesthood. "I kept my two eyes open," he said in old age, "and worked as he never worked since."[105] Without him there would have been no Seton Hall; none, at any rate, that would have lasted.

CHAPTER 3

The Michael Corrigan Years

A New President

McQuaid's successor was Father Michael Corrigan, who had been director of the seminary and vice president of the college since 1864. Only twenty-eight years old at the time of his appointment and hardly more senior than some of the boys, he was nevertheless an inspired choice: "a wonderful little man," Bayley described him, with "no end of work in him."[1] Corrigan was one of the most accomplished clerics of his generation, an example of the Church's knack of seizing upon talents of high order and developing them "for great usefulness."[2] His ability was a byword. "Mr. Corrigan, has, as usual, distinguished himself," Robert Seton wrote to Bayley from Rome in 1862,[3] echoing a general if not always generally welcome sentiment. One contemporary called him an "infernal prig,"[4] but even his enemies conceded his "tireless energy . . . indomitable will [and] extreme affability."[5] Corrigan's "innate talent of administration," his "gift of knowing men," his "charming blend of gentleness and strength" were notable, as was his waspish sense of humor. (Of the same Robert Seton, Corrigan once wrote that he "preached in *cappa magna* on the transitory glory of worldlings.")[6] But he was his own sharpest critic. In the seminary "he laid the deep foundations of that humility and sanctity which would serve him so well in the lofty offices which awaited him."[7] "Dr. Corrigan," Bayley said, "has learning enough for five bishops and sanctity enough for ten."[8] No-one was neutral about him.

Corrigan had cause for gratitude when he took up the presidency of Seton Hall, a college which provided him with domestic life, companionship, and a sense of purpose in the first years of his priesthood. "Seton Hall is and always has been very dear to me," he wrote in 1880. "I began to love it, I may say, even before I saw it, for when I left this country to begin my studies in Rome the ground for the college had not yet been purchased. [Even then I looked] upon it as my future home."[9] Born in Newark in 1839 of Irish parents, he was one of four brothers, of whom three became priests and the fourth a doctor. His father, Thomas, had made a fortune in the liquor business, substantial sums of it later funneled, by way of his sons, to Seton Hall. The family was respectable to a fault, laying the foundation for his lifelong social conservatism.[10]

Educated in Wilmington and Mount Saint Mary's at Emmitsburg, he completed studies for the priesthood as a member of the first class of seminarians at the North American College in Rome and was ordained at Saint John Lateran in September 1863. He finished his doctorate in Rome, "a most excellent young priest," Bayley thought, before being recalled to America in September 1864 to become professor of dogmatic theology in the seminary and vice-president of the college.[11] He arrived as a replacement for the equally clever but less reliable Henry Brann, who had begun promisingly at Seton Hall ("Dr. Brann is doing very well in the Seminary," McQuaid reported of him to Bayley)[12] but had fallen out of favor by 1865, seeming "only . . . to make trouble."[13] It was Brann himself who had pushed for him, laying "great stress on young Corrigan" coming to Seton Hall in 1863 when it was "flourishing"[14] and getting more than he bargained for when he arrived. "Rev. Mr Corrigan must come home," Bayley wrote to William McCloskey, rector of the North American College. "Our finances all going to the dogs, and the country with them for a few years at least."[15] Whether he could fix the country is doubtful: but he was expected to fix the school.

His immediate challenge was to serve as deputy to McQuaid. Newly ordained, with family money, intellectually self-sufficient, he was the kind of priest McQuaid could eat for breakfast. In fact, they got along well, not least because Corrigan knew how to defer to ecclesiastical authority and because he saw that McQuaid, with his "all-absorbing interest in the College," was not the kind of man who brooked much contradiction.[16] For his part, McQuaid recognized talent when he saw it. "Dr. Corrigan, when professor at Seton Hall, studied eight hours a day. He knew the matter of all the theologies and of Canon Law and of the Holy Scriptures . . . also the form in which to give adequate expression to his knowledge."[17] His major recommendation was that he was not Henry Brann. McQuaid was tough as nails, Corrigan epicene, but together they were formidable.

As president, Corrigan relied on McQuaid, now in Rochester, for moral support. "Be of good cheer, my dear doctor! You will begin with a fine school and I promise you with God's help, splendid success. Do not worry or be frightened at difficulties. When you cannot ride the waves let them break over you: they will do you no harm."[18] McQuaid also helped practically, sending Rochester seminarians to Seton Hall (six in 1868) to boost business. "[I am] *pro tempore* book-keeper as well as a great many other things in this establishment," Corrigan told him in 1870, one of the "great many things" that constituted a college president's life, among them the need to cultivate his predecessor and a member of the Board of Trustees.

If McQuaid was enthusiastic in 1868, he turned sour on Seton Hall (or at least its patron) in 1870. The reason was another row with Bayley about the latter's decision to deny entry to Rochester seminarians: "I know the capacity of Seton Hall, and I know that, with only a little over one hundred boys in the College, my six students might have been accommodated with ease and without injury to discipline . . . To make matters worse, your letter had scarcely reached me when I was struck dumb at hearing that Dr. Brann had been appointed to a Professorship at Troy. I don't know what to do. I fear to seem to persecute him, and yet I cannot bear the thought of having my students under his influence."[19]

Relations between Bayley and McQuaid never recovered, although McQuaid always admired Corrigan. McQuaid later founded and directed his own seminary, St. Bernard's in Rochester (in 1893) applying the lessons he had learned at Seton Hall thirty years earlier. In 1870, he was right: Seton Hall *did* enjoy "certain advantages" not found elsewhere.

Seton Hall in Plain and Hidden View

The college thus flourished under Corrigan. He enhanced its appearance and safety, building walks on the grounds, improving the gas and steam heating system, adding equipment to classrooms, carrying out repairs to the college building. He revised the curriculum in 1870, reducing the number of classes but adding more detail to remaining ones, slightly shifting the emphasis from classics to history and English. He expanded the library (helped by Bayley, who donated two hundred books and a collection of coins, and by Father Patrick Moran, who bequeathed his library and a burse of $6,000). He established prizes in philosophy, Christian doctrine, oratory, natural science, ethics, history, English, and scripture. With his brothers Father James Corrigan and Dr. Joseph Corrigan, he gave $5,000 to the college to tide things over when money was tight.[20] Bayley got a good return on his investment when he appointed him.

But Seton Hall operated very close to the margins in its early decades. After the fire, McQuaid had to argue to keep it open, later remarking that "when the proposition [to close] was made informally to me . . . I laughed at it. I had labored and made great sacrifices to build up a great diocesan institution, never dreaming that so many children of the household [i.e., Father Doane and friends] stood ready to tear it down."[21] The speed with which fund-raising was started quashed further talk of selling but the fire could easily have finished it.

What was speculative in 1866 became a matter for formal discussion five years later. In 1870 and 1871, both college and diocesan finances were in a dreadful state, prompting panic. Seeing rising property prices in South Orange, Bayley sought a buyer—any buyer—for the school: a religious order to keep it open or an individual who, if he wanted, could tear it down. The most likely purchasers were the Christian Brothers of Manhattan College. Corrigan wrote to Orestes Brownson, telling him that the Board of Trustees would meet on April 18, 1871, "to consider the question of continuing the College as at present or of passing it over to a Religious Corporation, viz., the Christian Brothers. You will understand that the importance of the interests involved requires absolute secrecy in the matter at present . . ." The case for selling was again made by Doane speaking on behalf of Bayley but, as before, his "argument in favor of discontinuing Seton Hall was so flimsy that no-one took the slightest heed of it."[22] Corrigan wrote to Brownson as soon as the meeting adjourned: "Only one person was in favor of making over the College to the Brothers; the nine other members of the Board who were present were strongly opposed to the plan proposed by the bishop. I presume, then, that we may consider the question as settled." He added a caution: "As the College is to continue under the present administration, it becomes more necessary than ever to keep secret the matter of the proposed sale, and to keep out of sight all signs of distress."[23]

A fortnight later, Father William McNulty, lately a professor at the college, wrote carpingly to McQuaid about Bayley's stewardship of the diocese. McNulty was a critic of Seton Hall (he thought it diverted money from parochial schools) but an even sharper one of Bayley, who was ready to sell the college "for one half its value—as you justly state" and with "no council . . . asked."[24] But if Seton Hall were so valuable, why sell it? The answer is that it was more attractive as land than as a school and could be liquidated to pay diocesan debts. Either Bayley was prepared to sell it too cheaply or the Christian Brothers were unwilling to buy it so expensively (it being still loss-making as a school). Whatever the reason, the episode became unmentionable in institutional memory, indeed almost eradicated from memory itself. Writing to Winand Wigger in 1882, Father James Corrigan advised him to "read over the minutes of the Board from its beginning." The record was complete, he said, except for "a part unrecorded at the request of Archbishop Bayley, and that is the meeting which related to the proposed sale of Seton Hall in 1870 and 1871."[25] No-one was to know that Seton Hall almost foundered because of the founder.

Bayley was too anxious to be rid of the college at a bargain basement price but it *did* constitute a drain on diocesan resources. When sale to the Christian Brothers was mooted, it had debts of $125,000 (offset by assets of around $263,000). Selling it would not have been unreasonable. At issue was the price, not the principle. Its debt was only manageable because the Corrigan family promised their own capital to support it. Without that guarantee, it might have closed. Those who wished to keep it open—Corrigan, McQuaid, and others—had only Seton Hall to think of. Bayley also had to think of the rest of the diocese. His desire to liquidate the asset should be seen in that context.

Even if the college stayed open, what was its relationship with the seminary? They shared a site, many of the same faculty, and were both under the direction of the Bishop of Newark, but were separate institutions serving distinct purposes. It did not follow that if the college were to remain in South Orange, the seminary should remain there also. "What may suit the education of youths destined for worldly pursuits," Father James Corrigan wrote to Bayley in October 1870, "may not be in harmony with what is required for those destined for the priesthood." Fearing the seminary could move to Newark, Corrigan made no attempt to disguise his preference for South Orange, which was healthy, spacious, had a suitable chapel, and was "sufficiently out of the way of public thoroughfares to preclude too much visiting from outsiders." Seminarians should be "free from outside nonsense" and seclusion would be good for professors too. In South Orange, they were unlikely to be interrupted by visitors and "consequently [would] have more time to prepare the lessons for their classes. If they do go out sometimes it is only at night and into the very best society." Newark was not a European city, Corrigan warned, "where seminarians can go out without danger of being insulted and stared to death." On the contrary, the "multitude of occasions [for] visiting, drinking etc which seminarians, precisely because being seminarians oftentimes easily fall into" ruled it out as a suitable location. "The professors would more or less frequently visit their friends at all hours throughout the day as well as in the night," he told Bayley, "and you will readily admit that the Newark Catholic society is not the most refined; hence the professors might sometimes come home in a state not over-edifying to the seminarians."[26] (Seton Hall was not unique in this respect. At Amherst College, Bayley's *alma mater*, the faculty worried about students frequenting groceries, taverns, and places "where the grossest dissipation may be indulged undiscovered.")[27] So the seminary stayed in South Orange, thanks to the anti-liquor arguments of the son of one of Newark's wealthiest liquor merchants.

Bayley played a poor part in the near-sale of Seton Hall in 1871 but he also rescued it from legal and fiscal jeopardy. The college had been granted tax-free status by the New Jersey legislature, a privilege resented by some tax-averse Protestants. The case against immunity was summarized by a correspondent of the *Newark Daily Advertiser*: "All the property of the institution including houses and lots in South Orange and lands on Orange Mountain, totally escape taxation, greatly to the prejudice of tax-payers generally. Were the college authorities to purchase the entire village and thousands of rich and fertile lands, not a penny could be assessed or collected . . ." The argument was answered by Bayley in the same paper: "The 'Houses and Lots' in South Orange . . . consist of a small piece of unimproved land which was purchased for a 'sandpit' and cost $800. The 'lands' on the Orange mountains cost $150 and were bought for the stone on them . . ."[28] The case against Seton Hall, Bayley insisted, was a threat to "all other similar institutions in the State" (such as the Drew Methodist seminary in Madison). The immunity remained but the episode was a reminder that local support for Catholic education could not be taken for granted.

Decades later, this argument came back to haunt Seton Hall in a famous legal case. But that was for the future.

Day to Day Seton Hall

Moments of near-death excepted, Seton Hall was reassuringly dull. It was a college, Michael Corrigan wrote to Orestes Brownson in September 1871, where "our students are now all at work and settling down for the year." The students were ignorant of its brushes with death, although not of death itself. (A popular young professor, Joseph Keany, "highly esteemed for his abilities as a teacher," was killed in a railway accident in September 1870.)[29] Corrigan's letter to Brownson, trying to persuade him to give a series of lectures, painted a modest picture: "As to the question of a house, the rents are very high in South Orange. I have heard of one or two places that are less objectionable in this regard. One is a cottage quite near the College, the rent of which would be three hundred dollars a year—but the house is rather small. Now as to the lectures, we are ready for you at any time. I enclose a time-table of trains from Newark to South Orange. The walk from the station is a long one and the road is miserable . . ."[30]

Brownson, a tough-minded spiritual wanderer,[31] had a high opinion of Seton Hall (as compared to Fordham).[32] It appealed to him because it was diocesan and rigorous and, for those reasons, he was prepared to overlook its ethnic origins. "I do not like in general our Irish population," he once complained. "They have no clear understanding of their religion."[33]

That he liked Seton Hall is not to immunize it from criticism. Brownson had astute things to say about Catholic schools, Seton Hall among them, in which moral formation turned easily to institutionalized brutality. Colleges conducting education "from its rudiments to the immediate preparation for . . . the learned professions" had to show "much more assiduous care" for those of "tender age." Corrigan had to raise children as well as teach them, bringing them from kindergarten to college and seminary. Younger students were left in the hands of prefects while priests and professors got on with teaching older boys and young men. Those who would rather have been in a parish thought of it as a quasimonastic Gothic prison: every day, week, month, and year regulated, every meal eaten in the same company, every fault magnified by familiarity. One or two may have gone quietly mad without anyone, even themselves, really noticing.

Brownson had another connection with the college in the form of his occasional correspondent, William Seton, Elizabeth Ann Seton's grandson. Novelist, traveler, and eccentric, Seton was spectacularly immune to the family's pious streak. Seeing the church as social comedy, he had no shortage of material at Seton Hall. "I hope my brother Robert comes to see you now and then," he wrote to Brownson in 1872, referring to Robert Seton, the first American priest to be made a Monsignor. "He is still like Old Mortality sitting on the tombstone playing with the moss and ivy. So are Bishop Bayley and Father Doane and all the rest of them. Verily must the Catholic Church be the true Church to be able to float with such a cargo."[34] Robert Seton exercised his own brand of *hauteur* on the college before decamping for Rome.

As president, Corrigan was able to persuade other notable Catholics to come to the college, among them Colonel James Maline, a civil war veteran and controversialist, who gave a series of lectures in 1872[35] and whose attacks on the English historian James Anthony Froude made his name in the Catholic world.[36] Another visitor was Cardinal McCloskey of New York, who recovered from serious illness there in 1876 and summered at the college in 1877. He was treated like royalty.

Student organizations prospered, notably the Bayley Literary Society, the Setonian Library Association, the Reading Room Society, the Setonian Brass Band and Vocal Chorus. The literary and library clubs were debating societies whose better speakers were dragooned into service during commencement. Of Corrigan's first commencement as president, the *Newark Daily Journal* noticed that "the specimens of oratory, three in number, were of *very* unequal degrees of merit: 'The Moral Influence of the Beautiful' was . . . beyond the culture of a very young college student; 'The Fables of History' would have been more highly appreciated had the delivery been better;" but both were redeemed by the "very fine" oration of C.H. Tiers, a "thoroughly educated graduate of a Catholic college." The brass band and chorus were trundled out on formal occasions when the solemnity of the event depended precariously on the competence of the performers. They seem to have done well enough.

Seton Hall's fourteenth graduation saw McQuaid return from Rochester to hand the baton to his successor. Speaking on the college's successes and failures, he blamed the latter on parents who should have kept their sons at school longer. But not even finger-wagging could darken a bright day: "Situated amid woods and fields of rare beauty, Seton Hall, now much enlarged, with the beautiful Gothic church hard by, presents a most picturesque appearance. Under the gentle but firm and able management of Dr. Corrigan we augur for it a steady continuance of the success which has hitherto marked its progress."[37]

When the crowds departed, Corrigan's biggest anxiety was money. Every day was an unequal struggle to ensure that more cash flowed in than flowed out. "We are very hard pressed this month to meet our indebtedness," wrote J. and R. Lamb, Church Furnishers of New York, in January 1871. "Will it be possible to let us have the balance of [our] account?"[38] (Fitting out the chapel was costing a fortune.) "Your account with us is now $315.23," wrote William F. Bailey and Company the same month.[39] "We do not desire to push you to hand, but think that you have had sufficient time on it, having run since August 1870 and the $100 you sent did not pay up the account to November." "The Gas Bill for Seton Hall College due January 10 has not been attended to," wrote the Orange Gas Company in February 1870. "Will you please remit the same at an early date as convenient for you: amount $588."[40] "Don't be too ready to spend money,"

McQuaid advised him. "Much as you need a sacristy, the money will be more useful in paying debts."[41] The chapel did without its sacristy for another generation.

In matters of debt, Corrigan was more victim than villain. "I am obliged to write asking your kind indulgence in the matter of Bernard's half yearly tuition," wrote a parent in 1872. "I am sorry to say I cannot meet [it] at present owing to the fact of my being out of work for the greater part of the winter."[42] "Please excuse me for not having sent you said bill before," explained another parent, "but the sugar market was so low that it may not be profitable to sell the crops."[43] The "property out of which [I] expected to be paid was not resold owing to the difficulties in Europe," a third parent wrote. "I am very sorry you are 'short' but that is so common at present that you would be an exception to the general rule were you free from it."[44] "Rest assured, dear Sir, that I have not forgotten my debt," explained a parent from Connecticut, "which may be discharged very soon if I have the good fortune to dispose of a Double Action precise Gothic Erana Harp . . . Perhaps your professor of music might find a purchaser for the same in which case I will allow him 10% commission."[45]

With hard times came haggling. A Mrs. Quinlan of Chicago bristled at "forty-three dollars for one month's board" for her son John. "Ten dollars per week would be considered an exhorbitant [sic] price . . . even in a first-class boarding house . . ."[46] The recently ordained Father Pierce McCarthy thought his final seminary bill was $100 more than it ought to have been.[47] "Your college won't get rich if you let bills stand so long before rendering them," one parent wrote. "I was not aware that anything was due."[48] Seton Hall accountancy could be slapdash.

Corrigan's faculty varied from the impressive to the improbable. In the first category was Sebastian Smith, D.D., who taught canon law in the seminary from 1868 to 1871. An alumnus of Seton Hall and the Pontifical North American College in Rome, Smith authored several best-selling books on ecclesiastical procedure (which came in handy during later spats with church authorities). He was an "able, chaste, and graceful writer" with "the promise of long years before him."[49] When he died, he left an estate estimated at between $50,000 and $75,000, very little of it accumulated from a Seton Hall salary.[50] Bombarded with applications, Corrigan came to know the desperate world of down-at-heel academics. From Elmira, New York came the offer to "teach any Latin class you would wish to give me, Mathematics or Greek . . . Please let me know what you can do for me."[51] From McAfee, Kentucky came the request "to be kept in remembrance . . . in regard to a situation as Professor of Mathematics."[52] From Dubuque, Iowa a dismissed seminarian called Corrigan, claiming to be a relation, and hoped "you will receive me into your diocese or at least give me some employment as a teacher in your college."[53] From New York, a graduate of the minuscule Catholic University of Ireland offered to "teach logic, metaphysics [and] classics." (His publications included a "History of the Catholic Church on Tory Island," a windswept speck off the Donegal coast with a population under a thousand.) From Middlebury, Vermont P. F. Burke was so anxious to teach anything that he offered to teach everything: "English, Philosophy, Rhetoric, the use of Globes, the Higher Mathematics, the Classics, etc."[54] A Mr. Maguire of Maynooth failed to get a job in 1868 because "it would be unfortunate to commence school with boyish prejudices of nationality against us."[55] (That also ruled out Martin O'Brennan, who offered to teach Irish, a subject for which there was zero demand in South Orange.)[56] A distinguished German grammarian, Caspar J. Beleke, was down on his luck when he wrote to Seton Hall. "Here I am in my old days, without a home, without money, without clothes, without a single book, without my manuscripts, without a position, a wanderer, a beggar."[57] A pedantic crank, forever telling students to "stick to de text," he gave the occasional lecture and then disappeared.[58]

Being in Corrigan's good books meant the difference between having a job or not, between a pleasant term or not, between living in decent digs or a hovel. "I see in the catalogue that we are to have English history next year," wrote N.J. O'Connell Ffrench during the summer vacation of 1872. "I will prepare some lectures." (O'Connell Ffrench was a professor of history and English literature.)[59] "Can I have either Mr. Hyde's or Mr. O'Reilly's room next year? I would prefer Mr. Hyde's. The extreme cold of the other room is I fear injurious to my sight."[60]

Would-be teachers came from all over the place. So did students. Many of the intake continued to be Cuban or Latin American, the well-to-do children of the English- or Spanish-speaking upper classes who wanted to board their children in the United States. Others came from California, the Carolinas, Kentucky, Louisiana, New England, and the Midwest. The majority were local or regional boys. For all of them, the college was part monastery, part finishing school, part boot camp. "The fact is, Willie is not a voluntary scholar," one parent told Corrigan. "I send him to school merely to keep him out of mischief." Parents had wide discretion in their children's schooling (or so they thought). "I find John is quite deficient in Arithmetic, Grammar and Spelling," complained one. "Knowing as I do the want of these branches in after life, I am most anxious that he be thorough in them, including grammar."[61] "Doctor," wrote another, "you would very much oblige me by having them speak pieces and be able to address an audience which would be very necessary for them thereafter."[62] "My boy started for Seton Hall last Saturday," wrote a third. "He has not time, neither do I think he has the requisite amount of application, to acquire a regular course. Therefore, I wish him to apply himself wholly to a good and thorough English education, principally to Mathematics, Chemistry, and Philosophy. I should like him to become a Civil Engineer or Architect."[63] One or two parents seemed surprised to discover that the college was Catholic. A father from Pennsylvania, noticing astronomy books in the library, warned against theology in the curriculum. "Had it not been for science, metaphy-sicians would probably have continued to burn witches to the present day . . . Such myths are not adapted to the American mind . . ."[64]

Hispanic parents worried about New Jersey winters—"in his letters he complains of suffering much from cold"[65]—or Latin American summers—"Manuel should not take any heavy clothing [home] with him since it would be of no use to him in Cuba."[66] Irish pupils had different priorities: "Thomas [requests permission] to come home on Saint Patrick's Day . . . Doctor, I do not wish them to come home now or any other time."[67] Most parents were interested in living conditions. "Please let him have a room by himself," ran one note. "He is much too much of a man to sleep in a dormitory with a lot of boys."[68] It was not easy "for two young men alone in one room not to interrupt each other in his studies, to which should be devoted all the time assigned to them."[69] A father demanded for his son "all the pure air day and night that he can possibly get . . . and two persons sleeping in such a small room would certainly be injurious to his health."[70] In winter, Seton Hall had all the fresh air anyone could have wished for.

Whatever the season, it was not a school for the squeamish: "The first time I was at the college, I went to my room to go to bed, and upon turning down the clothes I saw some cockroaches and spiders run from under them, but thinking I could stand them for one night, I went to bed, and hardly closed my eyes from the trouble occasioned by the aforesaid bugs."[71]

Corrigan accumulated enough sick notes to paper a generously proportioned sani-tarium, the complaints ranging from bronchitis to poor eyesight to indigestion. The wheeziness may have been due to Spanish sensitivity to New Jersey winters. Myopia put parents in the odd position of paying for a son's education and hoping he would do as little reading as possible. (The solution of spectacles did not seem to occur to them.) "My son Walter complains of the injurious effects of gaslight in his room and says one of the students has a separate room . . . in which some attachment to the gas fixture makes the light in that room much better and pleasanter to study by."[72] Dietary dif-ficulties were disguised demands for a better menu. "Victor's digestive organs are in a state of derangement," wrote a father from Pennsylvania. "He becomes feverish in the afternoon."[73] "My boy is not well," wrote another from New York. "He must have good plain substantial food . . . Meat so as to have plenty of nourishing elements left, with blood."[74] Here was Corrigan as head waiter, pencil at the ready. But some prob-lems were beyond him. "I learn by inquiry that there is no privacy for a boy of costive habit who may wish to use a cold-water syringe. Consequently he may go three or four days without an evacuation."[75] And what to do when a boy had to be excused lessons "owing to neuralgia caused by friction from an artificial eye too old for use"?[76]

For fit and unfit, teachers as well as students, Seton Hall was tough. Parents saying goodbye to children in September were alarmed when they returned in June. "Don't push him either in his studies or getting out of bed early. He is a mere skeleton, only skin and bones. I was surprised at this when [he was] here a few days ago."[77] "We are pained to observe a great change in his physical health," wrote a father from Pennsylvania. "He is thin and complains of continual sore throat and pains in the chest. Had you not noticed anything of the kind in his general appearance?"[78] If Corrigan had not noticed, it was because almost *every* parent or professor seemed to demand special treatment. Being a college president could be a dog's life. He was unusually suited to it.

CHAPTER 4

Another Corrigan, Another Fire

Three Characters

When on best behavior for commencements, solemn masses, and holy days, Seton Hall was a formidable place. Listen to *The New York Times* of June 21, 1872:

> The annual Commencement of Seton Hall College, South Orange, N.J., was held yesterday in a large tent adjoining the institute.
>
> A large number of the clergymen of the diocese occupied seats on the platform with the graduating classes, Faculty and officers of the College and seminary. The following were among the number, viz: Right Reverend James Roosevelt Bayley, of the Diocese of Newark; Right Reverend Bishop McQuaid, of the Diocese of Rochester; Right Reverend Bishop McFarland, of the Diocese of Hartford; Very Reverend George H. Doane. The Faculty of the Ecclesiastical Seminary, viz: Very Reverend M.A. Corrigan, D.D., V.G., President; Rev. J.H. Corrigan, Vice-President; Rev. Louis Schneider, D.D.; Rev. Father Messmer and Rev. William Salt. The following were the orators of the day: Mr. Jos. Tiers, of Philadelphia, on the "Development of Nations;" Mr. J. Carruanna on "Fascinating Tendencies;" Mr. Robert Emmet Burke, on "The Life, Character, Energies and Piety of Cardinal Ximenes of Spain;" Mr. Patrick McCabe, on "Political Depravity," an essay on the present aspect of national ideas and tendencies; Mr. John Sheppard, on "The Glad Tidings of Joy" . . . Degrees were conferred . . .

There was less to these "degrees conferred" than met the eye. Getting an MA required little more than writing a begging letter to the president, a practice about which Corrigan (who received all kinds of requests in the course of a year) rightly had qualms. Still, the college had earned the right to be taken seriously, boasting prelates, priests, a new seminary, a chapel, and lovely grounds. It had come through local opposition, a Civil War, a fire, and two proposed sales. Among its graduates was Joseph Flynn (future priest and author of the *History of the Catholic Church in New Jersey*) who had seen active service with Company B, 37th New Jersey Volunteers at the Siege of Petersburg in June 1864.[1] On the platform was Father William Salt, also a Civil War veteran (on the Confederate side). The faculty and graduates were survivors. So was the college.

Seton Hall remained a commercial enterprise and, in some ways, a precarious one. A month before, Bayley had sent Corrigan a check for $2,000 "with which I trust you will be able to get around the corner . . . if I can back some of my loans I will let you have more."[2] Too much grandiosity could price the school out of the market. "I was out at your College on Tuesday with the intention of sending my boy to your college," a parent wrote to Corrigan in September 1871, "but as I am not very wealthy and of small means I cannot afford to pay so much." All the same, "I was satisfied for my journey on seeing such a grand institution and if I could afford to pay your price I would not hesitate one moment. . . . It's little the people of New York know of such a grand college so near New York."[3] (Corrigan knew an appeal for reduced rates when he saw one.) "Seton Hall College, South Orange—Health, Comfortable, Modern," ran a notice in the *New Ulm Weekly Review* in Minnesota, one of many papers across the country in which the college advertised. (Above and below were two other ads which put it in commercial context: "Guns. Revolvers. Price List Free. Address Great Gun Works, Pittsburg, PA"; "12 sewing machine needles for any machine sent by mail for 35 cents.")[4]

June 25, 1873 saw the seventeenth commencement, "a delightful day," Corrigan thought, with a "fresh breeze [and] green grass after heavy rains," everything "pass[ing] off capitally."[5] Newark now had a college and seminary whose purpose (among other things) was to allow the bishop to show off. "Building is heated by steam, lighted by Gas, and thoroughly ventilated . . . Discipline strict, kind and gentle, with refinements of home."[6] Seton Hall was a kind of diocesan front parlor into which guests could be ushered and entertained, a local church dressing up. A delegation from Rome in May 1873 enjoyed "festivities at the College, which . . . were by far the pleasantest" Corrigan could ever recall.[7] And being "well ventilated" meant it was salubrious. Among competitor institutions were Mount Saint Mary's, Emmitsburg ("far removed from all malarial influences . . . renowned for the health, happiness and studious habits of its students"), Villanova College ("lofty and beautiful"), and Saint John's College, Fordham ("spacious and thoroughly ventilated").[8] Fresh air was the 11th commandment in most boarding schools.

To critics, there were too many such schools. "In the State of New York alone there are seven [Catholic colleges or universities]," wrote one. "Two of these are in New York City and two in Brooklyn. Then there is another at South Orange, in New Jersey, making five Catholic colleges in one neighborhood. Not one of these institutions has ever been so overcrowded as to render the others necessary, and yet they were established." This was untrue—Bayley regularly refused seminarians for lack of space or money— but the complaint was plausible: "Do the Jesuits distrust the Christian Brothers? If the Congregation of the Mission found a college, must the Benedictines have one too?

Surely, such a rivalry as this is not the best thing for the advancement of learning."[9] Seton Hall met educational needs but its additional value as status symbol is undeniable. One reason for not selling it to the Christian Brothers in 1871 was loss of face.

That America had too many Catholic colleges was another way of saying that some of them were not very good. They did one thing well—"teaching students to teach and speak the Latin language"—but otherwise critics refused to be impressed:

> In scientific studies, however, the Catholic colleges are inexcusably weak . . . The work of instruction is carried on by priests, whose knowledge of science is almost certainly meager and one sided. . . . At Seton Hall College, where the teaching force numbers sixteen, a single professor has to cope with mathematics and natural science. In Manhattan College, near New York, there are three men to teach Latin and Greek, and but one to deal with all the natural sciences. . . . But these examples are feeble compared with one offered by St. Vincent's College, in Pennsylvania. In this home of learning a single unfortunate man has to carry the title of "professor of logic, metaphysics, mathematics, astronomy, natural philosophy, and chemistry!" Why didn't they call him professor of polyology, and have done with it?[10]

This was to find fault with schools not being the Institutes of Technology they never claimed to be. Seton Hall had problems, but it was no worse than other colleges and in some respects it was markedly better.

Consider for example its national and international reputation. *Le Progres de Catholicisme Parmi Les Peuples D'Origine Anglo-Saxonne Depuis L'Année 1857* (published in Louvain in 1878) offered Seton Hall as proof of the advance of the Church in the United States (although crediting its foundation to Jesuits).[11] Of 152 students in 1873, fifty came from New Jersey, the rest from Spain (seven), the Yucatan Peninsula (five), Colombia (two), Cuba (three), Florida, Illinois, Kentucky, Louisiana, Ohio, Vermont, and Wisconsin. By any standards this was impressive.[12]

It was also acquiring institutional memory. "Saint Joseph's Day was celebrated as usual at the College," Corrigan wrote in his journal for March 19, 1874, the "as usual" conveying an invented tradition taking root.[13] The feast was the biggest day of the year, with classes cancelled, a High Mass, and, after 1871, a "Junior Night" in which, Corrigan's editors report, without apparent irony, "members of the . . . class demonstrated their musical, dramatic, and oratorical skills for the entertainment of the community."[14]

College characters reinforced the sense of community. Despite low salaries and difficult work, the lay faculty was solid: "Mr. William Joseph Philipps . . . professor of English literature at Seton Hall College, New Jersey, will deliver his interesting lecture on 'The Model Wife' under the auspices of the Young Catholics' Friends society, at

Tallmadge Hall on next Sunday evening. Professor Phillips is reported an excellent lecturer, a truly eloquent speaker, and a scholarly gentleman."[15]

The clerical faculty had eccentrics. Monsignor Robert Seton, cousin of Bishop Bayley, grandson of Elizabeth Ann Seton, was the subject of a vignette by another cousin, the novelist William Seton. Born in 1839 in Italy and educated at Emmitsburg and the North American College in Rome, Seton was ordained in 1865. Between 1867 and 1876, he lectured exactingly at Seton Hall. Expert in archaeology, theology, and canon law, he could bore people in Greek, Latin, Hebrew, Italian, French, Spanish, and German. Seton added *brio*, but his main function was to provide stories to be told behind his back. Corrigan thought him "odd" but "[he] knows how to maintain his dignity on occasion."[16] In 1888 Winand Wigger (by now Bishop of Newark) advised him "not to continue to speak out against the priests that come out from Seton Hall . . . Many priests of the diocese are beginning to inquire if Dr. Seton, after all, is so very perfect. . . ."[17] Seton demurred, claiming have been "grossly insulted at my own table by assistants from Seton Hall" but promising not to insult them in front of New York priests.[18] He was a reactionary figure of fun, the "anti-kissing pastor" of Jersey City,[19] who could be charming, witty, and, on his day, good company. The trick was to find the day.

Swiss-born Father Sebastian Messmer, professor of scripture, canon law, and moral and dogmatic theology, was educated at Innsbruck and captured for Newark by Father George Doane, who met him at the Oberammergau Passion Play. Messmer came to Seton Hall with two disadvantages (a heavy accent and unusual English) but also serious credentials as a scholar, gentleness, patience, and humility. In the classroom, he was soft, outside it an archconservative.[20] In 1888 he was appointed to the chair of Canon Law at the recently formed Catholic University of America, by which stage he had been at Seton Hall for eighteen years. Messmer was its best scholar, "a prodigy of learning and of industry."[21] Later, as fourth archbishop of Milwaukee, he played a vital role in "Americanizing" the archdiocese.[22]

Seton was a snob, Messmer almost a saint. Father William Salt was a star. No-one better personified the multifariousness of Newark in the second half of the nineteenth century. Born in Brooklyn of Baptist parents, Salt had been at various times a carpenter, Episcopalian seminarian, confederate soldier, Episcopalian deacon, Catholic convert, Seton Hall student, seminarian at the North American College in Rome, and volunteer member of the papal army.[23] Ordained in 1871, he was appointed to Seton Hall. Having been in uniform for Jefferson Davis and Pius IX—a rare double—he made the most of the anticlimax of being a college teacher, turning his hand to ecclesiastical history, political economy, civil polity, Christian evidences, mathematics, physics, and chemistry,[24] also serving as college treasurer. To students, Salt was frightening. To colleagues, he was hard to know. To Corrigan, he had "solid common sense and unaffected piety," a person to whom he would "rather entrust the management of diocesan affairs . . . than to any other priest now residing in New Jersey."[25] Salt never became a bishop but spent his priesthood in the relative obscurity of Seton Hall, dying suddenly of a hemorrhage in October 1890 as he was walking to breakfast. Seventy priests attended the funeral in the college chapel as did, poignantly, his parents.

A Bishop Briefly at the Helm

In February 1873, with Bayley now Archbishop of Baltimore, Corrigan was named Bishop of Newark. He continued to serve (increasingly nominally) as president for another four years and lived at Seton Hall after relinquishing the reins to his brother, James. "I will be glad to see you," he wrote to a former student in 1876. "It is so quiet here at times and so lonely that it is a relief to have a friend look in on us."[26] Enrollment reached 162 in 1874. Morale was high, finances secure, the curriculum in place, the alumni loyal, the staff more or less well behaved. Bayley died in St. Patrick's Pro-Cathedral Rectory in Newark in October 1877. He returned to South Orange as often as possible, much preferring it to Baltimore. His contribution to the church in New Jersey and the United States had been enormous.

Simultaneously running a diocese and directing a college was too much even for Michael Corrigan, who relied on his brother James to see to Seton Hall. He formalized the arrangement in June 1876 by resigning in his favor.[27] James Corrigan, although not as brilliant, was capable in his own right. Born in Newark in 1844 and educated at Emmitsburg, he trained in Rome and was ordained at Seton Hall in October 1867, serving as professor and director of the seminary before becoming vice-president and, at 32, president.

An alumni association was another sign of coming of age. The idea was mooted as early as 1871,[28] but nothing much happened until the late 1870s.[29] Only three people turned up for the inaugural meeting in June 1879. A formal dinner at Pinard's in New York in February 1881 was more successful, with sixty "active" and nearly fifty "associate" members in attendance. (Active members held a diploma or degree from Seton Hall. Associate members had attended the school for two years.) With a sprinkling of lawyers, businessmen, and priests representing eleven graduation classes, the 1881 dinner was a social and financial success, bringing enough funds to think of constructing Alumni Hall, the next building to appear on the campus (and still one of the best). Bishops Corrigan and Wigger each gave $500, as did Father James Corrigan and Eugene Kelly, the latter one of the wealthiest Catholics in New York, whose estate in South Orange abutted Seton Hall. Enough had been raised by July 1883 (a total of $5,695) to enable groundbreaking.[30] The cornerstone was laid on October 25, 1883 and the building opened on November 5, 1884. A two-story stone structure in plain gothic, seventy feet long, sixty feet high, forty feet wide, an attractive companion piece to the larger chapel to the west and the college building to the east, it allowed Seton Hall to expand, giving it a cultural as well as physical spaciousness. The lower level housed a library and recreation room for theological students.[31] The upper level was a gymnasium and concert room. Setting it off was a piazza between the college building, the chapel, and the hall.[32] (The library was mostly made up of volumes brought from Europe by Bayley on his many trips there.) Total cost was slightly over $15,000, of which just under $10,000 was contributed by alumni and other supporters. "For me, personally, every stone in the new structure is, and will be, eloquent," said James Corrigan.[33]

Generosity aside, it was Corrigan's misfortune to take charge of the college during economic difficulties. "The times are just terrible," a parent had written to Michael Corrigan, "and fathers are unable to send their sons to College." Within a year of his becoming president, the economy was in the grip of recession "I hope Father James has the courage to meet the matter fairly and squarely and try to keep the outlay in some relation to the income."[34] His solution was to reduce fees by $80 per year to keep the college competitive. "The tone and character of Seton Hall will remain unchanged," he explained to parents. "There will be the same staff of Professors, the same table, and the same attention to the health and progress of the students."[35] (The "same table" was nothing to boast about). The salaries of clerical faculty were reduced by 50 percent, Corrigan taking his cut with the rest.[36]

These economies brought relief but no long-term solution. "Heavy losses at the College, debts increasing," Bishop Corrigan wrote to McQuaid in 1878. "All these matters *entre nous*. But they worry F. Doane and myself immensely."[37] (Doane feared that "any unpleasant news brings on an attack of sickness.")[38] The retrenchment began a period of prolonged difficulty and deeper reflection on the nature of the entire enterprise. Seton Hall wanted to prosper but the first goal was to survive. Heavily mortgaged, at the mercy of rising interest rates and falling demand, a missed payment to it or by it could be fatal. The seminary was indebted to the college and to the diocese. The seminary relied on the college for staff and students. The assets of one were in effect the assets of the other. In good times, no-one cared that the college seemed to exist academically and financially to make the work of the seminary possible, but in bad times what exactly was the point of Seton Hall? To educate priests? To train laymen? To turn a profit? It was not clear.

Thanks to Michael Corrigan, a brilliant financial manager, between 1868 and 1877 the college's mortgage was reduced from $75,000 at 7 percent to $60,000 at 5 percent, easing pressure while never allowing the school entirely to escape debt. (A debt-free life was for the birds anyway.) Interest on the original mortgage, $75,000 from 1868 to 1880, came to almost $60,000. As James Corrigan put it, a sum "sufficient to erect a handsome building was paid for what was practically the mere rental of Seton Hall for these years."[39] Corrigan accepted students prepared to pay the fees. When the bailiffs beckoned, academic nicety went out the window.

It was little consolation that other colleges were also in difficulties. Mount Saint Mary's in Emmitsburg was in worse shape: "the debt is said to be fully $100,000," Michael Corrigan told McQuaid, "of which about $60,000 must be floating!"[40] "All this makes me reflect on the expediency of active measures for reducing the indebtedness of Seton Hall," Corrigan thought. "After the new Bishop comes, I hope something may be done."[41] The "new bishop" was his as yet unknown replacement as Bishop of Newark, Corrigan having been appointed coadjutor Archbishop of New York in 1880. In the event, he was succeeded by Winand Wigger in 1881, a "faithful, systematic, conscientious, [and] hard-working [man but also] somewhat lacking in courage and not sufficiently expansive to be generally acceptable."[42] It was an odd choice, Wigger neither strong enough physically or temperamentally for the job. On the other hand, he knew Seton Hall from the inside and was aware that it needed reform. He also knew, as James Corrigan reported to him in May 1882, that the cost of the seminary bore no relation to revenue: "For a short time the annual charge for a Seminarian was $250; but in 1879 it was reduced to $200—a charge that does not cover the cost of board and maintenance here. In addition to this, large deductions are allowed for ecclesiastical students in the College Department. Since my appointment to the Presidency in 1877 to the end of the present session, these deductions amount to $6,890, while during this time four ecclesiastical students, each for one year, were kept gratis. Their places filled by lay Collegians would have brought in $1,400." Then there were special privileges: "The Seminarians have better accommodations, and a somewhat better table; whereas the salaries of the Theological Professors, the wages of servants attending the seminarians' rooms and clothes, the furnishing of their rooms, together with heat and light, are paid out of College revenues. But while the College contributes largely to the Seminary's support, it carries, at the same time, a debt that is oppressive. . . . The thought of [this arrangement] continuing from year to year," Corrigan concluded, was "disheartening."[43]

One solution would have been to raise income, another to lower expenditure, a third to admit day pupils to increase revenues "without adding any new expenditure."[44] (This would have changed the character of the school and there were not enough pupils to make it feasible.) The fourth solution would have been to close down the college. To Corrigan, the seminary was supported by the college and not, as he thought it should have been, by the diocese. Common sense argued for some sort of separation. As for expenditure, that had already been pared to the bone: "The Teachers' salaries are about as low as they can be, and we could not manage with fewer teachers. The table and the service required for keeping everything neat and in good order are expensive. The farm this year will be a source of loss, as the dry weather and the burning of the stables last year did extensive damage; but the farm has been in some years a source of profit."[45]

Michael Corrigan had never taken a salary as president and James Corrigan, by teaching as well as performing administrative duties, saved $1,000 a year of a layman's salary. When all was said and done, Seton Hall, if not "in a bankrupt state and going a begging," hovered close to it. "We have taken things as we found them," James Corrigan wrote to Wigger, "and have tried to make the most of them in our fulfillment of duty . . . There has been an improvement in every department, so that the Seton Hall of today is unlike the Seton Hall of old."[46] But this could only be maintained if the college were allowed to flourish on its own. Corrigan thought the academic connection between seminary and college was mutually advantageous. He was not a "separatist": he simply wanted more support from the diocese for its seminary.

Wigger had the more radical idea of getting rid of the school entirely. Seton Hall was, in James Corrigan's words, "[un]popular [with many local priests] and [un]fitted to attain [its] ends,"[47] so why not let the Jesuits run it, or the Dominicans, or the Benedictines? Wigger thought likewise. "When in Philadelphia last week," Michael Corrigan told Bernard McQuaid in November 1882, "I was informed (and there was no secrecy about it) that during the visit of Monsignor Wigger to St. Vincent's in the summer it was the common talk of the house that he had gone there to offer Seton Hall to the Benedictines. This was stated by a layman who was on the premises at the time."[48] "Seton Hall College was offered to me again recently," wrote Abbot Boniface Wimmer of Saint Vincent's Arch Abbey to Abbot Alexius Edelbrock of St. John's Abbey, Collegeville, Minnesota in November 1882.[49] There was even talk of a price: $200, 000 or (as Michael Corrigan put it to McQuaid) "about $100,000 surplus over liabilities."[50] But the Benedictines were not biting. Saint Vincent's was a kind of Benedictine Seton Hall, with four clearly defined courses of study: ecclesiastical, classical, commercial, and elementary.[51] But this similarity was not enough for Wimmer, who thought there was "nothing in it" for his congregation and who knew that "of course, the bishop wants to get rid of the college because it does not pay."[52] No other order expressed an interest in Seton Hall and so it remained in Newark's hands.

Wigger was the second bishop, Bayley the first, who saw Seton Hall as a financial albatross. Between them were Michael Corrigan and Bernard McQuaid who, as presidents and bishops, were its advocates and rescuers. The college was lucky in its critics and its friends. Corrigan and McQuaid were more than a match for Wigger, a woeful negotiator who had no idea of what he wanted except to be relieved of his property at almost any price. Convinced that if someone wanted to buy it, then perhaps he should not sell, he also thought that if no-one wished to buy, then perhaps a sale was all the more necessary. This was bizarre logic. Trying to sell it twice, he persuaded possible purchasers not to buy precisely because of his urgency to offload it. With no particular attachment to it (one reason McQuaid had objected to his becoming bishop of Newark),[53] his desire to sell had the perverse effect of making it unsellable.

In the Benedictines, Wigger had met men at once more worldly and unworldly than himself: worldly enough to see it as a troubled school and to wish to have no part of it; unworldly enough not to notice that the land was worth more than the asking price and could have been sold off handsomely. Neither side wanted a property whose value neither understood. Like two archetypes of the middle ages, the German monk confronted the German bishop, the monk winning hands down.

A Catholic University of America?

These debates were known to few. Beyond the walls, though, another argument was developing that foreshadowed a very different future for Seton Hall. The debate had to do with the creation of a Catholic University of America, a kind of church-run version of Ivy League schools like Harvard and Yale. Its strongest supporter was Bishop John Spalding of Peoria, Illinois, its strongest critic Bishop Bernard McQuaid (who envisaged three Catholic universities in America, one in the East, one in the Mississippi Valley, and one for the Pacific coast).[54] Somewhere in the middle was Archbishop James Gibbons of Baltimore.[55] To its supporters, a Catholic University was a sign of the American Church's coming of age. To its critics, it was an act of hubris. To Seton Hall, it was a fleeting moment of opportunity.

Largely theoretical in the 1870s, the conversation turned practical in the 1880s as Gibbons attempted to implement the decrees of the Third Plenary Council of Baltimore in 1884, the single most significant meeting of American Catholic bishops in the nineteenth century. (Catholics of a certain generation still think of the Baltimore Catechism as a guarantee of orthodoxy.) Before the bishops met, Gibbons had been bombarded with manifestoes for and against a Catholic University, making a decision on the question almost unavoidable. Then came the news that a wealthy New York Catholic convert, Mary Gwendoline Caldwell, had promised to provide $300,000 for it, which settled the matter. In December 1884, "the American hierarchy . . . committed [itself] to a university for the American Church."[56] Difficulties remained—a site, the endowment of chairs, lines of authority—but the project itself was now fixed.

Mary Gwendoline Caldwell, twenty-one at the time of the donation, made the gift to fulfill a stipulation of her father's will that she use a third of her inheritance to help build the Church in America. Gibbons, eager to get the university under way, wanted the money as soon as possible. He should have cooled his heels. Caldwell would not deliver until certain conditions were met, one of them that she should have a say in the location of the school. Gibbons favored Seton Hall as a possible site: it was up and running, close to New York, connected to other centers of Catholic life, attractive. Its only disadvantage was "the terrible Jersey mosquitoes."[57]

An argument behind closed doors now took place; several arguments, in fact, behind several closed doors. A subcommittee of the Council was empaneled to work out details, with Archbishop Michael Corrigan one of the members. Wigger wrote to him in January 1885 outlining the financial state of Seton Hall, a bizarre letter in that its details had been earlier supplied by Corrigan himself or simply made up by Wigger.[58] A week later, at the committee's first meeting, Corrigan indicated that Wigger was prepared to sell Seton Hall for $250,000. At the same meeting, Eugene Kelly, executor of the Caldwell estate, proposed that it be bought. The following day, Wigger reduced his asking price to $200,000 and the committee agreed to buy it, with Corrigan and Spalding deputized to get Caldwell to agree.

And so, for the second time in half a decade, Wigger was involved in negotiations for the sale of Seton Hall; and, once again, he was so eager to be shot of it that he knocked $50,000 off the asking price before the ink was dry on the initial proposal. But the sides were subtly different this time around. Wigger insisted that the idea to sell was not his but Spalding's and that his willingness to reduce the price was because he wished to see a Catholic university thrive. He was doing a favor to the committee, not the other way around. Corrigan for his part was willing to facilitate the conveyance, no longer acting as Seton Hall's protector but as its betrayer, or, looking at the case from a different angle, its savior. What did he want? To see Seton Hall thrive? (That was never in doubt: before and after the proposed sale he supported it handsomely.)[59] Or to support a national university in a Northern rather than Southern setting? Or to help his archdiocese, which was close to the proposed site and likely to benefit from it? All that can be said is that he was prepared to facilitate the sale, bringing the college he had once led to glory or extinction. As for McQuaid, it was a "mystery" that Wigger was "willing to part with such a property" for $200,000 (a "great bargain") but, if he did, Seton Hall offered "many advantages" as a site for the Catholic university, having "easy . . . access from Newark, New York, and Philadelphia" and its "healthfulness" (that perennial theme) being "all that could be desired."[60]

But the negotiations came to nothing. Caldwell was unpersuaded of the case for South Orange, in the first place because she did not want to support an existing institution and, secondly, because she visited Seton Hall and found it a "broken-down college" unsuitable for her purposes. The nation's capital, she thought, was the obvious place for a national institution. (Presumably, it also boasted a better class of mosquito.) As late as May 1885, Gibbons thought he could prevail upon Wigger to sell Seton Hall, and upon Caldwell to accept it as the site for the university. (His persistence was perverse. On April 21, Spalding told him that "she prefers Washington but would I think consent to almost any site except Seton Hall.")[61] Most of his colleagues agreed with Caldwell that it should go to Washington and such, on May 7, 1885, was their decision.

Was Seton Hall ever seriously in the running to be the new Catholic University of America? Probably not. Its chief supporter, Gibbons, was less ardent in favor than those against. The blessing of the Archbishop of Baltimore counted for something. On the other hand, Caldwell saw its weakness, insisting that "taking Seton Hall would be rather like continuing an old institution than founding a new one." (She was also annoyed that bishops were taking her money for granted.) In any event, not being chosen may have been a blessing in disguise. Seton Hall as such would have disappeared, providing merely the site and some of the buildings of a wholly different creation. The name would have gone, leaving only a trace, if that, of the history it enshrined. To be under new management would have meant the end of what Bayley, McQuaid, and Corrigan had created. It took a twenty-one year old heiress to keep their vision alive.

Better Times

The brush with national destiny was soon forgotten. Eventually the recession eased and with it, some of the financial pressures under which the college had struggled for much of the 1880s. By the middle of the decade, the books looked healthier. In 1885 Wigger proposed a parish-by-parish seminary "tax" which caused one pastor publicly, and others privately, to complain that working men had to subsidize a professional man's school. (The levy was modest—$10,000—and was standard practice in other dioceses.)

Perhaps the cloistered existence of a Seton Hall priest inclined fellow clerics to feel sorry for him. Few relished the prospect of living there: "Priests coming from other Dioceses, or in trouble, may fancy Seminary or College life for a while, but only as a temporary position—a stepping stone to something else. It is of rare occurrence that Clergymen ordained for our Diocese relish the work to be done in the Seminary or the College."[62]

Corrigan was president of the college but never fully in charge of it, Wigger often treating him like a misbehaving student: "By taking your supper privately, an hour or two after we have taken ours, you caused great disorder, put the girls and Sisters to much unnecessary trouble, and increased the expenses of the house . . . I must therefore insist on your taking your meals with us in future."[63] Seton Hall, supposed to turn boys into men, also had the effect of turning men into boys. Corrigan had ability, social standing, was the brother of an archbishop. Who could blame him for bristling?

There were certainly troubled priests. Father John Francis Duffy, appointed dean of discipline in 1884, had as much discipline as some of the boys in his charge. "You are not to make use of intoxicating liquors," Wigger told him. "You are on no account even to visit or correspond with Miss McCabe of Newark . . . You are never to stay away from Seton Hall overnight, except on Saturdays, when you go to Caldwell [to say

Mass]."[64] Duffy fell off the wagon again in 1887: "I have not seen anything in the papers regarding your recent escapade in Far Rockaway . . . I am consequently willing to let you remain at Seton Hall as Prefect and Professor. I again remind you of the fact that Seton Hall is the only place where you can be employed. No Rector of the Diocese will have you as assistant on account of the scandal formerly given."[65] Duffy's alcoholism was a tragedy, Seton Hall's job to cover for it. The college was sometimes a home for clerical errors.

Lay men could also prove trouble-makers. George Quackenbos, professor of Latin, drawing, and rhetoric, was a highly intelligent malcontent. "We are dealing with an eccentric and unscrupulous fellow," Father William Marshall wrote to Wigger in 1892, when Quackenbos threatened suit for nonpayment of salary. "He has maniacal tendencies and deals largely in firearms . . . We are dealing with a freak."[66] He was certainly colorful: eventually he left Seton Hall to become a police sergeant specializing in sign language for nonnative deaf mutes.[67]

Setonia Literary Association

Seton Hall tolerated difference only up to a point. With debating societies, where variety was of the essence, speech was regulated in subtle and concealed ways. The full gamut of opinion was allowed from A to B. When the Setonia Literary Association was revived in 1886 (lasting until 1888) it was mainly a vehicle for schoolboy facetiousness. The inaugural debate (October 6, 1886) considered Chinese immigration to the United States. The level of argument may be inferred from the minutes: "It was clearly shown that this child of Asia is not and could not be a benefit to the United States. That while they clean the country of rats, they clean it also of money and introduce the custom of opium-smoking as a substitute for tobacco . . . Our honored President who in laconic style gave his judgment by saying: 'Melican man must stay home'."[68] Whether America should have a Catholic University was also debated: "Mr. Joseph Farmer opened the debate [with] a strong argument in favor of the University. He mentioned that America would thereby be raised to an equal footing with European countries . . . Mr. Charles Fitzpatrick [in the negative] declared it foolish and absurd to have a University in America where education is so dearly purchased when in foreign countries the highest education can be had for a mere pittance. He received prolonged applause. . . ."[69] The motion was carried.

The subject for January 27, 1887 was whether hanging was the appropriate form of execution for women: "Mr. Peter J. Walsh . . . declared that hanging should not at all be used as a capital punishment. That something more in conformity with civilization should take its place . . . Others . . . declared that Woman is weak. She showed her weakness in yielding to the dictates of the serpent in the garden of Paradise . . . Woman can commit a crime as dastard as ever perpetrated by man . . ."[70] The question was not put to a vote. A later debate (February 9, 1887)—"Which is the more laughable spectacle to behold—a man threading a needle or a woman driving a nail?"—was similarly inconclusive. Seton Hall was not awash with feminists.

Resolving that strikes were harmful to the laboring classes, that classical languages remained valid in the modern world, that the South had produced as many great men as the North, that wealth more than learning guaranteed entry to polite society, the Setonia Literary Association allowed articulate students to imitate the conventional views of their elders. Only with immigration did light-heartedness slip to reveal uglier views: views, indeed, that, directed against Catholics forty years before, had caused Bayley to found Seton Hall in the first place.

Disaster and New Beginnings

Seton Hall could survive student debaters but not another disaster. Right on cue, as if on a twenty-year cycle, another disaster happened. On the afternoon of March 9, 1886 the college building burned to the ground. There had been a fairly serious fire on the farm in September 1881: "Poor old Fanny, and the black mare and mule were lost. The farm house was saved. The fire came, they suppose, from tramps smoking . . . Loss of about $3000 above the insurance."[71] But this latest fire was much worse than those either of 1881 or 1866. The blaze started at lunchtime and ended a few hours later with the building that had been put up in 1860 and extended in 1863 laying in ruins. Next day, *The New York Times* recorded a curious fact: "The Reverend Dr. Corrigan, President of Seton Hall College, recently returned from Florida, and was entertained by the Alumni of the College at Pinard's on Monday evening. He started for the College at South Orange yesterday afternoon to renew his labors. While on the train the conductor, recognizing the President, said as he collected his ticket: "Spose you're going out to the fire.' 'Fire! Fire!' repeated the reverend gentleman. 'What do you mean?' 'I mean,' answered the conductor, 'that Seton Hall is in flames.'"

At first, students tried to put it out: "A small hose was attached to a pump and the students worked with might and main to extinguish the flames. Bucket brigades were formed under the command of Prefect D. Clancy and the plucky little fellows, hatless and coatless, rushed up the stairs to the roof and poured water wherever they saw fire." Then came the professionals: "In spite of their efforts the fire gained headway and when the engine company from Orange arrived the entire building was on fire." But it took an engine from Newark to bring it under control: "[When Chief Kiersted of Newark] took charge he saw that it was useless to attempt to save the college and he turned his attention to the seminary. That building was on fire in four places at one time, but after an hour's fight, at the end of which the firemen were assisted by a change in the wind, they concluded that the seminary was safe. Then they went to work at the college, and in a short time had the fire under control. While streams of water were being poured on the fire the walls of the building cracked and tottered and large fragments fell into the burning interior. At five o'clock the fire was entirely extinguished but nothing remained of the college except the four walls."[72] The *Newark Daily Advertiser* reported a make-shift chain of students and teachers, "some removing valuable books on the lower floors, while others took such means as were at their disposal to check the rapid advance . . . The lawn about the building was littered with such documents as could be removed." The cause was never established but it probably started in a dormitory as the result of a faulty flue. No-one was injured.

On the day of the fire, Seton Hall had eighty-three students with another eighteen at the seminary, all taught by a faculty of thirteen. Fifteen Sisters of Mercy occupied a house beside the college to attend to domestic needs. At least $35,000 worth of damage was caused (the *Newark Daily Advertiser* reckoned the figure between $45,000 and $50,000), of which only $18,000 was covered by insurance. The school had liabilities of over $120,000. Revenue from tuition came to $27,000, from boarding fees, $25,000, and from other sources, $6,000. Cash in hand amounted to $700. These figures pointed in an ominous direction. A week after the fire, with classes conducted in the upper floor of Alumni Hall and the lower floor used as a dormitory, the Board considered closure of the college. "It was agreed upon unanimously to continue the College, at least for another year," record the minutes.[73] After that, who could tell? There was no question of closing the seminary, which was intact.

The decision to continue "at least for another year" was, in effect, a decision to continue for longer than that. If the college were to have closed, it would have closed immediately. Instead, the fire presented an opportunity for another year of church door appeals, special dinners, circular letters, and anxious calls on charity. A diocesan collection raised slightly less than $8,000, roughly in keeping with other amounts raised over the years and indicating local goodwill. "Having selected Seton Hall as the best college in this part of the country," wrote Thomas Weston, a New York doctor and guardian of a Latin American student, and being "personally known to all the wealthy families of Nicaragua and Costa Rica . . . [I] shall not fail to recommend the renowned Institution of South Orange to those sending boys here for education."[74] With patience, a new Seton Hall might emerge from the embers.

And so, almost indestructible despite wars, depressions, fires, heiresses, and episcopal caprice, Seton Hall survived. Plans were approved for a new college building on June 1, 1886 and it was up the following January and in use as a dormitory the following May. At times of crisis, Seton Hall could act with astonishing speed.

Father James Corrigan circularized the diocese with requests for help but his heart, almost literally, was not in it. For much of his presidency he suffered from chronic digestive problems and "a marked tendency to obesity." (Perhaps this is why he pre-ferred to eat away from the common table.) His "mode of life," his doctor thought, was "utterly unsuited . . . to College work."[75] At the best of times, he was a reluctant presi-dent, and these were not the best of times. It was a relief when Wigger appointed him pastor of St. Mary's, Elizabeth. Father William Marshall, his vice-president, replaced him as president in 1888, becoming at the age of 40 the college's fifth man in charge. Cor-rigan died in 1891 and was buried from the college chapel. Seeing the college through two crises—the abortive sale and the fire—he deserves credit for performing uncon-genial tasks. Seton Hall always did well by the Corrigans. In 1891, Archbishop Michael Corrigan, resigning from the Board, donated $10,000 for the "education of young men to the priesthood."[76] James, less brilliant, was nevertheless a worthy successor.

Toward the End of the Century: Marshall, Wigger, and Synott

Father William Marshall's presidency was almost a refoundation. Before studying for the priesthood at Mount Saint Mary's in Emmitsburg, he attended a law and busi-ness college in Philadelphia and worked in real estate. Ordained in 1881 in the new Saint Patrick's Cathedral, New York, he was appointed a Seton Hall professor and, thereafter, treasurer, vice-president, and president of the college. Most of his work was drudgery: preparing bills, dealing with parents, haggling with tradesmen. He was, almost literally, a nuts-and-bolts man. (An architect complained that his specification called "for nails and cloth hooks etc. put up in the dormitories [but] Father Marshall did not want any put up.")[77] "Father Marshall fits his place excellently," James Corrigan reported in 1882, "and there is no priest in this Diocese that, to my knowledge, could be substituted for him."[78]

By the end of his time, the college had certainly improved. The diocese itself was in decent shape and as Newark thrived so did Seton Hall.[79] Some of the improvement had happened at the end of Corrigan's tenure but that, too, was the result of Marshall's management as vice-president. The debt of over $120,000 at the time of the fire was reduced to less than $93,000 fifteen months later. The mortgage on the seminary build-ing was rescheduled on more favorable terms. (A mortgage of $60,000 obtained in 1879 at 5 percent was paid off by borrowing $50,000 from the Mutual Life Insurance Com-pany of New York, with Wigger supplying the remaining $10,000. This loan was itself paid off by 1895.) For all practical purposes, Seton Hall was debt-free as it approached the end of the century.

Academically, the faculty was stronger, with "noted scholars both American and European" bringing "a maturity of approach" to the classroom.[80] Literary clubs flour-ished. Enrollment was good. "Things are going well at the College," Wigger wrote in

1895. "We have about 130 pupils. The Seminary is also full, having 34 young men."[81] "Our student body was less than a hundred," recalled a member of the class of 1895. "When we reached one hundred, as we occasionally did, we were given a holiday in celebration."[82] But not everyone was happy. Father Leo Thebaud, one of the first students of 1856, left Seton Hall out of his will,[83] and when James Farnham Edwards, a manuscript collector, visited in 1888 he was "disappointed." "Nothing to see except dormitories, studies, refectory, etc. Nothing pertaining to college work."[84] This judgment lacked charity and perspective. Seton Hall had been through the mill: Edwards could have been kinder.

Students were reasonably content. Eugene Kinkead of Jersey City entered as a fifteen-year-old freshman in 1891. He remembered "a hedge of cedars to the west and beyond that a field of ripened corn . . . to the east were two or three tennis courts edging the football field, and to the north the baseball diamond. The main sandstone building was partially hidden by beautiful broad maples. [It] was given over to the Seminarians and contained the offices of the President and rooms of the teaching priests and lay professors." Among his friends were two brothers from Ecuador, Carlos and Louis Arosemena, part of the large contingent of well-to-do students from Central and South America who were such a feature of the school's early history. Carlos Arosemena entered the College for a year in September 1901 and it left a mark: in 1947 he was elected President of Ecuador, where some of his "happiest memories" were of Seton Hall and "the principles of democracy" he had learned there.[85]

Actors Lionel and John Barrymore attended from 1889 to 1890 and from 1891 to 1892 respectively. Lionel remembered Seton Hall as "among the happiest days of my life," marked, in his case, by almost complete absence of scholastic achievement. Most of the time was spent in the gym.[86] "John tried out the parallel bars and several odd items fell from his pockets including a set of brass knuckles, a pack of cigarettes and a half pint of cheap whiskey."[87] It was at Seton Hall where he heard "the most amazing understatement of all time": "There was a football player who was unfortunately required to go to class. One morning, our instructor, forgetting to treat the great with proper consideration, called on this athlete and demanded of him that he give a short talk on the music of Robert Schumann. Our hero arose, shifted from one foot to the other, looked desperately about, and uttered this classic: "Well, Schumann, this Schumann, well, he was *all right*." And sat down."[88]

Not everyone enjoyed the school. In 1897 the *Philadelphia Inquirer*, reported the "Queer Antics of a Student": "Jersey City, April 21. A half-clad young man was captured by the crew of a Pennsylvania Railroad freight train early this morning while he was smashing signal lamps along the railroad with his bare fists. He gave his name as John J. Farrell, a student at Seton Hall College, Orange, and appeared to be demented."[89]

Happier characters included "Cap" Smith (the grounds man) who allowed seniors to play checkers in the furnace room, enthralling them "with tales of former Setonians who built homes in trees;"[90] "Swamp" Corrigan from Florida and "Beans" Riley from Massachusetts who led an abortive student strike; an Irish maid who announced that "the hot water is cold today"; and a student, later a priest, who defended the adultery of Irish statesman Charles Stewart Parnell.

Military science was introduced in August 1893 when Lieutenant Michael Lenihan, a West Point graduate, was appointed professor of military science and tactics. The government supplied equipment and an instructor—Lenihan—and Seton Hall provided a venue and recruits. Land in the Orange Mountains was set aside for "Camp Lenihan," Lenihan turning up for work in September, his equipment following in November. "The professorship being a new one, it was necessary to begin with a raw mass and work out an organization," wrote Inspector General Colonel R.P. Hughes in May 1894: "The college possesses a large tract of land and is in much better condition to carry out practical military instruction than most of the colleges in this inspection. The discipline of the Military department is enforced by the college authorities in the same general way that pertains to all other departments."[91]

In June 1894, cadets gave their first demonstration of skill at commencement. "The Catholics appear to be introducing military drill into their schools," complained James P. Guild of the American Proscription Association, suspecting a plot to seize the country: "Up at St. Francis Xavier College they have a regular company of cadets. At Seton Hall College I believe they are drilling some of the students too . . . The Catholics are only about one-eighth of the population and they would be foolish to engage in a contest in which they would be wiped out."[92]

Lenihan, surviving this lunatic fringe, was succeeded by Lieutenant W.G. Rafferty in May 1894. (Both became brigadier generals in the World War I.) The Department of Military Science and Tactics, disbanded at the outbreak of the Spanish-American War in 1898,[93] was considered, on the whole, an unhappy experiment. "The boys had outgrown their uniforms," the Board of Trustees was told, "and the institution was most unpopular with the students."[94]

As president, Marshall was on the receiving end of Wigger's petty advice, the latter being, at times, more headmaster than bishop: "All the Professors and teachers should be told never to give the pupils more marks than they deserve. Whoever gives a pupil more marks than he has merited simply writes down a falsehood . . ."[95] With an opinion on everything, from decent literature (in favor) to ball games on Saturdays (against) to nuns playing the organ in church (against), he nagged his subordinates almost literally to death. A professor demanding sick payment was told to find a substitute during a period of absence.[96] "We are already running some risk in engaging you who have no experience in teaching," he told a new staff member. "I think very few institutions would do that and offer you a salary."[97]

Many stayed for life, others bolted. General Eliakim Parker Scammon was professor of mathematics and history from 1875 to 1885, appointed to the post at the age of fifty-nine. Scammon was a veteran of three wars, a convert, a West Point graduate, a professor of history, geography and ethics at that institution, where he had tutored Ulysses S. Grant,[98] a former prisoner, an explorer and geographer. Another oddity was Francis J. Cummings, professor of Greek and rhetoric, who lasted a year before becoming principal of Brooklyn High School. He later fell to his death from the third floor of a New York hotel.[99] There was a slightly rackety quality to some faculty. "Ernest Joies, formerly professor of music at Seton Hall College, was arrested at 11.30 o'clock on warrants charging him with obtaining money on false pretenses. When approached by the policeman with the warrants he attempted to shoot himself."[100] Mostly, though, the school was sober. "Ever since I left the beautiful place of Seton Hall where I spent so many happy and cheerful days," a former student wrote to Wigger, "I kept a loving remembrance of all its gentle and amiable inmates, but principally of its supreme, kind pastor and bishop."[101]

John O'Connor, John Stafford, and Joseph Synott were the ablest priests of the diocese and all did duty in South Orange. "There is not one of us who ever sat under you," a graduate told O'Connor, "but will remember with grateful affection your manner of treating seminarians." O'Connor himself had been supported by Corrigan when, as a student in Louvain in 1877, his father's business collapsed.[102] O'Connor succeeded Wigger as bishop of Newark in 1901. Synott, the first American to hold a doctorate from Innsbruck, the first priest to hold an honorary MA from Yale, was professor of moral theology, canon law, and Hebrew. He was a formidable controversialist, in 1893 defending Wigger against Father Patrick Corrigan, who blamed him for the allegedly Germanizing tendencies of the American Church,[103] comprehensively destroying the argument.[104] Synott became rector of the seminary, succeeding O'Connor in 1895.

Marshall, never fully fit and in 1890 seriously ill with rheumatism, resigned as president in June 1897,[105] having long pined for release. "Please give . . . all . . . my best regards," he wrote from Florida in 1892, "and offer any one of them the treasury or presidency of the College."[106] In retirement, he lived in France and California, translating the French classics, working on a history of Abyssinia, and, belying illness, living to an advanced old age. An alumnus visiting in 1931 found him "old and wrinkled [with] a fine high forehead [and] a thin fluffy beard . . . He showed me a well-kept, old-fashioned watch. With the impersonal detachment of the aged, he pointed out the date—1879—and told me how . . . the 'boys' presented [it to] him."[107] Marshall preserved the traditions of the school, surviving long enough to become one himself.

Wigger did not think twice before making Synott president (although technically the choice lay with the Board).[108] Beloved at the seminary,[109] he was a sensible administrator who reorganized the curriculum to allow greater distinction among the senior school, the college, and seminary. Hiving off the high school from the rest of the college, creating what was to become Seton Hall Preparatory School, he enhanced at a stroke the academic standing of both. Seton Hall High School and Seton Hall College were now distinct entities. Under him, Seton Hall degrees were recognized by the New York Board of Regents and the State Department of Education in Rhode Island, an important development for the future when accreditation would be a concern.

He also built. The Board decided in March 1897 that "more rooms [were] needed for the Annual Clerical Retreat; Library; Rooms and Classrooms for the seminarians; a new kitchen, et cetera,"[110] plans that were reduced within three months to a library. Jeremiah O'Rourke proposed a one-story building at the cost of $17,000, prompting the suggestion that a grander building could be had at little extra cost. (As it turned out, a library twice the size cost, unsurprisingly, twice the amount.) He then offered a second set of plans, this time for a two-story building, leaving Wigger to decide between them.[111] He chose the more spacious proposal, helped in his expansiveness by a bequest of $5,000 from Monsignor Januarius de Concilio "towards the erection of the new library." (De Concilio's testy association with Seton Hall thus ended more or less happily.)[112] Empowered to spend $30,000 and to raise $20,000 of it in a mortgage, the Board showed remarkable confidence in Seton Hall when other buildings were going up (a laundry at $8,000) and when many students were taking courses without actually paying for them.[113]

O'Rourke was now one of the leading figures in his profession, having served a stint as supervising architect of the U.S. Treasury.[114] Changing his signature neo-Gothic style, this time he presented plans in the Americanized Florentine style first popularized in the Astor Library in New York and evident in some local churches. Seventy feet in length and two and a half stories high, built of pressed brick with cut stone and terra cotta trimmings, the library had a capacity of 40,000 books but could accommodate twice that number if necessary. Completed in 1898, it was an exotic addition to the gothic ensemble that surrounded it.

In distinguishing between the high school and the college, in winning external recognition for its degrees, in building a library, Synott was positioning Seton Hall to withstand the commercial pressures that all Catholic schools had to face. At the same time, he recognized that competitor colleges were also colleagues in the shared enterprise of religious education. Seton Hall was represented at an 1894 meeting of the Alumni Association of St. John's College, Fordham when "the question of forming a general association of all the Catholic colleges of the East" was discussed. (The Seton Hall delegate was Father James F. Mooney, later president of the College.)[115] Speaking in Chicago in April 1899 at what was hailed as the first conference of heads of American Catholic schools and colleges, Monsignor Thomas Conaty, rector of the Catholic University of America, insisted that "we want . . . to fit our young men for professional as well as ecclesiastical life."[116] Fifty delegates attended, including Father George F. Brown, vice-president of Seton Hall. Father John Murphy of the Holy Ghost College, Pittsburg gave the opening address—"The Typical Catholic College: What Should It Teach?"—to which Brown gave the response. Brown's presence signaled Wigger's wish that Seton Hall take the lead in curricular reform, not least because Catholic students were increasingly choosing not to attend Catholic colleges at all.[117]

Synott died in March 1899 aged thirty-six. "He was so young and strong! So good and useful a priest! I feel his loss very keenly—daily more so," said Wigger.[118] Seton Hall felt it too. Popular with colleagues and respected by students, his reorganization of the college, building on Marshall's steadying of the finances, was a worthy legacy.

CHAPTER 5

A New Century

A New Generation

Synott was a transitional president, as, in their way, are all presidents. He was the guardian of a tradition, a sustainer of what others had created. Yet what he did was important. Distinguishing the College from the High School and the Seminary enhanced all three. He knew that standards had to be improved if budgets were to be met. Catholic educators might meet together in solidarity—at Fordham in 1894, Chicago in 1899—but they were rivals as well as colleagues, each hoping to exploit the market for good students, good teachers, good priests, good professors, and, not least, good parents (who would pay their bills on time and keep their sons in school). The Catholic world was small enough for word of mouth about a failing school to become self-fulfilling. The quest for improvement took on new purpose under Synott and, had he lived, Seton Hall might have become a stronger institution. He was a reformer given only a limited time to reform.

The pioneering generation was also passing from the scene. Bayley was dead. McQuaid was a bishop, Corrigan an archbishop. The other figures of Seton Hall's early history, Daniel Fisher and Alfred Young, were scarcely memories to the staff who patrolled the corridors in their place. Wigger died in January 1901 of pneumonia after a visit to Egypt, North Africa, and Rome. A gifted linguist and musician, as a bishop he was a martinet, too insistent on his dignity to seem entirely dignified. The young priest who risked cholera in 1866 to tend to the dying had long since disappeared behind a protective wall of purple, idealism encrusted by canon law. Wigger led Newark as well as his abilities allowed, keeping clergy and people more or less content, limiting scandal to a minimum and taking extreme interest in a school he had twice tried to sell. Seton Hall's masculine domesticity gave him the only home he knew. Wigger was "firm because he was just," Henry Brann remembered. "It would have been . . . easier . . . to move the Orange mountains . . . than to move him from [the Catholic faith]."[1] He took Seton Hall seriously, offering generally sensible advice, appointing worthy priests, defending it in public, taking pride in its reputation, and bathing it in the golden memories of youth. "Ever since I left the beautiful place of Seton Hall where

I spent so many happy and cheerful days," wrote Bishop Otto Zardetti to him, "I kept a loving remembrance of all its gentle and amiable inmates [sic]" of whom Wigger was the kindest.[2] At his death, the Trustees paid tribute to his "intense interest" in the College, his "fatherly supervision over each department, Ecclesiastical and Collegiate, his long residence within the College precincts, and his strong individual influence for its welfare and prosperity."[3] "The college was in a sound condition from every point of view," wrote one obituarist, "and days of sunshine had followed the financial gloom which had enveloped it in the earlier days of his episcopate."[4]

As for the rest of the founding generation, Michael Corrigan died on May 5, 1902 aged sixty-two. At Seton Hall, said Brann, laying it on, "he was the lily white of all the flowers of the garden. [As] priest, bishop and archbishop the whiteness of his life was unstained and the fragrance of his virtues was universally diffused."[5] Brann's nemesis, Bernard McQuaid, served as Bishop of Rochester for forty-one years and died on January 18, 1909, aged eighty-five, prompting a lugubrious and less fragrant tribute from the Board.[6]

If all presidencies are transitional, some are more transitional than others. Viewed comparatively, Seton Hall had more presidential stability than other schools. In its first sixty years, Georgetown had twenty-two presidents. Gonzaga College in Washington, DC had twelve between 1850 and 1890. The College of Saint Francis Xavier in New York had twelve between 1847 and 1897. Notre Dame had fifteen in its first century. Creighton University had nine in twenty-five years.[7] In each case, the intersection of institutional and personal history is unique, making it impossible to establish meaningful norms. Seton Hall was unusual in having long presidencies interrupted by briefer ones. The fact that it was a diocesan college made a difference. Under the eye of a resident bishop, there was no canonical reason for a successful president not to serve for as long as the bishop wished.[8] Seton Hall was saved the disadvantages of frequent presidencies (such as having a new man to train and different policies to pursue). On the other hand, a man long in the job could lose his appetite for it. Most of the duties of a president were dull; a mediocrity could have performed them, and sometimes did.

Larger transitions were also under way. Half a century of growth had transformed the diocese of Newark, making it unrecognizable from the pioneering days of Bayley and McQuaid. Bishop John O'Connor, ruling it from Seton Hall, summarized the social revolution: "The twenty-five churches of 1853 have so multiplied that there are in the diocese of Newark 155, and in the diocese of Trenton [established in 1881] 114, a total of 269 in the state. The number of priests has increased from 25 to 387. In the two dioceses there are now 150 parochial schools, with an attendance of nearly 50,000 children . . . There are at present [1902] in the diocese of Newark alone 300,000 Catholics."[9]

Seton Hall served these first- and second-generation immigrants and was itself a first-generation school, founded during one of the greatest waves of immigration the

United States had ever seen. It was made by a community and was itself the making of that community. It was the American Catholic Church in miniature.

By the turn of the century, education for immigrants was no longer a matter of teaching the basics but also of adding social polish. Parochial schools did the basics. Diocesan colleges like Seton Hall did the polishing. Catholic parents wanted for their children a few years of lecture halls, libraries, debating clubs, Latin and Greek, and, then, the career advantages that were thought to come with them. Even women—another transition—sought diplomas. In 1860, when Seton Hall vacated it, the Sisters of Charity established a convent and motherhouse at the college's first site at Madison. In 1899 the Sisters received permission to turn their school into a degree-awarding institution, making the College of Saint Elizabeth the first female Catholic college in the United States. "It is only of late that our Catholic girls are going to College," McQuaid wrote in 1903, intrigued that higher education for women had become "a sort of fad." "Nearly all [the young women] go to non-Catholic Colleges . . . I am setting my face against their attendance at these." McQuaid was no feminist but he believed that women had brains and should use them. "Music and art are very necessary for a school of young ladies but these accomplishments do not make a College . . . Latin, Greek, Mathematics and Scientific Studies are the requirement of a college . . . Severe training, it is true, but [it] will be the making of the place." "You will need professors of French, German, Italian, and Spanish," he told the College's first president, Sister Mary Pauline Kelligar. "Even Polish must not be despised." From polish to Polish might serve as a metaphor for the social transformation of female education in the first decades of the twentieth century. On the other hand, too much learning could be dangerous. "Your mission is not to dignify the walks of public life, or to dazzle the multitude with . . . eloquence or to pursue the devious paths of politics," Bishop John O'Connor told Saint Elizabeth's first graduating class in 1903. "Yours to fulfill duties more sacred than these—to adorn and ennoble the Christian home"[10] The church wanted to advance women but it drew the line at Advanced Women.

New Beginnings, Old Problems

Synott was replaced as president by Father John Stafford in May 1899, Wigger as bishop by Father John O'Connor in 1901. Stafford served until 1907 and O'Connor until his death in 1927. For seventeen years a professor of theology and philosophy in the seminary, O'Connor continued to live at Seton Hall, maintaining an arrangement established by Bishops Corrigan and Wigger. A house and estate abutting the campus once belonging to the late Eugene Kelly of New York was bought for him. The house was substantial, coming with a cottage and a retainer (whom O'Connor did not wish to retain), furniture, accoutrements, farm implements, and a cow. Thus Eugene Kelly's son Thomas to O'Connor, sealing the deal: "If you do not intend to get your milk sent over from the College, I know [James Brown the farmhand] would be glad to keep on the cow which does no harm to the lawn . . .")[11] Stout and square-headed in his prime, white-haired in his decline, O'Connor was a disciplinarian (forbidding priests, except those living in rural parishes, to own motor cars) but also "the most lovable of men."[12]

A thirty-eight-year-old native of Jersey City and a graduate of Seton Hall and the North American College, Stafford was a popular president. The *New York Daily Tribune* described him as "young in years [but] with a wise head on his shoulders," with "great personal charm of manner," "infectious enthusiasm," and common sense. Stafford wanted Seton Hall to be known for excellence and, indeed, to *be* excellent. He tried to cut costs, not corners. Turning the "raw material of youth" into "educated and cultured" gentlemen took time: "The mania for abbreviated courses is contagious . . . Seton Hall College deplores that tendency and will do everything to maintain its present high standard."[13] This anti-utilitarian argument was paradoxically useful, justifying lengthy education and the continuing existence of colleges such as Seton Hall to provide it.

That said, he was concerned that standards were slipping. Seton Hall still took students from Cuba and Latin America, although fewer than in previous years. (At least one student, Macy King, not himself Cuban, may have fought in the Cuban War of Independence against Spain.)[14] Too much time was devoted to remedial work; to deal with the problem, Stafford created a separate elementary school in 1901 to "take students at an earlier age and give them a thorough grammar school course . . . [this] in addition [facilitating] the more difficult work of the High School."[15] This so-called Bayley Hall had sixth, seventh, and eighth grade teachers and, grandiloquently, a professor of "penmanship." It was "rather amusing," wrote John Talbot Smith, a critic of American Catholic higher education, "to enter the imposing vestibule of a Catholic university, whose doctors and masters parade their degree in society, and to see in the distance the knickerbockers of boyhood or to hear the shrieks of the young savages protesting against the horrors of the bath."[16] He could have been describing Seton Hall.

The challenge was to take boys and turn them into men. The College Catalogue of 1911–1912 explained how this was done: "The occupations of every hour have been so apportioned that mind and body are given useful work and healthy play from the morning bell at half-past six to the last bell at half-past eight . . . The discipline is firm, as discipline must always be; but harshness is never permitted to mar the relations of teacher and pupil . . . No pains are spared to lay the foundations of that combination of culture and religious virtue which constitutes the Christian gentleman . . ."[17] Parents entrusted their children to Seton Hall because it offered a good education at a decent price and because it trained character.

Outwardly the school flourished but the private reality was less rosy. Deficits were a way of life, with debt being carried over from year to year like a cough that could not be shaken. With overheads fixed and income variable, borrowing was needed to balance the books at the end of the year, an unsustainable state of affairs. A teacher's contract might not be renewed, a banker's note renegotiated, a building left unpainted: all of this was standard practice (and not only at Seton Hall). What was needed was predictable income and expenditure, yet nothing resembling a business plan was ever drawn up. Enrollment, the ratio of seminarians to collegians, the number of students who paid full freight, the number of students "off the books": these changed from year to year. When even Bayley had been slow to pay bills to the college he founded, what likelihood that others would be more forthcoming? Seton Hall imposed tough discipline on others but, financially, it never imposed it on itself.

Take 1905. Each collegian and seminarian cost on average $291.40 to educate and board. Priests, nuns, some lay faculty, domestic staff, farmhands, handymen, and furnace-tenders had to be housed and fed at a cost of $103 per head. Based on receipts for financial year 1903–1904, Stafford reckoned that Seton Hall's total expenditure for 1904–1905 would come to $39,950.20. Income only amounted to $33,638.00. The resulting deficit, $6,312.20, had to be carried over to the next financial year. On paper, the gap was over $6,300. In reality, it was nearer $11,300 because insurance rates had risen between 1903 and 1905. Previously Seton Hall paid $1,200 per year to insure its buildings and contents to the value of $202,000. Now it was asked to pay $3,500 for the same coverage. O'Connor and Stafford reduced the premiums, thinking that as long as there was a "safe indemnity in case of fire" they could live with the risk. Seton Hall found itself paying higher premiums (although not as high as they might have been) to buy lower coverage. Even to qualify for reduced coverage it had to improve fire safety. The result was another $2,000 for construction costs and $1,000 for the cost of "horse and hose carriage." When those monies had been found, nearly $1,980 still had to be paid for the premium itself.

Seton Hall also charged different rates for different students, rates that bore little resemblance to fees quoted in the catalog or costs incurred in the classroom. Collegians subsidized seminarians and collegians intending to become seminarians were themselves subsidized by other collegians. Individual students were charged individual rates depending on family circumstances. Hard cases (there were a few every year) were kept on the house, making Seton Hall a quasicharity, a fact that was to have legal implications a decade later. Stafford captured the confusion in a letter to O'Connor:

> The actual cost of boarding and educating a student . . . amounts to $291.40 per capita. Now what amount of tuition is paid by the students? The catalogue rates are $380.00 per annum. The diocese pays the treasurer $250.00 per annum for each student in the seminary which sum is $41.40 per capita less than the actual cost of boarding and educating said students. Add to this the fact that there are in the College forty-two

students or about one half the number registered who propose to become priests and who according to an ancient tradition must be educated at the same rates as those who are actually in the seminary, namely $250.00 or $41.40 per capita less than the actual cost of their education and maintenance. [Thus] the number of students in the College who pay full rates is very small and is confined chiefly to the Spanish-speaking students. The average tuition we receive from students who do not intend to embrace the ecclesiastical state amounts to $317.00, a sum somewhat above the actual cost per capita but in no way adequate to meet the cost incurred by clerical rates.

Balancing Seton Hall's books meant understanding them. No-one did.

But *was* Seton Hall a business? In a sense, it was not a commercial but a spiritual enterprise. Its purpose (in the bishop's eyes) was to produce priests, not profits. Year after year, Stafford complained, it educated Newark's clerics at reduced prices and got little thanks in return. (Indeed, some priests resented the college when it came looking for gifts and legacies.) Stafford reckoned that between 1893 and 1903 the diocese "paid $4100.00 less than the amount actually expended to support and educate the seminarians." The number of seminarians during that period was 316, nearly 32 a year. Seton Hall's financial problems began and ended with the bishop and it was up to the bishop, Stafford thought, to sort them out.

So, what exactly was Seton Hall *for*? To serve the diocese? To educate the laity? To support the state by producing good citizens? It did all of things but, Stafford bluntly wondered, in what order of priority?

If I am not mistaken, the College was founded as an aid to support the diocesan Seminary. If such be the fact, it seems scarcely just to force the corporation as such to increase its debt in order that the seminarians and ecclesiastical students may be housed, fed and educated. When the College has lent all the aid in its power the deficit, it seems to me, should be supplied by the diocese either by direct assessment on the various parishes or by any other means you and the diocesan council may suggest.

If I am mistaken as to the motive for founding the College and the argument be advanced that the institution was established as a business enterprise, then charity should not figure in its management and all students, whether seminarians, ecclesiastical or lay, should pay the stipulated pension as advertised in the catalogue, viz. $380.00 a scholastic year.

In fact, the relationship between diocese and college was one of mutual dependency. Take away students intending to study for the priesthood and a good chunk of the college's clientele disappeared. That was never going to happen, but Stafford entertained the idea to show the perversity of financial arrangements in which Seton Hall acted as a charity in constant need of the charity of the body it supported.

Diocesan and college money was fungible. Announcing a capital campaign for 1906, O'Connor made no distinction between "the golden jubilee of our diocesan college and seminary" (although the seminary dated from 1860 not 1856), reasoning that the "heavy expenses" involved in conducting "a large educational institution, the tuitions of the college students and annual assessments for the seminary" were the same. Under Synott and Stafford, some $95,000 had been spent in the years leading up to the jubilee, a huge sum paying for a new library, a new heating system, a laundry and infirmary for the seminary. (In his begging letter, O'Connor reminded pastors that "a considerable portion of this outlay was caused by the need of providing better accommodations for the clergy at the annual retreats.")[18] Stafford and other priests members of the faculty visited parishes of the diocese on two successive Sundays, first to appeal, then to collect.[19] Coming on top of other demands (Peter's Pence, the Catholic University of America, the new cathedral in Newark, parochial schools), these requests indicated Seton Hall's continued dependence on the goodwill of far from wealthy New Jersey Catholics. Without them as donors and customers, it could not have survived.

Problems about money were always about more than money. Balance sheets revealed a loss of competitive edge:

Twenty-five years ago or I may say fifteen years ago Seton Hall was as good in material equipment and educational appliances as the average Catholic College but we cannot make the same boast today. There has been a notable advance both in construction and equipment, particularly in the Scientific, Commercial, and Athletic departments, and Seton Hall, through lack of resources, has not kept up with the procession. A graduate of our classical department who proposes to take up the study of medicine, for instance, is handicapped at the very threshold of his professional studies by his elementary knowledge of Chemistry . . . A graduate of the Commercial department of our High School has learned the theory of commercial work but the practical application of his knowledge in filling the various offices of a banking or a commercial house, a feature in Commercial Colleges today, is not furnished our students, and is a sad defect in our system.

Captious critics take advantage of our weakness in this respect and without a knowledge of our difficulties form judgments prejudicial to Seton Hall.

Seton Hall was not as good as it claimed to be. Living from year to year meant dying from year to year. If other colleges could improve facilities or pay decent wages, Seton Hall had to do the same.

Institutional identity was a factor here. "Our sister colleges pay no salary," Stafford complained, thinking of schools run by religious orders, where nuns contributed their services for next to nothing. "The board and clothing of professors and a nominal sum for pocket money and car fare [are] the only expenses [they incur]." Seton Hall by contrast had an "enormous" bill of sixteen thousand dollars a year for faculty. "In the science of cutting rates our competitors outclass us," he thought, "practically" disqualifying it from matching them in "soliciting patronage." Seton Hall was too grand for some, not grand enough for others. Keeping costs low meant a second-rate faculty which made the school unattractive, a vicious circle. Rendered as a single budgetary item, Seton Hall's salaries were high. Rendered as a series of weekly checks, they were low. The College paid more for less, rival schools less for more: "Colleges conducted by religious orders train their professors for special lines of work. Particularly is this the case with the Jesuits who conduct most of our Catholic colleges. The consequence is that they are up to date in their knowledge, methods, and equipment. Seton Hall on the contrary must be content with an inferior staff of lay teachers because it cannot sufficiently remunerate professors of acknowledged ability and experience."

The College faced competition from parochial schools offering a good education at lower rates. It also failed to make the most of its centrality. "Our location adjacent to the great metropolis [of New York] with the populous cities of Newark and Jersey City at our very doors should ensure a large registration," Stafford thought. Publicly he boasted of the school's smallness and intimacy. Privately he worried about it.

Seton Hall's problem, in other words, was that it was neither one thing nor the other. It was either too pricey or too cheap, too much a finishing school for parents who wanted their children to have a trade, too much a trade school for parents who wanted their children to have some finish. Socially it straddled the hinterland between the well-to-do and the petty bourgeoisie. "The wealthier class . . . favor a University training for their sons after they have graduated from the public High Schools while the middle and poorer class rush their sons into the professional schools of the City whose doors are thrown wide open to the fortunate possessors of a high school certificate." As a result, it never fitted any niche: "There is an ambition inherent in young men today to take up professional work, complete it, and start hurriedly in the search for the mighty dollar. It matters not to them that their education is incomplete or that their minds lack that development which is the golden recompense of a thorough classical and sound philosophical education. This ambition coupled with the extraordinary facilities afforded by the State for the realization of its ideals is to my mind a death blow to the smaller college.

Stafford was eager for dollars but getting them often had little to do with education. In nine cases out of ten, he said, when parents had a son ready for college, "his choice will be largely influenced by the efficiency or weakness of the Athletics Department."[20]

Home Truths about Seton Hall

Belying these anxieties, Seton Hall remained apparently unchanged at the turn of the century. New Jersey Catholics were proud to have their own college and seminary. True, Seton Hall's austerity left something to be desired: but what Catholic school was not like that? Priests returning as grown men discovered that twenty years of adulthood meant nothing to college authorities who still saw them as children. One cleric, not himself a graduate of Seton Hall, found the atmosphere so infantilizing he vowed never to return. "Please book me for the first retreat," he wrote to the diocesan secretary in 1903: "I would also respectfully request that in view of my thirty-three years of priesthood a decent room be assigned to me . . . I have never complained when I did not even have a chair to sit upon, but a school bench. I never said anything unkind when I had to room with that loquacious old woman called Father Miller. I never complained when I had to sleep under a window with a pane of glass broken. It gave a cold that ended in [my] being laid up by rheumatism . . . I never complained when I was put alone in a hot box and was annoyed late into the night by the Young Bloods. . . ."[21] For a noncomplainer, he had a lot of complaints. Behind the gate, Seton Hall was a college less magnificent but more human than its publicity suggested.

Reunions recreated worlds that had never gone away. A visitor from Corrigan's time would have recognized the school he had left behind thirty years before. Almost everything was the same. A prefect or a professor was always around to insure good conduct. A student still spent hours studying Aquinas, Augustine, Euclid, Archimedes, Shakespeare, and Sallust. Memorization got him through one week only to see the next looming ahead, a race that never ended. For some it was too much. "Breaks Down from Study," reported the *New York Times* in 1903. "Seton Hall Graduate a Mental Wreck in an Indiana Hospital." The scholar was one John McGowan of Orange, "an indefatigable student" [who] "took all his books with him" on a trip out West.[22] Few of his contemporaries seem to have suffered similar prostration from overwork.

The regime relaxed at Christmas, Easter, and the Feast of Saint Joseph (March 19), when classes gave way to concerts and supervised levity. Stafford, who had a good voice, sang at Christmas parties. The 1906 commencement, the fiftieth anniversary of the foundation, was the first to be held indoors, taking place in the Newark Theatre to accommodate an audience of over 1,200. Bishop McQuaid, the last link with the earliest days, expatiated on the college's origins and the current state of Catholic education. It was like old times, a moralist remembering better days, as moralists often do.

Stafford stepped down as president in January 1907 to become pastor of St. Paul of the Cross Church in Jersey City. (He died in 1913.) "The College [is] in a very prosperous condition," recorded the Trustees in 1908, one reason being the generosity of donors. Mary O'Brien, a domestic servant, left $4,000 of her $10,000 life savings to Seton

Hall "for the education of priests."[23] Mary E. Carroll of Newark gave jewels to the value of $50,000 to three Roman Catholic institutions, of which Seton Hall was one. In the Seton Hall collection was a diamond-studded bracelet once belonging to Marie Antoinette and fashioned into a chalice after her death.[24] The New York publisher Peter Collier, cultivated by Seton Hall with an LLD and membership of the Board of Trustees, left the College a paltry $5,000 out of an estate of nearly $5 million.[25]

That the College was "growing and prospering" meant constant updating. Building on excellence was the theme: "Greater success could easily be attained if the institution were adequately endowed. Chief among its needs may be mentioned a new College dormitory, with private rooms for the senior students; a science building and music hall; more elaborate scientific apparatus, and more extensive geological and historical collections."[26] Not all these schemes came to pass but among Stafford's achievements were improvements in the chapel and the construction of a brownstone cloister uniting it with the seminary. He also built an Infirmary and residence for the Sisters of Charity who attended to the domestic needs of the college and seminary.[27] (After the Sisters departed, the Infirmary served as a dormitory for boarders and an academic building. It is now known as McQuaid Hall.)

Seton Hall had good enrollments, a clear curriculum of studies, and a well-stocked library (or so the catalog claimed) of nearly forty thousand volumes with room for more.[28] Justice Luke Stapleton of the Supreme Court of New York, addressing the class of 1907, praised the college as an "effective and generous if not an opulent mother,"[29] which hit the nail on the head. "The training of the heart and the formation of character under the guiding influence of Christian principles," said the catalog, "the awakening of the intellectual faculties, the arousing and strengthening of laudable ambition, the acquiring of habits of logical thought, correct methods of study, self-discipline and refinement, the realization, in a word, of the highest ideals of excellence in the cultured Christian gentleman—these are the ends that Seton Hall keeps steadily in view."[30]

Students were instructed in the doctrines of the Church, given "an intelligent faith" able "to withstand the manifold attacks" which awaited "after . . . college days are ended." But the interior life was also important: "The ceremonial of the Church is carried out with all possible solemnity and in its complete beauty in the College Chapel. Solemn Mass, during which a short instruction is delivered, is celebrated every Sunday of the school year and is attended by the students in a body. At vespers and Benediction, on Sunday afternoons, the Psalms and hymns are sung by the students. . . . Non-Catholics will be received, provided their parents or guardians are willing to have them placed under the influence of a Catholic institution. No efforts at proselytizing are made, but no exceptions in the order of the house are made in favor of non-Catholic students."[31]

Fifty years and counting, Seton Hall thought itself as good as any institution in the country. Father Charles Mackel, professor of ethics, metaphysics, and sociology, wrote to Michael Mulligan, a recent graduate studying in Rome, that he would "feel very ashamed if any one of you should return without having completed his course and obtained his doctorate . . . The students of our college are [not] inferior to any others."[32] Mackel alternated between vicarious pleasure at Seton Hall's achievements and resentment that he was stuck there. "For the past ten years I have been working night and day to render myself . . . qualified to fill a position for which I am not now competent and for which I was quite unfitted when it was imposed upon me by the supreme authority of the diocese . . . My projected work in ten volumes on 'The metaphysical essence of abstract ideas formally in the mind and fundamentally in the mud,' will remain forever more a shadow."[33] For some, Seton Hall was the place where dreams went to die. Professor John Johnson resigned to become a policeman (and was known for the rest of his career as the "scholar cop.") "His language in presenting his cases at court abounded with Latin quotations, to the great mystification of the other members of the force and the edification of lawyers and others in the courtroom."[34] Johnson escaped. Mackel was a lifer.

A New Man, a New Disaster

Stafford's successor was Father James Mooney, a New Yorker who graduated from Seton Hall in 1884 and who had studied for the priesthood in Brignole-Sale in Genoa, Italy. Ordained in 1889, Mooney was appointed to the Hall in 1902 where he wore many hats as professor of English and Latin in the College, and vice-rector and professor of theology and canon law in the Seminary. With two doctorates, one in divinity from Brignole-Sale, the other in law awarded *honoris causa* by Mount Saint Mary's, his scholarship was impressive. So, too, was his self-sufficiency. "He built the walls which kept other people from him," a colleague recalled. "You could respect him. You could feel a reverence for the ascetic life he had chosen. But he never encouraged you to like him."[35] To Will Durant, though, Mooney was a saintly figure: "I have never forgotten how, as my mother seemed near death, he hurried up from the rectory a mile away, knelt beside her bed, and prayed aloud while my father and the doctor stood aside, and how Mother seemed to take strength and courage from his prayers. From that day, I loved Father Mooney . . ."[36] His "ever vigilant and most adamant" discipline was what most people remembered.[37] For fifteen years, "there was never a time that he did not have the institution under complete control."[38]

It was good that Mooney was equipped for leadership because it was soon needed. On Sunday, March 27, 1909, between midnight and one in the morning, fire broke out in the basement of the College building and by dawn the structure lay in ruins. First to notice trouble was Austin Gibbon, professor of Latin and History in the High School, returning home after an evening out. Seeing a glow from the lower windows of the hall, he discovered that fire had taken hold of the lower level of the building and was rapidly spreading to the levels above. Gibbon alerted Mooney and together they evacuated the boys who were asleep on the third and fourth floors, then began to rescue books from the library. By the time the South Orange Village Fire Department arrived, the flames had intensified, forcing firemen to get help from Orange and Newark. It was three o'clock in the morning before the fire was under control, by which time the college building was destroyed. Damage to the library was slight.

In the middle of the night all was noise and excitement but at dawn, with rain falling and the boys homeless, it was a wretched sight: "Straw hats, overalls, bandanna handkerchiefs and other nondescript articles of clothing were in evidence . . . Students [asked] those more fortunate and even . . . the employees at the College for sufficient covering to enable them to get home . . . Trolleys and trains were filled with students wearing clothing too large or too small, and misfit shoes, but they did not seem much concerned at their losses . . ."[39]

The fire made national news. *The Washington Times* reported that the flames had destroyed "an historic college" with students barely escaping with their lives. O'Connor and Mooney "together with the priests of the seminary, rushed into the burning building and directed firemen to save books and manuscripts of almost priceless value." (The manuscripts were unspecified: insurance policies perhaps.)[40] "Seton Hall College Burns" ran *The Alliance Herald* of Box Butte County, Nebraska, its readers informed that the college was "the foremost training school for the Catholic priesthood in New Jersey." (The fire jostled with other stories: "Indians Surrounded: Posse closing in on Crazy Snake's Force near Pierce" and "Powers Solve Balkan Crisis: Reach Agreement regarding Austria and Servia.")[41]

Normality was proclaimed almost at once. "Of course, it is a great calamity and we deplore it very much," O'Connor assured reporters. "The College will be rebuilt: that is certain."[42] In fact, it was not certain at all. The seminary was squeezed to provide extra classrooms. Alumni Hall and the infirmary were fitted up as dormitories. As with the fires of 1866 and 1886, these improvisations implied that the school would continue come what may. Some favored closing the college as a way of keeping the seminary going, reversing the argument made by Stafford a few years before that the seminary's viability depended on funds from the college. O'Connor forced the issue by assuming the outcome. "Trustees of Seton Hall meet to discuss rebuilding," recorded Monsignor John Sheppard, a member of the Board, on April 6, 1909. "The meeting a little stormy."[43] In fact, the meeting was one of the sharpest in the Board's history: "Fr.

Kelly i.e. Mgr. maintained [the college] should not be rebuilt, just go on as we are with the Seminary. I believe we should have a good substantial building which will become in time a preparatory seminary."[44]

This was not an argument for abandoning the college but reducing it to fit new circumstances: for making permanent the temporary arrangements of the previous week. The case for rebuilding was emotional and practical. With Seton Hall's prospects good and local esteem high, a properly equipped college was still needed to train future priests. The key voice was O'Connor, who instructed Mooney to take immediate steps "in all matters relative to the rebuilding of the College." It was resolved "to leave to the Bishop the choice of location & cost of same." With that blank check, the crisis passed.[45]

Work began on the new building in May 1909 and finished (after some legal difficulty)[46] eleven months later. It opened in September 1910. An auditorium was fashioned from the surviving exterior walls of the old building, which in time came to be called Stafford Hall. (It survived until 2013.) The new building (now called Mooney Hall) was built of white brick, stone, and terra cotta, with an interior of reinforced concrete and a frontage of 180 feet and a depth of 80 feet, with classrooms, living rooms, study halls, a dining hall, and dormitories. Total cost, including renovation of the shell of the old building and repair of fire damage, was $131,000. With insurance, church collections, and other revenue, the College was rebuilt with an outstanding debt of $58,000. Bishop O'Connor gave $1,000. Father P.E. Smyth of St. Joseph's, Jersey City, gave $500 (and his parishioners $1,000). Saint Michael's in Jersey City gave $1,500, as did St. John's in Orange. Lesser gifts had a quirky specificity. Our Lady of Mount Carmel, Boonton, gave $59.19. St. Bernard's, Mount Hope, gave $9.29.[47] Everyone lent a hand, not least students themselves, one of them Will Durant: "We made cement, and hammered nails, and built chairs and desks, and painted walls and floors, and for a month or two exchanged the intellectual for the practical life . . . To this day I pass it (safely anonymous) with a strange feeling of affection and pride."[48] Seton Hall was rescued by the people it was intended to serve.

The renovation gave O'Connor an opportunity to implement a long-contemplated plan "to establish a Preparatory Seminary at Seton Hall." A bigger College building meant that future seminarians could enter Seton Hall as boarders or day students (in some instances as very young boys) at relatively little expense. Until September 1911, they had had to come as boarders, placing an "impossible burden, in many instances, on parents." O'Connor outlined his thinking in July 1911:

Within the last year or two, the number of day-students at Seton Hall has so increased that I have been led to consider the feasibility of instituting a Junior Seminary for day-students [who] can attend Seton Hall daily, without marked inconvenience, from such distant points as Paterson, Hoboken, Jersey City, Plainfield, Dover, Morristown, and the contiguous suburban towns. Moreover, the President of the College finds it practicable not only to introduce a schedule of religious exercises that will tend to enlighten and strengthen these students in their vocation, but also to so reduce the cost of tuition and of a warm lunch as to place the advantage of the Preparatory Seminary within the reach of students of the most moderate means.[49]

Pastors were now "to direct all the younger aspirants to the priesthood to Seton Hall, not merely for the continuation of studies already begun, but for the very beginning of their studies."[50]

A new College building meant that Bayley Hall Grammar School could move out of the rough brownstone building in which it had been originally housed into a building of its own. No trace of this older building now exists, but it seems to have been in the vicinity of the "Wash House" close to the seminary building. The Wash House is also defunct.[51] The new building was known as Bayley Hall or (for a time) "the new Bayley Hall building." Coming close on the heels of the pricey College Building, it required yet more expenditure. A mortgage of $25,000 was taken out, to which the diocese added another $25,000 in a loan.[52] Building got under way in 1913. The architect was J.T. Rowland of Jersey City (who received $2,640.25). The contractor was J.J. Egan (who received $53, 117.24). Total cost came to $56, 613.07, for which Seton Hall got its money's worth. Bayley Hall was two stories high with an attic and a deep basement, the exterior in the collegiate style, of light brick trimmed with limestone, the roof of slate and copper. Inside was a large basement recreation room, with a kitchen, pantries, and a dining room. The main floor comprised a large study hall, three classrooms, a recitation room, and prefects' rooms, also wardrobes, washrooms, toilets, and showers. The second floor had a large dormitory and living quarters for the Headmaster (a sitting room and bedroom). Basement to top floor were connected by two wide flights of steel and stone staircases, with the whole building fireproof. "It stands well isolated from the other buildings and yet forms a part of the general college group," stated the catalog. "It is well equipped for about eighty or ninety boys."[53]

Bayley Hall Grammar School graduated classes until 1926, when the presence of very young students on campus began to seem out of place. As a school, it gave "a very good account of itself in both scholastic and athletic prowess,"[54] producing at least one legendary teacher, Edward Jennings, who was "justly regarded by all former Bayley Hall students, as well as by his wider range of friends, as a rare guide in reaching the highest ideals of life."[55] After Bayley Hall closed, the building became the "College Lecture Hall" and was used in the high-sounding manner that the name suggests. It is now, once again, Bayley Hall.

Seton Hall and the Supreme Court

These institutional transformations amounted to a quiet revolution in the first twelve or thirteen years of the twentieth century. What Synott and Stafford dreamed of, Mooney accomplished. A quiet and reserved man, he was more interested in the cultivation of his interior life than in day-to-day administration of a college. On the other hand, when Seton Hall was attacked, he defended it; in 1916 that defense went all the way to the Supreme Court of the United States. Thanks to Mooney, Seton Hall has a place in the legal history of the United States.[56]

The origins of the story are remote, going back to the foundation of the college, also trivial. But important points of law were at stake, and Mooney did not let them go uncontested. As a result, he found himself devoting two years of his life to an arduous contest at the end of which some clarity was achieved with respect to Seton Hall's standing as a corporation and charitable entity. It turned out to be an expensive argument.

At first, nothing seemed amiss. In 1861, as we have seen, Seton Hall was incorporated by special act of the New Jersey Legislature (Laws 1861, p. 198) which granted a charter for advancing the purposes of education and which enabled it "to purchase, take, and hold real estate, provided the value thereof shall not exceed the sum of one hundred thousand dollars." In 1868, Drew Theological Seminary was also incorporated as an educational body (Laws 1868, p. 4) and it, too, was allowed to purchase property, the only difference being that "the property of the said corporation real and personal" was to be "exempt from assessment and taxation." This distinction was plainly unfair to Seton Hall. Accordingly, by a law of 1870 (Laws of 1870, p. 596), Seton Hall's original charter was amended so that it, too, and in precisely similar language, could enjoy the same exemption from taxation and assessment as enjoyed by its Methodist neighbor up the road. There was no provision in the act incorporating Seton Hall College giving it immunity from assessment and taxation; that arose under the 1870 act.

Meanwhile, one of the purchases made under the terms of Seton Hall's original charter was a farm bought in 1864 and registered with Essex County in 1865, its sole purpose being to supply the College and Seminary with vegetables and dairy products. As it had no commercial aspect, no-one thought any more of the purchase, then or for years to come. Nor was thought given to the fact that, to improve it, buildings and outhouses were added over the course of time. That the farm was at a small physical distance from Seton Hall but within the village of South Orange was also neither here nor there. The matter of tax did not arise because there was nothing to tax and, after 1870, there was legislative immunity from taxation anyway.

So far, so good. Unfortunately, the exemptions provided for in these charters proved less permanent than at first appeared. For one thing, by Mooney's time, even within the terms of the original charter, Seton Hall held real and personal property

substantially in excess of $100,000 in value. For another thing, the New Jersey Consti-
tution, passed in 1875 and subsequently amended, directed that property in the state
was to be "assessed for taxes under general laws and by uniform rules according to
its true value." A third consideration was that certain decisions of the New Jersey Supreme Court and the Court of Errors had held that "under our present Constitution"
there could be "no exemption of property from taxation by force of special or local
statutes, except, of course, in case of contract which the amendment of the organic law
could not reach." As a result, exemptions contained in charters granted prior to 1875
were repealed, unless the charter was in the nature of an irrepealable contract. Given
subsequent New Jersey case law, some of it dealing with religious and educational bodies, it was unlikely that Seton Hall's charter as granted in 1861 and amended in 1870
constituted such a contract. Indeed, decisions of the courts made clear that the 1861
act creating Seton Hall as a corporation, and the subsequent amendment to it in 1870,
did *not* constitute an irrepealable contract, and that College property *was* subject to
taxation at the will of the legislature. It was probably only a matter of time before the
tax man came calling.

There the matter rested until 1911, when the Village Tax Collector of South Orange
did knock on the door. Citing a Tax Law of 1903[57] which exempted from taxation all
buildings and lands "actually and exclusively used for colleges, schools, academies, and
seminaries" up to "five acres in extent" but including those above that amount, the Village authorities assessed the rest of Seton Hall's land (including the farm not physically
within the College grounds but adjacent to it) at a valuation of $35,000. (The same stat-
ute of 1903[58] exempted from taxation all buildings, lands, and personal property used
exclusively for purposes considered charitable under the common law.) This came as
a shock to Mooney, who refused to accept the assessment, claiming that the College
had acted fully within the terms of its original and amended charter in purchasing
and improving land and that it was therefore not liable to tax. After the passage of the
amended charter and before the enactment of the Constitution of 1875, he said, Seton
Hall had erected buildings, barns, stables, and dwellings on lands within and adjacent
to the College, which fell wholly within the terms of the Charter and were intended
not only for educational but also for charitable purposes at common law. The lands in
question, he said, from which the College derived "no pecuniary profit," were used
"solely as pasture lands for cows," with the dwellings thereon used to house the farm
hands; the farm produced only "milk, butter, and dairy products . . . used exclusively
at the table of the . . . College," with none of it sold, given away, or otherwise disposed
of; without these "absolutely essential and necessary" products the College would be
compelled to purchase the same. The farm was not a commercial enterprise any more
than Seton Hall was a commercial enterprise. The operation of one was essential to
the operation of the other.

To this outlandish claim, Mooney added another argument, hoping that if one failed the other might succeed. Since its foundation, Seton Hall had been conducted for the education of young men, some of them destined for ordination to the Roman Catholic priesthood. Of its students both clerical and lay, he said, some paid "no tuition or boarding fees whatever" and were admitted "as charity students." In teaching them, as in teaching all other students, the College did not "conduct its business for profit" and, in any case, it did not in fact make a profit. The tax demand would not and, he implied, could not be paid, because Seton Hall (its property now valued well in excess of $100,000) was without resources to pay what it plainly should not have to pay.

The argument that Seton Hall was chartered for charitable as well as educational purposes was intended to shelter it within New Jersey case law that looked benevolently upon eleemosynary enterprises. Thus the Sisters of Charity at Convent Station had claimed immunity from taxation in 1890 on the grounds that their buildings were used exclusively for purposes considered charitable at common law, that their charter was thus in the nature of an irrepealable contract and so unaffected by the property tax provisions of the 1875 Constitution, and that, for both these reasons, although their property exceeded five acres, it was not taxable. The claim was upheld because it was demonstrably sound. The charter of the Sisters showed that their purposes were to educate youth, to build and maintain a hospital for the sick and destitute, and to afford assistance to the poor and destitute. The Sisters were easily able to show that they did this.

The problem with Mooney's second argument, that Seton Hall enjoyed charitable immunity from state and local taxes derived from its charter, was that Seton Hall was *not* chartered for charitable purposes. In any case, the tax immunity contained in the amended charter of 1870 was most likely repealed by the Constitution of 1875 and subsequent court decisions. That the College acted charitably did not make it a charity. Indeed, to the extent that some students were enjoying free board and tuition and others were not meant that the latter were underwriting the former. Seton Hall's terms of incorporation in 1861 were nowhere near as broad as those of the Sisters of Charity, its original purpose being, let us remind ourselves, "the advancement of education" and not the granting of gratuities to otherwise unprovided-for students and their families. True, the argument could have been made that the education of priests was a charitable purpose at common law; but that would have been to contradict the plain intent of the 1903 act, which was to narrow, not broaden, the range of charitable exemptions. The act distinguished between, on the one hand, lands, buildings, and personal property "actually and exclusively used for colleges, schools, academies, and seminaries not conducted for profit" and, on the other, lands, buildings, and personal property used "exclusively" for purposes considered charitable under the common law. It was hard to see how Seton Hall fell into the latter category.

It was also hard to see how the College was immunized against taxation on the grounds that all its land was necessary for the fair enjoyment of the buildings and the uses to which they were put. (The tax demanded by South Orange village was leviable only on the value of land exceeding five acres exclusive of buildings.) That exclusion plausibly operated as far as the College campus was concerned (so that, for instance, Bishop O'Connor's house, situated on the grounds of the College, was probably exempt from taxation in that it was necessary for him to reside at Seton Hall in order to perform his duties as president of the Board of Trustees). Could it reasonably be said to work as far as a farm on the north side of South Orange Avenue was concerned? That provided an income—in the form of money saved that would otherwise have been spent on the purchase of farm products—not exclusively or even substantially used for charitable purposes, Mooney's claim to the contrary notwithstanding.

For all these reasons, Seton Hall needed better arguments to avoid the reach of the tax man.

As it turned out, there was another, although slender, argument to hand. What state law denied, federal law might permit; and two cases gave Mooney grounds for hope. In 1865, the state of Missouri adopted a Constitution which authorized the legislature to impose certain taxes; and subsequently the legislature did indeed tax the real property of a charitable body called the Home of the Friendless. The Home had been incorporated by an act of the Missouri legislature in 1853. Twenty years before the passage of the Constitution, in 1845, Missouri had passed a statute relating to corporations, the sixth, seventh, and eighth sections of which provided for the possible alteration, suspension, or repeal of a charter at the discretion of the legislature. However, the 1853 act incorporating the Friends of the Homeless exempted it from taxation and specifically excluded it from the operation of sixth, seventh, and eighth sections of the 1845 act. The question, therefore, was whether the charter of 1853 was a contract never to tax: the Home asserted that it was, the State that it was not. When the Home was assessed for tax, a Home whose objects included the care of destitute women, the assessment was disputed all the way to the United States Supreme Court. The Court held that the 1853 terms of incorporation, which stated that "all property of said corporation shall be exempt from taxation," were sufficiently explicit to require no further statement of legislature intent. The 1853 charter, in other words, was a contract never to tax, and as such it was unaffected by the 1865 Constitution. The tax assessment was therefore void.

A second Missouri case—Washington University v. Rouse—was also promising. There, the charter was similar to that of the Home of the Friendless and, into the bargain, the terms of incorporation indicated no limitation as to the right to acquire further property. The question then arose (when an assessment for tax was made) whether the university might acquire property beyond its legitimate wants. The court held that this fear was more imaginary than real. The corporation was created specifically to promote the endowment of a seminary, and it was not to be presumed that the corporation would ever act in such a manner as to jeopardize its corporate rights. If ever a case arose in the future where a corporation seemed to pursue a line of conduct different from that provided for in its terms of incorporation, then was the time to decide it. In the meantime, the Court set aside the assessment on the university as an impairment of the state's contractual obligation not to tax it.

Mooney had a choice. It seemed plain that state law was against him, that New Jersey courts would consider Seton Hall's charter not an irrepealable contract, and that the College was therefore subject to taxation at the discretion of the legislature. On the other hand, cases before the federal court had tended to take a contrary view or no view at all. The law was unsettled and, perhaps, it could be settled in Seton Hall's favor. For that to happen, the United States Supreme Court would have to overturn any decisions made against the College by state courts. Indeed, even if it were held that the charter of 1861, amended in 1870, *was* an irrepealable contract, then the difficulty remained that under the terms of that contract the College was immune from taxation only on property up to $100,000 in value. All property in excess of $100,000 in value, the Court would most likely decide, would still be taxable. Mooney decided to fight.

The progress of the case may now be described. On March 12, 1912, Seton Hall filed a petition with the Board of Equalization of Taxes of New Jersey seeking annulment and cancellation of taxes assessed on its property within the Village of South Orange; that is to say, on its farm and farm buildings, but not on the land upon which the College itself was built. The grounds for the petition were that the assessment was "unlawful and erroneous, and made through error and mistake," the College being exempt from tax under the terms of the original and amended charters of 1861 and 1870. On April 18, 1912, the Board held in favor of Seton Hall. On June 11, 1912, however, the Village filed for the reopening of the case on the ground that the assessor who had consented to the cancelation of the assessment had done so without having first sought the agreement of village Board of Trustees, who now sought reinstatement of the original assessment on the grounds that it was validly made. This argument was accepted and the matter was reopened.

The argument did not go so well for Seton Hall. Citing both the Constitution of 1875 and the Tax Act of 1903, the Board of Equalization of Taxes held that Seton Hall could only claim exemption from taxes under the amended 1870 charter if that charter were considered an irrevocable contract. There were good reasons for thinking that it was not so. For example, if the exemption were claimed under the terms of the amended charter, it failed because that charter had been passed long after an earlier act (1846) by which the New Jersey Legislature reserved for itself the right to alter, suspend, or repeal the terms of any and every charter it might thereafter grant. Likewise, if the exemption were claimed under the terms of the original charter, that, too, hardly amounted to an irrepealable contract because there was nothing in its language which suggested a binding contract between the State and the College. When it was passed, Seton Hall had been in existence for several years, it had purchased lands and erected buildings, and it was carrying out the purposes for which it had been incorporated. Even if its work were deemed charitable and thus exempt from taxation, there was nothing to show that such work would be discontinued if the legislature failed to grant it immunity. True, the argument could be made that, exempt from taxation, it could extend its field of operations as an educational institution and so increase the extent of its benefits to society. Any such extension would be purely voluntary, however, and was in no case conditioned upon the enjoyment of a tax exemption. Finally, there was the question of a state binding itself by means of irrevocable contracts. The presumption had to be that it was not in a state's interests so to bind itself. Thus in an earlier case before the Court of Errors and Appeals, it had been ruled that "a contract that disables the State from exercising the sovereign power of taxation, with respect to the property of a given corporation, is in derogation of common right, and, do far as it goes, is subversive of the power of government itself. Every reasonable intendment is against the existence of such a contract. He who comes into Court asserting its existence must be prepared to show that, in fact, it was made as alleged, and that its terms are such as to reasonably admit of no other interpretation than that claimed." For all these reasons, on September 17, 1912, the Board of Equalization of Taxes, reconsidering its earlier judgment, held that the 1870 Act amending Seton Hall's 1861 charter was not an irrepealable contract but was, rather, a gratuitous privilege extended to the College by the public and subject to revocation. The assessment for taxes was thus upheld.

Seton Hall promptly appealed this judgment to the New Jersey Supreme Court, claiming that it had been decided on "unjust, illegal, and erroneous" grounds and that its exemption from taxation was no gratuity but was in the nature of an irrepealable contract. It also insisted that its educational work was conducted without profit and was properly considered as charitable at common law. Finally, the College reiterated its claim that an exemption from taxation on the land in question was necessary for the fair use and enjoyment of the buildings on the land and for the general purposes for which the institution had been established.

It is hard to miss a sense of diminishing returns at this stage. These were not new arguments, merely the old arguments that had failed before. And, predictably enough, they failed yet again. The New Jersey Supreme Court, no more receptive to them than the lower court, dismissed the appeal.

Stymied at state level, Mooney had one of two options: either to accept the court decisions and abandon the fight or contest them at federal level and hope for a more favorable outcome. He had, as we have seen, at least some grounds for hope that an unsettled matter of law might be settled in his favor. What was at stake? Essentially this: that by insisting upon the revocability of Seton Hall's charters, the New Jersey courts had violated article 1, section 10 of the Constitution of the United States by which Seton Hall was entitled to enjoy unimpaired its contractual rights as established by those charters. Neither the New Jersey Constitution of 1875 nor the Tax Act of 1903 could undo that prior federal entitlement to contractual inviolability.

So Seton Hall argued before the United States Supreme Court; and so the Supreme Court refused to accept. Finding against the College at every level—in effect, reinstating every unfavorable judgment against it of the New Jersey lower courts—the highest court in the land closed off any further hope of redress. Mr. Justice William Rufus Day, in delivering the opinion, neatly summarized the legal basis upon which Seton Hall had conducted its business for over half a century,[59] noting that the court's task was to decide whether the college's charter, original and amended, constituted an irrevocable charter whose terms had been violated by 1875 Constitution of New Jersey (allowing for property to be assessed for taxation according to its true value under general laws and uniform rules) and by the 1903 act of the New Jersey legislature (4 N.J. Comp. Stat. 5079) which provided that all property not therein expressly exempted should be subject to taxation, and that all acts, general and special, inconsistent with its provision, were repealed. Day noted that although the court had indeed made such determination in the past, decisions of state courts in construing their own statutes were "entitled to much consideration and respect." He was unpersuaded of the applicability of the Home of the Friendless case to Seton Hall, upon which Seton Hall had placed "much reliance," noting that, in the Missouri case, the U.S. Supreme Court had held that the corporation was expressly withdrawn from the authority of the general act giving a right to alter, suspend, and repeal and, as such, its charter constituted a contract which could not be repealed. That was not the case with respect to Seton Hall. On the contrary, when the alleged contract was made exempting Seton Hall from taxation, the New Jersey act of 1846 was in force, providing that "the charter of every corporation which shall hereafter be granted by the legislature shall be subject to the alteration, suspension, and repeal in the discretion of the legislature." "It is only reasonable to assume," Day concluded, that the New Jersey legislature extended immunity from taxation to Seton Hall "subject to the right of alteration and repeal reserved in the act of 1846."

For a state to surrender its power to tax, a power which long-settled jurisprudence had held to be essential to its sovereign authority, the surrender had to be shown in language which could not be otherwise reasonably construed. Moreover, all cases of doubt had to be resolved in favor of the state. This spelled doom for Seton Hall. The state court was right to conclude that there was no binding contract exempting the college from taxation:

The college was incorporated under no promise of such exemption, and could not have relied upon it in undertaking the work for which it was organized. After the privilege of the act in favor of the Drew Seminary was extended to it, it made no new promises and assumed no new burdens. It is true it has been kept in operation, and it has doubtless continued and expanded its usefulness, but we fail to discover from anything in this record that it would not have done so except in reliance upon the tax exemption extended to it by the legislature. By the terms of that act, the state court has held that a revocable privilege was extended, and no irrepealable contract was entered into. Bearing in mind our own right of independent examination of questions of this character, we are unable to say that the conclusion reached is not well founded in law and fact.

It follows that the judgment of the state court must be affirmed.[60]

Mooney's adventure as a jurist thus ended in ignominy. He had argued his case in every court available to him and in each of them, with one exception, he had lost. Moreover, he had argued in a scattershot way, throwing this idea at the bench, then that, then throwing them all at once in, as it were, a louder voice. Was the effort courageous or quixotic? Here the verdict must be mixed. As early as 1911 he had been warned by his attorney that state law was against him. Still, it was worth giving it a go. A tax assessment of $35,000 was no small matter and a charter exemption was a charter exemption. It made sense to test the matter at law. He had also been told by the same attorney, but with no great confidence, that he might prevail at federal level, if only because case law relating to irrevocable contracts remained unsettled. It was Mooney's distinction—not a happy one—to have helped to settle it. Perhaps he might have been better advised to keep his own counsel.

Seton Hall as a Community

After a fire, a rebuilding program, and a Supreme Court reversal, Seton Hall survived because the Catholics of New Jersey wanted it to survive. Bishop O'Connor was a child of Irish immigrants for whom Seton Hall represented the possibility of a better life. James Kelley from Kearny, his father an Edinburgh-raised Dubliner, entered the college in 1916, and he, too, saw Seton Hall as the gateway to a wider world, in his case, as it turned out, the presidency of Seton Hall itself. LeRoy McWilliams entered the College in 1911 and the Seminary four years later, passing most of his life as a priest in Jersey City. "I spent from 1916 to 1949 under her aegis," wrote Kelley in his old age, "the finest thirty-three years of my life."[61] McWilliams, less romantic, acknowledged Seton Hall's faults, but its Irish classmates and professors, a collection of Bolands, McNultys, Flanagans, Barretts, Mooneys, McLaughlins, and McHughs, made him feel at home. (A few non-Irish also made the grade. The most remark-able German was Francis Charles Schreiner, who joined the staff in 1881 at twenty and was still teaching music fifty-three years later as "Professor of Piano, Violin, and Banjo.") If its limitations could be endured, Seton Hall was as good a place as any to spend a life, or part of one.

Some constraints made little sense. There were four prefects of disciple, one for each class, and on Thursdays (a day off) the biggest treat was to take a long walk with one. McWilliams baulked at this "holdover from ancient seminarian discipline" which was no fun for anyone.[62] On the other hand, students remembered affectionately the eccentricity of their teachers. Father Clarence McClary, the College vice-president, was tight-fisted. Father Thomas McLaughlin taught English so severely that the prose of Cardinal Newman, surreptitiously incorporated into exercises, came back corrected. (He "lacerated . . . sentences until . . . papers looked like a cross section of the venous system of a frog.")[63] Father Frank McHugh, Professor of Psychology and Ethics, wore a wig. (After his death, the Board of Commissioners of Newark offered O'Connor con-dolences on the loss of "a great student and scholar" dedicated to "the betterment of mankind.")[64] Mooney was "Pum-Pum," the best approximation of his cough as he did his rounds.[65] James ("Pop") Cloherty, a Christian Brother turned priest, was professor of English and mathematics, proud of his reputation as a teaching machine. Father John Dauenhauer, who taught history, economics, and Greek, was "Dingle." Father John Duffy was grandiloquent ("golden-tongued, sagacious, and winning")[66] but also frightening ("any-one who asked a question risked being drawn and quartered . . . the sarcasm that followed . . . would scorch paint").[67] On his day off he walked twelve miles to visit his mother.[68] He later became a bishop.

It took stamina to survive. Indeed, survival was not guaranteed. In April 1912, Charles English, eleven, a student of the Preparatory School, died of diphtheria. Sev-eral other students came down with it and the college had to close for fumigation. That was a rare break in the routine. Otherwise during the winter months, "liter-ary and musical entertainments, lectures, billiard tournaments and skating relieve the monotony of the season."[69] In reality, "Two students shared each room and shared a gaslight between two desks. The floor was bare. Each student had his own washstand, bowl and pitcher. If you roomed in the front of the house, in the winter, you wore a bathrobe as you studied, and it was common to wake up mornings and find ice in the pitcher. There was one room that was colder than all the others. We called it 'the freezer.' And one sub-zero afternoon, some-one hung a red ball outside the door and a sign that said, 'Skating here today'."[70]

For seminarians, the day began at 5:30 and by 6 they were in chapel, supposedly at prayer, some half asleep. Mass was at 6:30, breakfast an hour later. Classes began at 9. The Angelus was recited at noon, followed by lunch, more classes, Rosary at 3:30, more classes, spiritual reading between 5 and 6 and a conference with the Rector. The hours between 7 PM and 9 were spent in study and the day ended, as it began, in the chapel. The one treat was a smoke in the recreation room (pipe, not cigarettes). "No-one ever had to sing a seminarian to sleep."[71]

A Collegian's life was also regimented. Edward "Dutch" Heine attended Seton Hall Preparatory School and College from 1911 to 1917, before serving in France in World War I:

> A bell would get us up at 6 AM and we would wash and make our beds. We'd either attend Mass or report to the study hall until breakfast at 7:30 AM. Then there was a free period of 45 minutes before classes started. Thursdays there were no classes and students could leave the grounds, but permission to leave was hard to get. In other words, your whole life was lived on campus.

> Under these conditions, what was a healthy kid to do? There was a lot of talent at the College. Quite a few boys could play the piano and sing well, and they'd put on shows (minstrel shows) while others would play sports just to get the exercise. Remember, there was only one building on the campus, for both Prep and College. We ate and slept there, those of us who were not "Day Hops" attended classes there. It was one, big family.[72]

In 1911, the senior class had built a log cabin "modeled after the hut in which Abraham Lincoln was born," a story carried by newspapers in Missouri: "It took the students eight months to do the work in spare moments . . . It still remains to build the fireplace [but] when the last finishing touch has been put on the proud builders will have a house-warming to which they will invite the president of the college, the Rev. Dr. James Mooney, and other notables."[73]

Students lived under a regime whose discipline acknowledged the disruptive power of adolescent urges. One of Mooney's rare public causes (apart from losing a case before the United States Supreme Court) was to urge that the Fourth of July be celebrated with fewer firecrackers.[74]

The most notable rebel was Will Durant, clever and intermittently devout, who repaid his debt to the college by immortalizing its professors in prose. Some never forgave him.[75] Durant entered Saint Peter's College, Jersey City in 1907, intending to study for the priesthood, and after graduation worked briefly as a reporter before accepting Mooney's offer of a place in the seminary and a job teaching Latin, French, and geometry. He began his career as a "professor" in September 1909 and the result of his brief stint was a *roman à clef* called *Transition* and a "dual autobiography" written many years later with his wife, Ariel. *Transition* is a coming-of-age story in which the narrator, taken under the wing of "Father Morley," discovers himself at "South Hall" as a student and professor. Mooney—"Father Morley"—is described affectionately, Seton Hall acerbically. At first sight the College was "a paradise":

> You approached it by wide gravel walks that ran apart and then came together before the entrance of the administration building. Every inch of the walks was shaded by generously spreading trees. To the right lay great fields of corn and wheat, which fed the college tables; at the left was a spacious playground where happy lads were tossing baseballs, basketballs, and handballs, and the other paraphernalia of youth. The buildings were of gray stone that had taken on the mellow shades of age; the chapel particularly was picturesque with its fine rose window and its graceful lines. Behind the administration building were dormitories, classrooms, recreation rooms, and the sleeping quarters of the teaching staff.[76]

His colleagues were "rather uninspiring"[77] but friendly enough. Durant "shared a room and a mouse" with another member of staff. *Transition* is an assault on childish belief which is in some ways as childish as the ideas it repudiates. "He enters the seminary, generally a skeptic," one reviewer put it, "yet in the hope that the mysterious charm of a Catholic atmosphere will stem the rising tide of indifference and doubt." [78]

Durant's seminary job was to look after the library, a position he used to read material on the Index of Forbidden Books. "As librarian of Seton Hall College, the discovery of Darwin, Spencer, Spinoza, and Anatole France hiding among thousands of tomes of theology, wrought his apostasy."[79] The library was otherwise somnolent:

> Were you the only other librarian on duty? Yes
> About how many volumes were available? About 10,000
> About how many books circulated per day? Four or five
> Did the library's resources seem adequate then for undergraduate study? Yes
> For seminary study? Yes
> What would you judge to be the strong and weak points of the library's resources then, in light of your considerable knowledge of books now? Absence of modern literature
> Were there any special collections considered important? Can't say
> Was library use considered a necessary part of college study then? Or were textbooks commonly used to "cover the subject"? The latter
> How well were the facilities of the library used? Very little
> How many hours a day was the library open? About five
> How many days a week? Six

Was the library considered as a place to study or merely the place to hold books? Chiefly the latter. Not used as a place of study.

Were there any magazines, newspapers, or quarterlies available? No

Please add any other information that you wish: I used it as a pleasant retreat and can't remember seeing any other soul in it in my day, September 1909–June 1911.[80]

The library was typical of most seminaries the world over. "A great world-shaking movement had been in progress for some years in Germany [and England]," wrote Walter MacDonald in his classic account of student days in Ireland's Maynooth. Meanwhile, "our professors went calmly on their way, with a shrug . . . or a sneer . . . We heard nothing of myths or redactions or . . . the Synoptic problem. Our strong, child-like faith kept us safe in the Middle Ages."[81] "Modern Civilization?" Durant has Mooney exclaim. "Civilization, that began with the Anabaptist riots and ended with a Europe armed for suicide? 'Modern'" thought?—which began with individual judgment in religion, passed to individualism in religion, and was ending in an orgy of devil-may-care immorality, childless marriages, and capitalistic greed? 'Modern' science?—which changed its dogmas every century . . . ?[82]

Gerald Sloyan was a Seton Hall undergraduate only half a generation later than Durant (he was born in 1919 and went on to ordination and a distinguished career as a theologian and educator). He too saw problems. "We must face the bitter truth," he said in 1960. "Every man-jack of us in this room was irreparably maimed in his education in its early stages."[83]

Reliance on theological manuals was not a sign of laziness but overwork. Mc-Clary, vice-president of the College, taught chemistry and physics in the High School. McLaughlin, professor of logic, Latin, and Greek in the College, taught sacred scripture in the Seminary. Duffy, professor of Latin and English in the College, taught ecclesiastical history in the Seminary. Dauenhauer, professor of Greek and political economy in the College, taught sacred liturgy in the Seminary. McHugh, professor of psychology in the College, taught dogmatic theology in the Seminary. Modernism was the last thing on their minds.

Seton Hall's claim of encouraging students to show "originality of thought and expression" was largely for show.[84] Originality of thought was what students were encouraged *not* to exhibit. Socialism was introduced into the curriculum in 1912 because it was "deserving of analysis and discussion" but also because it threatened "the future stability of government and order" and needed to be understood before being refuted. (The course considered "the implications of socialism; the effects on progress in general; the decay of individual initiative; the supremacy of labor; the neglect of the arts and sciences; the disorganization of the family; the destruction of religion.")[85]

Seton Hall's task was to keep subversion at bay, whether in the form of high-spiritedness or skepticism. That job was easier said than done,[86] but generally it was done.

The Great War and After

In 1914, as war broke out in Europe, nothing troubled Seton Hall. In 1915, commencement speakers considered the "literary, social, and religious tendencies in recent thought" with no suggestion of the Western Front. In 1916, on the eve of the Battle of the Somme, the commencement talk was devoted to the church in mediaeval Europe.

When America entered the war in April 1917, 200 students and faculty joined a Carnegie Hall rally of 10,000 collegians pledging support for Wilson as Commander-in-Chief.[87] But these demonstrations of loyalty took a toll on student numbers. In 1911, Seton Hall had a combined total of students in the seminary, college, and preparatory school of 239, the bulk of them came from New Jersey, with others from New York and handful from Connecticut, Massachusetts, and Pennsylvania. The rest from came Cuba, Colombia, Mexico, and Brazil.[88] Many of these boys, of course, were not fighting age. By 1916, the college (excluding the Seminary and the preparatory School) was down to 105. By 1920, only 81 students were on the college books. For years, enrollment hovered around one hundred. During and immediately after the war, average enrollment was 94.[89]

The most immediate effect of war was death. In the last push on the Western Front in November 1918 a Seton Hall man, Lieutenant Daniel A. Dugan of Orange, was killed. The son of Judge Daniel Dugan, the younger Dugan came from a family with close connections with Seton Hall and New Jersey politics.[90]

By this stage, Mooney was past his best. In 1908, thinking to share power with the faculty, he introduced "Standing Committees" to advise on curricular matters, although it is unclear whether he listened the advice. In his decline he seemed exhausted. When a deputation from a local parish sought reduced fees for graduates of its high school, he was confined to bed by doctor's orders and received them in his bedroom. "Being in a languid state physically and mentally I agreed to [their] terms. In my better senses I realized at once that the tuition was absurdly low—ruinous if extended to other parishes—and was by no means to be duplicated."[91] Seton Hall, too, was in a languid state. The books were in balance, the debt had been reduced, cash was on hand for investment in high-yielding accounts. On the other hand, capital expenditure had stuttered to a halt. In 1920, the Board of Trustees mandated a new seminary building "to accommodate at least one hundred seminarians and provide rooms for the professors."[92] A year later, it mandated the same.[93] In 1922 it sold its farm on the north side of South Orange Avenue to raise money for the new building (and to avoid the tax which the Supreme Court had said it should pay on it). Still nothing happened. By the time he gave up the presidency, Mooney had become a caretaker who did not seem to care very much.

He resigned in August 1922—"tearfully . . . under the most unfair pressures"[94]—and died in 1928. O'Connor wanted a firmer hand and in Father Thomas McLaughlin, Mooney's successor, he got it. Mooney's last days were a mixture of illness and boredom but the final verdict must be positive. He left Seton Hall free of the debt he had inherited, its endowments intact, and with two new buildings, the College Building and Bayley Hall. Under him, Seton Hall had literally come through fire and survived. That was achievement enough.

CHAPTER 6

McLaughlin at the Helm

Germanic Efficiency

With McLaughlin at the helm, the drift of Mooney's last years came to an end. Before he took charge, the college had struck John Francis Neylan, a member of the class of 1903, as mediocre: "The old place looked down at the heel, and I have been sad whenever I have thought of it since, and wondered how those in authority could be so shortsighted as not to have built substantially and permanently on the foundations which existed a quarter of a century ago for a great institution."[1]

This was a sharp intuition. At the turn of the century, the college should have funded capital projects not in reaction to events (fires) but in anticipation of them (competition from other colleges and the growing Catholic population). Stafford had been baffled that a college so close to New York was not doing better, concluding that Seton Hall's chronically confusing finances held it back. By the time he resigned it was almost too late. Mooney had a sharp mind but he directed it inward not outward. Balancing the books, albeit by selling land and shrinking numbers, gave his successors a legacy to build on: but for much longer? "I took a day off and ran out to Seton Hall," Neylan wrote, and "was impressed by the utter indifference of those in charge."[2] (When McLaughlin got in touch, it was "the first word" he had received "from the high school and college where I spent six good years.") "I would have been delighted to have had a plate of the old stew. However, the reception was as chilly as the weather outside."[3] Seton Hall should have been cultivating Neylan, not turning him away. When it did, the effort was rewarded.[4]

McLaughlin's first act as president was to write to local priests telling them that Seton Hall could be "the equal of any institution dedicated to the imparting of sound knowledge and Catholic virtue." He wanted Seton Hall to be noticed, and no-one could fail to notice him. Born in New York in 1881 and raised in Montclair, he studied for the priesthood at Innsbruck, where he was ordained in 1904, completing doctoral studies in theology in 1908. At Seton Hall, he taught almost everything: English, Latin, Greek, psychology, philosophy, ethics, and public speaking in the College, dogmatic theology, sacred scripture, homiletics, and canon law in the Seminary. He also served as vice-president and dean of discipline in the college and vice-rector of the seminary. Such versatility was intended to save money but it also taught a lesson in the oneness of Truth (and McLaughlin's belief that he possessed almost the entirety of it). He enjoyed a joshing relationship with Bishop O'Connor, who left him to run the show.[5]

McLaughlin contained multitudes; or, rather, he failed to contain them. Booming and erudite, tall and *soigné*, he looked like a Hollenzollern portrait come to life. Germany obsessed him: there was more Munich than Montclair in his accent. (Will Durant captured him in *Transition* as "Father Farrell," with his 'tendency to speak English with queer Teutonic idioms—ending every fifth sentence with 'the same.'")[6] Everyone else called him "Schlitz." McLaughlin spouted information like water from a tap: hot, cold, muddy, clear, unstoppable. As a professor, he was inept.[7] Substituting for absent colleagues, he entered the room with an imperative "give me the book," the command establishing his authority to teach until it became clear that he could not. "No persiflaging!" he bawled at talkative students, the word itself rendering them speechless. His moralism was severe. The 1931 College Yearbook was banned from the seminary because the wrestling team was photographed insufficiently clad. A student seeking admission to the seminary was rejected because, sporting a moustache, he exhibited a certain "lightness of mind." Seminarians wishing to swim were told to wear costumes "usque ad genua et extenens" (down to the knees and beyond). Modesty was insisted upon, with seminarians in the six-man dorm rooms required to dress and undress behind small screens. (Most of them ignored this as impractical.)[8] Ordinands drinking beer to celebrate his appointment as Protonotary Apostolic were told that "into my cup of joy some wormwood has crept." (McLaughlin knew he was a character and played up to it.) But there was anxiety, too. A 1926 freshman, John J. Dougherty, remembered that "you were sort of in fear of authority and persons." Even as "young men [we thought] that some of the decisions were arbitrary, personal or not well reasoned. But we did nothing in the way of protest."[9] Resistance was futile. McLaughlin was possibly wrong but never in doubt.[10] "Prefects must take more pains to keep their own rooms in order," he wrote in his diary in 1924. "No cigarettes. Must insist in season and out of season on order. Must make them understand they are not lords on whom all must dance attendance but clerics who are willing to sacrifice their own concerns . . . They are permitted to read papers and magazines only in reference to matters in which B.H. [Bayley Hall] is concerned."[11]

"Must insist in season and out of season on order." Here was his world view in a nutshell.

McLaughlin set the tone, made the system work, and articulated the governing philosophy. Addressing priests and faculty at the beginning of the academic year in 1927, he struck a characteristic note, telling them that "on account of the present condition in which I must continue to guide both [the College and the Seminary] . . . all will help to make the burden easier by accepting conditions as we find them and being contented":

> Let us try to make this college by our mutual sacrifices and inspirations for men what St. Elizabeth is for women. Especially stress Catholic culture.
> Please do not make any changes without consultation . . .
> Promptness in regard to the monthly marks the senior professor of each class or division will see that they are in the hands of the registrar before the morning 8.30 of the last Thursday of the month . . .[12]

Recently appointed teachers were reminded that teaching at Seton Hall was a spiritual calling. "All professors should realize that they are working here not for a mere livelihood but actually are fulfilling a sublime mission in their own lives while they are co-operating in the development of the minds and hearts of the boys according to the Plans of Divine Providence." "Young teachers," he said, "should never be unduly critical of their superiors and other ecclesiastical authorities" and, as far as the Church was concerned, they should not investigate its history "except through the channels provided for in canon law."[13] If they chafed, they could resign. "The practice of being out late frequently is hardly compatible with successful teaching, especially if in addition to carrying your classes you may be engaged in extra work [to supplement, he did not add, the meagre salary]. Anything that would reflect upon the character of the institution or its personnel would call for a severance of relations."[14]

"Be boosters, not knockers," he urged. "Do not lend a ready ear to complaints on the part of students or outsiders or be a party to disgruntled criticism . . . Avoid, especially before the students, comparisons between institutions which may be odious."

Loyalty was important, too: "Some of you no doubt intend to pursue or engage in other occupations not inconsistent with your work here. We are not opposed to this. In fact we rather welcome it. It indicates laudable ambition . . . Should, however, it become apparent that anyone is only going through the motions of teaching I must not only in the interest of the student body but of the reputation of the institution and the cause of Catholic education plainly state that we shall have to dispense with the services of such."[15]

Teaching came first, scholarship second (if at all). "Preserve discipline . . . through the creation and sustaining of the students' interest . . . This presupposes interest on the part of the teacher as well as a certain degree of mastery." Confidence was important but so also an awareness of different abilities:

> A professor's utility is over when the students are able to remark among themselves "he does not know much more about the subject than we do." When you perceive

a student displaying little or no interest, before reproving him study the causes in order that you may apply the proper remedies . . . We are not to blame for variation in mental equipment dependent [on] previous preparation, character of schools previously attended, native ability, home environment, etc. What we are concerned with is the fact of the group as we find them. It would be as unfair as unpedagogical to devote oneself solely to the gifted and those who are fully up to grade. In most instances the individual himself is not to blame for the lack of mental equipment . . . Nor will it do to throw up one's hands and say we cannot do anything with this or that section . . . [16]

McLaughlin saw the danger of too close an association between pupils and teachers: "boys must never become the companions of the professors . . . [They] are not to be permitted to visit [their] rooms except for . . . direction in study and then only with the consent of the disciplinary authorities." Beginning and ending each class with prayer ("devout recitations of the Ave"), attending the sacraments frequently, a professor had to live an edifying, quasimonastic life.

Religion teachers, in particular, had to avoid any taint of positivism: "We consider the class in religion to be not only from a spiritual but from an educational standpoint the most important class in the curriculum . . . It must not be a purely informative class, nor one in moral casuistry, nor a forum for curious questions, but one in which the student will consciously grasp the need of living in accordance with our holy religion inspired with an idealism for the most sacred things . . . [17] That truth grasped, all would be well.

Seton Hall Renewed

McLaughlin's expansive vision required, for the first time in a generation, a serious capital campaign. Writing to local clergy and through them to their parishioners, he envisaged chemistry, physics, and biology laboratories at a cost of $15,000. Another $6,000 would see to blackboards, desks, and maps; $5,000 were earmarked for the library, $10,000 for gymnastic equipment, $11,000 for a house for the groundskeeper, $8,000 for renovation of the chapel in addition to (price unknown) a new organ. Altogether, $65,000 would put Seton Hall on its feet. The sum was exaggerated to encourage generosity but without some such figure the College could not compete with "public institutions of learning, even . . . the elementary schools." The next generation needed a "proper appreciation of Science and Literature [uncontaminated] by skepticism"[18] and Seton Hall could provide it.

Neylan from California responded with $5,000 for the gymnasium (leaving McLaughlin to wonder how much would have given had he been approached sooner).

Other sums accrued so that in June 1923 the Board of Trustees congratulated itself on "the highly prosperous condition of the College." (Seton Hall owned $125,000 worth of United States Liberty Bonds that summer.)[19] By 1924, nearly $55,000 had been raised, allowing Alumni Hall and the Seminary to be gutted and repaired, classrooms repainted, the chapel given a new organ and a facelift.[20] A new kitchen and heating plant were installed, and an iron fence around the boundaries of the college (except at the front on South Orange Avenue).[21] The laboratories and gymnasium were renovated from top to bottom. The campaign realized $52, 872, the refurbishments costing $79,333.[22] The difference would be covered by improvements paying for themselves over years.

The Quest for Respectability

Apart from physical neglect, Seton Hall was also *ad hoc* in its academic organization. Mooney's "Standing Committees" concealed the reality that power resided with the president and bishop. Departments, offices, secretaries, structures of promotion, encouragements to scholarship: these things simply did not exist. Reputation in the "profession" meant nothing to faculty. They had no *profession*. They had a job.

McLaughlin realized that this amateurism had to change. In the early 1920s, Seton Hall graduates wishing to become teachers took courses in educational psychology, secondary education, and the philosophy of education; courses which did not qualify them to teach in public schools. Professional bodies did not recognize Seton Hall degrees, meaning that would-be teachers had to undergo additional examination by state boards to be certified. McLaughlin resented this intrusion into his autonomy. "The views of non-Catholics on these subjects are . . . fundamentally divergent from ours," he wrote in 1924. "To pass such examinations Catholics [are] compelled to study works . . . noxious to Catholic faith and moral principles, while in the field of history the glorious work of the Church, when not misrepresented, is ignored."[23] But enrollment would suffer if students discovered that they were studying for a degree which did not advance their careers. Accreditation by a Catholic organization might answer the difficulty.

Bayley and McQuaid had founded Seton Hall to escape the interference of others, but fifty years of the administrative state—court decisions, tort law, statutory requirements, duties of care, expanding federal government—put paid to the notion that any corporate entity could be, or should be, free of outside control. A school could not be a self-governing island. Under the terms of the Immigration Act (1924), for example, Seton Hall required the approval of the Secretary of Labor "as an institution of learning for immigrant students." This was granted in September 1924. (The first student to benefit was Hugh Meenan from Ireland whose visa request was handled personally by McLaughlin.)[24] Successive presidents regarded outside agencies as nuisances but now they could no longer be kept at a distance. Since 1898, the academic work of the Seton Hall Preparatory School had been recognized by the Regents of the University of the State of New York "as the equivalent of a four-year high school course."[25] Seton Hall College's BA and BS degrees gained approval by the same body in 1909.[26] But when McLaughlin asked the New York Regents to approve the degree of PhB (Bachelor of Philosophy) he was told that for years those Regents had sent Seton Hall forms to renew its accreditation and, for years, those forms had gone unanswered. Mooney simply ignored them, perhaps not even opening the letter. The result was potentially disastrous. "We may lose our rights to confer degrees of any kind which would be recognized in New York State," McLaughlin informed O'Connor, and with it the likelihood of students from that state enrolling at the College. The forms were not hard to fill out, requiring financial information, lists of salaries, numbers of students, qualifications of the faculty, and the like, but collating the information would show how underpaid were Seton Hall teachers and how run-down its physical plant. McLaughlin reckoned that Seton Hall's business was nobody else's business. In this he was mistaken.

Failure to abide by New York regulations was an argument for accreditation by *some* outside organization. "If we wish to retain our place as a recognized institution," he told Bishop O'Connor, "it seems that something ought to be done towards approval and standardization . . . Technically we [do] not meet all the requirements for standardization but that we might be able to tide over matters for a year and . . . make such adjustments as would enable us to present at least a satisfactory Arts course, if not in Science."[27]

The agency he had in mind was the Catholic Educational Association, to which he made application for membership in August 1923. Tracing its origins to 1899, the CEA did not formally come into existence until 1904, its purpose to provide standards for parochial schools, high schools, and colleges. Many Catholic colleges were linked physically to preparatory and high schools that shared their premises. For most people this posed no problem, but for educational reformers it was reason for concern. The CEA, created to impose academic and financial discipline on schools and colleges that lacked common standards, revolutionized Catholic education. Schools like Holy Cross College in Worcester, Massachusetts eliminated their preparatory schools early. Other places took longer. But some definition of a Catholic college was needed and, in 1915, the CEA provided it. A "standard" college had to have at least seven departments, each with a full-time professor holding a college degree or its equivalent. A college also had to meet rules regarding library assets, teaching loads, credit requirements, laboratory equipment, and so on. By the early 1920s Catholic colleges had much to gain by the CEA's imprimatur and much to lose by its withdrawal.[28]

Some standards were common sense. "A college should demand for admission the satisfactory completion of a four-year course in [an approved] secondary school . . .

the financial status of each college should be judged in relation to its educational system . . . a college should have . . . a library of at least 8,000 volumes." Seton Hall had no trouble with that. On the other hand, the rule that "for a college of approximately a hundred students, the faculty should consist of at least eight heads of departments devoted full time to college work" posed a problem. Seton Hall had no heads of departments because it had no departments. "A college should not maintain a preparatory school as part of its . . . organization. If a school is maintained under the college charter, it should be kept rigidly distinct from the college in students, faculty, buildings and discipline." Synott had begun to tackle that problem a generation earlier, but Seton Hall was still dependent on its preparatory school, as was the preparatory school on Seton Hall. These difficulties notwithstanding, McLaughlin thought he could satisfy the CEA.

He should not have been so confident. McLaughlin traveled to Milwaukee in June 1924 to attend the annual meeting of the CEA, but the Accrediting Committee of the CEA had scheduled no meeting at that time, a fact of which he had not bothered to inform himself. The application was deferred until 1925, two years after the original submission. But the trip was not wasted. Before leaving Milwaukee, McLaughlin met with Father Albert Fox, S.J., chairman of the Accrediting Committee, and Father J.W. Maguire, the secretary who had failed to read the application. Both men pointed out weaknesses that would have doomed it, chiefly Seton Hall's lack of departments, the fact that some instructors taught in the High School and the College, and the fact that the college lacked accreditation with local boards of education. Thinking on his feet, McLaughlin offered answers to these difficulties, not believing them himself. "I told them that [lack of departments] might be remedied," he wrote to O'Connor, "though personally at this moment I do not see how." State approval was touchier. "We are not accredited with our local standardizing agency. To this I replied that our degrees are recognized in New York and New Jersey (though I knew that this did not count)." The biggest problem was faculty. "With very few exceptions, the degrees of our professors were our own," they complained. "This irritated me, and I retorted 'How about a certain religious order whose members, practically all, pursue their studies in their own houses, and teach without any degree at all.'"[29] Glimpsing McLaughlin the Headmaster, the Jesuit chairman beat a retreat.

Without abandoning the CEA application, indeed recognizing one of its stipulations, another option was to seek accreditation from the Middle States Association of Colleges and Secondary Schools. This body originated in an 1887 effort by some Pennsylvania colleges to lessen the impact of taxation on property used for educational purposes. It became the College Association of the Middle States and Maryland in 1889, publishing its first list of accredited colleges in 1921.[30] As McLaughlin explained to O'Connor, Seton Hall could not hold itself aloof even from secular bodies. "Either we must give up our autonomy to some extent and arrange our work as these people dictate, being subject to visitation every five years, answering questionnaires every three years, or proceed as we have been doing independently, allowing our students to take their chances of admission to professional schools or practice . . . Several times I have been placed in the embarrassing position of having had to evade the question on student blanks 'with what standardizing agency are you accredited?' Unless we are accredited we cannot compete on equal terms with other Colleges, even those of our own faith."[31] O'Connor agreed that Seton Hall should apply both to the CEA and the Middle States Association.

Finance played a part in the reluctance to bow to outside pressure. By CEA standards, a department could consist of "one leading professor for each particular subject," which did not preclude, but acknowledged, the possibility of one-person departments.[32] But a "leading professor" meant a professor who would teach nothing but that subject and (self-evidently) one who was capable of teaching it. In classics and theology, in which every priest on the faculty was competent, this was no problem. In science or mathematics, on the other hand, an expensive layman, or laymen, might have to be hired (or a priest especially trained) to take charge. To establish departments, in other words, meant finding money. Eight new professors (one each in English, classics, history and social science, religion, natural sciences and mathematics, and education, and two in philosophy) would mean an extra $6,400 per annum if priests were appointed to head them and more if they were staffed by laymen. No science or mathematics teacher could be had for less than $2,000 a year.

Seton Hall could not afford such sums. The "College department as such is not a paying proposition," McLaughlin told O'Connor. There were 119 students doing college work in 1924. Of these, half were boarders and half day boys. Of the boarders, only five paid full freight. The rest were clerical students on reduced fees. The Seminary was subsidized by the College and the College was subsidized by the High School and all (in some sense) were supported by the diocese as sponsor and customer. To the CEA's insistence that "a college should not maintain a preparatory school as part of its organization," McLaughlin responded that most Catholic colleges and seminaries would cease if the stipulation were strictly enforced. The CEA knew this too. Its requirement that schools and colleges be distinct "in students, faculty, buildings, and discipline" said nothing about shared sites or revenue. High schools might still support colleges and seminaries if the rules were read generously.

Indeed, a rosier picture of the Seton Hall's finances could be painted with a little manipulation. What if priests could be considered as a kind of "living-endowment," with their low salaries considered as a gift-in-kind to the school? The difference between a clerical and lay salary could be calculated as a dollar amount. In fact, in 1924 McLaughlin reckoned the figure to be $54,780.97, a preposterous but ingenious way of turning poverty into wealth.[33] Financial autonomy was obviously in the eyes of the beholder. Seton Hall thus won CEA accreditation in 1925.

But what of Middle States? In 1922, McLaughlin had been approached by it with a view to joining, an overture he resisted.[34] Five years later, he continued to have qualms. "We do not intend to sit idly by and allow a privately formed organization to hinder our work," he told E.D. Grizzell of the University of Pennsylvania, chairman of the association. "It will not be necessary to send any inspector to Seton Hall."[35] But this was bravado. By 1928, McLaughlin realized that its approval really did carry weight.

It took another five years for Seton Hall to win Middle States accreditation, and for a simple reason. The accreditors asked questions in 1927 that revealed the chasm between their idea of a college and McLaughlin's. "Is the Chief Librarian profession-ally educated? Where?" *Chief* librarian? How about *any* Librarian? McLaughlin was bemused:

> How long have . . . entrance requirements been in force? Since 1922
> Who administers the entrance requirements? The President.
> Are the entrance records kept on file subject to inspection? Yes
> In how far does the work of the first college year articulate with the second-ary schools? Inasmuch as it is the continuation of the usual Classical and Latin-scientific curriculum.

These answers were deceptively coherent. The continuation of the usual classical and scientific curriculum meant that a boy could leave Seton Hall Preparatory School in June and begin at Seton Hall College in September and hardly notice the difference in surroundings, classmates, and teachers. Keeping entrance records subject to inspec-tion was easy when the only inspector was McLaughlin. Other questions produced bluff or ignorance or both:

> Number of College Buildings? 5
> Number of Classrooms? 8
> Average student capacity of each? 35
> Are the hygienic conditions excellent? Yes
> Value of Scientific apparatus in your institution? $40,000
> What percentage of this do you rate as effective? 100%
> Annual expenditure for the chemical laboratory? $500
> Biological laboratory? [blank]
> Physical laboratory? [blank]
> Others? [blank]
> Amount of the library fee? $5

Annual appropriation for library? [blank]

Annual expenditure for books and periodicals? [blank]

Number of librarians and assistants? 3

Salaries of librarians and assistants [blank]

Number of volumes exclusive of public documents? [blank]

What percentage of these do you rate as effective? [blank]

Number of public documents? [blank]

Number of periodicals subscribed for? 9

Student capacity of college library? 5

How many hours a day in the library open? 3

Technically truthful answers were practically false: "Can candidates from your institution enter graduate schools of high standing such as Harvard, Yale, Columbia, Cornell, Chicago, Johns Hopkins, Princeton, and the University of Pennsylvania? Yes." (Seton Hall did not send students to such places.) Occasionally only the unvarnished truth would do: "Salaries of Professors? Associate Professors? Assistant Professors? Instructors? The professors, with two exceptions, are Catholic clergymen, devoting their time exclusively to education, and receive a moderate competence." That being so, other questions answered themselves: "Give on a separate sheet a list of the recent books, articles, reports, published experiments, and original researches of the members of your faculty. [Blank]"[36] McLaughlin was a schoolboy doing an exam for which he had not done the revision.

Yet dozens of other colleges were in the same position. After all, there would have been no need of accrediting agencies if everyone miraculously maintained high standards. Middle States knew this. It also knew that its own future depended on having as many colleges as possible accept its membership, which is why Seton Hall was invited to apply in 1922. And so, in May 1932, Dr. George Chambers of the University of Pennsylvania visited Seton Hall on behalf of the Association. He found lax admission standards, an inbred faculty, unimaginative teaching, an underfunded library, overcrowded classrooms, shaky finances, and poor salaries. Some students had "entrance records of a doubtful character." Of fourteen teachers in South Orange,[37] only one had a PhD (teaching eighty-seven students packed into one room once a week). Most had MAs from the seminary, with one or two having only a bachelor's degree. A "considerable number" of classes exceeded thirty students. Some lectures were dictated and taken down verbatim. Language was taught "by individual recitations." Too many teachers taught too many subjects. (Mathematics and biology, for example, were taught by one man.) Laboratory facilities for chemistry were "ample" but for biology inadequate: five microscopes. The library had 14,000 volumes and 50 seats but "no large dictionary" and poor collections in mathematics, biology, and astronomy. The periodical collection was "meager" in arts and nonexistent in science. On the positive side, Bayley Hall contained "four good sized, well lighted and well-furnished rooms for lecture and recitation work."[38]

Some of these complaints were unfair. To deplore language teaching by rote was to condemn standard practice. To disparage Seton Hall's preference for its own graduates was to ignore part of its *raison d'etre*. To complain of low admission standards was to forget that even mediocre high school pupils deserved a chance. But enough was right about Seton Hall to suggest that what was wrong with it could be fixed. Five months after the report, and with promises to repair deficiencies, the Middle States Association accepted Seton Hall's application for membership.

McLaughlin had already embarked on reform of the curriculum, in 1926 introducing a "pre-medical" program:

> Seton Hall College presents three curricula, Classical, Scientific, and Pre-Medical. Courses in Education, recognized by the New Jersey State Board of Education are also presented in the Junior and Senior Years.
>
> Classical. The studies in this curriculum lead to the degree of Bachelor of Arts. The Arts course is especially recommended as providing the best training for any special scientific, professional or literary work that may be undertaken.
>
> Scientific. The Scientific curriculum leads to the degree of Bachelor of Science and is intended for those who have pursued a scientific course in an accredited high school and who are reflecting either on pursuing scientific work in later life or desire to secure that general knowledge and culture which can be derived from the study of the natural sciences, modern language, and philosophy.
>
> Pre-Medical. The Pre-Medical course as such is not something distinct and apart from regular collegiate work. Practically all medical schools today prefer to receive students who have secured their baccalaureate. Students reflecting on medicine should pursue in their courses definite studies in Chemistry, Biology, Physics and Modern Languages, preferably German or French.[39]

"Pre-med" was marketing, a way of making undersubscribed science classes more appealing while satisfying state requirements for teaching future medical students. It was not a new program. More telling was the *rationale* for Latin and Greek, once good in themselves, now merely ways of "training" the mind. That was new.

Other changes were harder. "The minimum salary to be paid to a head of department is $3,500 if he is married; and $2,500 if we board an unmarried man," McLaughlin reported to the Board of Trustees following the Middle States visit. The sums required would be "impossible to meet in view of the depression and the financial [state of the college]."[40] The money would be found through loans, gifts, and diocesan support.

Only the "certitude of a subvention for at least four years in the amount of approximately $30,000 per year" could allow the new salary structure to be put in place. As with the CEA, McLaughlin's anxiety was loss of autonomy. "It will not be advisable to grant many honorary degrees, as this is looked upon askance by accrediting agencies," he told Bishop Thomas Walsh (now Bishop of Newark since O'Connor's death in 1927). The days of the easy doctorate were over.

Priests were cheaper to employ than laymen and so it made sense for the diocese to identify academically talented clerics for advanced study, expecting them to teach at Seton Hall and perhaps spend the rest of their lives there. Aquinas House of Studies (1931) was the result. "The simplest type of college must have on its staff professors possessing the degree of Doctor of Philosophy in specific branches for at least seven departments . . . This necessitates special university graduate work, and . . . to avoid the dangers that might accrue to young priests from promiscuous attendance without proper supervision, this House of Studies has been established."[41] The purchase of a house in Ward Place, South Orange allowed the Institute to open in June 1931. "Institute" was a grand term for a household of young priests of differing aptitudes and personalities. McLaughlin required them on June 28, 1931 to "report" for supper before fixing their assignments:

> Reverend John J. Outwater to Fordham: Education and History
> Reverend Leo Martin to Columbia: Natural Sciences and Math
> Reverend James McCarthy to Columbia: English and French

The Aquinas Institute had high ambition—

> July 2: Father Outwater registers at Fordham for Education
> Father Martin at Columbia for Physics and Calculus
> Father McCarthy for English

followed by dawning reality—

> July 13: Rev Leo Martin and James McCarthy discontinue Columbia, the work being entirely beyond them.

Famed for his wit, Martin survived the Columbia embarrassment by matriculating at Fordham to study Classical Languages (although he later left because of a breakdown in health). McCarthy abandoned doctoral ambitions and became a pastor.

Aquinas House was quasimonastic, its priests McLaughlin's spiritual children. "I at a meeting of Aquinas House Fathers emphasized the necessity of no outside engagements, reporting for supper at 6 PM every night, cost of expenses namely 50 [cents] for dinner, commutation ticket, regular Sunday work. Delivered a pep talk—they should master their subject—satisfaction from such mastery and a great gain for Seton Hall to have men (priests) who excel in each branch. . . ." If infantilizing, the venture was nonetheless a marker of seriousness, an effort to appease the accreditors. To that extent it succeeded, even if some of its inmates failed.

McLaughlin fostered talent by sending priests to the Ivy League. He also tried to bring the Ivy League to Seton Hall. Recruiting professors from Columbia, Yale, and Harvard could lead to non-Catholics teaching Catholic students but he was able to "secure a very good group of gentlemen," six in all, from leading graduate schools to head the recently established departments.[42] Only two were Catholic but all were "in sympathy with our viewpoint and promised to conform to our regulations . . . in the matter of principles and readings . . . I have found [them] courteous and deferential, ready to carry out every wish." One of them, James Lackey of Columbia, professor of natural science, was married to a Catholic "and is raising his little family in our religion." Another had reportedly spoken "disparagingly of a Catholic Author" but this "was not verified on investigation."

The hires were impressive. As head of classical languages, John Joseph Savage of Harvard published in *Speculum*, the major journal of medieval studies. He left after a couple of years and was replaced by James F. O'Donnell of Holy Cross and Catholic University, author of significant work on the Latinity of Saint Gregory the Great. Allen Woodall, head of English, produced a fine translation of Horace. Milton Proctor, head of the department of education, had written for the *Journal of Educational Sociology*. Lawrence McGrath, with graduate degrees from Harvard and Stanford, headed the new department of social science (which included history).

The men came to "departments" which had not yet developed a sense of their own importance. The study of education was optional and "recommended only to those who intended to enter the teaching profession."[43] Proctor's department gathered together a group of courses (philosophy of education, philosophy of secondary education, methods of teaching with observation, educational psychology) that enabled a student to obtain a teacher's certificate from the state of New Jersey. Of these, the most important was the first, which presented "the fundamental principles of philosophy underlying the true concept of education" and criticized "prevailing modern systems of thought."[44] The department of English, giving students "such mastery over his language as will enable him to use it . . . with correctness, clearness, grace and force," also taught how "to distinguish between the good and the bad in literature," with emphasis on "the masterpieces of British and American literature" and "the Irish contribution to English literature." The textbooks were *English Literature* by Brother Leo, F.S.C, and *The Stream of English Literature* by Sister Eleanor Carver.

The department of history and social science offered only two history courses—History of the Christian Era I (for freshmen) and History of the Christian Era II (for sophomores). The first ended and the second began with the "Outbreak of the Protestant Revolution, 1517." Sociology was its other area, applying "sound principles of Catholic philosophy and theology to all social problems of family, state marriage, population, eugenics, morality and the child, education, crime, ownership, employment and wages." The encyclicals of Pope Leo XIII were used "to refute the errors that were started in the name of sociology by the various socialistic, evolutionistic, materialistic, or rationalistic schools, and which have great influence in the writings of many modern sociologists."[45]

The department of modern languages enabled the student "to read at sight any selection from ordinary literature . . . conversation is also stressed." As well as French, German, Spanish, and Italian (the last of these taught in the seminary at Darlington), there were classes in Polish, Slovak, and Lithuanian. Although the training was rudimentary, Seton Hall was a pioneer in teaching the languages of Eastern Europe. Nearly twenty years later, in 1951, only nineteen universities and thirteen colleges throughout the United States offered courses in Polish.[46]

The department of music remained, as for years, under the direction of Francis C.L. Schreiner, who taught all resident students one period a week (in effect a rehearsal for Sunday vespers) and was available for optional study and private lessons if desired. The department of public speaking offered Principles of Vocal Expression, Principles of Visible Expression, Extemporaneous Speaking, and various other courses aimed at turning out "young men well trained in the art of public address."

The departments of religion and classical languages were vital to the work of the college, the latter for future priests, the former "to make the faith of the student an intelligent faith, and to provide him with the knowledge necessary to withstand the manifold attacks which religious belief may encounter after college days are ended . . . Non-Catholics will be received provided their parents or guardians are willing to have them placed under the influence of a Catholic Institution. No efforts at proselytizing are made, but no exceptions in the order of the house are made in favor of non-Catholic students."[47]

Religion was not so much a department as an all-encompassing worldview. But religious knowledge could not be assumed: it, too, had to be taught, and in an intellectually rigorous and spiritually sound way. The department of religion offered a course in Christian Evidence—"a reasoned exposition and demonstration of the dogmas of the Catholic faith"—required of all students. Freshmen took two periods a week of Christian Morality; sophomores, two periods a week of Christian Dogma; juniors, two periods a week of Salvation as Realized in the Individual; and seniors, two periods a week of Apologetics ("The Truth of the Catholic Religion, Revelation, pre-Christian and

Christian, the Church, Scripture, Tradition, and the Rule of Faith.") Religious instruction was a subject of debate among Catholic educators in the 1930s, who divided into opposing camps of theologians, philosophers, and pietists. McLaughlin's instruction that religion class was not to be "purely informative" or an exercise in "moral casuistry" or a "forum for curious questions" but a foundation for "character development" and "idealism for the most sacred things" was not pious anti-intellectualism, but it approached it.

Latin was compulsory in the freshman and sophomore years of the Arts course. Greek came later, consisting of translation of Plato, Demosthenes, and Aeschylus. Upper-level courses were geared for future seminarians: in Latin, the writings of the Early Fathers, in Greek, the works of Saint Basil.

The department of mathematics aimed to developed "concise and independent reasoning and to inspire habits of original thought . . . Any tendency to make the study a matter of memory is discouraged at the outset." Seven courses were offered, with emphasis on algebra, differential and integral calculus, trigonometry, and astronomy. The department of natural science offered students a chance "to become acquainted with the facts of modern science and the special forms of reasoning and method applied thereto." It offered four courses in chemistry, one in physics, one in biology, one in general anatomy, and one in hygiene and public health.

Seton Hall's quest for respectability bore fruit. "We opened in September [1932] with a registry in the College of seventy-five boarders, 212 day scholars, total 287," McLaughlin reported to the Trustees. "On May 1ˢᵗ 1933 we had on our roll 70 boarders and 199 day scholars, total 269, leaving a difference of 18—a rather small percentage." "The type of a student [now] entering the College is rather high and we have the advantage of having a student body of generally serious students," he continued, "due to the strict requirements of the Middle States Association."[48] The accreditors had done Seton Hall a favor, forcing it to confront faults and fix them, raising its standards by making it meet the standards of others.

Seton Hall's World

Every self-respecting college needs a newspaper. *The Setonian* first appeared on March 15, 1924, running to four pages of three columns each, well written, serious, and dull. The aim was to "[diffuse] knowledge of Setonian activities among the students and [to unite] them in loyalty and devotion towards their Alma Mater."[49] If the writers seemed more solemn than their professors, that was because some of the writing was done by professors themselves or by students eager to impress them. The first story told how the paper was "called forth from the world of possibilities into the regions of reality." A freshman called John O'Brien, approaching Mooney in 1922 for permission to start a paper, was turned down. Later, as a senior, he approached McLaughlin and was given "every encouragement and support."[50] The result was a professionally produced and attractive journal "keen to . . . influence the moral [and] mental education of the student." Initial enthusiasm gave way to apathy—"Setonians!! We have noticed a decided drop in the circulation . . . due to forgetfulness and other matters"—largely because *The Setonian* was the work often or twelve students who carried the load for the rest.

Appearing every month (it became a quarterly in money-pressed 1931), the paper was indisputably Catholic: "Junior Night. Yes! Over fifty years have slipped away since this noble tradition had its inception. What a glorious record! Especially in our day when everywhere outside the Catholic Church tradition is being thrown to the four winds of heaven or trampled underfoot as some much rubbish."[51] Most writers were future clerics (John O'Brien, Walter Jarvais, Leo Martin, and William Furlong), the job of the moderator being to moderate their baroque prose. Devotion to Our Lady competed for space with football. Cartoons (nicely drawn) made an appearance within a couple of issues. The glory of the priesthood was a stock-in-trade: "On Saturday morning, March 7th [1925], in the ivy-trellised chapel of the Immaculate Conception, within whose walls so many gallant heroes of the Standard of the Cross have received their distinguished insignia in the ranks of the anointed, six young and generous hearts prostrate themselves before the Rt. Reverend Bishop, pledged themselves to a life of toil and sacrifice wherever and with whomsoever obedience should direct them."[52] Walter Jarvais, later a popular English professor, insisted on the Catholic origins of America: "Let us condemn and override prejudice. Let us despise and reject religious bigotry, scatter the indecencies masked under a cloak of simulated American patriotism, but in reality perpetrated by those who, like moths, work in the dark, gnawing our flag thread from thread and devouring its sacred strands as their only food."[53]

To the extent that the politics of Seton Hall may be inferred from the politics of *The Setonian*, the college was isolationist. The League of Nations was a joke.[54] A World Court was folly.[55] Immigration should be banned.[56] Prohibition was "utopian imbecility."[57] The depression was caused by "a falling away from God."[58] The New Deal was a sham. Other than Mussolini,[59] the Pope was the only Italian *The Setonian* seemed to like. Never sure if its purpose was to embrace modernity or laugh at it, the paper relied on the Catholic certainties of commencement addresses over the years. Those certainties wore thin after a while. There were two sides to every story; *The Setonian* usually saw only one.

Darlington

In the last three years of the Mooney era, from 1919 to 1921, the Board of Trustees considered but deferred the transfer of clerical students to a site on the South Orange campus or another beyond it. The idea was not novel. Indeed, establishing a physically and institutionally separate seminary had been the intention from the beginning, first with Bayley's foundation of the college in Madison in 1856, then with his transfer of it to South Orange in 1860, allowing the seminary proper to begin. South Orange, to Bayley, was always judged in terms of suitability for a seminary. Its attractiveness as a location for a college was a bonus. That the college and the seminary had grown up side-by-side was an accident. Sharing a site confirmed but confused their connection. By the time McLaughlin completed his curricular reforms of 1926, strengthening practical subjects and slightly diluting classical ones, it made sense for college and seminary to go their separate ways. That had been intention of the reforms.

Seminary enrollments were steady (fifty-three in 1922, forty-five in 1924, forty-nine in 1926). Although seminarians could have been accommodated in the existing building (what is now called Presidents Hall, in those days Immaculate Conception Seminary or, simply, "the Seminary"), its age and architecture made expansion impossible. Were the seminary to move to new premises, the college could take over the vacated building, allowing the high school to have use of the college building. Transferring the seminary to a new site would allow fifty or more new students to enroll in the college, enhancing revenue at a time when every dollar counted. "We are the only Catholic College for men functioning in New Jersey," McLaughlin wrote. "We must be in a position to extend our facilities and so attract the Catholic students who are not studying for the priesthood." He envisaged "a common purchasing agency for both institutions" and a farm "to maintain cattle and perhaps produce certain staples." The question was whether the new site should be in South Orange or elsewhere. That McLaughlin envisaged a farm supplying staples for both suggests that he saw South Orange as the site for a new seminary, but soon it was realized that that would have cost at least $850,000, a counterproductively expensive proposition given that one of the motivations was to increase college revenue.

Cost was not the only consideration. A seminary required peace and quiet, maybe a rural setting. One reason for establishing the seminary in South Orange in 1861—proximity to Newark—was now a reason for its removal. Seton Hall, wrote McLaughlin, could no longer "ensure the privacy . . . requisite for proper seminary training" because it was turning "more and more [into] a day college." The code of canon law of 1917 required that seminarians be taught apart from other students.[60] Pope Pius XI insisted that seminary professors of scripture possess degrees from the Pontifical Biblical Institute. The North American church took these instructions seriously. As Monsignor Robert Wister points out in his superb history of Immaculate Conception Seminary, "the idea of relocation was not unique to Newark. Kenrick Seminary in St. Louis moved to a suburban area in 1916. Cincinnati's Mount Saint Mary's of the West moved to Norwood in 1923. Saint Mary's Seminary, the first United States seminary, moved to a new and expanded location in Roland Park, a

Baltimore suburb, in 1925. In 1931, the Pontifical College Josephinum moved from Columbus, Ohio to a semi-rural setting."[61] With Rome pushing for seminaries to be located in isolated settings, Immaculate Conception Seminary looked anomalous. It also damaged Seton Hall's reputation (in an era of accreditors) that seminarians were expected to act as junior professors despite being "only two years removed" from the men they taught.

In 1925 a firm of local architects provided a design for a new seminary building in South Orange that was quickly seen as unfeasible. A larger structure on separate site was the only option. Scouting around for suitable properties, McLaughlin found a mansion and estate in Hohokus (now Mahwah) township in the Ramapo Mountains. Owned by the heirs of the one Emerson McMillan and set in 1,100 acres of rolling woodland, this Darlington Estate (so-called after its previous owner, A.B. Darling) offered dignity, scale, and dramatic proof (were it to be used as a seminary) of the social advance of Roman Catholicism in twentieth century New Jersey. (The realtor did not reveal to the vendor its ultimate purpose.) The estate's mansion, a neo-Jacobean masterpiece designed by James Brite and built between 1901 and 1907, was magnificent. In June 1926, the estate was secured for almost half a million dollars.[62] By October 1926, the "Darlington Mansion" (quickly shortened to "Darlington") was being used for diocesan functions. In April 1927, with the addition of classrooms, dormitories, and a chapel, the first seminarians took up residence.

Removal did not mean the severing of ties. On June 9, 1926, when the Board of Trustees ratified the contract signed a week before between the diocese and the heirs of Emerson McMillan, it made explicit the continuing connection. "The faculty of the Seminary of the Immaculate Conception," the Trustees insisted, "as well as the student body, constitute, in educational matters, covered by the charter of Seton Hall College, an integral part of said institution." The rector of the Seminary would be a member of the College's Board of Trustees. To be sure, a major change had occurred. "Seminary accounts [were to be] kept separate and distinct from Seton Hall College, according to the provisions of canon law," the Board continued, which meant that nearly $172,000 in seminary scholarships would have to be transferred to a separate seminary account within the diocese.[63] The college and seminary remained academically connected—future seminarians taking undergraduate courses in the college before transferring to the seminary—but financially distinct. The connection was made flesh in the form of McLaughlin as Rector and President who lived in Darlington from Monday to Wednesday and in South Orange for the rest of the week.

Yet something monumental had happened. With the sense of one chapter closing and another opening, McLaughlin recorded in his diary the last days of Immaculate Conception Seminary in South Orange:

April 15. Last conference to seminarians at South Orange. General directions for way to Darlington and the proper spirit of entry therein.

April 16. Seminarians left to go to cathedral to go to Darlington, Thursday, April 21, 1927.

April 17. Took all seminarian registers and documents pertaining to Seminary and new seal to Darlington, thus closing Seminary at South Orange after 66 years on that spot. May God bless the seminarians and successors in new home.[64]

Bayley's vision was at last fulfilled.

Ringing the Changes in South Orange

There were other transitions. Bishop John J. O'Connor died on May 27, 1927, at Seton Hall. His last appearance had been the dedication of the new seminary on October 12, 1926. In failing health for some time (bronchial asthma), he delegated many of the tasks of his office to Monsignor John Duffy. O'Connor was replaced by Bishop Thomas J. Walsh of Trenton, an appointment that "disappointed" those who had hoped to get Duffy.[65] But Walsh was formidable, a "gentle yet determined and driving"[66] man with a "highly individualistic and idiosyncratic cast of mind."[67] He was far from bland.

And so, Seton Hall experienced its most significant institutional change since 1860. Moving into the old seminary building, Seton Hall College attained institutional adulthood. With the former college building to itself, the High School also developed physically and psychologically. (Their proximity had one unexpected consequence. In 1928, both had to close because of an outbreak of scarlet fever.)[68] The High School was separated from the College, with Father David Mulcahy appointed headmaster, assisted by Fathers William Bradley and Eugene Gallagher as prefects of discipline and athletics moderator respectively. Final decisions remained with the president of the college and the bishop. Seton Hall "Prep" remained very much part of the college as a whole.

McLaughlin continued to serve as rector of the seminary and president of the college, combining the roles eccentrically. A few years after the move to Darlington, a catalogue of spoke of Seton Hall College as comprising

The College of Arts and Sciences at South Orange
The School of Philosophy at the Immaculate Conception Seminary, Darlington
The School of Theology at the latter place

assuming the seminary to be a constituent element of the college, as indeed the Board had stipulated it should be. McLaughlin considered his duties as rector and president as separate yet indistinguishable, "an exacting executive, yet a kindly disciplinarian," said a local newspaper, who enjoyed the "friendship and affection of the hundreds who have come under his jurisdiction."[69] (The words may have come from McLaughlin himself.) As rector of the seminary, he had to write to the president of the college. As president of the college, he had to reply. These letters winged their way from South Orange to Darlington and back, author and recipient one and the same. A seminarian discovering his Seton Hall diploma had not been signed by McLaughlin as president asked him in Darlington to make good the omission. The response that he could not do so since only the President could sign diplomas came with the promise that he would bring the paper to South Orange and take up the matter with the President when he arrived.[70] Such was Schliztophrenia.

If McLaughlin's personality reflected the ambiguous relationship between college and seminary, the separation meant quasi-independence for each. Apart from future seminarians studying for their bachelor's degrees, the South Orange campus now comprised students who never gave Darlington a thought. The small group of professors who traveled between the two, teaching scripture in one, Latin and Greek in the other, were exceptions, keeping alive a tenuous connection. (The arrangement lasted only a few months.) Except McLaughlin, still wearing two hats in 1933, all clerical faculty lived either at the college or the seminary. Priests, remembering student days at Seton Hall and Darlington, distinguished between the two, as did everyone else.

Taking Stock

Bowing to social, educational, financial, and canonical reality, Seton Hall celebrated its seventy-fifth anniversary in June 1931 with McLaughlin still in charge. He had rationalized the finances, improved the tone, overseen the move of the seminary from South Orange to Darlington, reformed the preparatory school, and gained the endorsements of the Catholic Educational Association and the Middle States Association. With these achievements to laud, the 75th Jubilee Commencement of June 4, 1931 was impressive. "Thousands of alumni from different parts of the United States, and some from Canada, Mexico and the Philippine Islands" were expected return to "renew the days of their youth at New Jersey's foremost Catholic institution of higher learning. Lawyers, Monsignors, doctors, merchants and representatives of all walks of life will rub elbows with today's students and will sing . . . the strains of *Old Setonia*."[71] Eighty-four degrees were conferred, along with seven honorary doctorates. Pope Pius XI communicated his Apostolic Blessing.

Among dignitaries on the day were Patrick Cardinal Hayes of New York, the New Jersey Commissioner of Education, and fifty representatives of colleges and universities, including Amherst College (Bayley's alma mater) and Rutgers. The authorities in South Orange asked residents to adorn their homes with flags giving "something of a general holiday air to the entire village." The quadrangle in front of the Administration Building was transformed into an open-air chapel for High Mass, the altar erected on the porch of Alumni Hall and adjoining it a large platform serving as the sanctuary. The sermon was delivered by Monsignor John Duffy, who praised the early pioneers, Bayley especially, who foresaw "the vast immigration of Catholics from Europe" and founded the college to keep the faith alive for them. Seton Hall had the one, true conception of education: "the development of character and power."[72] All the rest amounted to "science without God, industry without heart, economics without soul."[73]

James O'Connell spoke on behalf of the graduating class, striking a standard if racially crude note: "The educated man enjoys and appreciates all that is good, all that is beautiful, all that is noble; but to the unlettered man literature has very little meaning and to him philosophical dissertations are impractical, time wasted. Now, it has always been the province of Seton Hall to educate along these lines. . . ."[74] (The crudity came by way of contrast: such education distinguished Seton Hall men from "Zulu boys in the darkness of their ignorance.")

Francis Meehan, president of the Alumni Association, praised McLaughlin's "untiring efforts and magnificent accomplishments." John Cleary, alumnus from the 1870s and editor of the *Trenton Times*, lauded the "venerable institution" that commanded "unwavering reverence and gratitude." Walsh spoke of "the educational, financial and spiritual success of the College."[75] A student, Thomas Gilhooley, produced doggerel:

I dreamed a dream the other night,
A dream of Seton Hall;
It was concerned with Jubilees—
I'll tell you of it all
It seems there was a big parade,
Of all Setonia's Sons—
Of those who were gray and stooped with age
And those who had just begun . . .[76]

Seton Hall had produced bishops and archbishops—Corrigan, McQuaid, Wigger, O'Connor, Messmer, and McFaul. It had produced a Rector of the North American College in Rome, Eugene Burke, graduate of the class of 1907. It had produced Joseph Corrigan (nephew of the archbishop), Chief Magistrate of New York in 1930. It had produced Congressman Eugene Kinkead, who served in the U.S. House of Representatives from 1909 to 1915. It had produced Thomas McCrann, class of 1896, former Attorney-General of New Jersey and widely known as an orator.[77] It had produced James Nugent, class of 1882, for twenty years the "Big Boss" of Democratic Party politics in New Jersey, a national figure.[78] It had produced Judge Thomas Riley of Massachusetts, prominent in that state's Democratic Party, former campaign manager for Woodrow Wilson.[79] It had produced Thomas H. Kelly, a chamberlain to every Pope since Leo XIII, and generous supporter of Irish political causes.[80] It had produced Will Durant, historian, philosopher, socialist, gadfly, and future recipient of the Pulitzer Prize and Presidential Medal of Freedom. It had produced (although hardly educated) John and Lionel Barrymore. It had produced Frank Wilstach, a major if eccentric figure in the motion picture industry.[81] It had even produced, in Henry O'Neill, its own film star, whose efforts included *From Headquarters*, *The World Changes*, *I Loved a Woman*, and *Bedside*.[82] At seventy-five years of age, Seton Hall was entitled to celebrate a successful three-quarters of a century.

CHAPTER 7

From McLaughlin to Monaghan to Kelley

A Bishop Speaks

When Bishop Walsh praised Seton Hall's financial success in 1931, he spoke of a budget more complicated than most people realized. At one level, the college provided a service to the diocese—it educated its priests—for which payment was due. At another level, the diocese was the patron and sponsor of the college and its most important customer. Who was underwriting whom? With the seminary no longer attached to the college, the latter's diocesan links might have become attenuated, with Seton Hall free to develop under Catholic sponsorship while thinking little of the sponsor itself. But the seminary's move to Darlington did not break the college's connection with the diocese; it strengthened and formalized it. The diocese still provided Seton Hall with its priests, its president, its Board of Trustees, and its governing philosophy. It also provided it with most of its students, not only future clerics also lay men from its parishes and schools.

Walsh counted for almost everything at Seton Hall and no-one knew this better than McLaughlin, who was extremely scrupulous about protocol.[1] Walsh was exacting, obsessive, and finicky,[2] and in McLaughlin he met a man equally colorful. Together they controlled Seton Hall for a third of a century. McLaughlin saw firsthand the alarming fiscal and academic realities that Walsh only saw at a distance. Only a year after Walsh had spoken of financial success and the Board had hailed its "prosperous" state, McLaughlin told trustees that "in view of the depression . . . unless subventions or temporary loans without interest are made to the college from some source, it will be impossible for us [to pay the faculty]."[3] He needed $30,000 a year for four years from the diocese. At Christmas, he asked for a $7,000 "to meet the December payroll before the holidays."[4] Walsh kept the college afloat, granting McLaughlin his annual $30,000 and later giving Monsignor Frank Monaghan, his successor, $15,000 a year for another three years. Without this "diocesan subsidy" Seton Hall would have been out of business.

When the bishop spoke, everyone listened. (This was literally so. If Walsh was unable to attend seminary events, he sent along voice recordings "to be played for the faculty assembled *in globo* or in smaller groups . . . There is also enclosed an especially prepared needle which will play 2,500 recordings perfectly.")[5] Little happened without his approval. "I hereby appoint you head of the Department of Philosophy in Seton Hall College," he wrote to Father James F. Kelley. "As you will teach Philosophy in both the College and the Seminary, I have instructed the Very Reverend President of Seton Hall College to purchase for you and your use a new Ford automobile at the cost of not over nine hundred dollars." "Since Reverend James F. Kelley has returned particularly qualified with the Academic degree of Doctor of Philosophy from Louvain, I respectfully request you to cede him the office of head of the department of philosophy," he told Father Peter Guterl, the displaced incumbent.[6] Although notionally in charge of teaching appointments, McLaughlin had no say in the assignments of diocesan clergy, who went where the bishop told them. Thus was Seton Hall staffed.

Walsh's academic preoccupations were equally quirky. Worried that priests would emerge ill equipped for the polyglot realities of parish life, he created the "Master School of Modern Languages of Seton Hall High School and Seton Hall College" to offer courses in Arabic, Armenian, French, German, Hungarian, Italian, Lithuanian, Polish, the Slavic languages, and Spanish. "May I recommend that every student learn one new word every day during all his years of school and study . . . May I recommend that every student look up every word in the dictionary signing the word looked up in every reference with the dot of a lead pencil . . ."[7] There was, indeed, something dotty about this.

Defending Seton Hall from the Challenge of Public Education

Other than finances, Seton Hall's greatest challenge of the 1930s was a political environment increasingly inhospitable to small, private colleges. Publicly funded higher education, insignificant at first, bulked larger in New Jersey in the middle of the twentieth century. The superiority of private education was a Seton Hall axiom. At the 1925 commencement exercises, Father William Griffin welcomed the U.S. Supreme Court's striking down of an Oregon law that would have required children between the ages of eight and sixteen to be educated at public school. "Every child has the right to attend the school he chooses," he argued, adding that the growing irreligion of the times was attributable to public education.[8] Before the 1930s, higher education in New Jersey was largely private and denominational. Chartered by the state, colleges were free to flourish or fail on their own. It was private schooling, McLaughlin believed, that made a "profound and lasting contribution to the culture and development of [the] state." Yet public policy was moving in the direction of tax-funded higher education. Before 1865, Rutgers College was a denominational school associated with the Dutch Reformed Church. After 1865, it was divided into Rutgers College and a separate Theological

Seminary (so that the former could qualify as a land grant college under post-Civil War federal legislation). In 1925, with the founding of the New Jersey College of Women, it changed from a college to a university overseen by a state Board of Regents. If higher education was a public good, it was difficult to maintain that it should not be supported by the state. The extent of that support, whether funding or merely legislative approval in the form of charters, was the question.

The answer became clearer in the 1930s. Advised by Albert Meredith of New York University, the state Board of Regents that oversaw Rutgers University in January 1932 offered a "Proposal for Discussion" that would have revolutionized higher education in New Jersey, transforming Rutgers into a federated body of constituent colleges controlled by the Governor and the Legislature. The idea was to bundle together a set of miscellaneous educational enterprises and direct them from Trenton.[9] Here, in embryo, was the State University of New Jersey that came into being with successive acts of the legislature in 1945 and 1956. The era of publicly funded and relatively cheap higher education would soon pose challenges for small, privately managed and comparatively under-funded colleges such as Seton Hall.

Meredith envisaged that the State Board of Regents could "purchase by annual contract with the trustees of any institution of higher education within the state . . . such higher educational services as the Regents may desire." The two exceptions were the component colleges of the University of New Jersey (whose services were contracted for already) and "institutions in which a religious doctrine or tenet may be taught." There would be no public money for religious institutions, although their degrees would enjoy state recognition. Obvious constitutional considerations lay behind the denial of state funding for religious schools, but it jarred with McLaughlin all the same. Insisting that "Seton Hall College is not primarily intended for the preparation of candidates for the priesthood but is a general college giving recognized courses in the arts and sciences,"[10] he argued that if some private colleges could receive public funding (for services rendered) but others, because religious, could not, it would be better if none were to receive money at all.

Why make difficulties for private colleges when they were already functioning well? In a memorandum submitted to the State Board of Regents, McLaughlin made the point in a welter of subordinate clauses. The "unwarranted" and "preposterous" possibility of "free university instruction" concerned him, as well it might. "It is not fair in a Democracy of our kind to use State money for the benefit of those who can well afford to provide themselves with an education from which they will receive the chief, if not the only emolument." He conceded that the state "has the right to supervise schools which claim to fit their students for practical walks of life," but beyond that, it had no power to determine "the inward thoughts, the sublimity of ideals, the prescription of a definite moral or practical philosophy of education."[11]

This was a standard but contradictory argument. To claim that a state university would "experiment and direct not only the education but the very thoughts, aspirations, and activities of the people" ran counter to the complaint that "righteous living, morality, and public conscience" had declined precisely because the state had abandoned its role as a moral instructor. "Young people today are not receiving enough spiritual training in the public schools," Father Griffin had complained at commencement half a decade before.[12] It was hard to insist on, then deplore, the government as a guardian of decency. Catholics, recognizing that the state had a legitimate interest in education, struggled to find a principle by which that interest might be limited. They were by no means hostile to government *per se*—read Aquinas to see why—but when government arrogated to itself duties properly in the domain of parents or civic associations, they began to worry. Some of the anxiety was institutional—keeping Catholic schools afloat—but at a deeper level it was about defending the spiritual life.

As it turned out, the fight would be fought by other warriors. In May 1933, citing declining health, McLaughlin resigned as president of the college, remaining as rector of the seminary. Weekly travel between South Orange and Darlington had taken a toll, as had his third job as Vicar General of the diocese. The Board of Trustees accepted the resignation "with deep regret," allowing it to come into effect after the commencement. Eleven years at the top was a good run by any standard. When McLaughlin assumed the presidency, the combined teaching staff of the College, the Seminary, and the High School was twenty-two. When he left, it was sixty-two. Defending Seton Hall from state centralism was among his last acts as president, but it was of a piece with what had gone before. Conscious of threats to Seton Hall's autonomy, he resisted interference from outsiders, only to recognize its inevitability. Recognizing the need for accreditation, he secured CEA and Middle States approval for the college's diplomas and degrees. Realizing the importance of curricular change, he promoted new programs. Conceding a measure of faculty self-governance, he organized academic departments. Raising substantial sums of money, he transformed the campus from dowdy to attractive. Noticing growing state interest in higher education, he defended the private sector intelligently. McLaughlin was one of Seton Hall's great presidents and characters. His "reasons of ill health" did not prevent him from becoming auxiliary bishop of Newark in 1935 and bishop of the newly formed diocese of Paterson in 1937, where, with undiminished eccentricity, he continued until his death in 1947.[13]

Marking Time with Monaghan

His successor was Father, later (in 1934) Monsignor, Frank Joseph Monaghan, the forty-three-year old professor of dogmatic theology and metaphysics at the seminary. After McLaughlin, Monaghan was an anticlimax. Born in Newark in 1890 and ordained in

1915, he attended Seton Hall High School and College and the Pontifical North Ameri-can College in Rome, completing doctoral work at the Propaganda Fide before being appointed to the Seton Hall faculty in 1926 and to the Seminary the following year. A stickler for standards, he taught at the Seminary "with honor and distinction" until he was promoted as President of the College. He was not Walsh's first choice, the job having been offered to Father William Lawlor of Bayonne, who refused it. (Walsh, in-furiated by this snub, denied Lawlor preferment for the rest of his career.)[14] Monaghan was worthy but dull, a dry stick. At the Seminary he insisted on "recitations" before ordinations, the notion of a moment of levity never occurring to him. His welcoming message to students was severe. "You should be busy now! You are at Seton Hall for study and work!"[15] (To be fair, Monaghan set aside three mornings a week when any student could come to see him.) "May your presidency [of] this splendid diocesan edu-cational institution be long, happy, fruitful and blessed," Walsh wrote to him.[16] It was not. Monaghan, a brilliant undergraduate, turned out to be an uninspired president. In 1936, aged 45, he became coadjutor bishop of Ogdensburg, New York, which was a promotion but also, in a way, a banishment.

Thanks to McLaughlin, and the occasional financial embarrassment notwithstand-ing, Seton Hall was solid. In 1932, McLaughlin's last full year in charge, its total expen-diture of nearly $450,000 consisted of professorial salaries ($157,000), food ($95,000), wages for servants ($48,000), grounds and maintenance ($49,000), administration and correspondence ($49,000), and utilities ($36,500). Smaller amounts were spent on the library and laboratories (almost $10,000) and laundry ($1,600).[17] Balancing these costs was an income derived from board and tuition ($353,000), the diocesan collec-tion ($65,000), interest on securities ($9700), various donations, legacies, and honoraria ($84,000), and a balance carried over from the previous year amounting to $84,000. In 1936, in addition to nonclerical students, there were ninety-one diocesan students in South Orange preparing to proceed to Darlington. In 1937, there were 119 (73 in the High School and 46 in the College) hoping to do the same. In 1938, there were 214 of them (117 in the High School and 97 in the College.[18] At the end of 1934, Seton Hall had a surplus of nearly $137,000. Of these sums, one calls for mention. Benny Savage, a grounds man known as "Old Benny," bequeathed nearly $11,000. "Benny came to Seton Hall in 1881, and has been 'on the job' ever since. And if you strike up a conversa-tion with him, you will find that in addition to his other accomplishments, Benny is also—a philosopher."[19]

Monaghan never realized that the point of money is to spend it. Deferred main-tenance made a mockery of cash in the bank. Nor did he understand bookkeeping. His successor as president, Father James Kelley, discovered "no system of accounting" when he took over. The annual financial report for the Board of Trustees was pre-pared by the cashier, not the President. "I found as many rates at Seton Hall as there were students," he complained. "A student could name his own price at Seton Hall . . . Every professor, both in the High School and the College, was paid [a] different salary . . . Accounts collectable had been neglected and in a period of only six years there was still on the books $57,662 of accounts receivable . . . Roofs were leaking and walls falling in . . ."[20]

Kelley's complaint was a way of promoting himself by demoting his predecessor, but Monaghan *did* let things slip. Fund-raising was negligible. Recruitment was unheard of. Marketing was minimal. "While we have canvassed the class very carefully," the principal of a local high school told the president of the Alumni Association, "at present we do not have any who are planning on Seton Hall next year. Perhaps it is the college's fault."[21] "Old Mr. Maloney on many occasions reiterated his intention of bestowing large sums upon Seton Hall," Monaghan wrote to Monsignor J.C. McClary. "He was a trustee of this institution . . . Anything you can do for us will be greatly appreciated." This was the fabulous wealthy Martin Maloney of Spring Lake, New Jersey, some of whose cash would have been welcome. It was not forthcoming.[22] A more energetic president would have landed this fish.

A ship seemingly becalmed was actually sinking. Enrollment in September 1933 was 251 students (189 day scholars and 62 boarders). Compared to 1932, this represented a drop of thirty-six students—twenty-three day boys and ten boarders. In September 1934, enrollment was 194. In the space of two years, the college lost nearly 50 percent of its student body. Not all or even most of this was Monaghan's fault (this was the depth of the Depression) but the trends were not good and passivity was not an answer to them.

Little happened from year to year. "The same faculty took charge of the classes [in September 1933]," Monaghan reported to the Board in May 1934, "with these four exceptions":

> The lower registration made it possible to drop one instructor, Mr. James O'Connell.
> Doctor Proctor who had headed the Department of Education [has] resigned.
> In his place I obtained the services of Dr. Elmer Kilmer, Ph.D., from New York University. He is an elderly gentleman and has proved very satisfactory.

Among other promises made to the Middle States Association in return for accreditation was one to replace the two medical doctors who taught inorganic chemistry by a person qualified to teach the subject. "I hired Professor Frederick Delmore, B.S., M.S., which degrees he obtained at Holy Cross . . . He has somewhat enthused the whole school by bringing here different lecturers in the field of Industrial Chemistry.

His last lecture was conducted by himself and its subject was this new 'heavy water'" so prominently mentioned in the daily papers. . . ."[23] The New York State Board submitted the college "to a very searching investigation" in November 1933 before it renewed recognition of its degrees. In an era of falling enrolments, no college could give potential students a reason for not attending, a lesson that Monaghan, like McLaughlin, was beginning to learn.

Seton Hall did not have many out-of-class clubs because boarders lived a regimented existence and because day "hops" preferred to go home. Monaghan was still able to report "an abundance of extracurricular activity" in 1934 with "at least an average of one affair a week":

> The Chemistry Club under Professor Delmore has had many lectures on Chemistry in Industry.
>
> The Art Club under Doctor Savage and Doctor Howald [has] made excursions to the Metropolitan Museum in New York.
>
> The Classical Club presented very successfully and entertainingly in modernized dress, "The Captivi" of Plautus.
>
> The Dramatic Club presented once in Jersey City and twice in Newark the play "Broken Dishes." They were supplemented by some members of St. Elizabeth's College who played the female roles. [The Club reciprocated] by playing the male roles in "Medea" at St. Elizabeth's.

A couple of students in the Radio Club received an operator's license to broadcast over the short wavelength. "We have had two such broadcasts," Monaghan reported. "This is all in line with the students' work in the physics laboratory."

Sport, which is treated elsewhere in this book, played an important role in student life. At their meeting of May 1933, McLaughlin's last as president, the Board of Trustees recommended the promotion of intramural athletics. "Athletics have cost more than $10,000 a year at Seton Hall and there is little student interest and practically no alumni interest," McLaughlin protested. But the Board insisted that a department of physical education be established and that students be encouraged to form intramural teams. "In basketball this was particularly successful," Monaghan reported, "and in football it was moderately successful; but in baseball (perhaps because examinations are so near?) it has not taken hold to any extent." Monaghan secured the services of "a first class Catholic man, Mr. John Colrick, A.B., of Notre Dame" to prepare varsity baseball, basketball, and freshman football teams for academic year 1934–1935. Harry Coates was hired as a track team coach for the high school and the college (his $400 salary came out of College funds). Together, Colrick and Coates built a program.[24]

A Local College

For Albert Hakim of Kearny, a 1937 freshman, going to Seton Hall was "the most prosaic thing imaginable." He had heard about the College from a friend, thought he would visit, took the bus, met Father Bill Duffy smoking outside the main building, asked him a few questions, and was then told that "that will be five bucks." What he took to be a conversation turned out to be an interview.[25] (He was even given a receipt signed by Stella Jasina, Seton Hall's secretary-cum-treasurer-cum-typist-cum-phone-operator-cum-mother-hen: what a later age would call the administration.) Seton Hall was Hakim's kind of place. "Were our needs brought home perhaps to Catholics of means," McLaughlin had written to pastors in 1928, "we would be in a position also to offer the advantages of education to gifted boys and young men who are not blessed with this world's goods."[26] It had clever students (like Hakim) and some not so clever. It had well-off boys and some not so well off. Catholics were supposed to look after each other and Seton Hall helped them do so.

Most students came from Catholic schools and households. "Did you enjoy the retreat?" gentle Father Walter Jarvais asked Hakim at the end of his first one. (The annual retreat was mandatory.) To the latter's surprise, the answer was "yes," thus beginning his journey to the priesthood. Cassocks were everywhere. With one or two exceptions, Seton Hall's priests were not scholars: most had MAs rather than doctorates. Their job was to teach, not publish, and this they did well. Father John Ryan, a fastidious anglophile, had an accent that wavered somewhere between Hoboken and the Home Counties. "The Lawst Maws," he announced, "will be a Low Maaas." Father Harold Dilger, an actual Englishman, was uncompromising. "Father, I don't believe in Hell," went one exchange. "Well, in that case, get the Hell out of here, Son!" Father Adrian Maine, aloof, well dressed, aristocratic, taught chemistry with dry humor. Away from the lab, he relaxed by playing the organ.[27] Father Mike Jaremczyk, another chemist, raised procrastination to a fine art. Students awaiting grades long after the end of the course joked he would be late for his own funeral.

Some priests made a bigger impression than others. Father Joseph Brady, with a Columbia doctorate in history, was exacting. "We shall always remember his ability to achieve the ultimate in scholastic attainments," his contemporaries remembered, "for he belonged to the intellectual aristocracy; yet we rather like to think of him as just Joe, a comrade and a gentleman."[28] Planning his classes to the last dot, his intelligence formidable, his strictness legendary, Brady's decency was hidden behind a mien of professorial severity. The realm of ignorance, where students dwelled, had to give way to the kingdom of knowledge, where he reigned supreme. For Brady, everything had to be in place: ideas, arguments, defenses of the faith, arranged with the formality of a pressed suit or a row of pencils in a case. If students missed the emotional reserve behind these masks of authority, Brady missed the impetuousness of youth that needed to let off steam. Illness was possibly one reason for the distance—he suffered from a heart condition—but he was a superb scholar in a college where scholarship was prized as an adjunct to teaching, not a substitute for it.[29] He was fifty-six when he died in 1961, having spent the last six years of his life as Rector of Immaculate Conception Seminary. "Students remember him," said Bishop Walter Curtis at his funeral, "as one whose intellectual honesty would permit him to certify their achievements only when there were achievements to certify."[30]

At the other end of the spectrum was Father Jim Carey, for many years director of athletics and advisor and mentor to hundreds of students. Carey made no claims to scholarship. Time in a classroom was a distraction from the more compelling world of sport. Small, colorful, noisy, smoking twenty to the dozen, "a loyal rooter at practically every basketball and baseball game,"[31] Carey was impossible to dislike. He knew who had to be encouraged, who had to be calmed down, who was struggling, who was marked for success. He "kept peace within the family," one alumnus recalled.[32] It was difficult to argue with a coach who distributed miraculous medals to the basketball team. Students short of cash came away with a name, address, and a contact for a summer job. Men dropped from the team were let go sympathetically. Carey started the Knights of Setonia, a weekly Mass and Communion followed by breakfast, which attracted hundreds of students. It is more than a play on words to say that Carey cared.

Father Walter Jarvais, small and benign, taught English and Religion. With a slightly odd mannerism (his speech sounded like a series of snorts) he might have been the butt of mockery but was well liked as an undergraduate and beloved as a teacher. "Often we sat in rapt amazement listening to him explain how we get our ideas, that is, if we ever had any. Majors and minors and conclusions just rippled from his tongue. Always quiet and calm in the classroom, 'poofs' and snorts never bothered him."[33]

In the same mold was Father William Halliwell, who taught classics. Gregarious, funny, and spiritual, Halliwell had a subversive streak that appealed to smarter students. One colleague, Father William Noé Field, offering a fatuous opinion of a book, found the volume removed from his hand and flung on the floor. Insisting on authenticity in art, religion, conversation, and personal relations, Halliwell could be blunt.

Father James ("Red") Hamilton, was a small, high-pitched man with a parrotlike voice and a nickname derived from his hair and temperament. Casual about teaching duties, he thought nothing of driving students to appointments and helping them find work. As a disciplinarian, he was incompetent. When students locked French professor Henri Petitjean out of his classroom, Hamilton read the riot act in circumstances that ended in farce. Petitjean, breaking in, aimed an ineffectual kick at the ringleader, whose mock indignation provoked a collapse of seriousness. Hamilton was popular without courting popularity, a good definition of what it means to be respected. Petitjean was a figure of fun.

Seton Hall had a good lay faculty. Tall, thin, and dignified, Frederick Cassidy knew chemistry better than anyone else on the staff. He saw students as human beings, not vessels to be filled with formulas and solutions. James O'Donnell, professor of Greek, lived and died for the classics. His erudition was intimidating. Allen Woodall, head of English, was winner in 1935 of the National Drama Contest of the American Classical League with his play, *A Friend of Maecenas*.[34] Laurence McGrath, professor of economics, was a member of President Roosevelt's Brain Trust. Howard Merity, professor of education, was intelligent and affable. Nicolas Montani, professor of music, never lost his temper with the most tuneless pupil. Devoting his life to teaching seminarians to sing, he knew purgatory firsthand. Louis Rausch, with a PhD in mathematics from the University of Chicago, was modest and dry. Inaudible to students in the back of the class, he offered a memorable solution: "You boys in the front go to the back. You boys in the back come to the front." During World War II, when many teachers left, Rauch ended up in California. The war long over, he applied for a position in the math department, thinking it would look like special pleading if he mentioned that he had taught at Seton Hall before. The job was offered, and he returned in 1963 after a gap of twenty years to spend the rest of his career at the university.[35]

Farewell to Monaghan

This was Monaghan's Seton Hall: a solid, unshowy place. The same adjectives might be applied to Monaghan himself, who did not want the job but who performed it dutifully. But he was a stopgap. McLaughlin had shown what could be done with flair and energy. Monaghan had shown what could happen when these qualities were lacking. His appointment as coadjutor bishop Ogdensburg eased him out. "To one and all this news came as a complete surprise accompanied by a deep feeling of regret," *The Setonian* reported. In fact, the person most pained was the bishop of Ogdensburg, Joseph Conroy, who refused to speak to Walsh, the engineer of the move, for two years. Monaghan began as president of Seton Hall with one annoyed bishop and he ended it with another. Walsh was happy to see him go, Conroy unhappy to see him arrive. He was everyone's second choice.

The story has a tragic epilogue. Monaghan was forty-five when he was promoted to Ogdensburg. Nine years later, in November 1942, he died in bizarre circumstances, suffering injuries in a freakish train accident. Passing from a coach to a Pullman, he was about to step across the platform when the Pullman disconnected, throwing him to the ground. He lingered for several weeks before succumbing to heart failure and cerebral hemorrhage. In death, as in life, Monaghan was a transitional figure who never quite made the connection.

CHAPTER 8

Resurgence

A New President

Seton Hall's new leader was Father James Kelley, the second youngest president in the college's history (after Corrigan) and at thirty-four the youngest college president in the country. Kelley was energetic, self-possessed, and visionary, a modern figure in a way that Monaghan was not. "Having seen the old place go downhill for a long time," John Francis Neylan wrote to him, "then having met you and the faculty you had gathered around you . . . it is a great pleasure to see how sound policy has fructified."[1] "I have known of Seton Hall over the years, but it takes a personal visit to the campus to really appreciate [its] spirit," wrote J. Edgar Hoover, signing himself Edgar and offering Kelley his "highest esteem and admiration."[2] (He had just received an honorary degree.) Kelley's tenure ended unhappily (with other, less friendly communications from the FBI) but for thirteen years he offered a master class in college presidency, turning a small, male college into a major urban institution and placing Seton Hall in the forefront of Catholic institutions in the nation. After Monaghan, he was a whirlwind.

Kelley was a local lad made good. He graduated from Seton Hall in 1924, studied for a year at Immaculate Conception Seminary, and then at Louvain, where he was ordained a priest in July 1928. His first assignment as a professor of French, religion, and education lasted for four years before Bishop Walsh returned him to Louvain for further study, where he received his PhD in 1935, completing a four-year course in two years and taking his licentiate in philosophy with highest honors. Kelley also worked at the Universities of Lille and Munich and at the Sorbonne. In Munich in 1933 when Hitler came to power, he also found time when in England to visit George Bernard Shaw, a distant maternal relation. "Jim Kelley is here in Paris and we have done our best to keep the American end up," wrote a friend to Father Joseph Brady (Kelley's colleague at Seton Hall). "He is doing well, and if he is not made Mayor or something, he should get back to Newark in good shape."[3]

Returning to Seton Hall in August 1935 as head of philosophy in the college and as lecturer in theology at the seminary, Kelley was given a sleepy assignment. The small faculty in South Orange consisted of his former professors, all older than he and some irritated at his slightly bumptious mission to "revise and revitalize" the teaching of philosophy.[4] But his stint lasted only a year when in April 1936 he was summoned to see Walsh at the Chancery Office: "The Archbishop brought me into a larger room. He said to the group of thirteen men who constituted the Board of Trustees, 'Here is our new President.' They all stood and applauded, and the Archbishop brought me over to the head of the table and said, 'Sit here and preside.' I was still then not thirty-three years of age, and brash, maybe a little foolish, but I said, 'Archbishop, don't I have anything to say about this?' He said, 'Sit down and you will have time later to express your gratitude.'"[5] "Where can I get a copy of the duties of the President of Seton Hall?' he asked Walsh. "They don't exist," he was told. They then improvised them on the spot."[6]

A Reformer in a Hurry

As president, Kelley inherited a venerable institution. "The oldest and only Board-ing Catholic College in New Jersey for Men," ran its advertisement in the *New York Times*. "Eighty Years of Education—Training Outstanding Citizens—Internationally recognized by foremost accrediting agencies—Every department under the direction of a Ph. D—41 Professors Assembled from leading universities for 300 students lead-ing to degrees of A.B, B.S., and Ph. B.—Tuition $100 per term—Board and Residence $175—Visit the campus at Your Convenience."[7] Expansion was to be his hallmark but at first the college's smallness was the selling point. "My purpose and policy is not by any means to produce a large enrollment," he said. "Seton Hall has always stood for quality rather than quantity. [My ambition] is to turn out good characters, fine upright citizens, not just good minds, because some of the best minds are behind bars."[8] "No college institution will make a profit. As a matter of fact, it shouldn't, for if you raise the tuition rates you get students whose only reason for being in college is that their parents have money and exclude others of ability who cannot afford the fee."[9]

If senior professors resented his flair for self-promotion (local newspapers routinely printed accounts of his brilliance), students liked him. (He had once been a boxer: it is hard to imagine Monaghan in a ring).[10] His established a student council chosen from members of each class with "authority in matters of importance on the cam-pus."[11] The matters were unimportant—organizing debates, running socials—but the gesture was noticed.[12] He started a department of student counseling to offer advice on courses and careers. He created a Dean's list. He established honors societies, the Cross and Crescent for those in college clubs and Phi Kappa Pi for education students.[13] He announced new courses in English, science, social science, finance, accounting, statistics, business law, and international trade. He strengthened pre-medical and pre-dental offerings by adding courses on entomology and histology. (Seton Hall was now to have a psychology laboratory: "[Experiments] will include the workings of memory and habit formation. White rats will figure greatly in the latter cases, with the aid of systems of mazes.")[14] He introduced journalism in 1938.[15] (The first instructor, William Considine, a graduate of Boston College and Harvard Law School and Seton Hall's director of publicity, connected students with local and national papers, getting them paid for their articles. He also brought speakers to campus.) Finally, Kelley introduced freshman orientation in 1939, when for three days the "general purposes and opportunities of a liberal arts college [were] fully explained and the specific aims of Seton Hall College are impressed upon every student."[16]

Most of this curricular revolution was common sense but behind it lay assumptions about the institution and the world that awaited its graduates. Seton Hall students were now to be equipped with useful knowledge, a fairly unobjectionable goal to which *The Setonian* nonetheless objected: "All the emphasis is on *doing*. Students learn to accomplish almost everything but they are never taught to *be* anything . . . And this crazy system becomes the crazier when we link it up with the current advance in mechanical and electrical science. Today we have electric eyes that do almost anything, and a recent invention has perfected a robot that speaks. Does it not seem that we shall soon have engines to accomplish human acts and skilled youths who can bring about any mechanical result? When men have forgotten how to think, a motor will do it for them. Humans and machines will have exchanged functions. Well, you must admit we are heading in that direction."[17]

We have arrived.

Americanism

Kelley's most notable innovation was a course called "Americanism," an attempt to promote a distinctively Catholic understanding of citizenship. Civics had been taught in public schools since 1919 and study of the Constitution had been compulsory since 1932.[18] Seton Hall was only catching up. "You impressed upon me the need of making better citizens out of our men," Kelley wrote in 1944 to John F. Neylan (whose idea it was). "It was then that I instituted the course on Americanism requiring eight credits on the subject, two for each of the four years, from every student seeking any of our degrees. We did produce a very fine type of old-fashioned Americanism among our own boys . . . I frequently have letters from them, out in the fox-holes, on the high seas and in the air."[19]

"America is not merely a member of the family of nations," Father John Cavanaugh of Notre Dame had said in 1919. "America is a condition of soul."[20] Cavanaugh overstated his case, but he spoke for Catholics who never thought themselves less American for being Catholic. Kelley likewise wanted to celebrate his country, although the course had a specifically Catholic tone that almost undermined the assimilation it intended to promote. But Kelley could be a critic, too. "Just as the idolatry of the sciences was the curse of the last century," he wrote, "so, too, in our own day . . . the idolatry of the technological or the application of the sciences to our everyday life has become a fetish." [21]

No-one noticed the oddity of mandatory instruction in freedom. Nor did undergraduates need lessons in patriotism. (It was they, not the faculty, who organized the Students' Crusade for Americanism, bringing businessmen and politicians to campus to speak on various aspects of modern industrial life.)[22] "We need men of good-will like yourself," a correspondent wrote to Kelley, to "preserve this country as a haven for religious liberty and democracy."[23] A group of Los Angeles veterans was "very much pleased" that "one of America's older colleges" had taken the lead in teaching patriotism and civic obligation.[24] "My Country, Tis of Thee?" asked one Californian, not so impressed. "Mr. Kelly [sic]: Teach your students . . . the only liberty they now have is to . . . hunt for a job and then, not being able to find [one], become a criminal."[25]

Contrarianism

Americanism was tempered by a kind of Catholic contrarianism. Under Kelley, Seton Hall emphasized Catholic difference as much as conformity. When Thomas J. Walsh was raised to archbishop of Newark in 1938, *The Setonian* noted "the dominance which Catholicity occupies in this country . . . Protestantism's only foundation is a memory; the entire religious system is a crumbling citadel built on the mere reflection that once God was theirs but they found His demands too exacting."[26]

For every article that stressed Catholic patriotism, another stressed Catholic peculiarity, suggesting a college, like Kelley, half critic, half celebrant, of its own country. Self-assurance bordering on bumptiousness marked *The Setonian's* politics, finding fault, for instance, with the "socialistic leanings of the New Deal" and condemning government programs as wasteful failures. Many students resented, or claimed to resent, the Social Security Administration, which threatened to replace mutual aid societies that had flourished as charitable organizations for over a century.[27] Monsignor Maurice Sheehy of Catholic University reckoned that in 1936, 103 of 106 American bishops voted for Roosevelt[28] but at Seton Hall, where social issues were understood as moral problems susceptible to moral (that is to say, personal) solutions, enthusiasm for FDR was limited. To be sure, the New Deal, in the guise of the National Youth Administration, allowed sixty students to defray tuition costs by working in the library, laboratories, and other places on campus.[29] Not every student was as hostile to the federal government as the paper required him to be.

The Setonian had views on foreign affairs, too, as if anyone cared. Mussolini pursued domestic policies that were "thoughtfully and sanely carried out" and hence "usually successful."[30] Hitler was "given to severe fits of melancholia and day-dreaming, holding the floor for hours" with very little "confidence in himself." Franco's opponents were "misguided" and "stupid" communist dupes. [31] Manuel Castello, a native of Valencia, joined the faculty in 1937 to teach Spanish and French. "While in Spain," he told *The Setonian*, "I beheld some of the worst tragedies imaginable," concluding that "the courage of the Catholics in defending their Faith will never be forgotten."[32]

Seton Hall was both engaged and isolated, opinionated but uninvolved. It regarded the world beyond its gates as insufficiently endowed with its own idiosyncratic wisdom. Only *The Setonian* could denounce Thanksgiving and almost get away with it: "We Catholics must tolerate [it] as part of the alien culture in which we, as a minority, are forced to live. No longer are our neighbors heretics, with whom we have much in common. They are pagans and atheists. Our lot is far worse in many ways than that of the imaginary Catholic who visited Salem. But our chief danger is that we do not realize how much worse it is . . ."[33] Compared to "abroad," Seton Hall preferred America—except at its most American.

A Formal Extension Unit: Nursing and Business

In December 1936, Kelley "called together the entire faculty and asked for their reaction to our starting a formal extension unit." The idea, approved unanimously, was his most significant innovation to date.

By the third decade of the twentieth century, heavy industry, mass transportation, and population growth had transformed Newark from a substantial town to a major city. The Trans Hudson Railroad, completed in 1911, linked it directly to New York City. The dredging of the harbor turned the bay into a deep-water port. By the 1920s, Newark had an airport. In 1935, the Pennsylvania Railroad station was completed. A few miles down the road, Jersey City was a Democratic fiefdom under Frank Hague, who kept the city going using state and federal money to reward followers with municipal employment. Seton Hall, a leafy college in a quiet town, was on the edge of an enormous market for educational services.

The "formal extension unit" meant in practice a set of adult education classes taught in Newark and Jersey City with the emphasis on nursing and business studies. Within a week of becoming president, Kelley had visited leading educationalists (including President Nicholas Murray Butler of Columbia University) "to obtain all the advice and assistance I could for my new position" and to learn how to start "other schools or departments in Business Administration, Pre-Medical studies, Physical Education and Education proper on the campus and . . . in Newark."[34] Seton Hall could offer degrees and certificates to women, even non-Catholics, boasting now of inclusivity. "I challenge anyone to investigate Seton Hall and find a single department where true learning does not proceed entirely unhampered by any religious dogma," he claimed,[35] sounding quite unlike his predecessors, for whom religious dogma was precisely the point of Seton Hall. There was at least one good practical reason for this newly insisted-upon nondenominationalism: Jews were generous supporters and Kelley did not wish to offend them. [36]

Many Catholic colleges, Seton Hall included, had enjoyed "tremendous growth" in the 1920s,[37] but this was different. McLaughlin had been a modernizer but modernization, for him, meant updating finances, administration, and the physical plant. It did not mean opening the doors to women or workers. Kelley had wider trends in mind, conscious that Catholic institutions attracted half of those Catholics who went to college, the other half going to public universities or to schools of other denominations.[38] The educational world was changing around him—even the Catholic educational world—and he needed to respond.

Kelley's extension campus was not the result of lengthy forethought. If it had been, it would have looked different. One story has it that when a prospective student remarked to him that Fordham had classes in accountancy whereas Seton Hall had none, Kelley hired a professor within a week and thereby created the School of Business Administration. (The student's name was Baiocchi, and he insisted on the truth of the story for the rest of his life.) Kelley certainly had little idea what he was doing. He simply appointed Howard Merity as director and Father Peter Francis Guterl as dean, and left both to get on with it. Merity, a Seton Hall graduate with a doctorate from NYU, had been school administrator of Cliffside, New Jersey for ten years. Guterl was a precise budget manager to whom fell the task of seeking permissions from state bodies to establish the Extension School and of canvassing local hospitals to establish a School of Nursing Education, which opened in August 1937. Talk of opening a law school in Newark got nowhere.

Classes began, farcically, in Newark in February 1937 in a renovated floor of St. Patrick's Pro-Cathedral School. (None of the students could fit the grammar school seats.) Initial enrollment saw 321 students taking 37 courses leading to the degrees of Bachelor and Master of Arts, and Bachelor of Science, the courses covering history, English, and mathematics, business administration and education. The faculty was strong. Dr. Walter Robinson, "distinguished traveler and lecturer," taught European government.[39] (Robinson was principal of Roosevelt School, Bayonne.) Mary C. Powers, a native of Jersey City and the first woman appointed to the faculty of Seton Hall, taught English and history. (Later she served as Director of Admissions.) Dorothy Mulgrave, assistant professor of English at New York University, accepted a similar appointment at Seton Hall. Also on the staff was Blanche Kelly, head of English at Mount Saint Vincent's College and the only woman on the editorial board of the Catholic Encyclopedia.[40] The faculty included George King, an attorney, who taught business law;

Sister Teresa Gertrude, a Benedictine nun and formerly professor of education at the Catholic University of America; Sister Aloysius, a Dominican with a Fordham PhD in philosophy; Father Gregory Schramm OSB, a chemistry teacher, lecturer in abnormal psychology, and expert on early childhood who had taught at the Catholic University of Peking[41]; Aileen O'Reilly, who taught Celtic literature at Hunter College[42] (whose appointment to Seton Hall made national news in Ireland)[43]; Father Virgil Stallbaumer, another Benedictine, joined as professor of English; Dr. Gerald Cetrulo, taught physiology (and fencing); Dr. John McCole, a *belle lettrist*, taught English.

Six months after opening in Newark, classes started in St. John's Parochial School, Jersey City. The numbers were good, with 305 students enrolled in courses leading to the same degrees on offer in Newark. By the end of the academic year, enrollment had reached 424, bringing the total in both branches to 729. Students in Newark and Jersey City paid the same tuition as in South Orange, although members of religious orders, mainly nuns, paid less. In the decade before Kelley became president, average annual enrollment in South Orange was 281. By the end of his first year, 297 students were taking classes there, by the end of his second year, 428.[44] The extension school, far from detracting from South Orange, helped it.

Saint Patrick's School in Newark (a small red schoolhouse built in 1888) proved inadequate, forcing Kelley to acquire a "beautiful" seven-story brick building (in fact, a far from lovely office block) at 31 Clinton Street, Newark in June 1938. On the main floor were offices, on the next five floors classrooms, on the sixth "an elaborate laboratory," and on the seventh a "penthouse and roof garden . . . converted into a library." The previous tenants had been the New Jersey Communist Party. "Our attendance in the building and our discovery of the actual nature of the activities going on in this one floor," Kelley recorded in his *Memoirs*, "caused the Party to withdraw within a month."[45]

The purpose of the extension campus was not to reproduce in Newark or Jersey City the curriculum of South Orange. It was geared to urban life. In all three places, students could study "the elements that once characterized all Christian literature." They could take Seneca or Historical Latin Grammar, examine "complex problems in religion, philosophy, economics, and science as found in Tennyson, Browning, Newman, and other Victorian writers," learn of the fusion of "Christian, Roman, and Germanic elements that make up the civilization of Europe," acquaint themselves with "the effect of individual differences and artificial modifications on the universal personality factors." But practicality was to the fore in the city. Business English I taught "correct and forceful English for business purposes, with special attention to vocabulary and good usage." Accounting III considered "factory cost allocation." Library Science introduced "the evaluation, study, and use of reference materials." The Legal Status of School Superintendents treated of "the foundation principles of proper conduct of School Board meetings."[46] (It sounds deadly.)

The extension campus was the institutional parent of what was to become the College of Nursing, which shall be examined in the next chapter. Seton Hall was later criticized for getting ahead of itself in the extension school, but with nursing education some improvisation was inevitable. Planning was often lacking at Seton Hall but in this case it was a virtue.

"Extensionsists" had a student council but the downtown campuses were not meant for fun. "Enthusiasm ran high as [the Council] debated plans for the 'Get-to-Gather' party and dance which is to be the first move in the establishment of a close friendship and fellowship between the students of the Jersey City branch and the Newark branch of the college."[47] Most students simply wanted to go home when class was over. These were city schools for city people. There was no point in pretending otherwise.

Matching the novelty of women faculty members were women students. Seton Hall's first coed was Mary Grace Dougherty of Newark, a would-be English teacher, whom The Setonian regarded as exotic, "a pretty lass about five foot five inches tall" who "likes the place very much." "I think it is a great honor to be the first co-ed at such a college as Seton Hall," she said.[48]

Considered in toto, the "Formal Extension Unit" was a success and an omen. When Kelley became president in 1936, 464 students were enrolled in Seton Hall College and Seton Hall Preparatory School. In 1938, enrollment in South Orange, Newark, and Jersey City amounted to 2,295. In 1941, the Newark and Jersey City enrollment was 3,200. These numbers give a misleading impression of vastness, most students and faculty being part-timers. Still, a revolution was under way. The fiction was maintained that Seton Hall remained unchanged. Despite good intentions, the urban division lacked definition, finances, and, frankly, students qualified for college-level work. The budget was chaotic.[49] Facilities were rudimentary. The faculty was makeshift. Planning was nil. Kelley reorganized the campuses in February 1938, hoping to meet Middle States standards but unsure if he would. In the extension school, Seton Hall overextended itself. The "professional division" was anything but professional.

Middle States inspectors were unhappy when they came to Seton Hall in 1940. The main campus—what had been, at the time of the last inspection, the only campus—was much as before. "Seton Hall at South Orange is a fairly typical, conservative Catholic college for prospective priests." Its primary purpose was to "supply higher education under Catholic supervision to the predominantly Catholic population of the Newark area."[50] This it did with a faculty of twenty priests and twenty-six laymen, sixteen with doctorates, fourteen with Master's degrees, and three with no degrees (who taught physical education).[51] Eight of the MAs were awarded by Seton Hall itself and "the college apologizes for these degrees." Apart from Marshall Library, which was physically and intellectually inadequate (it closed when the librarian, Father Charles Murphy, went to teach class), the college had good classrooms, clean laboratories, attractive

grounds, and a "splendid" new gymnasium. The biology department lacked equipment, materials for teaching physics were "minimal," but otherwise most needs were
well supplied. A "good deal of the curriculum [was] prescribed," leading to overem-
phasis on memorization, but graduation rates were good and success beyond college,
as measured by entrance into graduate school, acceptable.[52] Financially, Seton Hall
was underwritten by the Archdiocese of Newark in the form of priests who taught for
modest salaries and students who attended the college with a view to studying for the
priesthood. Otherwise, it depended on tuition, fees, and gifts.

Turning to the extension division, the inspectors were withering. Jersey City and
Newark were "very poor apologies for educational institutions . . . If they are not
abandoned they should at least stop all graduate work, and the $10,000 or $15,000
necessary to equip them with laboratories and libraries should be made available immediately." Newark's library had only 1,700 volumes, Jersey City's "one medium-sized
bookcase with perhaps 150 . . . reference books." Courses in English, history, government, and sociology were weak, the rest little better. The urban division was so poor
there was no reason why Seton Hall "should not be dropped from the accepted list of
the Middle States Association." In 1938, Kelley bluffed the Association. In 1940, the
bluff was called.[53]

The report, intended to shock, succeeded. Privately, the inspectors were more relaxed, recognizing that Seton Hall was not the first college to run before it could walk.
The problems were fixable: remove undersubscribed or redundant courses; demand
higher admission standards; hire decent administrators; keep track of students; buy
books for the library; make graduate students write a thesis. "Okay," "yes," "coming,"
"correct," Kelley scribbled on the letter containing these recommendations, patheti-
cally grateful for a second chance.

When inspectors returned two years later, they were full of praise (although they
wondered what was the point of teaching Latin and Greek to trainee nurses, as the
trainee nurses also wondered).[54] The "formal extension campus" eventually produced
the College of Nursing, the School of Education and Human Services, and the School
of Business. It was Kelley's biggest gamble and his biggest success. For a while, though,
it threatened to be his biggest failure.

The Decade Ends

Kelley weathered his first crisis by panicking. But not every day was so fraught. He
was a delegator, relying on Fathers John F. Davis, William F. Furlong, and Charles
Murphy to do routine business for him. Davis, an exceptionally bright young priest,
combined the pastoral qualities of a preacher with the practical skills of an accountant.
Furlong had a certain ethereality, walking to chapel in winter, students joked, leaving

no footprints in the snow. His nickname was "Plu" (short for pluperfect). Murphy, when not teaching English, was the librarian whose meager domain was patronized in winter "not because the students wanted books but because it was warm." It was also heavy with the "almost daily aromas which ascend from the kitchen."[55]

Kelley also relied on the College's many friends. Rose Kehoe, a spinster of Jersey City, left Seton Hall $28,000 in her will.[56] "We are organizing a ladies unit comprising the relatives of alumni and the present student body," announced a group of supporters from Bayonne and the Oranges, "first, for their own social and intellectual activities; and, secondly, to lend social and cultural influence to the college campus." Some 210 women answered the call. In April 1939, the name "Bayley-Seton League" was adopted and within three years, it had become "the outstanding women's society in New Jersey," its "splendid womanly influence" as important as the cash it raised.[57]

There was a final flourish as the 1930s went out. Kelley, a sportsman, believed in healthy bodies in healthy minds. The drive for a new gymnasium had begun in February 1935 with Bishop Walsh taking the lead. The old gymnasium was the former College Building which had been destroyed by fire in 1909, leaving nothing standing but the walls.[58] Rebuilt as a one-story auditorium-gymnasium and by the 1930s plainly inadequate as a gym, this building (later known as Stafford Hall) was refurbished in 1937.[59] But Seton Hall needed a proper gymnasium. The idea was to raise $250,000 by public subscription (Walsh donated $5,000) so that "Seton Hall may be equally accredited in the athletic line as in the academic lines."[60] Ground was broken in June 1939, the cornerstone laid in October, the building completed the following April. Costing $850,000 and built on a grand scale, it was modeled on gymnasia in the Universities of Oregon, Chicago, and Wisconsin, combining facilities for swimming, basketball, squash, bowling, boxing, billiards, and gymnastics, with a theater for 400 people. "Only in the Americas could such an event as this cornerstone laying at Seton Hall be taking place today," said Arthur Sinnott, editor of the *Newark Evening News*. "Elsewhere in the world the lights of civilization are out or going out. Elsewhere in the world intolerance and persecution have taken the place of tolerance and humanness. This ceremony can be held, this building can be dedicated, to Christian education because the people of this nation are dedicated to tolerance, to respect for the opinions of mankind, and to reverence for God and His truths."[61]

It was a heavy burden for a gymnasium to bear.

CHAPTER 9

Seton Hall at War

A Crisis of Numbers

Photographed at the center of his faculty in 1937, the youngest of a graying group, Kelley seemed a man with the world at his feet. "Father Kelley dictates letters, composes manuscripts . . . writes speeches and reports" from the back of his car, wrote one credulous journalist.[1] At his desk by eleven at night, he enjoyed for another three hours the "the meager time for the scholar's life he loves so well." He was urbane, apparently owning a car once belonging to Wendell Wilkie and a rug belonging to Pius XII (whom he had taught to speak English).[2] He was friendly with Spencer Tracy and Thomas Edison (who lived locally) and an expert on eye operations (which may have been true: Kelley did suffer from poor eyesight). Some of these claims his fellow priests took with a pinch of salt. Kelley's job was to promote Seton Hall by promoting himself and he was good at doing both. Kelley enjoyed flattery too much but he was on nodding terms with some notable figures. "I am not, of course, intimately familiar with Seton Hall," Wilkie wrote to him, "but I am fully aware of the splendid educational work done by the Catholic clergy at many institutions throughout the land. I regard these educators as one of the great bulwarks against the spread of Communism, Nazism, and other subversive doctrines which threaten the preservation of America's personal and political liberties."[3] Kelley was simply the president of a small Catholic college in New Jersey; others inhabited a grander world he could only dream about. Seton Hall was "venerable," said church historian Peter Guilday in 1938.[4] It was now under new, less elderly, management.

Kelley could be capricious: friendly then rude then friendly again. Most complaints had to do with his aloofness, the difficulty of getting meetings with him, his preference for the gym over the office, his unseemly interest in receipts at sporting events, and his failure to take seriously questions of faculty rank and salary.[5] There were "two or three inevitable trouble-makers" in any college, he thought, although at Seton Hall "pure, unadulterated gossip [of] Ivory Soap proportions" seemed to prevail over fact by a ratio of 98 to 2.[6] It was no different from anywhere else, in short.

The glamour of being boss appealed to him more than the grind. Committees would be impaneled, then ignored. Kelley's vice president, Father James Hamilton, was little more than a secretary: "he will open and sort the general mail of the College and will have such mail answered by the respective departments. . . . He will receive visitors and will accept phone calls of anyone who may have called for the President."[7] The administration of the school was subcontracted to an impressive-sounding bureaucracy—the Executive Advisory Committee, the Heads of Department Committee, the Admissions Committee, the Vocational Guidance Committee, the Catalog and Schedule Committee, the Committee on Tests and Measurements, the Library Committee, the Committee on Academic Standing—whose function was to preserve the fiction of faculty governance when the reality was presidential decree.[8] If they caused trouble, Kelley ignored them.

On the other hand, he could not ignore the day-to-day bureaucratic details. "I find we are suffering a very bad name among our creditors for failure to promptly meet our bills," he complained in 1941.[9] McQuaid or Corrigan could have written the same eighty years before. He was also irritated by Seton Hall's bad habit of keeping tuition low, then making up for it by hidden fees.[10] But other problems were of more recent vintage. Seton Hall had become larger and more complex, no longer manageable along the informal lines of his predecessors. Kelley insisted against the evidence that the administration was still small enough to be handled by a president, vice president, and secretary, only reluctantly conceding the need for change. Instead of a personal reply from Kelley to applicants came a form letter. Instead of customized responses came a college catalog. Instead of a presidential decision came a Committee on Admissions meeting twice in April, three times in May, four times in June, July, and August, and twice in early September. Kelley was wise (or idle) enough to realize he should not do all this work himself.[11]

More serious was the relationship between the Extension schools and the main campus, particularly the slapdash methods of the former as compared to the rigorous program of the latter. "Here we give the student a coherent, progressive course," Father Joseph Brady wrote to Kelley in late 1939. "In the Extension School, there has been manifest[ly] a 'hit-or-miss' system of taking courses, not in any sequence, but whenever it happens to be convenient." Two students could emerge from Seton Hall with the same degree having had substantially different academic experiences.[12] Seton Hall's urban division was an administrative shambles, with most courses given for two credits, not three as in South Orange. How was the difference to be adjusted when arranging transfers? South Orange had academic departments and was the better for them. The urban division had none, which meant that faculty knew nothing of a student beyond the fact that he or she was "taking this or that course with them individually."[13]

Brady wondered about having an Executive Advisory Committee when its advice was unheeded.[14] Kelley's tautological response was that its role was merely advisory.[15] When minutes of its meetings were written to reflect Kelley's apparently progressive intentions, Brady annotated them acerbically: "Dr. Kelley said nothing of the kind" to the notion that he would establish an Admissions Committee for the urban division, and an extravagantly scrawled "White-Wash" to the idea that he was in favor of "the highest possible standards" for athletes.[16]

The years leading up to Pearl Harbor saw Kelley deal with trivialities. The occasional quarrel at a social event or a bit of vandalism on a Saturday night were the worst of his problems. The headmaster of Saint Benedict's Preparatory School, Newark complained in 1940 of the "yearly offenses" of Seton Hall students pulling down goalposts and destroying field markers.[17] In the week before the Ribbentrop-Molotov Pact, Father Thomas Gilhooley was trying to improve student elocution. "Every freshman will be required to take a phonographic test for his speech upon entering school in September."[18] In the weeks after the fall of Poland, Kelley was "earnestly" requesting that "every professor exclude from his class any student not wearing a coat and tie" and that a course be given "to all non-Catholic students on Character Formation."[19] "In drawing up next year's schedule," it was decided, "the Christmas date should be advanced because of the fact that many of the students work in post offices during this period of the year."[20]

The freshmen who gathered in September 1940 to begin their college careers were introduced to each other in a two-day series of exercises whose regimentation was itself the most accurate indicator of what lay ahead:

Thursday September 12th:
    9 AM: Mass in the College Chapel
    Sermon: The Spiritual Side of College
    Reverend Harold Dilger, Head of the Department of Religion
    10 AM Little Theater (New Gymnasium Building)
    College Opportunities and Responsibilities
    Address of Welcome: Very Reverend James F. Kelley, President
    What Seton Hall Expects of You: Reverend James Hamilton, Dean
    The Cultural Growth of the College Man: Dr James F. O'Donnell, Head of the Department of Classical Languages. . . .

A healthy mind in a healthy body was Seton Hall's goal and, in some ways, its entrance requirement. To look at freshmen classes of the late 1930s is to see certain physical deficiencies, some remediable, some not, all now the responsibility of the college. Eager to justify the new gymnasium, the physical education department described a student body exhibiting "many glaring defects unknown to the individual student" and an "obvious need for development from either skeletal, muscular, coordinative, or postural point of view." Students fell into one of six categories, with many students apparently unaware that they suffered from "bad hearing, poor vision, carious teeth, and infected throats":

A . . . . Athletes—Athletic build

N . . . . Normal health and normal physical condition

D . . . . Development group necessitating corrective or special exercises for muscular, skeletal, postural or coordinative development

R . . . . Restricted group—Cardiacs and defectives

F . . . . Follow-up group necessitating medical or dental care through family physician or dentist.

The physical education department and the Division of Student Counsel developed a program by which faculty were to be given a list of "R" and "F" freshman and sophomore students and told to watch out for them. Professors were reminded that failing or inferior performance in the classroom might have had medical roots. Student absences were to be reported to the health department. The aim was to "insure a healthy body, prepared not only to cope attentively with scholastic requirements, but prepared to cope with the future demands of competitive life."[21]

Seton Hall was a school, not a sanitarium, but here, too, pressure for change was building. Undergraduates in the urban division were "largely interested in preparation for specific fields, namely Education, Business Administration, Nursing Education, [and] Social Studies," Ernest Bowles of the Middle States Association told Kelley in May 1941. "They do not seem to be interested in the Arts Division as such."[22] Kelley had earlier responded to such demands by creating schools of nursing education and business administration, but now he decided that what Seton Hall needed was a school of engineering, which would contribute to the local economy, keep Seton Hall's name in the news, and diversify academic offerings at a perilous time for the country and for small colleges. The Board of Trustees approved, Kelley drew up a curriculum, arranged to hire teachers, even visited a number of schools in New England to see how their engineering programs operated. Then the idea was dropped. The war killed it: the same war, had timing been better, that might have been the making of it. The school of engineering died, as did an American way of life, on December 7, 1941. Seton Hall did not know what was about to hit it.

Even before Pearl Harbor, Kelley had warned of "extremely dark days . . . ahead for the American college." Encouraging numbers in the extension campuses concealed the fact that part-time students made enrollment seem bigger than it was. To Kelley, South

Orange was where the action, or inaction, was. In September 1941, the college stood to lose sixty-two students, or about 11 percent of the freshman, sophomore, and junior classes. If Congress lowered the draft age to eighteen, four of five students would have been eligible, threatening closure of the school. One solution might have been to have minor seminarians classified as ineligible—major seminarians were already so— which would have kept at least some students on campus. "Anyone who understands the process of training young men for the priesthood," Kelley wrote to the Newark Draft Board in May 1941, "will readily agree that the small number of students who have actually declared and signed up for their studies for the priesthood . . . [should] come under Class 4D . . . These years at Seton Hall are a necessary probation and an integral part of his theological training."[23] Five students were allowed to remain.[24] Another possibility was to seek new students to provide, as Kelley put it, "some core for survival" if war were to break out. He had the school of engineering in mind. Another resort was "some financial aid [from the archdiocese] in order to weather the storm," but that, Kelley informed the Board, "may not materialize until 1943."[25] Colleges like Seton Hall that emphasized the humanities could seem inessential and, in Kelley's words, "decidedly inferior to technical and professional training schools," not only for the duration of the war but long thereafter. Stories "are now trickling out of Washington," he told the Board in June 1941, "that Federal subsidy will now be granted to key colleges in each locality to force out of existence superfluous colleges, where several now exist."[26] Even if they did survived, colleges could not continue as before. "Occasionally we hear our leaders like Churchill and Roosevelt remind us that we have to win the peace as well as the war," Kelley told the Board in 1942. In reality, "emphasis is now placed on skill, amounting almost to an idolatry of the technological." "President Roosevelt [expects] many of the Liberal Arts colleges [to] be forced into bankruptcy and out of existence, thus proving their unimportance and their uselessness to the nation."[27] Seton Hall, opened by one Roosevelt, might have been closed by another. On December 7, 1942, the first anniversary of Pearl Harbor, the seriousness of the College's financial situation was plain for all to see: "A discussion was had [at a meeting of the Faculty Advisory Committee] with regard to Jap evacuees and the statute passed by the Government, enabling japs [sic] who are loyal to the United States Government to leave their camps of internment and attend school, paying their own tuition, and it was decided to delegate Father Lillis to write to the proper authorities in this regard."[28] Nothing came of it.

Kelley wanted to keep enrollments healthy but not so healthy as to draw attention to them. The 4D exemption did not cover ecclesiastical aspirants studying outside Seton Hall, prompting him to suggest in 1942 that "it might be called to the attention of any parish priest who has boys that are beginning studies for the priesthood . . . that these students will not be exempt from the draft unless they are attending Seton

Hall Preparatory School." "It might be better not to gamble on such a move since it would look like an evasion, crowding Seton Hall with people seeking exemptions."[29] War reveals the divided social personalities of those caught up in it, and Kelley was as divided as the next, a priest who wished to train priests, a patriot who wished the best for his country, a president who wished to protect his college. These desires were not easily reconciled.

The conflict did not hit home immediately. Numbers reached record highs in academic year 1941–1942, with 704 men and women taking courses in South Orange, 1,545 in Newark and Jersey City, and 602 enrolled in the summer session: a total of 2,851. Ten years before, as Kelley remarked, "one quarter of that figure would have been considered phenomenal."[30] But "taking a course" did not mean being a full-time student. In 1942, South Orange lost 166 students to the armed forces or industry, over 20 percent of the body in a year. Newark and Jersey City lost 413. Professors of fighting age were drafted or joined the war effort in a civilian capacity, playing "unusual havoc" with the "exceptionally fine faculty" painstakingly assembled during the previous five years.[31] In September 1941, Seton Hall had a faculty of fifty-six (twenty-four priests and thirty-two laymen). Nine months later, sixteen of them were gone, three priests (Revv. Peter Rush, John Feeley, and James Carey) who volunteered as military chaplains and thirteen laymen drafted into the army, working for the FBI, or (in the case of two Spanish professors) acting as civilian censors.

As he complained to the Board of loss of staff, so Kelly also complained somewhat disingenuously to the archdiocese of loss of students. "As is happening to all colleges, we have had a tremendous drop in student enrollment in the past six months," he wrote to Vicar-General Monsignor John McClary, "and we have had to carry on with the same professorial staff and the same current expenses . . . I have not even the funds to pay the current salaries of my professors."[32] By his own admission a few weeks later, he did *not* have the "same professorial staff" although plainly he lacked the funds to pay even those who remained. In beggary any argument will do and Kelley, at this stage, was desperate. Tradesmen had taken to sending their unpaid Seton Hall bills directly to the Archbishop. In September 1942 Stella Jasina resigned, unable to cope with the "general upset condition" of the books and the "unjust treatment and insults" she had endured since Kelley had become president.[33] The same month, the comptroller, Father Joseph Tuite, was on the verge of "hysteria"—Kelley's phrase—because of shortage of cash and inability to pay salaries.[34] In the end, thanks to the archdiocese, the faculty and creditors got their money, but Tuite's worry was reasonable. Kelley was good at blaming the war for troubles of which he was principal author.

Within a year of the outbreak of war, then, Seton Hall faced financial catastrophe. In September 1942 there were 563 students on the books, of whom 60 were boarders and 503 day boys. By February 1943 the number was down to 451 and, by June 1943, to

298. "I personally believe that with a proper drive for collection of delinquent student accounts there should be no real problem," Kelley assured McClary, as if the problem were one of accountancy.[35] But disappearing, not delinquent students, was the difficulty. Of 50 seniors who returned to Seton Hall in September 1942, "only 14," Kelley reported to the Board, "will be in cap and gown to receive their degrees." In June 1943, only sixteen priests and thirteen laymen remained on the faculty. By September, total enrollment amounted to 165. By May 1944 only 140 students remained on campus, taught by 12 priests and 1 layman. "With only two exceptions," Kelley reported to the Board, "the priests obediently and willingly concurred in the extra duties imposed upon them under war-time necessity."[36]

Some students were drafted, others took "lucrative employment in defense production where they are exempt from the draft." (The "present business boom" was "devastating to college enrollment.") Many "under the enthusiasm of wartime and because of the opportunities of training for commissions volunteered for service even though exempt from the Draft." Almost every absence was war related. Neighboring colleges faced similar difficulties, with Columbia University running an annual deficit of over $200,000 and Upsala College in East Orange forced into "a very unsavory and unsatisfactory arrangement" with the Newark College of Engineering whereby each agreed to exchange students. (It is hard to see what was so unsavory about this arrangement. Kelley would have done the same himself.) Faced with difficulties, Kelley insisted on "absolute economy."[37] There would be no investment in laboratory equipment, no expansion or alteration of buildings, no purchases of books for the library, no repairs to the physical plant. This had its comic side. "Another plan which we have been considering, but which the war has forced us to abandon for the time being," he told the Board in 1942, "is Secretarial Studies." The curriculum involved "the setting up of a room with typewriters [but] unfortunately typewriters are not available at the present time."[38] In Newark, classroom heat was "not only poor but extremely uncertain." The good news that more women were taking courses was offset by the bad news that in Newark there were no toilets for them.

Newark and Jersey City kept their numbers better than South Orange, even turning a profit.[39] Most students in Newark and Jersey City were women, a high percentage of them future nurses. Religious orders supplied novices studying for state-mandated certificates in general and elementary education.[40] The success of the urban division in Newark led to a breakdown of relations between Guterl and Kelley, with Guterl deploring the inadequacy of the facilities and wanting to move to "an adequate and dignified location where we can expand after the war or even during [it]," and Kelley refusing to envisage new expenditures at a time of extreme shortage. In May 1944 the Board, taking Kelley's side, "unanimously and absolutely" refused to fund a new building in Newark. Kelley resented Guterl's "contempt of, and disregard of, all authorities."[41] Guterl resented Kelley's "very insulting and contumelious manner,"[42] his "twisted truths, vicious half-truths, malicious insinuations and downright lies, some of them 'whoppers.'"[43] Walsh took Kelley's side and appointed Guterl to a parish, Dr. Charles Elliot, former New Jersey Commissioner for Education, replacing him.

Life on the Home Front

War brought other changes. *The Setonian* ceased publication. Its postwar editor, Edmund Rezetko, remembered nothing newsworthy about his Seton Hall days except the successes of the basketball and fencing teams. In 1942, he abandoned his studies to spend forty-four months in Iceland, England, and the Continent, returning in 1947 as a junior with a Silver Star for gallantry in action.[44] Classes ran with fewer students or were cancelled. "Americanism" survived but some subjects were scrapped and others (air raid protection) added. Professor Felix Italiano, coordinator of a new Civil Aeronautics course, brought a single-propeller plane to campus in May 1942, demonstrating its controls before allowing students to fly it to an airfield in Warwick, New York.[45] Italiano, a mathematician, was subject of an admiring profile in *The Newark Star-Ledger* for his work on putting Seton Hall on a war footing.[46] (Kelley did not share the admiration because most of his teaching was done by a student.)[47] Kelley's ambition, the *Star-Ledger* reported, was "to put the South Orange institution on a wartime basis . . . Today that program is in full swing . . . Students are taught map-reading and topographical drawing, surveying and navigation and nautical astronomy . . . The finger-printing of students at Seton Hall for identification in Washington has been completed. [This extended to the faculty. Done by the FBI, its purpose was to identify air-raid victims.] A first aid course for all students has been arranged, and rifle practice in the school's modern range is offered as many students as possible."[48]

Victor Di Filippo, director of physical education, inherited "no major students, [no full-time colleagues], no materials, no equipment, no books . . . no Gym (unless you can call the space which is now a library a Gym)" when he came to Seton Hall in 1937.[49] The physical fitness movement toughened students for battles ahead, although "tap dancing, folk dancing, social dancing, badminton, bowling and golf" were unlikely to stop the Third Reich in its tracks.[50]

War accelerated, while attenuating, the business of getting a degree. With many students leaving in the middle of studies, Kelley worried that some might receive no degree at all. To avoid this, he offered a speeded-up wartime degree approved by the Board in May 1943 by which a student would be granted full credit for the semester during which he was called into active service "on condition that he can pass satisfactorily a comprehensive examination before a Faculty Committee appointed for that purpose."[51] The scheme worked well without solving, indeed in some ways exacerbating, the problem of falling numbers. Kelley even considered admitting students with only three years of high school work, but the idea was shelved.

Summer school kept Seton Hall going, also cheerful:

Enjoyable movies were shown every week in the Little Theatre and played to well-filled houses. The nuns had a picnic in the Auditorium-Gymnasium that was the best ever but, more than that, they discovered the pool for the first time and were delighted with it . . .

Events were climaxed by the double performance of an old-fashioned melodrama, *Her Fatal Beauty* or *A Shop-Girl's Honor* . . . a fitting conclusion to a summer school of serious purpose but of pleasant surroundings and associations . . . [52]

Better days ahead would surely look like this.

Fighting Seton Hall

Seton Hall's contribution to the war effort was substantial. At least three alumni saw the Japanese attack on Pearl Harbor, none losing their lives. One was in hospital suffering from a football injury. Another, Father William Maguire, was about to board the flagship of the fleet to say Mass and was widely credited with the words "Praise the Lord and pass the Ammunition" which were turned by Frank Loesser into the most patriotic song of the war. "I don't recall saying [them]," he admitted when he returned to Seton Hall in November 1942, "but I rather hope I did." Addressing the assembled student body, he told them that "the Jap [is] a good warrior . . . the American fighter's sense of sportsmanship and fair play is unknown to the Nipponese."[53] If Maguire was unfamiliar to most students, better known was Father James Carey, assistant athletic director, who was commissioned in May 1942 as a first lieutenant to serve as a chaplain to the U.S. Army Eighth Armored Division. Carey was probably the most popular man on campus.

Well over 1500 alumni, undergraduates, and faculty fought in the services. Of that number at least twenty-one were killed, two in Normandy in 1944.[54] "We have had reports," one correspondent wrote to the Bayley-Seton League, "of reunions in the Hawaiian Islands, the Gilberts, England, Ireland, and in fact from almost every part of the globe." "The offensive in the South Pacific was on! And our Alumni were on the spot . . . The battle of North Africa was initiated and the sands . . . became a Seton Hall outpost . . . The air war over Europe has been the work of many Setonians . . . Our men have been active in the landings on Nassau Bay, Lae, Finchaven, Arawe, Saidor, Cape Gloucester, Taraw and word has reached us that one of the boys from the Hall has been wounded on Saipan . . . The China front is also on our list." The reality was sobering. "At least four have been shot down from their planes and taken prisoner . . . at least two [have landed] in Sicily . . . There isn't much Seton Hall in China but what there is, I'm sure, has brought much fame to the Hall in the sight of God":

[Jerry Moore and Ed Arliss] are now Passionist Missionaries [in China]. I met them one night at Mass a few months ago. You can imagine how I felt when I heard they were Hall boys. Their home mission had been burned down by the Japs a short time ago, so they moved into my neck of the woods. All three of us were together at Mass on Christmas.

"The Alumni Bulletin for Men in Service is sent to all Setonians in the armed forces every month [and] have provoked many letters from the men relating their experiences, all of them interesting to us. One related the incident of two classmates meeting at Mass in the jungles of India. They hadn't seen each other since graduation. To complete the picture, the Chaplain saying the Mass was a Setonian!" Seeing a home-town face was good reason for giving thanks: "each letter we receive contains the wish to be back on the campus in South Orange."[55]

Seton Hall's most conspicuous hero was Father John Washington, a member of the class of 1931, who studied for the priesthood at Immaculate Conception Seminary and was ordained in June 1935. Washington was one of four US chaplains who died in the sinking of the USAT[56] Dorchester off the coast of Greenland in February 1943. With nine hundred sleeping men on board, the ship was torpedoed by a Nazi U-boat in the middle of the night. Taking the initiative, the chaplains led soldiers to the life jackets, dispensing them until the supply was depleted. Then each of them – Washington, two Protestant ministers, and a rabbi – offered his life-jacket to four GIs, telling them to jump. The ship went down twenty-five minutes later. Survivors recalled the chaplains linked arm-in-arm in prayer as they died.[57] In May 1948 their sacrifice was marked by a commemorative US postage stamp. In 1961, in one of his last acts as President, Dwight D. Eisenhower presented their families with special medals authorized by Congress.[58]

The Alumni Bulletin for Men in Service did not please the Office of Censorship in Washington, DC. "Our attention has been directed to your issue for February [1943], which contains, unintentionally, of course, certain information which might be of value to our enemies." Careless talk cost lives.[59] Within these constraints, editor Daniel McCormick, maintained correspondence with Seton Hall men on overseas duty, reporting on their deeds and keeping up morale.

Students and staff who survived returned with stories to tell. Dean Cetrulo (who went on to win an Olympic bronze medal in fencing in 1948 and of whom more in a later chapter) had a war that was "the stuff of Hollywood drama." A captain in the US 8th Army Air Force, a winner of the Purple Heart, Cetrulo was shot down over enemy territory in Italy in 1944 and, captured, escaped from a German prisoner of war camp, avoiding recapture by his ability to speak Italian. On the run for months, he made his way toward Allied lines until dramatically reunited with his older brother Guido "who had sought leave from his post in Sicily to search for [him] on the Naples-Anzio front." When he died in 2010 aged 91, Cetrulo was remembered as an Olympic champion, "a

Broadway actor with Hollywood good looks, the subject of a Hardy Boys mystery *The Clue of the Broken Blade*, a war hero and an educator."[60]

Letter after letter, some censored by the War Department to save lives, others by the Alumni Association association to save blushes, told of day-to-day duties of war. There were pleasures: "October 29, 1944. Frank Spatuzzi and Father Reilly were up to visit me while I was in hospital. I came back on a hospital ship which had a gal from Newark as a nurse. I was telling Spats about her and lo and behold she was an old friend of his. I don't know how he made out because I haven't seen him since."[61] And sorrows: "I am very sorry to hear of, and read of, the deaths of the Hallers. No matter what year they graduated, they were all real Catholic American gentlemen. I am positive all gave a good account of themselves before going to meet our God."[62] But laughter: "How about those pinochle sessions up in Father Powers' room? Are they disbanded now or three handed now? Give my regards to the Padres and all of the boys, especially '41. Till the next issue . . ."[63]

From an undisclosed location in January 1945, Father Jim Carey was able to put war into perspective: "Can't tell you much about myself right now. Was assured of a Combat Tank or Inf[antry] Div[ision]. I hope they put me to work before my waistline equals that of the Dean of the Divinity School."[64] From France in February 1945, Private Bill Waldron was able to look on the bright side: "We are billeted in the hay loft of a barn. It isn't what I would call nice, but I at least it is very much better than sleeping in the mud, rain, and cold."[65]

Little was nice about northern France in early 1945: "I received the Alumni news bulletin the other day and it certainly makes darn interesting reading but I certainly don't like to read a long list of names of men who have been killed each time. You get hardened to a lot of things in the army but never to reading about someone getting it . . . Looks like Bert and I are going in opposite directions from New Jersey. Maybe I will meet him when we take a cruise to the Pacific after this war ends in a year or two. Never let anyone tell you the war in Europe is over by a long shot."[66]

But when war ended, the optimism of these dispatches was one reason for victory: "Well, Dan, tell me, has the Hall changed much during the past three years? I've been living in Italy so long that the spaghetti-benders have made me an honorary citizen. After spending 31 months of hedge-hopping from one spot to another, I'm really ripe for that long-awaited boat ride to civilization. Brother, I've had it! Sooooooo, if all goes well for this Sad Sack, I should be tripping the light fantastic sometime in April. Arriverderci, bona serra, Chow, bona note, and all that sort of confusion, from Jack Erikson."[67]

Here was the voice of Seton Hall at war: humorous, serious, and brave. Such men had no need of courses in Americanism: they personified it.

CHAPTER 10

A New Beginning

Making the Future

To the casual visitor, Seton Hall in 1945 looked like a college from an earlier time. It was small, rustic, faintly dilapidated, a place with few residents (sixty in 1940)[1] and even fewer prospects. Only the extension campuses showed signs of life. South Orange was moribund. "There was no such thing as a gate," remembered William Dunham, appointed to teach political science at the end of the war, "merely a narrow road, half dirt, half paved, only big enough for two cars."[2] A tree-lined path formed an arch from the entrance on South Orange Avenue to the Administration Building, the chapel, Bayley Hall, the Preparatory School (in Mooney Hall), Alumni Hall, the Marshall Library, and the gymnasium. Seton Hall was mostly grass and fields, one of hundreds of small colleges built for the nineteenth century and unsure of how to cope with the challenges of the twentieth. Its virtual abandonment during the war, except for summer schools and a handful of students and priests, gave it the appearance of a gothic morgue. The war had shown Seton Hall's decency, bravery, and improvisation, but also—in Kelley's efforts to make ends meet, in his warning that technology would make or break small colleges, in his uncertainty about state support for private education—its challenges and limitations.[3] Unless numbers picked up, the future was doubtful. Even if they did pick up, the future would be different from the past.

In fact, numbers picked up spectacularly. Kelley's wartime dreams of postwar growth were, if anything, modest. Beyond the half-paved, half-dirt road lay spreading suburbs and returning GIs: new fields, almost literally, to conquer. Seton Hall was about to embark on the greatest transformation in its history. Dunham's two cars were soon twenty, then two hundred, then two thousand. (They also became a metaphor for a college on the move and a source of complaint for those who thought it was moving too fast.)[4] "For the past four years, due to the national emergency, many customs and traditions here at Seton Hall have been shelved," *The Setonian* editorialized in November 1945.[5] "Already the camp-to-campus movement has changed our college, [now] bustling with activity and a new found look . . . The time has come to expand our college [and to attain the goal of university status]." "Seton Hall College will accept all applicants, veterans and non-veterans alike, provided they can meet the require-ments," Kelley announced,[6] avoiding the question of whether Seton Hall itself could meet the requirements. After war came peace, but not peace and quiet.

Seton Hall was not alone. "The immediate postwar period was the golden age of higher education,"[7] Paul Clemens has written, during which the nation committed itself to social renewal by way of third-level education. Colleges and universities would "smooth the transition to a postwar economy, provide tools to win the Cold War, and open career paths for an expanding middle class."[8] More intangibly, a college educa-tion came to be understood as a right and a social passport. In Europe, universities were ivory towers from which society could be viewed or ordered but not invited in. America developed a more democratic "national consensus" that students should be educated beyond their high school years.[9] It took other countries—Britain, for exam-ple—another two generations to reach the same conclusion.

"Your outline of the growth of Seton Hall has amazed me," wrote John Francis Neylan to Kelley in 1946. "I did not have the slightest realization of such an enormous growth [achieved] without any sacrifice of entrance requirements or standards."[10] Ney-lan was impressed but also slightly troubled: "Although preliminary information had prepared me for a great change in Seton Hall, my visit there left me rather bewildered. Of course, the story is one of the most amazing in the history of American educational institutions. Even with readjustments . . . you have laid the foundations for one of the qualitative colleges of the country."[11]

If Seton Hall retained its religious character, he thought, it would succeed; other-wise, not. Kelley was keen to stress pluralism. It was not "generally known," he told the *Newark Star-Ledger* in April 1946, "that we have about two hundred Jewish and Protestant boys. One of our best athletes was a lad whose mother asked us to make sure he attended Methodist services every Sunday. And one of the smartest lads we ever had is a Jewish lad who has just been graduated from the medical school of the University of North Carolina."[12] But mostly the student body was Catholic. Neylan had no need to fear for the school's religious identity.

And so, between 1936 and 1946, Seton Hall expanded, then contracted, then ex-panded again. There were 902 newcomers in February 1946, up from 140 the previous year. By October 1946 the number was 2,500 spread over Newark, Jersey City, and South Orange, 1,300 of them squeezed into the last of these. "Newark has been dipped in the culture and traditions of Seton Hall and so far it has proven itself worthy . . . A few coats of paint; some new lights; and a general old-fashioned house-cleaning trans-formed the building into a college . . . With faith in our captains and full co-operation, we need not worry about the future of the Urban Division."[13]

"The big student body commands a respect and an ear from universities through-out the country," said *The Setonian*. "Within a few years Seton Hall will be a power to reckon with in the collegiate world."[14] Over 90 percent of the growth was made up of men who had served in the armed forces.[15] When, on June 22, 1944, Roosevelt signed into law the GI Bill of Rights (officially the Servicemen's Readjustments Act), no-one could have known the revolution about to be take place. One of the great pieces of legislation of the century, the act provided federal assistance to returning veterans for help with hospital treatment, purchase of homes and businesses, and education, the government pledging to cover the cost of tuition, living expenses, books, and equipment: a promise redeemed by eight million veterans in the seven years following the passage of the legislation. Some 2.3 million people opted to attend college or university, while 3.5 million received a high school education, and another 3.4 million some form of job training. The cost was enormous—roughly $14 billion between 1944 and 1951—but the cost of not passing the bill, in disappointed hopes and unrealized potential, would have been greater; it was a domestic Marshall Plan, an answer to pent-up social expectations produced and postponed by the war. The "craving for higher learning" presented "a crisis throughout the land," claimed Seton Hall's department of public relations in 1947. "Something had to be done—and quickly."[16] A "vast new segment of the American population"[17] came to regard college as a natural destination after high school, this in turn creating demand for college teachers, for graduate schools in which to train them, for administrators and bureaucrats to organize them. Higher education was where blue collars could be turned white.

Soon Kelley was boasting of numbers that ten years before he had deplored. "Seton Hall's enrollment of 4,192 in February 1948," he told the Board, "represents a new record in the history of the College." Combined with enrollment in Newark and Jersey City, registration came to 8,124, making Seton Hall "the largest Catholic college in the United States." Including 2,767 summer school students and 68 seminarians at Darlington, enrollment for 1947–1948 was 10,969. Seton Hall, Kelley assured the Board, pointing to a survey in *America* in January 1948, was "the seventh largest Catholic educational institution in the nation and the largest Catholic liberal arts college."[18] While impressive, the numbers were also unsustainable. In 1948, when 57 percent of the student body was composed of veterans, only 48 percent of the freshmen class was drawn from GIs, suggesting that a peak had been reached and that any shortfall would have to be made up from high school graduates. Archbishop Walsh privately wondered if the very notion of universal college education had been oversold. "I might say this in confidence, Johnny, and I do not think I have ever repeated it to anyone," Kelley wrote to John McNulty on December 3, 1949, "it is the attitude of the Archbishop that there are too many of our youth going to college because of free tuition opportunities, while at the same time the same individuals will suffer from the fact that they would not be able to absorb a college education, that many of them may endure or acquire a defeatist attitude because of that failure, but more important because the professions and trades that do not require educated men will be neglected. That is certainly true in the case of housing here in our country."[19] In expansive, expensive, egalitarian postwar America, those sentiments were best kept to himself.

Walsh's doubts notwithstanding, the scale of the achievement is hard to overstate. The Church of the 1950s, through its school system, was an instrument of upward social mobility for millions. Bishops, priests, and nuns enjoyed the loyalty of their people. Parishes were often the only point of contact between immigrants and the American world. The Church created a Catholic elite through colleges, seminaries, and lay communities dedicated to social justice, family life, international peace, and spiritual perfection.[20] In this sense, Seton Hall played a role in two postwar stories, first by funneling tens of thousands of Catholics into the mainstream of American life through an educational experience that remained thoroughly Catholic well into the 1960s and, secondly, by helping to create a Catholic lay elite whose loyalty to the Church would only come under strain as it confronted new forms of modernity after the Second Vatican Council. As with many revolutions, the implications were only imperfectly understood at the time, but it *was* a revolution.

For Seton Hall, the GI Bill was both an opportunity and a difficulty, opening up an enormous market for educational services but, equally, also opening it up to rival institutions. "In the postwar chaos that will certainly result when ten million boys come marching home," Kelley told the Board in 1943, "and after another ten million are released are released from industry . . . when there is no employment [for them], religious schools will be more vitally needed than ever before . . . [That is why] this institution will be kept going during these trying times."[21] When the war ended, he claimed vindication: "During the academic year 1946, there were 44,800 [students in New Jersey], almost three times the normal number of students. During the academic year 1949, there will be, according to estimates, 50,577 students . . . Education is contagious. The present overcrowded conditions here on campus will continue for some years to come . . ."[22]

How to proceed? First came a building program to cost $325,000 that would allow the student population to reach 2,600.[23] Three "small and compact" buildings were to be constructed, each with six classrooms for up to sixty students. One of the buildings (now called Duffy Hall) was ready for occupation by October 1946. Throughout spring and summer of 1946, large numbers of applicants took accelerated courses in English and mathematics to prepare for the opening of school in September. In July, Kelley acquired thirteen surplus army housing units from the Federal Public Housing Authority to be used as dormitories, and in August they were brought from Camp Shanks, New York and erected in a corner of the campus known as "Veterans Village." (It was opened with marching bands and an address by film actor Pat O'Brien.)[24] The first veterans building was dedicated to Lieutenant John Ruthenberg, who had been killed in action in the war. Students otherwise unhoused were billeted in the gymnasium.

What Kelley called the "little inconveniences . . . owing to temporary crowding" represented a return to military life, not an escape from it, including sleeping in an emptied swimming pool and storing clothes in the gym. "It's going to be hard, it's going to be tough, but we are going to try it anyway," said Father William Furlong to 1,300 freshmen in September 1946. "We don't cater to cranks and chronic complainers," warned *The Setonian*, "and there are always quite a few of them."[25]

A Campus Transformed

The challenges were cultural as much as physical. Former soldiers, sailors, and marines could not be treated as overgrown schoolboys. "The days of hazing are apparently over," thought *The Setonian*. "Previously a freshman was . . . obliged to wear an idiotic cap, address his superiors with deference, and in general act in awe of sophomores, juniors, and seniors. Today he stands in awe of no-one." As it turned out, it took more than Hitler to kill off hazing,[26] but for a while it looked as idiotic as it was. To students who had remained in school for the duration of the war, the new men offered "an awesome remembrance to carry away."[27] They also represented a great social experiment. "This assembled body," Kelley told the incoming class, "composed of every race, color, and creed will frankly be a testing ground to prove the value and wisdom of the policy of Americanism which was instituted for the first time on any American campus here at Seton Hall ten years ago."[28] A few days after Pearl Harbor he had called together "a monster rally of our students [and] made an appeal to every [one of them] to lay aside any individual opinions and unite solidly behind out commander-in-chief and the armed forces of our country: there must be no divided allegiance, and no questioning of the policies of our leaders, no internal debates, no pacifists."[29] Now the emphasis was on diversity, not uniformity. Americanism was a versatile creed.

Many students were married with children, and most had no experience of college life. "All of them should get married," said Arthur Hertz, professor of German. "They will study better."[30] Jesus Fernandez, professor of Spanish, thought that "it depends on the kind of wife a man has. She can either be a help and an inspiration or a hindrance. The right kind of wife can help a man tremendously, but the wrong kind can destroy his chances completely." Paul Jordan, professor of English, held that "married men make honest and serious students since they realize there is more at stake."[31] Married or single, everyone had to negotiate forms, lines, and officialdom "Here is a simple and clear system of computing quality credits," said *The Setonian*. "You take the number of courses which you are carrying, divide it by your age, subtract the amount of change in your left coat pocket, multiply by the number of days in the month, and then add 4.2. The result will equal the number of quality credits needed . . . to get a degree from the college."[32] Bureaucracy, as much as the classes made possible by it, became the bonding experience.

Some veterans needed basic training, others found the pace too slow. The majority fell in between. *The Setonian* invented a composite freshman, Sam, who may have been typical: "Sam leaped nimbly from the pads at 8:13 AM. He dressed, threw talcum powder on his day-old beard and raced madly down the stairs . . . just in time to miss the 8:27 bus. After a short wait, he caught a bus and was driven comfortably to the Seton Hall campus. His first class was English and Sam managed to discover the location of the room by 8:49. As the lecture started, Sam realized with a grim little smile that he had neglected to bring his notebook. With a good deal of initiative, he scratched his notes on the back of a Summons which he was carrying with him. He had no pencil but his fingernails were long and his spirit was willing . . ."[33] Seton Hall had its share of the frivolous, the immature, the unserious, but most students were conscientious because they could not afford not to be.

Frivolity was out of place when memories of war were recent and deep. Asked in December 1946 how they had spent previous Christmases, veterans told their stories:

> Christmas of 1944 will always stay in my mind. It was a very cold day and we were in the midst of the Battle of the Bulge. I spent Christmas Day with 2nd Armored Division who were chasing German motor columns.
>
> We celebrated our Christmas in the midst of a hot Panamanian summer. In addition to the GIs in our congregation, we also had a large crowd of Indians . . . Many of the Indian children came into church completely naked; however, the chaplain solved this problem by handing out towels for them to wear during services.
>
> I'll probably never forget the Christmas I spent on Saipan. After Midnight Mass, while we were listening to a choir made up of Japanese prisoners sing Christmas carols, the Japanese Air Force started bombing us. . . . Our Christmas dinner was not like the ones mother used to make.[34]

After such sights and worse,[35] Seton Hall was reassuringly dull.

Being there also meant mastering a new vocabulary of social aspiration. "What are you doing in college at your age?" asked John Whalen, a veteran in his late twenties, addressing the question as much to himself as his readers. "You're here because you found out in the service what an education meant when you watched your buddies shove off for OCS because they had that little magic key of a B.S. or A.B. We're here for the same reason. Uncle Sam gave us a chance to catch up with a lots of guys who were way ahead of us before the shooting started. We're here for an EDUCATION." This "school deal is strictly . . . business . . . with us," he insisted. "Some of us are married, others have kids, and. . . . some . . . pushing thirty [find] the old earning capacity isn't on the upswing." Veterans were aware of benefits they could obtain from government,[36] which may have prevented some of them from seeing education as an end in itself. Yet Howard

Leahy, director of admissions, returning from a conference in Colorado, reported that the "universal opinion" was that veterans were "far more studious and purposeful" than nonveterans. He also reported that Seton Hall was "maintaining higher standards of admission than other colleges of its type" and was less overcrowded.[37]

Among the student body, the immature competed with those who were old before their time. Analyzing the social transformations of war and peace, the latter brought the tools of a Catholic sociology that had not changed much over the years: "The war not only produced immoral motion pictures glorifying crimes and criminals but was responsible for the mass juvenile delinquency that spread over the land. Mothers working in war plants helped break up the family life so integral to the growing person; bobby-soxers springing forth full-grown in this environment turned to drink, smoking and other vices as an escape, or in an effort to keep up with the decaying world. Now, with an end to war, conditions, it is to be hoped, will soon return to normal . . ."[38]

Most students, though, were determined to see the bright side. "I like the great spirit that prevails at Seton Hall. Now that more fellows are coming back from the service . . . there seems to be a great air of friendliness and co-operation." That Seton Hall was "so near home" was "an asset." "Though it is relatively near the city [it] has maintained a real college atmosphere." "I marvel at the size, the beauty, and the excellent facilities of the gymnasium."[39] "We are thoroughly sick of this namby-pamby guff," wrote *The Setonian*. "The Hall isn't perfect. You know it. We know it. And the priests in the Administration building know it. The Hall is our School. Let's Start Boosting It."[40]

GIs turned the college, almost literally, into a barracks. Students were hanging from the rafters. Teachers were giving classes with no space to spare. Priests said Mass to overflow congregations. Young husbands went home to wives and children after a day or evening of classes. It was a remarkable adventure in Catholic social democracy.

Institutional Revolution

Equally remarkably, Seton Hall provided a home for European intellectuals displaced by war. As the student body was transformed, so was the faculty. Norman Lubasz and C.A. Schuster were both appointed in 1946. Lubasz received a doctorate in law from the University of Vienna. Schuster was a graduate of the University of Zurich. Both taught modern languages. Graduating at the top of his class in Vienna, Lubasz obtained the Imperial Ring, the highest academic honor of the Austrian Empire awarded to doctoral candidates. He practiced law in Vienna until 1939, fleeing to London following the Anschluss, surviving the Blitz, and making a living as a teacher and a translator for the Polish Government in exile He came to the United States after VE-Day. "Ever since I arrived in this country I have been deeply impressed by its beauty, its power, and its dynamic mode of life." Seton Hall compared favorably with European universities, he said. It "is doing a splendid job and has a fine future."[41]

Also from Europe was Friederic (Fred) Elston. Born in Berlin in 1895, Elston graduated from Mommsen Gymnasium and the Universities of Freiburg, Berlin, and Breslau, a mathematician by training with a passion for number theory. (He taught logic at his home when Jewish professors and students were banned from Berlin University.) Elston served as a judge until debarred as a "non-Aryan Christian" in 1938. He came to the United States in 1941 and from 1946 until his death in 1956 he taught German at Seton Hall. (Indeed, he died in the classroom.) "I have the feeling that contact between student and teacher is far better here at Seton Hall than it is at the universities of Europe. Here there is not only a willingness between student and teacher to get to know each other better, but the feeling of mutual co-operation. . . . It would be a lifetime study to determine what America is, but . . . I am certain that in these times I would want to be a citizen of no other country in the world."[42]

Nicholas Czyrowski, born and raised in Galicia in Poland, had a doctorate in law and a masters in economics, but in 1941 he was forced to work in a German war factory. Emigrating to the United States in 1949 and teaching business, he "noticed a distinction between students here and in Europe. The students over here are 'better hearted.' Education in Europe is limited and specialized but over here it is more general and all-inclusive." Czyrowski spoke five languages—Polish, German, Russian, Ukrainian, and "a little English." He had "an extensive English vocabulary" but had "some difficulty with our unique American pronunciation."[43]

Baron Jose M. De Vinck, who taught philosophy, was a character from the pages of a Chesterton novel. Born in Brussels, he had a doctorate from Louvain. His *Cantique de la Vie* (1943) won the highest prize for literature from the Belgian Royal Academy. When not teaching philosophy, he gave lectures on Belgian history (a minority interest at Seton Hall).[44] Later, he founded Alleluia Press, which published in the Byzantine liturgical tradition. His last distinction was to live to the age of 100.

Not every new teacher was a European émigré. Thirty-five-year-old Francis Hammond was the first African American appointed to the faculty, hired to teach philosophy. "Precedence has been shattered," reported *The Setonian*. A "Negro educator, the first of his race, has accepted a position."[45] Canadian by birth, Hammond graduated with a BS from Xavier University in New Orleans, a licentiate in philosophy from Louvain, and a doctorate from Laval University in Quebec in 1943. His commitment to racial equality, grounded in a Catholic understanding of human dignity, was the defining fact of his life. "If we all practiced [the Church's] principles," he believed, "the solution of our problems of race, color, and creed would be assured."[46] Hammond—"a very bright, well liked man who maintained a sense of loyalty to Seton Hall after he left"[47]—was the beginning of a wave of heightened racial awareness at the college. In 1949, the Inter-Racial

Council of Seton Hall aimed to "deal heavy blows to intolerance and prejudice"; among its projects was a radio play, *In Henry's Backyard*, which explored racial prejudice.[48] "The field of inter-racial justice is one of the most important and urgently needed areas of activity in the world," Hammond said. "American Catholics must get over their timidity and reluctance to understand that their attitude towards the Negro tests the sincerity of the Church's spiritual message . . . We are here on the proving grounds and, I might say, the firing line of Democracy."[49] Hammond was ahead of his time.

From John Allegra who taught modern languages to Andrew Yockers who taught philosophy, the faculty was, alphabetically, as diverse as America. Irving Alpert taught accounting. Charles Baatz was a philosopher. Joseph Caruso taught social sciences. Nicholas de Prospo taught biology. Jesus de Fernandez, Arthur Hertz, and Julius Lombardi taught modern languages. Sidney Glusman taught mathematics. Robert Kautzmann taught business. Some of the postwar intake lasted a year, others a lifetime. (Among the latter were Ed Henry in Modern Languages, Gerry Keenan and Paul Ochojski in English, Joe Cunningham in Education, and Nick Menza in Physical Education.) In 1947, their starting salary would have been $2,200, increasing to $2,400 for newly hired instructors in 1948.

The rush to find new professors produced some mediocrities. "Some college instructors," complained Howard Leahy, "are carried away by the thought that their high degree of specialization makes them immune to criticism. . . . The idea of 'academic freedom' [was] used to excuse their unwillingness to welcome inquiries concerning classroom methods."[50] Leahy thought that inexperienced teachers should visit the classes of good ones; that seminars in teaching should be required of all graduate students wishing to teach at the college level; and that "in every college and university, provisions should be made for the promotion of good teachers in salary and rank."[51] He found an ear in Kelley, who introduced faculty evaluation by heads of departments in 1948, requiring them to assess "preparation, methods of teaching, ability to stimulate and inspire young men, knowledge of subject matter, etc."[52] "To avoid censure by the accrediting agency," the Board of Trustees was told in 1949, "readjustment of teaching loads" was necessary. By then Kelley was gone, leaving his successor to deal with staff teaching twenty-five periods a week rather than the Middle States-mandated fifteen.

Campus Ethos

Culture

The main campus in South Orange was all-male. The urban division had women students, future nurses and teachers, but with a good all-female Catholic school in the College of Saint Elizabeth, Seton Hall felt little pressure to open its doors to women.

As a result, the student body had something of the barracks about it—literally so in "Veterans' Village." Humor could be crudely misogynistic.[53]

The college did not lack culture. A department of communication arts was established in 1948, and vital to its success was a student-run radio station, WSOU, which offered a "varied range of educational, [cultural] and religious programs for the benefit of the community, friends, and alumni of Seton Hall."[54] Tom Parnham was chief engineer from opening night in 1948 until his death in 1994.[55] Monsignor Thomas Gilhooley charmed money from friends in New York to make it possible.[56] (Rumor had it that WSOU got its start when he got a radio mast from a defunct station in Harrisburg, Pennsylvania and set it up in South Orange without permission.) Students could take courses in Speech for the Radio (with "attention directed to the development of clear, intelligible diction and acceptable pronunciation of American English"), Radio Announcing, Sound Effects, and Radio Programs for Children ("a study will be made of existing programs").[57] For a time, WSOU was the only student-run FM station in the country. Of its three studios, one was used for live broadcasts "such as piano and vocal shows, round table discussions etc.," another "for disk jockey shows," and the third for station breaks and announcements. Some material was heavy—Miriam Rooney on natural law, John Abbo on political philosophy—but "disk jockey shows" predominated. "Above the studios is a record library which contains over 5,000 pop records, 110,000 special broadcasting transcription records, and 500 albums and a comparable amount of long-playing classical records: all this contributing to making WSOU one of the best set-up collegiate stations in the nation and the only one of its type in New Jersey."[58]

Nostalgia was a stock-in-trade. The station gave a platform to a student, James McGlone, later a faculty member in the department of communication arts, a born broadcaster and talker: "Every once in a while we like to think back a few years to the Gay Nineties, the Roaring Twenties, Tin Pan Alley, and reminisce a while . . . It all comes to an end when you hear 'Take Out those Old Records' playing in the background and Jim McGlone says 'An inaudible and noiseless foot of time treads lightly on our fondest memories and it takes but a song, a word, to help us relive them.'"[59]

Cold War

Postwar Seton Hall fought the Cold War with vigor, as did other Catholic schools throughout the country.[60] When Archbishop Stepinac of Yugoslavia was sentenced in 1946 to sixteen years hard labor for demanding freedom of religion, 2,600 students telegrammed President Truman in protest.[61] Communism, Kelley warned, had "already made inroads in our own country" thanks to the "Russian fifth column" and the "quislings" who supported it.[62] His five-point plan to defeat the Soviets included understanding and appreciating "the great blessings of our own Christian Democracy," promoting American ideals, exposing "the whole traitorous action on the part of Russia" as it enslaved Eastern Europe, refusing to ship machinery and tools "that might easily be used in the production of atomic weapons against ourselves or the rest of the world, and standing united, prepared and strong so that we may never again invite a Pearl Harbor."[63] Students virtually unanimously said that "Russia should be stopped" and that war should be declared "if Russia persists in 'grabbing' the rest of Europe." When a major in government was launched in 1949, its emphasis was on "the importance of maintaining American Democracy in a world beset with many false philosophies and ideologies."[64] A student between 1949 and 1953, Robert Conley, found the atmosphere "childish," "stilted," and "authoritarian."[65] But Conley (later a professor of chemistry and Seton Hall president) was in a minority. Seton Hall was no more authoritarian than other Catholic schools. It took its tone from its clientele.

The threat, after all, was real. Vratislav Busek from Czechoslovakia taught European history in Newark. Arrested by the Nazis in 1942, he spent the rest of the war in Mauthausen concentration camp. In 1948, sentenced to death by communists as a former associate of Edward Benes, he escaped to France before the sentence was carried out. He came to Seton Hall in 1950. Asked what it meant to be in America, he replied, "wonderful, just wonderful."[66]

The expanded teaching staff contained anti-communists but also communists. Kelley's 1947–1948 report to the Board of Trustees may be recorded without commentary:

Mr. S. McKee, Special Agent in charge of New Jersey FBI [reported] that in Mr. Allen [Samuel G. Allen, instructor in business] we had one of the highest paid organizers of the Communist party. He declared that there are 760 Communist organizers in American Colleges and Universities at the present moment.

An FBI agent was put into the class of Mr. Allen as a student. Because he was in the field of Business Administration and was teaching objective mathematical courses, it was felt that he could do little harm. On the other hand, to discharge him for the issue of Communism might give him the publicity he was seeking. He might seek legal action against the violation of the breaking of his contract, or he might go to the Liberal National Educational Association, and make an issue of the reason for his discharge. It was decided, therefore, to keep a close watch on him and leave him on the campus, and then not to renew his contract next year.[67]

Such was Cold War Seton Hall.

Scandal

For nearly a decade and a half, as Seton Hall grew and shrank, Kelley rode his luck. He turned a small Catholic college in New Jersey into a major force in American higher education and turned himself, in the process, into something of a hero. In 1949, his luck ran out.

All was well in May 1946 when the Board of Trustees congratulated him on his "excellent report and splendid administration," authorizing him "to act as agent of [the college] with the United States Government or its proper agent for the procurement or transfer of Government properties to Seton Hall." In a human sense, Seton Hall was already coming down with army surplus, such a high percentage of its students being veterans, but soon it grew cluttered with material having nothing to do with higher education. The government was happy to be rid of it, stipulating only that it be used by those who received it, but how many ex-army mattresses and rolls of wire did a college need? Liquidating the assets made more sense. Therein lay the problem.

The materials were obtained by Seton Hall under Public Law 697 (passed in 1946 as an educational aid for the benefit of veterans) and distributed to it on the basis of a declaration that the College expected to have 2,697 veterans out of a student body of 4,000. The materials, including motors, generators, power machines, desks, chairs, typewriters, and office supplies, were delivered between fall 1946 and fall 1948. William D. Jones of the New York Office of the Federal Works Agency placed their "fair sale" value at $770,000. Seton Hall also received lesser amounts of goods from the War Assets Administration at a discount rate or as a donation. Under the 1946 Act, some 271 colleges and universities in eight eastern states were supplied by the Federal Works Agency with goods to the value of $16.7 million, of which $14.8 million worth was distributed free. Although there was no reason to think that materials were used for purposes other than those intended, the FWA decided to launch an investigation in spring 1948 when a number of New Jersey merchants began to complain that war surplus was appearing in local retail outlets, injuring their business. (Reports had army blankets sold to a Newark department store and desks and chairs to furniture dealers.) Another New Jersey college was investigated but, according to Jones, "it came up with a clean sheet." Seton Hall was less fortunate.

Administrative incompetence, or something worse, compounded the problem. In October 1948, an auditor complained of "the deplorable condition of the general accounting records" at Seton Hall (a complaint sharpened by the college's failure to pay his own bill).[68] Paul De Brienza, purchasing agent and veterans' coordinator, kept two sets of books, one including monies raised by the sale of army surplus, the other not. The difference between the two, and the whereabouts of the sums involved, caused concern. After a forensic examination in which none of the parties volunteered useful information, John Conlin, an accountant brought in by Archbishop Walsh to audit the accounts, discovered discrepancies in income received from the cafeteria, the bookstore, the college shop, the athletics department, from basketball games at Madison Square Garden, from tennis matches, and from tickets to the Metropolitan Opera. The stated income from the cafeteria, book store, and campus shop for 1946–1947 was $7,989.74, for 1947–1948, $8,450.32, and for 1948–1949 a suddenly larger $52,339.28. Of that last amount, over $50,000 turned up only after Conlin began his investigation. Income derived from athletics ticket sales in 1946–1947 was $25,727.84, but the amount turned in to the college was only $17,572.14. Ticket sales for a 1948 basketball game at Madison Square Garden amounted to $10,025, of which Seton Hall saw only $2,335.98.

War surplus attracted most attention because the amounts were large and because the federal government was involved. There were two issues: possibly fraudulent acquisition of materials based on false declarations as to need and use; and likely embezzlement of monies obtained by their resale. The FBI was interested in answers to both questions. How was government property released to Seton Hall without approval of the United States Office of Education? Were authorizations forged? Was there a ring involved that including representatives of the College, the Federal Works Agency, and the War Assets Administration? Did some schools get priority on certain goods and switch them to another without telling the government? Who received the goods? How were they funneled into the market? When one P. James Pellechia, Jr. was arrested on suspicion of embezzlement in 1948, an investigation revealed that he had obtained storage space in Newark garages for equipment obtained from the government by Seton Hall. Sentenced to ten to fifteen years in state prison for embezzlement, Pellechia had awkwardly close links to Seton Hall. "When all the details of this are ferreted out," said one FWA official, "it will be a fair way of becoming a major scandal."

Kelley and Brienza were questioned by FWA agents about orders for goods and their subsequent resale. Kelley professed ignorance of the scheme and Brienza that he had mistakenly but sincerely believed that the college had the authority to resell the material. Frederick J. Gassert, Seton Hall's counsel, admitted that the college had sold "certain quantities of surplus, due to a misunderstanding of the FWA limitations on their resale" and promised that the money would be repaid. Andrew Crummy, Seton Hall's counsel when the investigation began, acknowledged that Brienza "while talking to Pellechia and two or three other men mentioned that he needed storage space for considerable quantities of war surplus materials purchased by the college." According to Crummy, there was "never any sale of goods by the college to Pellechia. All material belonging to the college is marked with the college's name and title to it rests with Seton Hall." Pellechia was nonetheless an odd associate for a college finance officer. Odder still were the arrangements for the acquisition and delivery of the goods. When the program was announced, Seton Hall filed an application with the War Asset Administration. If a finding of need was approved by the Federal Works Authority, a transfer order was issued to the WAA to deliver the goods. Later, it seemed, shipments were made by the WAA after oral contact with government employees, with the paperwork only completed after the goods had been delivered. In these negotiations, according to Gassert, government officials decided the need, not the college. (Thus the suspicion of a ring.) By September 1948, the process was thoroughly compromised, with "substantial amounts" (in Gassert's phrase) being shipped to the college for which the college had made no direct application. The goods arrived in such quantities and at such odd times—Sunday afternoons, for instance—that campus storage facilities were overwhelmed, making it impossible to keep a check on materials received. (That is when Pellechia and his garages entered the picture.) At one point, the basement of a South Orange church was used for storage. When the FWA began checking, it found that unsigned-for shipments had been sent to Seton Hall and that receipts were executed although the college had no way of telling whether the goods had been delivered or not. The purpose of the FWA check was to discover what had been delivered, what had been sold and, of the remainder, whether Seton Hall had need of it.

The quantity and quality of items received by the College was staggering. Some of the material had academic or secretarial value—chemicals, laboratory equipment, stationery, filing cabinets—but a well-stocked Woolworth's might have been a better destination for most of it:

Mattress covers	710
Sunburn Lotion	192 bottles
Toothpaste	3,360 tubes
Shoe Laces	1,000 pairs
Barber's aprons	144
Barber's chair	1
Lace	30 yards
Nail Files	720
Bone Drills	4
Teeth	4,143 sets
Spectacle Frames	4,258
Sextant	1
Ammunition Pouches	200
Dummy Rifles	500
Marine Toilet	1
Candy-and-Cigar stand	2
Bed pans	7
Lift Rafts	2
Screws	20,199

By the time the materials had arrived (there were seven pages of inventory), the College Treasurer might well have had need for Alcohol (500 pints), some Operating Tables (5), an Anvil (18), a Rolling Pin (21), and a Hospital Restraint apparatus (81).[69]

If goods *had* been received under false pretenses and subsequently sold, what had become of the money? All that was certain was that Seton Hall had seen very little of it. In 1948–1949, the cost of materials purchased from the War Assets Administration was $43,408.58 and the cost of their trucking and storage $94,738.55, making a total of $138,147.13. Cash turned in to the College from the sale of the assets was only $114,785.98, representing a shortfall of $23,361.15. "I found," Conlin reported to the Archbishop, that "trucking, storage expense, and cost of materials were charged on the books to College Office, Housekeeping, and 'Gym' expenses in an apparent effort to 'bury.'" Other discrepancies may well have been accidental but were also troubling: "In 1941 there was a chest of valuable coins in Monsignor Kelley's room, left to the College by a friend. They were to have been appraised. . . . At the present time this chest of coins is not at the college." [70]

Kelley had not profited from the arrangements but the appearance of impropriety was undeniable. Archbishop Walsh summoned him to the Chancery Office on March 3, 1949 and requested his resignation. (Brienza submitted his resignation the following day.) Kelley claimed that he had been trying to resign for years, a somewhat unlikely notion,[71] but, whatever of that, the dismissal came as a shock—first of all to Kelley, then to everyone else. There was indeed a conspiracy, Kelley thought, but he and Brienza were its victims, not its perpetrators. "Apparently the combination of the *Newark News*, the renegade Mr. Crummy, and the anti-Catholic people of the F.W.A. are still trying to cause trouble for Seton Hall's former agent Mr. Brienza," he later wrote. "Fortunately, I had no more to do with these matters than the man on the moon, although they apparently lied otherwise to the Archbishop."[72] That was the story he told himself, and others, for the rest of his life. As for the immediate reaction, Father Albert Hakim was typical. Hakim, who had come to Seton Hall as a freshman just as Kelley was arriving as president, heard about it at lunch. Late to enter the priests' dining room he was greeted by silence. Asking the reason, he was told that "Kelley has been fired." He burst into tears. "The news of Monsignor Kelley's resignation stunned many," reported *The Setonian*, "but the effect was greatest among the students, who regarded the Monsignor as more than their president. They regarded him as a friend."[73]

Assessment

To compare the institution Kelley inherited to the one he bequeathed is to see two different places. Monaghan's small college, recently accredited, heavily theological, financially uncertain, set in its ways, could not have offered a stronger contrast to Kelley's multisited, educationally innovative, bursting-at-the-seams, quasi-university. Students who attended Monaghan's Seton Hall came from homes with books in them and with a certain amount of money in their pockets. Half a generation and a war later, students who attended Kelley's Seton Hall were mostly veterans, many from homes where not much reading was done. Few had given college a moment's thought until, thanks to the government, the opportunity arose to attend one. They only realized what Kelley meant to them when he was gone: "When most colleges closed their doors to the ex-GIs because they were overcrowded, the Monsignor did everything humanly possible to get the veterans started on the road back to normalcy . . . This was the beginning of a great friendship between the students and Monsignor Kelley."[74] Seton Hall may well have undergone its institutional revolution without him, but it would have missed his panache and self-assurance.

The inattention to detail was bound to tell in the end. Kelley turned Seton Hall from a backwater in 1937 to a powerhouse in 1949, but he trusted people who should not have been trusted and rewarded those who should have been kept at arm's length. "[I have] learned from my own bitter experience of the past few months how even the best intended actions can be misrepresented," he wrote to his successor in 1949.[75] For all his *savoir faire*, there was a kind of innocence to him. He had a license to teach psychology: his own was a study in itself.

CHAPTER 11

A New University

A Change of Style

Kelley's dismissal was the largest scandal in the college's history but the only one of real consequence. The generous view was that he had been hard done by, the ungenerous one that he was lucky to get away with it. There was, said the chairman of the Middle States Association, "an air of mystery now curtaining the College." Seton Hall, he thought, should go on record "as saying that it has nothing to hide."[1] In the end, Kelley was publicly humiliated but only privately exonerated. It took two years for a federal investigation to conclude that no action would be taken against officers of the university and by then the reputational damage was done.[2] Unfortunately it has stuck.

His successor could hardly have been more different. Born in New York in 1899, Father John McNulty was one of two brothers who became priests, both ordained on the same day. (The other, James, later became Bishop of Paterson.) A Seton Hall graduate, John McNulty studied at Louvain and after ordination taught French and religion at Seton Hall Preparatory School before becoming head of modern languages in the college in 1935, the year he received his doctorate. In 1943 he was named dean of the urban division and, six years later, president of the college (and given the title Monsignor). Kelley was slight, lively, and charming. McNulty was stately and plump, a man, Father Albert Hakim recalled, of "kindly smile, inimitable wit, contagious enthusiasm, and ever-welcome inspiration."[3] "I hope that when you walk out of here four years from now," McNulty told the freshmen of 1949, "your feet will be on the ground—and your eyes on eternity."[4] A passionate Francophile, heroically frugal, addicted to what his critics called "Louvain Logic," McNulty liked students and faculty to act as his chauffeurs, resenting all the while the low tuition paid by "the damned divinity students." A philosophy professor who bought a car was said to have used "Seton Hall's money" to do so: in other words, to have spent his own salary. Insisting on smaller portions in the priests' dining room, an economy not evident from his own girth, McNulty stopped serving fruit at lunchtime, claiming that "apples don't grow on trees, you know." Priests saying Mass in local parishes were to be fed at parish expense: "ubi missa, ibi mensa." Yet he also oversaw the greatest expansion in Seton

Hall's history, spending on buildings and programs, opening a law school and a college of medicine and dentistry, strengthening the schools of business administration and nursing, funding a science building and a library, adding a dormitory, improving the faculty, expanding the administration, and raising academic standards. Bishop Fulton Sheen, a friend from Louvain, considered him "the greatest college president in the country."[5] Under McNulty, Seton Hall College became Seton Hall University. He was a transformative president, one of the most significant in the institution's history.

A New University

By 1949, Seton Hall was no longer in any recognizable sense a liberal arts college. Producing nurses, teachers, businessmen, and (in association with the seminary in Darlington) clerics, it was a university in all but name, lacking only the title and an institutional commitment to research to place it in that category. When more than half of all undergraduates studied business, physical education, or nursing; when the endowment stood at over half a million dollars;[6] when more students[7] and faculty[8] pursued or taught more courses than before; when one "department"—graduate studies—had more than 850 students; when "Seton Hall" existed in Newark and Jersey City as well as in South Orange; when larger sums of federal money were being funneled to it; when tighter control and accountability were more necessary than ever; when alumni now included significant numbers of professional men and women; when South Orange had changed beyond recognition to cope with its postwar expansion: when all these things happened at once, Seton Hall was a "college" in name only.

Nursing, for instance, had become a serious component of academic life. When established in 1937, the School of Nursing Education (technically, a specialism within the department of education) offered programs in nursing education and public health nursing. In 1940, eight women received bachelor's degrees. One of them, Ann Murphy, became the school's director, marking the first college-level program of nursing education in New Jersey for graduates of diploma schools of nursing. In 1942, the public health nursing program was accredited by the National Organization for Public Health Nursing. In 1945, industrial nursing was added and, briefly, psychiatric nursing. The "dean" of the school of nursing education, a title accorded by the College Bulletin of 1945–1946, was Mary V. Barrett.

The School of Nursing Education flourished after the war thanks to large numbers of veterans who either wished to enroll in courses or who themselves needed the services of nurses. Caroline Di Donato, professor of public health nursing, became director in 1947, Mary Barrett's title and term as dean having ended as mysteriously as it had begun. Di Donato created two majors, in nursing education and in public health nursing. When the School of Nursing Education became the School of Nursing in 1950, all undergraduate nursing education programs were terminated. The number of students who earned the degree of Bachelor of Science in Nursing Education was 311; in Education, 147; in Public Health Nursing, 156; and in Industrial Nursing, 8. The last students to earn these degrees graduated in 1956.[9]

Business also struggled to find a niche in "Seton Hall College" but might have flourished in "Seton Hall University." Only when university status was conferred did a School of Business Administration came into existence. Before then, various courses in accountancy, economics, and mathematics were offered in the extension campuses in Newark and Jersey City. Lumped together with nurses and elementary education majors, business students (and teachers) had no sense of themselves as engaged in a distinctive academic enterprise. In 1950, "there was in reality no School. In the Urban Division of the University there was a dean, a curriculum, and the title of School, lacking, however, an organization. On the Campus was a department of business which offered a separate curriculum. There was no coordination between the two branches of the University."[10] Kelley's lack of planning was now beginning to show. In fairness, Kelley himself had been "more convinced than ever" in 1948 of the "very insistent demand" that Seton Hall become a university, claiming that "a large body of the population" was demanding it.[11]

Other factors played a role. In 1924, Rutgers College had become Rutgers University, starting a process by which Seton Hall could also change status. Designated the State University of New Jersey in 1945, Rutgers incorporated the old University of Newark in 1946 and the old College of South Jersey in Camden in 1950. Seton Hall's five-year spurt of growth, modest by comparison, reflected a similar trend towards consolidation. More immediately, Seton Hall's graduate diplomas (conferred in Newark) were accepted by the New Jersey Department of Education as certification for high school teachers but by no other body. Some universities refused Seton Hall MAs into their graduate programs because Seton Hall was not a member of the Association of American Universities. By becoming a university, Seton Hall would qualify for membership of that organization, remedying the problem of unmarketable qualifications and forcing it to take more seriously its own graduate degrees in history, English, and modern languages. As a university, Seton Hall's constituent "colleges" could become semiautonomous units within a larger structure, enjoying greater freedom, clearer demarcation of authority, and more localized decision-making.

There had been talk of university status in 1937[12] and again in 1945–1946, when a five-man in-house committee had suggested expansion in education, business administration, nursing, law, and possibly engineering. There was also a model to follow. Marquette University in Wisconsin had been chartered as a college by an act of the Wisconsin legislature in 1864. In 1906, an amendment to that act changed the location of the college. In 1907, by another amendment, the college was changed into a university.

Amending Seton Hall's legal status seemed very do-able. "Seton Hall College [must soon decide] whether it will remain . . . as it is now or . . . plan to become the Catholic University in the Newark area," said Frank Bowles of the Middle States Association in 1948. "I think the time is very near when the change to university status and university ideals and objectives is a logical one." Bowles, a powerful figure in the educational establishment, thought an "early change-over to university organization and operation" would allow professional schools to develop in Newark and Jersey City, leaving liberal arts to South Orange.[13] To make that happen, Seton Hall would have to have a better library, faculty, and administration, and a more serious approach to hiring, especially in the School of Education.[14] The college was still "shockingly below the minimum standard for recognition" in 1949 and "would have been summarily dropped" had not McNulty taken steps to improve it. "Only . . . the most generous possible interpretation of the Commission's views" allowed it to remain accredited in the early days of his presidency.[15]

As for academic and administrative standards, Kelley's dash for growth in 1945 had been too fast. The "insufficiency" of the library was "very serious." Teaching loads were deplorable. The Jersey City campus was too small. Boarding students in South Orange lived in a barracks. The biology, physics, and psychology labs were dilapidated.[16] If Seton Hall did not become a university it might (paradoxically) lose its accreditation as a college. "It is at the instigation of Mr. Bowles and the Middle States Association that we have put so much time and study [into] the thought of a university structure," McNulty told the Board in September 1949. "We do not know whether they think that the college has expanded so much that it cannot maintain its accrediting or whether it has grown so much that it is better to put it into this new thought [sic] and new structure before we seek accrediting."[17] That Seton Hall should have become a university to please accreditors who did not know whether it should remain a college is odd, but that was how it was.

Building on Kelley's groundwork, McNulty empaneled a number of committees to consider what Seton Hall College would look like were it to become Seton Hall University. Everything was on the table, from the curriculum to the relationship between South Orange and the urban division, from the balance between graduate and undergraduate students to the size of the library, from the status of the faculty to the state of the campus. The results were presented to the Board in June 1949, and in late September McNulty, Father William Furlong (vice president), and Father Thomas Cunningham (head of the English department) took the "Educational Reorganization Plan" to New Jersey Commissioner of Higher Education Robert Morrison. Five weeks later, it had his blessing. In effect, by preparing in 1949 for Middle States inspectors who visited in 1950, Seton Hall prepared itself to become a university. A vigorous spring cleaning took place, the library dubiously enhanced,[18] teaching improved,[19] and the faculty treated more professionally.[20] Seton Hall was on the move.

McNulty received advice from Edward Cratsley of St. Lawrence University, John Welsh of Syracuse University, William Conley of Loyola University in Chicago, and Cornelius Moynihan of Boston College Law School. Cratsley, visiting twice, found "a definite sense of progress" between his first and his second trips.[21] The college could become a university but chaotic budgeting would jeopardize the transition.[22] The curriculum was coherent, with every student taking courses in English literature, social studies, philosophy, religion, language, and science. On the other hand, the core was heavily prescriptive, leaving little room for electives. In that, Seton Hall was typical of many other places.[23]

Technically, the title "university" was conferred on June 2, 1950, when the New Jersey state legislature passed an act to that effect. "Seton Hall [College] has [had] many, many friends," said Archbishop Thomas Walsh two days later, "and we earnestly hope for their continued friendship in the honest promotion of the academic welfare of Seton Hall University."[24] In Walsh's telling, the university began with 3,700 students in South Orange and 5,400 in Newark and Jersey City, making a total of 9,100. Seventy-two professors had doctorates, 143 assistant professors had MAs. These figures conflated full-time and part-time staff and students, but there was no arguing that Seton Hall, unlike other schools, continued to grow throughout the 1950s.[25]

On paper, the new university looked formidable, with an array of colleges, divisions, and departments ready to do battle with the forces of ignorance. In terms of governance, first came the Archbishop of Newark, the Board of Trustees, and the president; then a vice-president of instruction who, "in addition to representing the President in his absence, shall act as intermediary between the President and the individual Deans of the various schools together with the individual administrative officers of the President's Council." Under the vice president of instruction was an "executive and advisory council [consisting] of the Deans of the Schools on the Campus, the Deans of the Schools of the Urban Division under the supervision of the Director and Dean of the Urban Division, together with the University librarian, the Dean of Administration, and the Director of Business Affairs." Seven schools, each controlled by a dean, were created: the College of Arts and Sciences, the School of Business Administration, the Divinity School, the School of Education, the School of Nursing (previously the School of Nursing Education), the School of Graduate Studies, and School of Adult Education. Of these, four constituted the Urban Division—Education, Nursing, Adult Education, Graduate Studies—under a director and dean. The College of Arts and Sciences, based in South Orange, was to have eleven departments—biology, classical languages, communication arts, English, mathematics, modern languages, philosophy, physical sciences, psychology, religion, social studies. The School of Business Administration was to comprise six departments—accounting, advertising, business management, economics, labor relations, and personnel administration. (This was more impressive on paper than reality but eventually reality caught up.)[26] The Divinity School in South Orange was composed of students intending to study for the priesthood who would begin their philosophical and classical studies in the university before completing their academic and spiritual work at the major seminary in Darlington. (Divinity students did classical languages in South Orange in their freshman and sophomore years, and philosophy at Darlington in their junior and senior years. The philosophy department at Darlington was part of Seton Hall.)

In Newark, the School of Education had departments of administration and supervision, elementary education, health and physical education, personnel and guidance, and secondary education. It offered courses leading to the degree of Master of Education. Under Joseph Connors, who came to Seton Hall in 1947 inspired by Kelley's vision to educate veterans, it flourished. The School of Nursing had departments of industrial nursing, nursing education, and public health nursing.[27] A School of Adult Education was to provide liberal arts and specialized courses to nonmatriculated students. The College of Graduate Studies offered courses leading to the MA in history, English, and modern languages. The campuses in Newark and Jersey City would henceforth be "University Colleges." A dean of administration was created, under whom would serve the directors of athletics, public information, and personnel services. These in turn supervised an admissions director, a registrar, a director of guidance, a dean of students, a medical officer, a veterans coordinator, a placement officer, an alumni secretary, and so on.

Inspectors returned in March 1952 to see how things were going. Frank Bowles noticed a "most gratifying [change] from the standpoint of the institution's intellectual growth and alertness to new ideas."[28] Father Edmund Cuneo came away with a "tremendous admiration" for McNulty's "breadth of vision."[29] Roy Deferrari of the Catholic University of America noticed "amazing good work" done by McNulty.[30] Robert Morrison was "deeply impressed by the splendid progress." [31] In 1955, reviewing his tenure as dean of the School of Business Administration, Austin Murphy reported that it enjoyed "the respect of many who were once our detractors."[32] Seton Hall was much better run as a university than it had been as a college.[33]

Governance

The Statutes of 1952 did not so much describe a new reality as bring it into being. Once duties, responsibilities, and obligations were written down, they had to be taken seriously. The days of improvisation were over. Kelley's legacy was that never again should things be done the Kelley way.

A Board of Trustees consisting of thirteen members remained the governing body, with vacancies filled by election of new members by old ones.[34] The Board had three officers—president, treasurer, and secretary. The president was the Archbishop of Newark, who presided over meetings, prepared the agenda, and "direct[ed] such studies as may be necessary to come to satisfactory decisions." The treasurer maintained records and presented statements of income and expenditure to the annual meeting in May. The secretary was the minute-taker and keeper of correspondence. Of these officers, the Archbishop was most important. "All acts of the Board, except the conferring of degrees," were subject to his approval. In cases of a tie, his was the deciding ballot. Even without a tie, he had a veto.

The Board of Trustees could request amendment of the Articles of Incorporation. It could amend the statutes. It fixed all fees and rates of tuition. It determined investment policies, sales and purchases of real estate, the incurring of debt "in due conformity to the protective provisions both of civil law and of canon law." It approved major agreements "between the university and other diocesan organizations" as well as legal acts concerning the university and the United States Government, the State of New Jersey, Essex County, and the City of Newark. The Board of Trustees was the legal person called Seton Hall University.

Below the Board, the University Council was in charge of day-to-day matters, deciding educational policies subject to Board approval and providing for "joint consideration of educational problems and plans" by administrators and faculty. Membership consisted of the president of the University (as chairman); the executive vice-president and vice-presidents in charge of Instruction, Student Personnel Services, and Business Affairs; the dean of each college and school, and all Regents; the University librarian; the director of athletics; the director of admissions; the director of guidance; the University registrar; the spiritual director; the director of public relations; the dean of men; the chairman of the Undergraduate Council; the chairman of the Graduate Council; and elected representatives from the faculty of each college and school, "one representative for each five hundred (full-time equivalent) students or fraction thereof." The University Council dealt with admissions, curriculum, academic standards, instruction, probation and dismissal of students, degree requirements, student services, research and publications, faculty employment, promotion, and welfare, the university library, and athletics.

The Council was less significant than two entities technically subordinate to it, the Graduate Council and the Undergraduate Council. These consisted, in the former instance, of the vice president in charge of instruction, the deans of each school offering graduate work (including the School of Law), and other members appointed at the discretion of the president; and, in the latter instance, of the vice president in charge of instruction, the dean of the College of Arts and Sciences, the dean of the School of

Business, the dean of the School of Education, the dean of the School of Nursing, the dean of University College, and one faculty representative from these schools.

Apart from the Archbishop, the president was the most significant figure in the university. As "chief administrative and executive officer," he conducted the internal and external administration of the university, developed sound educational programs, and promoted Seton Hall to the public while "interpreting" its "philosophy, purposes, programs and problems" to the Board, faculty, students and alumni. He was custodian of university property, making contracts and agreements in the name of the university, appointing and removing vice presidents, hiring, promoting, and (subject to contractual constraints) firing faculty, appointing and removing chairmen of committees and councils, and approving or vetoing any modification or amendment to the Statutes. "If in his judgment any policy submitted [by the University Council] is contrary to the welfare of the University, the mind of the Board of Trustees, or the Statutes of the University, he may return the policy . . . or veto [it]." (That his deputy was called a regent who would act as "his personal representative in a school, institute or office [and be] directly responsible" to him confirmed this quasimonarchical status. A regent also had to be a priest.) Between the president and a regent stood the executive vice president, whose task was to "supervise the execution of University policy," reporting to the president and "responsible for the effective communication of all policies and policy refinements to all members of the staff." The executive vice president represented the president during any absence.

The Vice President in Charge of Instruction supervised "a program of improving instruction through departments, schools, library, and the University as a whole." He appointed deans and departmental chairmen, drew up the instructional budget, developed long-range plans for building the teaching staff, and was "responsible for the selection and promotion of all faculty." No department chairman would have hired a teacher without his permission. He was supposed to "stimulate faculty growth and creative work," although how this happened day-to-day depended on personality of the man himself. For most of McNulty's presidency, the Vice President in charge of Instruction was Monsignor Thomas Cunningham, who also served as dean of the College of Arts and Sciences.

Deans coordinated the academic activities of their respective schools. A dean could visit any class, recommend the withdrawal of textbooks, and insist on the removal "of library holdings . . . contrary to University policy." A dean could also determine, in a comically ambiguous phrase, "the sectioning of students."

Arranging classes and finding teachers was the job of the department chairman. Most days his time was taken up with minutiae—determining majors, minors, course sequences, and prerequisites; preparing catalog copy; assigning teaching; maintaining standards between and within courses; keeping spending under control; organizing departmental meetings (two per semester). Chairmen (there were as yet no women) could hire and promote, approve textbooks and syllabi, and "visit classes of any member of the department at any time." A good chairman made the difference between a pleasant life and a miserable one.

Of faculty ranks, the lowest was graduate assistant instructor, of whom the only requirement was a bachelor's degree. The first academic rank proper was instructor, a nontenured position for which a Master's degree was the usual qualification, although "in a few cases" a person could be appointed who had "comparable preparation." (Some instructors had no degrees.) Next came assistant professors, who were supposed to have doctorates (although many did not). Associate professors and professors stood at the top of the scale. To be appointed to either rank required, in the former case, "sound scholarship, creative ability, and effective teaching" and, in the latter case, all these plus "distinguished service" and "a reputation among members of his field." Associate professors were selected "with utmost care . . . Men [sic] of outstanding ability may be appointed from other institutions to the rank for a specified period after which the appointment becomes permanent." Professors were few and far between. Attracting and keeping "men of outstanding ability from other institutions" conceded that Seton Hall had to judge itself by standards made by others, not itself. It took time before the implications of this were understood.

Professors dealt with the mind. Other university officials dealt with body and soul. The spiritual director, the dean of men, the dean of women, the dean of freshmen, the director of guidance, the director of student affairs, the director of medical services, were significant figures. The spiritual director supervised religious activities for "the students' moral and spiritual advantage." The dean of men dealt with discipline, enjoying "exclusive authority" to determine "the sufficiency of all excuses submitted for absence from class, the annual retreat and all other required activities." He also assigned the boarders' rooms, issued keys and meal tickets, enforced parking rules, delivered (not personally) student mail, and made "regular inspections of the living quarters of boarding students" to ensure "good order at all times." Dress, hair, and deportment came under his jurisdiction.

The dean of women, her office mandated by Middle States inspectors in 1950,[35] was not so much enforcer as encourager, a personification of Seton Hall's softer side: "She shall be responsible for fostering the general welfare of women students, and shall be in a special way their friend and adviser. . . . She shall be responsible for aiding students in overcoming personality difficulties, in developing desirable personality traits, and in acquiring poise and acceptable standards of social behavior . . . personal appearance, dress and speech."[36]

The dean of men was never "in a special way" anyone's friend; the dean of women, at least in theory, was supposed to be. Her role was complicated by the surreptitious presence of women on the South Orange campus (nursing students from Newark coming to do laboratory work) and by the crude attitude of men to women in their midst.[37] On the whole, though, women were more than capable of looking after themselves.

A Catholic School

That the university was a religious institution was self-evident. "Knowledge for knowledge's sake is unworthy of a Seton Hall student," McNulty thought. "It tends to inflate the ego and manufacture little deities in human form."[38] Seton Hall had its complement of the spiritually lazy, the theologically indifferent, and the intellectually unconvinced, but no-one could miss its Catholicism: "Daily Mass is offered in the campus chapel during all academic terms and vacation periods. All students are encouraged to receive Holy Communion as often as possible. Day students are provided with special opportunities in this regard by the Knights of Setonia organization, which sponsors later morning Masses for their convenience. Confessions are held daily."[39]

The Setonian's headline at the opening of the 1951–1952 school year was "Holy Father Calls for Aid through the Rosary."[40] "1,400 men receive as retreat ends," was its story on October 27, 1955, the reception in question being Holy Communion.[41] "It's not easy being on God's track team," said Father James Carey, moderator of the Knights of Setonia. "You must have proper food for your soul, and that means the Body and Blood of Christ."[42] When Pope Pius XII turned eighty in 1956, students gave him a birthday present of 20,850 aspirations, 2,609 Masses, 2,518 rosaries, 1,978 communions, 904 recitations of the Stations of the Cross, and 2,294 visits to the Blessed Sacrament.[43]

South Orange had boarders but most students were commuters. Come five or six o'clock, the university went quiet. Life was defined by Mass, class, and the bus. For boarders, instead of the bus there was Boland Hall, which many referred to as "the Big Barrack" and which one priest called "Radio City."[44] In 1954, Father Edward Larkin, appointed dean of men in September 1953, issued "Rules and Regulations in accordance with the aims of Seton Hall University."[45] Most were sensible, some odd:

All students are to exercise due consideration for the rights of others in the matter of excessive noise: such as, loud talk, hollering or singing, the banging of doors and loud playing of radios.

Female visitors are allowed only in the lobby of the first floor and the three visiting parlors off the lobby: young women, whether relatives or not, are never to be permitted in the building, except with specific permission.

Rooms must be kept . . . clean, neat, and orderly and . . . will be subject to very frequent and unscheduled inspections. When lights are on in the rooms, the shades must be turned down at least three quarters of the way . . . Freshmen must have lights out and be in bed at 11.00 p.m. Students will not be permitted in the halls in shorts or without tops . . . It is absolutely forbidden to break into the meal line . . . When going to showers . . . students must be dressed.

Rules could encourage the animal spirits they were supposed to quell. Monsignor Thomas Cunningham thought campus life had deteriorated: "As for us priests, we have . . . noticed the wee small hours return of many boarders (usually 12:30 AM to 1:15 AM) with great noise and car gyrations. There is also . . . drink and gambling on campus and in neighboring 'pubs' where our boys are known and from which reports are slipping back to us."[46]

Paul's Tavern in Newark, colloquially Pauly's, was a favored watering hole offering cheap beer well into the night. Students thrown out of it in the 1950s later achieved eminence as historians and lawyers; at least one became a judge. Horseplay, almost literally, was never far away. One Christmas, a student worse for wear failed to guard the animals of the "living crib" that had been a Seton Hall tradition since 1939. The escaping sheep and donkey made their way onto South Orange Avenue and were eventually arrested. Evidently the donkey, Amos by name, chewed tobacco. His companions, a heifer, calf, a sheep, had no bad habits.[47]

In later telling, the 1950s combined high spirits with low farce. "One night I found myself in a big black Buick heading through Newark to New York," recalled Frank Leonard, '54. "I was going to a Hall basketball game at Madison Square Garden. Driving the car was a fellow student who boarded in the next room. His father was the biggest mob boss in the country. The Buick was his father's car. A federal anti-crime committee was avidly seeking the father." "Ah, you'll love it here at the Hall" was the verdict.[48] "When *Peyton Place*, *Playboy*, Brigitte Bardot and their like appeal to the tastes of our 'men,'" thought Father James Sullivan, "things have reached a sorry state. Seton Hall would be well rid of this type of 'gentleman.'"[49]

Not everybody wanted to make spiritual bouquets for the pope. "The Puritans would have loved Seton Hall," complained *The Setonian* in 1950. "The student body as a group presents a quiet, unemotional, chilling exterior that is superb if you're reading old Cotton Mather but appears a bit frazzled at a basketball game."[50] In theory, a boarder's life was sedate:

Study period is from 7:20 to 9:30 every day from Monday to Thursday except the evenings preceding a holiday.

During study periods there is to be complete silence throughout the building. There is to be no congregation in rooms for the purpose of recreation, etc.

During study periods radios are not to be played at all.

During study period the doors of all rooms are to stand completely open.

Study periods are to be used for study exclusively.

High spirits were a way of letting off steam. Most students, even those turfed out of Pauly's, turned out all right.

Undergraduates were ardent cold warriors. In November 1951 a young man from Czechoslovakia, John Hvasta, brother of student Stephen Hvasta, was sentenced to seven years imprisonment in that country for "spying" for the United States. "Reds Imprison Setonian's Kin" was *The Setonian*'s headline.[51] In December 1951, students were urged not to forget "thousands of [Korean] kids roaming the streets in freezing temperatures."[52] One student, Stephen Drabik, urged opposition to Soviet Communism in language strangely nostalgic for the Third Reich. "The United States has a moral obligation to maintain the security of the German people," he said. "In World War II, the United States wiped from the face of the map of Europe the only force capable of crushing Russian communism, then unjustly tried the leaders of that proud nation as 'war criminals.' We have devastated the German Fatherland, the one citadel of strength that could have saved Europe from the Russian Marxist scourge. We cannot surrender our bastion of resistance in Germany."[53]

The Reserve Officer Training Corps (ROTC) came to campus in April 1950, resuming Seton Hall's connection with military training starting with "Camp Lenihan" in 1893 and discontinued in 1898 with the Spanish American War.[54] Under Lieutenant-Colonel Louis Mark, the unit, one of the largest in the country, proved popular.[55] With war in the Korean peninsula, ROTC was mandatory for freshmen, three classes a week, uniforms compulsory, drill twice a week at 7:30 AM rain or shine.[56] Some enjoyed it.[57]

A Better Faculty, a Better School

As a university, Seton Hall had to take research and publication seriously, but it took years for a culture of scholarship to develop. Not every teacher could publish; some had no desire to, others no talent, others no time. Most were too busy with classes to visit a library that was in any case ill-suited for producing original work. No-one spoke of a "teaching load" as if to distinguish teaching from other activity. "The members of an instructional staff in a university must be concerned first with effective teaching and secondly with creative work," William Conley reported, but "a faculty that does no creative work soon becomes mediocre, even in its teaching."[58] Lack of faculty creativity would have to be addressed, but these were not days of publish or perish. A person who published on top of teaching could well have perished in the process. There were limits.

Even as a college, Seton Hall had had good scholars (Fathers Joseph Brady and Ralph Glover, to name but two). As a university it had more. Some publications were in-house but none the worse for that. The first issue of *The Seton Review* appeared in November 1951, edited by Father William Noé Field of the English department, another of those priests who lived his whole life at the Hall. With an editorial board of Brady and Milton Conover of the social sciences department, Father Thomas Cunningham of English, Monsignor John Abbo, professor of political science, and Julius Lombardy of modern languages, *The Seton Review*, said Field, was "dedicated to contemporary thought." Inaugural articles included "Tradition and Saint Thomas More" by Cunningham, "Some Concepts of Confucius" by John Wu, a review by Father John Davis of *Hear My Heart* (a book of poems by Field), and "Economic Progress in the Belgian Congo 1940–1950" by Jean Comhaire.[59] Conover, with four books and eighteen articles to his name, had an academic background that included stints at Harvard, Yale, Princeton, Oxford, and the University of Paris.[60] John Wu had an international reputation as a jurist and translator. John Abbo was a canon lawyer whose jointly authored two-volume commentary, *The Sacred Canons* (Herder 1952), came to nearly two thousand pages. Cunningham was not a scholar, but he later published a book, *Saints Off Pedestals*, "a welcome hobby among his many official duties."[61]

Seton Hall gave postwar America two of its most distinguished theologians and religious educators, Gerard Sloyan and Edward Synan. As professor and chairman of the religion department at Catholic University and later at Temple University, Sloyan had an enormous impact on theology as a college discipline. A graduate of Seton Hall and Immaculate Conception Seminary, he was ordained a priest in 1944. Synan graduated from Seton Hall in 1938 and was ordained in 1942. Receiving his doctorate from the Pontifical Institute in Toronto in 1952, he returned to Seton Hall to chair the department of philosophy until he was appointed to the Pontifical Institute in 1959. Synan, expert in early fourteenth-century logic, ontology, and science, "truly embodied the Catholic intellectual spirit" described by Newman in *The Idea of a University.*[62]

Seton Hall was beginning to make its mark in other fields. Biology had Nicholas DeProspo, a highly competent teacher, researcher, and administrator. Chemistry was headed by Father Joseph Jaremezuk, who appointed Ellis V. Brown to a professorship in 1953. Jaremezuk, an old Seton Hall hand, had done graduate work in chemistry at Fordham and Columbia, but Brown was the driving force of the program.[63] Head of research and development for Pfizer during the war, holder of ten patents, author of more than thirty-five scientific papers, he was the kind of person that a new science building was intended to attract.[64]

Teaching was the bread-and-butter work, but it is not to be assumed that everyone was good at it. Some professors were dire. Too often, thought Tom Cunningham, the university was "a Red Cross agency for teachers who cannot fit in anywhere else," a "psychiatric" hospital for those who should have been nowhere near a classroom.[65] "The University faculty has improved a great deal in recent years," wrote Frank Bowles in 1952, "but during the immediate postwar period . . . a considerable number of people were added whose main qualifications were the possession of doctor's degrees rather than the possession of either good teaching ability or the traits of a good colleague."[66] (This was an exasperating criticism: it was Bowles who had insisted on the doctorate in the first place.) Money was another problem. Salaries were intentionally low, as if poverty were proof of a teacher's loyalty. "Do you want us to ignore or answer it?" Cunningham asked McNulty when Middle States asked what Seton Hall paid its faculty. "This type of continual bombardment for statistics in order to keep these petty researchers in jobs does get a bit aggravating."[67] Obsequiousness was an advantage when looking for a raise. ("I humbly pray to God that I might be able to do justice to the responsibilities of a teacher of philosophy and the trust you place in me," wrote Frank Caminiti, whose later career was not so conformist.)[68] Failing that, there was cheek. William Dunham, who taught government, planned to "ask [Monsignor McNulty] to increase my salary to $6,800." Then, "as I picked myself up off of the floor and as the Monsignor descended from the ceiling, I planned to tell him that I was willing to compromise for $6,200."[69] Pushiness could be counter-productive.[70] One principle never varied: men earned more than women.

As for promotion, it helped to get a doctorate,[71] have publications, show ability in the classroom, or simply get older. By the middle of the 1950s, efforts were made to tighten procedures, not least because agencies noticed how sloppy they were.[72] Promotion for length of service reduced its value as an incentive, and promotion with no increase in pay (for sentimental reasons, in other words) kept average salaries low. It made no sense not to pay teachers properly: the better ones would leave, the mediocre ones stay.

Professors varied in appeal and ability. In the School of Business Administration, located in Newark but holding some evening classes in South Orange, Anthony D'Amato was "extremely competent and well informed" in transportation economics. William Seaman in accounting had an exceptionally keen mind. William Nesbitt in finance was enthusiastic and lively. William Doerflinger in management was an addition to "the fine caliber of teachers."[73] John Deehan, an accountant, was "a thorough workman, a teacher of infinite patience, [with] talent as an administrator."[74] Lawrence McGrath, a Harvard and Stanford graduate who had taught at Seton Hall before the war, returned to teach banking, law, and finance. Marco Baeza, a Cuban with an undergraduate degree from Cornell, taught marketing. Anthony Trimakas, from Lithuania, taught economics. Raymond Wilhelm, a Fordham graduate, taught management.[75]

Departments also varied. Education was a sought-after degree, in some ways too popular for its own good. (The "abnormally high grades" in the School of Education gave the impression "that our MA students were all geniuses.")[76] The department of psychology failed to attract students and in Cunningham's view should have been "abolished or reduced to a minor level." Cunningham would also have done away with the department of mathematics because of "low registration [and] other problems," but kept it, knowing that a university without one was an absurdity.[77] Not even mathematicians of the caliber of the Ukrainian Joseph Andrushiv or the existence of a slightly forlorn Mathematics Club generated enthusiasm.[78] (The president of the latter, John Saccoman, went on to become a brilliant and long-serving professor in the department.)

The department of modern languages was a French department in all but name (although German, Italian, Spanish, Russian, and Polish were also taught). Its best scholars were war veteran Edward Henry, with graduate degrees from Fordham and New York University who had studied at the University of Paris, and Julius Lombardy, head of the department since 1946 and on the faculty since 1937. "The marking system of our department [has] been much too optimistic," Lombardy noted in 1952. "C is still . . . very honorable."[79] In addition, French teachers worried that fewer language requirements would "weaken the scholastic prestige of the University" (although their concern, only spoken behind closed doors, was that it would "put many department members out of employment.")[80] Lombardy started an Italian Institute in 1952 to encourage Italian cultural activities and promote Italian as a subject in local high schools. Charles Baretski launched the Institute of Polish Culture in 1953 as a "worthwhile adjunct for the adult education of the one-third million Polish-Americans living in the state of New Jersey." The Institute proclaimed "the traditional friendship between the United States of America and Free Poland."[81]

The department occasionally offered Irish as a subject (taught in Newark and Jersey City along with classes in Irish folk dancing and music.)[82] An Institute of Irish Culture was created in October 1952 to promote Irish history and literature (and provide economic assistance to Ireland). McNulty was proud of his Irish roots—his mother came from Navan, his father from Carrick-on-Shannon—and the Institute generated good publicity for the university in Ireland when he visited the country in 1954.

A Campus Transformed

What Kelley started in 1946 with the classroom building known as 'B Building' (renamed "Corrigan Hall" in March 1960),[83] McNulty completed in the early 1950s with a new dormitory, science building, and library. He wanted "splendid" structures[84] to give physical proof of Seton Hall as a university on the move. The science building and the library were effective additions, with the administration building and the chapel gathered around a common "green" remaining the visual centerpieces of the campus.

The program cost $8 million dollars, and it showed. The dormitory, known informally as Bishop's Hall, was "a showplace of modern collegiate campus living." (It is now called "Old Boland" or "West Res.") With room for four hundred students, designed by Gerald Phelan and built by Robert E. Hewer, it proclaimed a stylish, modern Catholicism: "One of the most spectacular features of the building will be a glass structure built in back of the altar and extending to the outer wall of the dormitory in the form of a cross. During the night this cross will be illuminated and clearly visible from South Orange Avenue."[85]

Replacing the library housed in Marshall Hall was a new building completed in 1955 and named McLaughlin Hall in 1960. Facing the administration building to its north and Bishop's Hall to its west, it was a strangely truncated three-story structure, its large circulation area opening to an impressive glass wall looking out on Bayley Hall. "Big reading rooms [intended] for general study and small individual rooms for intense graduate study" completed the effect.[86] With room for 300,000 volumes, it housed a stock of 70,000 books carried by conscripted students from the old library to the new over the course of a weekend. Its "majestic splendor" showed Seton Hall's "vivid eye for the future." A "unique feature" was its "elaborate communication and sound system" consisting of "an A.M./F.M. radio record player and a tape recorder." An auditorium seated one hundred people. Typing rooms and private carrels were available for students.[87] Everything was modern, up-to-date, the stuff of science fiction. "We will see electrical recordings of notes on record or tape, a visual device showing photos on a screen for clearer conception, and probably an electric brain that will do some of our work."[88]

The new science building, later named McNulty Hall, was equally *au courant*. For years, science at Seton Hall had been an afterthought. No more. The building was conceived as the home of a future Seton Hall School of Medicine and Dentistry, a project that eventually saw the light of day not in South Orange but Jersey City. State-of-the art classrooms and laboratories were topped off with a 250-seat amphitheater taking up an entire side of the building. Along with McLaughlin Library and Corrigan Hall, it formed a kind of second quadrangle for the university (also providing the setting for graduation ceremonies). "It heralds a new day," wrote historian John Cunningham in 1956.[89] Sixty years on, renovated and expanded, it remains the center of Seton Hall science.

A Campus in Paterson

The half-decade between 1949 and 1954 thus saw the greatest growth in the shortest time in Seton Hall's history. But campuses in Newark and Jersey City did not satisfy McNulty's expansive appetite. Indeed, the declining Catholic population in Jersey City was already beginning to show that postwar growth was not limitless.[90] When the Diocese of Paterson was created out of the Diocese of Newark in 1937, the Catholic population of Morris, Sussex, and Passaic Counties numbered 128,961. By 1947, it had risen to 167,032. In his early years as bishop, Thomas McLaughlin liked to leave Paterson in the morning, drive through the diocese looking at sites for future parishes, then build them in his own mind. His successor, Thomas A. Boland, created or built four parishes, three high schools, seven parochial schools, and five churches between 1947 and 1953.[91] Boland's successor, James A. McNulty, continued the work. Paterson was a textile city that had seen better days but that was not a reason to abandon it: rather the opposite. When Bishop James McNulty invited his brother to establish a branch campus of the university in his diocese, he could hardly refuse. Paterson's population of middle- and lower-income people wanting to better themselves was Seton Hall's world. John McNulty's ambition had its limits (in 1957, he refused to establish a campus in Camden),[92] but it was substantial.

McNulty told the faculty early in 1954 of his decision to open a branch in Paterson, inviting suggestions but not debate. Should the campus be coeducational? Should there be a four-year program or only an associate degree? What about the ratio of evening to daytime classes? Should Paterson be financially autonomous? What about ROTC? (This was not a small point. Daytime male students had to be given the opportunity to join the ROTC, otherwise they would have been eligible for the draft.) Cunningham urged caution, thinking a full four-year degree program would duplicate work done in South Orange, Newark, and Jersey City, that business and science degrees would not work, and that "innumerable" courses in education would be "headaches." He saw Paterson as a small school with a few students doing a handful of courses in social studies, English, and business.[93] But McNulty was more daring. Science had to be taught (he set aside $33,000 for building laboratories) along with a full curriculum in elementary education. He also wanted nursing, with the liberal arts component of the degree taught by day and practical training in the evening. There was also to be a daytime degree in business administration (management), with economics, marketing, and accounting courses at night. A "Community College" would offer business and secretarial courses leading to a two-year associate's degree and a "Liberal Arts College" would offer majors in social studies, English, and general science. Evening classes would include "special advanced courses as needed" and "teachers' equivalency, etc."[94] The "etc." was telling. As with Kelley's early "formal extension campus," this was a make-it-up-as-you-go-along effort.

Thus summoned out of nowhere, "Seton Hall Paterson" opened in September 1954 in St. John's Cathedral High School and at St. Joseph's Hospital (for nursing students). Afterwards it moved to 151 Ellison Street, bought from the Elks Club and renovated at the cost of $258,000. "We bring you a school accredited as highly as any in the country,"

McNulty said. "Nothing on campus will measure the man except the man himself."[95] By January 1955, the school was fully operational:

> The combined co-educational program embraces courses leading to the following degrees:
>> A.M. Administration and Supervision
>> A.M. General Education
>> A.M. Personnel and Guidance
>> A.B. Liberal Arts (Social Studies or English)
>> B.S. Business Administration (Management)
>> B.S. Elementary Education
>> B.S. Secondary Education
>> B.S. Nursing
>> A.A. General Business.[96]

From a standing start, this was impressive.

In charge was Monsignor Thomas Gillhooley, a convivial character who often conducted business in the Alexander Hamilton Hotel. Paterson was largely in the hands of his second-in-command, Edward Fitzgibbon, who on formal occasions was equally orotund.[97]

Within a year, the campus had one hundred day students and six hundred evening students. Within three years, it had many more. Paterson was not an ivory tower. It offered practical, down-to-earth courses to determinedly cheerful students: "We [are] the proud possessors of an active Student Council, a 'rarin'-to-go' basketball team and a gay social life! A 'first' activity of the organization was the BURN THE BEANIE dance . . . The class of 59 emerged from their beanies and their shells."[98]

Peripheral to South Orange, it held its own academically, its best students, women. (One of them, Ann Longstreet, went on to win a Woodrow Wilson scholarship.) The university thus had a commitment to coeducation long before the main campus formally inaugurated it in 1968. Because of its size, an extraordinary amount of faculty/ student interaction was possible in basketball and softball games and in the form of a journal—*History*—in which students published lively, sometimes outstanding papers. Among notable speakers to come to Paterson was Dorothy Day (who recorded a hostile reception in her journal). Faculty and students worked together to protest racial discrimination, signing petitions "supporting the Negro in his efforts to gain recognition of his natural and constitutional rights."[99] (Most students and faculty were Democrats.)[100] Those who taught in Paterson remembered it with fondness.

The campus—if one building may be so described—was not grand. The library was a large room, quiet and welcoming, supervised by mild-mannered Laura Frazier.

Faculty had no offices, taught three days a week and were expected to be around for four, and had five courses day and night. (Some faculty taught full-time in Paterson; others divided their time.) Lack of variety was a problem, with political scientist Richard Adinaro, for instance, teaching the same courses over and over again. (Students joked that they majored in Adinaro rather than his subject.) On the other hand, Adinaro also developed important relationships with the Paterson City government, leading to what was, in effect, Seton Hall's first internship program. Other teachers included James McGlone, John Botti, Joan Nourse, Emil Hensler, Nathaniel Thompson, James Perrone, Frank Sullivan, and Father Charles Stengel, who "found the students excellent."[101]

Paterson had problems not of its own making. In 1959, with 1,100 students, mostly women taking evening classes, it had only sixteen full-time teachers. The library was "most inadequate." Science equipment was "pitifully meager." The "whole Paterson program" needed urgent reconsideration.[102] Not even Gillhooly's gift of the gab could conceal weaknesses in a campus that had opened too quickly and was never adequately funded. Teachers such as Adinaro worked hard, but Paterson showed the dangers, as well as the possibilities, of putting together an operation without a plan to support it. It produced some of Seton Hall's best students, taught by some of its best teachers, but it was done on the cheap.

Two Institutes

The creation of two Institutes indicated Seton Hall's commitment to research. Each would eventually give Seton Hall an international reputation. One was politically conservative. The other was theologically liberal. Together, they were institutionally transformative.

The Institute of Far Eastern Studies

The Institute of Far Eastern Studies began in 1951 as a way of fostering "better understanding and relationships" in a "Catholic spirit" between the peoples of Asia and the United States.[103] Originally to be called the "Institute of Asiatic Culture" (the adjective was dropped as offensive), the idea was suggested to Archbishop Walsh by Cardinal Paul Yu-Pin and, through him, to McNulty. The State Department helped to fund it. Anti-communism was its abiding principle.

The Institute's first courses, taught to forty students, included The Far East Today, China in Modern Times, American Foreign Policy in China, Elementary Chinese, and Korea, Her Land, Her People, and Her International Relations (for which no-one signed up, the outbreak of the Korean War notwithstanding). Senator William F.

Knowland of California; You Chan Yang, Korean Ambassador to the United States; and Hu Shih, former Chinese Ambassador to the United States, gave lectures. Father Raymond de Jaeger and John Wu lectured on the Catholic Church in China. The Institute's director, Paul K. T. Sih, author of the classic *From Confucius to Christ* (Sheed and Ward, 1952) edited *How to Make Democracy Work in the Far East*. With contributions from Kotaro Tanaka, Chief Justice of the Supreme Court of Japan, the book was a notable piece of work.

As a convert, Sih bridged East and West using Catholicism as a coping stone. In that sense, he personified the spirit of the Institute itself. With John Wu, whose work in the Law School is treated elsewhere, he put Seton Hall in a different league. The Institute gave the university standing "across the seas in the diplomatic meetings of various nations whose interests lie in the orient."[104]

The faculty, strong in teaching and research, was stronger in ideological commitment. Typical was *A Chinese-English Dictionary of Simplified Words and Phrases Used in Communist China*: "Being frenzied by Soviet Russia's influence, Communist China has begun to coin a great number of new, Sovietized words, thus causing a deluge of Sovietized phrases and expressions. Mangled, amputated words . . . are being spread far and wide over the mainland and will gradually supplant the time-honored Chinese writings and the traditional lexicons."[105]

The Institute put scholarship at the service of American ideals. "Your unselfish and bold stand against Communism . . . will forever emblazon the escutcheon of Liberty, Justice, and Love of God," McNulty told President Ngo Dinh-Diem of Vietnam in 1956, offering him an honorary doctorate. "You have brought your country from chaos to peace . . . single-handed with only the teachings of our Lord Jesus Christ and a firm belief in Divine Guidance."[106] Diem accepted the degree as a "signal honor to the entire Vietnamese people."[107]

The Far Eastern Institute was one of the success stories of the 1950s. Later, when it became the department of Asian studies in the College of Arts and Sciences, it remained one of the best academic units in the university and, indeed, the country.[108] Only in the 1970s, when President Nixon went to China, did it lose favor with a state department now weary of its anti-Maoism. Until then, it fought the cold war with dictionaries and Dictaphones and may even have helped to win it.

The Institute of Judaeo-Christian Studies

Another bridge to international scholarship was the Institute of Judaeo-Christian Studies, which appeared in the early 1950s. "Monsignor McNulty . . . announced the opening of a new Institute of Judeo-Christian Studies under the Regency of Father [John] Dougherty of the seminary and under the Directorship of the Rev. John M.

Oesterreicher, a Jewish convert. This Institute was officially made a part of the University on the Feast of the Annunciation, March 25, 1953. The Institute shall be a center of research, education, and publication to promote interest and scholarship in the Judaeo-Christian heritage."[109]

Behind these words lay a remarkable story. The guiding spirit of the Institute was John Oesterreicher, a convert Jew, priest, and refugee from the Nazis who was to leave a major mark on Seton Hall and the Church. The work of the Institute—"to promote interest and scholarship in the Judaeo-Christian heritage"—bore fruit in October 1965 with the Second Vatican Council's denunciation of anti-Semitism, *Nostra Aetate*, a document substantially penned by Oesterreicher. "Never in its history," writes John Connelly, leading historian of the document, had the Church "looked upon Jews in the ways specified in *Nostra Aetate*."[110] For that "path-breaking"[111] achievement, Oesterreicher deserves credit, as does, indirectly, the university for giving him a home. Before, during, and after the Council, Seton Hall was at the heart of a conversation that may be said to have changed the church and the world.

Oesterreicher's life was intellectually and politically adventurous. Born in 1904 in northern Moravia, as a high school student in Olmutz he discovered the gospels and was swept up by "the majesty and gentleness of Christ."[112] As a still committedly Jewish medical student in Vienna in 1920, he read Kierkegaard and Newman to know more of the central claims of Christianity. He was baptized by the ecumenist Father Max Josef Metzger in the sacristy of Graz cathedral in 1924. Abandoning medical school, he then entered the seminary and was ordained a priest in July 1927, never ceasing to consider himself Jewish.[113]

Oesterreicher's early work as a priest in Gloggnitz and Vienna showed him the extent of Austrian racism, some of it expressed by churchmen not usually associated with the cruder forms of anti-Semitism.[114] Through his editorship of an ecumenical journal called *Missionruf*, he came in contact with intellectuals, of whom the most important were Protestant converts from Judaism, Karl Thieme and Dietrich von Hildebrand.

Oesterreicher was a formidable personality. Von Hildebrand considered him a man of "iron will." Yves Congar, meeting him at the Vatican Council, found him aware of his own importance. Connelly sees him as "opinionated, difficult, intellectually capacious, vulnerable but absolutely certain in moral judgments, tireless, and by turns flexible and uncompromising."[115] First in Austria before the war; then in Paris, where he wrote the ground-breaking study *Racisme—antisémitisme, antichristianisme* and from where broadcast sermons fiercely critical of Hitler;[116] then in Switzerland;[117] then in Paris again, where his identity as Hitler's critic became known to the Gestapo; then in the United States where he landed, by way of Portugal after the fall of France, in November 1940; then at the Church of the Assumption in West 49th Street, New York, no longer "Johannes Oesterreicher" but John M. Oesterreicher, American Catholic expert on the Jews";[118] then, after 1953, at Seton Hall: during all these turns he was a powerful prophetic voice.

The Institute of Judaeo-Christian Studies and Oesterreicher were interchangeable. Well-connected and intellectually courageous, bringing to the Institute and its annual publication *The Bridge* his probing and restless spirit of inquiry, he was almost too bright a star for Seton Hall. (Once at a meeting of priests, McNulty told him that he was "too big for this kind of thing" and told him to leave. Realizing his bad manners, he sent him an orange as an apology.)[119] No-one doubted his firepower. In 1960, Cardinal Augustin Bea asked Oesterreicher (along with Fathers Gregory Baum and Leo Rudloff) to act as a theological adviser in formulating a document on the Church's relations with the Jews. To Anton Ramselaar, a Dutch priest who came to know him at the Council, Oesterreicher was "always more a fighter than a thinker."[120] Perhaps so, but being a fighter is no bad thing in a fight.

The Institute of Judaeo-Christian Studies was Seton Hall's most intellectual significant enterprise of the 1950s. *The Bridge*, first published in 1956, received favorable notice in England, France, Germany, Austria, Italy, and the newly created state of Israel. Archbishop Richard Cushing of Boston acclaimed it as "an auspicious beginning." *Time* magazine gave it "unprecedentedly friendly" coverage.[121]

The Bridge was, for some, a bridge too far. Jews were conspicuous by their absence from its pages, some resenting what they saw as its call for them to convert. Even progressive Catholics gave Oesterreicher a wide berth.[122] On the other hand, by the end of the 1950s it was publishing daring work: "refutations of the Elders of Zion myth, Charles Journet's ideas on Israel's destiny, an exposé on antisemitism in the Soviet Union, and essays on contemporary Jewish thought."[123] Oesterreicher also attracted major Catholic scholars to Seton Hall, notably the Dominican Sister Rose Thering and Fathers Edward Flannery and Lawrence Frizzell, whose advocacy of better relations between Christians and Jews was to be the hallmark of the Institute for the remainder of Oesterreicher's life and after his death.

A Centenary to Celebrate, a Legacy to Leave

As 1956 approached, Seton Hall had reason to look forward to its centenary.[124] It had achieved university status. It had campuses in South Orange, Newark, Jersey City, and Paterson. It had a Law School and a School of Medicine and Dentistry. It had thousands of students. The university had reached, in the words of its commemorative history, "the summit of a century." A birthday party was in order.

The celebration began on the Feast of the Immaculate Conception, December 8, 1955, with a dinner in the Waldorf Astoria addressed by Bishop Fulton Sheen and Robert Murphy, assistant secretary of state. The year ended twelve months later with another $100 meal in the same place. In between came a high school seniors day, a performance of Italian music, and a day of Irish activities,[125] a High Mass and a series of academic convocations addressed by figures from business, politics, and the law. President Eisenhower sent "warm greetings and congratulations" on a century of "inspired service to the advancement of learning and to the development of responsible citizens."[126] There was even a centenary song, so bad as almost to be good:

> Seton Hall, a rapid growing university,
> A learning center where there's constantly
> Operation—
> Furthering education—
> The schools are fine;
> Instructors rank the very best in line;
> Yes, I can name a million reasons why
> We've acquired
> A rating that's all time high.[127]

Such was the summit of a century.

The heart of the celebration came on March 6, 1956, a wet and miserable day in Newark, with solemn Mass celebrated by Archbishop Amleto Giovanni Cicognani, apostolic delegate to the United States. Preaching, Archbishop Boland hailed Seton Hall's "wondrous history," its role in defeating Marxism and Darwinism, its opposition to atheistic science, its foundation at a "critical period of our nation, even of the history of the world." At luncheon following Mass, Bishop Justin McCarthy spoke of Seton Hall as part of a "natural [cycle] in the evolutionary process [coming] to complete fruition in the hands of the archbishop." (Between Mass and lunch, Darwin had evidently been forgiven.) McNulty praised Seton Hall's "priestly and religious alumni . . . they have been her staff and sinew."

The academic convocations—which were command performances—heard talks on law, agriculture, pharmaceuticals, trades unionism, and the American presidency. "I have been connected with the Department of Labor and Industry of the State of New Jersey in the administration of wage laws . . . for almost twenty years," wrote one audience member who had listened to George Meany of the AFL-CIO. "Here was evidence of real Catholic action in the field of social justice."[128] Supreme Court Justice William Brennan, a Newarker, spoke in November 1956 and "no-one," McNulty told him, "created a more favorable atmosphere."[129]

To compete with better-funded public and private schools such as Rutgers and Princeton, Seton Hall needed to build and maintain capital. McNulty conceived the notion of a centenary Scholarship Fund supported by local parishes to function an endowment for the university and an investment for the parishes themselves. Pastors were asked for $25,000 payable over four years, the interest to be set aside for the education of students from their parishes, the fund giving the university working capital and encouraging Catholic students to attend the school. In return, all academic fees were included, the student's only responsibility his or her living expenses. "Seton Hall belongs in a special way to the Priests of the Archdiocese," said Father Charles Murphy, coordinating the drive, "and since it cannot be an up and going university without the support of our priests, we must all work for her as best we can."[130] Murphy visited almost every parish of the diocese, carefully recording the warmth or otherwise of his reception. He charmed his friends into generosity, as if not asking for, but bestowing, favors. When the centenary was over, this was its best executed achievement.

A Catholic Intellectual Life?

Seton Hall's postwar expansion was among the most ambitious and successful transformations in American Catholic higher education. Its significance, however, is not that it was unique but that it was typical. Archbishop Walsh, remembering an earlier Seton Hall, was not alone in worry about mass education. The church historian Monsignor John Tracy Ellis questioned American Catholic commitment to the life of the mind as such, as did Cambridge historian Denis W. Brogan, who argued that "in no Western society" was "the intellectual prestige of Catholicism" lower than in the United States. On the face of it, these criticisms are hard to square with the fact that so many Catholics were getting a third-level education, but it was the alleged nature of that education—heavily prescriptive, textbook driven, uncritical of Church teaching and clerical authority—that made the argument plausible.

Part of John Tracy Ellis's complaint concerned the notion that Catholics had retreated into a cultural redoubt they never wished to leave, happy in their own parishes, grammar schools, high schools, colleges, and universities. Indifferent to the life of the mind, perhaps even hostile to it because already in possession of the Truth,[131] they shared the general anti-intellectualism of American culture,[132] preferring material success to serious books. "The chief blame, I firmly believe, lies with Catholics themselves," Ellis said. "It lies in their frequently self-imposed ghetto mentality which prevents them from mingling as they should with their non-Catholic colleagues." Their "lack of industry and habit of work" explained why American Catholic scholars had "not measured up to the incomparable tradition of which they are the direct heirs."[133] All the Seton Halls in the world would not make them better: in some ways, they would make them worse.

Given as a talk in Maryville College in Saint Louis, then as an article in *Thought* magazine in the fall of 1955, Ellis's critique caused a sensation. Indeed, the reaction almost confounded the thesis, with Catholics for a while thinking of nothing other than their own reluctance to think. Bishop John J. Wright of Worcester, Massachusetts spoke of a "great debate" in the Catholic press for the next two years. "If you were to have asked [the] question as of 1885," Ellis said towards the end of his life, "I would have agreed that the lack of intellectual achievement among Catholics was excusable. Ethnic roots and anti-Catholicism severely limited what could reasonably be expected of Catholic intellectual life in the late nineteenth century. But by 1955 these limitations were largely gone; Catholics were among the leaders in business, politics and other fields save the intellectual life. Our dismal performance was not so excusable in 1955, and today [1985] we have no excuse at all."[134]

Catholic anti-intellectualism existed, but the "ghetto" was livelier than its critics allowed.   The notion that American Catholics preferred "closed" systems of thought is absurd. Colleges and universities, Seton Hall among them, obsessed about the need for integrated courses of studies to bind together disparate disciplines, not to simplify the world but to acknowledge its complexity. At a workshop held at Catholic University of America in 1952, *Theology, Philosophy and History as Integrating Disciplines in the Catholic College of Liberal Arts*, lively Catholic minds engaged with business, the arts, the sciences, and the humanities,[135] Seton Hall was represented by Fathers John Cain and John Davis.[136] (Davis was coauthor of *Catholic Transcription Series*, one of the strangest books ever published by a Seton Hall faculty member, perhaps making Ellis's point: "a new concept in modern shorthand instruction integrated with Catholic thought in the field of secretarial science.")[137]

Seton Hall had bright students eager to get on, but "getting on" was understood as the acquisition of what critics condescendingly called "passports to suburbia"[138] and what others called, unironically, "living the American dream." If the intellectual life as such was less of a priority than material success, students were bright enough to recognize when they were being patronized by cultural commentators whose hostility to American materialism had not prevented them from doing well out of it themselves. Ellis's generalizations assume, in their own way, a world knowable and known: the Catholic "ghetto." Thinking went on there, too.

Thomas Sugrue, in *An American Catholic Speaks His Mind* (1952), lamented the insularity, cultural isolation, defensiveness, and clericalism of American Catholics. Thomas O'Dea, in *American Catholic Dilemma: An Inquiry into the Intellectual Life* (1958), claimed that Catholics suffered five "basic characteristics [inhibiting] the development of mature intellectual activity": formalism, authoritarianism, clericalism, moralism, and defensiveness. "We didn't have different outlooks because we never asked questions," remembered Peter Ahr, a Seton Hall freshman of the 1950s, confirming O'Dea's argument. "Going along with things was like walking with your feet on the ground and your head in the air."[139] O'Dea argued that the American Catholic was a "divided man" simultaneously incorporated into, and alienated from, American culture.[140] "On the one side is a firm identification with American society and strong loyalty to and love for its basic institutions. On the other is an alienation from the intellectual and spiritual experiences which . . . were central to those of Protestant background.[141]

At Seton Hall, the overidentification manifested itself as anti-communism and flashy Americanism: "The taste for automobiles, the styles of clothing and hairdressing and use of cosmetics, the felt necessity for radio and television, the interest in movies and sports—in short, all the other indices of superficial conformity—seem to be quite visible in the American Catholic scene."[142] There were plenty of cars at Seton Hall in the 1950s but some critics of them, too. Postwar expansion of the university would have been impossible without them. Only the affluent tend to complain of consumerism and only then when they have bought the idea—consumed it—from someone else.

Crucial to O'Dea's argument was that "defensiveness" about the world inhibited the development of intellectual life among lay people. The "defensiveness" was theological (the world seen as the realm of nature to be subordinated to and made sacred by the realm of grace) and historical (the medieval division between the clerical and lay "apostolates" carried over to the modern era).[143] Catholics should have embraced science but found ways of avoiding it. They should have transcended cultural boundaries but stayed within them.[144] The "ghetto" was thus not a social but a philosophical problem:

> While the modern world has been engaged upon the great adventure of science, Catholic thought has often tended to regard such developments as a series of "problems" and "difficulties" to be withstood and met with cautious, apologetic compromise . . . Unless it is possible for a Catholic youth to understand his faith, to know what faith really is, and maintain his faith, without having on the one hand to be spoon fed when genuine difficulties are involved, and, on the other, having his head jammed with ready-made formulae memorized in religion and philosophy classes, there really is no hope for the development of an intellectual life among Catholics . . .[145]

O'Dea was not referring to Seton Hall when he spoke of American Catholicism of the 1950s as "neo-Jansenism grafted on to a lower-middle class mentality"[146] but he could have been.

Consider, finally, John D. Donovan, whose 1964 book *The Academic Man in the Catholic College* provided evidence of the "dependent, submissive, pietistic and intellectually uncurious" attitudes in Catholic colleges leading up to the Second Vatican Council. (This before-and-after-the-Council trope has been repudiated: see, for example, James McCartin's *Prayers of the Faithful*.) Donovan's subject was the Catholic college professor, "the central figure in the American Catholic Church's unique venture into the field of higher education."[147] Historically, the Catholic college professor was almost always a priest assigned to teach by, and responsible for what he taught only to, his religious superiors. "The organization, growth, and spirit of Catholic higher education was thus, in American educational terms, unusual, the curriculum following classical models of European secondary schools and seminaries [and emphasizing] the integrity of the person at the expense of the subject-matter." But with the GI Bill, the need for more college-educated citizens, with lay professors assuming greater teaching responsibility and trained to higher professional standards, with renewed attention on the curriculum, above all with changes in the church itself, Catholic colleges could not afford to remain as they were. The postwar years marked their transition from "a prolonged intellectual adolescence to a point where they can face the challenges of maturity."[148]

Donovan and O'Dea personified the phenomenon they explored, being sophisticated laymen looking for new ways of expressing their faith in a world different from that of their parents. Yet even the notion of a "lay apostolate" was a theological expression of a sociological truth—the existence of an educated laity—that had been made possible in part by the very Catholic colleges they criticized. As Eugene D. McCarraher has written, running down Catholic higher education was "something of a sport" among Catholic intellectuals after the war: "Once-feared school administrators became philistine blockheads. Clerical professors were routinely pilloried as incompetent, lazy, and intellectually antediluvian. The Catholic college graduate was depicted leaving school as a toxic compound of ignorance and triumphalist smugness. . . . Not even seminary teachers escaped derision: Michael Novak recalled that one of his instructors was credited with having 'one of the finest minds of the fifteenth century.'"[149]

McCarraher is right. The over-articulated anxieties of Ellis and others were ideological. "Always on the lookout for signs and portents of popular irrationality, many Catholic intellectuals began moonlighting as cultural policemen walking the Catholic beat."[150] Their qualifications for the job were self-awarded.

An Assessment

Seton Hall in the fifteen years after the end of World War II offers partial corroboration of some of the claims of Ellis, Sugrue, O'Dea, and Donovan. A time of expansion, confidence, and theological certainty seemed to justify McNulty's baroque rhetoric. Good scholarship meant Catholic scholarship. Good teaching meant Catholic teaching. Good philosophy meant Catholic philosophy. Future elementary teachers were taught Apologetics, the Life of Christ, Moral Guidance I and II, God and the World, Incarnation and Redemption, Sacraments of the Church, Christian Marriage, Logic, Epistemology, Metaphysics, Rational Psychology, Moral Philosophy: Elements, Moral

Philosophy: Applications. Eventually, they studied those subjects which would bring them into contact with schoolchildren. Future nurses learned that obstetric nursing had as its objective "the family as the basic unit of society; its rights, privileges and responsibility to God and society."[151] Business majors attended seminars that began with "the existence of God, man [as] body-soul fused [and] created in [His] image and likeness, and original sin [as] the first fact to be dealt with in human experience and management," and ended with "getting results through the combined efforts of ourselves and those we lead."[152] Psychologists graduated from a department that placed "special emphasis . . . on the study of the normal human adult personality." William Noé Field, head of English, told his faculty to "draw a distinction between the matter and form of literature [so that] certain famed works by Voltaire or Rousseau or Moravia can be admitted to have good form but bad matter, sufficiently bad to warrant their exclusion from reading lists."[153]

"What is the naturalist view of philosophy?" Albert Hakim asked at his department's annual colloquium honoring St. Thomas Aquinas. A naturalist "denies the existence of a supernatural being of any kind and doubts the validity of metaphysics . . . he is a recent type of materialist . . . Father Hakim systematically pointed out the fallacies of this position and explained the foolishness of accepting naturalism as a starting point of philosophy."[154] (By way of contrast, students in the Rutgers Philosophean Society discussed Voltaire's *Candide* and John Stuart Mill's *On Liberty*.)[155]

History courses included Religious Movements of the Sixteenth Century ("a survey of the origins, development, and import of the religious revolution of the sixteenth century, stressing the disruption of the unity of Christendom"); Medieval Europe ("the fusion of the Christian, Roman, and Germanic influences that formed the civilization of Europe"); The Development of Political Thought ("ancient, medieval, and modern philosophers of the state, with special attention to . . . the preservation of fundamental human rights as opposed to absolutism and totalitarian philosophies");[156] and United States History (aiming "to make the student of today the better citizen of tomorrow by improving his knowledge of yesterday").[157]

In Newark and Jersey City, journalism professor Louis Budenz, former managing editor of the New York *Daily Worker*, taught a course on The Techniques of Communism, including lectures on "Communist Phraseology," "Invading Education," "Use and Abuse of Minority Groups: The Negro, the Mexican-American, Anti-Semitism," and "Knowledge and Facts as Weapons." He had been recommended to McNulty by Fulton Sheen. "Seton Hall is Concerned to bring this series of lectures to the attention of as wide an audience as possible; its subject is of acute interest not only to the University community but to every American citizen."[158]

"What is Success?" asked *The Setonian* at the beginning of the decade. The answer held good at the end: "Science has become a religion practiced both individually and nationally; the individuals striving to accumulate the largest pile of mechanical junk; the nations striving to secure a monopoly of the best scientific brains, processes and weapons. The humanities are the safety valves of men . . . Without their Homeric capacity for expression, the fertility of the human mind would be limited to a play toy absorption in the dynamos, pistons, and equally insignificant paraphernalia of a mechanic-crazed generation."[159]

Critics of Catholic anti-intellectualism were worried about closed systems of thought. That did not worry students, who, to borrow a line from Chesterton, wanted to know only if those systems closed in on the Truth. McNulty's Seton Hall gave them ways of finding out.

CHAPTER 12

A Law School for the City

The Origins of Seton Hall Law

Making a Case for Law

McNulty saw the university through its greatest expansion, adding buildings, schools, faculty, and students, while never forgetting that Seton Hall's ultimate purpose was to instill certain dispositions of mind, heart, and spirit in its graduates. In his down-to-earth way, he turned young men and women into teachers, businessmen, and nurses of whom their parents and church could be proud. But why stop at these professions? McNulty saw no reason why Seton Hall should not also have its own law school, and bringing this about was another of his acts of faith in a decade which saw many of them.

The story of American legal education need not be retold here.[1] A "law school" of sorts existed in Litchfield, Connecticut in the later eighteenth century and distinctive legal education as part of a college curriculum may be seen in Maryland and Virginia in the early national period. Harvard's law school began in 1817 (although by 1827 it had only one faculty member). After two false starts in 1825 and 1835, Princeton established a law school in 1846 run by local judges and practitioners but abandoned it six years later, having produced only six graduates.[2] America was famously a land of lawyers but not of law schools. Apprenticeship, not possession of a degree, was the normal way of entry into the legal profession until well into the nineteenth century. This began to change, as did notions of the profession itself, when the American Bar Association, formed in 1878, began to insist on postgraduate qualifications for membership of the bar, and when the American Association of Law Schools in 1906 stipulated that those qualifications should take a minimum of three years to acquire. Admission to the bar—"once practically the natural right of every citizen"[3]—began to be controlled by formal standards. By 1890, a period of study or apprenticeship before bar admission was required by twenty-three of thirty-nine jurisdictions in the United States.[4] As a result, law schools began to proliferate, some affiliated with universities, others self-standing, with Harvard the leader in the field. Setting the style, determining the curriculum, establishing standards, and teaching by case method, Harvard was confident in its own matchless superiority. The Harvard method, which dominated legal teaching for decades, prized facts and arguments, with the classroom as a court and the professor as a judge, decisions seen in terms of legal "rightness,"[5] and, finally, with law understood as a way of resolving disputes, not a field of moral speculation for its own sake.

By the time Seton Hall got around to starting a law school, it was late to a game that other Catholic institutions had been playing for nearly a century. Notre Dame established one in 1869; Georgetown in 1870; Catholic University in 1895; Creighton in 1904; Fordham in 1905; Marquette, Saint Louis, and Loyola (Chicago) in 1908; Duquesne and Santa Clara in 1911; the University of San Francisco, De Paul, and the University of Detroit in 1912; Gongaza in 1913; Loyola (New Orleans) in 1914; Loyola (Los Angeles) in 1920; Saint John's (Brooklyn) in 1925; Boston College in 1929; and Saint Mary's (San Antonio) in 1934. Of its Catholic rivals, only Villanova (1953) came later.[6] Seton Hall may have had ambitions to be in this first wave of schools, to become thereby a more significant force in higher education. Thus *The Sun* (New York) in June 1901: "Seton Hall College, South Orange, has purchased the country place of the late Eugene Kelly, the New York millionaire. The property embraces five acres of land and adjoins the ground already owed by the college. Within the next two years a law school will be added to the college. Eventually other schools will be added, so that the college will be an active competitor of the universities."[7] Nothing came of the idea but here in embryo was the university that Seton Hall became half a century later.

Catholic law schools were not especially impressive (and some failed) but they were at least animated by a desire to teach "immutable principles of reason and justice . . . governing the conduct of men in view of their relation to God, the state and one another."[8] They were not, that is to say, trade schools conducted under Catholic auspices but institutions thoroughly Catholic in their understanding of the law itself. Yet there *was* something of the trade school about them: the profit motive was more or less explicit. Georgetown Law School was initially intended to be selective but rapidly became "one of the largest and most lucrative part-time programs in the nation" because of pressure to lower its standards.[9] When it was later mooted that Georgetown's law and medical schools be transferred to the Catholic University of America, the reaction of the rector was that they were not good enough.[10]

Law schools could be highly profitable—thus their proliferation—and some were little better than secretarial colleges. The invention of the typewriter and the rise of gas and electric lighting, allowing for evening classes, also helped their growth.[11] From twenty-eight schools with 1,600 students in 1870, by 1890 the United States had fifty-four law schools with 6,000 students. There were one hundred schools with 13,000 students ten years later.[12] Alarmed by this unregulated expansion, in 1899 the American Bar Association demanded an organization of "reputable" law schools to regulate entry into the profession, leading to the foundation of the Association of American Law Schools in 1900. Together, the ABA and the AALS campaigned for proper accreditation of schools, their motivations self-serving and far from altruistic. (Keeping Jews and Catholics from the practice of law was part of it.[13] Elihu Root, president of the ABA, complained that 15 percent of New York lawyers were foreign-born, whose alien influences must be "expelled by the spirit of American institutions."[14] Harlan Stone, later Chief Justice of the United States, worried about "the influx to the bar of greater numbers of the unfit" who exhibited "racial tendencies toward study by memorization" and displayed "a mind almost Oriental in its fidelity to the minutiae of the subject without regard to any controlling rule or reason.")[15] In 1921, the campaign for exclusivity reached a conclusion when the ABA stipulated that only a law school could provide adequate legal education, that two years of college was required for admission to such a school, and that night schools would be accredited only if they became four-year institutions.

Higher standards—*any* standards—were welcome signs of growing professionalism. "The quality of the law school directly determines the quality of our bar, the quality of our bench and, considering the number of lawyers in executive, administrative, and legislative offices, the quality of our government," editorialized the *New Jersey Law Journal* in 1947. An ABA-approved school had to have adequate facilities and maintain a sound educational policy, admitting students who had completed at least half of the work required for a Bachelor's degree at a four-year college or university. A law degree would now take three years of full-time study (a year being thirty weeks) or four years of part-time study (a year being thirty-six weeks). The library of an accredited school had to have at least 7,500 volumes and be kept up to date (with at least $1,000 a year spent on books), with at least one full-time instructor for every hundred students (and at least three full-time instructors altogether). No school could operate as a commercial enterprise or allow administrative and teaching positions to depend upon the number of students enrolled or fees received (This seemed to contradict the 1:100 ratio). There had to be a full-time dean.[16] Secretarial colleges masquerading as law schools were doomed.[17]

Where does Seton Hall stand in this story? Its law school came into being at the end of the period between 1945 and 1950 that saw the greatest change in the training of lawyers in New Jersey history. One institution went out of business, the John Marshall School of Law in Jersey City. Another, Rutgers University, took over the University of Newark and the College of South Jersey in 1946 and 1950, creating out of them two new law schools. The New Jersey Supreme Court changed its rules in 1947 to require any law school offering professional qualifications to be accredited by the American Bar Association. (With the exception of students who had already begun their studies, after September 1, 1948 no-one would receive credit for work done at a school failing to meet ABA standards.) Once started, there was no stopping this push toward the professionalization of legal education. McNulty's aim, to produce Catholic lawyers, chimed with the bench's aim, to produce better ones.

This second impulse was bad news for the John Marshall School of Law. Founded and incorporated in 1928 by Alexander Ormsby, a former Hudson County judge, it opened for business in September 1929 under Dean James F. Minturn, recently retired after twenty-one years of service on the New Jersey Supreme Court. Apart from law, other subjects taught in "the College" included English, history, psychology, economics, and accounting. Some students had degrees (from Seton Hall, Notre Dame, and Holy Cross), others did not. In effect, John Marshall was a junior college and self-styled "graduate" law school rolled into one, its advantage a halfway decent library, its disadvantage no full-time legal faculty. It sold itself as "the University in the City" catering to "ambitious American Young People [wishing] to Earn-and-Learn." Often "supporting an idle father, even a wife and children, they carried their books to the office or shop, to class after five o'clock, and then home to prepare, in the wee small hours, next day's assignments. . . . Some new Horatio Alger may yet tell their story."[18]

It flourished even in the teeth of the Depression and World War II, but changes to rules of the New Jersey Supreme Court sealed its fate. The only school in the state besides the College of South Jersey without an affiliation with an accredited college or university, it attempted but failed to win ABA approval in in June 1948. A petition to the New Jersey Supreme Court for more time to remedy its defects was also denied. Accordingly, on July 1, 1948 its graduates were prevented from taking the bar examination. Further efforts at remediation, including the acquisition of a new library in April 1949, were also unsuccessful.

These reverses were unsurprising. The college's chief purpose was to make money for its owner by offering a variety of "college" courses in economics, accounting, secretarial skills, and law. Its "graduate" faculty were practicing and retired attorneys of modest academic ambitions, men who would have blushed to call themselves professors of law. ("A faculty member has written a valuable income-tax pamphlet which may be had on request.")[19] John Marshall had a certain school spirit (glee clubs and debating societies) and an undeniably enthusiastic owner, but as a serious law school it was a nonstarter. "The John Marshall School is done for as far as recognition by the American Bar Association goes," Judge John A. Matthews, former advisory master of the court of chancery of New Jersey, told McNulty in April 1950. "Alex *is* the school . . . he has made "a barrel of dough" out of it . . . he is "very tight" . . . his "trustees are Charlie McCarthys" . . . he "carries the school in his vest pocket" . . ."who owns the school library is the real question" . . . Alex will be impelled by "pocket patriotism when it comes to parting with his baby."[20] There lay McNulty's opportunity. Ormbsy was unwilling to reveal the assets of the school and the salary he paid himself as its proprietor and could never have satisfied the ABA of the quality of his enterprise. Short of a miracle, John Marshall's days were done. Perhaps, though, its assets could be transferred to Seton Hall, allowing it to have a kind of academic afterlife under new management.

Seton Hall lacked specific entitlement to open a law school, but under the terms of the 1861 charter it did not need additional approval from the state to create one from scratch. As long as it could be shown to fall within the educational purposes for which the first charter was granted, further legal action was unnecessary. Under the rules of the New Jersey Supreme Court (1: 8-2 [f]), any applicant for the bar was required to have attended an ABA-approved law school, the ABA withholding approval of schools until they had graduated their first class. How to attract students to a school as yet unapproved was solved by gaining provisional ABA approval. But how to give John Marshall a decent burial without dancing on its grave? McNulty wanted to buy its library and put it in storage until Seton Hall could inaugurate a school of its own, and a delegation of lawyers friendly to Seton Hall put precisely that proposal to Ormsby in 1949. They were told that he had no intention of selling the library or the school. But once Ormsby realized that John Marshall could never win accreditation, he agreed to transfer the library to Seton Hall as a kind of dowry for a future marriage between the two entities. The gesture occurred unexpectedly as he and McNulty were strolling along the boardwalk in Atlantic City during a meeting of the Middle States Association. "Why don't you give that library of yours to Seton Hall College?" McNulty asked. "Since he [was] a great friend of the Archbishop," he agreed.[21] John Marshall College held its twenty-third and final commencement on June 29, 1950, granting diplomas to a class of sixty-three students, not all of them law graduates.

To Ormsby, the school was not dead but reborn. There was "no safer repository in which to place the future progress of the aims, policies, tradition, and spirit of John Marshall College" than Seton Hall. Privately, McNulty was more realistic:

All academic work at John Marshall has ceased, and there is no obligation on Seton Hall to take any student. There are no students in the law School, so all we received from that is a marvelous physical beginning of a law library. [Ormsby's] junior college has gone down to approximately nothing because the students knew that there was no transfer to the law School. These students have been told that they are to transfer to the college of their choice, and I understand that the maximum would be about forty freshmen.

We are going to close the academic building and take the laboratory, the library, and the physical equipment to Seton Hall. We shall sublet the space to someone else. We are maintaining the lease on 40 Journal Square, the building where the Law School is; and the Archbishop is appointing a committee of outstanding lawyers to set up a graduate law school. We do not expect to do anything about that except study it for the coming scholastic year so that when it begins it shall be worthy of the University and also worthy of the effort that we are putting in to make a strong base here at Seton Hall.[22]

McNulty wanted a new and "a very splendid set-up"[23] and that, more or less, is what he got.

The Seton Hall School of Law began where the John Marshall College of Law ended, in Journal Square, Jersey City. Otherwise, "John Marshall Law School is dead," reported Cornelius Moynihan of Boston College, advising McNulty on how to set up a school of his own. An "entirely new atmosphere should be created," he said, by taking down signs, repainting walls, rebuilding offices, and erasing all indications (other than the library) of the previous life. Intellectually, it was a matter of getting a dean who was "a sincere Catholic, preferably a graduate of a Catholic college, and a graduate of a recognized Law School," and a faculty composed of "men [sic] of unquestioned character and mental stature" willing to publish across the spectrum of legal scholarship. In an unexpected way, Moynihan got his wish. The dean *was* a Catholic and a distinguished product of Catholic schooling. The dean was also a woman.

Miriam Rooney, Thomas Reardon, and John Wu

McNulty's choice for dean was Miriam Rooney, professor of law at the Catholic University of America since 1948 and the first female dean of a law school in the United States. From 1939 until 1948 she was a member, and three times chair, of the Philosophy of Law section of the American Catholic Philosophical Association. She was also associate editor of *The New Scholasticism*. Asked to take charge, Rooney recalled her first task as recruiting "a faculty and a student body, most of whom had never so much as glimpsed the vision of what a law school under Catholic auspices could be, [shifting] their sights towards hitherto undreamed galaxies." Devoutly Catholic and a committed Thomist, Rooney attended Harvard between 1926 and 1928 before transferring to the Catholic University of America, where she graduated BA, MA, and PhD. Her doctoral dissertation, *Law, Lawlessness, and Sanction*, published in 1937, examined theories of legal sanction in Jeremy Bentham, Sir Henry Maine, and Oliver Wendell Holmes, comparing them with Henry de Bracton, the thirteenth-century founder of the common law. Subsequent studies of Justices Brandeis and Cardozo appeared in various law reviews.

To Rooney and McNulty, the purpose of a Catholic law school was to produce Catholic lawyers; and for Rooney in particular this was more than prospectus: it was a passion. To her critics, among them attorneys she recruited to the faculty, she was more theologian than jurist, carried away with airy possibilities: "A great deal needs to be said regarding the relationship between law and theology which a sound philosophy of law could clarify. From the revelations to Moses, the attempt to Christianize Justinian's Code under the name of the Trinity, the implications of the Brehon Laws for the monks of the West, the Saxon renaissance and the patronage of Matilda of Saxony, . . . [the works of] Gratian . . . and Henry de Bracton in the development of Anglo-American jurisprudence: all these and more must become known not only in our law schools but in our seminaries."[24]

Natural law was foundational to her jurisprudence and, she hoped, to the school she was inaugurating. "It is a source of continued embarrassment," she wrote, "that in a century which has arrived at a rejection of positivism consequent upon the trials at Nuremburg, and at a distrust of sociological jurisprudence because of the use of the theory of communism as an instrument of tyranny by the Marx-Lenin-Stalin regime, no adequate contemporary literature is available about the natural law . . . The prevailing gobbledygook will eventually be cut away."[25] (Rooney wrote, one critic noticed, with "considerable self-assurance.")[26] Natural law was useful for trying war criminals but was otherwise a "parochial concept that enjoyed limited supported outside of a few Catholic law schools," according to one historian.[27] Rooney disagreed. Without it, statutes and constitutions were merely morally arbitrary rules. Seton Hall, she believed, could aim higher than that.

Rooney created a curriculum of contracts, tort, criminal law, equity, evidence, civil procedure, constitutional law, family and administrative law, and philosophy of law, with defined courses in the first year and some flexibility thereafter. What made the school different was its unapologetically Catholic jurisprudence in an era of positivism. That, and Rooney herself. She was a formidable woman in a man's world, "stern . . . but very passionate about the law and the school,"[28] practical and far from a soft touch.[29] "The law field is only crowded at the bottom," she said. "There is a great demand for good lawyers at the upper strata"[30]—where, she believed, Seton Hall people ought to be. Apart from a bachelor's degree, the school had no specific entrance requirements, although competence in mathematics, physics, chemistry, biology, modern languages, anything requiring "precision of thought, exact observation, and careful evaluation," was preferred.[31] In teaching, McNulty wanted to combine the Harvard research method and "the purely practical approach" of New York University, Fordham, and Rutgers. Seton Hall would be "one of the few institutions to adapt its textbooks and its teachers to this combination." He also wanted international law "as a basic requirement."[32]

Rooney did none of this alone. Father Thomas Reardon was appointed the law school's regent in December 1950, adding a certain glamor to the administration. (A regent was, in effect, the president's representative, his eyes and ears, at the school.) Reardon was a war hero, the "fighting chaplain" of Guadalcanal and later the subject of a motion picture for his exploits in that sphere of combat.[33] Ordained in 1934, he had served in Newark and Jersey City before enlisting as a naval chaplain shortly before Pearl Harbor. On August 7, 1942, he landed with the third wave of marines under fire at Guadalcanal, the first chaplain to go ashore. Four months later, he collapsed from malaria. In the film *Guadalcanal Diary*, the role of Reardon ("Father Donnelly") was played by Preston Foster. Rooney had an exceptionally high opinion of "Tommy" Reardon, praising his "loyalty to the Archdiocese of Newark and to the Seton Hall idea, his bravery under fire and miraculous survival on the battlefield, his experience in dealing with men under every possible circumstance in military and civilian life, his unending post-graduate education in sociology, social work and the law."[34]

Rooney aside, the most distinguished teacher was John Wu, who arrived from Honolulu in July 1951 after an extraordinary public and private career. Wu has been called many things—one of the twentieth century's greatest converts to Catholicism, a "top legal scholar and a representative of the old literati class,"[35] a bridge between East and West, a "Chinese Chesterton,"[36] a man, in Frank Sheed's words, "totally Catholic, totally Chinese, and totally himself."[37] He was a friend of Jacques Maritain; a correspondent of Justice Oliver Wendell Holmes; an admirer of, and admired by, Justice Felix Frankfurter, who called him "that amazing Chinese philosopher in the law"; a translator of the New Testament and Psalms into Chinese[38]; "one of the giants of post-Imperial Chinese law, philosophy, education, and religion";[39] a Doctor, as he jokingly called himself, of "Jurisimprudence."[40] Add to these his authorship of a memoir, *Beyond East and West*, which Maritain considered "a masterpiece"; add also his work as a translator into English of the Dao De Jing (*The Classic of the Way*); add the remark of Father John Hardon, S.J., to whom it was "not too much to see in this Chinese sage the promise of a glorious future for the Gospel in the East"[41]; add the extraordinary breadth of his acquaintanceships—from Chiang Kai-Shek to Pius XII to Dorothy Day to (later) Thomas Merton to Leo Strauss; add, finally, his manifest goodness as a family man, a Catholic, and a man of prayer, and the result was a remarkable addition to the school. "Everybody admired in him a rare combination of human and spiritual virtues," wrote Maritain, his "fervent faith, freshness of heart, refined simplicity, piety, courtesy, and true love of wisdom."

Wu and Seton Hall were in one sense mismatched. With degrees from the Soochow University School of Comparative Law and the University of Michigan (where he had shown "extraordinary ability . . . a real capacity in everything he did"),[42] Wu was a jurist of world renown. In 1927 he was appointed by the Jiangshu Provincial Government as a judge on the Shanghai Provisional Court, later serving as its chief justice and president. In 1929 he resigned to take up an appointment as Rosenthal Lecturer at Northwestern Law School. In 1930 he accepted a research fellowship at Harvard. Returning to Shanghai in 1930, he practiced law until, becoming a Catholic in 1937, he embarked on a career as a translator and diplomat (while not ignoring the law). Wu was principal author of the 1946 Chinese Constitution, based on an earlier draft (still known as the "Wu Draft") of 1933. After serving as Chinese minister to the Vatican in 1946 and 1947, he returned to Shanghai in February 1949 and was invited to become minister of justice, an appointment that proved abortive with the fall of the Guomindang government and Chang Kai-shek's exile to Taiwan. In March 1949, he left China for the last time, teaching at the University of Hawaii before coming to Seton Hall in 1951.

Mismatched in some ways, Wu and the Law School were well matched in others. The university was a kind of homecoming for him, reminding him of his own student days in China when "the students were mostly grown-up people who had work to do in the daytime . . . I was the youngest." "I went to see the dormitory and met a sopho-more student, who asked me, 'What are *you* doing here?'" he wrote in *Beyond East and West*. "I told him that I was just admitted. 'What!' he said, 'Look at these big text-books and case-book. We have to read a hundred pages a day. How can you catch up with the assignments, a young boy like you?'" [43]

Rooney and Wu were giants but the rest of the school was solid. John Thomas Fitzgerald and John Kean were the other full-time teachers. Frank Coughlin, who taught torts, was joined by two young lawyers, John P. Loftus and John J. Gibbons. Family law was taught by Harold McNeice, assistant dean of St. John's University School of Law, who sat as special master for the U.S. District Court for the Eastern District of New York. Joseph Larkin, assistant general counsel of Merck and Company, offered a course on Torts. Raymond del Tufo, a Newark attorney, taught Modern Procedure. Introduction to Law was taught by Rodman Herman, a Seton Hall graduate with a law degree from Harvard. [44] The librarian was John Kuhn, assisted by Arthur Murphy, a holdover from John Marshall days, and Ann Picinich, who also doubled as the secretary. The director of admissions was Ann Hari. Eighty-eight people applied for admission between February and June 1951; eighty-one were successful and seventy-two eventually enrolled. Only two of those seventy-two were out of state, only six of them women. There were fifty-six veterans, forty admitted under the GI Bill. The Law School had two divisions, Morning and Evening, with twice as many students in the latter as the former. It was off to a good start.

Early Days

Rooney, convening her first faculty meeting in February 1951, wanted nothing shoddy or second-rate. There was to be no smoking, typing, or talking in the library. Students "should be on time, [wearing] collars, ties, and jackets." They "should stand when reciting as an aid to thinking on their feet." A "crucifix [was] to be on display in every classroom" and classes were to begin with the Our Father. "The first half would be recited by the faculty member or a student, and the class would answer the second half. This would make provision for non-Catholic students to say the Our Father in accordance with their religion. It would also give those who preferred not to say the prayer an opportunity to remain silent . . ." Grades should be low. "The standard of scholarship in the School would not be judged favorably if As and Bs were numerous. As a matter of fact, in the first-year law class Cs, Ds, and Fs should predominate in order that only those indicating ability at legal analysis should be encouraged to continue studying law." John Loftus worried that "an A man [might not always] be an ethical man and a good lawyer." Kean thought that mere mention of an A should "of course [be] prohibited." Coughlin, the wit of the faculty, mused that "A men make judges, B men teachers, C men, money." Reardon wanted high standards humanely enforced. Loftus warned that easy grades could Seton Hall "notorious as a refuge for outcasts from other . . . schools." "We are running a law school," Gibbons noted, "not a charitable institution."[45]

Coughlin was a wag. In hypothetical tort cases, he offered his mother-in-law as the victim.[46] Fitzgerald was "a real curmudgeon, but also brilliant." One student, forty-five minutes late for a contract examination because his son had been born an hour before, was told "you better get busy, you only have an hour to finish."[47] One student arriving in his room "looking woozy" was "in no physical or mental condition to get into any arguments with you tonight." Reardon suspected that some students were in school "largely for the purpose of avoiding the draft."[48] "If anyone had told me a year ago," one said, "that I would be studying eight hours a day, I'd tell him he was crazy."[49] For a man with thirteen children, Wu saw law school monastically: "Professor Coughlin asked about students who wanted to take early examinations to get married, etc., to which Dr. Wu replied: 'Marriage is controllable and should have the permission of the Dean.' No decision was reached . . ."[50]

Rooney was as tough on the staff as on the students, insisting that they understood themselves as part of a unit "carrying forward the distinctive program of this law school [in] close collaboration [and] regardless of physical circumstances."[51] Expected to show up for extra-curricular events, they struggled to mimic enthusiasm. "Dr. Rooney wondered whether we could bring in the Catholic Lawyers' Guild . . . and show some films suitable for lawyers . . . Mr. [Robert] Colquhoun wanted to know if this were to be compulsory, since otherwise they would not attend in great numbers."[52] After a day in court or an office, teaching at night was a good way of supplementing income. Most of her faculty were unexcited by the academic life *per se*. At one point, Rooney thought of having them sign in and out for class but decided against, wisely seeing it as demeaning. "Coaching for the New Jersey bar," Rooney said, "is not the goal of a first-class law school." Her colleagues, too polite or intimidated to demur, failed to offer the counterargument that Seton Hall was not, as yet, such a school. "We are training national leaders," she insisted, "not merely students for the Bar." Gibbons thought her more interested in producing theologians than lawyers, but her vision of Seton Hall as the leading Catholic law school in the United States remained intact. Asked how long that might take, she replied "fifty years."[53] "Our secret partner is God," said Reardon, "and with His help we shall go on."[54]

God worked through committees, of which the most important dealt with admissions, consisting of Rooney "and any other three professors available *ad hoc*."[55] Rooney and Reardon made most decisions, with Wu chiming in as a respected senior jurist. Other decisions had to do with the conduct of meetings—Robert's Rules as Holy Writ—and the application of modern technology to the law. Loftus thought that parliamentary procedure was important "because most communists . . . are conversant with it . . . and it is often used as a club . . . for good or evil."[56] As for the day-to-day life of the school, public lectures in the evening were a waste of time "in view of the hesitancy of people to leave their homes . . . in this TV age." (Among the hesitant were the faculty.) Lawyers were "not too strong for listening to lectures" unless "the speeches show [them] how to make money."[57]When Rooney proposed a conference on natural law, Coughlin thought the subject too remote for New Jersey attorneys.[58] Gibbons, asked how students might find placements, said they should wear a shirt and tie and write a resumé.[59] When the honor system was proposed for exams, Coughlin, demurred, pointing out that classes always began with "Lead us not into temptation."[60]

Everyone had ideas about teaching law. McNulty set some of the text books to be used in class.[61] Chief Justice Vanderbilt thought that law graduates emerged from their training insufficiently equipped with legal skills (ironic for a man who had done his best to end the apprenticeship system). "Judging by some of his latest decisions," Wu complained, "it would be a good thing for him to take a course in legal skills himself."[62] Frank Coughlin offered that "a man might take seventy-five courses but still he is no match for the practical man with experience,"[63] a line of argument calling into question the efficacy of law school itself and implying a return to apprenticeship. No-one wanted to go that far.

The Law School moved from 31 to 40 Clinton Street, Newark in August 1951. The school's temporary home, 31 Clinton Street, was taken over by the other operations of Seton Hall's extension campus. The new home, 40 Clinton Street, was an eight-story office block of which the law school occupied the first five and the eighth floors. A month later, it was provisionally approved by the ABA, subject to annual inspections for three years, after which it was entitled to apply for membership in the Association of American Law Schools. The school underwent ABA inspection in April 1953 and was found to be "in good order" but with a detailed list of anxieties about students on probation, special students, library expenditure, course offerings, new courses, faculty loads, faculty committees, and rates of success in the bar exam.[64] Rooney was inclined to see the glass half full when the ABA saw it half empty. Full ABA approval came on August 26, 1955.

Rooney defended the school in public while being privately critical of it, conceding in 1954 that it needed "a student body more intellectually alert."[65] In 1955, a Pre-Legal Education Committee found much of the teaching in South Orange (a feeder for the school) "deplorable, especially in English . . . The bulk of the students could not properly write, read . . . or talk or think."[66] In 1956, following disappointing bar exam results, Rooney toughened admission standards and placed more students on probation. In 1957, Daniel Degnan suggested that admissions needed to be "cut down considerably to a more promising group no matter [the] cost."[67] There was no arguing with the bar exam, a sure indicator of whether the school was as good as it claimed to be. Students with genuine difficulties were treated leniently,[68] but even a scholastically competent student could be dismissed "for failure to demonstrate the character and integrity of a learned profession." Students of dubious morals were unwelcome. (One man "showed evidence of . . . studying the law to learn how to circumvent it.")[69] Rooney argued for the right to dismiss on character grounds,[70] convinced that intellect alone was insufficient qualification to become a lawyer. The ABA worried about communists.[71] Reardon worried about divorcés.[72] Rooney worried about pragmatists and positivists.

Attracting faculty was difficult. No-one imagined that Seton Hall would pay large, or even adequate, salaries from the beginning, but with the national median income for law professors at $6,300 a year, the university came nowhere close. (Most of the faculty, of course, had income from legal practice.) Reardon thought that "the high financial demands placed upon approved schools"[73] would lead to "educational piracy" (poaching top professors with higher salaries), an astute prediction for the future. For the time being, Seton Hall hoped that institutional loyalty would trump individual ambition.[74] McNulty canvassed other schools as to their salary scales, but when none responded he had to come up with a figure off the top of his head—a head never much inclined to generosity when it came to faculty compensation. Flying blind, Seton Hall came second to last in the salary scale of schools inspected by the ABA. To be fair, the schools that refused to tell McNulty what they paid their professors also refused to tell the ABA unless those amounts remained secret. In effect, the ABA told Seton Hall to improve standards without saying what the standards were. The Law School, John Wu thought, had "something that cannot be bought for money,"[75] which was true, but money would have helped.

None of the faculty except Rooney and Wu had an academic profile or any sense of how to win one. Most were practicing lawyers with other interests. Attending conferences, making connections, churning out articles and reviews were the last things on their minds. Rooney advised them to attend professional meetings to "acquire a national reputation." Reardon reminded them "to publish articles in national law reviews since a reputation for competence upon the national level is also obtained in this way."[76] But Rooney had no wish to buy a better faculty or any reason to do so. The faculty was decent as it was, with "a reasonable amount of spirit, intellectual vigor, and sincere pedagogical interest in the problems of legal education." Some had even produced "several volumes of apparent merit." The Law School was off to a solid start.[77]

John Wu and Fountain of Justice

Of those volumes "of apparent merit" one deserves mention. Rooney's passion was that Seton Hall should produce lawyers acquainted with the Catholic Christian and natural law roots of Anglo-American jurisprudence. In this ambition she had a soulmate in John Wu. Wu's book *Fountain of Justice: A Study of the Natural Law* (1955) was the most significant intellectual product of Seton Hall Law in its first twenty years of existence. Even in its every-day character, Wu said, law contains "an echo of the infinite. . . . a hint of the universal law."[78] *Fountain of Justice*, the most mature expression of Wu's Catholic jurisprudence, is a legal masterpiece. "This is a very good book written by a remarkable man," said the *Cambridge Law Journal* in 1959.[79] "Purity of heart, independence of spirit, the ethics of decision-making," wrote Bishop James A. Pike in *The Christian Scholar*: "lawyers, teachers and students will be better prepared to face such questions . . . if they read books like *Fountain of Justice*."[80] It was also very much a Seton Hall book, conceived almost as an inspiration during Mass "in the lovely chapel" of the university.[81] To Rooney, he owed his serious interest in Bracton, which began with her "remarkable book" *Law, Lawlessness, and Sanction*. Father Edward Synan helped with translation. Monsignor John Oesterreicher suggested the distinction between "lawyers" in the Biblical sense and "lawyers" in the popular sense. (Wu repaid the debt by helping Oesterreicher establish the Institute of Judaeo-Christian Studies in 1953.)[82] But Wu's greatest debt was to John McNulty, without whose guidance and encouragement the book could never have been written.[83]

One reading of Wu sees him as him a relativist and historicist, seeking "to harmonize conflicting schools of thought in jurisprudence and political theory, religion, and culture."[84] Even if true of his earlier work on the Chinese constitution, such a view misreads his later jurisprudence, in which historicism was the very principle that rescued him from relativism. "The principles of the natural law are permanent and comprehensive; but just because they are comprehensive, they have an elasticity when they come to be applied . . . Because [they] are broad and elastic in their application, many a superficial jurist is led to deny their intrinsic immutability."[85] Wu was steeped in two great traditions of law, the Chinese and the Christian, finding no difficulty in quoting Confucius or Mencius in support of Aquinas. In *Fountain of Justice* and, later, in

Christian Humanism and Chinese Spirituality (1965), he insisted that echoes of the infinite may be heard everywhere if our ears are sufficiently attuned. Infinity, by definition, is not confined by time and space.

The End of the Decade

Wu and his friends inaugurated a golden age for Catholic intellectual life at Seton Hall at the Law School and on the main campus in South Orange. He saw himself, and was seen, as a bridge-builder. Rooney, too, wished to span modernity and medievalism, the former unaware of its debt to the latter. Paul Sih, one of Wu's "dearest godchildren"[86] who directed the Institute of Far Eastern Studies in South Orange, wished to link Confucius and Christ, showing how in "the peculiar circumstances of his own life . . . the traditions of east and west were united."[87] John Oesterreicher wished to connect Christians and Jews and did so, appropriately, in *The Bridge*.

The other bridge was Seton Hall itself. It was an act of brilliant showmanship for McNulty to gather Wu, Rooney, Synan, and Oesterreicher to enable them to conduct a conversation greater than the sum of its parts. Wu himself, who left off teaching law in 1961 to teach Chinese language and thought in South Orange, left an ineradicable impression on generations of students. He was a notable figure on campus, traditionally attired in Chinese fashion, slightly stooped, walking to Mass followed by a gaggle of children.[88] Ralph Walz, an undergraduate at the university in the early 1950s, later a professor of history, remembered him as a vivid representative of several worlds, an "illustrious refugee from Red China . . . He and his wife, in the exotic garb of Old China, walked (she a few paces behind him), across the campus from their home somewhere behind the gym to the chapel to 'assist' at Mass. Theirs was a daily routine and one could set one's watch by their regular appearance. I never exchanged a word with this couple but if our paths actually crossed, a slight bow said it all."[89]

Meantime, the work of the law school continued. The best efforts of Rooney notwithstanding, not every student did justice to the training he received. Only one in four graduates passed the New Jersey bar first time round, a figure below the national average but not a calamity. (The more important question was how many would pass the second time.) The eagerness of students to practice the law told against them. "Those not quite poor enough to be dismissed, but no better than the run of the mill in other law schools, insist on rushing into bar examinations before they have properly reviewed, with disastrous results to our reputation, as well as to their own," Rooney remarked in 1955.[90] "The burden placed upon this faculty of producing graduates comparable to those prepared in other first-class law schools is a heavy one."[91] But by 1956, according to inspectors from the AALS, the school was flourishing. Students participated "fairly well" in class, were "reasonably business-like" in habits, good in "appearance and conduct", and "much as . . . students of other law schools," studying in "small and informal" classes and making use of a library that was adequate, even impressive.[92] By 1959, bar pass rates were higher, a tribute to good teaching, unsentimental grading, and better recruitment. (Averaged out, 80 percent of Seton Hall law graduates between 1954 and 1958 passed the bar in New Jersey, New York, the District of Columbia, or Pennsylvania. In 1960, 100 out of 183 graduates passed the New Jersey bar at the first attempt.)[93] Maintaining standards became an obsession even to the point of absurdity: "one student maintained an average of 73.9 and another 73.95. It was suggested that they be given practically equal rank in the class list but after long and vigorous discussion it was voted to let their permanent rank stand as their original records even to the second decimal place."[94] (Law professors could also be unfeeling: "Voted: not to admit an applicant for special study who is recovering from a brain tumor operation to take only one course.")[95] As a result, grades became more predictive of success in the bar exam than scores on the LSATs, suggesting either the low value of the latter as a measurement of aptitude or the high value of the degree as qualification for the profession.

Toward the end of the decade Seton Hall marketed itself no longer as a new law school but as a successful one. Its closeness to New York was a draw (although most graduates practiced in New Jersey).[96] It tried to recruit in Princeton among Catholic students.[97] A hike in fees in 1957 did not discourage applications from graduates in the top 10 percent of their class.[98] Whatever it was doing, it was doing something right. It had a library of 40,000 volumes, a faculty of twenty-three (ten full time), an active alumni association, a cohort of graduates making their way in the profession, a better qualified student body, and a respectable pass rate at the bar. Its curriculum was stable to the point of stagnancy.[99] It had been founded in 1951 to provide a Catholic alternative to "legal positivism, economic materialism, and sociological pragmatism."[100] There was every reason to believe that it had succeeded.

SETON-HALL COLLEGE,
Madison, Morris Co. N.J.
Sept. 1856.

1. The original site of Seton Hall College at Madison, New Jersey, in 1856. Source: SHU e-Repository.

2. The Elphinstone Mansion in South Orange in the early 1860s. Source: SHU e-Repository, 1931 Setonian History.

3. James Roosevelt Bayley, bishop of Newark (1853) and founder of Seton Hall College. Source: 1931 Setonian History.

4. Bernard McQuaid, first president of Seton Hall College, later bishop of Rochester (1868). Source: 1931 Setonian History.

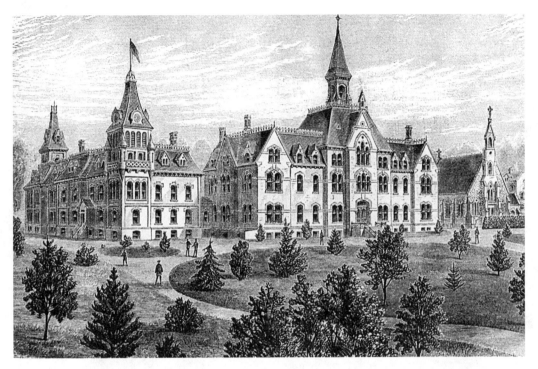

5. Left, the College Building, expanded in 1863; center, the Seminary Building (now Presidents Hall), completed in 1867; right, the Chapel, built in 1863, the oldest building on campus. Source: 1931 Setonian History.

6. Michael Corrigan, third president of Seton Hall, later bishop of Newark (1872) and archbishop of New York (1880). Source: SHU Hallmark Alumni Magazine, fall 1968.

7. Alumni Hall. Source: SHU Photograph Collection.

8. The class of 1889. Source: 1951 *Galleon* Yearbook.

9. Father William Marshall, president of Seton Hall (1888–1897).
Source: 1931 Setonian History.

10. Monsignor James Mooney, president of Seton Hall (1907–1922). Source: 1931 Setonian History.

11. Seton Hall cadet officers in 1896. Source: 1931 Setonian History.

12. Seton Hall Glee Club, early 1900s. Source: SHU 125th Anniversary History.

13. The early Bayley Hall. Source: SHU Postcard Collection.

14. The colorful Monsignor Thomas McLaughlin, president of Seton Hall College (1922–1933), rector of Immaculate Conception Seminary, later bishop of Paterson (1937–1947). Source: ADN Collection.

15. The science laboratory in Alumni Hall. Source: 1931 Setonian History.

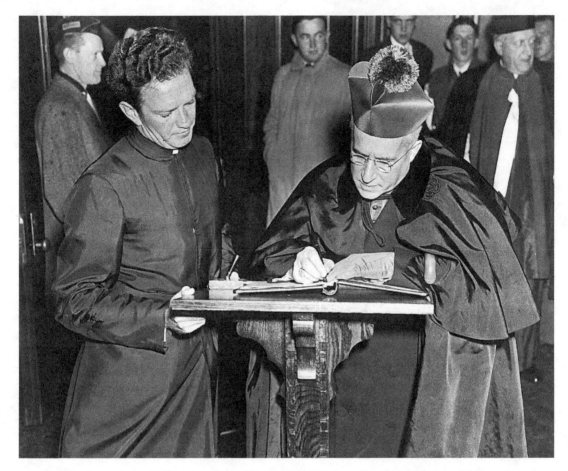

16. Monsignor James Kelley, president of Seton Hall (1936–1949) with Archbishop Thomas J. Walsh of Newark. Source: SHU Photograph Collection—Handy & Boesser of Newark.

17. Monsignor John McNulty, president of Seton Hall (1949–1959). Source: ADN Collection.

18. Francis Hammond, professor of philosophy, Seton Hall's first African-American faculty member. Source: 1951 *Galleon* Yearbook.

19. Undergraduate life in 1951. Source: 1951 *Galleon Yearbook*.

20. Andy Stanfield, "the world's fastest human," twice an Olympic gold medalist in Helsinki in 1952, and a silver medalist in Melbourne in 1956. Source: SHU
Athletics Collection.

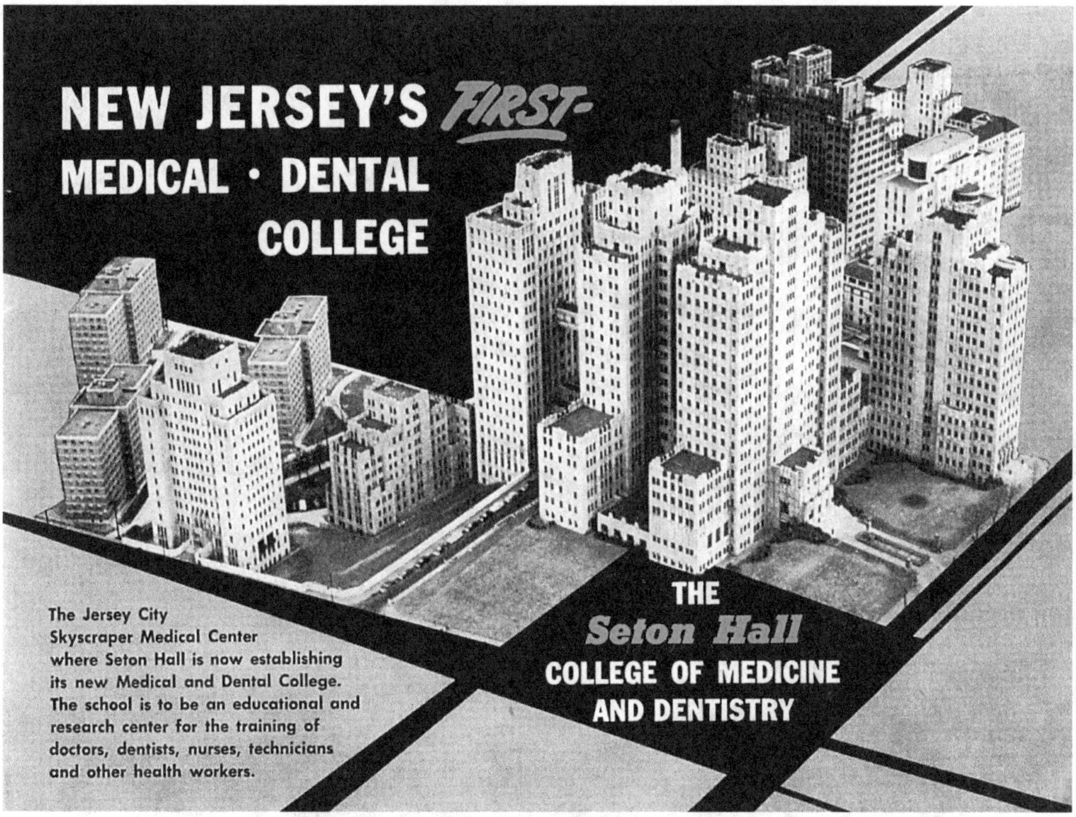
NEW JERSEY'S FIRST-
MEDICAL · DENTAL
COLLEGE
The Jersey City
Skyscraper Medical Center
where Seton Hall is now establishing
its new Medical and Dental College.
The school is to be an educational and
research center for the training of
doctors, dentists, nurses, technicians
and other health workers.
THE
Seton Hall
COLLEGE OF MEDICINE
AND DENTISTRY

21. Promotional material for Seton Hall's ultramodern College of Medicine and Dentistry. Source: SHU Vertical File, College of Medicine & Dentistry Papers.

22. Seton Hall School of Law in Newark in the early 1950s. Source: Centennial History, 1956.

23. Miriam Rooney, first woman dean of a law school in the United States. Source: 1956 *Galleon* Yearbook.

24. Professor John Wu, early star of the law school.
Source: SHU Photograph Collection.

25. The compulsory annual retreat of 1950. Source: 1950 *Galleon* Yearbook.

SISTER MARY HUMILLIA HADUCH,
FEL. O. S. F.

Bachelor of Science   Education

Immaculate Conception Convent

South Main Street, Lodi, New Jersey

SISTER MARY HUMILIS JAKIELEWICZ,
FEL. O. S. F.

Bachelor of Science   Education

Immaculate Conception Convent

South Main Street, Lodi, New Jersey

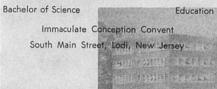

SISTER MARY THERENIA KOWALSKA,
FEL. O. S. F.

Bachelor of Science   Elementary Education

Immaculate Conception Convent

South Main Street, Lodi, New Jersey

SISTER MARY MICHAELA LIS
FEL. O. S. F.

Bachelor of Science   Education

Immaculate Conception Convent

South Main Street, Lodi, New Jersey

26. Nuns intending to become elementary teachers were an important element of the student body in the Newark campus. Source: 1952 *Galleon* Yearbook.

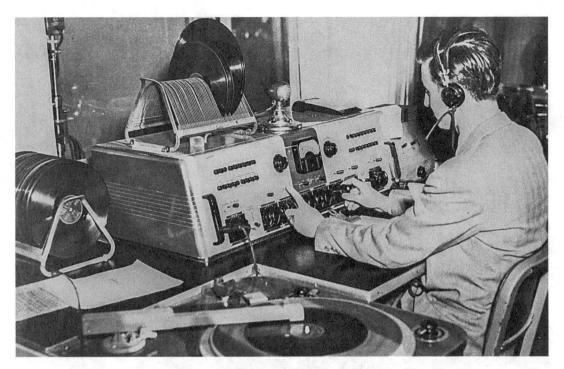

27. WSOU in the 1950s. Source: 1950 *Galleon* Yearbook.

28. The Institute for Far Eastern Studies. Source: 1953 *Galleon* Yearbook and 1951 Setonian.

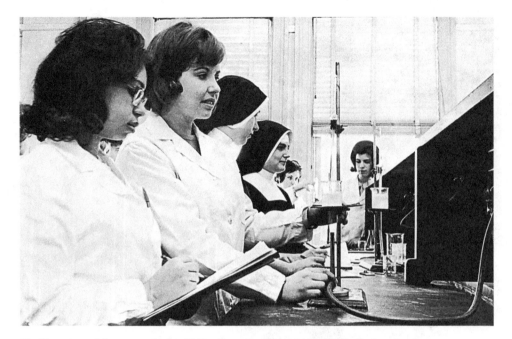

29. Chemistry laboratory in the 1960s. Source: 1965–1966 SHU Bulletin.

30. Archbishop Thomas Boland blesses the foundation stone of the Humanities Building watched by, from his right, Bishop John Dougherty (president 1959–1969), Father Albert Hakim (dean of the College of Arts and Sciences 1960–1972), and Father Thomas Fahy, president (1970–1976). Source: SHU e-Repository.

JOHN R. KELLER
PH.D.
Biology

CHRYSANTHY M. KEHAYES
M.A.
English

Mr. G. Devine . . .
University College.

REV. WILLIAM KELLER
M.A.
History and Political Science

TADASHI KIKUOKA
M.A.
Asian Studies

REV. ECKHARD KOEHLE
PH.D.
Philosophy

HERBERT C. KRAFT
M.A.
Anthropology

A. PAUL KLOSE
M.A.
Communication Arts, Chairman

ELIOT KRAUSE
M.S.
Biology

31. Faculty members, 1967. The sole female in the picture, Chrysanthy Kehayes, had a pioneering career as chair of the English department and acting dean of Arts and Sciences and the Library. Source: 1967 *Galleon* Yearbook.

32. Learning computer science in 1967. Source: 1965–1966 Seton Hall Bulletin.

33. The university senate in 1971. Source: SHU Photograph Collection.

34. Monsignor Edward Fleming, acting president (1969–1970), faced mounting unrest.
Source: SHU Photograph Collection.

35. Student protests, 1970. Source: 1970 *Galleon* Yearbook.

36. Women students in 1972 changed the face of the South Orange campus. Source: 1972 *Galleon* Yearbook.

37. The Community House in 1975—radicalism in the form of cheap tuna sandwiches.
Source: 1975 *Galleon* Yearbook.

38. Professor David Abalos, Department of Religious Studies, addressed a student rally outside Presidents Hall in 1975. Source: 1975 *Galleon* Yearbook.

39. Professor John Sweeney, Department of English, was a much-loved campus figure. Source: 1975 *Galleon* Yearbook.

40. John Conley, president (1977–1979), faced severe financial pressure and was unable to deal with it. Source: SHU Photograph Collection.

41. The law school played an increasingly prominent role in the legal profession in New Jersey and beyond. From left in 1984, Monsignor John Petillo, Chief Justice Robert Wilentz, Edward D'Alessio, governor and former Chief Justice Richard Hughes, Father Daniel Degnan, SJ, dean of the law school. Source: SHU Photograph Collection.

42. President Ronald Reagan addressed the graduating class of 1983. Source: SHU Photograph Collection.

43. Peter ("P.J.") Carlesimo coached the Seton Hall Pirates to the NCAA Final Four in 1989.
Source: 1989 *Galleon* Yearbook

44. Father Thomas Peterson OP, chancellor of Seton Hall (1990–1995). Source: 1996 *Galleon* Yearbook.

45. Monsignor Robert Sheeran, president of Seton Hall (1995–2010). Source: 2001 *Galleon* Yearbook.

Frank Caltabilota

John Giunta

Aaron Karol

46. Aaron Karol, Frank Caltabilota, and John Giunta lost their lives in the Boland Hall fire of January 19, 2000. Source: 2000 *Galleon* Yearbook.

CHAPTER 13

A Revolution under Dougherty

A New President

John McNulty died of a heart attack while on retreat at Darlington in May 1959, only sixty and in fine spirits a few months before when he celebrated ten years as president. "I've never seen a group of people more shocked," said Professor Joseph Cunningham. "He was like a father to us." With the exception of his seminary days in Louvain, Mc-Nulty's life had been spent almost entirely at Seton Hall as a schoolboy, student, priest, professor, and president. He became president when the Kelley scandal suggested a ramshackle institution. Now, with a law school, a medical school, an undergraduate operation across four campuses, and a greatly enlarged faculty, it was indisputably a force in Catholic higher education. "The Church has lost a great priest, the community a great leader, Seton Hall a great president, and many thousands a sincere, self-sacrificing friend" said Father Albert Hakim.[1] Leonard Dreyfuss thought McNulty "remarkable": "Seton Hall became one of the great universities of the United States under his amiable and down-to-earth stewardship."[2]

Monsignor John J. Dougherty, professor of Sacred Scripture at Immaculate Conception Seminary for the past twenty-two years, succeeded him as the thirteenth president in December 1959. (The story goes that he was given the job by Archbishop Thomas Boland when in Rome for the centennial celebrations of the North American College, both men vesting for Mass at the time.) Dougherty came from an "average Irish Catholic middle-class family" in Jersey City, the kind of people for whom Seton Hall was made. Graduating from the College, he studied for the priesthood in Rome, was ordained in 1933, and continued his studies at the Pontifical Biblical Institute, later doing research in the Holy Land. In 1936, he returned to teach at Darlington, where he remained, with a year of absence to complete his doctorate, until his appointment as president. Dougherty came of age at a fertile time for biblical studies, when a new generation of scholars had begun to argue that the Bible was more than a book of quotations for use in theological dispute, its historicity itself an aspect of revelation. Dougherty, of similar mind, was first and last a seminary professor, a teacher of future priests, not an upsetter of orthodoxy. He was also a popular evangelist, in the mid-1940s appearing on *The Catholic Hour* and, as television came into its own, developing a similar program from which came *Rome Eternal*. He was a member of the Vatican Commission on Radio and Television. Dougherty was a man of parts: a former athlete, he found time as president to work out on barbells, to walk, swim, and play tennis.[3] He was also fluent in French, German, Italian, Spanish, Latin, Greek, Arabic, Aramaic, Hebrew, and Sanskrit, a man of culture, warmth, and eloquence.

"We are conscious that presidents are passing," he observed on his installation in April 1960 (the first time a president began with a formal academic ceremony, and one for which the campus received a spring-cleaning).[4] "It is the presidency that remains." The remark captured Dougherty's commitment to institutions and offices, his recognition of traditions larger than himself, his modesty in the face of history, and his belief that the presidency and the university *would* remain for another generation. Yet to assert continuity was to acknowledge the reality of change. Under McNulty, Seton Hall had seen a decade "of outstanding progress."[5] Under Dougherty, the change continued, dramatic and unsettling. Although progressive in many of his views, he was not to know how rapidly the world he took for granted would disappear. McNulty's Seton Hall was expansive, confident, and typical of the Catholic moment of the 1950s. Dougherty's was modern, turbulent, and typical of the Catholic moment of the 1960s. McNulty and Dougherty were different personalities leading at different times. What they had in common was a sense that the cultural currents they were negotiating could sweep them away.

For Dougherty, Seton Hall was a "fellowship of educated men," a home for "inquiring spirits," a "living community of scholars." He spoke of a future "when . . . secularism [will have been] found wanting and religion [will be] restored to its rightful place of honor in our nation as the mother and the queen of culture." Seton Hall was to play its part in that restoration. McNulty was a bricks-and-mortar man: Dougherty was grandiloquent. His aim was to dedicate Seton Hall "to the cause of Catholic higher education in the tradition of the liberal arts . . . to create a . . . community of scholars educated in American and European universities; to restore university theology to a position of influence and prestige; to be truly Catholic and truly American . . ."[6] Such liberal humanism proved too refined for the problems he was to face. Students, he believed, were "hungering for answers to burning theological questions raised in the classroom or on the campus." Theological questions did burn brightly, but the kindling was provided by theology itself.[7] The Second Vatican Council (which Dougherty attended as Auxiliary Bishop of Newark)[8] began a series of social and political renewals both overdue and (to some) overdone. Endorsing religious liberty, ecumenism, and better relations with nonbelievers, promoting a people-of-God ecclesiology, episcopal collegiality, and greater Catholic openness to the world, the Council was nothing short of a Catholic revolution. At the same time, the modern world itself was more fractured, torn apart by assassination, racial violence, sexual revolution, and war.[9] Seton Hall played its part in these changes. The president of the Alumni Association saw in 1966 "a noticeable deterioration at Seton Hall of student demeanor, religious activity, social graces, and enlightened discipline—all of which one has a right to expect of any great Catholic university."[10] "One of the most tantalizing paradoxes of human experience," Dougherty said in 1969, "is man's deep existential yearning for peace and his apparent inability to achieve it."[11] He could have been describing his own campus.

Dougherty's nostalgia for his "average Irish middle class family" reflected what David O'Brien has called the "Americanized Catholicism" that replaced the "immigrant church" of the nineteenth century. For O'Brien, American Catholics increasingly lacked a supporting subculture,[12] with immigrants, as they assimilated, vulnerable to loss of identity and acceptance of alien cultural values. In one sense, Seton Hall epitomized "Americanized Catholicism." (Students voted for the Catholic Kennedy over the Quaker Nixon in 1960.)[13] But Seton Hall also resisted that culture, faulting its materialism and secularism. The transformed social composition of American Catholics, O'Brien argued, meant "enormous pressures for change" even had there been no Second Vatican Council. Seton Hall was part of that story. Its "supporting subculture" almost disappeared in the 1960s, making it less deferential and weakening its clerical mentality. Dougherty was a progressive swept away by his own progressivism.

Dougherty's last years as president were unhappy, but academically the university was stronger at the end of the 1960s than the beginning. Father Andrew Greeley, Chicago sociologist and novelist, visited South Orange in 1966 and discovered "one of the most interesting and exciting schools" he ever encountered, "[a] high point . . . of American Catholic higher education."[14] Seton Hall was unrecognizable in 1970 from 1960 but so also was American Catholic higher education. Excellence was the buzzword of the day and Seton Hall joined the "binge" along with everyone else.[15]

Uncertain Future

Seton Hall improved under McNulty, but when Dougherty became president its reputation needed repair. "Frankly, I am worried about the state of our relations with the alumni," wrote Ben Thompson, newly appointed director of public relations and development in 1961, noting "widespread antagonism" among World War II veterans and those who felt that the medical school drained funds from general education.[16] Seton Hall, tuition-driven and lacking a large endowment, admitted some marginal students, academically weak high schoolers from modest backgrounds who deserved a chance. Professors were hard pressed to keep up. Facilities were overstretched. "Faculty morale is low," wrote Thompson, "partly due to the average teaching load of 15 hours per week, partly to salaries low enough to force many into overtime teaching or moonlighting, partly to the Administration's reluctance to improve health and TIAA benefits, partly to the absence of seemingly minor services as personal mail delivery."[17] Clerical and lay faculty were separated at academic processions. No-one had an office (some not a desk). Faculty had to undergo bag searches as they left the library.[18] There was no common room. Prompted by the Middle States Association, the university aggressively sought teachers with PhDs and began to grant sabbaticals and help with publication. Even so, "we will have difficulty," Thompson thought, "in attracting first-rate teachers and scholars to Seton Hall."[19] Faculty salaries rose throughout the 1960s but from a low base;[20] and as salaries rose so did workload.[21]

Thompson was not alone. When Father Albert Hakim became dean of the College of Arts and Sciences in 1961, he removed over thirty faculty members, some without degrees, allowing him to appoint scholars who remained at Seton Hall for the rest of their careers. Hakim was genial but unsentimental. "Reportedly uninspired plodder, not a college-level teacher," he wrote of one colleague. "Suggest he be kicked upstairs to full-time public relations work." "Good background but erratic and rambling in lectures," he wrote of another. "[Recommend we] transfer him to full-time evening staff in Newark." "Tries hard," he wrote of a third. "[Recommend] that he tries harder."[22] These assessments came from the gentlest of men on his way to becoming a Seton Hall institution. He had reason to be unsentimental: "The problem of seniors who cannot graduate is embarrassing," concluded one report. "A student who exhibits poor scholarship should be redirected into other fields." "The function of the teacher should be restricted to academic counseling . . . Emotionally disturbed students should be referred to adequate counseling."[23]

The satellite campuses were also in difficulties. Dougherty inherited a sprawling, quasifederated university whose urban division had grown too quickly and, in another sense, had not really grown at all. When Hakim wanted rid of an inadequate South Orange professor, he recommended him for "full time evening staff in Newark," an assessment not only of the teacher but also of Newark. Father Charles Murphy as librarian wanted "emphasis on . . . South Orange first, secondly on Paterson and Newark."[24] Jersey City, weakest of the satellites, closed on July 1, 1961, having struggled with poor classrooms, an inadequate library, insufficient laboratory space, and a limited curriculum, its closure "another step in [the University's] path towards academic excellence," claimed The Setonian, making the best of an embarrassing admission of failure. The 1,100 students who took courses there were mostly absorbed into South Orange, Newark, and Paterson. The original site of the Seton Hall School of Nursing, the Jersey City campus represented the university's inclusiveness, unpretentiousness, and willingness to take a risk. Its students and faculty genuinely lamented the loss. "Very few [Jersey City students] consider it a hardship to travel to Newark by tube trains," wrote Father Edward Fleming, defending the closure. Nearly 90 percent of Jersey City students, given a choice, wished to transfer to Newark and nearly 30 percent of Newark students, given the same choice, wished to transfer to South Orange. The major factor was convenience.[25] "Students using automobiles will appreciate the ample parking facilities at our South Orange division," Fleming continued. "The excellent facilities of Saint Peter's College will continue to meet the needs of many Hudson County students . . . We can take care of the demand for the next few years with our facilities at South Orange, Newark, and Paterson. We anticipate a need for a new facility for students in Hudson and Bergen counties."[26]

The closure of Jersey City drew attention to the inadequacy of the other campuses. Monsignor Thomas Gillhooley thought that in Paterson the "excellence binge" had a way to go.[27] The intellectual life of 31 Clinton Street in Newark also left much to be desired, many of the students tired after a day's work, taught by part-timers, lacking a decent library in which to work.[28] As an urban college, it reflected urban more than academic life.

Adding to the challenge was the extraordinary growth of community colleges, putting cheaper higher education within the reach of millions. Nationally, some 457 community colleges were established in the 1960s. Locally, the New Jersey County College Act (1962) got the ball rolling, allowing freeholders to establish county colleges to be funded by the state. New Jersey's first four community colleges were founded in 1966,[29] six more in 1968. The colleges were regulated by the New Jersey Higher Education Act (1967), which brought "sweeping changes" to the state's higher education landscape, establishing a separate Board of Higher Education, the office of chancellor, and the Department of Higher Education.[30] This institutional revolution caught Seton Hall off guard, in one way jeopardizing its supply of students, in another way encouraging it (in the form of those completing their degrees there). "We cannot oppose the community colleges," Fleming thought. "Perhaps they will serve a purpose."[31] As yet, no-one knew.

Solutions

Poor public relations, loss of morale, overstretched facilities, low salaries, and a weak urban division were not problems of Dougherty's making. Nor could he solve them alone. In 1962, he established a senate to "study and make recommendations to the University Council concerning educational policy and faculty welfare," an important advance in governance reflecting his democratizing instincts.[32] "A large and complex institution such as Seton Hall . . . needs the best thinking of all its staff members," he reasoned.[33] The new body, partly elective and partly appointive,[34] was not especially powerful, although its notional jurisdiction was substantial. Under the terms of the amended University Statutes, its "greatest competence" lay in making recommendations concerning

> [the] objectives of the university; the common curriculum; library services; research and publications; testing and examinations; the evaluation of proposals for new services, new departments, new schools and new centers; standards for appointment, induction, retention and promotion of university teachers; standards for admission, orientation, retention and graduation of students; faculty meetings; programs for upgrading faculty members; teaching loads; public relations; rules and regulations concerning absence because of illness, leave for study or other purposes, group insurance, retirement allowances, and fringe benefits; acceptance by faculty members of outside employment; grievances.

These were vital responsibilities if handled well.

The closure of Jersey City was the down payment. Soon, other ideas emerged: that a new campus be developed at Saddle Brook, New Jersey (where the university purchased 180 acres of land in 1962); that a campus be developed in Newark (for which architectural plans were drawn up); that, rather than develop Newark, the campus there should be closed; that the law school be moved to South Orange; and so on.[35]

Everything was in flux. And why not? The American Catholic college or university of the 1960s was organizationally hard to define.[36] Indeed, it was not clear how many Catholic colleges and universities there actually were in the United States, and how many Catholics went to them. (Many Catholics took degrees in public or non-Catholic schools.) The Committee of Higher Education of the NCEA reported 457 Catholic institutions of higher learning in the United States in 1969, 200 of them seminaries of one sort or another, 257 of them colleges or universities for lay men and women. To the extent that the statistics are reliable, by the middle 1960s, fewer than 30 percent of college-going Catholics (roughly 430,000) attended in Church-sponsored institutions, the remainder going to other private colleges or, the majority, graduating from the burgeoning public university system.[37] Between 9 and 12 percent of bachelor's degrees awarded in the United States were awarded by Catholic institutions and over 90 percent of these degrees were awarded to Catholics.[38] In other words, very few non-Catholics attended Catholic schools. With Seton Hall, Catholic numbers remained strong throughout the decade, but this was no guarantee they would continue that way. In fact, there was no guarantee that overall numbers would remain strong. The biggest concern was that the campus would be renewed but that there would be fewer students around to enjoy it. Enrollment had been steadily declining since 1956, reported *The Setonian* misleadingly.[39] In fact, in 1965, the university welcomed a freshman class of 825, the largest in twenty years.[40] Still, many feared loss of denominational identity, the quest for "excellence" possibly entailing a loss of localism. In addition, the disparity between Catholic schools was wide, many lacking regional accreditation while others (Notre Dame, Georgetown, Boston College, Fordham) enjoyed international reputations. By the end of the 1960s, only six Catholic colleges and universities were affiliated with Phi Beta Kappa. Notre Dame was an academic powerhouse,[41] able to attract and keep outstandingly good teachers and students.[42] Seton Hall was only beginning to realize that it had to do likewise.

Dougherty's Seton Hall or, more precisely, McNulty's, was typical of "the rest" rather than "the best," being solid but not brilliant. Describing American Catholic higher education at the end of the 1960s, Robert Hassenger captured Seton Hall at the beginning: "Basic student freedoms were not preserved, and there was considerable regulation of students' lives. Academically, the colleges seemed characterized by a rather anti-intellectual vocationalism, with relatively little interest in liberalizing courses and experiences. Passports to suburbia were being purchased."[43] Saint John's University in New York attracted students like Seton Hall's—aspirant, impatient, a bit rough around the edges.[44] Seton Hall was good at reinforcing lessons taught in strongly religious households but not so good at taking students from less devout households and making them more devout. In this, too, it was typical.[45] Many colleges were social and philosophical extensions of high schools and parishes; Seton Hall certainly was.

An Academic Revolution:
The College of Arts and Sciences

In 1960, the office of dean of the college of arts and sciences was separated from the office of vice president in charge of instruction. (For several years both had been held by Monsignor Thomas Cunningham.) The former position was filled until August 1961 by Charles O'Neill, an Aquinas scholar from Marquette University, when Father Albert Hakim of the department of philosophy was appointed to the post. Hakim was a transformational figure who professionalized the college, encouraging excellence, eliminating or attempting to eliminate the shoddy and the second-rate, introducing higher standards for appointment and promotion, reviving undergraduate programs, and introducing new graduate degrees. Cunningham had been "ultra-conservative"—his own description—in matters of academic policy.[46] Hakim was cheerful, sympathetic, and humane, a progressive who disarmed both traditionalists and radicals by negotiating a middle ground between continuity and change. His goodwill, intelligence, and devotion to the university were manifest. "I view my tenure . . . with a certain amount of incredulity," he wrote in 1973. "Janus-like, it looks back on the traditional way of 'doing education' towards the present, with all the disturbing ideological and political transformations in between."[47] His friend Father Larry Murphy summarized his significance many years later. "Institutions often have frail memories," Murphy wrote, "and I wonder how many people realize that Al was the prime mover during the turbulent 1960s in leading Seton Hall into the world of respectable academic stature."[48] Fresh and alert, Hakim welcomed new ideas while holding to first principles, always ready to offer an opinion about contemporary trends.[49] He was a model dean for a college of arts and sciences in a Catholic university.

The change was spectacular. In 1960, the twelve departments of the College of Arts and Sciences offered fifteen undergraduate degrees and four Master's degrees. In 1965, fourteen departments offered seventeen undergraduate degrees, six Master's degrees, and the PhD in chemistry. Asian studies, physics, and sociology became departments, with military science and tactics becoming another unit of the university. In 1960, there were 124 full-time faculty members, of whom about a third (43) had doctorates. In 1965, there were 173 full-timers, of whom almost a half (82) had doctorates. The improvement was achieved by natural wastage, dismissal of the incompetent, good appointments, and encouragement to publication. "We are attempting to get more PhDs," wrote Father Edward Fleming, "especially with the Middle States on our trail."[50] The attempt succeeded. This was a golden age for hiring. Jobs were to be had almost for the asking. Seton Hall was about to acquire some young and up-and-coming scholars from the luckiest generation in American academic history.

Departments

An assessment of the English department in 1961 revealed one professor who was "incompetent, digressive [and] barely adequate," another "unambitious because he has other income," a third "totally ineffectual, almost deaf," a fourth "over seventy, drawing a pension already."[51] (Hakim justified a $100 raise for a long-standing faculty member as "a kind gesture: no MA.")[52] The faculty had its share of eccentrics, among them Gerry Keenan, a bachelor, European traveler, and nonstop talker. Keenan, a graduate of Middlebury College in Vermont, lived in an apartment behind the university, walked everywhere, and shared his meals with old Russian emigrés. Appointments such as John Sweeney (a "Modern Renaissance Man"),[53] Laurence MacPhee (who had spent a year at the University of Lausanne in Switzerland),[54] and John Harrington (an ex-seminarian and another nonstop talker) showed flair. Sweeney was fluent in Latin and Greek, played flute and bagpipes, had painted over forty theater sets, built and ran toy train sets, and (at the time of his appointment) was writing a play for CBS. He was one of that generation for whom academic work was available in abundance: before coming to Seton Hall he had thirteen job offers.

Weak at the beginning of the decade, English was strong at the end. Sweeney, MacPhee, and Harrington were joined by David Rogers, a poet; Tom Duff, a

Shakespeare scholar; and James Paris, an expert on film. Ranjee Shahani, author of *Shakespeare through Eastern Eyes* and biographer of Gandhi, struck some students as a sage.[55] The Catholic literary magazine *Spirit* came to Seton Hall in 1969, and under David Rogers it published special issues to the poetry of Scotland, Wales, Sweden, Italy, and (especially) Australia. With readers in England, Israel, and Italy, for nearly ten years until it ceased publication *Spirit* placed Seton Hall in the forefront of Catholic poetry in America.

Asian studies, chemistry, history, and social studies were among the best departments in the university, and the first of these among the best in the nation. They "seem to have the spirit," wrote a visitor from the University of Pennsylvania in 1965, a "faculty composed in large and refreshing part of young men of promise."[56] Asian studies was created as a department in 1961, Chinese and Japanese having been taught by the Institute of Far Eastern Studies, McNulty's Cold War creation of the 1950s. (It was to be the department of Asiatic studies until the "depreciatory and pejorative" connotations of the adjective were noticed.)[57] Its success was extraordinary. In 1965, every qualified teacher of Japanese in a secondary school in the continental United States was Seton Hall-trained, as were half the teachers of Chinese. The department was responsible for a twelve-volume series of Chinese language textbooks used in high schools and colleges throughout the country. The extraordinary John Wu transferred his allegiance from the law school to teach in it. John Tsu, chair of the department, was "the most outstanding Chinese linguist in the world," his work required reading at leading universities.[58] Tsu was later connected to the Nixon administration and the State Department, where the department's national reputation rested heavily on him.[59] By the end of Dougherty's presidency, Tsu had assembled a remarkable faculty, attracted gifted students, developed strong graduate and undergraduate curricula, and, as Hakim remarked, encouraged a "vast number of scholarly publications."[60]

Of these, the most notable was the multivolume Chinese language series. Its chief author, John De Francis, was an outstanding Sinologist whose career reads like an adventure story. A Yale-trained economist who graduated in 1933 and found it impossible to get work, he went to China where, abandoning a business career for librarianship, he immersed himself in books about China and the Chinese. In 1935, aged twenty-three, he and a companion retraced the route of Genghis Khan, a journey recounted in his 1993 book *In the Footsteps of Genghis Khan*, describing a trek of a thousand miles by camel across the Gobi Desert followed by twelve hundred miles down the Yellow River on a raft of inflated sheepskins.

Returning to the United States in 1936, De Francis enrolled as the first PhD student in Chinese studies at Yale, later transferring to Columbia. His first academic post, and almost his last, was as assistant professor in the Paige School of International Relations at Johns Hopkins University. When the director of the school, Owen Lattimore,

was targeted by Senator Joseph McCarthy as America's leading communist agita-
tor, De Francis defended him, losing his job as a result. He abandoned Sinology for
a job as a vacuum-cleaner salesman and a mathematics teacher at a private school in
Connecticut.

John Tsu and Seton Hall rescued him. With the creation of the Asian studies department and the Red Scare abating, Tsu offered him a six-month contract to write
a first-year textbook of Mandarin Chinese. The manuscript delivered, Tsu then used
the book to obtain federal funding for a more advanced text. Eventually, Tsu and De
Francis received hundreds of thousands of dollars of federal support for the project,
Beginning, Intermediate, and *Advanced Chinese,* popularly known as "the De Francis series." De Francis left Seton Hall in 1966 for the University of Hawaii, from which he
retired in 1976. When he died in his late nineties in 2009, he was a giant in the field. His
association with Seton Hall was brief, but without John Tsu's intervention in 1961 this
extraordinary scholar might have been lost to Asian studies.[61]

Another star was John Montanaro, a formidable teacher of Chinese who began
his career at Seton Hall before leaving for Yale in 1974. Wong Fang-yu ("Fred" Wong)
came to the United States from mainland China after the Communist takeover in
1949. His version of the classic story *The Lady in The Painting* remained a standard text
for years. (Yale University recognized him with an honorary LLD). Later, Winston
Yang came to the department, bringing with him a wealth of contacts. One graduate
of the program, recalling her first visit to China in 1982, found that Seton Hall was
recognized wherever she went.[62] For this, the university had John Tsu, John Wu, John
DeFrancis, John Montanaro, and Fred Wong to thank and, more remotely, John Mc-
Nulty and the CIA.[63]

The department of history was formed out of the social studies and political science department in 1968, and within five years it had become as good a department
as any comparably sized one in the country.[64] In 1960 social studies had two PhDs in
a faculty of twenty. In 1965, history and political science had eleven PhDs in a faculty
of twenty-three. In 1960, only one faculty member had published a book. In 1965, the
number of books stood at eleven. History and political science (with over 400 majors,
Seton Hall's largest department) at one point thought of establishing a PhD program
which, although abortive, suggested confidence,[65] as did the introduction of a Russian
area studies program under James O'Donnell in September 1964.[66] Most of the credit
for history's resurgence went to the chairman, George Reilly, who snapped up talented
historians and made them feel wanted: Ralph Walz, a Seton Hall graduate with a doctorate from New York University, a fine Germanist; Bernard Sternsher, an authority
on the New Deal; Bernhard Scholz, a superb mediaevalist from Germany; Joseph Mahoney, expert on the progressive period in New Jersey history; John Duff, a twentieth-
century immigration historian; Carl Prince, who wrote on early colonial America;

Peter Mitchell, an Americanist from Iowa by way of Colorado; William Mathes, a Columbia-trained expert on Russian universities; Phyllis Stock, a Yale-educated Europeanist specializing in French intellectual and educational history;[67] Edwin Lewinson, who, blind from birth, nevertheless completed a Columbia PhD in twentieth-century American history. (In a minor way, Lewinson made history as well as wrote it. A political activist, he was familiar to the police and occasionally the courts.)[68] They made a cheerful group. Only historians, considering course offerings, could vote "that the French Revolution be changed to Saturday morning."[69] Reilly, a widely published specialist on Britain, Ireland, and Catholic history, was humorous, intelligent, and slightly distracted. John Tracy Ellis, dean of American Catholic historians, admired him as a "fine fellow" and "a great credit to Seton Hall."[70] His house in South Orange became a salon for the talkative and thirsty of his flock. Few did more to raise the profile of Seton Hall or more engagingly personify it.

Although not a member of the history department, Herbert Kraft was an archaeologist specializing in native American cultures and the country's leading expert on the Lenni Lenape Indians. Kraft joined the university in 1960 as curator of a newly formed Natural History Museum.[71] Kraft was enthusiastic, knowledgeable, and curious. The university did not make as much of its collection as it should have, but not for want of energy on Kraft's part.

The historians epitomized the good luck of academics who came of age in the 1960s, many from modest social backgrounds. Peter Mitchell, born in the depths of the Depression when the birth rate was low, came of age when the Boomers had to be taught. Before coming to Seton Hall, he was interviewed by sixteen other schools. Even without a finished doctorate he was offered a position at $7,200 a year. "My father was amazed. He retired a decade earlier and made ten grand in his final year as managing editor of our daily newspaper."[72]

Because the department was big and the disciplines different, political science eventually broke from history. In 1965, out of a total of twenty-three full-time professors in the department of history and political science, six were political scientists. In 1966, the university inaugurated a political science major, attracting 194 majors within a year. In December 1967, the University Council endorsed the creation of a department of government. The departments remained close through ties of friendship and interest, but the separation was beneficial for both.

Elsewhere, the department of communication arts was "in excellent shape," with a "splendidly devised" journalism curriculum, with mass communications "imaginatively . . . taught," and with a student newspaper providing "a fine laboratory" for would-be reporters.[73] The chairman of the department, Al Klose, with vast experience in Midwest radio stations, had been on the faculty since 1953, pioneering curricular developments that later bore fruit.[74] If anything, communication arts was a victim of its own success, growing faster than the university as a whole and accounting for nearly 10 percent of undergraduate enrollment in 1974. A greatly expanded faculty found itself squeezed for space in the basement of a new humanities building, which was poor as far as teaching basic journalism was concerned. Of this building, more later.

For a Catholic university where things of beauty are supposed to matter, Seton Hall was surprisingly deficient in visual arts, having no full-time instructor in art in 1960 and only one course to cover all Western and non-Western traditions in music, painting, sculpture, and architecture. In 1961, the university hired its first full-time instructor in art history and added a course in Italian painting of the renaissance. Over the next years, the classical, medieval, renaissance, baroque, rococo, and modern periods were also covered, a studio was opened in Paterson and in 1968 a department of art and music was established in South Orange, gathering together some altogether impressive people: Louis De Crenascol and Barbara Kaufman to teach art, and Walter Cohrssen and Julius Zsako to teach music. De Crenascol, Cohrssen, and Zsako were all European imports, De Crenascol from Italy, Cohrssen from Germany,[75] Zsako from Hungary. De Crenascol had been director of the Museum of Fine Arts at Lodi and a Fulbright scholar at Harvard before coming to Seton Hall in 1961.[76] A lawyer by training, he had standards almost too much high for American egalitarian taste.[77] Cohrssen was Seton Hall's only music teacher for a time (and the only one ever to have his own string quartet performed at Carnegie Hall). "The art of hearing classical music is one thing the Seton Hall student has too long ignored," he said.[78] To remedy this deficiency he had support from Dougherty, an opera fan and friend of opera singers, who invited the Amadeus Quartet to the university in 1961 and Leopold Stokowski and the American Symphony Orchestra in 1963.[79] These efforts to improve the tone prompted some hostile reviews. Father Edward Fleming thought that "too many chamber concerts can be as bad as too many hootenannies . . . [they] are activities which are on the fringe of the objectives of the University . . . Our students are notoriously unenthusiastic about chamber music . . . Therefore we have to hit our faculty or our house priests or have the university pick up the tab."[80] In 1973, the art component of the department of art and music moved to the Arts Center, the renovated Carriage House close to South Orange Avenue, a rehearsal room and storehouse and singularly unsuited for any purpose other than that for which it was originally built in the nineteenth century.[81] (It was de Crenascol's idea to transform the Carriage House and have it registered as a national landmark. He found the funds to do so.) The musicians worked in Corrigan Hall.

The department of classical languages, vital for divinity students, flourished during Hakim's deanship. It suffered a blow with the death of Monsignor Joseph Christopher in September 1964 (an outstanding Latinist), but with Fathers Vincent Monella, Gerald

O'Sullivan, James Sullivan and Eugene Cotter it remained in good hands. Cotter was a slight figure of a man, funny, energetic, and clever, full of good stories, mostly against himself. The finest scholar in the department was Basil Steciuk, a Ukrainian fluent in English, Latin, Greek, Polish, Russian, Ukrainian, Czech, and Slovak. With two doctorates and over thirty books and articles to his name, courtly, dignified, warm, and never boring, Steciuk was, according to fellow classicist Tom Fahy, "exceptional" as a man and scholar.[82] The department was "a tremendous improvement over the former part-time system."[83]

Few scientists took Seton Hall seriously during the McNulty years (even after the construction of McNulty Hall in 1953, which was custom built for them). But Hakim's undergraduate training in physical sciences made him an energetic promoter. Physics scarcely existed as a subject in 1960, being a handful of courses, mainly geological in nature, taught by Father Hubert Funk of the department of mathematics. (Funk was another Seton Hall character: one of the last priests to smoke cigars and to wear a cassock on which the remains of his breakfast were all too visible.) Seton Hall "should and could [have been] a major factor" in physics, said one graduate, but was "looked down at" by employers who tended to choose products of the better-funded state universities for their intake.[84] A department of physics was created in 1962 under Eugene Petrik, a Columbia-trained algebraist who complained of "its meager resources just now struggling to reach the point of respectability."[85] His colleagues were Funk and Dr. Henry Miller. By 1965, the department, now more demanding,[86] had grown to six professors who, although not yet distinguished in research, produced many of the high school science teachers in the state. Petrik did not stay to see the department achieve the honors it would later win, but he gave it a respectable start.

A small biology faculty in 1960 became, in 1965, a department of seven PhDs with twenty years of teaching or industrial research between them.[87] Biology did not count highly at the beginning of the decade, consisting of eight courses, one program, poor facilities, and rudimentary laboratory work. Father Mike Fronczak, a capable teacher of general science, was distracted by administrative duties. In 1960, the combined facilities and faculty consisted of one laboratory, one PhD, three teachers, thirty microscopes and, presumably, several dead frogs and mice. Only one faculty member, Nicholas de Prospo, engaged (with great ability) in research. Five years later, with better students and more programs,[88] De Prospo was determined to see his discipline taken seriously. Thanks to Hakim, it was.

Chemistry was the success story of the decade. New Jersey needed chemists and Seton Hall produced them. The seeds of the department were sown in the 1950s when McNulty decided that priests properly trained in hard sciences should teach in his new medical school. The growing pharmaceutical industry in New Jersey also played a

role. Two brilliant priests, Al Celiano and Owen Garrigan, initially trained in classical languages, were retrained to doctoral level in chemistry, Celiano one of the first
men of the Archdiocese of Newark to undertake full-time work towards a PhD in a
nontheological subject,[89] Garrigan one of few to study at Columbia University. (Garrigan contributed science articles to the *New Catholic Encyclopedia*.) McNulty looked to
Celiano for leadership of the department in 1959, but within a semester of his arrival
three faculty members had resigned, complaining that McNulty had reneged on his
promise to offer a doctoral program in the subject. Celiano was forced to create what
was in effect a second department almost from scratch. By the middle of the 1960s,
a department of eight full-time faculty members, six with doctorates, had grown to
one with thirteen full-timers, twelve doctorates, and a PhD program (offered for the
first time in September 1963). The department's best researchers were Robert Conley,
Robert Augustine, Paul Ander and, later, Roland Hirsch, a cohesive if occasionally
self-enamored group, conscious of its superiority over other departments in research
and publication.[90] In 1960, fewer than 20 percent of Seton Hall's chemistry graduates
went on to graduate work. Five years later, the number was 75 percent, half in a PhD
program. The majority of chemists no longer graduated "with an attitude that they
have been short-changed . . . They . . . have been given . . . a first-rate education which
prepares them well for continued studies and careers in industry."[91] Celiano raised the
department from mediocrity to excellence. Chemistry was the most successful fund-
raising department in the College of Arts and Sciences[92] and Seton Hall chemistry
graduates among the most accomplished alumni of the university. Apart from those
who landed scholarships to top-notch medical schools, Bolesh Skutnik earned his doctorate at Yale and joined the faculty at Brandeis; Robert Shine did his PhD at Penn
State and became a professor at Trinity College in Washington; Lawrence Chapoy did
a doctorate at Princeton and took a position as at the University of Uppsala Institute of
Physical Chemistry in Sweden. Seton Hall, said Chapoy, was "a vital part of my education," giving him "the independence and creativity" expected of scientists.[93]

Balancing successes were difficulties. "The faculty of the department of sociology
is uniformally [*sic*] non-descript and non-productive," wrote its chairman in 1970. "Few
do anything professional beyond the call of duty."[94] The "Barracks is still very unsatisfactory," he complained, teaching sociology in a classroom that was itself a sociological study. "From utter chaos it has improved to the status of quite unbelievable."[95]
New blood at the beginning of the decade in the form of Brigitte Sys, appointed to
teach French in 1960,[96] did little to lessen the anemia of the department of modern
languages, where only Eden Sarot had a noteworthy scholarly record. The department
regarded itself as "a poor relation" to the rest of the university, an assessment the rest
of the university shared.[97] The "prevalence of smoking in some of the classrooms"
made serious work difficult,[98] as did student immaturity.[99] Visitors were impressed

by students who were "courteous, articulate, knowledgeable, and [really loyal] to the university,"[100] but the view from the trenches was not always kind.

Religion and Philosophy

Nowhere was Hakim's academic revolution more apparent than in religion and philosophy. The search for a core curriculum, for some courses or integrative principle to hold together the work of different classrooms, had been the quest of Catholic education for years. Should theology be at the center? Or philosophy? Or catechism? Or religious instruction? Or moral formation? John Henry Newman gave priority to theology in *The Idea of a University* (1845), which conceded that it was impossible to do theology without cultivating a "philosophic habit of mind." But "religion" broadly defined as personally transformative knowledge was also important. In 1929, the Catholic University of America established a department of religious education under Father John Montgomery Cooper, its purpose to deepen students' awareness of faith in their daily lives.[101] The Thomist, Father Walter Farrell, O.P., condemned the experiment as a dilution of the subject. "The offices of professor, retreat-master, preacher, and confessor" should not be confused, he said: theology should retain primacy in Catholic colleges.[102] The English Catholic historian Christopher Dawson proposed Christian culture as another integrative principle, culture itself understood as incarnational, part of the continuing revelation of Christ in time. The notion of Western European civilization as essentially Catholic and Christian was an appealing idea to many. Catholic educators could teach a broad range of subjects—history, literature, art, music—in a way that honored their uniqueness while stressing their interconnectedness and revelatory power.

To help colleagues think more clearly about these questions, Hakim invited guests from other institutions to share their experiences. Barry Ulanov of Barnard College urged "a greater revolution than the revolution created by Pope John," arguing that the thirteenth century "disjunction between philosophy and theology" had been "catastrophic" for Catholic intellectual life, leading to a delimiting of experience and a false compartmentalizing of knowledge. "As we teach religion now in the Catholic college or university," he said, "I think we build up a whole series of firm membranes against any understanding of religion, against religious experience which is even more important." His recommendation was that "you should teach religion and not theology, because theology leads to that kind of rationalistic vocabulary, out of Thomism, from which Catholics can ultimately suffocate." The teaching of theology as religion was harmful. A proper religion department, he said, "should offer either by itself or by working with anthropology departments, sociology departments, and other departments in which this sort of scholarship would be encouraged."

There was a fallacy in Ulanov's argument (he was comparing apples and oranges) but his enthusiasm appealed to David Rogers of English, another enthusiast, who complained of "frozen theology" driving "the potentially brightest student" out of the classroom. "Taken to its extreme," Hakim thought, Ulanov's position was implied that "all reality is united and therefore [there should be] no departments—[no] one college in which reality is 'taught' and [another in which] reality is experienced." Ulanov was only proposing an interdisciplinary approach to religion and the liberal arts that owed something to Jacques Maritain's notion of integral humanism but this was more ideal than reality. "We all like to say, 'let's start from zero, Cartesian-wise, and let's build a college from the ground up',"[103] said Hakim, but as a working dean he did not have that luxury.

He was, nonetheless, a serious reformer. Hakim worried that there was such a plethora of low credit courses in philosophy and religion "as to induce academic ane-mia." He urged a reduction in their number and an increase in their value. (That said, philosophy benefited from his hiring spree, with Gerard Dalcourt and William Radtke appointed in 1962, Dalcourt never wavering from the Thomism he was appointed to teach, Radtke branching out.) Hakim thought the department of religion should change its name to theology "in keeping with the desire to tone-up scholastic interest in revealed truth." He even thought of combining both subjects into a department of Christian wisdom but abandoned the idea as "doctrinally and administratively unfea-sible." Theology as "the rational elaboration of the data of revelation" should hold a special place within a Catholic university, he argued.[104] But Father Edward O'Toole, his replacement as chair of philosophy, feared that what Hakim took to be tidying up, others would take as a wholesale change to the curriculum itself. "Some [faculty] are de-emphasizing the importance of Saint Thomas in the regular core courses," O'Toole announced to a departmental meeting in 1962. "This practice will have to stop."[105] O'Toole's response was less to defend Thomism than to enforce it (which was a pity, because O'Toole was a fine defender of Thomas.)[106] Aquinas had become a trademark of a certain kind of Catholicism. At Seton Hall, no-one was supposed to speak when Aquinas was in the room. More precisely, no-one was supposed to speak, not even Aquinas, when O'Toole had the floor. His department had to teach scholastic philoso-phy whatever the taste of the teacher, making it dry and disliked.

Once its unusual language had been mastered, Thomism represented a way of looking at the world. Everything depended on how well it was taught. "Most instruc-tors," complained one student, "either completely ignore the text or are hopelessly tied to it . . . the errors of each philosopher are graphically pointed out and [then], for the ninth time, the 'complete' answer of St. Thomas is retold in all its celestial glory." At best, it was versatile, beautiful, and clear. At worst, it was jargon-choked and dull.

Graduating philosophy seniors wishing to do postgraduate work had to take an-other year of undergraduate philosophy before other colleges would enroll them,[107] suggesting a program either old-fashioned or in need of repair. "Official approval of a certain line of thought could and did produce a party-spirit which was narrow and polemical," even Frederick Copleston could write. "In many ecclesiastical insti-tutions Thomism, or what was considered such, came to be taught in a dogmatic manner analogous to that in which Marxism-Leninism is taught in Communist-dominated education."[108]

Not the least reason for teaching St. Thomas was that alternatives to him were dire. One member of the philosophy department argued that philosophers "whose program is to guide . . . and enlarge the horizons of life" should take LSD.[109] Another instructed his class on how to break into the Pentagon, providing blackboard diagrams of the building.[110] Compared to that, the *Summa Contra Gentiles* was not so bad after all.

The philosophers modified their curriculum, scrapping one credit courses and abandoning exclusive reliance on Thomism. The de-emphasis on Thomism was man-dated by a new core curriculum in 1969 that reduced the combined philosophy and theology load from twenty-four credits to nine. Thomism had kept the department alive, providing large and captive audiences. Once its monopoly was broken, students began to notice "the personality problems of some teachers, the abstract nature of phi-losophy itself, [and] the long-standing accusation of bad teaching on the part of some of our full-time staff."[111] The philosophers should have thought of that sooner.

The new 1969 curriculum also made a difference to theology. A department of theology was created out of the department of religion in 1961. The old department was hardly a department at all, with only one full-time teacher and many part-timers[112] teaching courses "suffocatingly dogmatic."[113] (In the 1950s, Father William Furlong re-dundantly urged priests teaching religion to take the oath against Modernism.)[114] This dogmatism changed in the late 1950s as a number of priests returning from graduate study at Notre Dame introduced new thinking into their teaching. Father Frank Nead became chair of the reconstituted department of theology in 1961, and in 1962 the first lay teacher, Vincent Zamoyta, was hired. For a time, the offerings of the department went down well (and compared favorably with those of philosophy). "The theology department has made considerable progress," said *The Setonian* in 1964. "Most teachers approach theology in a healthy way—to draw religion out of man, not to pour it in to him."[115] But the department enjoyed only a brief life before it, too, acquired the itch for reinvention. The "kerygmatic" approach to theology gave way to "pre-evangelization" (preparing students to receive the message, or "kerygma" of Christ) before this was abandoned as insufficiently attentive to cultural, historical, sociological, and anthro-pological approaches to religion. In the middle 1960s, Hakim was convinced that theology had to choose between being "dead and neglected" or taking "the pressure of the times [to] live; but if choose life, it has need of three things: a university setting, lay participation, and the Ecumenical dialogue."[116] Even as the department became less clerical, he worried that the university showed "lamentable lack of commitment to the training and preparation of personnel" for new responsibilities.[117]

By the end of the decade, reflecting changes in wider academic world, the department adopted "a . . . scientific or objective [approach to the subject, offering] systematic, critical, and historical study of religion . . . as a given confessional position."[118] In July 1967, the Land O' Lakes conference (a group of Catholic educators meeting under the auspices of the International Federation of Catholic Universities) declared that theological faculties should "engage directly in exploring the depths of Christian tradition and the total religious heritage of the world" to "come to the best possible understanding of religion and revelation, of man in all his varied relationships to God." The purpose was no longer to provide religious instruction or moral formation but to explore religion as a multicomplex phenomenon. By 1969, the department committed itself to providing "liberal education in the Catholic tradition," no longer comfortable with the "traditional . . . connotations of piety" of religion and theology.[119] This departure "gravely concerned" a couple of traditionalists who did not "not like to think of . . . theological innocents wandering aimlessly from course to course in theologies which must be considered exotic in the western world."[120] Edward Fleming regretted that theology, now "the weakest and most unsettled" department in the university, was in "turmoil" because of its introduction of "the 'new' theology."[121] Mostly, the new major offered serious courses taught in a serious way, but even the liberal-minded Hakim later conceded that some changes went too far, with syncretism much in vogue and "being Catholic less important . . . than being religious."[122]

What happened with philosophy and theology was of a piece with what was happening in the rest of the Church.[123] In 1968, some of Seton Hall's theologians publicly dissented from *Humanae Vitae*, Pope Paul VI's encyclical forbidding artificial means of birth control. Given the departmental turmoil of the previous decade, such dissent might have been predicted. More surprising was the response of the Board of Trustees, which was to take "no specific action . . . at this time," preferring to "seek from the members of the department agreements as to limitations upon expressions of their dissent from the Encyclical both in the classroom and in any public forum." The Board further expressed concern for Catholics and non-Catholics alike "who might be confused or worried by this situation."[124] Few were more confused, it seemed, than the Board itself. Progressives had little to fear, and traditionalists little to hope, from such timidity. A year later, Thomas Melady, chairman of department of Asian studies and U.S. Ambassador-designate to the Vatican, warned Cardinal Cooke of New York that Seton Hall was "undergoing some tensions" with "a very small but articulate clique . . . out to break [its] essential Catholic nature." [125] At least they were articulate.

What constituted the "essential Catholic nature" of the university was a component of the larger question of what constituted the essential Catholic nature of the church. To that question, many answers were offered in a decade in which, as Philip Gleason suggests, the Second Vatican Council caused the Thomistic edifice to topple "almost overnight" like "a house of cards."[126]

Seton Hall was one of a thousand schools, parishes, and families to experience the same bewilderment. Many students rejected the Church as an institution (according to the university chaplain in 1969) while being "open and warmly receptive to the priest as a person." Traditional attitudes were "often rejected without inspection or evaluation" while attendance at Sunday Mass remained "good."[127] There was no easy way, at Seton Hall or elsewhere, to interpret these confusingly contradictory signs of the times.

An Honors Program

Revitalizing old subjects and old teachers while giving students an opportunity to stretch themselves was the reason Hakim inaugurated a humanities honors program in September 1962, one of about 200 such programs in the country. Its purpose, said *The Setonian*, offering a mildly eugenicist token of approval, was to "draw a higher type of student to the university."[128] The program's progenitors were Father William Keller of the social studies department and John Harrington of the department of English. The two made a formidable if oddly matched team: Keller quiet, reserved, and exceptionally well-read, Harrington larger than life, literature-obsessed, and incapable of one word when a hundred would do. Seton Hall's best students, they felt, were poorly served by professors plodding their way through the usual dull textbooks. When such students applied to graduate or professional schools, they were lost in the shuffle, undistinguished from the rest of the pack. Using Columbia University's Western civilization program as a model, Keller and Harrington created a curriculum examining the Western experience as a whole, beginning with the ancient and classical civilizations and ending in the contemporary world, the emphasis on the mutual dependence of philosophy, literature, art, and religion. Together, students would gain "a perception not only of the past-ness of the past, but of its presence . . . The liberally educated man is truly a free man, liberated from prejudices and preconceptions, capable and thinking and judging for himself in the light of the traditions of the past. He possesses a full conviction of humanity's uniqueness and of its vast potential in this world and ultimate goal in the next world." Human liberation was to be achieved, bathetically, by "frequent use . . . of audio-visual aids, films, plays, concerts, recordings, [and] television."

Asked to evaluate the program after two semesters, students praised "a fine idea at a school which had previously been renowned only for its basketball" and the "only thing that makes going to Seton Hall worthwhile." The objective was achieved, Keller believed, "if not with total success, [then] with some measure of satisfaction."[129] Although Keller and Harrington saw themselves as pioneers, the program was not universally loved. "Father Keller stopped by to ask about women on campus who have been dropped from the Honors Program," Edward Fleming wrote in 1964. "All these girls seem to gravitate to the beatnik type of boys (boys who, incidentally, could not possibly qualify for Honors Programs)."[130] Hoping to attract "the higher type of student," the program represented the struggle on every campus to raise the academic tone. When the philosopher Anton Pegis gave a talk on "Philosophy and the Middle Ages" he was "annoyed by [one] student reading a newspaper."[131]

Pegis's talk, the first of what was to become a series commemorating the granting of Seton Hall's charter in 1861,[132] recalled an earlier appearance at the NCEA conference in 1960 where he lent his reputation to the Catholic quest for "excellence." Yet Catholic colleges, as Philip Gleason has pointed out, "were not in a position to *define* academic excellence." They had "to look elsewhere for models to emulate—places like Harvard, Columbia, and the University of California."[133] When the Honors Program took Columbia as its model, it borrowed a standard of academic quality at the cost of its own curricular distinctiveness. "The liberally educated man" may have been liberated from "the prejudices and preconceptions of the past" but that goal, when not merely a cliché, ran counter to Seton Hall's custodianship of the Catholic intellectual tradition which was itself both liberating and hemmed in by history. If Catholics could not be sure they had a distinctive intellectual vision, perhaps Seton Hall's honors program was an example not of confidence but the opposite.

Keller and Harrington were highly strung, unwilling to compromise with student indifference and, ultimately, with each other. The honors program lapsed in 1970–1971 (to be revived in 1978 under Bernhard Scholz of history and John Sweeney of English). Short-lived, the first iteration of the program left a significant legacy. In 1962, Keller and Harrington created a literary and film series called "Commentary" which lasted five years despite "almost insuperable" faculty apathy.[134] Harrington later revived it as "Poetry in the Round," bringing major writers to campus and winning Seton Hall a national reputation as a venue for intelligent literary conversation. The reputation was already evident in 1963, when the university hosted the annual meeting of the Catholic Renascence Society, among the speakers Bishop (later Cardinal) John J. Wright of Pittsburgh, the novelist Paul Horgan, the psychiatrist Karl Stern, Father Ernan McMullen of Notre Dame and, from Seton Hall itself, Monsignor John Oesterreicher. (Two weeks later, the university welcomed Archbishop John Heenan of Liverpool, future Cardinal Archbishop of Westminster.)[135] The honors program, which continues today, was an important component of the intellectual and cultural revival of Seton Hall in the 1960s.[136]

Division for Humanistic Studies

In the fall of 1966, Hakim created the division of humanistic studies, its aim to acquaint students and faculty with the latest thinking about feminism, war, peace, and human liberation. Under Robert Pollock, a retired professor of philosophy at Fordham University, and his assistant Francis Caminiti of Seton Hall's department of philosophy, humanistic studies offered courses with a "human component" conveying "deeper understanding of contemporary man." Hakim considered Pollock an "original and passionate exponent of Christian humanism . . . always contemporary and 'turned on' . . . helping young people break out of a mood of alienation by locating them in a world of meaning." With "startling acuteness" he had a "vibrant feeling for *homo americanus*."[137] After Harvard, Toronto, Bowdoin College, and Notre Dame, Pollock spent most of his career at Fordham, where he represented an intellectually important attempt to bring Catholics to terms with mid-twentieth century thought.[138] "I would say that in most of our university class, there is little communication," he told a seminar in 1965. "It's minimum, it's a waste of words . . . There's nothing to dig into . . . I want a person who is alive himself and I find that he is making me alive."[139] "Consciousness evolves, experience evolves," he said, risking laughter, "from pre-historic man to students in South Orange today."[140]

If it was odd that Seton Hall should hire a pensioner to explain modern youth to itself, Pollock made good on his agenda. "The Contemporary Dialogue between Christians and Marxists" could have been offered in many universities in the later 1960s, but for Seton Hall it was a novelty. Also typical were "The Phenomenon of Women" and "The Meaning of Death," the first in homage to Teilhard de Chardin, the second an attempt to speak about the meaning of life without recourse to such a title. (The inventor of "The Phenomenon of Women" was Nancy Rambusch, a pioneer in early childhood education who antedated by several years the wave of women's studies of the early 1970s.) More daring were "Psychotheology" and "The Meaning of Aspiration," the first a combination of phenomenology and psychology promising psychedelic experience but delivering only sociology, the second an exploration of the "strains of thought" of "Emerson, William James, Paul Tillich, Bob Dylan, and the Beatles," a few traditionalists (such as James McGlone of the department of communication) straining to find in the last two any connected thought at all. The spirit was captured in "Perspectives in Mind Expansion," a study of "the way in which contemporary man views the problems of the expansion of our mental universe through subjectivity, experience taken in its multidimensionality, the development of awareness, nonverbal experience, and the expansion of perceptiveness." Celebrating nonverbal experience with extreme verbosity, the course collapsed under the weight of its own weightlessness.

Humanistic studies annoyed faculty members who felt patronized by its favored status and by Pollock's pose as a guru even as he pretended to disclaim the role. ("We must break down the image of the teacher as figure of authority, the father image," he claimed. He and Caminiti, who hero-worshipped him,[141] were known as "the Doctor and his assistant.")[142] At best, humanistic studies was exploratory and adventurous. At worst, it was amorphous and vague. "He was recognized by colleagues and students as a vibrant teacher who had a way of turning students into disciples," recalled Hakim of Caminiti. "As a person, he was friendly, gregarious and warm. As a philosopher and teacher, he was definitely a mystic."[143] Pollock and his associates saved the careers of some floundering students, but when Hakim left the deanship in 1973 to assume directorship of what was, by then, the Center for Humanistic Studies, the venture had become marginal, with even those teaching in it recognizing its inadequacies. Thomas Cahill, later to achieve fame as author of works of popular history, skewered it: "I have a gnawing fear that we are misleading them—and ourselves. We cannot teach them about the NOW—*they* are the NOW, much more than we are . . . How can we compete with The Grateful Dead, Ken Kesey, Dennis Hopper, and the Whole Earth Catalog?"[144] How indeed?

The Core Curriculum and New Styles of Learning

Underpinning arguments about new and old ways of looking at the world was a sense that the core curriculum of the College of Arts and Sciences (which constituted a *de facto* core for the university) needed reform. According to a 1967 report of an *ad hoc* committee of the college, "the traditional ideals of a liberal education and the need to encourage intellectual curiosity" rendered the existing core obsolete. The only schools with "larger and more rigid core curriculum requirements were . . . weaker Roman Catholic institutions." This claim begged several questions. In one or two cases, the boredom of the instructor may have been projected onto the student. It was also odd that a coherent program of logic and epistemology should have been seen as a sign of intellectual inadequacy. Be that as it may, a revolution on behalf of student choice was presented as a *fait accompli* to students who had no choice in the matter. From the history department, George Reilly argued that the existing curriculum was "too rigid and contains paternalism that is the hallmark of high school." From the department of government, Richard Connors urged "a gradual loosening up" of requirements. From modern languages, Edward Henry wanted a "minimum" core. Students were also un-happy. "This is not a factory and we are not automobiles," said one. The "stuffy old philosophy and theology requirements" irritated another.[145]

The key figures in the reform were Hakim as dean and Owen Garrigan of the department of chemistry. The result was a radical reordering of the curriculum, with theology and philosophy reduced to six and three credits respectively, and with increasing priority given to electives. The new curriculum was "quite conservative in comparison with existing practices at institutions other than Roman Catholic ones," but Seton Hall's traditionalists took little comfort from the comparison.[146] Student arguments in favor of the new core were alarmingly dismissive of the old one, repudiating its "outdated educational philosophy," its assumption that a "liberally educated man must know something of the basic elements which runs through his society's cultural thought." James McGlone considered the new core an academic free-for-all: "There has been some cosmetic work done on course titles, and certain departments have been willing to woo students with extra time on their hands with strange sounding studies. The religious studies department (theology) in particular has offerings in Religious Dimensions of Media Experience and a course in Theology and Sexuality!"[147]

The impressively named Student Senate Undergraduate Educational Policy Committee (an example of the young imitating their elders just as their elders were imitating the young) railed against memorization, examinations, grades, and "antiquated teaching methods." "No area of knowledge [was to be] preferred over another," its rhetorical certainty at odds with its epistemological skepticism: "The lecture-examination-grade method, regardless of its intention, must stifle the individual's growth. The student must be made to behave passively if the lecture material is to be covered. When the ever-present bell signals the beginning of the period, everyone must submerge their [sic] individuality into the stagnant puddle called the class . . . As a result of this passivity the student grows apathetic, like a spectator at a dull ball game." "We are at the dawning of a new age," wrote one faculty member. "An age of world community, an age of the global village, an age in which men are discovering how close they are to one another not only in kind but also in space, an age in which the communiversity [sic] is struggling to be born."[148] Aquarius was winning out over Aquinas.

"I'm an old guy who tries to mind his own business," complained a physicist, "but I am shocked at what is developing . . . This year [1969] the undergraduate program is going to hell on a bandwagon."[149] For ultra-progressives, the new core was insufficient; for traditionalists, it was (almost literally) the end of Western Civilization as they knew it. Tucked away in a corner of campus was Community House, where the "Free University" made its home. It seemed to vindicate both claims: "The Free University is a service extension of the Community House. The Free University is called 'free' [because] we have tried to free ourselves from the bureaucratic paraphrenalia [sic] which surrounds the 'un-free' University . . ."[150]

Community House attracted notable visitors over the years (Saul Alinsky and Nat Hentoff)[151] but it offered mainly self-parody: "We are free of teaching requirements;

anyone wishing to teach a course or organize an action-oriented program is welcome and encouraged to do so . . . Since we believe that a person has a right to explore any avenue leading to a new knowledge and experience, we must conclude that if any person organizes a course or program on *any* subject and can attract a number of people to his [*sic*] course, that course has justified its existence . . ."[152] The Free University ended in bathos. "When people mention the Free University or Community House, people think of tuna fish [said Father Robert Antczak, its director]. 'It's kind of sad. I've never envisioned the alternative society being defined by a 35¢ tuna sandwich.'"[153]

In place of the "lecture–examination–grade" method came the "dorm course," whereby a few teachers met the students in their natural habitat, seeking themselves to blend in. It was unclear what a "dorm course" meant but the history department tried to come up with a definition:

> Driscoll: This will be a dorm course but it will take place in a classroom.
> Mitchell: If it is in a classroom, how can it be a dorm course?
> Lewinson: I propose that we rename it a student-initiated course.
> Markoff: I propose that we rename it a glorified bull session.[154]

No-one pointed out that dormitories were places for consciousness-lowering, not the opposite. The idea was discontinued.

An Academic Revolution:
Business, Education, Nursing, and a Library

Within three years of Dougherty's becoming president, Seton Hall's faculty was better trained and more productive, its administration more professional, its physical plant updated, its academic reputation on the rise. In 1957, the School of Education had thirteen full-time faculty members, all located in Newark. By 1963, with all graduate work now consolidated on the South Orange campus, the number had increased to thirty-one. The School added a four-year daytime program in elementary education in Newark and a department of special education in South Orange, the latter to improve student reading and speaking skills. A program in audiology and speech pathology started in September 1962. In John Callan, the School of Education had a strong dean, in Bernard Duffy an excellent assistant then associate dean. Duffy came to Seton Hall in 1961 as a professor of secondary education and served for thirty-five years as "one of the most student-oriented administrators in the entire faculty."[155] The teaching staff were "sincere, dedicated, hardworking, and uncomplaining." On the other hand, too many courses were textbook taught, teachers spent too long commuting between campuses, and salaries were low. "There seems to be a passion in general for good teaching," concluded the Middle States report in 1964, "but little excitement in the pursuit of, or the adventure in, new ideas in education."[156] Still, the movement was in the right direction. In 1967, there were forty-three full-time faculty members, almost half of them holding terminal degrees. The office of educational media and practice under Ruth Cornfield was a boon and the division of education research under Albert Reiners was a clearinghouse for best practices in the field. "The greatest evidence of our coming of age," said Callan, "is the respect that is recorded to the School of Education by the professional community in New Jersey."[157]

The School of Nursing, still in Newark, was graduating bright students. In the cheerfully discriminatory language of the day, nursing students had to give evidence not only of "better than average intelligence" but also of "good health, emotional and social maturity, good breeding, pleasing appearance, [and] proper motivation."[158] Strong teeth also helped.[159]

Many "well-qualified, alert, and stable" faculty were engaged in graduate study.[160] Tucked away in Newark, the faculty wished to relocate to South Orange to enjoy closer communication with colleagues in physical, biological, and social sciences. That would have to wait, but by the beginning of the 1960s the need was becoming more urgent. The other problem was Newark's lack of laboratories. With the best will in the world, no-one could seriously train to be a nurse in Clinton Street alone.

The School of Business Administration, with more full-time and fewer part-time teachers, was more professional by the mid-1960s, much of the credit going to Robert Senkier, who arrived as dean from Columbia University in January 1962 and who, like Hakim, refused to renew contracts of inadequate teachers. (Senkier, a veteran, was present at the signing of the Atlantic Charter between Roosevelt and Churchill in August 1941.)[161] His appointment coincided with the publication of two reports on business education in the United States, both faulting the "descriptive and excessively specialized" courses offered by most schools. One of Senkier's aims was revise the curriculum (he had written a book on the subject)[162] to give greater attention to English, psychology, government, sociology, history, mathematics, and physical and natural sciences. "What the public expects of business has risen dramatically since the end of the Second World War. The Seton Hall School of Business Administration [has] an important responsibility in this area, whether we like it or not, because the large corporate enterprise in America has become an instrument of national policy."[163]

Senkier understood his role expansively. Businessmen had social responsibilities and Seton Hall had a duty to teach them. Computers would relieve middle managers of routine functions, giving them "additional time for community welfare work." (He failed to notice that computers might also relieve middle managers of their jobs.) He worried about "a narrowing of vision and an over-concern with vocation," never defining the difference.

At the beginning of Senkier's tenure, the School of Business Administration was mediocre, its scholarly reputation low, its local engagement minimal. In 1962 he launched the semiannual *Journal of Business*. He also established an Institute of International Business, offering MBA candidates a certificate in international business to take advantage of Seton Hall's proximity to Port Newark and Newark Airport. He created an alumni association, started a Middle Management Development Program, and established a Business School Advisory Council to improve links between students, teachers and administration. Above all, he argued for a new facility for the School in South Orange as the only way to make permanent the improvements he sought.

Within five years of his appointment, the undergraduate program was essentially the same as programs offered at the Wharton School at the University of Pennsylvania and at Boston College. The MBA program was comparable to those at Stanford, Harvard, and Columbia.[164] Eighty percent of graduate students came from outside Seton Hall and undergraduate applications were "slightly better" than before.[165] Less than 40 percent of the faculty had terminal degrees in 1964. By 1966, 56 percent had doctorates or the equivalent. Only 30 percent of the faculty had an article or book to their name in 1966 (not bad compared with other schools). Salaries were modestly on the up although it was normal for business faculty to have second jobs (and some of them menial).[166]

The School of Business Administration had characters. Gordon Dippel, a bachelor who lived above a funeral parlor, came from Villanova by way of doctoral work at Columbia to teach finance in 1962. He never left (even after retirement). Irving Alpert, one of few accounting professors with a PhD, was one of the most effective teachers in the school. Bill Dineen was casual, easy-going, and popular (perhaps because he gave the same final exam every year). Emil Hensel, an accountant, was happier playing music. Of the school's five departments—economics, finance, marketing, management, and accounting—accounting was the best and economics the most influential.[167] But the School *did* lag behind the competition. When Dippel went to academic conventions, no-one would talk to him because Seton Hall's salaries and its Catholicism marked him as suspect. A panel of assessors reported in 1964 that "thirty-five faculty members share ten desks in one room in the library."[168] Only in the 1970s, with a new academic building in South Orange, did that change.

Rounding out the decade, the library flourished under Monsignor William Noé Field. Since the opening of the McLaughlin Library in 1955, holdings had doubled and the staff had become more professional.[169] The collection was strong in philosophy, theology, history, political science, classical languages, and mathematics, adequate in English and American literature, weak in education, geography, sociology, fine arts, music, and foreign languages. "What we don't have," Field admitted in 1966 "is terrifying." Against this were a good reference section, the MacManus and Murphy collections (of Irish and American Civil War materials respectively), and well-developed reader services.

As librarian, Field was idiosyncratic. "In the early summer I requested [revision] of the rules for classroom dress so that women might be permitted to wear slacks in the library."[170] This complaint made its way to the authorities in November. "I cannot reveal my long-range plans, which are frequently intelligent . . ."[171] Of a colleague seeking promotion, he wrote that "she has been engaged in the selection . . . of books to combat Communist propaganda."[172] Of new trends in social science scholarship, he wrote that "[we need] to beef up our collection either by, or about, blacks."[173] Material on the Index of Forbidden Books had to be kept separately and "closed to general use" (an exclusion applying only to Catholics). The philosopher and physicist Father Stanley Jaki, requiring his students to read Descartes, was told that "the book which you have requested . . . is on the Index. The Library is not permitted to make these books available to the Catholic student body."[174] (Jaki went on to win the Templeton Prize for Religion.) Students may have wondered about a regime that in one class urged them to read as much as possible and in another urged them not to read at all.

An Institutional Revolution: Campus Development

In November 1962 Dougherty appointed a university development commission under Father Edward Fleming "for the purpose of formulating plans for the future expansion of the university."[175] Asked to imagine Seton Hall in ten years' time, they realized that biggest problems were shortage of classroom and office space, inadequate residences for priests, insufficient dormitories, and the university's modest academic ambitions. South Orange was at or near capacity in 1963, with enrollment of 4,315 daytime students. In the next ten years, an anticipated 10,000 students would need to be housed, taught, and fed in a facility designed for a tenth of that number. More and better students, more and better teachers, meant more and better buildings such as, for example, a Life Sciences and Arts building for the College of Arts and Sciences; the conversion of the second and third floors of McNulty Hall for physics and chemistry; a building for the School of Business Administration; a new library; proper dining facilities. Construction to the tune of $11.5 million would be needed to bring Seton Hall into the second half of the twentieth century.[176]

Some ideas appeared and disappeared with the regularity of migratory birds (better science facilities was a particular favorite),[177] but within the decade Dougherty had started or completed new dormitories, a student center, offices and classrooms for the College of Nursing, the School of Business Administration, and the College of Arts and Sciences. A previously bucolic campus began to seem crowded and filled in. In that sense, Seton Hall resembled the rapidly growing state as a whole, and its plans for expansion mirrored those of neighboring institutions such as Rutgers.[178]

The dormitory was called New Boland, a large, modern extension to Bishop's Hall (or "Old Boland"), which dominated the South Orange Avenue frontage of the university. Begun in September 1965, it was built in 1966 and 1967 at a cost of $2,350,000, funded mostly from federal grants and loans.[179] Not yet complete, it opened in March 1967 with room for more than 700 students, doubling the residential capacity of the university.[180]

The new student center was announced in 1961, begun in 1962, and completed in 1963. Part of the funding came from the Bayley-Seton League, which contributed $25,000.[181] All chrome, glass, and awkward angles, it had a theater, a main lounge, a huge dining area, a bookstore, a corridor-cum-art gallery, and other nooks and crannies. The Student Center defined the "new heart" of Seton Hall, claimed *The Setonian*.[182] Dougherty thought every ear should "tingle" at its name.[183] Students liked it but conceded that it took getting used to.[184] The most notable feature was a theater-in-the-round that was to see hundreds of plays performed thousands of times, directed by Professors James McGlone and Gil Rathbun.[185] Rathbun called it the Workshop Theater. (McGlone did not). The first production, directed by Rathbun, was Henri Gheon's *The Comedian*, which opened in December 1963, dealing with the conversion and martyrdom of Saint Genesius, patron saint of actors.[186] "It is true that 'all the world's a stage,'" Dougherty wrote, "but as far back as classical Greece the stage has been confined to a much more restricted space . . . I have wandered through the ruins of theatres in Athens, Ephesus, and elsewhere. Back home in South Orange, sitting in the President's chair and planning the Student Center, I was able to realize a dream. My hope for the Theater-in-the-Round is that it will not only move the 'conscience of the king' but also move the general audience to laughter and tears."[187]

The student center was only the beginning. Designed by Swiss-born architect Emil Schmidlin, the Humanities Building (later called Fahy Hall) was begun in 1966 and dedicated in 1968 at a cost of $2.5 million.[188] (Construction was delayed by a strike of building workers).[189] A brick-faced warren of classrooms, offices, lecture theaters, and a television studio, it won no prizes for beauty or functionality. The Humanities Building was home to the College of Arts and Sciences, with philosophers, historians, and literary people on one floor, linguists and classicists on another, mathematicians and theater types consigned to the basement.

The most pressing need was for a home for the School of Business Administration, which moved to South Orange in 1968. "In 1962 . . . when nobody had adequate facilities except the Law School and Science faculty members, no serious criticism was heard," Senkier reported in 1968. "Now that the Humanities . . . and the School of Education . . . have been taken care of, the School of Business faculty finds itself at the bottom of the barrel."[190] Senkier exploited his connections to find funds, chief among his supporters W. Paul Stillman, head of two of the state's largest corporations. With a gift of over $310,000, Stillman was the building's most generous ·patron (not bad for a man who had reached the top without benefit of a college education, let alone a business degree). The Board of Trustees agreed to the construction in February 1968, the building to be located between the Student Center and the Humanities Building. Designed to accommodate 1,500 students with offices for 60 professors,[191] it cost $2.1 million. A tribute to Stillman, the building was also a tribute to Senkier, who, when he resigned in 1974 to go to Fordham, said that his twelve years at Seton Hall had been "the happiest and most productive" of his life.[192]

The needs of the School of Nursing outstripped even those of the School of Business Administration. In 1937, when the first batch of eight students began classes, they did so in rented rooms in St. Patrick's School, Newark, the headquarters of the university's Urban Division. Its progress thereafter has already been detailed. In 1968, the school moved to South Orange under Dean Agnes Reinkemeyer, a Franciscan Sister of Mary who was appointed to raise money for a proper facility. Born into modest circumstances in rural Missouri, Reinkemeyer graduated in nursing from St. Louis University and completed a doctorate at the University of California at Berkeley, one of only 500 people nationally to hold the degree at the time. Within three years of coming to Seton Hall, she had raised $1 million from the federal government, corporations, foundations, and individuals. The School of Nursing became a College in 1971. Reinkeymer was supported by Mrs. Caroline Schwartz, née Di Donato, who had been closely associated with Seton Hall nursing from earliest days. In 1969 she became the first woman to serve on the University's Board of Trustees. Schwartz and her husband were among the most generous benefactors in the College's history. Sister Agnes remained dean of the College until 1977.[193]

The nursing and business schools shared a conjoined double building opened in May 1973, which housed offices, classrooms, and lecture theaters. Low-lying and irregular, constructed of marble and glass, it cost slightly over $3 million, the nursing side of the building requiring two-thirds of that amount, the business side one third. To mark the opening, the School of Business Administration was formally renamed the W. Paul Stillman School of Business, making Stillman the first layman so to be recognized at Seton Hall. The nursing building was named for Caroline Schwartz.

Finance

Dougherty spent money he did not have. All presidents do. Capital expenditure came out of a capital account made up of loans and mortgages and other forms of indebtedness. He was not the first president, nor the last, to hope that buildings would attract the students who would ultimately pay for them. The transformation of the campus suggested a healthy ledger, but day-to-day finances suggested otherwise. As the student center was opening, Dougherty was told by his vice president for business affairs, the aptly named Robert DeValue,[194] that the "overall financial condition of the University" was "bleak," that Seton Hall had "no reserve to fall back on," that its cash situation was "precarious" and "critical," that deficits were inevitable, and that failure to remedy the problem "would mean we will soon be in a position where we could not meet our payrolls." *"This is a critical situation,"* De Value emphasized. "I need not tell Your Excellency here what the results of this situation would be."[195]

It was foolish to run a deficit of nearly $700,000 in 1963–1964 and another in excess of $500,000 for 1964–1965 as if there would be no consequences. *"We must put the University on a pay as you go basis,"* he told Dougherty,[196] suggesting not so much an end to long-term debt (which was manageable) as to short-term deficits (which were not). Seton Hall's problem was not that it was borrowing too much for the long term or that it was spending too much in the short term (although it was), but that it did not know the extent of its immediate liabilities and was thus was living beyond its means because it did not know how to live any other way.

Fixing the problem was easier said than done. The University could boost its income, reduce its expenditure, or do both. To do the first meant a hike in tuition, which was never easy in a university with a moral and historical commitment to provide education to the less well-off. To do the second meant a smaller operation, such as the possible closure of Newark and Paterson. To do both ran the danger of giving the public less and charging them more for it. To do nothing meant disaster.

Complicating the situation was the university's relationship with the archdiocese, which was one of codependency and, occasionally, mutual resentment.[197] "Since we are a University of the Archdiocese, I do not think it improper to receive aid from the Archdiocese," De Value thought. "Obtaining [its] support . . . to cover any cash deficit" was vital. On the other hand, such support was not a gratuity. (If anything, the indebtedness ran in the other direction. In 1964, for example, De Value reckoned that the Archdiocese owed the University $1,095,000, from a loan of $1 million given to the Archdiocese by the University in 1950). Seton Hall provided services to the Archdiocese for which payment was due: educating nuns and clergy at 50 percent discount, a subsidy extended to other dioceses who pocketed the gift and offered little in return; providing offices free of charge in 31 Clinton Street, Newark for a score of diocesan agencies; allowing the use of facilities such as the gymnasium to diocesan personnel who, paying nothing, contributed nothing to their upkeep and maintenance; and so on. To be fair, the archdiocese returned the favor by providing modestly remunerated clergy in large numbers to teach and work at the university. So who, precisely, was subsidizing whom? (It was a question as old as Seton Hall.) "If they do not permit us to raise tuition fees," De Value wrote to Dougherty of the Archdiocese, then "aid" from them "would be almost mandated,"[198] as if somehow the University had to ask permission from an outside body before setting its prices. But, of course, the Archdiocese was not an outside body. It was the sponsoring institution.

The crisis passed, but it prompted reflection not so much on the tangled financial relationship between Archdiocese and University—that was a fact of life—as on the inadequacy of Seton Hall accountancy—another fact of life. Some of the endowment was in a noninterest-bearing checking account.[199] There were no manuals defining the policies, procedures, and reporting relationships of the university. There was no uniformity of bookkeeping practice between South Orange, Newark, and Paterson. The annual budget bore little relationship to monthly expenditures. No-one knew how much money, if any, was being made by the four bookstores run by the university. Some business activities (athletics, for example) did not come under the business manager at all.

Any management consultant could—and did[200]—point out multiple failings. Competitive bids were not sought for large purchase items. Bank balances were not reconciled to the general ledger. Payroll filing systems were inadequate. Students not fully paid up for courses could complete them. ("Professors should be instructed to prohibit these students from taking final examinations," a management consultant said.)[201] Certain student loans were repayable to the wrong office. Accounts receivable were not received. Invoices and purchase orders were often discrepant. Some offices were understaffed. (In Paterson and the Law School, the latter a budgetary law unto itself, only one person was responsible for receiving cash, maintaining student financial records, preparing monthly statements of accruals and cash summaries, and making bank deposits.)

In themselves, these were small problems. Together, however, they represented a major challenge that posed almost as many difficulties as untangling the University's relationship with the Archdiocese. To their credit, senior administrators were increasingly insistent that Seton Hall be run more professionally. Relative prosperity (such as enjoyed in McNulty's last years) concealed, and made possible, the lax standards. Tighter times meant tighter procedures. Under Dougherty, sensible improvements were made and fat trimmed. But similar complaints recurred decade after decade.

University Governance

When Dougherty became president, deans and departmental chairmen were unchallenged in their domains, with faculty members enjoying little formal (although much informal) power over hiring and firing. This had to change.[202] The way to make faculty more responsible was to give them more responsibility, a "dangerous innovation,"

Father Tom Fahy drily noted. Fahy urged that department chairmen be chosen by departments because "it is better in the long run to yield a measure of control to the faculty [gradually] than to allow pressure to build up to a crisis."[203] The Board of Trustees agreed, although Archbishop Boland remained dubious. In October 1967, at his prompting, it had a "lengthy" discussion "on the question of the faculty's role in the University."[204] The creation of a Faculty Senate that year, reconstituted from the older senate of 1964, addressed the question of governance, but the Board had to be persuaded. "Problems . . . might arise," it was told, "from this new participation of the faculty in educational policy making . . . such a radical change [was] predicated on the Board's approval of faculty participation in educational policy making [but] the faculty should have a voice . . . and the University should benefit from their participation insomuch as the faculty are the professionals in this field."[205]

Throughout the decade, some power shifted from the administration to faculty and students, although most decisions remained with the president (who chaired meetings of the senate and wielded a veto). "The Faculty Senate never serves to originate ideas," a student noted, "except when they want a pay increase."[206] But to the extent that administrators came to complain of it, faculty power was becoming a reality. It took another generation for a reconstituted Faculty Senate to achieve significance in the 1990s, but the effort of 1967 was a down payment.

Coeducation

By 1966, as the university approached its 110th birthday, 95 percent of Seton Hall students came from New Jersey. (In 1962, to illustrate the point, a mere 90 percent of Rutgers students came from New Jersey. Seton Hall was more of a state university than the state university itself.) Ninety-two percent of undergraduates in South Orange were Catholic. The number for Newark was 93 percent, for Paterson 88 percent, for graduate students and law school students 74 and 58 percent respectively. "The primary mission of this university is, almost certainly will continue to be, and in our judgment should remain, service to New Jersey Catholics," the Board of Trustees insisted.[207] In one sense, though, overwhelmingly Catholic Seton Hall was not Catholic enough. Fully one half of the Catholic population—women—were largely ignored by it. "Girls" could take classes in Newark and Paterson, but South Orange remained a male preserve. In that, it was little different from other Catholic colleges, which were either all male or all female, segregated by gender for moral, practical, and physical reasons. But a gender revolution was soon to break out in higher education, and Seton Hall was to play its part in it. "When women first arrived on formerly male campuses," Leslie Miller-Bernal and Susan Poulson have written, "they faced a culture that had no established place for them, which had no process of acculturation for women, and few mentors or role models. [They] faced the challenge of redefining those subtle, quiet norms, in the minds of others as well as in their own."[208] As with the nation, so with Seton Hall.

Between 1954 and 1966, the number of women in third-level education in the United States increased by 143 percent. In September 1963, more than 40 percent of all New Jersey residents in full-time college education were women (the figure was 39,414). Assuming that roughly 40 percent of the population of New Jersey was Catholic, at least 15,765 New Jersey Catholic women attended college somewhere in the United States. Most of them did not attend New Jersey colleges. In fact, only 2,149 New Jersey women attended Catholic schools full time in the state, and even if all these women were Catholic, as they were not, it meant that only 14 percent of New Jersey Catholic women who attended college full time did so in a New Jersey Catholic college. A demand existed and Seton Hall could satisfy it.

Yet why coeducation and not simply more Catholic women's colleges? One reason was that, given a choice between women-only Catholic colleges and coeducational schools, many Catholic women chose the latter. A substantial number even preferred non-Catholic over Catholic schools as long as they were of mixed sex. (This preference for coeducation was true for men also and was evident elsewhere: at Notre Dame, for example.)[209] Coed women were also better prepared academically than men. It was "easier to get intellectually superior girls than boys," Edward Fleming noted in 1963. "At the present time, try as we may, we are having difficulty maintaining admission standards. We can't seem to attract intellectually superior boys in any numbers."[210] One argument for coeducation, that it was good for women, concealed the subtler argument that it was also good for men, forcing them to compete academically and to improve their manners. At other Catholic colleges such as Georgetown, similar arguments were heard: that the way to improve an all-male school academically was to allow women to attend it.[211]

Over the years, Newark had seen many women go through its doors to be taught by a partly female faculty. In Paterson, women did well as teachers and as students. Did these facts argue for making the satellite campuses, not South Orange, the vehicle for Seton Hall's coeducational ventures? No. Condescension marked the attitude of the main campus to the satellites (so that, for example, a member of the Board of Trustees could write that "there seems to be an operation in Paterson—I'm not clear what this school does but I have the impression it is a business school.")[212] Newark's daytime programs were restricted to nursing and elementary education, Paterson's to social studies, English, and philosophy. Science was hardly taught at all. Both campuses, Newark especially, lay in problem neighborhoods, so that a staff of Pinkerton guards had to be hired in Newark in 1966 to protect female students from molestation. If the argument for moving freshman and sophomore courses to South Orange was strong, the case for making Newark and Paterson Seton Hall's only coeducational campuses was weak.

In any case, nursing students had to do laboratory work in South Orange and no-one seemed to mind as long as they came in the evening. Administrators favored co-education, with some provisos. ("Since certain difficulties may be foreseen in view of the presence of the Divinity School, it is observed that Divinity students attend separate classes.")[213] Edward Fleming was "personally" in support of coeducation. John Callan thought it "highly desirable." Robert Senkier insisted on "the important place for women in American business and industry." (Women could take courses in ac-counting, finance, marketing, economics, and business in South Orange but only in the evening and only if such courses could not be taken elsewhere. Paterson offered day-time courses for women; Newark operated in the late afternoon and evening.)[214] Albert Hakim, arguing in favor, pointed out that "after all, women aren't freaks."[215] There were objections, of course. The fact that women were already part of the univer-sity became, eccentrically, an argument for having one campus, South Orange, remain male-only. It was foolish (the reasoning ran) to discriminate against men to appease a phantom grievance of women. Then came the problem. "Most . . . college men . . . agree that girls [have] a distracting effect upon their male counterparts. I'm definitely pro-girls—but not on campus."[216] In universities such as Rutgers, the admission of women was often seen as a matter of civil rights, the next step in a long revolution to put an end to all forms of discrimination and segregation.[217] For Seton Hall, the ques-tion was not articulated so grandly, but for many faculty and administrators that was the implication and the desire. At Seton Hall, as at Georgetown, women had already been part of the university for some years, so that it might be more accurate to speak of an evolution rather than a revolution. Either way, the transition in both schools seemed natural, not forced.[218]

By the middle of the 1960s, then, Seton Hall had a strong school of nursing and a growing school of education but a poor liberal arts program to attract women. Its physical plant was designed with men in mind. Its satellite campuses, especially Newark, posed security problems. The main challenge was cultural rather than aca-demic, the need to overcome the notion that women went to college largely to find husbands, a view sometimes expressed by women themselves. "Our Catholic women students meet our men in a limited way in 'glamorous' set-ups—dances, social, etc.," noticed a committee of female faculty members in 1960. "Our Catholic philosophy should force us to show concern for the fragility of today's marriages. Part of the Catholic women's education, particularly on college level, should take place with the men of her own background. This should be the natural state of affairs rather than awaiting social events to bring Catholic men and women together."[219] Articulating

"Seton Hall's responsibility to its women," the committee, quoting Saint Paul, insisted that man is "the image and glory of God: but women is the glory of man," drawing the conclusion that "our Catholic women can be guided into understanding her [sic] role to be complementary not competitive." Such a view did not appeal to all women. At Rutgers, opponents of coeducation feared that bringing young men and women together would lead to early marriages and a population explosion.[220] Perhaps, as Poulson and Miller-Bernal have argued, the "virtual collapse of sexual segregation in formerly men's colleges undermined the gender ideals of traditional Catholicism," making "Catholic higher education more like other colleges and universities."[221] Seton Hall did not shy away from articulating those ideals or from using coeducation as a way of restating them.

Women were to be admitted in a trickle, with numbers restricted to 125 a year to keep disturbance to a minimum. "If we were to go co-ed on the South Orange campus," wrote Fleming in 1963, "it would only be on a dayhop basis. We would need no residence halls for women in the foreseeable future."[222] "Men will [still] outnumber women by at least three to one on the campus," the Board of Trustees was told in 1967.[223] When women arrived *en masse* in February 1968—640 of them—the result was an anticlimax. "Right now, the presence of girls on campus simply improves the scenery" was one fairly typical adolescent response, repeated in hundreds of campuses across the country. "Most of the fellows were annoyed by the congestion in the parking lots."[224] "The university was unprepared for the girls," said Carole Pasquale, a chemistry student, "but that's not unusual because they're generally unprepared for everything."[225] "Very little advanced planning went into the move from Newark to here," conceded Edward Hendrikson, director of student affairs.[226] "We don't have much contact with boys," observed a nursing student. "We're mostly homogenous groups, always together except for liberal arts courses." One administrator noted that women rarely joined in "apart from a few cake bakes and fraternity mixers." "The guys on campus have a dorm to unite them . . . the girls have no tie that binds. [They] are [as] estranged from the University [as] the male day hops." [227] Dougherty reported to the Board of Trustees in 1968 as if the fuss had been about nothing. "The young ladies integrated into the academic life of the campus with remarkable ease and smoothness. Their presence here seems entirely natural and wholesome."[228]

Women were expected literally to muck in. Chris Carlson, a nursing student, liked the campus but objected to "tramping through mud to classes—it gets rather messy." "My only objection is the amount of mud that seems to have an affinity for nylons," echoed Ilona Fisher. "The atmosphere is friendlier than many of us had expected," said Elaine Lusardi. "It's nice to go to a college that has a campus instead of an office building surrounding it," said Judy Barberio. "It's certainly a lot cleaner here," said Pat Gahan, "and it's nice to see trees and grass instead of empty booze bottles on the sidewalks." Betty Davis, an education major, "appreciated the spaciousness of the library," a "big improvement over the one in Newark." "The eating facilities are much better. In Newark we always went out to eat." The men were friendly, said Cathie Bylinksi, "but if you don't join a club of activity you are out of it." [229] Men made concessions but still tended to think of the university as their own territory. The idea of women as guests, not equals, was hard to shake. "The ties and jackets that were worn the first couple of weeks have disappeared and the girls have stopped setting their hair every night. Seton Hall has settled into the groove of a co-educational institution." [230]

Blending in yet standing out, women arrived on a campus increasingly divided along political lines. Among the first to arrive was Vicki Mezzo, who, bucking one trend by coming to a largely male campus, bucked another by identifying with ROTC. "Picture the times. Anti-war protests and the Vietnam War going on. Some of us brave gals were willing . . . to strike out in new direction, because we loved our country then as now, and because we supported, then and now, the guys/gals who defend us." It was tough work. "We practiced in the parking lot where the Walsh Gym stood, [the] majority of us commuters . . . Morning after morning, sharing the time and space with the guys . . . Talk about early morning wake up. The crisp air and the drills had us ready for our 8 AM classes!" [231]

Coeducation presumed, perhaps overconfidently, a degree of maturity on the part of students at first unused to each other's company. Professor Hirsch Silverman of the College of Education saw the miniskirt as a sign of servility and long hair, in men, an indication of sexual inadequacy. "Girls who try to advertise their femininity only by vast exposure of the erogenous zone may be psychologically or emotionally poor," and men with "abundant hair" and "superfluous gaudy clothing" were probably "in need of psychotherapeutic help." [232] Poised between old and new moralities, The Setonian embraced both. In March 1968, it carried advertisements for the Paulist Fathers ("Be Yourself—Individuality is an integral element in the life of a Paulist") [233] and, in April, for Belle de Jour ("Luis Bunuel's Masterpiece of Erotica!"). [234]

One fear, that coeducation would keep men out, proved illusory. In fact, as Fleming acknowledged, no man was deprived of a slot by a woman: in 1968 "we accepted every male applicant who met the . . . requirements." Women enhanced the academic profile of the university, gravitating towards sociology, communication arts, psychology, and secondary education, and making those disciplines better by their presence. They made better mathematicians than the men. [235] "Women students on the campus have had a wholesome effect," one committee reported, stating the obvious. [236]

Female faculty members found it hard going at first. Chrysanthy Kehayes, who taught English, was told by a colleague that she had deprived a male breadwinner of a slot. (Her answer, that she was sole breadwinner of her own extended family, broke the ice and began a lifelong friendship.) Amelia Klepp complained that women were treated as second-class citizens, a view dismissed by Fleming as "kittenish nonsense,"[237] the refutation of the argument vindicating it. Some women were undoubtedly lonely.

Newark

Linked to coeducation was the future of Newark, where overcrowding and underfunding had been evident for years. The possibility of closure had been discussed in 1961 (and made plausible by the closure of Jersey City). A "strictly confidential" meeting of university vice presidents in November 1961 "agreed that Seton Hall should concentrate as much as possible in an area where unit costs are lowest" and that "thoughtful consideration be given to the transferral of all courses from the Newark Division to the South Orange Division."[238] (This did not include the Law School.) In 1964 the "unanimous consensus of the vice presidents" was that the university "phase out of the Newark operation."[239] Even with 2,200 students in day and night programs and 600 women day students doing nursing and elementary education, Newark was increasingly unfeasible, losing money.[240] Accordingly, its closure was announced in March 1967, for reasons of "prohibitively high" costs and the "unjustified duplication of facilities already available or under construction on the South Orange campus."[241] The "city of Newark can be served better at its South Orange campus," the Board of Trustees claimed, "which actually borders on Newark and is only four miles from Broad and Market Streets."[242]

The curtain came down with little fuss. The Board granted permission for "approximately 100 girls to be enrolled in courses in secondary education, the College of Arts and Sciences and the School of Business" "in connection with the move of the University College from 31 Clinton Street, Newark to the South Orange campus."[243] Thirty-One Clinton Street was leased to Essex County Community College for three years for an annual rent of $200,000, with a right of first refusal if the university decided to sell. (The following year, it was sold outright for $800,000.) McQuaid Hall, built in the early twentieth century as an infirmary and for several years an overcrowded men's dormitory, was earmarked as the home for the School of Education and $170,000 set aside for its renovation. (The renovation was difficult—its walls were sixteen inches thick[244]—and far from perfect. Forty-three faculty members had to fit into twenty rooms.)[245]

Seton Hall Preparatory School

The closure of Jersey City and Newark, the coming of women, the air of institutional renovation, all pointed to serious discussion about the future of Seton Hall Preparatory School on campus. The school was linked to the university not only as a feeder of some of its ablest students but also as the home of many diocesan priests who were

often themselves products of the school, the university, and the seminary at Darlington. It was common for a man to teach at the high school, then transfer to the university, so that prep school priests, who lived on campus, were as much part of the Seton
Hall "family" as their university counterparts. One half of the graduating class of the
prep went to the university, the transition as natural as moving, quite literally, from
one room or building to another.

The Prep was funded from tuition payments, but the university also subsidized it
to the tune of approximately $90,000 per year, part of which represented the cost of
maintaining Mooney and Duffy Halls, the school's classroom buildings. When the
school ran a deficit, the university balanced the books. The tangible and intangible
benefits of having the school on campus were important to both institutions. But one
year's deficit could be absorbed; a multiyear deficit could not. The Prep had been a
deficit operation for several years, and by the middle 1960s the university's patience
was wearing thin. Moving off campus became more likely in 1967 with the possible
purchase of a site in North Caldwell, New Jersey for that purpose. Another possibility
was for a financial restructuring of the school. A third approach would be for the Prep
to distance itself academically as well as financially from the university, becoming (as
the minutes of one Board meeting rather unfortunately put it) "a 'quality' school" with
higher tuition and standards and with the aim of placing its graduates in more competitive universities. The last option was to close it down.

Removing the Prep from campus was impossible. Purchasing a site and constructing new facilities meant a capital expenditure of $2 million, an amount beyond it.[246]
"Give them financial independence," DeValue, wrote to Dougherty in 1967. "Let them
have their own business operation. I do not see why our university students should
subsidize the Prep School."[247] But "financial independence" meant raising tuition costs
to cover expenses, an idea that gave the Board of Trustees pause. Conscious of the
school's "original purpose" to serve students of modest means,[248] the Board wanted to
make a Seton Hall education as affordable as possible.[249]

In the end, the Board settled for a full study and report into the school's operation
and prospects, deciding a few months later that the school should stay on campus "for
the foreseeable future." The subsidy continued pending the establishment of a separate
accounting system so that the financial situation of the school could be determined.[250]
The Preparatory School remained in South Orange.

The foreseeable future turned out to be longer than many imagined. Seton Hall
Preparatory School remained on the South Orange campus until 1985, when it moved
to facilities bought from the old West Orange High School. In its new location it
thrived as an academic powerhouse thanks largely to the exceptional leadership of
Monsignor Michael Kelly (who knew thousands of students by name). One or two
of its priest-teachers remained resident on the South Orange campus, notably Father

Joseph Wortmann, famously enthusiastic for all things German. Although the move was best for both institutions, something was lost as well as gained when the Prep left for West Orange. For the first time since 1861, no schoolboys were seen on the South Orange campus, a kind of historical fracture.

Student Life

Seton Hall's curriculum, faculty, and campus underwent a revolution in the 1960s. By contrast the student body, often thought of as the most revolutionary element in any 1960s university, was conservative or—what sometimes amounted to the same thing—indifferent to political engagement of any kind. Students were more attuned to their parents' cultural world than that of their professors. "He never said the prayer before the class," complained one student of an economics teacher in 1963, "nor did he even bless himself" before—worst offense of all—he taught the "really heretical" free-market theories of Ludwig von Mises.[251]

Conservatives could be contrarian. In 1961, a student invitation to William F. Buckley, editor of *National Review*, was rescinded by Alfred Donovan, vice president for student affairs, who baulked at his criticism of Pope John XXIII. (Buckley had attacked the encyclical *Mater et Magistra*, calling it a "venture in triviality" and, using a phrase he came later to regret, spoke of his own position as "mater si, magistra non.")[252] "I am not against controversy," Donovan said, "but to invite Mr. Buckley now might be construed as condoning his stand."[253] In 1963, the Edmund Burke Society invited Professor Andrew Speigel of C.W. Post College, Long Island, to speak on "Edmund Burke and the French Revolution" with part of his honorarium to be paid by the Intercollegiate Society of Individualists (ISI), a conservative tax-exempt foundation. The invitation was withdrawn at the last moment (Spiegel was told at the behest of the administration, in fact at the behest of students), which prompted conservative author Russell Kirk to question Dougherty's integrity and his knowledge of Burke. "If Catholic university presidents set to work discriminating against both conservatives and liberals," he said, "what will become of academic standards on those campuses?" None of these imputations were true and, threatened with legal action, Kirk retracted them.[254]

The Edmund Burke Society was untypical of Seton Hall students, whose conservatism was Burkean to the extent that it was suspicious of ideas as such, even those of Burke. The small minority who proclaimed themselves conservatives (as opposed to the larger majority who *were* conservative) were figures of fun. *The Setonian*'s stock figure was Marvin Moneywater, whose resemblance to Barry Goldwater was so heavy-handed that even liberals may have winced at the crudity of the satire.[255] In the early 1960s, with a young, Democratic, Catholic president in the White House, Seton Hall students were mainly conservative by habit and instinct, which is, of course, a good conservative habit and instinct. Burke, Kirk, and Buckley were for the tweed jacket crowd, but mostly students were indifferent to them. For students who were conservative by intellectual commitment as well as temperament, the atmosphere at Seton Hall was beginning to change.

What passed for liberalism was largely cheek. Students long complained of the dress code and the prohibition of alcohol. The chief bugbear was Father Stephen Lynch (appointed dean of men in September 1963) who was more suited to seminary than university life. "Shorts, dungarees, T-shirts etc. are not considered proper attire for gentlemen . . . Shorts and slacks are not considered proper attire for ladies . . . Students are to be denied admission to class who appear without suit, jacket, and tie."[256] Behavior in the dormitory was a problem because students were "confined during study period with nothing to do with their time." Father Joseph Russell, a classicist, was bemused: "Pardon me, I thought they were supposed to be studying. In the city of Newark, people who make noise by having loud, boisterous parties, loud radios or TVs after eleven o'clock at night are reported to the police. . . . If we did this at the dorm here, the South Orange police would deserve a bonus for working overtime or, I think, they would drop dead from exhaustion."[257] Comparing the reality with the ideal—evening prayers at 7 PM, students at their desks with room doors open between 7:30 until 10:15, absences recorded on an index card, all residents in the rooms at 11:30 PM, lights out at midnight—suggested that authorities were fighting a losing battle. The rules were relaxed in 1965, and Lynch (his health poor) was replaced as dean of men by Father Robert Antzcak,[258] then Father John Ballweg, both more liberal.[259] "I have begged the Sacred Heart to make Himself known and loved to the young men of Seton Hall," Lynch wrote to Dougherty. "I have failed."[260]

In February 1964, two students were threatened with expulsion for having beards,[261] prompting Robert Conley, professor of chemistry, to express support for "the carefree idolistic [sic] young" and to notice that "we have a shortage of unkempt geniuses and aren't doing anything about it." "Notice to all Students," The Setonian announced, protesting the proposed expulsions:

> As of 20th of February, 1964, the following rules will take effect
> All individuality must be lost on joining the Seton Hall family. Strive to be a cog in the machine.
> Students must dress as uncomfortably as possible, i.e., suit jacket and tie must be worn to class.
> Students must shave daily. Hair may be no longer than 2.31 inches (Found to be the average length at Princeton.)
> Food complaints are to be written on a 3x5 card and placed in the nearest garbage container. In this manner they can be most effectively evaluated.

Absolutely no females are permitted in off campus apartments. This includes mothers, nuns, sisters, wives, cafeteria workers and Mrs. Bayer. . . . [262]

Dougherty suspended the paper for this "unwholesome spirit of cynicism,"[263] an affront to "the philosophy and theology to which the University [was] committed."[264] Six hundred students then blocked traffic on South Orange Avenue until forced back onto campus by policing using a low-pressure hose. "These students are very resentful of discipline," wrote one alumnus to Dougherty. "If I were in your shoes I would be very stern with them."[265] "Pietro, Pastore, Pignatelli, Risimini [the students who ran *The Setonian*] [are] all Sicilians and perhaps related to Cosa Nostra!" "That . . . half-Protestant, revolutionary priest 'Father' Finnerty [a member of the Theology Department who supported the students] should be transferred to some post where his usual talents for inciting to riot will be less productive." More sensibly, Father Tom Fahy, vice president for instruction, thought it a "grave mistake" not to resume the paper because its suspension distracted from the normal functions of the University.[266] In the end, *The Setonian* returned armed with a new constitution and pledges of journalistic responsibility on the part of contributors. "We were not radicals or activists," recalled the editor Rocco De Pietro. "The things that we protested, other schools would not have tolerated . . . The administration ran the show."[267] But the show was changing. In 1966, when the annual student retreat was made voluntary,[268] only 15 percent of students registered for it, turning it into a five-day holiday for the rest.[269] In 1967, it was done away with and replaced by two "Days of Recollection."

ROTC was another cause for grumbling. "I'm here . . . for an education—not drill practices," one recruit complained. "Visitors to the campus might get the idea that this is a military academy."[270] Some students enjoyed regimentation for its own sake and others accepted it as a fact of life. One or two noticed its comedic aspects. (In 1966 those exempted from ROTC included five who had flat feet, one who had acne, one who had gout, and five deemed "too big for uniform.")[271] But ROTC was a serious matter, undoubtedly helping to save lives when alumni served in Vietnam.[272] It also built lasting bonds of affection for the university. Nonetheless, in 1968, as Vietnam took its toll on national morale, dividing student from student and faculty from faculty, ROTC became voluntary. As a quasi-alternative to it, the Peace Corps came to Seton Hall in May 1961 attracting students who wished to serve their country overseas.[273] No-one objected to such service, but the fact remained that some Seton Hall men served their country by dying for it.[274]

Most students were indifferent to ideology. A survey in 1965 found little evidence of enthusiasm for the liberal arts, wondering whether the faculty and administration bore some responsibility "for the absence of a stimulating and scholarly environment."[275] Compared to other Catholic universities, Seton Hall students were more rebellious, impulsive, and intolerant of academic pretension. (They were also guilty of using "alcoholic beverages on the last day of class," of "revelry and wanton destruction," and of "conduct unbecoming university gentlemen.")[276] But even as rebels they tended to be conservative. The "system" against which they railed was the world of forms, registration, and lines, what one wit called *Setonopoly*: "a game intended for people from 18 to adult, although anyone over age 4 should have no trouble floundering . . . The object . . . is to get out . . ."[277] Seton Hall could be frustrating, but it rarely turned conformists into rebels.

Race

These minor matters were as nothing compared to the question of race. Seton Hall appointed its first Black faculty member, Francis Hammond, in 1946. In the 1950s, the South Orange campus had a handful of Black students (among them women), but their small numbers only drew attention to the university's overwhelming Whiteness. "My father fought racism all his life," recalled Hammond's daughter Bertha after his death, "fearless" in his belief in human dignity.[278] Equally courageous were early African American students, among them the scholar-athlete Philip Thigpen of the Class of 1953 who remembered that "the only Black people I saw around here were the ones working in the kitchen," while acknowledging that he himself "had the respect of everyone at school . . . racism never happened overtly." African American women had a double strike against them, race and gender, among them Dorothy Herbert and Laura Frazier of the Class of 1956, the former addressed several times by a professor using a racial epithet until formally reprimanded by the university president, John McNulty, for doing so.[279] It would be wrong to think of the university as a tinderbox, but the invisibility of race in McNulty's day was less a sign of success than of failure; a failure in which most of the nation shared. In July 1967, when Newark experienced one of the worst race riots in American history, the university was unprepared. Following the arrest and beating of a Black cab driver, crowds attacked the police and commercial buildings, prompting the deployment of the New Jersey State Police and the National Guard. Twenty-three people died, over 700 were injured and nearly 1,500 were arrested. Parts of Newark looked like a war zone. "White Flight" (already under way) became unstoppable.

With segregation and poverty daily realities for thousands of African Americans, the university could not ignore the large community on its doorstep. Including satellite campuses, Seton Hall had a student population of over 9,700, of whom fewer than 2 percent were Black near a city that was 73 percent African American. Father Edwin Sullivan of the department of sociology conducted a survey in 1963 in which eighty local Black and White families visited each other's homes to discuss racial matters and, perhaps, to become friends. A tentative and unscientific effort, the survey hinted at the need for major change: 51 percent of the respondents recorded no change in attitude; the rest were willing to think more favorably of their hosts.[280] In 1965, 250 administrators, faculty, and students walked down South Orange Avenue to Newark in support of the Selma to Montgomery Freedom March,[281] an "ordered, well-executed manifestation of public sympathy"[282] encouraged by Dougherty and addressed by faculty members.[283] Dougherty was liberal-minded. "We felt more human because of Martin Luther King," he said when King was assassinated in 1968. "We all felt more Christ-like and noble."[284]

One idea was to promote race-based academic and social programs (leaving aside for the moment whether these should be self-eliminating remedies to an immediate problem or permanent features of the university landscape). "Both scholarship and the times demand a new approach to the problem of the Negro in America," wrote Sullivan after the assassination of Martin Luther King. "There is ample justification for a course which will offer to the non-Negro insight into the way of life of over twenty million Americans. I would suggest that the course be taught or supervised by a Negro."[285] "In the Commencement procession on Saturday I counted the following Negroes," wrote Alfred Donovan, finding a total of twenty. (Donovan was referring not to the number of Black graduates, still relatively few, but to those who showed up to receive their degree.) "All things considered, I don't think this is bad."[286] All things considered, it was disastrous.

To some, America's race crisis was an urban *jacquerie*, to others, lawlessness, to yet more, a bizarre case of psychopathology. "The Negro people are now looking for an identity," suggested Joseph Spiegel, Seton Hall's director of counseling. "The submissive, dependent, and childlike manner of Negroes from the era of the feudal South was conducive to [the] role of slave." But these were stereotypes rewritten as science, the condescension palpable, the analysis ludicrous. Such a system apparently predisposed "the Negro to express himself in movement, laughter, song, and easy conversation." [287] Monsignor William Noé Field proposed a course in Black merchandising underwritten by Bamberger's, a Newark department store.[288] Alfred Donovan favored "a Black Institute . . . if such leadership and programs . . . would be of genuine benefit to Black people and not just those who receive stipends for working in it."[289] Edward Fleming saw "no value [in] reducing our standards as a university . . . we are doing too much in the area of community relations."[290] Thomas Melady worried that a Black Institute would become "a breeding ground for extremists."[291] A speaker invited to address the biology department in the early 1960s announced, as if making a concession, that "negroes [are] indubitably of the same species" as Whites.[292]

Yet there was another side to the story. Thomas Fahy thought the problems of minority groups so overwhelming that no institution could really say that it was doing

enough. He was proud to be associated with a university which "did not have to integrate" before it became politically fashionable or legally required. Seton Hall, he insisted, accepted "without question students from any racial, religious, or ethnic group
when they felt they were ready for college."[293] In 1969 twenty diocesan priests accused
Archbishop Boland of racism, prompting Dougherty to point to his "inspiring leadership" under which Seton Hall had opened Head Start programs that helped hundreds
of youngsters from ethnic minorities prepare for college.[294] The Martin Luther King
Scholarship program, established in March 1969 by Dougherty and reaffirmed two
years later by Fahy, increased minority enrollment through regular admissions. The
Equal Opportunity Program, established in 1968, encouraged culturally and economically deprived students to enroll at the university. When it began, there were approximately fifty African-American and Puerto Rican students on campus. By 1974, there
600.[295] Many of Seton Hall's minority students recorded superb academic achievements. (The first Seton Hall student to win a scholarship to Harvard Medical School
was Vilma Ruddock, a citizen of Jamaica.)[296] Dougherty responded generously to the
"Black Student League," an *ad hoc* group of African American students who, complaining that the "present system of education at Seton Hall University does not truly affirm
the dignity and integrity of the Black Man in America," proposed that a quarter of the
freshman class be composed of African Americans, that a full-time admissions officer
be appointed "to direct the year round recruitment of Black students," that there be
more Black faculty, administrators, and coaches, that there be a Black Institute, and
that an African American be appointed to the Board of Trustees. Dougherty agreed
in principle to the demands while acknowledging the practical difficulties of the first,
commending the league "for the reasonableness of their requests and the spirit with
which they were presented." Seton Hall, he said, was "dedicated to the dignity of *all*
men" and to meeting "the needs of our time in a manner worthy of the university
tradition and American democracy."[297] Most colleges, thought Tom Fahy, "would be
delighted to have a proposal as moderate and sensible as the one submitted by our
Black Student League."[298]

   The university inaugurated a Black studies program in 1969, out of which emerged
a Center for African American Studies under George Jackson assisted by Julia Miller,
who later succeeded him as director. Initially small, the Center grew to offer sixteen
courses taught by five full-time and six part-time faculty members, although student
numbers—four Black studies majors in 1972—remained modest. The library set aside
funds to purchase "Black material" including the *Journal of Negro History*, the *Journal
of Negro Education*, "*Phylon*, a Black literary journal," *A Documentary History of the Negro
People in the U.S.*, and *The Black Power Revolt*.[299] "The Black scholar working in Black
Studies is accountable to Black people," the catalog announced, articulating the apart-
heid the program was supposed to combat. "Active participation in the struggle for

social justice and freedom for Black people and thus all peoples" was the goal. This was too edgy for many[300] and often the Center ignored university procedures.[301] Eventually it was replaced by a department of African American studies housed in the College of Arts and Sciences.

The panicky quality to these measures made Seton Hall no different from most other campuses. For all that, and given their limited ambition, they seemed to work. "The problem of accommodating large numbers of minority students has been successfully solved at Seton Hall to an impressive degree," a 1973 visitor thought, having "rarely" seen "so much success in assimilating a large group of minority students."[302] As an interim verdict, this was encouraging.

An Era Ends

Dougherty submitted his resignation to the Board of Trustees on May 7, 1969. His last official act was to confer 1,900 degrees at the commencement ceremony a month later. Combining his duties as auxiliary Bishop of Newark and president of the university, as well as his commitment to the National Conference of Catholic Bishops, had become "too burdensome for one man to bear."[303] For all his liberalism, Dougherty seemed out of place, a figure from an earlier age of clerical paternalism. If the balance of power shifted from an omnicompetent administration to a more questioning faculty and to less passive students, Seton Hall remained a churchy place, its collective life still shaped by priests and bishops. No-one doubted, however, the revolutionary nature of the Dougherty Decade: "The year 1959 was pre-Student Center, Boland Hall annex, and Humanities Building. There was no discussion of communal baths versus private ones for the girls' dormitory; there were no female students at all on the South Orange campus. ROTC was mandatory for freshmen and sophomores. Curfews were in effect for Boland Hall residents. Alcohol on campus was forbidden. Eighteen credits of philosophy were required, as were night prayers. This was a time prior to the discussion of a tri-partite government or student-faculty screening committees to choose the president of the university."[304]

Ten years later, the university was unrecognizable. Presiding over the changes, Dougherty gave them the appearance of continuity, which was his greatest achievement. Because of his participation in the Second Vatican Council, his chairmanship of the United States Bishops Committee for Work, Justice, and Peace, his involvement in the work of the United Nations, his embrace of ecumenism, his criticism of Vietnam, his skill as a broadcaster, his power of personality, his cheerful eloquence, and his profound love of the arts, he drew a wide audience to Seton Hall. As the 1960s closed, more people had heard of it than before and most of what they heard was good. "I remember many things about Seton Hall in the 60s," recalled Robert Sheeran, then a divinity student. "I often think of Bishop Dougherty and the upbeat and confident tone he set on campus during those days. I recall his walking around campus after supper; preaching Lenten services in the chapel; showing us his latest NBC shows; and his involvement in the United Nations, always encouraging us students to see a larger, exciting world outside our gates. Best, I remember his warm, infectious smile. It always captured the friendly, welcoming tone that I remember as an undergraduate at Seton Hall."[305] It seemed a more innocent age then, unaware of forces about to be unleashed. [306] Albert Hakim—himself a transitional figure—put it best. Dougherty, he said, "wanted to be a liberal but didn't know how."[307]

CHAPTER 14

Noble Dream

*The Seton Hall University School
of Medicine and Dentistry*

Rising Demand

Under Kelley and McNulty, Seton Hall produced the priests, nurses, teachers, and businessmen who served mid-twentieth century America. It was a college, like its students, on the way up. But why stop there? The greatest generation which won the war and their Baby-Boomer children demanded the best of everything, and "everything" increasingly included proper healthcare. Higher incomes and educational attainment, wider participation in private insurance schemes, greater awareness of disease and its causes: all of these had transformed social attitudes and cultural expectations. Between 1940 and 1965, the average number of physician visits per individual in the United States doubled. The healthier Americans became, the more doctors they needed, a paradox of affluence unresolved even today.

Where would these doctors and dentists come from? Locally and nationally, supply nowhere met demand. In 1950, New Jersey had no medical school. Its doctors came from out-of-state in that those who practiced medicine in New Jersey had qualified elsewhere, including men and women who had left the state to study before returning home to practice. In 1959 the Bane Report on Medical Education in the United States would later identify a need for at least twenty-one new medical schools in the United States, mostly in areas of high population where demand for medical services and the desire to enter the medical professions were high. Later studies suggested that by 1970 New Jersey should have two such schools. By 1956, one had already opened: the Seton Hall College of Medicine and Dentistry. McNulty's dream to add medicine to law as a profession for which Seton Hall would prepare students was realized half a decade after the opening of Law School, making these the most dramatic growth years in the university's history. The College of Medicine and Dentistry marked the last great achievement of Seton Hall's first one hundred years. "This humanitarian project alone," said Father Arthur Griffith (who led the fund-raising), "has caused Seton Hall to be ranked in prestige second to no other university in the country."[1] Nothing seemed beyond Seton Hall in its centennial year.

The idea did not come out of the blue. For nearly twenty years Seton Hall had pioneered medical education in New Jersey. The School of Nursing began in 1937 with courses preparing registered nurses for teaching, supervision, and administration in hospitals. The public health program was accredited in 1942. In 1953 the School of Nursing inaugurated a four-year academic course in professional nursing for high-school graduates. By the time the College of Medicine and Dentistry was conceived, Seton Hall was a local leader in public health with a solid record of achievement, conducting one of the largest degree programs in nursing in the eastern United States and the only university in the state to offer degrees in public health and nursing education, graduating more than 350 nurses. It had an enrollment of over 550 undergraduate and graduate nursing students. In 1946, it had established a program in a graduate medical education which offered over 200 separate courses to more than 6,000 doctors, the faculty coming from leading Columbia, Cornell, New York University, Jefferson, Temple, and Penn, the cooperating hospitals, Martland Medical Center, Beth Israel, Saint Michael's, and Jersey City Medical Center. The College of Medicine and Dentistry ("a new school with an old heritage")[2] was built on good foundations.

The College was also built on a philosophy that stressed that local needs should be met by local institutions. The university (and Seton Hall College before it) was "started by the people and has been supported by them," proclaimed one brochure. "No single benefactor or small group of philanthropists has sustained her through the years."[3] But "the people" in the case of the medical school was defined to include "the government," which complicated things. A private university seeking to do a public good has to rely on a public that put its own needs first. Without state and municipal backing, the school was inconceivable. Without support from the courts it would have been stillborn. Without private financial backing it would not have grown. Medical education did not, and does not, come cheap and, in New Jersey, it became entangled in the very localism that McNulty proclaimed as a virtue. Everyone had an interest in the school but not everyone had the same interest. McNulty came to that realization too late.

Public or private, medical schools were enormously expensive, and the really good ones, leaders in research, cost the earth. In 1954 a New Jersey state referendum called for expenditure of $25 million on construction of, and equipment for, a future medical school, and an annual subsidy of $3 million to help keep it going. In fact, the bond issue was defeated, in part because the church mobilized opposition to it. McNulty thought he could do it for less, promising $5 million for Seton Hall's effort and thinking he could run it with a smaller subsidy by relying on grants and private generosity. Never before had the university pledged itself to find huge sums year on year to maintain an operation that could only break even. "An educator resembles a man with a hole in his pocket," McNulty told Hudson County businessmen in 1954. "Every time he reaches there's nothing left. He is dependent on philanthropy to patch the hole."[4] (It was a misleading metaphor. Seton Hall was sewing a suit with a hole deliberately left in it.) The benefits were obvious (even if it was not obvious that Seton Hall should be the one to supply them): New Jersey students could study for the medical professions at home; they would have preference for admission to the school; local hospitals would have more trainees for internships and residencies; the Medical Center in Jersey City could become a leader in research and patient care; jobs could be created. But these benefits would only accrue if the school had an endowment to cover the costs. With help from the National Fund for Medical Education and from the Ford Foundation (which had earmarked $90 million nationally for the support of medical schools), the College of Medicine and Dentistry might succeed. But it could also fail. (In March 1957, the Ford Foundation granted the College $800,000 to be invested as an endowment to help pay medical school salaries.)

Succeed or fail, it came to life quickly. On March 17, 1954 McNulty announced that Seton Hall was considering the possibility of setting up a College of Medicine and Dentistry in the Jersey City Medical Center. Four days later, Dr. John Hirschboeck, dean of Marquette University School of Medicine, surveyed the center and pronounced it suitable for the creation of "one of the finest medical schools in the nation." On May 12, the Board of Trustees endorsed the plan and on August 6, 1954 incorporation papers were filed in Trenton for the creation of an entity separate from Seton Hall University to shield the university from financial and legal exposure and to make fund-raising easier. On August 11, the Seton Hall University College of Medicine and Dentistry was formally inaugurated in a ceremony in the Medical Center attended by 400 educators, officials, doctors, dentists, nurses, and guests. McNulty spoke glowingly: "Financially we are in a very splendid condition; and since the Diocese has guaranteed complete financial backing for the medical and dental school, plus the cooperation of the civil authorities in this area, we feel confident that no burden shall come to the University through the inauguration of the new school."[5]

With only faintly detectable sleight of hand, he promised that funding for the Seton Hall College of Medicine and Dentistry would not come from Seton Hall University, of which it was not, technically, a part. Whether that distinction would indemnify the university against loss remained to be seen. Morally, it made no difference. This was Seton Hall's medical school and everyone understood it as such.

Words were cheaper than wards. McNulty had never launched, still less run, a medical school and in some basic ways he was naïve, not knowing, for instance, that the approval of both the American Medical Association and the Association of American

Medical Colleges was necessary for the launch of a school. To be fair, some of the technical details were very technical,[6] and McNulty was a fast learner, but getting to know things he should have known in the first place was a risky way to launch any venture.

To prepare for opening day, in October 1954 McNulty, Father Mike Fronczak, and a representative of the mayor of Jersey City traveled to Chicago to meet Dr. Dean Smiley, secretary of the AAMC, and Dr. Walter Wiggins, representing the AMA's Council on Medical Education and Hospitals. Fronczak, a science professor and Seton Hall's pre-medical academic advisor, was liaison between the university and the new school. Smiley and Wiggins offered crucial advice. McNulty and Fronczak had envisaged a specific set of admissions requirements, including courses in comparative vertebrate anatomy and vertebrate embryology, but Smiley and Wiggins said that these would exclude all but the most advanced biology majors. They were therefore dropped, as were many "recommended" courses which, Smiley and Wiggins noted, often became requirements in all but name. As to the politics of the school, which were always likely to be complicated, Smiley and Wiggins urged completion of negotiations with Jersey City before choosing a dean (who should be a lay person). This was good advice because nothing about the politics of Jersey City or Seton Hall was ever simple. In the appointment or dismissal of faculty, they said, staff in wards used for teaching purposes and those employed in ancillary services such as x-ray and clinical and pathological laboratories had to be under the control of the medical school, not the city. The Jersey City representative agreed with this stipulation, promising "to co-operate 100% with Seton Hall University to establish an A1 school."[7] The immediate need was to appoint heads of department in the first year (anatomy, physiology, and biochemistry) and other staff thereafter. The first intake of students should take place in September 1956, unless by "extraordinary good fortune" good appointments had been made before then.[8]

The sequence unfolded quickly. On November 5, 1954 Seton Hall received a license to operate the College of Medicine and Dentistry from the New Jersey Department of Education. Eleven days later the Jersey City Commission unanimously approved the leasing of the Clinical Building of the Medical Center for the use of the College. On November 30, the New Jersey State Dental Society named a liaison committee to assist in the establishment of the College, Dr. William A. Giblin, state president, acting as its chairman. On December 10, Seton Hall signed the lease for the use of the Clinical Building in Jersey City Medical Center as the site of the school. Under the terms of the agreement, to remain in force for fifty years, the College undertook to rent the Clinical Building from Jersey City for $275,000 annually.

The Center was the largest in the state and one of the largest in the country. With bed space close to 1,700 and annual admissions approaching 18,000, it comprised sixteen buildings, including the Jersey City General Hospital, the Berthold S. Pollak

Hospital for Chest Diseases, and the Margaret Hague Maternity Hospital. Its more than 100,000 outpatient visits per year, 50,000 emergency room cases, 6,300 operations, and 275,000 laboratory examinations offered a rich field of clinical experience. Already it conducted a School of Nursing and a School for X-Ray Technicians and was accredited for internships and residencies in internal medicine, ophthalmology, otolaryngology, gynecology, obstetrics, pathology, pediatrics, pulmonary diseases, radiology, general surgery, thoracic surgery, and urology. Well supplied with a large amphitheater, offices, and conference rooms, it was easily adaptable for Seton Hall's purposes. The agreement provided for the College of Medicine and Dentistry to take over the entire sixteen-clinic complex, but as renovation progressed it became clear that moving emergency, x-ray, and outpatient facilities would be prohibitively expensive. The largely unused isolation building next to the clinic contained essentially the same floor space and so it was decided to trade these areas and locate the Dental School there with no basic change in the agreement with the city. Seton Hall would thus occupy part of one and the entirety of another building.

On January 12, 1955, McNulty announced the appointment of Charles L. Brown, dean of Hahnemann Medical College in Philadelphia, as dean of the College of Medicine. (He assumed his duties on July 1.) "He was a kind of Atomic explosion at Hahnemann," his successor said of him, "the chain effects of which are even now being felt."[9] Five days later, on January 17, Merritte M.J. Maxwell, former chief of dental services at the San Diego Naval Hospital, was named as dean of the College of Dentistry. Together, they were welcomed by the Jersey City Chamber of Commerce at a dinner attended by 400 businessmen on February 21, 1955. In the following months they put together their team. Heading the department of anatomy was Pinckney Harmon of Georgetown and Yale, whose interests lay in experimental pathology. Under him were Charles Berry of Northwestern working in electrophysiology; May Hollinshead of Columbia, an experimental embryologist; Christian Hovde of Columbia, an electrophysiologist; Joseph Tassoni of New York University, interested in general physiology; and Robin Curtis of Brown, an expert on multiple sclerosis. These appointments were matched by impressive hires in the department of physiology. Under David Opdyke, who came to Seton Hall from the Merck Institute for Therapeutic Research, the department's remit was to cover as broad a range of investigative interests as possible. Arthur Kahn of New York University and Georgetown studied muscular physiology. Richard Mason of the Merck Institute was an endocrinologist. Charles Smith of the University of Michigan specialized in respiratory physiology. The department of biochemistry was led by Raymond Garner, who had gained his doctorate at Johns Hopkins in 1932. His colleagues were William Burke, formerly a fellow of the Atomic Energy Commission, who worked in liver perfusion studies, and John Glick of St. Louis University, whose field was lipid and steroid chemistry. The department of medicine, initially small, was led by Harold

Jeghers, who had held a similar post at Georgetown, assisted by John J. Calabro, formerly chief medical resident on the Harvard Service at Boston City Hospital. The plan
was to hire another seven to ten professors and, eventually, to subdivide the department into neurology, dermatology, industrial medicine, and psychiatry. Dean Brown,
a medical history buff, appointed Morris Saffron to teach a course in medical history.[10]

On March 27, 1955, a year and ten days after McNulty's announcement that Seton
Hall was to open a medical school, the college received its first grant, from the International Academy of Proctology. On May 2, the New Jersey State legislature unanimously
passed a bill safeguarding the college's legal status, Governor Robert B. Meyner signing it into law two weeks later. On June 5, 1955 the college unveiled its first educational
offering, a four-day postgraduate course for orthodontists under the auspices of the
Hudson County Dental Society. (Twenty-three students enrolled.) On June 11, Dr. Edward J. McCormick, past president of the American Medical Association, delivering
Seton Hall's commencement address, urged New Jerseyans to support the College. Finally, on November 2, 1955, the postgraduate department began a program of thirteen
courses with an enrollment of more than 400 doctors. "Recent Advances in Pediatrics,"
conducted under the auspices of the New Jersey State Department of Health and the
New Jersey Medical Society, had over seventy doctors enrolled.

Behind these public events were significant private arrangements with the potential to make or break the school. The college was incorporated separately from the
university to facilitate fund-raising, to prevent undue financial exposure, and to avoid
the difficulties of university and medical faculty receiving widely divergent salaries.
The president of Seton Hall University was to be president of the College of Medicine
and Dentistry, the plan being to have separate Boards of Trustees for the college and
university with overlapping membership, the Archbishop of Newark serving as chairman of both. Such separation would ensure that the interests of the city would be represented on the College's Board, interests which were apparent from the beginning.
The annual payment for use of the medical and dental school buildings was arrived
at by assigning to Seton Hall a rental charge of 5 percent of the appraised value of the
two buildings plus an annual charge of $125,000 for maintenance. In addition, Seton
Hall was responsible for construction expenses connected with adapting the buildings
for academic uses. An initial estimate of $1.5 million to fit out the facility was revised
upwards to $2.5 million by November 1956. The "agreement in principle" was hazy,
but when the picture cleared, the costs for which Seton Hall was committed were substantially greater than first envisaged by McNulty. With an annual payment to Jersey
City of $275,000 and with an estimated budget of $600,000 for the school of dentistry
and $1,486,000 for the school of medicine, Seton Hall faced a yearly bill of $2,361,667 to
keep the College of Medicine and Dentistry going.[11]

These were frightening figures but enthusiasm kept the ship kept afloat. "To have achieved your goal under normal circumstances would have given reason for highest commendation," a friend wrote to McNulty in September 1956. "Yours, however, was no ordinary procedure. Seton Hall now takes the lead as the outstanding university in the state of New Jersey."[12] "Many individuals interested in the health problems of the nation will watch further growth with great interest," wrote Walter Wiggins. "It is particularly heartening," he said, "that this development has taken place in heavily populated New Jersey which until now has not had a stable and adequate institution for medical education."[13] What struck most observers was the school's speedy open- ing, the rigor but generosity of its admission standards, the intelligence of its faculty, and the commitment of Archbishop Thomas Boland of Newark to make a success of it.

Of an entering class of 120 men and women selected from a pool of nearly 900, eighty were medical and forty were dental students, very slightly over half of them from New Jersey, among them ten Jews, four African-Americans, and eight women. The Medical Center was nonreligious, with devotional paraphernalia to suggest Cath- olic sponsorship, but the College insisted on a clear code of behavior. "Conduct your- self, especially in local restaurants and similar establishments, in such a way that Seton Hall students will be always welcome":

Dress appropriately. A shirt, tie, and jacket are always in good taste, but season and occasion may make more informal attire perfectly acceptable . . .

Do not talk shop, particularly about dissections or animal experiments, in the presence of lay people [sic].

Male students are not permitted in the Women's lounges (or vice versa!)[14]

Seton Hall's trainee-doctors, poised between adolescence and adulthood, were little different from medical students the world over.

Meeting the Demand

The College of Medicine and Dentistry admitted its first class in September 1956, a century almost to the day from the opening of Seton Hall College. There was little in place to teach second-year students because there were no second years to teach. Finding additional staff and improving facilities was so urgent that as early (or late) as November 1956 Wiggins was pressing for the "immediate" appointment of basic science faculty for the second year if the College were not to be "jeopardized." The faculty were good, although anatomy, physiology, and biochemistry had to be taught more by lecture than demonstration and covered in a shorter period of time than

otherwise desirable. Staff shortages and limitations of space necessitated a "block system" of teaching. Charles Brown designed the freshman curriculum, consisting of two
eighteen-week semesters, the first devoted to gross and microscopic anatomy, the second to physiology and biochemistry.

Space was never enough. There were four lecture rooms, five seminar rooms, six
student laboratories, along with offices and storage facilities and the wards and clinics
of the hospital itself. A new library was needed to replace the Jersey City Medical Center Library, with its collection of 3,000 textbooks and nearly 8,000 bound periodicals.
Without something bigger and better, the College's research ambitions were risible.
Wiggins worried that the "investigative activities of the staff," put to one side to get
the College up and running, would never be resumed if laboratories and teaching load
were not improved. But these were fixable problems. What was important was that the
College *was* up and running. Something remarkable had been achieved.

Eager to get the show on the road, the university and the municipal authorities
left certain matters unresolved. As these revealed themselves, Seton Hall rather than
City Hall was seen to have had the poorer end of the bargain. Senior medics were paid
by the university for services essentially rendered to the city (which was not how it
was done in teaching hospitals in Boston, Buffalo, Baltimore, Milwaukee, Colorado
and, especially, Los Angeles, whose arrangements were a model for the rest of the
country). Seton Hall and Jersey City should have conducted their partnership similarly,
but because the "long-range monetary support" of the College had not been thought
through, a disproportionate burden was placed on the university.[15] Jersey City got its
teaching hospital on the cheap, and McNulty was only beginning to discover the cost
of Seton Hall's name in front of it. Other sources of support could be called upon—the
local medical profession, the archdiocese, business and labor groups, all those with a
moral and practical interest in Seton Hall's success—but it remained unclear if Jersey
City, the medical school's biggest supporter and beneficiary, would match its deeds to
its words.

The university had only itself to blame for this state of affairs. McNulty announced
in April 1956:

> Seton Hall will finance the College of Medicine and Dentistry out of its own collat-
> eral . . . [relying on] aid from the industries and labor organizations which sponsored
> the medical school . . . grants from private foundations . . . [and] gifts from alumni
> and friends. . . .
>
>   Seton Hall University is an instrument of the Archdiocese of Newark. The Arch-
> bishop of the diocese is the President of the Board of trustees of the College of
> Medicine and Dentistry. Therefore, the collateral of the archdiocese is the primary
> base upon which the financial structure of the University is built. Seton Hall is one

hundred years old and during the course of its history has not received financial aid or loan, either from the State or the National Government.

The physical assets of the University are estimated at twenty-seven million dollars (real and financial). The University is without debt of any kind, even in the construction of its newest buildings.

In its final prognostications . . . Seton Hall does not anticipate any aid from the State of New Jersey but hopefully looks forward to the day when similar to the philosophy of the State of Pennsylvania, medical education will become part of the legislative wisdom of New Jersey.[16]

McNulty's bluff was called. Convincing politicians of his *bona fides* made it easier for the same politicians to withhold support. A man cannot play Dives and Lazarus at the same time. Of organized labor, the Teamsters Union was the school's most generous patron, handing over a check for $96,000 in November 1956,[17] but even that came at a price. (Beds had to be set aside for members of the union at the Margaret Hague Hospital.) "All the hard liquor industries" failed to support the school, McNulty noticed, an ironic complaint from a prominent supporter of Alcoholics Anonymous.[18] The hole in his suit was getting bigger.

Money was one problem, governance another. Earl Halligan, medical director of the Center and chief of surgical services, was answerable to the mayor of Jersey City. Charles Brown, dean of the College of Medicine, was answerable to the president of Seton Hall and the Archbishop of Newark. With Meritte Maxwell, dean of the College of Dentistry, Brown served on the nine-member medical board of the Center. The two units of the Medical Center under Hudson County rather than Jersey City control, the Pollock Hospital (dealing with chest illnesses) and the Margaret Hague Maternity Hospital, each had a lay administrator, with Halligan serving on their supervisory board. To add to the confusion, the clinical staff of the Medical Center had agreed to resign if requested by Brown to do so, an unlikely but notional possibility. Brown wanted to hold on to as many of the existing staff as he could, using them as part-time or voluntary clinical faculty selected on the basis of academic qualifications and willingness to teach medical students. Those ineligible to teach could stay as clinical staff with the privilege of admitting and caring for patients on the private service.

The assumption that the clinical department chairmen of the medical school would become chiefs of their respective services within the Center was just that—an assumption. The roles of the mayor and city commissioners of Jersey City were also unclear. The mayor's rights of appointment and dismissal of the medical staff (freely exercised in the past) seemed constrained by the new management structure. But was there a management structure at all as opposed to a set of *ad hoc* arrangements depending on good will? The mayor was paymaster for the hospital. He sat on the various boards of management. He regarded the College as a tenant and provider of services rather than as an independent entity exercising authority over some of his domain. With nothing on paper as to the practical management of the hospitals, these ambiguities were potentially lethal.

Dangers Ahead

In 1956 and 1957, with clinical work only on the horizon, the jurisdictional uncertainties seemed inconsequential. By 1958, however, they could not be ignored. In July, with the 1956 intake weeks away from clinical training, Jersey City and Seton Hall finally hammered out an agreement under which the city promised full access to the hospital for private staff, faculty, and qualified students and use of its facilities for teaching and research. In return for payments by the city to the college, certain services were to be provided to the Medical Center under the supervision of the city's medical director. The college agreed to advise in setting up and staffing various departments of the hospital, promising to submit to the city the names of persons to be appointed to the professional staff of the hospital, and undertaking to advise in the recruitment and training of nurses, residents, and interns. It committed to help the city establish specialist laboratories for diagnosis, treatment, and research and to arrange for services to be rendered to the hospital by its qualified third- and fourth-year medical students as specified by the medical director, the city not required to compensate them for it. The college agreed to spend $25,000 a year in medical or dental research and not less than $100,000 to equip an outpatient dental clinic. The city promised to make available a total of fifteen beds without charge for indigent patients of Jersey City selected by the college for purposes of teaching and research, the only guaranteed teaching beds out of a total of nearly 1,700 beds in the Medical Center mentioned in the affiliation agreement. The college agreed that faculty would confine their care of patients in all existing and any future clinics or departments to the medically indigent or those referred to them by private physicians. Finally, the city undertook to cover half of the cost of the clinical departments, 20 percent of the cost of the preclinical departments of pathology and bacteriology, 10 percent of the preclinical department of biochemistry, and 5 percent of the preclinical departments of pharmacology, physiology, and anatomy. Total payment by the city to the college was not to exceed 8 percent of the cost of the Jersey City Medical Center.

This was game, set, and match to the mayor. He alone, through the medical director, was to enjoy complete discretion of appointment to professional positions. He alone, in any argument about qualifications, would have the last word. He alone, were he so minded, could make the dean's position untenable by questioning his hiring decisions and disputing his costs. He alone controlled the teaching beds. Other medical centers preferred that elected officials with limited time in office would not exercise long-term control over policy and personnel. Not so in Jersey City, where mayors stayed in office for as long as possible and where graft did not refer to a skin operation. To the liaison committee, this deference to political power was an "unfortunate" development, requiring "every effort" to give "more authority for the professional aspects of the Medical Center to the College of Medicine." William Kellow of the University of Illinois College of Medicine, acknowledging the mayor's proper oversight of public funds, had the "rather firm impression" that the dean of the medical school was not master in his own household. By 1960 the arrangement was so unsatisfactory, notwithstanding the apparent willingness of the mayor to give "sympathetic consideration" to the school,[19] that the AMA and AAMC withheld full accreditation, giving only provisional approval pending another inspection the following year.

By then the college had suffered two further blows. McNulty died in May 1959 and Charles Brown in December. McNulty's successor, John J. Dougherty, was committed to the college's success but may have been less afraid, because he was not its progenitor, of failure. Brown's replacement as dean was Hugh Grady of the department of pathology, an interim appointment. The loss of Brown was serious because his ability to recruit a first-rate faculty and his vision of the college had been vital to its early success. He would be hard to replace.

Academically the College was solid. In four years, the faculty (not all full-time university teachers, of course) had grown from six professorial heads of department in February 1958 to eleven in 1959 (along with thirty-two other professors); from four associate professors to sixty-one; from nine assistant professors to ninety-two (along with thirty-two senior instructors, seventy instructors, and twenty-two assistants in medicine.) These numbers reflected growth in the student body but also confidence in the institution. Recruitment lay in the hands of the dean and an executive committee made up of the six chairmen of the science departments and the five chairmen of the clinical departments functioning as a kind of collective associate dean.[20] When the AMA and AAMC visited in 1959, they found ambiguous tenure policies and few incentives for older professors to retire, but these were problems of success, not failure. The curriculum was idiosyncratic and *ad hoc* because some professors taught what they liked, not what they should have taught. There was too much lecturing in the first two years and not enough hands-on demonstration. Electives were scarce. The third- and fourth-year curricula were not well integrated, with insufficient on-the-job-training for fourth-years. There were no full-time chairmen of the departments of obstetrics and gynecology and surgery. Surgery was taught curiously, with students not routinely reviewing x-ray findings or reporting the results of surgical procedures.[21] The library was mediocre. But none of these difficulties was insuperable. The college had a "fine" faculty, well organized, hard-working, decently paid, and making a "significant contribution" to healthcare in New Jersey.

Recruiting classes from the best graduates of New York University, Rutgers, Seton Hall, Saint Peter's College, and thirty-eight other pre-medical colleges, the school was attractive and competitive. Slightly over half the entering class came from New Jersey (forty-six out of eighty in 1959) with New York in second place (twenty-three), Connecticut (five), Massachusetts (three) and Pennsylvania (three) far behind. It was not a safety school, although it was easier for New Jerseyans than others to enter.[22] Attrition was low. (Medical students who survived their first year usually survived to the end.) The college did little for students except teach them, taking for granted that they could organize their extracurricular lives themselves, although housing, finance, and social welfare eventually became matters of concern.[23] An impressive postgraduate program rounded out the picture, with refresher courses for general practitioners and specialists.

Yet the Seton Hall College of Medicine and Dentistry labored under two burdens. The first was the affiliation agreement with Jersey City. The second was a growing deficit. The operating budget increased dramatically as the college grew: $767,548 in 1957–1958 and $1,308,100 in 1958–1959. Only a small amount of income ($385,000) was covered by fees. The rest came from the endowment (which was trivial), from gifts and grants (which were larger), and, finally, from "general university funds" (which amounted to nearly $300,000 in 1959). Sums on this scale caused McNulty sleepless nights. After his death (hastened by such worries, perhaps), with "every evidence" the university would continue the subsidy, income from other sources was clearly needed.[24] Every expenditure item had to be submitted to Father Fronczak, the liaison officer, but in typical Seton Hall fashion, there was no budget as such, making planning impossible. Department chairs thought the university's wallet was wide open when it was rapidly emptying. Seton Hall had the makings of a "superb and progressive medical school" if these problems could be ironed out. If they could not be ironed out, its success was its greatest threat.[25]

A Gathering Crisis

By 1962, a new dean, James McCormack, faced these difficulties. McCormack, vigorous and experienced, saw that what was right about the college was being undermined by what was wrong. What he did not see, but soon discovered, was that the local medical profession was turning against Seton Hall, exhibiting "innumerable instances of callousness, of mercenary attitude, and of obstructive behavior" towards a school they once pledged to support.[26] (The reason for their hostility was that they

were underpaid by it.) Nor could McCormack have known that the college's relationship with Jersey City would worsen and that its dealings with Hudson County would
collapse altogether.

The affiliation agreement was rapidly unraveling. McCormack thought that Jersey
City respected the letter but ignored the spirit of the arrangements. In fact, the problem
was not breach of contract but the contract itself, which violated "almost every known
academic principle"[27] and which allowed successive mayors of Jersey City to exercise
powers of patronage which had more to do with politics than medicine. No one should
have been surprised when Mayor Thomas Gangemi appointed an Italian American
as director of the Medical Center despite the objections of Seton Hall and despite his
"complete lack of any qualification" for the job. (Gangemi was unqualified for his own
job: he was later forced to resign when it transpired that, Italian-born, he was not a nat-
uralized U.S. citizen.) Lacking academic experience, Gangemi's appointee had been in
private general practice and, although apparently well-disposed to Seton Hall, his chief
interest was to ensure that the affiliation agreement continued to work "to the city's
advantage."[28] As a result, day-to-day cooperation between the Medical Center and the
Medical School broke down. The orthopedic and urology units were headed by men
of whom McCormack knew nothing until they were hired. Gangemi denied faculty
control over standards of practice in the private and semiprivate areas of the hospital,
rewriting the terms of reference of an inquiry to protect "the incompetence (or worse)
of doctors on the private staff." He treated the Hudson County Medical Society with
more deference than Seton Hall. He refused to enforce the city's financial obligation to
the college. He was, claimed McCormack, "increasingly overt" in his hostility to Seton
Hall in private and semiprivate conversation. He insisted on appointing two surgeons
to the Medical Center who had been dismissed from other hospitals for incompetence.
"We cannot fail to be contaminated by this kind of practitioner even though they are
not members of the Seton Hall faculty," McCormack wrote to Archbishop Boland.

The closer one looked at the Jersey City Medical Center, the more alarming it became. The department of pathology was "sadly deficient," the department of radiology "grossly inadequate," the laboratories of the department of medicine "completely
inadequate." In obstetrics and gynecology, it was impossible to know who was treating
whom. In pediatrics, a "unique and unethical arrangement" allowed care to be given
by medical school staff but patients to be billed by and for the benefit of private physicians. Worst of all, "non-professional people played key roles in the performance of
autopsies"—a good description of Jersey City voting practices down the years.[29]

Gangemi and his friends were not personally corrupt so much as participants in a
corrupt system. Division of the spoils was dictated by the world in which they moved.
But even by those standards, health care in Jersey City was spectacularly tainted. At
one point, there had been one medical director for the three hospitals connected with

Seton Hall: the Jersey City Medical Center, the Pollak Hospital, and the Margaret Hague Maternity Hospital. Now each hospital had its own director, multiplying by three the possibilities of favoritism. Complicating the picture, the second and third of these hospitals came under the jurisdiction of Hudson County, not Jersey City. Although the College of Medicine and Dentistry had no contractual connection with Hudson County, the university anticipated that it would exercise broad control over the clinical practices of the two institutions. In fact, Hudson County Democratic boss John Kenny, initially well disposed, turned hostile to Seton Hall, showing himself more interested in patronage than patient care. Under him, the Pollak Hospital became "a haven for those so-called surgeons" whose operating privileges had been limited elsewhere, the kind of "incompetent and unqualified people" that Seton Hall's professor of surgery, Kenneth Judy, had been attempting to remove from the facility but who seemed to return year after year. The Teamsters' Union had a block of beds set aside at the Pollak Hospital for the use of its members, an arrangement negotiated by the colorful Anthony Provenzano ("Tony Pro"), a character more out of Damon Runyan than Doctor Kildare. Kenny ran the hospital so cheaply that funding agencies refused to take it seriously, and Seton Hall unable to hold on to teaching staff when many were tempted elsewhere. "If we lose a few faculty members," McCormack told Boland, "this may start a chain reaction of resignations . . . It is the consensus of our faculty that we cannot survive in Jersey City." Even removed from the grubbiness of local politics, Hudson County may not have been the best place for a teaching hospital. Of all counties in the state, it was the only one (thanks to flight to the suburbs) to have suffered a net loss of population in the preceding ten years. Lamenting the "complex and sordid" politics of Jersey City, McCormack sounded like a man who, expecting fresh air, found himself coughing in the middle of a smoke-filled room.

The irony was that, educationally, the Medical School was doing more things right than wrong. Some faculty could command better salaries elsewhere (the quality of the school, in other words, was working against its interests). Everyone saw the difficulty of not having a proper endowment (which made it dependent on municipal authorities and on the rapidly depleting general funds of the university).[30] The school continued to attract impressive teachers and students, ranking forty-ninth among medical schools in size of entering class (eighty a year) but eleventh in the number of applications received. Academically it thrived. Politically it was in terrible shape.

The AMA and AAMC watched these developments with alarm. In March 1962 a team from the AAMC urged that the contract with the city be renegotiated. Failing this, they suggested that the by-laws of the Jersey City hospital be changed to give the college more say in clinical matters. That was unlikely but not impossible. Finally, they pressed for the Liaison Office to be closed to give the college greater institutional and financial autonomy. (This was implemented at the end of 1962.) At the close of the year, another team discovered that efforts to develop a better relationship with the city had proved "completely fruitless." The hospitals themselves, placed under probation in 1961 and 1962, were "not operating at acceptable hospital standards," with the college having "very little control of the medical care on which its clinical teaching program [was] dependent." "Not only has little improvement taken place since the last survey," the AAMC suggested, "but no plan has been presented which shows real promise of improving existing circumstances." Accordingly, the College of Medicine and Dentistry was placed on public probation beginning in June 1963, having already been on confidential probation until that point. Failure to remedy its "staggering array of problems"[31] would result in forfeiture of its accreditation as a medical school in June 1965.

Dougherty responded that although the situation had not improved and might even have deteriorated, Seton Hall planned to remove students from at least two clinical services in the hospital to induce the city to cooperate.[32] He knew, though, that reconciliation was "almost doomed to failure." In February 1962 he had sounded out John O'Connor, president of Merck, who told him to give "serious consideration" to the possibility of having the College become a state-managed institution. "Quite frankly," O'Connor told him, "I don't see how Seton Hall can continue to attempt to finance and manage the Medical School . . ." As a trustee of Syracuse University, he was able to report that when that university faced similar difficulties, its medical school eventually becoming part of the SUNY system, the benefits of handing over to the state were immediate and long-lasting. "Relief from the growing financial burdens of the Medical School enabled to University to advance more soundly in other educational fields, particularly at the graduate level."[33] The ground was thus laid for divorce. In June 1962, sensing the irretrievable breakdown of the relationship with Jersey City, Dougherty contacted Governor Richard Hughes to explore the possibility of a state takeover of the medical school, ensuring in this way, he told the AAMC, that "the local political difficulties will be overcome." Several confidential meetings followed with the Commissioner of Education, it being in no-one's interest that the College's status be known to be under negotiation with the state when it was under renegotiation with the city.

Would the state wish to assume responsibility for the school? From Seton Hall's point of view, the advantage was that the state would take control of the assets and liabilities as well as operating responsibility. Since the assets were intangible—goodwill depleting by the day—and since the liabilities amounted to a debt of about $5 million and an annual operating deficit of $1 million, the state would have to think hard before committing itself. Another possibility, favored by the faculty, was for Seton Hall to build its own medical center or at least its own teaching hospital. But four difficulties argued against this notion—the vast sums required, the university's modest history of professional fund-raising, the fact that the university's capital ambitions were committed elsewhere, and, finally, the fact that Dougherty had no time for the idea. If not that, then, how about a state subsidy? Here the objection was that Seton Hall operated under Catholic auspices, raising questions of separation of church and state. If not subsidy, then, why not place the students elsewhere and close the school? Pride argued against this, as did Dougherty himself, a Jersey City native. Besides, the original case for a Jersey City school remained strong, as did the school itself. If not a takeover, then, or a capital campaign, or a subsidy, or closure, how about restructuring the College from a four-year to a two-year school? That idea, although unprecedented in the history of medical colleges, had a certain appeal, in its favor the fact that it would allow the school to maintain its integrity while enabling it to improve, against it the fact that almost all the clinical faculty would have to be dismissed and provision made for current clinical students. Of all possible solutions—takeover, subsidy, campaign, closure—the notion of restructuring was the one most favored by the AAMC.[34]

By the spring and early summer of 1963, Dougherty's hopes of renegotiating terms with the city while exploring other avenues with the state were stalled. To the bemusement of the AAMC, he offered public assurances that existing by-laws of the hospital could guarantee the College academic and clinical autonomy, a view he privately doubted.[35] Negotiations with the state were delicately balanced between the interests of Seton Hall, the governor, and, potentially, Rutgers University, which was planning to open its own medical school in September 1966. What would happen if the state of New Jersey were willing to assume control of the College but unwilling to assume its existing obligations? Dougherty thought that Seton Hall could probably go along with that. As for a future Rutgers Medical School jeopardizing any takeover of Seton Hall, Dougherty reminded Hughes that he himself had argued for at least two medical schools in the state. There was always a chance that Seton Hall could go it alone, relying on financial support from the archdiocese, whose building fund stood at $32 million and which might have been used along with a levy on parishes to establish an endowment. But this was a long shot.

What Dougherty needed was time, and that was running out. By April 1963 he was even suggesting that the AAMC might itself intervene with the city to make the case that the medical school remained viable in its current guise—a bizarre idea. The best he could hope for, because it might bring the city to its senses, was that the College be put on probation, a rare instance of a president wishing for the humiliation of his own school. But that wish, soon granted, could encourage existing students to leave while discourage others from applying, bringing about the disaster it was supposed to prevent.

Meanwhile the College bled money. The dispute with Jersey City, ostensibly about appointments, patronage, and clinical practice, was also about unpaid debt. Payment by the city to the college for clinical services came in dribs and drabs, long after the services had been rendered and frequently the subject of dispute because of the complicated formula by which the payment was calculated. A system of fixed and agreed annual payments would have enabled both sides to draw up budgets in advance of need, but that never happened. By 1963, the city owed the college $414,000 for medical services, a debt unlikely to be paid. Arguing that an immediate demand for repayment would cause "great financial hardship [to] the City," the city's lawyer, Jeremiah O'Callaghan, persuaded Dougherty and Boland to accept 65 percent (or $267,000) in full payment, the amount to be liquidated, with interest, in a series of annual installments ending in 1972. This at least was a start but the city's hardship was as nothing compared to the university's. The College's deficit for 1962–1963 was $820,400, the estimated deficit for 1963–1964 $714,600. The reduced deficit from 1963 to 1964 was the result of reduced services—unfilled faculty lines—and nonrecurring research grants from federal sources. The shortfall in the operating budget was due to heavy debt service. As for the debt itself, building up for a decade and representing the undischarged start-up costs of the College and its accumulating deficits, the College owed the banks some $7,050,000, and this after a decade in which the university's total investment in it amounted to some $20 million. To cap it all, the College owned none of the buildings it occupied, being merely a tenant of Jersey City. Seton Hall was paying a bigger and bigger mortgage for the pleasure of living in someone else's house and doing the dishes for him.

In truth, medical schools in the United States were beyond the pockets of all but the best-heeled private institutions. "Every medical school has to run at a deficit in order to run good facilities," James McCormick argued. "But unless a private school has massive endowments, it simply cannot keep going today . . . The future of the schools lies with the states."[36] Between public and private colleges of medicine in the United States a rough parity obtained—forty-five private and forty-two public in 1964—but of those in the planning stage, the heavy preponderance, eleven out of thirteen, lay in the public sector. Even those remaining private were so reliant on federal grants and awards that they enjoyed a kind of quasipublic status, never free, or desiring to be free, of some degree of external control. Some simply changed from being private to public, three in New York state alone in the 1950s. Nor was there any reason why a medical school, public or private, needed a university affiliation in the first place. Of five medical colleges in Philadelphia, three had no corporate relationship with a university. Of six medical colleges in New York City, one was independent, one (Cornell) was hundreds of miles away from its parent university, and a third (Downstate Medical Center) was part of a SUNY system which was more a board of control than a university in the normally understood sense of the word. Other colleges were for all practical purposes only nominally affiliated with a university: Harvard Medical Center in Boston was miles from Cambridge; Columbia Presbyterian Medical Center was half a city away from Columbia University; Johns Hopkins Medical School was distant from the parent campus; none of the three medical schools of the University of Texas were on the main campus at Austin. The Seton Hall College of Medicine and Dentistry thus looked anomalous, affiliated at ruinous cost with a small, private university when other schools were only nominally affiliated with large public or private institutions or were entirely in public hands.[37]

Meanwhile, the association with Jersey City had a final course to run. The reform-minded Kenneth Judy, director of surgery of the Medical Center and chairman of the medical school's surgery department, was dismissed in February 1964 by Mayor Thomas Whelan, to be replaced by a favored son of the Hudson County Democratic Party. (This was par for the course. In June 1971, Whelan was convicted of federal extortion conspiracy charges and sentenced to fifteen years in jail.) Judy's ouster prompted a substantial number of physicians serving as faculty members and members of the medical center staff to resign and it also persuaded sixty juniors and seniors from the College not to seek surgical clerkships. Whelan was as tired of the college and the center as they were of him, hoping the state would absorb the debt of the center (with its annual deficit of $5 million) even as he hoped that Seton Hall would forgive city's debt to it. The dismissal was a breach of contract, and the College's Board of Trustees lost no time in notifying the city of the fact.

Faced with this shambles, a nonpartisan Seton Hall Fact-Finding Committee appointed in March 1964 by Hughes and the New Jersey State Legislature to look into "the Seton Hall problem" concluded that some sort of state takeover was inevitable. The public policy argument for a medical college remained compelling—New Jersey needed an additional 400 physicians a year to maintain existing doctor-patient ratios. (People under fifteen and over sixty, the two groups most in need of medical attention, constituted 42 percent of New Jersey's population in 1964.) Maintaining dentist-patient ratios required an additional one hundred dentists per year. This was to say nothing of the need for postgraduate training of currently licensed doctors and dentists, or of the benefit to New Jersey's pharmaceutical industry of the scientific and medical research conducted under the auspices of the school. Those interviewed by the fact-finding committee unanimously thought the loss of the school would be "catastrophic" and would constitute "a serious reflection on the State of New Jersey." Taking it into public ownership would gain the state an established, accredited institution "that took ten years and cost $20 million to bring to its present stage." Of course, the state would also inherit certain problems, "the correction of which [would] require time, brains, and money."[38] The committee reported its findings on July 28, 1964.

And so, the end approached. Hughes's fact-finders recommended that the College be taken immediately into state ownership to prevent any interruption in its work. The state should pay $4 million for the property and intangible assets of the College while assuming none of its debts or other obligations. A new board would be constituted for a new college of medicine (its name open for negotiation). There would also be a new set of arrangements between the state and, respectively, the Jersey City Medical Center and Rutgers University. If the Medical Center were to continue as a teaching hospital, the state would acquire unequivocal control of those aspects of its operation. By the same token, Rutgers University, which had proposed that the Seton Hall College of Medicine and Dentistry be incorporated into its medical school in New Brunswick, which was due to open in 1966, would have to be persuaded of the impossibility of that idea but also assured that its own medical school remained on track. As for short- and long-term costs, "the state must be prepared to make an annual appropriation for the support of the College" and, if a new facility were needed, federal funds could cover perhaps 40 percent of any capital outlay. With such help, the Committee concluded, "it will not be difficult to design and build facilities to meet high standard but at a reasonable cost."[39]

This was the penultimate act of the drama. The *coup de grace* was delivered by the AMA and the AAMC. The College had been happy with an agreement in 1963 by which the city agreed to a new set of hospital by-laws giving the college professional control of the hospital, but Judy's departure showed that the agreement was worthless, the *furore* it caused prompting the AMA and AAMC to visit the College in September 1964. After three days of probing, they concluded that the College should be put on public probation. Only the possibility of a state take-over persuaded them to postpone the implementation of the recommendation until February 1965.[40]

The Seton Hall University College of Medicine and Dentistry, conceived in 1954, thus prepared to close in 1964. Under the terms of the New Jersey Medical and Dental College Act, 1964, the legislature of New Jersey created the New Jersey College of Medicine and Dentistry, and it was this entity that on January 1, 1965 entered an agreement to purchase the Seton Hall University College of Medicine and Dentistry for $4 million, the purchase itself finally executed on May 3, 1965. (The State also appropriated $300,000 to cover the College's operating deficit for the first six months of 1965.) On January 31, 1966 Jersey City and the practically defunct but still legally incorporated Seton Hall College of Medicine and Dentistry agreed to settle any outstanding future claims against each other for a dollar.[41] (The city also agreed to pay $75,000 to settle its unpaid debts to the college, a sum far below the amounted owed.)[42] When the possibility of a takeover was mooted in 1962, and in all subsequent discussions, it was on the basis of the new State Medical College taking over not only the assets but also the liabilities of the Seton Hall University College of Medicine and Dentistry. In 1962, those debts, primarily in the form of bank loans, amounted to roughly $5.5 million. By May 1965, when the purchase was executed, the medical school's debts exceeded $7.5 million. In the end, the State bought the tangible and intangible assets of the College but left it up to Seton Hall to find the money to pay off the difference between debts owed and the purchase price to be received.

The medical school ended, as it began, with a group of medical bureaucrats persuading themselves of the need to spend large amounts of other people's money. In the
interim, the financial and political cost to Seton Hall was enormous. Medical schools
were open pits into which wheelbarrows of cash had to be poured year after year.
Symbolizing an era when the Church thought itself capable of almost any educational
venture, the medical school expressed Seton Hall's commitment to, and capacity for,
urban education in the middle of the twentieth century. For nearly a decade, the school
allowed some of New Jersey's brightest faculty to teach some of its brightest students.
It advanced medical knowledge in key areas. It laid the foundation for another institution, the University of Medicine and Dentistry of New Jersey. All the Medical School
needed was luck and, in the end, it ran out of it.

CHAPTER 15

Dangerous Decade

Seton Hall in the 1970s

Dramatic Interlude

Following Dougherty's resignation, Edward Fleming became acting president, serving from 1969 to 1970. A graduate of Seton Hall College and Saint John's University, Fleming was appointed to the faculty in 1949, teaching Latin at the Prep before serving as director of student affairs, dean of the university colleges in Newark and Jersey City, and (in 1960) executive vice president. He was named Monsignor in 1962. Tall, athletic, and handsome, Fleming made possible many of the changes of the postwar era and, in a different time, might have made an outstanding president. But an intemperate homily at the beginning of the school year undid him and, had it not been for that, he might have lasted longer.

The trouble had been building for years. "The old ways worked well and will continue to work perhaps for a few short years more. But the old ways are beginning to break down and will ultimately break down completely. The present period is transitional." So thought Michael Valente of the department of theology, himself an exotic flowering of those seeds of change.[1] Fleming, a social and religious conservative, took a different view. The old ways were good enough for him and he had dedicated his life to them. The purpose of Catholic universities, he said, was "to bear witness to the incarnation of the Son of God," a theme he developed during the 1969 Mass of the Holy Spirit. It was a dramatic *démarche*: "Those who would refashion our society, the church, and specifically Seton Hall into something of their own image, no matter how sincere or well-intentioned they may be, must be confronted with the fact that there are real basic principles which will cannot and will not compromise until hell freezes over."[2] The sermon was the most memorable act of his time in office, representing ten years of frustration spilling out in ten minutes.

Some thought the remarks overdue, others that they were unfair. "The institution which once stood in high regard has sunk to the depths of degradation," wrote a local pastor. "In this area it is known as Seton Hall Motel."[3] "If a rock is thrown into a pack of dogs," said Father Virgil Stallbaumer, professor of English, "the ones hit will yelp."[4] Fleming's defenders worked themselves into a fever of clichés, demanding the removal of "heretical theology professors who instigate revolt against His Holiness the Pope" and the immediate expulsion of students "organizing demonstrations against established rules and regulations of the University." (The national anthem was also to be restored at sporting events.)[5] Fleming's critics complained that his remarks were inaccurate but also that the behavior in question was legitimate. His defenders sounded parodies of outraged patriotism. Fleming himself, refusing to apologize, was eventually ferried to hospital, suffering, like the university, from hypertension.

The response to the homily strangely vindicated it. Mass meetings and demonstrations indicated that respect for authority had indeed broken down. Yet Fleming himself was also at fault, his remarks designedly provocative, a gauntlet thrown down. Writing to the Board of Trustees, he found "ample evidence" that students were "both incapable of and disinclined toward any type of responsible self-regulation."[6] The university chaplain was gloomy about Seton Hall's "monumental" problems, lamenting the difficulty of protecting "the Catholic in a Catholic university."[7] The old order was visibly passing away.

Worse was to follow. The killing of four students at Kent State University in May 1970 brought Seton Hall to a halt. On May 5, the headquarters of ROTC were ransacked and nearly torched and, a few hours later, a group of students calling themselves "The Coalition" occupied and vandalized Bayley Hall, demanding that ROTC be removed from campus pending the end of the war in Indo-China. The Faculty Senate expressed "grave concern" about the "despair, hatred, and strife" caused by "the policies of the national government."[8] Not everyone was radicalized[9] and the cancellation of examinations did not sit well with nursing and law students who needed to satisfy professional requirements. In July 1970, a deans' meeting considered changes to the application form for academic employment. "Religion" became "Religious Preference." Another question was dropped: whether the applicant had ever been a member of an organization advocating the overthrow of the United States government by violence.[10] A few days later, Father Tom Fahy announced that he did not "intend to permit any more burning of buildings—especially of those with people living in them."[11]

Fund-raising suffered. Only 2 percent of alumni responded positively to an appeal for donations in December 1970. A letter to 300 special gifts prospects produced one gift of $50. A letter to the presidents of 800 corporations produced seven gifts, five from vendors who dealt with the university. "Adverse reactions to campus disturbances, a bearish stock market, the reaction of older people to student hair and clothing styles" all caused decreased contributions to the school.[12]

A President for the Seventies

Fleming soothed these tensions by resigning. (He returned to campus nearly twenty years later, as director of development of Immaculate Conception Seminary, proclaiming vindication.)[13] Tom Fahy succeeded him, the contrast between the two men vast. Born in Jersey City in 1922, ordained in 1947, with a doctorate from Fordham, Fahy had taught Greek and Latin in the preparatory school and the university while also serving at various times as director of athletics, dean of men, and vice president of instruction. Dark circles under his eyes, down-to-earth, older than his years, Fahy was a breath of smoky air, an ordinary man with an extraordinary sense of social justice. As a young priest, he had organized a rent strike at a federal housing facility in Newark. He also supported the United Farm Workers in their campaign to improve living conditions of migrant farm workers in New Jersey.[14] As president, he took the side of the overlooked and marginalized, criticizing the School of Business for aiming "at middle and upper management" while ignoring "smaller . . . operations."[15] "I'm not the big-shot type, right?" he told *The New York Times*.[16] Sitting on the steps of Presidents Hall with a senior administrator when Vietnam was at its height, both noticed a passing student with an army greatcoat, rings on his hands and ears, and semi-dyed hair. "Get a load of this guy," said the administrator. "That's my nephew," replied Fahy.[17] He was "the epitome of what a clergyman should be—sensitive, decent, concerned for people."[18]

Chosen in April 1970 (the first president to be appointed after a search), Fahy was inaugurated in October. Ten years before, Dougherty had spoken of a "fellowship of educated men," a home for "inquiring spirits," a "living community of scholars." Fahy by contrast spoke of "binding up . . . wounds," of establishing "some kind of . . . relationship" with the police, of ensuring that "casualties should be kept to a minimum." "Without a spirit of high adventure such as impels young men to . . . go over Niagara Falls in a barrel," a paper remarked, "it is desirable to avoid a college presidency."[19] But Fahy was untroubled: "We have been turning out generations of students who can be generally complacent . . . when the Blacks and Puerto Ricans of our rat-infested city ghettoes, or the poor whites of Appalachia, or the deprived Mexican-Americans of the South-West utter as much as a murmur of complaint . . . [But] Catholic colleges have a strong tradition of offering moral value-judgments and offer more quickly what students seem to want . . . This is only one of many reasons why I think Seton Hall can survive only as she is—an independent, private, Catholic university."[20] In a few sentences, he changed the tone, saying nothing that Fleming could not have said but saying it in a way more likely to appeal to Fleming's critics. War and peace remained contentious but for a few minutes he emptied them of their poison.

Fahy was an old Latin teacher. The classics moved him deeply, as did train time-tables and baseball scores. (He once took a vacation to St. Louis and, asked why, he explained it was the first train available.)[21] Standing outside Presidents Hall smoking twenty to the dozen, his arm arched over his head in a gesture that became his trade-mark, he did good by stealth. "You made me extremely happy by your wonderful kindness to me at your inauguration yesterday," Monsignor James Kelley wrote to him. "You brought me back home again after an absence of twenty-one years—back to a campus where I had come as an enthusiastic youngster in 1916 and had left quite wearied and embattled in 1949."[22] Stories abounded among faculty of extra cash at the birth of a child[23] or, in the case of a history professor, a letter out of the blue stating that his salary was too low and was being increased. The professor in question, Scott Morton, had been a Presbyterian missionary in China. Fahy was a practical Christian, exasperated by Seton Hall's amateurishness but in the best way personifying it. If rules could be bent, he was first to bend them. His model for university presidency was the Beatitudes: "There is no blessing for the tough guy, the executioner, or insensitive people. You only find it for the poor in spirit, the merciful, or the peacemakers. That's what Christianity and Catholic education is all about."[24]

Midterm Report

Fahy, president from 1970 to 1977, began with the opening of a long-planned (and de-layed) women's dormitory in December 1971. Many women students, either commut-ers or living in rented accommodation, wished to live on campus but were unable to do so. Dougherty had feared that any dormitory, male or female, might dilute the number of New Jerseyans at Seton Hall by attracting out-of-staters to the university. By the late 1960s that anxiety had been allayed (75 percent of residential students came from within the state) but another worry took its place, namely that without a wom-en's dormitory Seton Hall would find itself at a competitive disadvantage. (In 1968, 63 percent of female nursing students admitted to Seton Hall chose not to attend, most of them choosing colleges with dormitories for women.)[25] "Some may deprecate [co-education]," a 1969 reported stated, but it was "a fact with which higher education will have to live, and Seton Hall University in particular will have to live."[26] Once women were allowed on to campus, they could not be denied a place to live.

Built at $2.5 million funded from federal loans (and intended to turn a profit), the dormitory occupied a corner of the campus where the old ROTC barracks had once been. In September 1971, 214 women students arrived to find sixty room rooms avail-able to them, forcing them to double up in Boland Hall (discomfiting the Archbishop after whom it was named). The Women's Dormitory (subsequently named West Res and Aquinas Hall) was ready in December 1971. By the end of the decade it housed 325 women students.[27] By 1981, it was coed.

This progressive start continued with a positive midterm report from the Middle States Association in November 1973. Fahy thought the assessment "surprisingly good," the adverb revealing.[28] Faculty, administrators, staff, and students were hailed as courteous, honest, and friendly, their affection for Seton Hall deep, the reputation of the university high but, outside New Jersey, not as high as it deserved to be. "We have a much finer institution here than many people realize," Provost John Duff reported. Concerns about generosity in granting tenure, the business office, the lack of long-range planning, and the poor organization of graduate programs did not diminish the strength of the overall verdict. "They were generally impressed with the progress that had been made over the years," said Duff, "whether this had been done through long-term planning or by the seat of our pants."[29]

How to explain the improvement? The passage of time helped, as did Fahy's personality, but institutional factors were also at work. Seton Hall had a reputation for loyalty to the people who had seen it through. In 1973, when the New Jersey Legislature provided a subsidy for private colleges after tuition fees had been set, the university (despite suffering a 3 percent fall in enrollment) reduced its previously announced charge for academic credit.[30] The student body was slightly below the national norm in the percentage of parents who had attended college; it met the norm in the percentage of students who had graduated in the top half of their schools; and it was above the norm in the number of colleges by which they were accepted. Seton Hall, in other words, had reasonably well-qualified students who wished to be there. Classes were small. The emphasis was on teaching rather than research. Most professors were happy in their work.[31]

Teaching and Scholarship

By one measure of health—undergraduate teaching—the university began to reap the rewards of the Dougherty era. Almost all subjects were well taught, some outstandingly so. History and classics were strong. The communications department had "noticeable vibrancy," with a small faculty teaching 340 majors in theater, television, radio, film, journalism, and speech. The English department was "reasonably good." The department of Asian studies, strongest of the interdisciplinary programs, remained a national leader. The sciences showed "considerable buoyancy" (with physics adapting to falling enrollments by branching into electronics and earth sciences). Chemistry had a powerful faculty, a solid research agenda, and impressive alumni. Its chairman, Roland Hirsch, spent 1975–1976 at Oxford University. His namesake, Jerry

Hirsch, was author of *Concepts in Theoretical Organic Chemistry*. The graduate program was small by the standards of major research universities—a total of sixty-six PhDs in chemistry between 1966 and 1974—but its alumni admired its "high quality faculty," its "prestige," its "unique" teaching excellence, its "vital" role in the chemical industry of northern New Jersey.[32]

The College of Nursing, housed in a new building in South Orange, had well-prepared instructors teaching well-qualified students in well-appointed facilities. Between 1972 and 1979 under Sister Agnes Reinkemeyer, its enrollment tripled from 340 to 916.[33] (Usually it hovered between 500 and 600.) Full-time faculty numbered twenty-four—all women—of whom five had doctorates. The College had a master's program in gerontology, one of only two in the country.[34] It streamlined its organization, establishing four departments (graduate nursing, adult health nursing, maternity-child nursing, and mental health psychiatric nursing).[35] Overwhelmingly, nursing students were women (98 percent in 1977), but a few men entered the field and found it welcoming.[36]

The School of Business had a new building and an energetic dean. Following its move from Newark, it was scattered across the campus, the administration on the second floor of Bayley Hall, then on the second floor of the library, then back to Bayley Hall. Faculty offices were in basement of Presidents Hall, with classes in Corrigan Hall and the old barracks. Undergraduate programs were unimaginative[37] but improving, and when the school celebrated its twenty-fifth anniversary, its new dean, Edward Mazze, had built on the advances made by Dean Robert Senkier. Senkier had established the *Journal of Business*; established a President's Advisory Council for the School of Business; inaugurated an accounting internship program; created an Institute of International Business; founded an Institute of Labor Relations; revised the undergraduate and MBA curricula to conform to AACSB standards; increased full-time undergraduate enrollment from 650 to 950 students and MBA enrollment from 200 to 850; recruited thirty faculty (of whom twenty-six remained); and raised funds for the new building.[38] "As these people grow, we will grow," Mazze said of the seven teachers he was able to hire in 1976.[39] Another two deans, John Sutherland and Philip Phillips, found themselves dealing with low salaries, accreditation, and faculty productivity, indicating that the school was far from perfect.[40] (Senkier declined to submit the school for AACSB accreditation in 1974, knowing that it would not receive it.)[41] But it was getting better.

Business flourished at the expense of Nursing. Nursing made the money that went more or less directly to Business to pay for the latter's accreditation. The administrator responsible for this transfer of funds, Peter Mitchell, was mildly embarrassed by it but kept his embarrassment to himself.[42]

The School of Education did a creditable job of preparing a moderately able student body, succeeding despite limited resources.[43] The faculty performed "over and above what is expected."[44]

With the exception of the Law School and the doctoral degree in chemistry, Seton Hall's graduate programs were a mess. With forty-six masters' degrees and no-one in charge of admission standards, the need for reform was urgent. Seton Hall was not the only institution where the graduate dean served as a rather "hapless coordinator" of courses and instructors over which he had little control. Indeed, the inadequacy of Catholic graduate education had been a topic of discussion for years.[45] Seton Hall saw a large future in graduate degrees, but it was an expectation that brought its own dangers.[46]

Business Blues

In Dougherty's day, Seton Hall's financial management was inadequate, a problem only partially remedied by the time Fahy became president. Budget-making was a model of what not to do, with few guidelines for requests and no overarching philosophy of income and expenditure. The job of the Budget Committee was to find revenue to meet financial obligations incurred by departments with no incentive to stop spending and every incentive to continue it. "At Seton Hall," the Middle States visitors noticed, "there is no systematic budget-planning more than a year in advance."[47] Making a budget only a year ahead was trying to tell the time by looking only at the minute hand. Long-term planning made people think, forcing them to become responsive and responsible.

External pressure brought extra urgency. With Catholics losing denominational solidarity, with public education offering cheaper alternatives, with local and national economies shrinking, and with demographic change in New Jersey high schools, Seton Hall faced serious challenges. A third of Catholic colleges in the country were in difficulty. Church-run colleges and universities (of all denominations) declined by 20 percent between 1965 and 1975, the vulnerable institutions being small private colleges without distinctive identity. Financial pressures on private schools, Seton Hall included, were inexorable. As the university assumed the cost of employee medical insurance, contributory pension plans, more competitive salaries, and financial aid for students, and with a heavily tenured faculty, Fahy presided over an institution academically robust but financially fragile.

As the decade progressed, balancing budgets grew fraught. Sometimes the reasons were beyond the university's control (the Middle East oil crisis). Sometimes they were not (poor management). Sometimes they simply suggested a jinx. Dennis Garbini recalled his first day as assistant bursar in 1972. "I saw someone walk into the back area [of the bursar's office] with a grocery bag. In one hand he had a gun but I assumed he was the Brink's guy because no-one seemed to care." He stole $34,000 from the university—funds eventually recovered. "I've been waiting for it to get as exciting as that ever since."[48] Finances were "essentially sound" in 1974, said John Cole, university treasurer, but rising costs meant a 3 percent budget cut across the board.[49] Seton Hall faced "a very difficult financial situation" in 1976, its "survival" depending on state and federal funds to undo inflation, recession, and "uncontrollable fuel costs."[50] "We must remain within the budgets. We must be budgetarily responsible. We have to stick to our budgets," said Cole, adding some verbal inflation of his own.[51] (To put this in perspective, the 1975 budget was $23.5 million, with tuition raised from $59 to $67 per credit.)[52] Fahy thought that Seton Hall had a "talent, if not genius" for surviving by "luck, skill, or divine intervention."[53] But signs of divine favor also included the services of a good accountant. Reduced state support brought a shortfall of $300,000 in February 1976 and the possibility of lay-offs.[54] A surcharge of two dollars per credit was added to cover fuel charges a few months later.[55] Declining undergraduate enrollment (down 5 percent between 1976 and 1977)[56] and rising deficits ($2.5 million by the fall of 1976)[57] made this a perilous time.

Tight budgets meant tough decisions and, to help him make them, Fahy called on Peter Mitchell and John Duff. As vice president for instruction from 1970 and provost from 1973,[58] Duff was senior to Mitchell, who was assistant vice president. In 1976, Mitchell succeeded Duff with the title vice president for academic affairs. (A word should be said about these confusing titles. "Executive vice president" was changed to "provost" in April 1972, the duties broadened to include primary responsibility for academic leadership. The title "vice president for instruction" was changed to vice president for academic affairs, the duties to include supervision of the Registrar's office and the Admissions Office. When Duff resigned as provost in 1976 to become president of the University of Lowell, he suggested that the position be abolished. In fact, it was left vacant for a year to save money, after which the title was given to Mitchell.[59] Mitchell was appointed to the combined position of vice president for academic affairs and provost in December 1977.)

With complementary personalities, Duff and Mitchell acted as a team. Mitchell's fellow historian Bernhard Scholz remembered his "lean and sparsely staffed office," his "effective" and "collegial" style of leadership, his "attention above all to the long-range problems and prospects of the university."[60] Duff, another historian and one of three brothers associated with Seton Hall,[61] was more of a bruiser. "I believe in administration by *tension*. Make people realize what will happen to them if the job *isn't* done."[62] "Acceptable facilities are one of the things we give the faculty instead of salaries," he admitted in 1974.[63] But he also knew that cost-cutting could also be comic. "The re-seeding of lawns is expensive," noticed one administrator. "How about approaching students and asking their cooperation in not walking on the grass?" "In some offices, the heat is on so high that the occupants may also turn on the air-conditioning."[64] Duff saw, or was made to see, the funny side of it. "How can you and we face the Middle States next November if we are harboring here [in the library] an old-age home instead of an academic staff?" "How can you explain an eighty-six-year-old cataloguer, eighty-three and eighty-two-year old clerks, a seventy-four years old branch librarian who may not even have a high school diploma?"[65] Sometimes he was, unintentionally, the funny side of it himself. "Last year, *The Setonian* agreed it [the granting of certain fees] would be the last demand they would make. This is like Hitler and Czechoslovakia!"[66]

Paterson

Seton Hall's last remaining satellite campus made clear this perennial tension between academics and finances. Open since 1954, Paterson enjoyed stable enrollments of 450 full-time day students during the academic bull market of the 1950s, but its clientele drifted away in the late 1960s and early 1970s to New Jersey's growing network of community colleges. Academic quality as measured by SAT scores and the ratio of full-time to part-time instructors was also in decline. The campus lacked facilities. The library was poor. There was no language laboratory or equipment for the study of the natural sciences. The parking lot was between a bar, a warehouse, and the Paterson Fire Department. Enrollment of 715 in September 1968 was down to 539 in September 1970. Although the campus was closer than South Orange to centers of population in Passaic and Bergen Counties, more daytime students from those counties chose to attend South Orange. "The sentiment was very strong for phasing Paterson out," said law professor Robert Diab. "Hardly anyone wants to keep it open, including the students."[67] "The school cannot possibly impart the benefits of a university education in light of its Lilliputian size and aesthetic shortcomings," said *The Setonian*.[68]

These weaknesses constituted an argument for either closure or improvement. A Paterson student paying the same tuition as a South Orange student was worse off, lacking indoor and outdoor recreational space, room to park, computer facilities, and the chance to meet faculty in their own offices. Precisely because the school was profitable, Fahy noticed, it was "a matter of conscience as to whether we have the right to take students' money under these circumstances."[69] "One way or another we're probably going to keep it open," he said in February 1972, "but maybe not as it is now."[70] Some were undisguisedly contemptuous of Paterson, others supportive.[71]

Turning the campus into an "Experimental Urban College" was mooted, which would have reduced its twelve majors to four divisions—a School of Natural Science and Mathematics; a School of Social and Behavioral Science; a School of Humanities and Arts; and a School of Language and Communications—but by the spring of 1972, with Paterson down to 335 students and 32 full-time and part-time professors, closure was all but inevitable. A small class was admitted for academic year 1973–1974 with assurances that qualified students could transfer to South Orange for the fall semester of 1974. For students already enrolled, limited courses were available with transfer to

South Orange of students and faculty already under way. When it opened, Paterson expressed Seton Hall's mission to educate the middle classes of New Jersey. When it died, part of the university's soul died with it. At its height in 1959, 1,138 students were enrolled. Nearly 10 percent of its graduates received honors, with quite a few of them going on to receive master's or doctoral degrees or some other form of professional qualification.[72] There was much to be proud of in such a record.

The New Professionalism

Thanks to Duff and Mitchell, Seton Hall became academically and professionally stronger in the 1970s. The improvement, however, was painful. As the Middle States inspectors noted, "a heavily over-tenured faculty [and] a restless and frustrated group of younger faculty for whom no tenure slots can be made available" was a recipe for both complacency and anger. Elizabeth Baumgartner, dean of nursing, complained that "Seton Hall is full of 'do nothings.'"[73] There were two forms of tenure: *de jure* (letters of commitment to some permanent faculty) and *de facto* (informal commitments to abide by AAUP guidelines concerning contracts of employment with long-term teachers). The university only began formal review of untenured faculty with six years of employment in 1971,[74] although a "Committee on Rank and Tenure" had been proposed by Dougherty ten years earlier.[75] In 1973, 70 percent of full-time teachers were tenured under one system or another. One solution to the problem of a heavily tenured faculty would be to encourage, and eventually to mandate, possession of the doctorate. Another would be to tighten standards for tenure and promotion, so that, in return for acceptance of those standards, those tenured *de facto* would be tenured *de jure*. (This was done by unanimous resolution of the Board of Trustees in March 1978.)[76] A final idea would be to impose stricter retirement dates.

"The toughest decisions should be made regarding tenure, then retirement; then promotion," Duff said. Instead, he complained, "promotion is hard to get; tenure sails right through."[77] Fahy also wanted tougher requirements but to have them introduced "humanely [and] delicately."[78] At Columbia, Duff's alma mater, only one in five gained tenure. At Seton Hall the ratio was four in five.[79] He and his successors Richard Connors and Peter Mitchell tightened requirements, but even under their new rules it sometimes seemed that only the "flagrantly poor" (in Mitchell's phrase) did not go through.[80] Between 1979 and 1988, 116 probationary professors applied for tenure, of whom 70 were successful and 46 not.[81] These were not ratios in the Columbia range but it *was* becoming harder to receive a permanent contract. As provost in 1979, Richard Connors urged "extreme caution" in granting tenure, recognizing the financial burden it placed on the university.[82]

University governance was another sign of new professionalism. Fahy inherited, then deepened, an institutional commitment to shared decision-making. In March 1969, the three major representative bodies of the university—the University Council, the Faculty Senate, and the Student Senate—resolved to create a Seton Hall University Committee on Decision Making consisting of five members from each of them. Dougherty charged the Committee with establishing a tripartite body with university-wide decision-making powers. From this emerged the idea of a University Senate to supersede the three existing bodies. Membership consisted of seventy-one representatives of administration, faculty, students, and alumni, its meetings to be public and held at least three times a semester, the president of the university to act as nonvoting chairman. The senate was "to consider, evaluate, and decide policies of education, student personnel services, and business at the University" but not to "supervise day-to-day operations." The President had veto power over any action of the University Senate within thirty days of official notification of its passage. A two-thirds majority (forty-eight votes out of seventy-one) could over-ride a presidential veto, with the action then submitted to the Board of Trustees for approval. If the Board refused approval, its reasons were to be transmitted to the Senate.

Fahy endorsed the proposal and the Board gave its approval on January 20, 1971. Elections were held in April 1971. Fahy hailed the University Senate as "the beginning of a new era in the governance of Seton Hall University."[83] In fact, it was too large to exercise real oversight and its power was chiefly to nudge rather than to demand. If anything, it slightly diminished a distinctive faculty voice in university affairs, because the faculty was now lumped together with the rest of the university. In December 1971, faculty representatives on the senate formed themselves into a smaller body to press for authority to vote on matters to do with their own concerns, but that idea got nowhere. The creation of the University Senate, by giving more constituencies a say in running Seton Hall, was a modest effort to improve collective governance.

Student Life, Catholic Life

Under Fahy, Seton Hall remained almost defiantly a local university. Ninety-five percent of Seton Hall's students came from New Jersey and, of these, 90 percent were between eighteen and twenty-four years old.[84] Forty percent of the fathers and 80 percent of mothers of the freshman class of 1971 had the equivalent of a high school diploma or better. Compared to national norms, this was slightly on the low side. Seventeen percent of Seton Hall fathers and 9 percent of mothers were college graduates: again, a shade behind the norm. Students were more likely to come from the second rank of their high school class and to rely on financial assistance.[85] Seton Hall was a college for families with little experience of college life. Some thought the school *too* local, wanting Seton Hall to look to a national, even an international, market. "The university must expand its recruitment base if we are to get numbers and quality," Nicholas DeProspo wrote. [86] Others believed that it was local or it was nothing.

Local or not, norms were changing. "A decade ago, the undergraduates . . . of Seton Hall were men who had to wear jackets and ties to class," wrote Fred Cicetti, class of 1963. "Today more than a third of the students . . . are women who don't have to wear bras."[87] "I don't think having a dress code makes that much difference," Fahy thought. "The students are happier without one and that is important to me." "Pot is very big in the high schools," said one student (missing his pun). "The trend [among freshmen] is definitely away from beer." In the women's dormitory, marijuana was not only smoked but grown.[88] Professors abandoned one uniform of pipe and tweeds for another of jeans and sandals. "You'll have a cop in every corner," complained a member of the sociology department. Why "should an individual's private conduct be subjugated [*sic*] to university approval when he is not an agent of the university when he is being arrested [*sic*]?"[89] Fleming's philippic of 1969 began to seem less unhinged than prophetic.

If the 1950s were not dead, they were dying. (A sign of their continuing life was that when a major in liberal arts was approved by the College of Arts and Sciences, one argument in favor was that it would appeal to women who will be "the wives of professional men in the area.") [90] In 1970, Elizabeth Baumgartner of the School of Nursing became first chair of WASHU (Women's Association of Seton Hall University). A three-day Conference on Women was held in March 1973 as part of Women's Week. Women's studies was launched in September 1973, consisting of the Sociology of Women taught by Lucinda San Giovanni and Lynn Atwater, Women in History taught by Phyllis Stock, The Phenomenon of Women taught by Miriam Luisi, and the Women's Movement taught, surprisingly, by Joseph Mahoney.[91] The Women's Action Alliance sought to "raise the collective consciousness of a conservative, middle-class suburban university"[92] by pointing out, among other things, how few women held authority in the university. A morally serious feminism and a morally frivolous campus seem oddly juxtaposed only if the former is not seen as a response to the latter.

Yet what was the nature of Seton Hall's religious identity if feminism and frivolity could flourish almost independently of each other? A university that once took Catholicism so much for granted that it never gave it a second thought now took it so little for granted that it thought about nothing else. Seton Hall talked more about faith in 1970, when it was weak, than in 1960, when it was strong. "Can a university be Catholic and a university?" *The Setonian* asked in 1969. "[It] is safe to say that no conclusion has been reached."[93] (Rather specific conclusions *had* been reached but unfortunately had yet to reach *The Setonian*.) "They do have a right to set up a college," thought Daniel Weeks, professor of chemistry ("they" being the Roman Catholic clergy). "However, there should be a point fairly early on in the history when the control is relinquished." "Dr. Weeks doesn't think there is any repression going on, at least not in the Chemistry Department . . . Unfortunately, we've been so concerned with being a Catholic university that we have forgotten to be a university . . . scholarship has been sacrificed along the way."[94] When a scientist without theological training set himself up as a theologian to disparage the claims of theology, trouble was on the way. Historians got in on the act, too. "A university can be Catholic and a university as long as the word catholic does not suggest ecclesiastical control or an orthodox point of view," Peter Mitchell argued, skewering a straw man. "If one thinks of a Catholic university as a teaching wing of the church, as a means of spreading doctrine, then it is not a university at all." "The University maintains a full range of encouragement for intellectual inquiry and for the development of concomitant community services appropriate to its teaching and research functions," concluded an assessment of the Law School in 1975. "The Judaeo-Christian principles which prompted its founding are evident in its assumed roles and tasks. In its execution of its tasks and in pursuit of its goals, only the finest traditions of this heritage is [sic] manifest. There is not the slightest evidence of the stifling of inquiry, teaching, or service by doctrinaire application of sectarianism."[95]

Intended as a compliment, this was an insult, congratulating Seton Hall for escaping its aboriginal obscurantism. Still, it warmed the heart of John Duff. "We have done away with Retreats, compulsory chapel, compulsory theology courses. We have opened the way to greater freedom. We are closer to Fordham than to Niagara [University], and this is good!"[96]

A sharper sense of the intellectual possibilities of faith in conversation with reason came from Father Eugene Cotter, a classicist, who proposed that "on the highest level, a Catholic university should be a place in which scholars of all disciplines, theology among them, should confront each other. [It] presents a corporate theological knowledge that one person could not acquire by himself." Father Kenneth O'Leary, professor of English, wanted "an intelligent and sound academic theology, a vigorous personal and social moral response, and an earnest and meaningful liturgical participation."[97] Cotter and O'Leary were sensible. So, too, was George Devine, Michael Valente's replacement as chairman of the department of theology, who saw two "liberalisms" at work at Seton Hall, one "genuine," the other "bogus." The first presumed mutual respect between different traditions. The second left "no stone standing" in order to upset traditional belief.[98] The most intolerant voices were on the left, not the right.

At one level, it was unsurprising that in 1973 the Middle States Association found "little that was Catholic about Seton Hall except a scattering of religious on campus."[99] In 1976, to fix the problem, an Office of Campus Ministry was created which, although a step forward, was itself occasionally problematic. (Among its offerings was a "clown ministry" in which assorted jesters for Jesus visited nursing homes and greeted down-and-outs, the last of these perhaps thinking that *delirium tremens* had reached its final stages).[100] At another level, Catholicism remained unavoidable, a grammar by which all reality could be understood, certainly a grammar by which all of Seton Hall could be understood. Even as eccentricity, as clowns or cassocks, it was a central fact of university life. Professors and students were either progressive or traditional, a dichotomy as much cultural and generational as theological and philosophical. One sociologist, representing the new guard, lamented a university whose intellectual life was conducted at the level of the Holy Name Society. Another deplored its attachment to "traditional morality."[101] Some "liberals" were priests. Some "conservatives" were laymen. "We claim 'Hazard Zet Forward' but are unwilling to hazard anything," complained Father Robert Antczak.[102] A Catholic university meant more than being "a nice 1940s–1950s Social Action Club wherein the social encyclicals are discussed and discarded."[103]

The traditionalist position was taken by Professor James McGlone of the department of communication, who urged colleagues to rediscover John Henry Newman and Joseph Pieper. "Even if our students are not noticeably holier, nor our language more genteel, our attire more modest than our secular counterparts, we at least have an idea what we ought to be, for we have an institutional set of values."[104] His views were shared by Joseph Mahoney and Ralph Walz of the department of history, Robert Herrera of philosophy, and Laurence MacPhee of English. From the Quaker tradition, David Rogers, also of English, insisted on Catholicism as a call to perfection, noticing that "the truly religious among the young have turned away from the church not because it is too spiritual but because it is not spiritual enough."[105]

Seton Hall was good at making urban Catholics suburban, in giving working-class students a leg up. Whether it was equally successful at keeping them Catholic was another matter. In that quandary, however, it was far from unique.

Securing a Legacy, Facing a Crisis

Fahy suffered a severe heart attack in July 1976 and succumbed to another one in October. The day before his death he told a colleague: "Don't worry about me. I'm not going anywhere. I'm going to die in this job."[106] Both laughed. At fifty-four (he looked older) he was the second Seton Hall president, after McNulty, to die in office. Inheriting a fractious university, he left it academically and administratively stronger. His predecessor as president, Bishop John Dougherty, remembered his "gifted mind, his unassuming manner, and his manly and unobtrusive piety," the times they had worked together, the "routine days and the febrile hours of crisis . . . He used the power of the institution well, in keeping with its long tradition, to serve those in need of education, in need of recognition, in need of dignity, in need of love."[107]

In an age of dissenting judgments, few dissented from that one.

Three Presidents in a Row

Conley

During the second half of Fahy's tenure, all the numbers moved in the wrong direction. His heart attack was brought on by smoking and overwork, but worry was also a factor. Facing a deficit of $3.3 million with declining enrollments, Seton Hall survived in part because John Cole (acting president after Fahy's first heart attack) capped salaries, stopped hiring, increased tuition, and deferred maintenance. Cole, an old Seton Hall hand,[108] saw an "absolute and grave" need for retrenchment.[109] The aim was to keep tuition low, but with overheads at nearly 70 percent, margins were extremely tight.[110] Cole was unfairly criticized for cutting costs wherever he could, critics forgetting that Fahy would have done the same.[111] Unless the situation were reversed, Seton Hall might no longer be a going concern.[112] He deserved credit for keeping the ship afloat. "I liked Cole a lot," Peter Mitchell recalled, "and he never interfered with my decisions after Fahy died."[113]

Another of Cole's contributions was to make it possible for the Board of Trustees to envision a layman as president. When a search committee was empaneled in November 1976 to choose Fahy's successor, two candidates stood out. Witty and gentle, Father Laurence Murphy was a Maryknoll priest, a graduate of the Naval Academy and Notre Dame, a professor of mathematics at Seton Hall after the war and of philosophy at Maryknoll and Notre Dame in the 1950s and 1960s. Articulate and forceful, Robert Conley was a chemistry graduate of Seton Hall and Princeton, a top-tier scientist with a solid career of administration in several Midwestern universities. The job went to Conley, who impressed the Board, Bishop Dougherty especially, with his vigor.[114] "He comes to us highly qualified and we look forward to great things from him,"[115] said Peter Gerety, chairman of the Board of Trustees and Archbishop of Newark since July 1974.

What ailed Seton Hall, Conley insisted, was not one big problem but a series of morale-sapping small ones.[116] Some of the latter were not so small. In the late 1970s the university opened its doors to large freshman classes that provided financial relief, but at the cost of reputation and comfort. Conditions in 1978 and 1979 were "horrendous."[117] The university's "physical unattractiveness," said Professor Peter Ahr, encouraged "people to treat it casually . . . Seton Hall must look more like a university and less like a parking lot surrounded by buildings. The difference between us and Princeton in this respect can be measured in oak trees and rhododendrons . . ."[118]

Some compared the grounds to a primeval tar-pit and the athletic fields to a training site for astronauts.[119] When not teaching in overcrowded classrooms, faculty wanted a common room. The best they had was the wood-paneled AFA club, which opened in 1974 but was later closed, having lost a fortune.[120] Meanwhile Conley's inauguration, in April 1978, was an unwitting metaphor for a university cheerfully spending its way to bankruptcy.[121] Two hundred waitresses served 3,700 guests a menu consisting of sliced filet of beef, fresh fruit cup, and parfait, with an open and conspicuously well-patronized bar.[122] A concert given by the Seton Hall University Chorus and Symphony Orchestra included numbers that turned out to be prophetic: "So Long, Farewell," "No Way to Stop It," "You're Away," and "Rhapsody in Blue."

Conley made good personnel decisions but was fixated on trivialities. He was also unlucky. A fire in November 1977 destroyed the basement of Walsh Gymnasium. A popular baseball player, Patrick O'Connor, died in his dormitory room in March 1978. Two priests, Joseph Wortmann and Martin Foran, were held up at gunpoint in front of the Humanities Building in October 1978.[123]

The deficit increased from $3,376,141 on June 30, 1977 to $4,792,124 on June 30, 1978. Short-term borrowing rose to $3,963,000 at June 30, 1978 from $1,950,000 the year before.[124] Peter Mitchell (who resigned as provost in June 1979) thought that university administration and finance were "in shambles," that student affairs had "serious morale problems," that the library was "in disarray," and that many administrators were inept. "I thought Conley was a bit crazy and it spurred me to leave the university," he recalled, a decision he came to regret but one that many others might like to have made.[125] The last straw was when Conley allowed anyone on the waitlist to enter the university if someone wrote a sponsoring letter.

The basic problem—year-on-year deficits, tuition dependency, and minimal endowment income—had plagued Seton Hall for years. Conley added some touches of his own, in his first budget forgetting to include the cost of fringe benefits, FICA payments, and the university's contribution to TIAA-CREF, a $2 million mistake only noticed at the last minute by Father John Horgan, university controller.[126] Contributed services by priests was entered as income but salary lines did not include expenditure to account for it, resulting in a net increase in the deficit. (It is hard to lose money by saving it, but Seton Hall succeeded.) Capital expenditures at the Law School were not budgeted, resulting in another deficit increase. Student enrollment was overestimated, resulting a shortfall in credit generation. Salaries and costs were not budgeted for in some offices (including the president's), again increasing the deficit. Conley described the finances in a series of baffling statements, claiming that he had inherited a deficit of $1.4 million,[127] that he had balanced the budget,[128] that the deficit was $1 million,[129] that it was $190,000 (but in reality $30,000 [sic]),[130] that it was $750,000 and rising.[131] In April 1979, he presented a set of figures that bore no resemblance to reality at all.[132] "I don't want accountants determining academics," he said.[133] Unfortunately, he did not want accountants determining accountancy either. In May 1979, Seton Hall reached its borrowing limit. In June, with faculty threatening to go on strike[134] and the deficit at $7.1 million, the university faced layoffs or protection under federal bankruptcy laws.[135]

Conley was forced out of office in July by Archbishop Gerety and his righthand man, Monsignor John Petillo, chancellor of administration for the Archdiocese of Newark and secretary of the Board of Trustees. A young priest of managerial brilliance, Petillo had been assuming greater authority in the day-to-day affairs of the university and now he engineered the removal of a man who had proven "a bit catastrophic" as president.[136] In his last year in office, Seton Hall had overestimated its revenue by $1 million and had overspent even that by another $1.1 million. Father Al Celiano blamed "poor procedures . . . people buying without purchase orders, people over-expending, no controls"[137]: a good epitaph for the era.

Murphy

Conley's replacement was Father Laurence Murphy, who had been approached to take over the job a week before he was ousted. (Conley had no idea he was to be replaced, telling a few faculty days before of his plans for the future.)[138] At the time, Murphy was an assistant professor in the humanistic program—quite a promotion. Inheriting an abysmal budget, a bloated middle management, a depressed faculty, a demoralized student body, a university lacking "identity and a [decent] concept of itself," he was now in charge of what Professor Joseph Mahoney called the "parthenogenic reproduction of administrators at Seton Hall."[139] Liz Hegy, a political science student, offered a dry assessment. "Seton Hall University has overcrowded dorms, overcrowded parking lots, a tuition that is too high for the services rendered, a bookstore that doesn't function, lousy food plus teachers who are unsatisfied with contracts. Other than this, Father Murphy has done a good job. I hope [he] believes in miracles."[140]

Murphy offered not miracles but moderation. "This is a sober and difficult time in the life of Seton Hall," he told the faculty, "but it is not a time of defeat or even decline." The deficit for fiscal year 1978–1979 was between $1.6 and $1.8 million, bringing the total deficit to $6.5 million. "We have been operating for some time spending considerably more than we took in. . . . We have no vice president for development and that we must find one at once. . . . Little things mount up: petty destruction and vandalism, litter, misuse of telephones, leaving lights on, open windows in winter, using Xerox when stencils would be just as good, and so forth."[141]

He was helped by Father Al Celiano, professor of chemistry, who served as vice president for administrative services. "If one person who should be credited for rescuing the university from financial shipwreck," claimed Peter Ahr, "it is Father Celiano."[142] Murphy appointed Richard Connors acting provost and vice president for academic affairs, Nicholas DeProspo acting vice president for planning, and Father Celiano acting dean of the arts and sciences. (He lasted about a month before becoming acting vice president for administrative affairs—thus the search for beds. His position at arts and sciences was taken by Bernhard Scholz, professor of history and director of the honors program).

Murphy drew on the Mexican writer Octavio Paz to describe Seton Hall's problems,[143] but the faculty was in no mood to hear musings about Western hedonism when their salaries had failed to keep pace with the cost of living. For Mary Boutilier, chair of the faculty council, the problem lay with "a Board of Trustees that acts as if it oversees a corporate enterprise rather than an educational institution . . . a Board that has veered between near total disinterest and lack of knowledge about the University to one that virtually dictates every decision and direction . . . a Board that has decided that the university is a business ledger which has only debits and assets, not humans, not values, not ideas."[144] It was hard to take some of these contradictory complaints seriously. Why was it acceptable for faculty to complain of financial devastation but not, apparently, for students, who paid faculty salaries? Why complain that the university was run as a business and that it was not? Still, Boutilier's grievances were symptomatic of serious disillusion.

Academic year 1979–1980 began without a budget. On June 30, 1979, as Conley was about to depart, Seton Hall's cash, temporary investments, and marketable securities amounted to $5,000.[145] In October 1979, a fiscal task force under Celiano rapidly identified a year's worth of financial cuts.[146] In November 1979, the university faced a shortfall of over $7 million, "a very grave though not hopelessly irreversible financial problem."[147] In January 1980, one of every six students registered for a course had paid nothing in tuition, a situation which, if unrectified, would have caused a deficit of $1.2 million and immediate budget cuts.[148]

Between the end of 1979 and the beginning of 1980, financial arrangements were entirely *ad hoc*. Delving into the weeds of Conley's budget, the Task Force found room for cuts in athletics, the president's office, and unfilled staff positions.[149] (They also discovered eye-watering abuse of the campus phone system.)[150] Celiano and Professor Jack Shannon, assistant dean of the school of business and a member of the task force, went round turning off lights and lowering thermostats to reduce costs. (Without a mild winter, Seton Hall's freeze, in every sense, would have been worse.) By leaving positions unfilled and winning favorable terms of debt service, they were able to turn a deficit at the beginning of the academic year into a small surplus at the end. "Right now we could use $30 million [from a fund drive]," said Murphy. "Our credit line won't be extended. Banks won't give us another penny. We're going to run a balanced budget or else."[151] The "or else" was closure.

Despite a cratering national economy and inflation running at 20 percent, Murphy refused to despair.[152] But relentless negativity took its toll. The Board of Trustees forced him to account for every decision he made no matter how trivial, wearing him down by petty indignities. (He resented having to account for travel expenses, as if he were not to be trusted.) The appointment in August 1980 of Edward D'Alessio as executive vice president was an implied vote of no confidence. D'Alessio was a former education professor with administrative experience in federal government. In the seven weeks that the arrangement lasted, the Board deferred to D'Alessio, prompting Celiano to resign from the Budget Committee in protest at the treatment of his friend and fellow priest, Murphy. At the same time, Murphy's assistant, Michael Murray, showed more loyalty to Petillo than to his nominal boss. Petillo appeared to be pulling most of the strings from his office in Newark.[153] The governing body of Seton Hall was riven with factions.

This is not to deny achievements. Murphy inherited a disaster and, thanks to Celiano, Shannon, and Petillo he bequeathed a going concern. Another legacy was also significant. In June 1980, university by-laws were changed to enable the thirteen-member Board of Trustees (Seton Hall's original corporation) to elect a twenty-five-member Board of Regents, the Trustees to act as custodians of the university's physical assets and Catholic identity, the Regents to have oversight of academic and financial management. (This was the brainchild of Nicholas De Prospo, vice president for planning.) Petillo served as first chairman of the Board of Regents. The Board of Trustees was to consist mainly of clergymen, the Regents mainly of lay people. Before the separation, the Trustees dealt with policy, strategy, budgets, and academic procedures, its horizons limited, its planning reactive. With two Boards, it was now possible to think in a less *ad hoc* way about academic and financial policy. The Board of Regents included lawyers, businessmen, and accountants who did not hesitate to insert themselves into university life. Within a couple of years, it became apparent that the Board of Regents, rather than the Board of Trustees, was the key governing body of the university, giving legal force to tenure decisions, civil contracts, and the like. The fact that the two Boards had overlapping memberships did not obscure the reality of their distinctive functions; the most important of those functions as far as day-to-day oversight university was concerned lay with the Regents.

Murphy resigned on August 29, 1980, citing age and ill health as his reasons, although he was only sixty-two.[154] (The anxiety was exaggerated: he died in 2021 at the age of 102.) Other than the university's survival, he could record successes: a statement on Catholicity which, although the work of a committee, expressed much of his own generous pluralism;[155] the establishment of a doctoral program in the School of Education; the signing of an exchange program with the People's Republic of China. On the day he told the cabinet of his resignation, asking them to continue his policies, he specified five areas of concern which, together, suggested a legacy. These were, first, the need to implement the statement on Catholicity; then, to insure "opportunities for blacks and other minorities to participate in the good of the university"; then, to "cherish and assist students"; then to expand the international dimension of education;

finally, to encourage a "marriage between competence and vision" in the faculty.[156] But these were aspirations, not achievements. At the same meeting at which he announced his departure, the difficulties he bequeathed were obvious, with the budget as yet un-approved and faculty morale "at rock bottom."[157]

Years later, when the dust had settled, Murphy looked back on his presidency with few regrets. "I think we did stabilize the university, put it back . . . There was a lot of dissatisfaction among the faculty. I got them feeling comfortable again, which I guess you can call a milestone."[158]

D'Alessio

Announcing his successor, Murphy said that Edward D'Alessio would "assume the administration of the university immediately. . . . There will be no Acting or Interim President." Aged forty-eight, D'Alessio had been a Seton Hall undergraduate in the early 1950s, a faculty member and assistant dean in the School of Education from 1958 to 1967, president of the College of Our Lady of the Elms in Chicopee, Massachusetts, and a midlevel administrator in the U.S. Department of Education. Already *in situ* as ex-ecutive vice president, he paid tribute to Murphy for having "stabilized" the university, insisting that it was now "on the brink of greatness."[159] (For some reason, he refused to have a conversation with Murphy, a snub which hurt.) Technically, D'Alessio was "chief operating officer" (a title which laconic Bernhard Scholz thought "may be . . . appropriate for a submarine or a tire factory but [not for a University]."[160] Soon into his stint, the university sold its 180-acre tract of land at Saddle Brook, New Jersey for $4.5 million; the land, purchased in 1960 with the intention of building a new campus, had lain undeveloped because of local objections. The windfall eased some financial pres-sure. In addition, an agreement was signed with the Beijing Institute of Foreign Trade allowing for faculty and student exchange between the two institutions,[161] the most important fruit of Murphy's visit to China in June 1980.

The "present arrangements" lasted for nearly a year, until D'Alessio was named president in June 1981. A faculty-led search committee was impaneled but its short-list, which did not include D'Alessio, was ignored by the Board of Regents, provoking unfulfilled threats of litigation. D'Alessio, untroubled by the prospect of legal action, stated the faculty was within its rights to file suit if it wished.[162] But John Petillo of the Board of Regents had the last word. "In naming D'Alessio," he said, "the Regents have selected an individual with outstanding academic credentials and an educator who is both known to the community and familiar with the university's administration and objectives."[163] Most faculty disliked the procedure or the outcome or both.[164]

Youngest of fourteen children of Italian immigrants, D'Alessio personified the mis-sion of the school. In some ways lucky—Conley's near fatal deficit of June 1979 was all but eliminated by June 1982[165]—in other ways he was unlucky. Saint Andrew's College Seminary, housed since 1976 in a former Episcopal church a short walk from campus, was destroyed by fire in March 1982.[166] Displaced students were relocated to Boland Hall (where "divvies" had once lived before moving to Saint Andrew's). Bayley Hall was damaged by fire a week later, leaving the roof in need of replacement.[167] Smaller fires (possibly deliberate) damaged Fahy Hall and McLaughlin Library in May 1982.[168] A series of bomb threats in late 1981 and early 1982 frayed nerves. Morale remained low.

Eventually D'Alessio hit his stride, appointing two supporters to vice presidencies, Michael Murray to administrative services,[169] Charles Dees to university affairs.[170] In a sense, D'Alessio was himself a vice president to Petillo, chair of the Board of Regents. Over $2 million were spent in capital improvements in his first year (some necessitated by the fires). Saint Andrew's College Seminary added rooms and an attractive chapel.[171] But the stakes were high. "I have a passionate desire to see your presidency succeed," wrote Monsignor John Oesterreicher to him. "Were it to flounder like that of your predecessors, Seton Hall would be finished."[172]

A new president did not mean an end to old problems. A year into his term, a team of auditors found a "chaotic approach to day-to-day problems," "lack of adequate supervision of staff," "computerized financial systems not understood by the people [who] use them," "serious problems in the payroll department," grant management "broken down almost completely," "totally erroneous" computer programs, and student attrition hovering around 20 percent. On the other hand, by the beginning of 1982 the financial situation of the university had turned around, thanks to Petillo and the Board of Regents. In 1978, when he became the Archdiocese of Newark's chancellor for administration, Petillo had "to salvage Seton Hall from the brink of bankruptcy."[173] By 1983, he had done a "remarkable job" in "overcoming deficits and returning Seton Hall to financial stability."[174] "If the deficit hadn't been turned around," said Robert Gentry, vice president for financial affairs, "this university could have been put out of existence."[175] In fact, after repaying debt, the university bought treasury notes using money from student tuition at the beginning of the semester and selling it at the end, thus generating interest income. A borrower had become a lender. "Despite the nation's economic stresses," said D'Alessio, "1982 was the best financial year in memory for Seton Hall," with no short-term debt and no outstanding notes payable for the first time since 1967. By April 1983, the unrestricted fund showed a surplus of $1.1 million.[176] D'Alessio, an accidental president, had accomplishments to his name.

CHAPTER 16

The Seton Hall Renaissance

Midlife Crisis

Under D'Alessio, Seton Hall survived but hardly thrived. The "manifest . . . good health" of the Fahy years, when "caring, kindness, [even] quiet euphoria" prevailed, was replaced by low morale,[1] "aimless drifting," "lack of purpose," and "inordinate preoccupation with budgetary matters."[2] Accreditation of schools and programs, more doctorates, stable enrollment, and better finances had failed to erase "feelings of distrust" among faculty and staff,[3] a kind of institutional midlife crisis leading only to despondency and gloom. (Indeed, the average age of a Seton Hall professor in 1982 was nearly forty-eight: one set of crises seemed almost to lead to another.) "Almost universally the faculty believes the administration is both top heavy and, in many cases, lacking in competence," wrote James O'Connor of the College of Education and Human Services.[4] "My highest priority will be to seek suitable employment elsewhere," wrote Jerry Hirsch, professor of chemistry[5] (who found it in 1987 as dean of the College of Arts and Sciences). "Since the days of Bishop Dougherty and Monsignor Fahy, times of trust, respect, appreciation, [and] love, faculty morale has been on a bobsled," wrote Albert Reiners, professor of education. "We knew we were a Catholic university—no slogans needed."[6] To a degree, morale was low because everyone said it was low, and, paradoxically, when that was agreed, everyone began to feel better. But there were objective reasons for concern. "If we delude ourselves into thinking that this institution can continue with the standard of living it has enjoyed through the sixties, seventies, and most of the eighties," said Nicholas DeProspo, "we are on a collision course with disaster . . . Many of our administrators . . . tend to meet crisis after crisis, putting out one brushfire after another."[7]

The problem was not only lack of money but of uncertainty of mission. "What is Seton Hall trying to be?" Larry Murphy asked in April 1980. "It cannot be Harvard," he answered, "but it is also not a county college."[8] Seton Hall's problems were thus not so much those of a financially struggling institution (although it was certainly that) as those of a culture and society trying to come to terms with a new identity. Andrew Greeley's description of American Catholicism in the early 1970s as "a period

341

of emotional exhaustion" comes to mind.[9] With Seton Hall, the fatigue reflected not so much dislike as exasperated affection for an institution that frequently flirted with failure. A 1980 survey reported "almost surrealistic" levels of enthusiasm for a university which, one alumnus put it, made it "very hard for you to love" but which did such a "good job [that I can't forget it] and I appreciate it."[10] Seton Hall oscillated between "an unfortunate but very discernible inferiority complex" and a conviction that it was "not just another college" but a "family" that did some things "uniquely well."[11]

This is not to deny bright moments. President Ronald Reagan coming to campus in 1983 to give the commencement address was one such. Seton Hall had never hosted a sitting president before (or any president, for that matter). Drenching rain gave way to sunshine as Reagan's helicopter came into view. The sodden campus cheered up as Pearl Bailey, also honored that day, delighted parents and, more likely, grandparents with her singing. Reagan spoke of school prayer, the right to life, and the need for educational tax vouchers: in every sense, vintage material. He was surprisingly nervous, a fact he confided to his diary but to no one else. D'Alessio had his difficulties as president but only he could claim to have delivered President Reagan.

Another Leader

Yet D'Alessio was never master in his own house. Shadowing him was Monsignor John Petillo, chancellor of administration for the Archdiocese of Newark, who ran the show, controlling Seton Hall's budget and thus the university itself. Petillo, a tough-minded child of Italian immigrants, proved one of the most significant figures in Seton Hall history, rescuing it from near-bankruptcy. Seton Hall opened doors for him and he returned the favor by keeping those doors open for others. In July 1983, at age thirty-six, he was appointed chancellor of the university, the appointment made because the reaffiliation of the seminary with the university had raised the canonical problem of a layman, as president, exercising jurisdiction over priestly formation. To deal with the difficulty, the Board of Trustees created the position of chancellor, to be held by a priest who would act as chief executive officer of the university and seminary, while also serving as chairman of the Board of Regents. The position of president was retained, open to a lay person (or priest) with responsibility for academic matters and day-to-day operations. This argument from canon law was a contrivance and indeed itself a violation of canon law. (No-one may come between a bishop and the rector of his seminary.) The real purpose of the appointment was to allow Petillo to deal with the "current demands on leadership in the University,"[12] a euphemism for D'Alessio's inadequacy. "The president will be dealing with me directly on everything that relates to his areas," said Petillo, raising the question of what those areas might be. In fact, it was "patently clear," the Middle States reported in 1983, that the presidential office had been "debased and eroded."[13] "Our difficulties," wrote Nicholas DeProspo years later, "stemmed from a lack of clarity between the roles of D'Alessio as president and Petillo as chancellor. The vice presidents of academic affairs, planning, and administration answered to D'Alessio, whereas the vice presidents of finance and university affairs answered to Petillo. . . . It was an awkward arrangement."[14] Later, the office of president was abolished,[15] only to be reinstated during the chancellorship of Father Thomas Peterson in the early 1990s. With these exceptions, Seton Hall has always been led by a president.

Whatever the title, Petillo had the power. "I see the need to improve our image, cultivate our friends and alumni, improve the facilities, and plan for the future," he said, leaving no doubt that he set the agenda.[16] "Higher education is in a crisis; we are a part of it . . . Trust is necessary to build a strong university."[17] Over the next half-decade, he won that trust, leaving Bernhard Scholz to think that the years between 1983 and 1988 represented "one of the most innovative and creative periods in the . . . history of Seton Hall."[18] Not all of the successes were due to Petillo but many of them were.

Planning and Building the Future

Seton Hall's problems were not all home grown or easily solved by the exercise of one man's will. In 1976, high school graduates in New Jersey peaked at 113,711. In September 1987, the number was projected to be less than 92,000. Seton Hall's traditional catchment areas, Bergen, Essex, Hudson, Passaic, and Union Counties, declined in population between 1976 and 1986[19] and Middlesex County, where population had risen, saw a fall in the White middle class which was Seton Hall's prime recruitment target.[20] Seton Hall went from a local to a regional university by necessity. Future students were "not going to be coming from East Orange or the North Ward (Newark) or Belleville or Nutley," said Petillo in 1985. "They are still going to come, but now we're going to get them from Monmouth, Ocean, and even as far down as Atlantic County and Cape May County."[21] Students over the age of twenty-five were no answer to falling high school numbers because older part-time students (who had their own costly needs) were insufficient to offset loss of revenue from declining full-time eighteen- to twenty-four-year-olds. African American and Hispanic populations were projected to rise dramatically, becoming a target for Seton Hall and other schools in the state and region. (In 1986, one third of all Catholics in the United States between the ages of eighteen and twenty-four were Hispanic.) Foreign students were another untapped market.[22] All these complex variables had to be understood to do basic planning that, for years, Seton Hall had shirked. Granting tenure meant a promise to employ a teacher for perhaps thirty years. What if there were no students to teach? Building a dormitory meant paying customers and willing pockets. What if the pockets were not willing? Or if students wanted to live at home? Or if they were financially willing but academically weak? These were real-world questions with real-world risks. In 1977, combined SAT scores for all Seton Hall students was 913. In 1982, it was 899. "Our incoming freshman class numbers 1,265," Petillo told faculty in September 1983. "If we had set a minimum combined SAT score at 1,000, [it] would have numbered 350."[23] Petillo did not give the impression of having sleepless nights, but these were problems to worry the most serene temperament.

Seton Hall also faced what Petillo called a "facilities war." Testifying in front of Congress in 1985, he explained that almost every private university in the nation faced decaying physical plant, uncertain revenue flow, and growing demand for expensive equipment: all the problems of a postwar expansion now rapidly losing energy. (A 1975 study estimated that 20 percent of college facilities throughout the country needed replacement at a cost of $50 billion.) Offering an interim account of his own stewardship, he told Congress that Seton Hall had led the way: "In the last five years we have built a new seminary, initiated steps to double our dormitory capacity, spent four million dollars catching up on long-deferred maintenance, and have begun construction of a recreation center . . . Most of our facilities are 45 to 50 years old. We need to spend nine million dollars to renovate and equip our science building . . . We need to spend one million dollars on our library building and two and a half million dollars for our main classroom building . . . A conservative estimate of our needs is twenty million dollars over the next five years."[24]

Under Petillo, the university changed beyond recognition, a transformation the more impressive for being achieved in the face of the local and national decline in student population. For every wealthy private or public university putting up a high-tech science center or a state-of-the-art sports arena, there were dozens of Seton Halls trying to meet twentieth-century needs in nineteenth-century buildings. Commanding an annual budget of $50 million in 1985, 90 percent of it derived from tuition and fees, Petillo argued that capital expenditure was necessary for basic survival. "There's an old adage in the building trade that 'you cannot cheat a house,'" he told faculty in October 1987. "We ought to know: we tried it for years. And we're learning how incredibly costly and time-consuming it is!"[25]

A Campus Renewed

The Return of the Seminary

Academically and architecturally, not to say spiritually, the most important project was the return of Immaculate Conception Seminary to South Orange in 1984. Having the seminary back on campus reintroduced Seton Hall to itself, a reminder to those who may have forgotten or may have wished to forget that it was, above all, a Catholic university. Although distinct from Seton Hall College, the seminary had always been part of it. The college came first, and then, in 1860, the seminary. The latter, enjoying separate status in canon law, was in civil law part of the corporation called Seton Hall College that was founded in 1856. That did not change even after the move to Darlington in 1927. Immaculate Conception Seminary was not civilly incorporated until August 1972.[26] Even when the seminary moved off campus to begin its independent life, the connection to Seton Hall remained and indeed was formally written into the minutes of the Board of Trustees on the occasion of the move. The theology department of the seminary granted its master's degree in Seton Hall's name until 1932. Seminarians continued to take their BAs in philosophy from the College. Generations of priests ordained in the middle decades of the century began their studies in South Orange as schoolboys or students and finished them miles away in Mahwah. Physical distance attenuated the emotional links between the seminary and the university but the academic links, although less obvious, remained intact.

These connections persisted in the postwar period. In the 1950s, divinity students preparing to enter the major seminary remained on campus, but by the 1960s and '70s these "divvies" lived in a university unsure of what to make of them, and they of it. The "Divinity School" preparing students for the major seminary formed an integral part of the university but, for that very reason, it also seemed distinct from the rest of the campus: "The Divinity School [said the university catalog] is an individual scholastic unit within the framework of the College of Arts and Sciences. It functions under its own Director, appointed by the Archbishop of Newark, President of the Board of Trustees of the University. [It] supervises the academic progress of its students during the initial two years of college spent on the South Orange campus, before entrance into the Major Philosophical-Theological Seminary of the Immaculate Conception, Darlington, New Jersey. The philosophy curriculum of the Seminary is an integral part of the College of Arts and Sciences of the University."[27] Divinity students concentrated on philosophy in their junior year, but their degree was in classical languages. They lived on a floor of Boland Hall and were similar to the ordinary run of undergraduates (a fact that caused concern when they transferred to Darlington in the 1960s). In 1968, following a recommendation of a joint committee of the university and seminary and with the approval of Archbishop Thomas Boland, divinity students began to pursue their entire four-year course on the South Orange campus and were free to choose any arts degree (although they needed the permission of the director of the Divinity School to major in science). This liberalization did not sit well with Monsignor Harold Darcy, rector of the seminary between 1972 and 1974, nor with Boland himself, both men worried about priestly formation and, in Boland's case, about the Catholic character of the university. By the early 1970s, then, Seton Hall had no major seminary, no graduate school of theology, and a Divinity School that was somewhere between a holding company for pious undergraduates and a directed program of common living. In 1973, Saint Andrew's College Seminary opened in South Center Street, South Orange, making use of a former Episcopalian church to create a more communitarian experience of spiritual discernment among divinity students.[28]

It would be wrong to imagine that the College Seminary produced students indistinguishable from other undergraduates who then had to be clericalized when they went to the major seminary. If anything, students leaving Seton Hall were more conservative than the faculty at Darlington who greeted them when they arrived. In 1978 Monsignor John O'Brien, secretary to the Board of Trustees of Immaculate Conception Seminary, reported "some uneasiness among the Seton Hall students concerning the liberal ideas purportedly espoused by this Seminary's faculty," which, he said, had "painful ramifications." In any given class, he said, "the seminarians from the Divinity School at Seton Hall are usually readily identifiable by position and/or practice."[29] In the 1970s, when the campus seemed to lose its way as far as Catholicity was concerned, the seminary's complaint was that it was producing candidates for the priesthood who were, if anything, too priestly, too assured about their vocations.[30]

Whatever of that, Darlington was too big for the slimmed-down needs of the 1970s when vocations declined and archdiocesan finances, poorly managed for years, began to give cause for alarm.[31] In 1972 the rector, Monsignor William Hogan, warned that "for the first time" enrollments were "reaching a dangerously low level."[32] Diocesan finances were also chaotic, with unsecured debt of $24.5 million and few plans to deal with it. "There's going to be some blood on the floor around here, but we can't help it," Gerety told officials in 1977.[33] By the middle of that year, the unsecured debt was reduced to $21.5 million, but with $1.8 million in annual interest charges. In December 1978, negotiations with the archdiocese's creditors took place in a frigidly cold room in the Chancery Office in Newark. (Asked why, the chairman explained that the archdiocese could not afford to heat it. In fact, someone had turned on the air-conditioning.) The result was a significantly improved loan agreement providing for a reduced annual rate of interest of 7 per cent.[34]

Darlington's closure was inevitable.[35] "I have continually said I do not want to destroy the seminary and I believe it will be destroyed if we do not affiliate [with Seton Hall]," Gerety told seminary faculty in September 1981. "On January 1, 1984, I have to face the banks again. We have been supporting this seminary over $600,000 a year. This cannot go on. A couple of years ago I served notice that the large subsidy has to end . . . The archdiocese owns it. The property is valued at millions of dollars."[36] Expressed thus, the decision seems purely financial but Gerety also believed that what was good for the seminary could also be good for the university: "My concern is about the catholicity of Seton Hall University. It seems to me that to have the seminary, with the scholars that are now on the faculty, immediately puts us in a position to have influence on the university scene."[37]

The idea was not only that Darlington be sold and the seminary move to Seton Hall, but that the new relationship be created between the two to the benefit of both. This had consequences for seminary faculty, who would now be connected to a larger academic community; for seminary administration, which would now be beholden in complicated ways to Seton Hall and the archdiocese; and for seminarians, who would now find themselves in a different setting from the one to which they were accustomed. But Gerety hoped that the biggest change would be for Seton Hall itself. "Seton Hall's Catholic character will be enhanced by the presence of seminary students and faculty, while the seminary will benefit from exposure to scholars from a broad spectrum of academic disciplines," he thought.[38] This was a hope, not a plan, but in many ways he was proved right.

The move was financially astute. By January 1984, the archdiocese had paid off the last of the $14 million it owed to the banks, and by December 1985, it completed the sale of the Darlington property for $8.6 million. Of that sum, $3 million was to be used for the construction of the new seminary building on the Seton Hall campus and the remainder used to endow a pension fund for retired archdiocesan priests. Additionally, a capital campaign for the seminary generated over $4.2 million in pledges, with the Kresge Foundation chipping in another $350,000.

Ground was broken for the new building in June 1983. Students arrived in October 1984 (having begun the academic year in in Darlington). Located between Presidents Hall, Alumni Hall and the baseball field, the seminary symbolized Seton Hall old and new. At one point during construction the roof collapsed, causing some $300,000 worth of damage,[39] but when completed the building was impressive. Alumni Hall (physically connected to the new building by a walkway) was converted into offices on the ground floor with a chapel on the first floor (a space that had been, over the course of a century, a billiards room, a laboratory, and a classroom). An attractive library on the lower level of the main building looked to the back of Presidents Hall. A cloistered garden defined the space between Immaculate Conception Chapel, Presidents Hall, Alumni Hall, Stafford Hall, and Marshall Library. A pleasant entrance foyer overlooked the baseball field, with offices and rooms to the left and right of a central atrium. There were 15 suites for priests, one 101 rooms for students, along with common rooms, a faculty lounge, and 2 dining areas, one for priests, the other for seminarians. Over the years, the newness of the building was softened by statues, windows, and other artifacts brought down from Darlington or out of storage in South Orange. Presidents Hall had been the seminary building from 1867 to 1927. Now, literally and metaphorically, the seminary could look back on the place where it started. As Ciuba wrote to Gerety on October 12, 1984:

On April 17, 1927, Msgr. Thomas McLaughlin, the rector of the seminary at South Orange, recorded the following in his diary: "Took all seminarian registers and documents pertaining to the seminary and new seal to Darlington, thus closing seminary at South Orange after 66 years in that spot. May God bless the seminarians and successors in new home." As I close this seminary at Darlington, on October 12, 1984, I too am taking all seminarian registers and documents pertaining to the seminary, thus closing the seminary in Mahwah, N.J. after fifty-seven years in that spot. May God bless the seminarians, faculty, and staff in our new home on the campus of Seton Hall University.[40]

What to call the new entity? After a few false starts—at one point it was to be called, absurdly, the Darlington Seminary of the Immaculate Conception Graduate School of Theology and Pastoral Ministry of Seton Hall University—in 1986 the name became the Immaculate Conception Seminary/School of Theology of Seton Hall University. In 1977, while still in Darlington, the seminary had become a degree-granting institution accredited by the Association of Theological Schools and the Middle States Association, an accreditation renewed for ten years in 1982. Under a new agreement, the university and the seminary remained legally distinct but mutually dependent entities, Seton Hall owning the seminary buildings and responsible for their maintenance, the seminary drawing up a budget in accordance with the financial policies of the university. The seminary operated at a loss of between $500,000 and $650,000 a year, with the archdiocese making up the shortfall. Seton Hall benefited by $2 million dollars from the archdiocese's fundraising between 1982 and 1992. Seminary faculty were to be appointed by the chancellor of the university (a priest) and, if priests, released for service by the archbishop or accepted into the diocese by him. There would be no tenure.[41] The university provost (almost always a layman) would exercise academic oversight, with the rector/dean of the seminary answerable to him on scholarly, pedagogic, and financial matters and answerable to the archbishop on spiritual and formational ones. In 1988 the arrangements were modified to allow the rector/dean certain rights not enjoyed by other deans and to require appointment to the faculty first by the archbishop and then by the university.[42]

There were grumbles. Religious studies professor John Mitchell complained that the Seminary/School of Theology wished to "enjoy the fruits of life within the University when this suits their ends but [also to] stand outside the processes of accountability required of other academic components of the university when this does not [sic] suit their purposes." Mitchell objected to the fact (as he saw it) that faculty members of the School of Theology did not enjoy academic freedom. "Neither the long-term intellectual vitality of Catholic theology nor the training of candidates for the priesthood are well served by a neo-conservative mentality which seeks to impose narrowly drawn tests for orthodoxy on those involved in the academic discipline of theology."[43] In fact, the School of Theology was impressive in the quantity and quality of its scholarship, the real reason for Mitchell's anxiety not lack of academic freedom but the seminary's intelligent exercise of it. Others struck a more positive note. For Peter Ahr, the return of the seminary would strengthen the university by bringing together seminary faculty, faculty of Religious studies, Judeo-Christian studies, and "our departments of Asian Studies, Sociology, Political Science, History, Counseling, and Psychology."[44] This vision was only partially realized, if at all, but it suggested a core of benevolence.

Goodwill was evident at the opening and blessing of the new building in April 1985, with Archbishop Pio Laghi, papal nuncio to the United States, presiding. (The building was named Lewis Hall in honor of Milton and Rita Lewis, its major benefactors.) Ciuba noted the "reconstitution of the mission on new soil . . . The seed has been planted in new and rich soil." To Gerety the presence of the papal nuncio indicated "our union with the Holy Father." Laghi was impressed by the standing ovation given to Ciuba, who was beloved by the seminary community.[45] The return of the seminary was one of the great days in Seton Hall history.

For all that, the era of good feelings was short lived and, for seminary faculty, the blame for its disappearance lay with Petillo and his provost, Bernhard Scholz, both of them more interested, it seemed, in asserting the claims of the university than in respecting the rights of the seminary. All sorts of issues complicated the relationship, from faculty contracts to faculty offices, from finances to the affiliation agreement, from the status of the seminary as a house of formation and as fully integrated academic entity within the university answerable to the provost. Monsignor Richard Liddy, Ciuba's unconfrontational and soft-spoken replacement as rector, suspected that, under the guise of academic freedom, certain Seton Hall faculty were "not friends of the Church."[46] (This was a masterpiece of understatement.) Symbolizing the tension was the courtyard area between Presidents Hall and the seminary, a space earmarked for the seminary's exclusive use, which in March 1987 was redesigned without notice with the intention of being made available to the whole university.[47] Petillo yielded, grudgingly. The affiliation agreement was eventually revised thanks to Liddy and two other members of the seminary faculty, Fathers Thomas Guarino and Robert Wister. Wister, the seminary's distinguished historian, summarizes that part of the history of which he had firsthand knowledge: "Officials of the university viewed the seminary simply as another academic unit. They were indifferent to its particular mission as a place for the formation of priests with a canonical connection to the archbishop. This may have been due to the efforts of the part of some university officials, like many of their contemporaries at other Catholic colleges at the time, to loosen ties with ecclesiastical authorities. The seminary and its faculty, however, were unwilling to make any concessions that would weaken its essential mission. Therefore, they were willing to sacrifice such academic privileges such as tenure."[48]

The revised affiliation agreement radically transformed the relationship for the better, seminary faculty now accorded status as university faculty and eligible to serve on all university committees except the University Rank and Tenure Committee. The seminary, writes Wister, "was now able to settle into its new home and to continue and expand its mission without the distractions of continual strife with the university administration. Of course, there would be occasional tensions but these resolved around issues that were part and parcel of daily university life—turf, facilities, and funding struggles."[49]

Two ironies are worth noting. It was a priest—Petillo—who seemed least attentive to the specific needs of priestly formation. His working relationship with the seminary in general and Liddy in particular was, for a time, hostile. Moreover, one motivation for returning to South Orange—that the seminary would strengthen the Catholic character of the university—almost ended with the university weakening the Catholic character of the seminary. Only the patience and vigilance of Liddy, Wister, Guarino and others ensured that that did not happen.

A Campus Rebuilt

The return of the seminary to South Orange was part of a sorely needed renewal of the campus. The deferred maintenance of the 1970s could be deferred no longer. When George Ring, a member of the Board of Regents, inspected the West Residence dormitory in 1987 ("a cave," he called it) he noticed closet rods, shower doors, curtains, soap dishes all missing, a microcosm of a more general culture of neglect.[50] The university needed "to retain students and successfully compete for [them] over the next ten years," noted the Board of Regents in 1984. Winning the "facilities war" was the only way to do it. A commuter school would become, more or less, residential, one of those risks that caused uneasy nights in many quarters. The greater risk was to do nothing at all. A new dormitory and teaching building were envisaged at a cost of $6,425,000[51] and a new Recreation Center at $9.4 million.[52] Rental income from dormitories would relieve reliance on tuition while helping to recruit better students. (That was the theory, but the argument worked both ways. Because such income was vital, filling the dormitories—tuition reliance by another name—became even more important.) Petillo reckoned that the university lost 300 students in 1984–1985 because it had nowhere to house them.[53] In 1980, Murphy had seen no future in new residences. In 1984, Petillo saw no future without them.

To finance the Recreation Center and student residence (provisionally "New Res" until named Xavier Hall in 1988), $42 million in low-interest loans were sought from the New Jersey Educational Facilities Authority (NJEFA).[54] The dormitory called for 2 three-story wings and a seven-story tower to accommodate 522 beds. (Students complained that the dormitory eliminated parking spaces, but it also reduced need for them.)[55] The Recreation Center reconfigured the Kelley-era gymnasium by adding a swimming pool, a field house, and fitness rooms. "When I see potential students," said Patricia Kuchon, vice chancellor for student affairs, "the things that excite them most are the things we are doing—the Rec. Center [and] the Residence Hall."[56] Both buildings were supposed to produce revenue simultaneously, but a projected income of $67,000 in the first year of operation turned into a loss of $732,000 as a result of higher-than-expected costs and debt service.[57] The Recreation Center was opened on University Day, October 24, 1987. New Res opened in fall 1986.

Construction began on three dormitories to the left and in front of the Humanities Building in September 1987. (The Humanities Building underwent extensive renovation at the same time and acquired a new name, Fahy Hall, in 1988.) "There is an incredible demand for on-campus housing," said Karen Flaster, director of Housing and Residence Life, "and research shows that living on campus makes a student happier and more well- adjusted."[58] The three residence halls, one a five-story building (Cabrini), the others three stories each (Serra[59] and Neumann), provided rooms for 500 students and apartments for resident priests. Although necessary, the construction cut off the east end of the campus from the rest of the university and made it difficult for students to get to the Humanities Building, where many of their classes were held. Getting from the Art Building (the old Carriage House) to other locations was almost impossible without leaving campus. "The only people who will benefit from the construction are the future resident students and the administration," noted *The Setonian* sourly.[60] Other projects included a new traffic entrance to the university, rerouting cars from the McNulty gate on South Orange Avenue to a new Farinella gate facing South Center Street. It was built in 1987–1988 at a cost of $250,000.[61] Money realized from the sale of off-campus housing was used to build a priests' residence behind Corrigan Hall on the site of some old garages. Named Gerety Hall (1988), this set of modern, self-contained, condominium-style apartments cost $600,000 to build.[62]

"A high school senior comes here and he sees a bulldozer," said Father Dennis Mahon, vice chancellor for policy and planning in 1988. It was "a sign of life," he said, but also "a risk . . . When we looked at the demographics of people born 18 years ago to Catholic families in the surrounding four counties who might come to Seton Hall as commuters, they weren't there. We came to the conclusion that once you get beyond a 45 minute or one hour commute, people are not going to come. We had to make the decision to move out there or make a provision for the students to be here . . . Without this construction Seton Hall would be in a very difficult situation to BE Seton Hall."[63]

"It used to be that you drove to school, parked your car, went to class, maybe the cafeteria, then went home," said Keith Meyers, director of the Recreation Center. [64] Those days were gone. As Serra, Neumann and Cabrini Halls were built (and so named in 1988), Xavier Hall became less a showpiece and more a familiar feature on the landscape. Completing the picture, the academic wing of the Seminary Building was named Alfieri Hall in honor of Dominick Alfieri, secretary of the Board of Regents. A large house just off campus was named the Ring Building after George M. Ring, also of the Board of Regents. It became headquarters of University Affairs (fund-raising).[65]

Essential for long-term survival, these capital projects could not conceal short-term embarrassment. In a replay of Dougherty's experience of 1964 when buildings went up as the university nearly failed to make its payroll, Petillo found that long-term loans were of little value for meeting immediate needs. Deepening deficits forced the elimination of 105 clerical, faculty, and administrative positions in December 1984, bringing savings of $2.2 million but generating bad publicity in the supposedly festive season.[66] The alternative would have been to raise student tuition by 18.5 percent which, even had it balanced the books (unlikely because of reduced demand), would also have underwritten Seton Hall's multiple inefficiencies. Forty-six of the terminated positions were already vacant, reducing the number of actual dismissals to fifty-nine, or 10 per cent of Seton Hall's employee positions.[67] "It is uncomfortable to have to separate people from the institution who have been very positive and friendly," said Petillo "but the reality and facts mandate that if we don't, the entire organization will be in jeopardy."[68]

Firing people was one solution, hiring them another. The appointment in January 1985 of James O. Allison as executive vice chancellor was an important step in improving the financial and administrative procedures of the university. A highly intelligent former marine, Allison came to Seton Hall from Duquesne University in Pittsburgh.[69] He was an excellent choice.

Academic Renewal

Finding Leaders for Institutional Change

Seton Hall was "not a research university," said Joseph Stetar, associate vice president for academic affairs in 1984. "Our faculty, with very few exceptions, were neither hired to direct basic research projects nor do we have the number and range of doctoral students to support major research efforts."[70] But research did get done, sometimes with the aid of federal or corporate dollars, sometimes without them. By one measurement of research vitality, outside funding, Seton Hall was not in the same league as

Boston College, which received $2.6 million in Department of Defense research grants alone. Richard Connors, who served as Provost in the early 1980s, emphasized the need "to analyze our grant support activities to see which are essential to the mission of the university [and which are not]."[71] If seed money could be found, Stetar thought, perhaps up to $3 million a year might be generated in outside support,[72] which was a small sum by the standards of competitor institutions but large by Seton Hall's historic standards. But with regionally declining student numbers, acute financial challenges facing tuition-dependent colleges, increased educational consumerism, and pressure from well-funded and research active public universities, Seton Hall could not afford to be complacent. It had to "confront the future with boldness and zest."[73]

Connors had been a fine provost in difficult circumstances but no-one begrudged him a return to the classroom. The appointment of a Franciscan priest, Reverend David Bossman, to replace him was meant to reinforce the university's Catholicism. Bossman came to Seton Hall from Saint Bonaventure University where, as professor of theology and dean of the graduate school, he edited the *Biblical Theology Bulletin*. However, his tenure was brief, his talents lying elsewhere. Assuming the position in June 1985 and relinquishing it a year later to return to the faculty, his legacy was an altered budget process, a completed Faculty Guide, and new guidelines for academic planning.

After a brief interlude with Nicholas DeProspo as interim provost, Bossman's permanent replacement was German-born Bernhard Scholz, a member of George Reilly's history department of the 1960s who had risen through the administrative ranks. The ideal provost, he thought, should be "a leader rather than a mere manager of higher education; a person with the right mixture of experiences, habits and talents; a [person with] a commitment to collegiality, tact . . . tolerance for petty annoyances . . . and the ability not to take himself or herself too seriously."[74] He satisfied his own criteria, although tact and collegiality were occasionally at odds with wit. (As dean of arts and sciences, he had complained of an administrator who had "no contact whatsoever with our clientele, students, or with our working ants, the faculty.")[75] Scholz always spoke his mind, which was formidable.

As provost, he insisted on tougher hiring and tenure rules as essential for academic rebuilding. Scholz thought that deans tended to shirk tough tenure decisions, leaving the University Rank and Tenure Committee and the provost to sort out the problem.[76] He also thought that tenure had been granted too readily in the past—this was certainly true—and that no more than 65 percent of the faculty should have permanent contracts. (He meant the percentage of tenured to untenured faculty, not the percentage of those who, applying for tenure, received it.) "Whenever possible," Scholz said, "we should seek alternatives to tenure-track positions when hiring new faculty" and be "more rigorous in stopping faculty on tenure-track" before they came up for permanent positions.[77] These positions were not guaranteed to win popularity, but in finding alternatives to tenure-track hiring he was ahead of his time.

Freshman Studies

Conley and D'Alessio enrolled large freshman classes only to see 20 percent of them leave after one or two semesters. By the end of eight semesters, between 36 and 41 percent were gone, an alarming rate, although in roughly keeping with national averages.[78] "For several years," Petillo told faculty in 1987, "we have been losing nearly two out of five students here at Seton Hall—including eighteen percent of our Freshmen. We didn't throw them out—they walked . . . We must face the fact that we play a part in a student's decision to leave."[79] "Students should be the true focal-point of the decision-making process on campus," said Lee Noel, author of *Increasing Student Retention*, who visited Seton Hall in 1987, not giving it high marks on the quality of its classroom teachers. In comparison to other institutions, he said bluntly, "you have got a situation you just can't tolerate."[80]

The numbers spoke for themselves. The entering class of 1985–1986 was below the targeted figure of 1,103, the result of tougher SAT requirements and the fact that Seton Hall looked like a building site that year. The School of Business had the highest retention, the School of Education the lowest.[81] By June 1987 the university was so worried that a program called freshman studies was inaugurated, not so much to improve retention as such as "to improve the entire university as a whole, which would then raise the retention rate."[82] It became a national model.

That freshmen should enjoy one-stop shopping for academic and social needs had been mooted as early as 1982 by Art Shriberg of the College of Education, who proposed a "freshman college" for nursing and education students.[83] Peter Ahr and David Abalos of the department of religious studies worried that the university lacked a structure "to integrate freshmen into the community of Seton Hall, give them a sense of the history of the University, link them with guides to the larger community, and foster in them from the beginning an understanding that they have become part of the larger whole that is Seton Hall."[84] Ahr and Abalos envisaged faculty members serving as full-time mentors to incoming students, with the Writing Center, the Center for Developmental Mathematics, and the Equal Opportunity Program coordinating their activities through the freshman studies program. The more involved college students were, the higher their chances for a completed degree.[85] Freshman studies was paradoxical. To eighteen-year-olds, Seton Hall had too many offices: the answer, it seemed, was to create another. Some of the program was oversold, some of it was infantilizing. Most freshmen were drawn to Seton Hall by its academic reputation, its convenience, and its Catholicism (a quarter of the incoming class, including non-Catholics,[86] chose it because it was Catholic[87]), but to the extent that freshman studies recognized that those who came for good reasons should also have good reasons to stay, it was one of the most important initiatives of the Petillo years. A friendlier campus was needed, not only to prevent attrition (of faculty as well as students) but because it was good in itself. It was almost as if the university itself were the freshman, finding its feet and walking unsteadily in an unfamiliar world.

The College of Arts and Sciences

Academic renewal happened one college, one department, one faculty member at a time. In the Arts and Sciences, Scholz thought that chemistry was "by far the most professional of the 30 academic departments," an assessment with which the chemists happily concurred.[88] Under Mort Gibian, its "vitality," "cohesiveness," and rate of productivity were "truly remarkable,"[89] not least because the faculty were "horrendously overburdened with teaching" and working in "a house of horrors"[90] called McNulty Hall. Linda Cline-Love, the first Seton Hall faculty member to file a patent application with the United States Patent and Trademark Office, received the Medal of the Society for Applied Spectroscopy. Robert Augustine enjoyed an international reputation.[91] Gibian, who died suddenly in 1987 aged forty-eight, was a National Institute of the Humanities Fellow and a member of the New Jersey Governor's Science Advisory Board.[92] Chemistry accounted for close to half of the College of Arts and Sciences' published scholarship in 1985.

In 1985 Petra Chu of Art and Music became the first Seton Hall professor to win a Guggenheim Fellowship. Daniel Leab of the department of history was Fulbright Senior Lecturer at the University of Cologne.[93] David Abalos was Herbert E. Garcia Visiting Professor in Chicano studies at Yale and New Jersey's Professor of the Year in 1987.[94] ("We must demand that every teacher strive to become a Dr. Abalos and every school a Seton Hall," said Governor Tom Kean, presenting the award.)[95] Robert Herrera in philosophy, James Lindroth in English, Edward Shapiro in history, Daniel Zalacain in modern languages, and Father Stanley Jaki in physics contributed significantly to published scholarship. Herrera served on the Board of the University of Dallas. Shapiro, a Harvard-educated historian of American Jewry, published prolifically, as did his colleague Leab. Lindroth was "amazingly productive," "a phenomenon . . . unmatched in Seton Hall's history,"[96] a powerhouse of essays and reviews.

Stanley Jaki deserves mention because his career culminated in 1987 with the award of the Templeton Prize for work probing the relationship between science and religion. Born in Hungary in 1924, Jaki entered the Benedictine Order in 1942 and, completing undergraduate training in philosophy, theology, and mathematics, did graduate work at the Pontifical Institute of San Anselmo in Rome. He was ordained priest in 1948 and he received a doctorate in 1950 for a dissertation published in 1956 under the title *Les tendances nouvelles de l'ecclesiologie* and reissued in 1963 during the Second Vatican Council. But it was as a scientist and philosopher of science that Jaki made his mark. Receiving a BS degree from Saint Vincent's College in Latrobe, Pennsylvania in 1954, he enrolled in the Graduate School of Fordham University to pursue doctoral work in physics under Victor Hess, the Nobel-prize winning discoverer of cosmic rays. The fruit of their collaboration was published in June 1958 in the *Journal of Geophysical Research* under the title "A Study of the Distribution of Radon, Thoron, and Their Decay Products above and below the Ground." Between 1958 and 1962 he was a research fellow in the history and philosophy of science at Stanford, Berkeley, and Princeton. After completing *The Relevance of Physics*, which *The American Scientist* acclaimed as "compulsory reading for all scientists, students and professors," he joined Seton Hall's faculty in 1965, becoming Distinguished University Professor in 1975. Thereafter, he published twenty-four books ranging from *Brain, Mind, and Computers* (1969) to *Planets and Planetarians* (1978), from *The Paradox of Olbers Paradox* (1969) to *Chesterton: Seer of Science* (1986); wrote multiple essays and edited volumes; gave the Gifford Lectures at Edinburgh University; and held visiting appointments at Oxford, Yale, Sydney, Princeton Theological Seminary, and the Institute of Advanced Study at Princeton. The fact that he made Seton Hall his home for half a century showed how it could attract and retain thinkers of the highest caliber. Jaki owed it "a great deal," he said. It "took me essentially on a research professorship basis with a very minimum of teaching at a time when my researches were just starting to be published."[97]

The College of Nursing

"Care must be exercised when viewing the College of Nursing," thought Paul Barnas, assistant provost in charge of finance, in 1985. "The situation lends itself to yellow journalism."[98] This characteristically wry assessment acknowledged successes and failures in a college in which the vital signs were mostly good. The nursing building was renovated. Funds were found for computerization. The master's program was thriving. Faculty were "extremely active" in state and national organizations. Almost all of them engaged in research and publication.[99] Two Seton Hall nursing professors spent ten weeks in China in June 1982 evaluating hospitals and teaching one hundred nurses and physicians in Zhejiang Province. The dean of the College, Dr. Kathleen Dirschel, was regularly elected president of the New Jersey State Board of Nursing, also serving on many other professional bodies.[100]

In the early 1980s, undergraduate enrollment fell (this was later reversed) and faculty with doctorates were poached by other institutions. In 1988, the College had a total undergraduate enrollment of 260 students, a figure far below the peak of 699 students in 1979–1980. "It used to be that women went into teaching and nursing," said Barbara Beeker, Dirschel's replacement as dean when the latter resigned in 1985. "But now women can go into any field." [101] The public image of nursing was misleading: "a lot of people think of the nurse as the handmaid of the physician [whereas] nursing is much more independent and autonomous than it was a number of years ago." Problems in public health (chiefly the AIDS crisis) disinclined some school-leavers from joining the profession.[102] Modest starting salaries were also a factor in declining enrollments.

By the end of the 1980s, as conditions improved, the faculty became more querulous, despite the fact (or perhaps because of it) that the College was the most successful unit in the university in receiving outside grants. In 1985 it was awarded $800,000 by the U.S. Department of Health and Human Services to develop a master's program for primary care of the young and the old. (Seton Hall was the only university in New Jersey to offer the program.)[103] Josephine Sienkiewicz and Janet Fickeissen won awards for work in community nursing, Sienkiewicz developing and managing a clinic serving 350 migrant and seasonal workers, Fickeissen awarded Seton Hall's Sara M. Errickson prize for leadership in professional organizations.[104] In 1988, the College received federal grants totaling over $1.1 million

All in all, the College of Nursing maintained an impressive profile while being serious about the Catholic mission of the university.[105] "The program is very hard, very rigid," said Kathy Berth, a senior nursing major in 1988. "But it is a very good program and you learn a lot. The professors are very helpful, personal."[106]

The W. Paul Stillman School of Business

The W. Paul Stillman School of Business had no illusions about the academic and financial climate in which it had to operate for most of the 1980s. Recruitment of qualified faculty was a "paramount concern"[107] causing the American Assembly of Collegiate Schools of Business (AACSB) to withhold accreditation in 1983. In accounting and computer sciences the shortage was more or less beyond Seton Hall's control, the result of higher-paying corporations in the metropolitan area poaching well-qualified faculty. (Better salaries eventually solved the problem.) But the AACSB also noticed internal problems: the rapid turnover of university presidents; the low priority given to the School of Business by the administration; inadequate scholarly activity on the part of senior professors; the need for curricular improvement.[108] Slowly, these concerns were addressed, so that by 1991–1992, the School was fully accredited. Enrollment remained a challenge—this was a national trend—but the appointment of a full-time director of graduate admissions helped. Improved productivity was also important, as was an innovative approach to international business, with close ties to business programs in

China, the USSR, Italy, Poland, and North Korea.[109] The school's flagship publication, *The Mid-Atlantic Journal of Business*, was strong.

College of Education and Human Services

The School of Education had more problems than it cared to admit but was in better health at the end of the decade than at the beginning. The most obvious difference came in 1984, with a change in title from the School of Education to the College of Education and Human Services, which was the idea of a new dean, Richard Ognibene, who replaced John Callan after the latter's long years of service. "[The new name] is a reflection of what is going to be happening in the future," Ognibene explained. "It tends to envelop the Counseling and Special Services Department, and not lose contact with what's going on now."[110] Variety and flexibility were crucial. In the early 1980s, as the undergraduate program declined alarmingly, its weakness was partly offset by high levels of student motivation and by a talented faculty. The pass rate for Seton Hall education majors on the National Teachers Examination was only between 50 and 60 percent, threatening the long-term viability of the program. Very few full-time faculty taught in the College's proliferating off-campus graduate programs and few tenured faculty supervised student teaching practice. On the credit side, graduate programs were strong, with a profusion of candidates (250 in two years at one stage) expressing an interest in, although not all receiving, the EdD degree.[111] The College offered good in-service training and was a leader in training science and mathematics teachers.[112]

Inheriting some ideas from his immediate predecessor, acting dean John Hampton, Ognibene saw administrative restructuring as essential if the College were to made good on its potential. The elementary, secondary, and general professional education departments and the health, physical education, and recreation departments were combined to form the department of educational studies. Offices of doctoral research (under Mel Shay) and continuing education (under Patricia Kuchon) were established in 1984. "An awful lot of our people are involved in *ad hoc* type formats," said Ognibene of the latter office. "This will be an organized effort to retain long-term relationships with schools and organizations." Such outreach, important for the reputation of the College, was an important way of generating revenue at a time of declining enrollments. "The team is in place and the projects are underway," said Ognibene in 1985, "and there are good people here."[113]

The changes bore fruit. In June 1985, the National Council for Accreditation of Teacher Education (NCATE) accredited all educational personnel programs submitted for review. According to Ognibene and Kuchon (who coordinated the NCATE visit), only 30 percent of colleges that applied for national accreditation received it. "Besides the benefits for the school as well as the students and faculty, it put pressure on us to keep our programs up to date," said Ognibene. "Seton Hall is one of the few colleges that require their students to take a course in special education," said Kuchon. NCATE was particularly impressed with preprofessional teacher training.[114] "It was an excellent program," said Andrea Verga, who graduated in secondary education in 1985 to become a mathematics teacher. "Until you're out there teaching you don't really know what it's like." "Courses at Seton Hall give you a lot of ideas and a very positive outlook in teaching," said Mike Wilbraham, studying to be a science teacher. "Then [as an intern] in the classroom you can see what works in one case but not in another."[115] These were encouraging verdicts.

Pedagogy itself (or at least its assessment) was a surprisingly low priority for a teaching university. Most faculty assumed that the best measure of their effectiveness was a student's ability to pass an examination set and graded by themselves. Scholz established a Center for College Teaching in 1987 to bring together faculty to consider what worked and what did not in the classroom. Under Marty Finkelstein of the College of Education and, later, Albert Hakim, the Center worked well, although Scholz considered it "somewhat amateurish" and even suspected it, in mock surprise, of "campus politics."[116]

Graduate Medical Education

Beginning with the College of Nursing in 1937 and continuing with the College of Medicine and Dentistry in 1956, Seton Hall's links with the medical profession were long and deep. Since the transfer of the medical school into state hands in 1964, the university was no longer in the business of teaching people to be doctors. But teaching doctors was another matter. Established by the Board of Regents in March 1987, the School of Graduate Medical Education forged links between Seton Hall and local Catholic hospitals, an arrangement that helped hospitals recruit students for residency programs while strengthening the university's connections with the archdiocese and the medical profession. The idea was that 300 graduate students serving residencies at three Catholic hospitals—Saint Joseph's Medical Center in Paterson, Saint Michael's Medical Center in Newark, and Saint Elizabeth's Hospital in Newark—would have the cost of their education borne by those hospitals, with Seton Hall validating their diplomas. The founding dean of the School was Nick DeProspo, until Dr. Jack Patterson, a dental surgeon, took over. The School's presence in South Orange was limited to the dean, an office, and a secretary. Its real life was in the hospitals where in-service teaching took place. As a relatively inexpensive way for Seton Hall to play a role in the medical life of New Jersey while protecting Catholic hospitals, it was an imaginative response to the vexed question of the Catholic presence in medical education.

Theodore McCarrick, who became Archbishop of Newark upon Peter Gerety's retirement in 1986, was a strong supporter.[117]

Never intended to replicate the College of Medicine and Dentistry, the School promoted "strong programs and research,"[118] especially in molecular biology. Its strengths lay in continuing education, bioethics, medical economics, and public health. Paterson wanted it "to carve out a position of eminence in [the] state"[119] and early in his tenure he identified the problems the School faced: poor facilities (in essence, one office on campus); tensions between the dean and CEOs of area hospitals; "formidable opposition" from the University of Medicine and Dentistry of New Jersey; and a faculty with marginal commitment to Seton Hall as opposed to the hospitals in which they worked. Some of these were teething troubles, some the inevitable consequence of a school that was of Seton Hall but not quite in it. Still, Graduate Medical Education was a significant and eventually successful initiative.

University Governance

Closely linked to academic renewal was the question of university governance. A faculty capable of good work in the classroom and library was also a faculty capable of looking after its own affairs. Governance loomed large in the Petillo years because an important legal case forced Seton Hall to consider the role played by the faculty in almost every aspect of university life. According to the U.S. Supreme Court's "Yeshiva Decision" in 1980,[120] faculty involved in university governance were "managerial employees" excluded from coverage by the National Labor Relations Act, meaning that certain private universities were not obliged to bargain with unionized representatives of the faculty. In 1982, when the American Federation of Teachers attempted to obtain certification as bargaining representative of Seton Hall's faculty, the university lodged an appeal with the National Labor Relations Board, which concluded that the faculty were indeed managerial employees under the terms of the Yeshiva decision and thus prevented from forming a union. This had significant implications. Because faculty controlled course offerings, the curriculum, degree requirements, admission standards, hiring and firing of teachers, and helped to the draw up budgets, the university was now required by law to continue its hitherto voluntary tradition of shared governance.[121] The alternative was a faculty union.

A substantial number of professors continued to press for a union, Yeshiva notwithstanding, but they met with resistance from Presidents Hall.[122] "Our major task," wrote one administrator, "is to erode the collective bargaining mentality which grips much of our faculty and develop mechanisms to ensure that faculty energies are constructively engaged for the good of the university rather than dissipated in negativism."[123] Some faculty preferred to sulk but others were more cooperative. The best case against unionization came from Angela Raimo, an attorney and professor of education, who pointed out that there was no guarantee that the university would recognize the American Federation of Teachers (AFT) as a bargaining unit, that the AFT had a long history of opposition to private education, that its dues were steep, and that the Faculty Council had been an adequate and respected vehicle for faculty representation over the years.[124] The best case for unionization was made by a number of history, English, philosophy, and communication professors who argued that the faculty at Seton Hall were not managers, that they were excluded from budgetary decisions, and that they had no say in the choosing of administrators or students.[125] (Indeed, administrators who lamented the collective bargaining mentality as essentially negative unwittingly revealed the need for it: they found it difficult to accept the good intentions of faculty and often presumed the worst.) Shared governance was not the be-all-and-end-all, but wise administrators realized it could sometimes save them from themselves. Scholz worried that faculty were happier striking attitudes than exercising responsibility. "I am well aware that uncooperative or ineffective chairpersons are a great burden on the University," he told John Hampton of the School of Business. "However, given Yeshiva, the hallowed principle of collegiality, and the idea of faculty participation in university governance, we have to put up with such chairpersons to a degree. As a wily and experienced dean you should not be seriously impeded by a single obstreperous chairman."[126] He tolerated "shared governance" but found it tiresome, preferring a faculty which agreed with him. (The faculty's ideal provost was one who did the same in reverse.) If shared governance meant self-discipline, he was for it; otherwise, not so much.

Catholic Life

Seton Hall's long conversation about faith and reason continued during the Petillo years, picking up where others had left off. Efforts to articulate the university's Catholic identity were pointless (because obvious) in the 1950s. They were urgent (because overdue) in the 1960s. They were almost played out (because endlessly repeated) in the 1970s. In the 1980s, they were self-referential: being Catholic meant talking about Seton Hall, not about Catholicism itself. "I don't think that Catholicism is weaker on campus, but I do think that it is different," said Father Philip Rotunno. "Yesterday, Catholicism was more external, but I don't know how many people were actually committed or how many people were just conforming . . . Today Catholicism has become more personal." In obvious ways, though, Catholicism *was* weaker. The return of the seminary was meant to strengthen it, implying that it needed strengthening. And the return did not immediately "take," with some faculty and administrators thinking of the seminary as an alien presence to be kept at arm's length. "I don't think that Seton

Hall will survive much into the next century if it does not maintain its Catholic identity," said historian George Reilly. "But if it does maintain its Catholicism, it has a good chance to be here for another 125 years!"[127] "I think there are those who have not been near us who quickly come to the conclusion that we're not Catholic, and that we've lost our identity," said Petillo in 1986. He seemed surprised by the idea but not surprised enough to wonder how it might have happened.[128] The more he protested that Seton Hall was Catholic, the more some wondered if it really was. Petillo was good at putting up buildings but was less sure-footed when it came to spiritual foundations.

Reilly and Rotunno, veterans of Seton Hall's culture wars, knew that, one way or another, Catholicism was the university's constitutive element, its verb "to be." Even in imprecisely defined ways, Seton Hall was Catholic, its endless cast of characters, its indulgence of eccentricity, its awareness of human frailty, its generosity of spirit, its inclination to see the best in people, its recognition that there was more to life than subcommittees—all signs, properly interpreted, of a university that was Catholic at its core. "The clergy are cool and in touch with us," said a student. "They're friends."[129] Indeed, many students resented the dilution of Catholicism across campus, wondering if some misplaced pluralism made all faiths, except that of the majority, welcome. Under its editor John T. Saccoman, later a mathematics professor at the university, *The Setonian* suspected that Catholicism was embarrassing to the administration, something best swept under the carpet. "Today is All Saints Day and it is unobserved as a university holiday . . . It is sad that Yom Kippur is listed on the Alumni Association calendar, along with Hanukkah, but Catholic holidays such as All Saints and [the] Feasts of the Assumption and Immaculate Conception remain unmentioned."[130] The paper was devotionally conservative. "For the last several years the Mass of the Holy Spirit has taken on a more 'modern' look. There have been clowns, dancers, and other nontraditional liturgical symbols integrated into the service. Chancellor Petillo has said that he does not oppose them . . . *The Setonian* respectfully disagrees."[131] *The Setonian* had a point. "'We tried to make the Mass more contemporary," said Rotunno. "The altar and surrounding areas were surrounded by red and white balloons and the Mass itself featured the 'Fountain Square Fools,' a Cincinnati-based mime group which seeks to unite the arts with the liturgy.'"[132] "It seems strange that with the communists of Eastern Europe forcefully banning all symbols of our Catholic faith from classrooms, this is also happening at Seton Hall," said business professor Jack Stukas. Newark-born of Lithuanian ancestry, Stukas spoke from the heart.[133]

Formal definitions of Seton Hall's Catholic life looked the era that produced them. *Seton Hall: A Catholic University* (1980) took a year and half to write during the Conley and Murphy presidencies, a collaborative effort that was eloquent in its own way but which failed to conceal fissures and fault-lines. Catholicism, said its authors, was not "a restrictive creed but an enabling vision" calling for what was "best and authentically human [in pursuit] of what is true and good . . . A university is not Catholic by proclamation but by the creative faith and love of its members. The Catholicity of Seton Hall is not a standard already achieved against which one is measured but a call to action and a commitment to a building of life that is faithful to the past and open to the future."[134]

Insisting that "because [the] university is free and autonomous, it has the right to make a religious option,"[135] the document reduced Seton Hall's Catholicism to thinned-out pluralism. The document was also prone to left-leaning *angst*: "How are the needs of national security balanced with a national concern for human rights? How can one choose a lifework as a vocation if one must compete for profits? Is a sexual relationship between a man and a woman right and proper only within marriage? What is the responsibility of industry for environmental pollution? Does agribusiness safeguard the health of consumers? All these are moral questions, all probe our values, none are simply answered."[136]

Some of these questions had been answered already, the third for instance, but on the whole *Seton Hall: A Catholic University* expressed an inclusive understanding of mission while showing that it was easier to abandon than build consensus. Agreeing on the importance of agreement was easier than reaching it.

Catholics on the faculty were supposed to "bear witness" to the university's mission in "their lives, learning, [and] enthusiasms," an aspiration easy to express but hard to formulate contractually. There was no proactive hiring of Catholics or much interest in the faith commitments of faculty once hired. A degree of self-selection took place among those applying for a position in a Catholic university: it may be assumed that some did not apply for work at Seton Hall thinking it, as Catholic, inhospitable to them. On the other hand, the same argument also applied to Catholics serious about their faith who may have concluded that Seton Hall's Catholic commitments were skin deep. Seton Hall was serious about its pluralism: was it as serious about its Catholicism? Joseph Mahoney of the history department thought it "highly desirable that non-Catholics work, teach, and study here" and "firmly" held that Seton Hall would be the loser if they did not. On the other hand, he thought that at some point a Catholic ethos could not be sustained without a critical mass of people "who share Catholicism as an informed and living faith," it being "self-evident" that the atmosphere of a Catholic university—"the commonality of goals, attitude, perceptions, assessments and reactions of the group of people who at any time constitute the university"—could only be Catholic if a substantial number of its citizens—staff, faculty, administration—were themselves Catholic.[137]

Joseph Maloy, a chemist, expressed the same view more trenchantly in 1987.

I left a tenured position at a state university in 1979 in order to accept the position I currently hold at Seton Hall. "I want to come here," I told [the provost who hired me] "because Seton Hall is a Catholic university."

I was wrong. Seton Hall is not a Catholic University. Seton Hall is a secular university that is operated by the Archdiocese of Newark. This affiliation with the archdiocese is its only claim to Catholicity. There is no particular reason for a Catholic to come to Seton Hall, either as a member of the faculty or as a student. In fact, to be a practicing Catholic at Seton Hall is to know alienation. I know this is true for me, and I fear it must be true of my students. . . .

At Seton Hall we seem to specialize in the cultivation of this rocky soil by catering to every class of nonbeliever . . . [138]

Maloy, a lonely crusader, was not alone. What he said, others thought. The problem was that those who thought it rarely got round to saying it.

Midway between Mahoney and Maloy was Dennis Mahon, chairman of the Task Force on Catholicity to which Maloy directed his philippic. To Mahon, Seton Hall drew its inspiration from many ambitions—a desire for excellence in teaching, the need to retain students, the demands of financial efficiency, an appreciation of the liberal arts and cultural diversity, the wish to develop a spirit of community—but none of these goals were in themselves particularly Catholic. Such motivations were "quite necessary for a Catholic university, but they are not sufficient." Mahon proposed instead a more substantial vision: "The constant inspiration and motivation of a Catholic university must be based on our belief that man is irrevocably related to the holy and that this absolute relationship supersedes, stands above, and judges all other motivations or ideologies. A Catholic university, of necessity, would not be only tolerant of the other motivations and ideologies but also welcoming of the freshness of such approaches. But Catholicism must be the norm on which all such ideologies are to be judged and evaluated."[139] Here was an eloquent summary of a long tradition.

Where did Petillo stand? "It is crucial that we not only understand what Catholic means," he told faculty in 1987, "Our catholicity goes beyond advocacy of values and curricular concerns, crucial as they are. It entails service—a sense of stewardship for others, beyond our university's walls."[140] This call to arms would have been more convincing if the Catholic mission *had* been translated into curricular concerns instead of being translated out of them. Petillo's Catholicism was activist, in keeping with his understanding of education itself: "We ought to keep in mind that people look at Seton Hall like a business, and measure our effectiveness by our product . . . in our case, our graduates. Are they leaders? Do they have a deep sense of social responsibility? And what did Seton Hall do to foster this leadership and social conscience during their college years?"[141] This anticipated one of the themes of a later president, Robert Sheeran, for whom "servant-leadership" was at Seton Hall's core. But activism itself was neutral: it needed an object. What cause was being served? Where did it lead? About that, Petillo was silent.

Others were not so mute. That Seton Hall was Catholic did not require it to have a Catholic curriculum, some faculty thought. Making an argument heard before,[142] one religious studies professor held that students should study religion as "a liberal art . . . and not as an extension of childhood catechesis." Anything "prescriptive of students' beliefs, values or behavior" was best left to "the chaplain's office. . . . A Catholic [university's] department of religious studies, therefore, is not a matter of Catholics teaching other Catholics what Catholics believe and why the other fellow is wrong . . . It is a department in which attention is focused on issues which are important in the Catholic and tradition and [how] these issues are explored from the Catholic and other Christian and even non-Christian points of view."[143] That departmental creed was less open-minded than it claimed. When Joseph Ratzinger was proposed for an honorary degree in 1986, a priest-member of the same department opposed it because "Seton Hall is a Catholic institution [and] we need to be aware of the implications and misunderstanding that can result when we honor people whose ideas and procedures are not just different from ours but at variance with an honest and open search for the truth."[144] Ratzinger's failure to graduate from Seton Hall did not harm his later career. That religion was a proper object of historical and anthropological inquiry was undisputed, but the demand for value-free empiricism was both contradictory (because empiricism itself was the value) and unwittingly theological (because it made assertions about the relationship between reason and revelation that had implications for both). It would have helped had Petillo given a lead on these matters, but he was a builder, not a theologian.

Being Catholic meant ultimately a commitment not to pluralism for its own sake but to the search for truth—for God—of which pluralism was a necessary manifestation. "The truth in all fields of learning, both secular and religious, leads to that summit of truth which is God, and consequently all fields of learning, both secular and religious, are rightly a part of a Catholic university's commitment," said Archbishop Pio Laghi, Apostolic Pro-Nuncio to the United States, addressing the university in February 1987. But with that freedom came responsibility. Asked to be specific, Laghi responded that "if a theologian is out of line, hey, you have to get him in." The modern world often emphasized freedom, but the same freedom "pluralizes attitudes, behaviors and ideologies. It is precisely the role of the Catholic university to overcome such pluralism and indifference and to point out the absolute values that are the essence and the honor of the human mind created in the image of God."[145]

The Volenski Case

These debates had consequences. The case of Leonard Volenski turned on Seton Hall's identity not only as a Catholic but also as a diocesan university, a distinction about which lawyers as well as theologians had things to say. Volenski was a priest of the archdiocese who joined the faculty as assistant professor of psychology in December 1977, gaining tenure in April 1981. By December 1983, he had decided to return to the lay state while remaining on the faculty, an idea to which Petillo made no objection but one which offended Gerety on the ground that that Volenski, tenured as a priest, could not remain tenured as a layman. Gerety undertook to find him "comparable employment at another university or college" but otherwise felt no obligation to him, certainly no obligation to retain him on the faculty. This did not satisfy Volenski, who indicated in May 1984 that he intended to continue teaching at the university as a tenured lay person. Gerety demurred. "I have decided that your continued presence at Seton Hall during these difficult times will be detrimental to the Catholic students and your fellow priests," he told him in June, reassigning him to work in the Chancery Office pending a decision on whether to grant him a leave of absence from the priest-hood. Meanwhile the university, proceeding on the assumption that he *would* continue to teach, even calculated his new salary as a lay person.

Volenski insisted, even as Gerety denied, that he had "resigned" as a priest. (Theo-logically and canonically, Gerety was on firmer ground in that argument.) Petillo then revoked his previous commitment to retain him as a member of the faculty, causing Volenski to sue for unfair dismissal on the grounds that his appointment and tenure had not been contingent upon continued good standing as a priest.[146] The university countered that the actions taken by the archbishop and administration were funda-mentally ecclesiastical in nature and beyond the jurisdiction of civil courts. "When a priest-professor is granted tenure," its brief argued, "it is his role as a priest that serves as one of the major determining factors":

> A priest is expected to play a proportionately larger part and bear a considerably larger burden in helping the university accomplish its goals of moral and religious emphasis in conjunction with the scholastic than an ordinary lay professor. Thus, a priest might be granted tenure solely on the basis of his clerical function, whereas an ordinary layman, with roughly the same academic background and credentials, would be denied tenure.
>
> Father Volenski's priesthood is a matter which goes to the essence of his employ-ment as a spiritual leader and motivator of the student population. The grant of ten-ure was implicitly and expressly [sic] conditioned on his continuance of not only his

educational function but his religious function as well. Priests are encouraged and expected to view their work as professors as part of a religious calling. Recruitment and tenure to priest-professor is done with this in view . . .

When Father Volenski was granted tenure by Seton Hall, both parties realized and knew that "continuation of the priesthood" was a term too obvious to need expression . . . The abdication of the priesthood will deprive Seton Hall of one of the major fruits of the contract—providing religious symbolism, example, and services to the students of the University . . . [147]

These were weak arguments. Tenure committees were explicitly instructed to evaluate clerical and lay faculty equally. To have done otherwise would have been to invite litigation. The claim that Volenski's priesthood was "too obvious" a stipulation of employment reflected poor understanding of the law of contract. Things understood have to be understood in writing. Priesthood was unmentioned in Volenski's or any other priest's letter of appointment not because it was "too obvious" but because the expression of it would have been to recognize at least the possibility of laicization, which is what Gerety wished to avoid. Moreover, "abdication of the priesthood" had not barred at least one faculty member, Albert Hakim, from continuing to serve the university (with distinction). Finally, Volenski was dismissed at the insistence of the archbishop (the university had been prepared to retain him until Gerety said no), which exposed Seton Hall to legal jeopardy. By reassigning him as a priest, even as Volenski insisted he was no longer one, Gerety deprived him of the procedural protections to which he was entitled under his terms of academic employment. By declaring Volenski unfit for further association with Seton Hall, in effect assuming the role of university employer as well as ecclesiastical superior, the archbishop violated his own previously expressed understanding of Seton Hall's proper relationship with the archdiocese. In 1982, during hearings held before the National Labor Relations Board to determine whether Seton Hall faculty could bargain collectively, the archdiocese's attorney had stated that "Archbishop Gerety is not the functional head of Seton Hall University, is not involved in the day-to-day affairs of the University, has no full-time position at the University, and has no direct knowledge of matters related to admissions policy, degree requirements, sabbaticals, tenure, grievance procedures, or with . . . any . . . factors of university administration . . ." His attitude to Volenski argued otherwise.

In June 1984, with Volenski pressing his claim to laicization and continued employment at the University, the Board of Regents passed a resolution pertaining to the academic tenure of priests and religious. In the event that tenure was granted to "any . . . clerical or religious [faculty] member," the resolution stipulated, "such tenure shall be contingent and conditioned upon (1) the member remaining a priest and/or religious in good standing; and (2) the continued release and approval of the member's Diocesan bishop or the Major Superior." This "priest tenure" seemed to close the loophole to which Volenski had drawn attention and as such Seton Hall should have been grateful to him for pointing it out. But did the new policy close it? One objection to "priest tenure" was that it permitted dismissal from the university without due process. The archbishop, or any other ecclesiastical superior, could insert himself in matters of internal university governance, albeit, through this resolution, with the permission of the university itself. And what of the rights of the dismissed party and of the departments and colleges forced to replace him? At least notionally, "priest tenure" may have solved one problem while creating others. Clerical faculty, particularly diocesan priests, could have felt pressure to conform to the wishes of the archbishop who (according to one reading of the situation) enjoyed "virtual veto power over that professor's freedom of expression."[148] That worry was exaggerated, but had a priest chosen to defy his ecclesiastical superior, the archbishop and the university had provided themselves with firm legal grounds for his dismissal.

The Volenski case revealed an anomaly: that an ex-priest could find it easier than a priest to get tenure at a Catholic university. What that in turn revealed was the sometimes prejudicial attitude toward priests in a university that had once cherished them and that could never have survived financially without them. Father Lawrence Frizzell regretted that the "morale" of the priest community hardly featured in decisions made by the Board of Regents.[149] Most priests wished to achieve tenure on their merits, rejecting the idea of special treatment. They were right to do so. By the end of the 1970s priests expected and were granted no favors from a lay faculty itself expected to perform at a higher level than before. The idea was sometimes heard that priests were either too intellectually compromised or pastorally overworked to function as scholars. The first argument was insultingly anti-Catholic. The second was plainly untrue. "At their most benign," thought Dennis Mahon, "faculty search committees look for the most impressive credentials, publications, and teaching experience . . . At their least benign [they] neither see the need for Newark Archdiocesan priests on the faculty of Seton Hall, or worse, see a need to diminish or eliminate [them]."[150] Two priests, one a musician, the other a sociologist, struggled to achieve tenure in the 1980s, prompting concerns of double standards. Bernhard Scholz conceded that one of them, Joseph Doyle, was the "victim of conflicting policies at Seton Hall University"—the desire, on the one hand, to maintain a priest faculty even by appointing those "far removed from the terminal degree" and the need, on the other, to apply the Faculty Guide to all applicants for tenure regardless of status.[151] Doyle was eventually tenured, but the other priest, Joseph Wozniak, left the university and, subsequently, the priesthood.[152] One way or another, Volenski was a watershed.

Pire Pressure

On the heels of the Volenski case came another controversy to do with abortion. In October 1984, Professor Gerald Pire of the Department of Religious Studies was one of several signatories of a statement sponsored by Catholics for a Free Choice arguing that a "diversity of opinion regarding abortion exists among committed Catholics" and that it was "therefore necessary that the Catholic community encourage candid and respectful discussion on this diversity of opinion within the Church." "I don't think this poses any real problems for me or for Seton Hall," Pire said. He was mistaken. To Mary K. Smith, president of the National Coalition Interstate Committee of Clergy and Laity, which claimed a national membership of between 5,000 and 6,000, Pire's action breached Canon 810 of the Code of Canon Law, which required that "teachers in Catholic universities be outstanding in their integrity of doctrine." If such commitment were lacking, it was the duty of competent ecclesial authority to remove the teacher from the classroom.

These were not well-framed arguments. Pire and Catholics for a Free Choice made a dubious factual claim and drew from it an unwarranted conclusion, imagining that the "diversity" of opinion of which they spoke (the evidence being their own dissent) was a warrant for unending discussion (and not a warrant for ending it). The notion that disagreement about the moral propriety of abortion proved that it was an open question was a *non sequitur*. Moreover, Pire's dismissal of Smith as wrong-headed contradicted his own demand for respectful discussion of the issue. On the other hand, Smith summoned canon law too quickly, allowing Pire's defenders to caricature her as authoritarian when her real demand was for institutional honesty. "Professor Pire has not claimed to be a spokesman for the university or its moral philosophy," said Petillo, dodging the issue. "He has acted entirely on his own volition and on his own responsibility. Seton Hall does not attempt to dictate personal beliefs. We do not agree with Professor Pire's position on the question of abortion and we re-emphasize our commitment to our Catholic tradition and teaching." Bernhard Scholz, then dean of arts and sciences, concurred: "Under the United States Constitution, and since the university subscribes to the principle of academic freedom, a faculty member is entitled to take a position on the issue."[153]

These arguments were incoherent. Petillo's claim that Pire was blameless because he had not identified himself as a spokesman for the university contradicted Scholz's claim that, even had he done so, no blame would attach to him because the university would underwrite his freedom "to take a position on the issue." What, precisely, was Pire's position on abortion? What, precisely, was Seton Hall's? What precisely would have happened if Pire had identified himself as a spokesman for the university? "The university educates, counsels, advises," said Petillo. "Acceptance of specific beliefs cannot be forced. We do not agree with Professor Pire's position on the question of abortion and we emphasize our commitment to our Catholic tradition and teaching." These were words in search of an idea. For Petillo and Scholz, Mary K. Smith was one of the awkward squad. Making her go away was what they really wanted. What did not go away was the question she asked: and one reason for that was that Petillo and Scholz had answered it glibly.

Eccentricity

Complaints notwithstanding, Seton Hall was still a place where people wanted to be. It attracted all sorts—the odd, the quirky, the eccentric—who gave it humanity. Among students, Denis Notari accumulated several hundred credits towards a degree but never took one. When eventually asked to leave he denied that he was, as the authorities claimed, a hindrance to the university. "That statement is simply ridiculous. I have been a student here for over seventeen years and no-one has ever said anything like that about me before."[154] Faculty oddballs included English professor Harold Petipas, who eventually cracked. "Because of his knowledge of God and of Cardinal Newman," wrote Peter Ahr, chronicling his final collapse, "he has volunteered his services as a consultant to the university . . . He [also] believes he . . . knows enough about numbers to be able to break the New Jersey lottery."[155] Another English department character was John Harrington, fascinated by Ivy League degrees, modern poetry, and a film called *Shave*. Tom Duff was a magnificent mimic, *bon vivant*, and wit. John Sweeney played the bagpipes, talked of toy trains, and provided the model for the label of Dewar's Scotch whiskey. (He took his payment in kind.)

Robert Herrera, a philosopher, tweaked his progressive colleagues by keeping a portrait of Antonio Salazar in his office. Francis Caminiti, formerly Robert Pollock's assistant in Humanistic Studies, abandoned three-piece suits for Buddhist bells. Bill Radtke, a third philosopher, had a fridge in his office; Bill Barlow, an historian, a bed. Bill Barto, a student in the 1980s and a faculty member in the 1990s, kept a gramophone in his office. Tom Hughes, also a 1980s student and 1990s faculty member, gave lectures dressed as Henry VIII. Gordon Dippel of the School of Business lived for many years above a funeral parlor. Eberhard Grosse, "dean" of university printing, looked as if he had strolled down the north face of the Eiger. Vincent Harder, university locksmith, was a published poet and novelist.[156] Father Francis Gavin was the last of his generation to wear a cassock. In the 1990s, he was accompanied by his Irish red setter, Tara, who never went to Mass, he said, because she was Protestant. Charles Engelhard, a member of the Board of Trustees, was the model of Ian Fleming's Goldfinger.

An Open Verdict

Anyone seeing Seton Hall at the beginning of the 1980s and returning at the end would have struggled to recognize the first in the second. Apart from the fact of its survival—easily the greatest of Petillo's achievements—the university was physically transformed. "What used to be parking lots and playing fields are now dormitories," said Kenneth Hoffman, a communications professor. "Ten years ago we were known as a local recruitment school," said Donald McKenna, also a professor of communications. "Now we are known as a regional, if not national residential university with an improving reputation." Frank Katz, associate dean of the college of arts and sciences, welcomed "major changes in the academic programs . . . for the better." Monsignor William Noé Field saw "a new emphasis on the Catholic outlook of the university" which had "a tremendous effect." The most thoughtful response came from Emma Quartaro of the department of social work, who noticed "a subtle change in the real mission of the university and a much better articulation of it in the documents. The change is moving us in the direction of a Catholic Ivy League identification, the implications of which are both good and bad."[157] Better students, higher name recognition, and greater prestige were good, but with the "renaissance" also came vague embarrassment about Seton Hall's proud parochialism. It had always catered for Catholics who lived a bus or train ride away. Would that remain the case? Petillo was good at laying foundations but what, precisely, had he built? That remained to be seen.

CHAPTER 17

Toward the New Millennium

A New Leader and a New Agenda for a New Century

By the late 1980s, Petillo had inherited a university in crisis and led it to financial and academic security, insisting against the evidence that its best days were yet to come. "Every [new] building on campus, I believe, saved the institution," he recalled. "At the point I got there, they were on the verge of bankruptcy, and when I left, we weren't."[1] This was the general view. "Petillo's . . . reputation as a manager, educator, religious leader and . . . economic thinker are all strong and viable," wrote one consultant. "His vision for the university . . . needs to be shared more broadly."[2] True, said the same observer, the speed of the change was more rapid "than most of Seton Hall's constituencies have been able to absorb."[3] But the alternative was dire. "John Petillo has been in every way the great architect of Seton Hall's renaissance," said Archbishop Theodore McCarrick. "He deserves my gratitude for his extraordinary leadership."

Being chancellor took its toll and in late 1988 Petillo received what was supposed to be a six-month sabbatical. The self-effacing Dennis Mahon, who had played a large role in the transformations for which Petillo received credit, replaced him as acting chancellor. Mahon did not have long to enjoy the position (but long enough to discover some quirks of Seton Hall accountancy which he tried unsuccessfully to remedy). Returning after three months to launch a capital campaign—his return oddly coincident with the success of the basketball team in the NCAA tournament—Petillo himself did not stay long in the position. On December 11, 1989 he submitted his resignation. "At times I have worked day and night, seven days a week, and, frankly, I'm tired. Maybe it was the luck of the dice but I was able to do more in five years than I might have thought I could in 10 or 15 years." During his term, Seton Hall had added 430,000 square feet of new building with another 200,000 under construction and 160,000 on the way. When he started, the average SAT score for incoming freshmen was 860. In 1989, it was 1005. In 1982, Seton Hall had 3,000 applicants, in 1989, nearly 6,000. In six and a half years, the university raised almost $86,000,000 (of which $52,000,000 had come recently). One way or another, he had left an indelible mark. Robert Brennan, chairman of the Board of Regents, referring to his "good friend," confirmed that "many of the great things that are happening at Seton Hall" owed to his leadership. (One of those good things was a Committee of 150 established in 1987 to prepare for Seton Hall's sesqui-centennial in 2006. Brennan contributed $10,000,000 to it.) He had "brilliant foresight," thought Newark attorney Donald Robinson; was a "tireless worker," according to Joseph La Sala, president of the alumni association; had a "selfless commitment" to the university, claimed Frank Walsh of the Board of Regents; and had "achieved national prominence for Seton Hall," said Larry Bathgate, also of the Board.[4]

But he was also controversial. At times Petillo looked more like a CEO than the leader of a university. Under him, Seton Hall could have been an insurance company or a hospital as much as a community of scholars. Indeed, after leaving Seton Hall, Petillo left the priesthood itself to begin a new career in charge of Blue Cross/Blue Shield of New Jersey, a seamless transition that seemed to shed retrospective light on his years at the university.

Monsignor Richard Liddy served as interim chancellor in 1990 while a permanent replacement was found. A Seton Hall graduate of 1960 who had studied for the priest-hood in Rome, Liddy was an internationally recognized authority on the thought of Bernard Lonergan, S.J., and although he preferred scholarship to administration, he enjoyed his brief time in charge, going to basketball games, shaking hands, riding in Robert Brennan's helicopter, and generally having fun.[5] Only a disputed tenure case interrupted the generally agreeable proceedings. His tour of duty over, Liddy went on sabbatical to write an acclaimed book on Lonergan, blinking his eyes as if it had all been a dream.

The permanent replacement was Father Tom Peterson, O.P., sixty-one, a Newarker who had decided to become a priest while an economics undergraduate at Providence College, Rhode Island. Trained as a Thomist, with a serious interest Buddhism and Confucianism and traveling and teaching in India and China to deepen his knowledge of them, Peterson enjoyed teaching and was good at it, a wry, laconic, slightly dis-tracted presence in the classroom. He also had administrative experience. As president of Providence from 1971 to 1985, he transformed the school from all-male to coed, introducing a lively and integrated curriculum in Western Civilization. "One thing he clearly had over all the other candidates, he has been president of a substantial college," said Joseph Mahoney, a member of the search committee. "For everybody else this would have been a step up. He had faced the pressures." "Father Peterson has the perfect combination of qualities to sustain the tremendous growth that has taken place over the past six years at Seton Hall," said Robert Brennan. "He brings experi-ence, maturity, and a record of successful leadership of a major Catholic university." For McCarrick (who may have preferred Liddy to remain in charge but who knew the value of flattery),[6] Peterson was "a great and wonderful priest, and a genius."[7] The best assessment came from Peterson himself. "I'm not an administrator first. I'm a priest first. The main lesson that all of us must learn together is the need to have God's values in our lives, and we as a Catholic university [must] place this in a very high priority."[8]

Unlike Petillo, an extrovert, Peterson lived an intense interior life and, except to close friends, was difficult to reach. He was more shy than university presidents are supposed to be. He was also always more a Dominican than a diocesan priest, as much an abbot as a chancellor. In public, he was everybody's affable uncle, making light of his honors and never taking himself too seriously. "I'm one of you," he said to the incoming class of 1994. "I'm a freshman, too."[9] Hearing of his appointment, President Howard Swearer of Brown University offered him a thermometer, thinking him in need of medical attention.[10] In private, he was a priest's priest, his best work done quietly if sometimes fussily. Yet for all his geniality, he never seemed entirely at home at Seton Hall. He came from an order and in the end, as illness overtook him, he returned to it. In the meantime, Seton Hall advanced as he declined.

A new leader meant no shortage of advice. "Academics is the thing," Father William Dettling, president of the Dominican House of Studies in Washington, DC told him. Seton Hall's "over-emphasis . . . upon athletics in general and intercollegiate basketball in particular" was a matter for regret.[11] Father Larry Murphy thought that "Seton Hall badly needs someone with academic competence and concern, after ten years of emphasis in other areas."[12] Others hoped he would arrest "the spiritual decline at Seton Hall and the archdiocese."[13] Retired archbishop Peter Gerety thought that taking charge of a major university in the twilight of a career was "an enormous challenge."[14] Yet Peterson seemed undaunted, insisting that the spirit of Seton Hall, as of any Catholic university, was one of "learning and of love and of laughter."[15] "The college curriculum of today needs to reflect the complexities of our world," he said at his inauguration (an unusual affair in which his speech was interspersed with musical numbers including "Let the River Run" and the love song from *The Phantom of the Opera*). "While it is true that truth is eternal . . . the roads that lead to this truth need redirection from time to time and even a bit of repaving."[16] After Petillo's bricks-and-mortar Renaissance, here was a Dominican-inspired Reformation. At the conclusion of his inauguration he planted a six-foot oak tree as a symbol of permanence in a changing world.

Peterson in Charge: Finances and Academics

Finances

Thanks to Petillo, the university was out of the woods by 1990. By 1995 it had "significant unexpended resources to prevent immediate short-term financial difficulty"[17] and "adequate working capital to meet its needs."[18] The university was unrecognizable from the struggling institution of a decade before and, with one exception, unimpeachable in its accountancy.[19] When Milton Lewis joined the Board of Regents in 1978, "he found there was no money to invest."[20] By November 1990, when Peterson, McCarrick, and Brennan launched the university capital campaign, they had a target figure of $100 million, insisting, Brennan said, that "this is not a time to be timid." The $100 million was to be shared as need demanded: $27 million to the endowment fund; $28 million to capital requirements; $12.3 million to the annual giving fund; and $32.7 million to grants and contracts requirements.[21] Much of the money would have come to Seton Hall anyway in the form of continuing grants, but the purpose was not only to raise money but also build institutional attachment. By December 1993, the campaign had raised $91 million. Between September and December 1993 over 400 alumni contributed to the university for the first time. Alumni chapters were formed in Chicago, Boston, and Atlanta. Seton Hall was named to the Chronicle of Philanthropy's Top 400 List, an annual compilation of charitable organizations that had received most in private donations. (The university was 341st.) Alumni who gave for the first time did not give a huge amount—$20,000— but the value of one campaign was that it laid a marker for another.

By 1994, the fund drive just shy of $106 million, the Council for the Advancement and Support of Education (CASE) recognized Seton Hall with its Circle of Excellence Award for outstanding fund-raising improvement in the preceding three years. Between July 1993 and July 1994, faculty and administrators obtained more than $6 million in external funding. The School of Business received a $1 million award from the W. Paul Stillman Terminating Trust for its Institute for International Business. The Foundation for Judaeo-Christian Studies contributed $300,000 to establish the H. Suzanne Jobert-Father James Sharp Endowment and to fund a memorial to Monsignor John Oesterreicher in the university library. The Class of 1994 presented a check for $1.1 million to Peterson at its reunion dinner.

Peterson could thus boast of a healthy balance sheet. In 1991, the endowment stood at $29,342,000. In 1993, it was $34,596,000. In 1993, it was $44,308,000. In 1994, it was $46,985,000. In 1995, it was $53,744,000.[22] The figures changed from quarter to quarter, indeed from day to day, but the trajectory was upwards. Between 1990 and 1995, the market value increased by 250 percent, with approximately 45 percent of the growth coming in the "quasi-endowment"—funds resulting from prior budget year surpluses which the Finance Committee of the Board of Regents permitted to be retained and invested. Indeed, the endowment grew faster than the university's total expense budget, indicating success in building capital through gifts, surpluses, and sound investments. Gift revenue was $800,000 in 1991 and 1992 but $2.5 million in 1993, $2.9 million in 1994, and $2.5 million in 1995.[23]

The current account was also solid. The university continued to rely on tuition and fees but any shortfall was made up from other sources. Seton Hall remained vulnerable to fluctuations in government revenue as a percentage of total revenue but was able to raise salaries and fringe benefits aggressively in the early 1990s while reducing overall cost of compensation as a proportion of general expenditure.[24] This was a far cry from the near bankruptcy of the Conley era.

From debt, Seton Hall had moved to surplus, from improvisation to planning. Once in the bottom third of peer institutions in terms of professors' salaries, it was now in the top third. The budget was now approved eight months earlier than previously, with audited financial statements presented to the Board of Regents six months earlier. The university was able to cope with two fiscal years (1985 and 1995) when the freshman class fell significantly short. Such changes were partly the result of a better economy and partly the result of overdue efficiencies (moving "from the dinosaur age" in computers or finding ways of earning more interest on capital).[25] By "reengineering" business practices, 15 percent could be cut from the discretionary budget.[26] Grumbles continued to be heard about quality-of-life issues[27] but, thanks to the foundations laid by Petillo, the good advice of portfolio managers, sensible economies in faculty recruitment and retention, phased retirements of expensive professors, a thoroughly professional capital campaign, greater alumni generosity, and not least a bull market in stocks and bonds such as the nation had rarely seen, Peterson proved an adept—and lucky—financial manager.

Academics

The Challenge of Diversity. Academically, the picture was reasonably encouraging. By the beginning of the 1990s, declining high school graduates and tighter competition among colleges meant that the yield of applicants to enrollments was on the rise, a sign that Seton Hall could not be as selective as it wished in putting together a freshman class. On the other hand, attrition had fallen from 24 percent (above the national norm) to a manageable 14 percent, SAT scores were up,[28] and incoming law students were the best on record. The university maintained a relatively constant faculty-to-student ratio between 1988 and 1992 and the faculty itself was better qualified and better paid in comparison with peer institutions ten years before. Tenured faculty represented a smaller fraction of the whole due to attrition and retirement.

"It remains an important goal," Scholz wrote to his deans in October 1991, "to have a diverse faculty, one that in its gender, ethnic, and racial makeup reasonably corresponds to the composition of the student body."[29] In that respect, the numbers were going in the wrong direction. In 1982, 33.7 percent of the faculty at Seton Hall were female. In 1989, the figure was 29.6 percent, the drop largely accounted for by drastic shrinkage in the College of Nursing, now half its former size.[30] By the early 1990s, female outnumbered male undergraduates and nearly a fifth of students belonged to a minority group, but these facts were poorly reflected in the demographic profile of those who taught them. Factors beyond Seton Hall's control made it hard to hire women even when that was the desire. Dean Jerry Hirsch of the College of Arts and Sciences argued that "in some applicant pools there are no women. . . . When the college had money from the Luce Foundation to hire women in the science field, it was difficult to find qualified applicants." Yet even he acknowledged "too few women full professors" and the need for "a clear directive to make an effort to hire women and minorities."[31] In 1993, of Seton Hall's nine academic officers, Barbara Beeker, dean of nursing, was the only woman. Only two women sat on the twenty-three-member Board of Regents, Eleanor McMahon of Brown University and Kent Manahan, a television anchor. Another woman, Eileen O'Kane Tauscher, resigned from the Board in 1990 because so few women were granted honorary degrees.[32] Of 52 governing positions at the university, only 5 were held by women compared with 28 out of 135 at Rutgers and 9 out of 72 at Saint Peter's College, Jersey City. "Women need to take responsibility in preparing themselves for these positions," said Patricia Kuchon, vice chancellor for student affairs, explaining that historically they had not been encouraged to do so. "I think Seton Hall University needs to seriously consider its diversity statement," said Michellene Davis, president of the Student Government Association. "They need to do what they've been saying [about diversity] and do it now."[33] Others were more sanguine. "Twenty-five years ago the concept of women on the campus of Seton Hall University was a novelty," said Lisa Candella, first woman president of the Student Government Association. "After twenty-five years, women have advanced into high administrative, staff and faculty role, [and] women students have taken on high leadership roles and have been very successful academically."[34] That was true. Notable additions included Lynn Atwater, who came to Seton Hall from Rutgers to teach sociology in 1972, remaining at the university and winning multiple prizes for teaching and scholarship until her death in 1994.[35] She "fought very hard in all her years at Seton Hall," said her colleague Lucinda San Giovanni, "for women's issues and students' issues." Mary Boutilier arrived in the early 1970s as a political science professor and made a mark as a member of the Title IX Committee, helping to implement the Higher Education Act of 1972 requiring gender equity in college-level sports programs. "The classroom provides access to more diversity than most people have in this country," she said, "and I want my students to have a social diversity as well as an academic diversity."[36]

As provost, Bernhard Scholz knew the difficulty and necessity of finding women and members of underrepresented racial and ethnic minorities for faculty positions. "In view of Seton Hall University's location, student composition, and commitment," he wrote somewhat grudgingly, "we have no choice but to be imaginative and enterprising in identifying and attracting women and minority candidates to new positions."[37] Insisting that deans and departments make positive efforts to hire women and minorities, he was pushing at a door that was open, or at least ajar.

In fall 1996 the university launched the Elizabeth Ann Seton Center for Women's Studies, a multidisciplinary program offering a minor in women's studies. The Center brought together courses taught in many departments (African American studies, anthropology, classical studies, English, history, philosophy, political science, psychology, religious studies, social work, and sociology) in an attempt to give a comprehensive account of the female experience of the world. The Center's inaugural teachers were Judith Stark of philosophy, Tracy Gottlieb of communication, and Elizabeth Milliken of history. "This has been the culmination of a two-year effort by women faculty in the College of Arts and Sciences," said Stark. "There has been a great deal of enthusiasm and dedication." "The program was named after Elizabeth Ann Seton because she was a feminist before the term was coined," said Gottlieb. "She was strong, and we think she was a strong role model for our students." Anchoring the minor was an introductory course on Women, Culture, and Society (taught by Gottlieb and Ilona Chessid of the department of modern languages) and Feminist Theories, a philosophy class taught by Stark. "Seton Hall's a little late in getting into this when other schools are celebrating their 20th and 25th anniversaries as women's studies programs, but it's better late than never," said Stark. "As a Catholic university, there is certainly the place for examining and rethinking the position of women in its tradition."[38]

The Challenge of Multiculturalism. The paradoxical assumption of these plans was that diversity meant similarity. Students were to be taught by a faculty that resembled them, not one different from them. Celebrating difference seemed to mean, in the end, celebrating sameness. This irony was less obvious when it came to the hiring of women, whose expertise was by no means confined to female matters, but it was clearer when the desideratum was racial harmony. Racial harmony was obviously good but it came with costs. Scholz worried that minorities experienced Seton Hall as "alien territory" and that, as he put it, "lose ten students and you lose $100,000 a year." There was an unsentimental calculus behind the idealism if, in Scholz's case, there was much idealism to begin with. At Seton Hall, conversations about race had to be handled delicately and honestly, two goals not easily combined. Peterson's achievement at Providence College had been a program in Western Civilization. At Seton Hall, his legacy was multiculturalism.

What was not to like about acceptance of human difference and diversity? Who was on the side of intolerance? But much of what passed for pluralism was platitude. "Let it Begin with You" was a week-long set of activities in 1992 designed to bring greater awareness of human difference, one of many such efforts whose reappearance every year seemed to indicate both necessity and futility. A "Celebration of Diversity" Mass was held in the Student Center to which all were invited. Flags were blessed. A diversity "suggestion box" was made available to those with suggestions, presumably constructive. Students were encouraged to visit infants with AIDS or teach English to Asian Americans. Some of the activities were contradictory (untonguing the Chinese by teaching them English) but the intentions were good. If harmony were to be willed into existence, there was both willingness and need in the Seton Hall of the early 1990s.

Not everybody was taken with the new style. Bishop James McHugh, a member of the Board of Trustees, thought that "racism was essentially a moral question" and that "courses and sensitivity training" were a waste of time.[39] Absent any deeper reflection on the nature of human persons, such courses were exercises in fashionable social catechism. When the fashion changed, so did the catechism. But when it came to minorities, McHugh was almost in a minority of one.

The solution was to apply balm. Under the chairmanship of Professor Daniel Leab, a distinguished historian of modern America who had come to Seton Hall from Columbia University twenty years before, a group of faculty put together a program devoted to "multicultural diversity," crafting a series of syllabi that attempted to satisfy Seton Hall's complex social and academic needs. Adventurous in some ways, conventional in others, the program was essentially an exploration of American immigration and ethnic history. In the words of associate provost Robert Sheeran, Leab's program was "as complete, balanced, and engaging" as any he had ever encountered, Leab himself "an enormously creative thinker with a wide range of experience [and] prodigious energy."[40] That energy was well deployed in the program, about which there was nothing radical or offensive or anything to suggest, in historian Arthur Schlesinger's criticism of multiculturalism, the "disuniting of America." The main criticism of multiculturalism was its exaggerated claim of novelty. Welcoming marginal groups had been Seton Hall's mission from the beginning. The groups had changed but the principle remained the same. In that sense, the Catholic Church was the most multicultural institution of all, also, in some ways, the most American, if by that is meant the assimilation and accommodation of difference within a framework of civil and juridical equality. Whether multiculturalism helped or hindered assimilation was another question, as was the notion of assimilation itself, with its obvious and subtle forms of social control. But those questions generally went unasked in a program whose task was to forestall sore feelings or to placate them.

Four Controversies: Jeffries, *Wilde!*, Parker, Euthanasia

Jeffries

These sincere, thoughtful, and humane efforts to deal with race could not conceal, but rather acknowledged, the fact that the issue itself remained fraught with peril. Race could bring the university together, as when the veteran anti-apartheid campaigner

Archbishop Desmond Tutu of South Africa gave a powerful address in September 1990.[41] But it could also pull it apart, as when a racial graffito was spray-painted on a student's door in 1991, stirring anger across campus and dividing the school along painfully predictable lines.[42] The slur was removed but the memory lingered. Peterson addressed a prayer vigil designed to restore calm, an improvised liturgy that seemed to succeed, but when the Black Student Union demanded that the victim be given a 4.0 GPA for the semester because "he cannot properly function academically under such circumstances," the idea rightly went nowhere.[43] In 1999, to make a chronological leap, Professor William Sales of the department of African-American studies received an anonymous and racially derogatory letter. Making the matter public, he complained that university policies on racial discrimination were inadequate and that having a Human Relations Council and similar organizations had not eliminated racism. "Structures and committees are just for show," he said,[44] forgetting that he had originally urged their creation. Even the best-intentioned efforts could flounder in the face of obduracy or amnesia or slogans.

The most difficult racial episode with which Peterson had to deal came in 1992, when the Black Student Union wished to invite to campus Professor Leonard Jeffries, chair of the City University of New York's African-American studies department. The university authorities demurred. According to critics, Jeffries was a hatemonger offering strange theories of "sun" and "ice" people mixed with social commentary that left many perplexed and some outraged. (In 1990, to give one example, Jeffries pronounced himself "sick and tired of having the damned Jews shoving the Holocaust down our throats.")[45] The invitation (which was never formally made) won support from some faculty and students on free speech grounds (although it is hard to reconcile what Jeffries had to say with freedom, let alone Catholicism). Donald McKenna, a communications professor, insisted that an "open, stimulating, exciting intellectual environment" could only exist when fueled by "diverse, even controversial ideas [and] . . . inflammatory thought."[46] "This university has no place for people who are not looking to build, just tear down," said vice chancellor Patricia Kuchon, putting the administration's case not very convincingly. Seton Hall, she said, strives towards "healing and reconciliation."[47] Edward Shapiro of the department of history put the argument more forcefully. "Professors are usually intolerant of their students' intellectual failings," he said, but an editorial in *The Setonian* advocating that Jeffries be invited to campus was

> incredibly sophomoric in equating freedom of speech with an obligation of Seton Hall to provide a platform for Leonard Jeffries words, and in claiming that the university has a duty to satisfy the students' "inalienable rights" to hear whomever they want . . . The idea that Seton Hall, by not allowing Jeffries on campus, is depriving our students of learning about one of the most notorious figures of our day is

ludicrous . . . Academic freedom involves the sanctity of the classroom and the publications of the faculty. It does not embrace the question of campus speakers. . . . [48]

Mr. Jeffries claim to fame is as an academic thug and an intellectual quack. His
presence at Seton Hall would add nothing of value to the scholarly life of the university and it would lend the university's prestige to his outlandish rantings . . . One
Seton Hall student, in attacking the university's decision, argued that Jeffries's appearance "will make people think." If so, then the intellectual level of American academia is even lower than the Japanese believe.[49]

Shapiro's tough-mindedness made counterproposals wilt. "We cannot continue to
keep "controversial" figures away by hiding behind our Catholicity," argued Fabio Fernandez of the Student Government Association, missing the point that Catholicity had
nothing to do with the Jeffries case, or, at least not in the way Fernandez imagined.
Peterson rebutted the argument that commitments of faith required suppression of
speech: "We do not 'hide behind our Catholicity' nor can we in any way minimize it.
While we do not wish to stand in the way of the intellectual development of our students, at the same time this development in no way demands that we provide a forum
for speakers whose past record has been judged by many as one of encouraging dis-
unity and of lacking proper respect for other groups within the community at large."[50]
Without realizing it, Jeffries had allowed the university to articulate a distinctively
Catholic multiculturalism that was both convincing and humane: "We welcome, as
part of our Catholic heritage, students of all races and ethnic origins. They are all equal
individuals of divine value and of great importance to our academic community."[51]

Archbishop McCarrick thought this "superb statement" was "truly something
which should be part of the life and work of the university."[52] By February 1995, when
Jeffries *did* come to campus, the event was dreary. (He took part a panel discussion on
the First Amendment at the law school. Sullen and implacable, he insisted that "in this
restricted atmosphere, it is doubtful that the dialogue we need can take place.")[53]

Wilde!

The year of Jeffries was also the year of *Wilde!*, a group of homosexual students seeking university recognition and funding for their association. When this recognition
was refused, sociologist Philip Kayal, the group's faculty advisor, protested that "gay
and lesbian students [were clearly unwelcome] at Seton Hall." Unmoved, Peterson appointed a "special task force" to "develop and recommend educational programs [and]
avenues of dialogue" between homosexual students and the rest of the university, a
standard strategy which usually meant much talk but not much dialogue. "At Seton

Hall," Peterson told a meeting of priests, "no decision will be reached that in anyway justifies or proliferates [sic] a homosexual lifestyle."[54] That should have ended the matter. In fact, there was more to be said and quite a few people prepared to say it. "Religious institutions cannot have it both ways," argued Jo Renée Formicola, an expert on Church-State relations. "They must either be willing to sacrifice federal monies . . . when their religious principles are compromised or . . . accommodate their immutable beliefs to national laws [and] state interests."[55] Like it or not, she argued, the claims of equality were likely to trump those of religious freedom in any institutions beholden to the federal government. But to Professor Joseph Varacalli of the Fellowship of Catholic Scholars,[56] the "suppression" of *Wilde!* was not an exercise in clerical authoritarianism but an opportunity "to affirm Seton Hall's commitment to Catholic roots." What was the point of a Seton Hall "renaissance," he wondered, when the real rebirth in Catholic higher education was taking place in smaller schools such as Christendom College in Virginia with a more complete understanding of the Catholic tradition? The controversy revealed Seton Hall as too Catholic (Kayal's point) or insufficiently so (Varacalli's). Peterson was caught in the middle.

Edward Shapiro, a Jewish teacher at a Catholic university, powerful in his denunciation of Leonard Jeffries, defended Peterson and testified to Seton Hall's tolerance:

> Members of the Seton Hall community—whether they be faculty, students, administrators or alumni—have a right to expect that Seton Hall will uphold academic freedom as it pertains to the teaching and publishing of its faculty, that its faculty will not propagandize in the classroom, and that its students will be intellectually challenged, evaluated fairly by the faculty, and treated as partners in that search for truth which is the defining mission of every university. Can Seton Hall truthfully be termed an academic community in which academic values processes and objectives are respected?
>
> Based on my experience of 24 years of teaching at Seton Hall, I believe the answer is a categorical "yes." I am unaware of any efforts by the administration during this period to stifle research or teaching . . . The university might not always make the right decision, but this is true of all academic institutions.
>
> Seton Hall, however, is not merely a university. It is a Catholic university. It is proper and to be expected that because of its religious character the Seton Hall community will differ in crucial respects from other academic communities such as Rutgers and Princeton . . . The university does not demand that non-Catholic students and employees convert to Roman Catholicism as a condition for enrollment or employment, but neither does the university assume that it has to modify its institutional character because of its openness. Speaking from personal experience, non-Catholics

are welcomed within the Seton Hall community. In return, they should respect the history and character of the university, and adopt an attitude of deferential silence when their own values come into conflict with those of the institution . . . The crux of the problem is not the status of homosexuals at Seton Hall, but rather the status of homosexuality. What the university does not welcome is the militant advocacy of homosexuality. Should this surprise anyone? Could you expect a Catholic university to do anything else?[57]

Only three other faculty members, Claire Rondeau Barrett of the College of Education and Human Services[58] and adjunct history professors William Barto and Thomas Hughes, spoke publicly in defense of the administration's position. Varacalli was right: most professors did not want to touch the issue. To be sure, Father Paul Holmes of the department of religious studies urged greater tolerance. "Last year it was Leonard Jeffries," he said. "This year it is *Wilde!* Neither is a trivial matter but next year it will be something else. The work we must do will not be easy. But before we allow sincere and well-meaning people, once again, to use Scripture, history, statistics and mission statements as weapons, before we can let each other stoop, once again, to name-calling, we should finally want to sit down, roll up our sleeves, and work out a compromise."[59] It was unclear what this "compromise of strategies" meant except, perhaps, an agreement to differ. Certain student organizations could or could not exist at Seton Hall. That was the issue and, in 1993, Peterson decided it.

Parker

Wilde! was a two-week wonder.[60] Sport was another matter. In 1995 a rising high school star from New York, Richie Parker, signed a letter of intent with Coach George Blaney to attend the university to play basketball. However, between signing and being admitted to Seton Hall, Parker was accused of, and pled guilty to, the felony charge of sexual abuse. "I don't think it changes anything," said Blaney. "We still think he's a good kid and he's somebody we want."[61] Others disagreed. The Faculty Senate "implored" Peterson to rescind the offer, arguing (with odd deafness to the actual charge) that Parker could "bring unfavorable publicity and strong criticism" to Seton Hall and "affect the recruiting of future applicants and students." Peterson agreed that "the common good and the integrity of Seton Hall" compelled him to withdraw the offer, while expressing "concern" for Parker's problems and wishing him well in solving them.[62] As it turned out, the conviction was to haunt Parker for the rest of his truncated career. Poor headlines, not the rights and wrongs of the matter, seem to have been Peterson's concern. While many applauded the decision, others denounced it, the *New York Post* noticing that Peterson had "buckled under intense pressure from media and alumni" to deny admission to a "star recruit."[63] Seeking to avoid poor publicity, he had managed to find it.

Euthanasia

By now, Peterson, his edge dulled by age and illness, was realizing that Seton Hall was a big, diverse, occasionally obstreperous place. In 1995, he had one more controversy to confront when Professor John Mitchell of the department of religious studies organized a conference on end-of-life issues, testing the limits of Seton Hall's capacity for dissent. Without consulting Mitchell, Peterson withdrew permission for the conference, prompting complaints of authoritarianism and infringement of academic freedom. In fact, the decision represented nothing of the sort. Insisting that the event be rearranged, not cancelled, and that it include a more balanced set of panelists, Peterson arrived at the defensible, indeed persuasive, position that some mention of Catholic teaching needed to be made at a conference in a Catholic university on a subject about which the Church had long held formed views. He had not infringed on freedom of speech: he wanted more of it. "The Catholic university is the place where the Church does its thinking," he pointed out, using a line from the Land O'Lakes declaration much loved by liberals. The conference, once rescheduled, should reflect that fact.[64] As it turned out, the rescheduled conference never took place and the row petered out. The irony was that Seton Hall *did* encourage and allow academic debate. The only oddity was that issues were hashed out before and after a cancelled conference and not in the conference itself.

The Catholic Question

These episodes had much to say about Seton Hall's Catholic identity, the endlessly debated question about which everyone had an opinion, intelligent or otherwise. When visitors from Middle States assessed the university in 1994, they wondered if Seton Hall's publicity and practice were in alignment. Rhetorical gestures towards Catholicism went largely untranslated into "the educational philosophies [and] programs of the university": "The easy 'fix' would be simply to insert statements of mission and catholicity in official institutional publications. This would simply be a minimal, extrinsic remedy. The real challenge is to mobilize administrators, and particularly faculty members, to incorporate these commitments into the goals and objectives of their schools and departments."[65]

In what sense could a university be Catholic if lacking a critical mass of Catholic faculty? And what constituted a "critical mass"? A head count of teachers? Of students? A willingness on the part of faculty and students to defend Catholic teaching? "The

university must explain more vigorously to itself and to others the Catholic and religious nature of the institution in a secular age," conceded the committee that prepared
the way for the Middle States visit. Specifically, it needed to "define more clearly what
is meant by the spirit of St. Elizabeth Ann Seton" and to "institute policies . . . to ensure
the continuity of [its] Catholic heritage"[66] including, perhaps, the affirmative hiring of
Catholics.[67] Even this concession was problematic. Seton Hall's Catholicism was often
taken to mean the preservation of institutional memory, as if being Catholic meant
safeguarding the "spirit" of Elizabeth Ann Seton. But preserving institutional memory
could become a form of historical *pietas* lacking Christian content of its own, a kind of
ancestor worship, little more. It would take time for a revitalized Catholicism to work
its way into classrooms, and the controversies of Peterson's chancellorship showed
how much needed to be done to make that happen.

Yet in other ways Seton Hall remained unmistakably Catholic. When Pope St. John
Paul II visited New Jersey in October 1995, three college seminarians served Mass in
the pouring rain at Giants Stadium. Peterson, concelebrating, met the Pope afterwards.
"He said to me: you are the Chancellor of a Catholic University. Tell your students to
love God and help one another."[68] Carrying with him a section of the cornerstone of
the new library (how he managed this is unclear) Peterson asked the Pope to bless it,
which he did.

It took a Jewish visitor, Professor Hadley Arkes of Amherst College, to insist on the
importance of Seton Hall's Catholicism in what he called a "dark time." In a sparkling
Charter Day address in 1994, Arkes argued that it had become almost uniquely the responsibility of Catholic universities to preserve the tradition of natural rights that lay
at the core of the American foundation. "Catholic schools as schools are as legitimate
as any other schools in this country."[69] Their moral beliefs must not be held as less
worthy of respect, or less binding upon their members, than those of public institutions. Arkes, who later became a Catholic, proposed that it was precisely Seton Hall's
Catholicism that gave it moral authority and a claim to legal respect and that it was
time that the university rediscovered it.

For some, then, Catholic identity was a heritage to be handed on, for others an
agenda to be acted upon, for yet others a nuisance. (Times had changed when *The
Setonian* could run the headline "Catholic Ideals Often Hinder Integrity of College
Papers.")[70] Harvard's Tom Landy thought that many Catholic universities, Seton Hall
included, framed the question poorly:

> One tendency is to locate Catholic identity outside the academic mission of the
> institution, in its service programs, campus ministry. Another is to discuss it in con-
> flictual terms about what the theology or philosophy departments ought to be doing.

Too many other times, we're content with platitudes about the role of faith in the academic mission.

[For me], the defining problem of Catholic identity in higher education is the lack of a well-developed, shared sense of what a Catholic intellectual life is about in a post-Vatican II context. Without a renewal of Catholic intellectual life, the conversation about Catholic identity will prove sterile.[71]

Angela Raimo, professor of education, preferred the old Seton Hall which "stood proudly for a family environment": "We shared so much in terms of Faith, community, caring, and concern. Priest-presidents would invite faculty and their families for Christmas parties. Father Fahy had a traditional Christmas Mass in the Main Lounge where children would all be invited to bring gifts to the altar for the poor."[72] As the family had eroded in our broader culture, she suggested, "it has somewhat eroded here."[73]

The conversation became more pointed when John Paul II's apostolic constitution on Catholic universities, *Ex Corde Ecclesiae* (*From the heart of the Church*), was the subject under discussion. *Ex Corde Ecclesiae* was an intellectually forthright document, a confident restatement of the dignity and importance of the Catholic university. It also had the canonical purpose of defining its norms and legal identity. In a series of dialogues in 1994 and 1995, Peterson heard the concerns of faculty who were committed to Seton Hall's Catholicism and its academic freedom but who wondered (as anyone would) what those terms meant in practice. He was aware, he said, that "the faculty thought bishops dominated and were involved in everything." The truth was more complex. Faculty members who feared episcopal interference (or who wanted more of it) tended to forget that bishops had other things to do. Nor did the bishops who served on Seton Hall's Board of Trustees speak with one voice. Bishop James McHugh of Camden thought that "previously bishops stood outside of everything . . . [Now] they must be more inside of everything . . . to do the necessary leading." Bishop Edward Hughes of Metuchen saw need to "[make] the effort with the faculty to understand our mission and to blend academic freedom with their teaching responsibility." Archbishop Theodore McCarrick thought there were three "moments" in any institution's life—the ideal, the actual, and the "becoming." Seton Hall was in the "becoming moment." "Most of us [bishops] lost control of hiring years ago," he said. "We have had people in key slots who did not share our ideal and there was no unanimity."[74] McCarrick took his role as academic custodian seriously, complaining (as many did) about the radio station[75] and even suggesting suitable reading for religion courses. (Father Richard McBrien's book *Catholicism* was "flawed' and "should not be used as a text in Religious Education even on the college level.")[76] But a bishop casually telling a president that he did not like a book was not the same as requiring him to drop it. The complaint was more an admission of powerlessness than power.

"People in key slots" assumed that willing professors were crucial in creating and sustaining Catholic identity. It did not follow that these professors had to be Catholic or that Catholic identity was a matter of denominational quotas. Professor William Toth of the School of Theology pointed to the deeper constitutive elements of a Catholic university, including an "assertive but unsectarian" commitment to Catholicity, a "sacramental" view of creation and the world, a commitment to community and to social responsibility, and to "the pursuit of truth, goodness and beauty in its many different forms."[77] For Father Dan Degnan S.J., a former dean of the law school, there was something to be said for *not* hiring Catholics. "We [need] to bring in non-Catholic educators," he told one symposium, "as they would be the strongest in helping us keep our Catholic identity."[78] His point was that Catholic hires were "imbued with academic freedom" whereas non-Catholics tended to be more respectful of mission and institutional memory. There was evidence for the second notion: see Edward Shapiro above. Several observant Jews on the faculty expressed disappointment that the university was less committedly Catholic than they had expected it to be. Few departments gave weight to denominational affiliation when they hired. Credentials, not creed, mattered most. Affirmative action for Catholics might have met with resistance or non-compliance, with claims that "academic freedom" had been compromised and departmental autonomy destroyed. The time for systematic Catholic hiring probably had gone.[79]

The deeper meaning of *Ex Corde Ecclesiae* for Seton Hall was well articulated by Robert Sheeran, soon to succeed Peterson at the helm. Sheeran thought that John Paul had proposed a double challenge: to transform structures and to transform hearts. How that double transformation was to occur, how it was to root itself in the actual and the ideal, how it was to enable the pursuit of truth in its multiple forms, how it was to speak in assertive but nonsectarian ways: that was the question. No-one, not even the Pope, claimed to know all the answers.

For all that, Seton Hall did offer *some* answers. "Any observer who looks at Seton Hall University from the outside," wrote Scholz in 1993, "must become aware not only of the thoroughly Catholic character of the institution but of a strong Catholic presence in our academic goals and activities."[80] Undergraduates took courses in ethics and religious dimensions of life. The faculty included scholars inspired by Catholic assumptions and concerns and by their own Catholic faith. Twenty-two members of the faculty were priests of the Archdiocese of Newark. The Institute of Judaeo-Christian Studies fostered understanding between Christians and Jews. "Rarely," said Scholz when John Oesterreicher died in 1993, "has a life over five decades been dedicated so single-mindedly to so necessary and noble a goal; and rare indeed must be the man in the Church whose concerns and hopes became, within his lifetime, the policies of popes and a General Council of the Church."[81]

The *Bulletin of Biblical Theology* was supported by the University. Father Stanley Jaki, Templeton prizewinner, held a distinguished professorship. The New Jersey Catholic Historical Records Commission was based at Seton Hall. The archives of the Archdiocese of Newark and other New Jersey dioceses were preserved in the university library. The Archbishop Peter L. Gerety lecture series addressed important questions of Catholic history. Major Catholic figures, cardinals, poets, philosophers, and activists came to campus. Seton Hall had exchange arrangements with the Catholic University of Puerto Rico, Sacred Heart University of Puerto Rico, Sophia University in Tokyo, and Sogang University in Seoul. It had strong links with local Catholic schools and hospitals. The Law School's Center for Social Justice provided free legal aid to 1,300 indigent clients in Newark every year. The Equal Opportunity Program, funded partly by the state and partly by the university, demonstrated Seton Hall's continuing commitment to social fairness. The Dr. Martin Luther King Jr. Scholarship program provided financial assistance to minority students. The Puerto Rican Institute had many ties to a local community that was largely Catholic. Monsignor Andrew Cusack's Institute for Priests had an international reputation, bringing contemporary thinking in theology, spirituality, psychology, and canon law to priests in pastoral ministry, a "vital ministry," thought Cardinal Paul Poupard, for "the overall life of the Catholic Church in the United States."[82] In 1995 alone, it hosted figures as diverse as Father Raymond Brown on contemporary biblical scholarship, Father Gerald O'Collins S.J. on the death and resurrection of Jesus, Father Bryan Hehir on Catholic social teaching, Father Walter Burghardt on the contemplative life in a parish setting, and Molly Scanlan Kelly on chastity.[83] Well over six feet tall and with a shock of white hair, Cusack looked like an Old Testament prophet. He was also a delight. (His driving, especially on Irish country roads, owed more to faith than reason.) In all sorts of ways, Scholz was right: Seton Hall's Catholicism was unmistakable.

These commitments spoke to an intellectual vitality that made Seton Hall special. Because of its affiliation with the Church, said Scholz, it necessarily reflected "tensions . . . evident in the Church today":

> In an institution that specifically embraces the 1940 statement on academic freedom of the American Association of University professors and that honors the freedom of faculty members in matters of research, publishing, taking a stand on public issues, and teaching, it would be surprising, and indeed disappointing, if controversial subjects were not raised at times and positions taken that are not in full agreement with what is generally accepted. Since its inception, the university, after all an invention of the Roman Catholic Church, and certainly the Catholic university, has

been a principal source of new ideas and interpretations that have led to controversy at times but as often to a more profound understanding of matters of the intellect and of faith. As a university, Seton Hall cannot function unless it possesses a certain latitude, openness, and willingness to take risks and accommodate unpopular views, and certainly in its academic efforts these qualities have not been absent in the past.[84]

Here was a good summary not only of Seton Hall but of the challenges facing Catholic higher education at the end of the twentieth century. For Scholz, Seton Hall's Catholicity had to be about "ideas and values that have always been held high in the Catholic tradition" which appealed to those outside the tradition. These ideas included "service, social responsibility, a high regard for the power of reason and the development of the intellect, a commitment to community, a readiness to think about ethical problems, and a willingness to adhere to certain moral values."[85] This was not to dilute Catholicism but to recognize its dynamism, its power to persuade, and its human appeal.

But to quantify the spiritual life is to miss its essence. At the end of the day, the Catholic identity of Seton Hall was not a matter of committee reports or spread sheets but a matter of lives—often priestly lives—lived in the light of the gospel and dedicated to bringing it to others. Among notable priests were John Mannion, spiritual director of the basketball team, who died saying Mass; the calm, sensible, Dan Murphy, retired professor of education; the brilliant linguist and loner Don Smith, assistant professor of modern languages and Phi Beta Kappa graduate of Princeton; the mordant Richard Nardone of religious studies, understated in all things except enthusiasm for Iceland; and the irrepressible Peter Lennon, professor of psychology, cheerful amidst ailments. These were the Catholic faces of a Catholic university.

Governance

University governance advanced despite difficulties during Peterson's time. As provost, Scholz thought that involving faculty in budgetary matters raised "unreasonable expectations and [generated] wish lists we [cannot] satisfy."[86] "We also don't want to invite them to approve everything under the sun."[87] But suspicion of faculty interference was unsustainable, not least because, after the Yeshiva decision, Seton Hall could not get away with the token efforts of an earlier generation. Shared governance had to be meaningful.

In 1990–1991 the Faculty Executive Committee and the Faculty Governance Coordinating Committee asked Peterson to establish a task force to study a new faculty governance structure. Nothing was done until May 1992, when the task force was formed, its recommendations submitted to the faculty for approval in the fall of that year. In December 1992, Seton Hall's newly elected senators held their first meeting, and the following spring they established committees, of which the most important were the Academic Policy and Core Curriculum Committee and the Compensation and Social Welfare Committee. The work was coordinated by an Executive Committee which met with the provost after each senate meeting.

The result was a revitalized faculty participation in university business coupled with occasional frustration when advice was sought but not accepted. For Professor Petra Chu, an advocate of unionization, the new senate was "a good beginning."[88] The senate acquired an impressive show of authority, committees for this, subcommittees for that, with some people seeming to serve on all of them. Occasionally senators thought themselves a parallel administration, but on the whole they did their work well. University governance presumed the goodwill that its structures sometimes undermined. From time to time the faculty senate overstepped its limits and the administration, for its part, did not always listen to legitimate concerns and constructive suggestions. The challenge was to see the senate as a partner, not a rival, a respected feature of Seton Hall's shared governance, not the loyal opposition.

Academic Challenges

The need for cooperation increased as academic challenges accumulated. At the level of individual schools and colleges, the university was doing much better than ten years before, with most indices going in the right direction. Strangely, this good news was not always reflected in faculty morale or in good relations between faculty and administration. In 1992, the College of Nursing was reaccredited with minor recommendations for improvement; new programs were developed; registered nurse enrollments and graduate enrollments had significantly increased; several off-site campus sites were added; salary savings from grants were returned to the college, substantial capital funds were released for computerization, and major renovations of the nursing building were carried out. For all that, Scholz noticed "with dismay" the "sudden expressions" of faculty discontent in the college. The reason was to be found in the rising expectations he had helped to bring about.[89]

The School of Graduate Medical Education was slapdash in its procedures. The semidetached nature of the School made it hard for Scholz to control, and its dean, John Patterson, was not at home in the world of committees and faculty guides, preferring to govern his scattered fiefdom in improvised, informal ways. Scholz and Paterson maintained good relations, but their understanding of academic administration was poles apart.

The W. Paul School of Business was accredited by the American Assembly of Collegiate Schools on the third attempt in 1992, the deferral due to the low percentage of the faculty with doctorates, the quantity and quality of their scholarship, the school's lack of computer and library facilities, and poor office space. Most of these difficulties had been addressed, if not fully solved, by 1992. "We are now faced with a new set of standards to be met, a new philosophy of accreditation," said Fred Kelly, dean of the college.[90] The new standards required more arts and sciences electives in the business curriculum. Although there were over 2,000 business programs in the country, only 280 were accredited, making the accreditation worth having. It was one thing to set standards, another to meet them. Despite accreditation, faculty morale was low and personal tensions high.[91]

Library

Peterson's greatest ambition was a new library. McLaughlin Library was "a memorable lady from the distant past . . . much beloved and much beleaguered," he said.[92] What was needed was "a star, a jewel of the campus." Chopped into cluttered areas, doors locked, corridors leading nowhere, only able to accommodate 13 percent of the under-graduate population, McLaughlin "utterly [defied] quick or easy understanding even by sophisticated library patrons."[93] When even the librarian spoke of "an environment generally inhospitable to both people and books"[94] its days were done. The argument for a new facility was technical and financial. Fixing McLaughlin Hall would have cost $7.5 million. A new building would have cost about $9.5 million. The additional $2 million amortized over thirty years was easily absorbed by a budget the size of Seton Hall's.[95] A new library would also act as the centerpiece of the capital campaign, which would be "significantly weakened," Peterson told the Board, if a decision were made not to build it.[96] McCarrick worried about more debt (among priests his reputation as a cheapskate was notorious), but Robert Brennan argued that not to build could result "in some of the worst forecasts becoming a reality."[97] Another regent, Thomas Shar-key, suggested that inaction would signal that the university's "renaissance" was over.

"We are trying to build a library which will be usable for fifty years," said Dennis Mahon. "We are trying to factor into the design the future of books. If in fifteen or twenty years, microforms or CDs are the desired form of information storage, then we want to build a building that would accommodate materials in any form." This up-to-dateness now seems itself out-of-date. The world of e-books, of libraries having fewer books and more portals, was invisible in 1992. The most exciting technical innovation was compact shelving.[98] But Seton Hall was going to be state-of-the-art, whatever that art might be.

The contract was signed with Alfieri Co. Inc. in April 1992 and the ground broken (between Mooney Hall and the Recreation Center) at the end of June. At 155,000 square feet, the library was much bigger than the one it replaced.[99] McLaughlin Hall was demolished in May 1995, not without a fight. (The wrecking crew discovered how stoutly it was put together.) Before it disappeared, it yielded a time capsule containing old catalogs and copies of *The Setonian*.[100] In a sense, the whole building was a time capsule.[101] The new library was made possible by the generosity of Frank Walsh,[102] whose joint gift, with Ray Chambers, of $5 million, helped defray costs. The State of New Jersey grant-funded it to the tune of almost $3 million.[103] Over four floors, with archives, special collections, an art gallery, a technology center, scholars' studies, and browsing room for periodicals, it was impressive. From a distance, its most striking feature was a huge, ten-paneled copper dome, thirty-five feet from top to bottom, designed and built by the Newark firm of Schlitter and Plevy (who had worked on Russian Orthodox churches, the Hoboken Ferry terminal, and Carnegie Hall).[104] "The 'Walsh Library'," Peterson wrote "will stand for long years to come as a statement in stone of Seton Hall's lasting commitment to academic excellence. It will be used by all who come here in order to seek to make their lives better by the sacred and secular learning which is imparted to them."[105] It opened on Monday August 29, 1994, the first student a senior from the School of Business, Jonathan Platell, and the first faculty member Leigh Steltzer, also from the School of Business, who presented a bottle of champagne (maintaining safe distance from the "No Food and Drink Allowed in the Library" sign). The first book transferred from McLaughlin Library to Walsh Library by way of a human chain of faculty and students was *The Summit of a Century*, Seton Hall's centennial history of 1956.[106]

"In McLaughlin it was extremely difficult for students just to find a place to sit down," said librarian Karen Mergurian. The new building in its public and private spaces could seat 1,100 people, a "vast size difference," over its predecessor.[107] Peter Ahr, dean of freshman studies, thought that McLaughlin Library "was designed to be a book warehouse, not allowing for browsing, hunting, and studying." By contrast, Walsh Library was "extremely inviting and congenial."[108] With significant internal and external funding to build up the collection (the latter especially from an NEH challenge grant designed to support humanities programs) the library was well stocked, well staffed, and well patronized.

Image and Reality

Under Peterson, Seton Hall tried to position itself as an old university with a new sense of possibility. Much of this "positioning" was marketing. Thomas Watson, founder of IBM, believed that to be great, companies had to act as if they were great already. This was the central idea of a Chancellor's Task Force on the Challenge of Excellence, which reported to Peterson in November 1994. The report was everything that is wrong when management consultants imagine themselves as philosophers. "We do not need excuses or complaints about the way things are or have been," it said. "We need to act and do something." The "something" turned out to be an apology for the university's religious identity. "Our promotion of Catholicity connotes restrictions (real or imagined) about the academic vitality and freedom of the university," it argued. "In one sense we open the door to diverse student population, in another we close the door in the strict, dogmatic portray of Catholicism."[109] Even Peterson sometimes seemed to think along these lines. "We have to say we are a Catholic college," he told one meeting of his Task Force on Adult Education in 1994, "but we do not have to flaunt it."[110]

From time to time, market analysis had its uses. It was important to know, for instance, that of 40,000 initial inquiries to Seton Hall from high school students in 1995, only 5,000 applied.[111] One school of thought held that it was "best to have the Seton Hall University name known as widely as possible in any positive manner, be it through academics, research, sports, alumni accomplishments or any other way."[112] But "rebranding" had strategic implications that needed to be thought through. Should the university become more selective? Should it rededicate itself to local, first-generation students? Should it develop a new model of educational "delivery" that combined conventional, campus-based programs with off-site approaches? What, precisely, was the Seton Hall "difference"? Unfortunately, no sooner had one marketer proposed that Seton Hall be distinctive than another urged that its distinctiveness, as Catholic and local, be downgraded or "played up."[113] Bombarded with contradictory advice, Peterson would have been better off saving his money. After so many Task Forces, "several members [of them] agreed that we have no idea of what people thought of us."[114] They hardly knew themselves.

One Task Forcer, Mary Meehan, had it right.[115] Perceived excellence would bring better students, she thought, but only real excellence would keep them. Meehan wanted the reality, not the image. What programs were good but could be great? Which needed to be eliminated? Was the university prepared to achieve excellence ("it could be done tomorrow") by setting higher SAT scores, by downsizing, by absorbing the short-term financial loss of fewer but better students? Meehan offered answers as well as questions. The quality of the faculty was more important than renown. (Seton Hall was fortunate to have teachers who enjoyed both.) The key was recruiting and retaining professors "invested in the mission and vision of the University" and removing those who were not. Donors could be identified to fund chairs in disciplines recognized as a "centers of excellence." The honors program could be expanded. Mentoring could be improved. Better use could be made of alumni to place graduates in employment. The campus could be made more attractive. None of the changes would happen overnight but, together, they would transform Seton Hall not only in perception but in fact. "If you build it, they will come."[116]

Whatever the perception, Seton Hall *did* have a good story to tell. Professors with an international reputation included Edward Shapiro, whose book *A Time for Healing: American Jewry since the Second World War* (Johns Hopkins University Press, 1992), was the fifth and final volume of the series *The Jewish People in America*; Elizabeth Defeis of the Law School, who helped draft the constitution of the Republic of Armenia (ratified in 1995);[117] and Father Richard Nardone, who published *The Story of the Christian Year* (Paulist Press, 1992) and was keynote speaker at the Fall Liturgy conference of the Archdiocese of Denver, Colorado in 1993.[118]

A New President and a Verdict

Four years into his chancellorship, Peterson's ability to deal with enormous challenges seemed increasingly doubtful. "All around us institutions are redefining themselves," Scholz told the faculty. "Our sister institutions . . . are already fierce competitors . . . We cannot do business as usual. . . . Is the campus really supportive of students? Is it tolerant and inclusive, vibrant and exciting? Or do we bore students to death, turn them off, irritate them?"[119]

The university needed to be responsive, but how responsive was Peterson? Slowly he began to decline, to the point that it was "almost impossible to ask one person to do everything," said Frank Walsh, chair of the Board of Regents, putting a kind face on his enfeeblement.[120] "Much charity has been extended to him," thought Scholz more astringently, "we cannot afford any more . . . The Board's love affair [with him] . . . has to come to an end now."[121] Only in his mid-sixties, by 1995 Peterson seemed an old man, shrinking physically by the day. His strengths (attention to detail) now seemed like weaknesses (fussiness about trivialities). (Dennis Mahon, who had experience of his style, called him not so much a micromanager as a nanomanager.) A man of intellectual gifts—a fluent Latin speaker, for example—he was less at ease in practical matters. His increasing debility seemed a threat to the university and an embarrassment to himself. "We need to tell the Seton Hall story to the outside world better," said Walsh. "We can do a lot better." The remark seemed to cast Peterson's tenure in the past rather than the future tense.

In December 1995, the Board of Regents appointed Monsignor Robert Sheeran as nineteenth president of Seton Hall. Peterson retained the title "chancellor" but was shunted aside. To replace the older for the younger man was an obvious although difficult decision. Twelve years before, when Petillo became chancellor, the effect had been to marginalize a president, D'Alessio. Now with Sheeran becoming president, the effect was to marginalize a chancellor. The intention in both cases was to replace a weak chief executive with a powerful one. "Seton Hall is now at a crossroads in which its future is one which it must itself create," Peterson said. "By adding additional and bold emphasis to both its internal and external administration, [it] enables itself to meet much more effectively the challenges that await in the twenty-first century."[122] The truth was more brutal. "Unless he recognizes himself what his new place is," Scholz wrote to Sheeran the day after Sheeran became president, "you have to be hard on him."[123] Peterson maintained his own secretariat and suite of offices but was reduced to putting in polite appearances at fund-raisers. "It is a real exciting time," Sheeran said on the day of his appointment. "We are building on strength to strength. This is part of a strategic transition of the university over the next five years."[124] A gracious manner, a winning optimism, and a manifest love for the institution, helped win over doubters. Sheeran was a known, and liked, quantity.

Peterson's leadership deserves to be remembered for its achievements rather than its disappointments. He built on Petillo's financial rescue while bringing a more urbane style. Never a Seton Hall booster as such, he was happier speaking generically of Catholic higher education and the university's place within it rather than of the institution of which he was leader. Despite growing up in its shadow and coming to it after a career elsewhere, Peterson was still partially a stranger to Seton Hall even at the end of his life. But the successes were undeniable—a new library, a more confident Catholicism, a more contemporary curriculum. Peterson was an introvert in an extrovert's job, a shy man more at home in the library than in a finance meeting. But he did well by Seton Hall and, for all his troubles, Seton Hall did well by him.

CHAPTER 18

A Law School for the City

Seton Hall Law from 1961

Toward Maturity: John Loftus as Dean 1961–1971

Rooney, Wu, Reardon, and their colleagues took the unaccredited John Marshall College and turned it into a fully functioning law school providing a solid legal education for the postwar generation. By the end of its first decade, it had a good library,[1] a talented faculty, intelligent students from a wide range of academic backgrounds,[2] a respectable bar pass rate, and active alumni making their ways in their professions. The school was never exclusive or sectarian but its Catholicism was unmistakable. Canceling class on holy days of obligation was axiomatic.[3] Rooney reminded colleagues that "for every hour spent in teaching an hour should be spent on one's knees before the Blessed Sacrament."[4] Nor was the school progressive. (A suggestion from New York University about a course on civil liberties was rebuffed.)[5] Rooney acknowledged the need to "meet the trends of the law in the industrial environment of urban areas" and that "constantly increasing demands" on lawyers could not be ignored.[6] That was as far as she would go. Juvenile delinquency and inner-city crime later became features of the curriculum but for now little disturbed its stable respectability.[7]

In 1961 Rooney gave up the deanship, returning to the faculty to teach and receiving high praise for her tenure.[8] Her successor John Loftus, not a philosopher-scholar in the same rank, was a competent teacher of property law[9] with an ability to quote cases down page number, almost as if memory alone could compensate for a certain lack of intellectual flair. His was a shoe-string operation (he even ran the elevator),[10] every chore falling to him[11] including hiring the faculty. That was a duty the faculty was happy to yield.[12]

But not even as conservative a figure as Loftus or as conservative a school as Seton Hall could resist forces beginning to impinge on them. Seton Hall was a law school for a city but was 1960s Newark a city for a law school? Crowded, noisy, and unsafe at night, Clinton Street was nothing to write home about. (Only Arnold's greasy spoon eatery warmed and perhaps clogged the heart.) The law school conceived itself as essentially urban in nature, but in the early 1960s, long before the riot of 1967, the university was thinking of moving some of its Newark operation elsewhere. (Female students in particular found the surroundings unsafe.) Why not also move the law school? It did not *have* to be in Newark: it could be anywhere.[13] Maybe it was not a city law school after all.

Then came the riot. Whatever the cause of that explosion—whether it was the result of poverty, racism, industrial dislocation, or human implacability; whether it was a disorganized political protest[14] or a self-inflicting wound;[15] whether it was due to African-American "clustering"[16] or because politicians exaggerated the potency of street protest[17]—the riot was a profoundly important moment for Newark and its people. Between 1964 and 1972, upwards of half a million African Americans participated in street violence across 300 American cities, during which there were 250 deaths, 60,000 arrests, and property damage totaling hundreds of millions of dollars. Black unemployment in Newark in 1967 was 12 percent; the school drop-out rate was 33 percent; some 40 percent of Black children lived in single-parent homes. Newark had the highest rate of infant mortality in the country, the highest number of new cases of tuberculosis; the seventh largest number of drug addicts; and some of the worst housing in the nation.[18]

How to conduct a law school in conditions of extreme lawlessness? Even a university historically committed to the transformative power of education could have been forgiven for leaving a city nearly destroyed by some of its own citizens. As it turned out, surprisingly little thought was given to leaving, not only because to abandon Newark was to abandon people who had done nothing to deserve their troubles, but also because it was unclear where the law school might go. Father Tom Fahy thought Seton Hall had a "moral obligation" to show solidarity with the city at its moment of greatest need,[19] the riot precisely the reason for *not* leaving.

Once the decision had been made to stay, the commitment to the city was wholehearted. Newark needed a law school not only to train future lawyers but also to explore the complex sociology that created lawlessness in the first place. Following a 1967 ruling of the New Jersey Supreme Court allowing third-year law students to work on legal aid cases, Professor Joseph Slowinski started a program handling small claims cases on behalf of the "legally poor." By the early 1970s the scheme was expanded to include not only the indigent but also those who, although slightly better off, were still unable to seek legal redress of their problems. By 1971, the Seton Hall Law School Legal Aid Clinic had developed into an official neighborhood law office of the Newark Legal Services Project, with sixty-two third-year students making 240 court appearances on behalf of clients in the Essex County Municipal Courts, the Juvenile and Domestic Relations Court, and the County District Court. Clinical programs introduced students to the lawyer as fact-finder, advisor, negotiator, draftsman, and advocate, increasing their sensitivity to unfairness in the legal system and encouraging them to seek solutions not only to individual cases but to the social problems that gave rise to them. In 1970–1971, the Legal Services Clinic dealt with a total of 674 cases.

Another venture was Patrick House in Jersey City. Founded in 1971 by Dr. Paul T. Jordan and Father Francis Schiller to help the estimated 5,000–7,000 heroin addicts in Hudson County, by 1973 Patrick House included legal, educational, economic, and psychiatric services for 1,200 people. Four hundred emergency criminal cases were handled by its over-worked part-time attorney who could only provide representation in criminal matters at municipal court level because, once indicted, an addict was transferred to the Office of Public Defender. Professor Mark Denbeaux, recently appointed to the faculty, proposed a Seton Hall Law Clinic for Patrick House to be staffed by third-year students working under supervision. The students' role in criminal matters was limited, most court-related work done by an attorney, but in civil matters they could handle cases involving landlord-tenant, debtor-creditor, and matrimonial problems.[20] The Patrick House Legal Clinic showed what a law school could do to help with real problems in real time.

And so, transformed by Newark and itself transforming it, Seton Hall Law stayed in the city. To Leon Jaworski, president of the American Bar Association, law was the "glamor profession" of the 1970s. That was not a word to describe 40 Clinton Street but, glamorous or not, under Loftus Seton Hall Law slowly improved, becoming a more confident, even pretentious, enterprise. In 1967, Theodore Meth started *Seton Hall Law Journal*. In 1968, following an ABA directive, the first Juris Doctor (JD) degree was conferred. In 1970, the *Seton Hall Law Review* was inaugurated, as was the more readable *Res Ipsa Loquitur*. The school thought of itself as quasi-independent, a view reinforced by physical distance from South Orange and by the fact that the ABA and the AALS required it to keep institutional distance from its sponsoring university. "A law school should be autonomous," said Professor John Wefing at a 1970 meeting with Academic Vice President John Duff, a view Rooney rejected and one that Duff thought unworkable but, to Wefing, simply a statement of AALS policy.[21] A few months before, Professor Reginald Stanton complained of "administrative authoritarianism of the worst kind" when the South Orange administration cancelled final examinations in the law school because of the Kent State killings.[22] As the 1960s gave way to the 1970s, the law school faculty was less deferential, finding fault with salaries, offices, and the state of the building. Lawyers are trained to argue, and some, unsurprisingly, turned out to be argumentative.

Students were also more demanding: "Although occasional horror stories still surface, most of the sociopaths who used to teach law under the theory that humiliation was somehow good for you have gone the way of Charles Dickens. Keep in mind that if you've done the reading, 'briefed' the cases, and tried to get at least some

understanding of why you were asked to read what you were asked to read, no professor is going to be able to destroy you, nor will he or she want to."[23]

Such satire suggested rueful affection but not everyone felt at home. Minority students held that the university was ungenerous in its aid to them.[24] Not every grievance
was justified nor indicative of systemic discrimination but one consequence of the 1967
riot was greater awareness of African American students and of the community from
which they came.

Toward Excellence: John Irving
and Daniel Degnan 1971–1983

Nothing in this urban activism contradicted the exalted visions of Rooney, whose repeated insistence on natural equity and Christian social teaching was now being fulfilled in unexpected ways. Training lawyers was not, at its core, a socially disruptive
enterprise. Under Loftus and his successors, John Irving and Daniel Degnan S.J., the
law school identified itself with the city, giving Newarkers reason for gratitude. New
Jersey was also in its debt. As first- and second-generation Seton Hall lawyers made
their way as attorneys, politicians, and judges, the state would have looked very different without them. People who never heard of John McNulty or Miriam Rooney had
their lives shaped by them.

Loftus retired in 1971 after ten years in charge, a turbulent decade for Newark,
a less turbulent but still troubled one for the school. The decade that followed saw
growth and growing pains in abundance. In 1973, the faculty numbered fifteen. By
1983, it stood at thirty-nine. In 1973, less than half of them had published a book or
article in the preceding five years. By 1983, almost all were actively publishing. The
Richard J. Hughes Chair in Constitutional and Public Law and Service was established,
it first occupant Richard J. Hughes himself, former governor and chief justice of New
Jersey. In 1978 the Monsignor Fahy Legal Education Opportunities Program (LEO)
was established to give disadvantaged students a chance at law school. In 1982, the
school's annual fund-drive was generating almost $100,000.[25] Deans John Irving from
1971 to 1977, Robert Diab from 1977 to 1978, and Daniel Degnan from 1978 to 1983,
oversaw the growth.

Irving, a graduate of Saint Peter's College, Jersey City, the Fordham Law School,
and the NYU Graduate School of Law, had served as law secretary to the New Jersey
Superior Court and as US Attorney for the National Labor Relations Board. "I knew
nothing about the university except my wife and I had been born and raised in Jersey
City. I knew there was a Seton Hall University. I knew they had a basketball team, and
there was some speculation that because I was tall that I was being brought in both
as a basketball coach and a law school dean, in effect to save money."[26] "We are not

distinguished, we need additional offices, our physical plant lacks humane principles, it is impersonal and cold," he told his colleagues at their first meeting. They, too, needed to shape up. ("Law school faculty with all sorts of degrees who are intolerable bores in the classroom," did not impress him.)[27] But he could also be charming, a man, one senior administrator noticed, with "a finely developed sense of P.R."[28] (He "much impressed" Fahy.)[29] "The faculty runs the law school," Irving said at his first encounter with his new colleagues, "not the students, not the campus, not the Alumni, nor the Chief Justice of New Jersey."[30] This was what they wanted to hear. Behind a gruff exterior, he was a romantic. "Love for the law and for obedience to its standards is caught and not taught. The heroes are there; we don't tell them enough about them."[31]

Irving was a man in a hurry, overseeing among other things a long-planned change in the required curriculum.[32] He came to a school with twelve full-time teachers plus two new members, himself included. Three more appointments came in 1972–1973, another three in 1973–1974, three more in 1974–1975, and five in 1975–1976. The full-time faculty doubled in five years to twenty-five, growth driven in part by pressure from the ABA.[33] "Since your arrival as Dean the law school seems to have undergone vast changes at all levels," one graduate wrote to him. "As [one] who has experienced the past and ushered in the new, I can accurately state that [your] efforts are much appreciated."[34]

Growth in student numbers was matched by growth in faculty quality. One or two eccentrics haunted the halls, but professors remained reasonably sane. (The eccentrics deserve mention. One greeted Irving's visit to his class by laying prone on the desk as in obeisance to a god. He was later fired.)[35] Christopher Clancy joined in 1973, having taught at Columbia and Texas Southern universities. His work involved complex questions of constitutional and labor law. Michael Risinger, a *magna cum laude* graduate of Yale and a *cum laude* graduate of Harvard Law School, also arrived in 1973, bringing an incisive mind to a range of legal, social, and literary matters. John Wefing shouldered heavy teaching while achieving advanced degrees, publishing, and chairing committees. Mark Denbeaux, with extensive public interest experience, was fascinated by student experience of law school.[36] E. Judson Jennings, a Princeton and Georgetown graduate who had taught at Columbia and New York Law School, numbered among his interests legal services for the elderly poor. Michael Ambrosio was an advocate of the natural law tradition. Ted Meth (*in situ* when Irving arrived) worked on animal rights. All brought intellectual heft to the school.

Irving was wry in his assessment of faculty-administration relations:

Why can't professors be more like their deans?
Deans are so decent, such regular guys,
Ready to help you, whatever your size,

Ready to buck you up whenever you are glum –
Why can't professors be a chum?[37]

Law professors, he thought, forgot that "money goes 'where the action is'," [38] as if he himself knew the whereabouts of that mysterious place. Not a scholar or a teacher, he was a bureaucrat, doing his work well and finding clever ways of hiring staff, generally by pleading pressure from accrediting agencies. Nor was he slow to share his views. The "three open wounds in the criminal justice," he told the U.S. House of Representatives Judiciary Committee in 1976, were municipal courts ("an outright cancer"); juvenile courts ("an absurdity"); and judicial selection ("so substandard and erratic . . . as to impede the entire court systems in most states.")[39] He was critical of New Jersey politics and thought a constitutional convention "urgently needed" to set matters right.[40] Rooney stuck to philosophy journals. Loftus made the lifts run on time. Irving thought his job was to opine. By this standard, he was an A-1 success.

In fairness, Irving also built the structure by which the law school moved from modesty to excellence. With the appointment of a dean of admissions, an academic dean, an assistant dean for registration, a director for procurement, and a financial aid director, it became a more complicated, if not more generous, place.[41] "There were no committees in those days," recalled Robert Diab of his early career. (He arrived at the school in 1958 and served as a sort of minister without portfolio to Loftus from 1961 to 1971.) "We were small then. It became more difficult in the early 1970s, when applications . . . began to rise and the school became larger. We were also tightening up on admission standards."[42] Minority recruitment became a priority, although with mixed results. Irving thought that minority recruitment meant going "to some colleges in the south, black colleges, and [trying] to excite interest in our law school."[43] It did not seem to occur to him that there was a large minority population outside his own front door.[44]

A New Law Center

If faculty, students and administrators agreed on nothing else, at least they agreed on the inadequacy of 40 Clinton Street as the premises for a law school. Only when leaving it did they begin to feel nostalgia for a building "remote and old and dirty and cramped . . . The old library gave us something to complain about, and was our excuse for not looking up cases outside of class. . . . There was no air-conditioning to filter out the smell of frying onions . . . Ours was probably the only bookstore in America with its own winding stone staircase . . . Somehow we'll miss working in semi-darkness, stepping over and sitting on boxes, and wading through the puddles that formed between the stacks on rainy days."[45] The frying onions came from Arnold's Bar and

Grill, for many years an unofficial student lounge where more law was settled, and unsettled, than in many classrooms.

It took an eternity to find somewhere better. In December 1968, the University and the Newark Housing Authority took steps to acquire 3.5 acres of land bounded by Raymond Boulevard, Mulberry and Park Streets, and McCarter Highway in downtown Newark on which to construct a new school. By 1971, the site remained undeveloped because, in the interim, the cheaper idea had been hatched of acquiring and renovating 500 Broad Street. In 1972, the original plan was back on the cards. In 1973, the building of the recently defunct *Newark Evening News* was offered to the university, but no-one seemed interested in spending half a million dollars to renovate it.[46] The Student Bar Association threatened "a tuition strike, a general strike, and a legal action against the University" unless a new facility were built.[47] It was certainly needed: not simply a new building but a new "Law Center"—vitally important, said Irving, so that "legal education not be entirely controlled by the state," so that the profession "be open to all segments of society," so that judges could be retrained for "New Jersey's war on crime and juvenile delinquency," so that (reaching the heights) "new legal theories [could be developed] to resolve the old problems that threaten the stability and solvency of our State and Nation."[48] None of this could be done to the smell of fried onions.

Irving proved a disappointing fund-raiser,[49] raising less than $220,000 for the new building by the end of 1975. His excuse—that "private donors give money to a number of worthwhile causes. Why give it to Seton Hall law school?"[50]—was hardly designed to win friends in the higher administration. Seton Hall Law was not mediocre, but some efforts on its behalf cut little ice with alumni who had no reason to feel warmly towards it.[51] Still, when it opened in 1976, Irving hailed the Law Center as a coming of age and, reasonably enough, he claimed credit for himself: "You know, nobody any longer feels embarrassed about being a student at Seton Hall Law School. . . . [Now] we have a magnificent building, and the law school, which cost an extraordinary commitment of time on my part, is now a very visible law school, locally so to speak, and nationally."[52]

The magnificence of the building was a matter of opinion. A temporary structure affectionately known as the Quonset hut was erected in 1972–1973 on approximately the spot where the current law school stands. All law school operations except the library (which stayed at 40 Clinton Street) were moved into it. A metal roof made audibility a problem during rainstorms. Faculty had cubicles rather than offices, with administrative offices a bit bigger. The student lounge and canteen were nondescript. It was a makeshift affair that lasted far longer than anyone imagined. The law school ran thus for three years until the fall of 1976, when the new building was completed. It was certainly an improvement, with modern tiered classrooms and brighter open spaces, but it lacked proper air-conditioning and the novelty quickly wore off. Nor was this the end of the old Quonset hut, which was made permanent by having an earth-colored brick skin applied to the outside walls and was then connected to the "new" facility by an open covered walkway about seventy-five feet long. Some years later, this walkway was enclosed. That was the layout until 1990, when the Quonset hut was torn down to make way for construction of the new building complex. (During construction of the latter, space was rented in 1080 Raymond Boulevard across the street, with students running back and forth for classes. When the present facility was finally ready for use, the old "new" building was torn down, having served for sixteen years.[53] The students, never slow with nicknames, captured its appearance with the moniker "McDonald's Law Center.")[54]

Irving was not denied his moment of glory. When he stepped down in 1977, the Law Center was his major achievement.[55] "The potential of the law school is enormous, absolutely enormous," he said. "I think the future is very bright for it."[56] Colleagues and students agreed. "We now have a new plant, an improved library, fine students, and a promising future," said Professor Harvey Sklaw. "Dean Irving is entitled to a major share of the credit for these achievements."[57] Irving, said Katharine Sweeney (later Hayden) who graduated in 1975, "swept Seton Hall Law School over the threshold toward the mainstream of legal education." A mother of two children, Hayden was the kind of nontraditional student Irving wished to attract. She went on to become, in 1997, Seton Hall's first federal judge.

Who was to succeed Irving? After a protracted search,[58] during which Robert Diab served as acting dean, in 1978 Father Daniel Degnan, S.J. was appointed to the position. Genial and wry, from a well-known local family, Degnan was a law graduate of Seton Hall (a member of the first class of 1954) and of Harvard (where he had taken his LLM in 1974). He had served as a member of the faculty in Rooney's time (1954–1957) after which he decided to become a priest. Before returning to Seton Hall, he taught law at Syracuse and Georgetown (his undergraduate *alma mater*). As a lawyer-cleric, Degnan had a foot in both camps but his affiliation was never in doubt. "I hope . . . I can turn the law school to assisting the work of the Church in the Diocese," he assured Archbishop Peter Gerety when he took up his appointment.[59] Not all of his colleagues saw his role, or theirs, in such terms.

As dean, Degnan dealt with the usual problems, his clerical status neither here nor there. He inherited difficulties that Irving had let accumulate and, in a piecemeal way, began to solve them. Struck by the casual way appointments and promotions were made, he tried to raise professional standards, causing some faculty to take offense, as if their judgment were being called into question (as it was). Allegations of racial discrimination in hiring and promotion were also thrown about, souring personal relationships.[60] On the other hand, Degnan could point to steadily improving finances during his time in charge due to the elimination of Conley's deficit by D'Alessio and Petillo and improved law school fund-raising.[61] The better it performed, making it a cash cow for the university as a whole, the more it annoyed faculty who thought that they enjoyed few of the benefits.

These were problems of success. Resigning as dean in June 1983 to return to the faculty, Degnan had taken a school which had drawn students largely from the Newark metropolitan area and had turned it into "a premier eastern law school,"[62] with significantly improved student quality and enhanced student diversity. "Normally a labor lawyer should not be sentimental," wrote Jerrold Glassman that year, "[but] when it comes to . . . the Law School, I am extremely sensitive. It gave me the education and the spiritual wherewithal to embark upon a new career."[63] Irving laid the foundations. Degnan built on them.

Crisis and Resolution:
Elizabeth Defeis and Ronald Riccio

Under the surface, however, all was not well. Degnan's successor was Elizabeth Defeis, a member of the faculty since 1971, having earned undergraduate and law degrees from St. John's University and New York University, who taught constitutional and communications law and a course on women and the law. Well liked by many, her appointment was contentious, with a substantial minority of the faculty against it and not slow, in the manner of the articulately aggrieved, to complain that their wishes had been ignored. Disgruntlement comes with the territory, but the depth of the divisions made the next five years the most critical and unpleasant half-decade in the school's history. In 1987, the school produced not one but *two* self-study reports for the American Bar Association, one an official version, the other a correction to it claiming that "we are a law school in crisis . . . torn by factionalism," a claim all too evidently demonstrated by the document itself. Without naming names, Provost Bernhard Scholz complained of a "lunatic fringe"[64] on the faculty, its membership no doubt differing according to taste.

At one level, the conflict was generational, at another cultural. Younger faculty members, impressively credentialed, found, when they arrived, a school with a growing but stymied reputation. (Nor were they impressed by the half-old, half-new Law Center, no doubt because some had never known Clinton Street at its worst.) Added to this were sectarian tensions, severe differences of opinion about to the extent to which the school should be defined by its Catholicism. Joseph Lynch, a long-standing faculty member, worried that the school was "very close" to ceasing to be Catholic, for which he blamed colleagues "open in [their] hostility to the Catholic administration."[65] (His solution was affirmative action for Catholics.) The explicitness of that hostility, and the hostility itself, are matters of debate, but there were certainly those whose vision of a Catholic law school was not that of Miriam Rooney.[66] The result was a disaster.

Appointments became impossible because neither group accepted the *bona fides* of the other; students were encouraged to take sides; colleagues were snubbed; a common social life was out of the question. What a law school did best—training people to argue—now became self-parodic. This was a law school at its worst.

To Lynch, the clash of generations was a clash of cultures, two visions of the law school in which death or victory were the only possible outcomes. He was scathing about his younger colleagues: "Their aim is, by force of numbers, finally to control the administration of the Law School. In this pursuit, they assiduously campaign against they consider likely to be sympathetic with the values of Catholicism or deferential to authority, and instead work to hire those like themselves: coldly rational and disrespectful or disregarding of authority."[67]

Lynch's committed Catholics were marginally in the majority, but they were also older, closer to retirement, and, in one case, ill. The disruptive minority (as he saw them) were younger, fresher, with time on their side. (Scholz thought that they were "arrested adolescents.")[68] The atmosphere became toxic. According to one of the younger faculty, who blamed the "inert and inept" administration, the law school was at "the edge of the abyss . . . and it is not the fault of the law faculty."[69]

Unsurprisingly, the ABA deplored this state of affairs. "The Law School currently has a number of problems, some [of them] acute," it found. "Significant student representation on key committees" led faculty to recruit students to their cause, some going "beyond the bounds of propriety" by leaking confidential data. The physical plant was "totally inadequate." Many students were more interested in working part-time than studying. Faculty with outside practices often cancelled classes with little or no notice. Fund raising was minimal. For all that, the law remained "a vibrant place . . . destined to play a key role in the future of the State of New Jersey," almost as if its very turbulence, the sharpness of its divisions, was an indicator of vigor.[70] But there was no denying that, in the words of Ronald Riccio, Defeis's successor as dean, the reaccreditation was "near disastrous."[71]

The troubles were partly those of success. "When I first came here," wrote Jud Jennings in 1986, "our faculty was housed in partitioned closets in the area currently occupied by the law review, and the library was still on Clinton Street. Today we are an accredited and prospering law school, with an excellent student body and a vigorous program."[72] Good things were happening despite the factionalism. Defeis spoke on the U.S. Constitution and on women's legal rights in Kenya, Uganda, Lesotho, and Malawi. Harvey Sklaw lectured in Siena, Pisa, Parma, and Florence. Lawrence Bershad traveled to Hong Kong and the People's Republic of China to meet lawyers and members of the judiciary. Martha Traylor spoke on Christianity and ecology in Indiana. Charles Sullivan and Michael Zimmer completed a major manuscript on employment discrimination. Paula Franzese excelled in every classroom she entered.[73]

"Take Seton Hall out of the statehouse," Governor Tom Kean remarked on a 1986 visit to the school, "and there isn't much left. I don't know of a Law School in the United States that has produced as much leadership in government as this one."[74] When she resigned as dean in 1988, Defeis was rightly praised by John Petillo for her "outstanding record of leadership and . . . service."[75]

The school was thus publicly successful and privately unhappy. The private unhappiness carried through to the choice of Defeis's successor, the subject of much back-and-forth at high levels, which turned out better than many imagined. "The Law School faculty is very independent," reported John Petillo to the Board of Trustees. "We need the ABA to be on the side of Seton Hall University, not the faculty."[76] These worries were shared by his ecclesiastical superior, who believed that the law school's "soul" needed to be "regained."[77] "This will be a very trying and challenging moment for all of us," wrote Archbishop Theodore McCarrick to Petillo. "I am sure that we will find a dean who is acceptable to a majority of the members of the faculty [but] if worse comes to worse, then it would be necessary for us to name an acting dean and to pursue that course until we see the appointment of a new dean within the vision . . . which now motivates the future mission of the university."[78] The argument went all the way to the Vatican, which sensibly kept its distance.[79]

Many wanted to make peace but had "no idea how to begin."[80] An excellent start was Ronald Riccio's appointment as dean, which improved the atmosphere. Critics claimed his chief qualification for the post was his friendship with the university's largest benefactor, Robert Brennan (as if that were somehow a disqualification), but Riccio also brought to the job a reputation as a solid, affable, highly intelligent lawyer from a respected firm, qualities which turned out to be "his most powerful tool."[81] He shared Brennan's enthusiasm for Seton Hall, boosting it at every turn. He was "very outgoing and likely to minimize personality conflicts," concluded Michael Ambrosio (who had not initially supported his candidacy). "Ron is doing much better than I anticipated," said Dan Degnan. "Ron is trying to do the right thing for the institution," agreed Michael Risinger. "You can accept a lot of disagreement when someone is basically pure in his motives." "If you go to the dean with a problem, he solves it," said Denbeaux. "If you go to the dean with an idea, he considers it; but if you go to him with some sort of negative or back-biting remark, he doesn't even hear it."[82] Riccio "has helped to heal division that only a short while ago seemed unhealable," Petillo reported to the ABA in 1988.[83]

The fight eventually burned itself. Indeed, the "near disastrous" reaccreditation may have turned out a blessing in disguise. Grievances aired in public seemed to lose their power, the act of confession bringing absolution. Once the factions got complaints off their chest they felt better. The process also forced the school to confront and remediate its inadequacies, the first of these being the need for a new facility, the second the need to clarify the financial relationship between the school and the rest of the university. As part of its pledge to secure reaccreditation, the university also committed itself to finding a new building. Of these, the last was most important. Installed in bright new offices, it was astonishing how pleasant former foes could be to one another.

A Law School for the Twenty-First Century

An era of good—or at least better—feelings broke out in the early 1990s. Riccio tended to side with his colleagues rather than the administration in South Orange (one reason his appointment had been resisted in that quarter)[84] but his real skill was to keep such fights to a minimum. Mostly the rows had to do with salaries[85] and the school's contribution to general funds,[86] but these were run-of-the-mill matters. The Catholic party (if such it was) was less vocal than before, if only because it thought itself less likely to be heard. Riccio was a lawyer, not a theologian. Religious fights did not interest him.[87] His major work was to build a new law school for the twenty-first century and to that task he brought passion and élan.

Building a new school raised an old question: where? Opened to applause only a decade before, the Law Center was cramped and depressing, and never intended as more than temporary anyway. Its drabness was at least partly responsible for the ill feelings of the mid-1980s. As a result, the ABA threatened to revoke accreditation unless it were substantially upgraded, even replaced, causing yet another round of speculation as to whether Seton Hall should move out of Newark. Although the property could have accommodated ABA-mandated improvements, the Board of Regents decided the site was too valuable, preferring to sell it and put the proceeds towards building a new school elsewhere.[88] Keeping the school going in the interim was the problem, because few developers would have wished to buy the site, then wait for two or three years while Seton Hall constructed its facility in another location.

As it turned out, one group, Bellmead Development Corporation, had interests that matched the university's. Bellmead had an office park in Roseland, New Jersey available for lease or purchase (a possible site for the law school) and were also interested in acquiring property for development in Newark. As a result, in October 1987 the Board of Regents decided to relocate the law school to Roseland if some sort of arrangement could be reached with Bellmead. In December, both parties tentatively agreed to a tax-free exchange of property, the Roseland office park to be conveyed to Seton Hall, the property in Newark to be conveyed to Bellmead, the Board assured that classes could begin on the new site in September 1988, and Bellmead that it could now build three office buildings and a parking garage in downtown Newark. But the news that Seton

Hall was to relocate to the suburbs caused consternation in Newark and, under political pressure, the university changed its mind, coming to an elaborate set of arrangements with Bellmead in January 1989 that would keep the school in place.

By deciding to build in the city, Seton Hall incurred approximately $25 million in costs (as opposed to $10 million for refurbishing Roseland property) to which the city might reasonably have been expected to make some contribution in kind. Recognizing this obligation, Newark agreed to a series of twenty-year tax abatements and waivers to the value of $10 million,[89] and in return Seton Hall agreed to $100,000 in annual scholarships for qualified residents of the city of Newark for the duration of the abatement. Seton Hall agreed to pay $24.5 million as a guaranteed maximum price to Bellmead to construct the new law school.

The university was not out of pocket for all these expenditures. On the contrary, it managed to win $5.3 million in federal funding in a classic piece of Jersey pork-barrel politics.[90] Leading the funding charge was former Congressmen Peter Rodino, assisted by Senator Frank Lautenberg (D-NJ) and Congressman Dean Gallo (R-NJ). Rodino, retired from Congress since January 1989, had been pressing the case for federal money for Seton Hall since spring 1988, when the university had committed itself to building a new law school. Lautenberg also wished it known that "at [his] request" funding had been secured "for this worthy project."[91] (For his pains, Seton Hall gave him a pair of cufflinks.)[92] Leading the opposition was Congresswoman Lynn Martin (R-Ill), who complained that House Rules had been bent to provide $15 million in appropriations for three projects, the law school being one of them. Seton Hall's $5.3 million was buried in a $15 million amendment to an Appropriations Bill whose purpose was to fund the Russell B. Long Federal Building and United States Courthouse in Baton Rouge, Louisiana. The amendment was never part of the House and Senate bills that had gone to the House-Senate conference for resolution, with the result that some members of the Appropriations Committee had no idea that the money was tucked into the bill.

Equally brazen was the lobbying by which the earmarks found their way to Newark. Rodino used his friendship with Neil Smith (D-Iowa), a key subcommittee chairman, to press the case. Seton Hall hired a well-connected Washington lobbyist. Dean Gallo took to the floor to urge $5.5 million in funding for the clinical law training program, never mentioning his personal and business connections to Bellmead. (It had contributed to his campaigns and his real-estate firm had earned brokerage commissions from it. He was also friendly with its executive vice president. Naturally, Bellemead exercised "absolutely no pressure" on him, according to his chief of staff.) "In the end," said *The New Jersey Law Journal*, "the battle on the House floor was not over the worthiness of clinics for the poor . . . The bill was simply pork barreling."[93]

The building opened in late 1991 and was dedicated in December 1993. Granite and glass, modern and practical, its most impressive feature was a five-story atrium offering views of the building's upper floors, sky walks, and balconies. "The thing that struck me most was the spaciousness," said Sheila Glackin, a third-year student. "It's provides a boost to the spirit after being in the cramped old building."[94] Dean Steven Frankino of Villanova University School of Law hailed it as "one of the best in American legal education . . . Dean Riccio and his faculty and staff deserve great credit for a major achievement."[95] "We may have traveled only a few short miles in distance from our birthplace but in achievement our journey has spanned light years," Riccio himself observed.[96] The centerpiece of the building was the three-story Peter W. Rodino, Jr. Library of more than 280,000 volumes. It also boasted two moot courtrooms, a computer room, student journal offices, a chapel, and a cafeteria. Only the old-timers could now remember Arnold's.

Toward the New Century

James Boskey, a long-standing faculty member, thought that American law schools fell into four categories.[97] The A level schools were national—Harvard, Yale, Stanford, Georgetown, Notre Dame, Michigan, and Chicago. The B+ schools were regional—Fordham, the University of Missouri at Columbia, Villanova, and the like. The B- schools were local—extremely traditional in curriculum, with a faculty not much interested in scholarship, and with graduates placed almost exclusively in smaller firms. Seton Hall in the 1970s, he thought, was such a school. How was it, he wondered, that Seton Hall had gone from a B- school to a B+ one? In the first instance, it had developed of "one of the most comprehensive clinical programs of any law school in the nation." Allowing students to act as practicing attorneys gave them a sense of the demands of the work while offering to the bar candidates who needed less "on-the-job" training. Seton Hall had also been able to attract "outstanding" teachers. The Richard J. Hughes Professorship enhanced the school's reputation.

Riccio's big personality was important in guiding the school to greater success, even opponents tending to forget differences when he was around. "Take the opportunity to publicly accent the positives of the Seton Hall Law experience," he told alumni, "and treat the negatives for what they were, namely, growing pains of an institution which is now beginning to reach its prime."[98] He was as good as his word. He dealt with all sorts of problems and never lost his enthusiasm for the job. One colleague well versed in theology thought he was a kind of saint.[99]

In September 1998 Riccio announced his decision to step down as dean in June 1999. Before he left, a very public row marred his last year. In November 1998 *Seton Hall Law Review* students decided to award Governor Christine Whitman their Sandra Day

O'Connor medal, angering many Catholics, among them law school alumni. (Whitman had vetoed a bill that would have banned partial-birth abortion; O'Connor had voted to uphold Roe vs. Wade.) University president Robert Sheeran conveyed his annoyance to Riccio, upsetting him.[100] Riccio, who thought that the students "were well within their rights and university policy" to present the medal to O'Connor, backed out of a university farewell tribute in his honor.[101] Whitman was eventually given her award off campus "so as not to imply an official university sanction of her position on abortion,"[102] a compromise that gave casuistry a bad name.

After a seven-month search, Patrick Hobbs was chosen as his replacement. Hobbs was Seton Hall through and through, graduating with a BS in Accounting in 1982 and a JD from the University of North Carolina in 1985 before returning to New Jersey to practice law and, in 1990, to take a teaching position at the law school. "Pat Hobbs is a superb choice," said Riccio. "He brings to the job the ability to continue the Law School's drive to national prominence while preserving its traditional role of service to the community."[103]

Hobbs, who could work a room with the practiced charm of a master, inherited some of Riccio's problems. In 2004, the *Seton Hall Law Review*, the Seton Hall Legislative Bureau, and the Seton Hall Women's Law Forum awarded the Sandra Day O'Connor Medal of Honor to Judge Maryanne Trump Barry, who had authored a decision overturning New Jersey's ban on late-term abortions. The award garnered strong criticism from pro-life groups throughout the country and a public rebuke from Archbishop John Myers, head of the Board of Trustees. "For those who were shocked and dismayed by the action, I can only say that I share your sentiments," he wrote in *The Catholic Advocate*, the archdiocesan newspaper. "I find this action profoundly offensive and contrary to the Catholic mission and identity of Seton Hall Law School, Seton Hall University, and the Archdiocese of Newark." "Seton Hall's commitment to the Gospel of Life is absolute," said a university spokesperson, Natalie Thigpen. "The conferral of awards to people who publicly espouse views that are contrary to the university's fundamental Catholic identity is a serious lapse." Thigpen promised a "thorough review" of the episode.[104]

Under Riccio and Hobbs, the law school was unrecognizable from the school Miriam Rooney and John McNulty had founded in 1951. So, too, was the culture in which it operated. But *mutatis mutandis* it was still a Catholic school. Even in dissent, it was Catholic. Even in argument, it could not forget its origins. "Students come here thinking there are clear-cut answers to legal issues," Professor Andrea Catania once remarked. "If there were you wouldn't need any lawyers."[105] Moral matters also had to be litigated and, for that task, the Church continued to provide the language. The most eloquent expression of those deeper purposes came from Theodore McCarrick, for whom the vision of Rooney still had power to move: "The presence of a Law School in a university, like that of a School of Theology, raises the institution to a completely new level of knowledge and demands that it focus on more than the ordinary considerations of academe. It demands that such a place of learning come face to face with the great realities of society—human law, divine law, justice, equity, and the right ordering of human relationships so that the common good may produce a harmonious civilization . . ."[106] Rooney would have agreed.

CHAPTER 19

The Sheeran Years

Sheeran in Charge

Robert Sheeran's appointment began one of the most consequential of Seton Hall's many presidencies. In length alone—fifteen years—his tenure surpassed that of most of his predecessors. In achievement, it was prodigious, in tragedy unparalleled. Guiding the university to its sesquicentennial year, he served as Seton Hall's leader for a tenth of its history, conscious of that history but aware that the future could not be held back by a lovingly embalmed past. Sheeran, a modernizer, saw that the pace of change is as important as change itself. He was also a traditionalist who understood tradition as a treasure to be explored, not a legacy to be hidden. Above all, he was a man of prayer[1] whose affection for the institution was reciprocated by those who recognized in him a priest whose life had been devoted to it. For him, the "university" was a parish as much as a school, the president a pastor, a source of support, encouragement, and occasional rebuke. As the head of a university with almost 1,300 employees, over 9,000 students, 65,000 alumni, and an annual budget close to $200 million, he never forgot the human duties of the office, sending thank-you notes, writing letters of condolence or congratulation, taking time to acknowledge a birth or bereavement.[2] His difficulties (personnel problems, a financial panic) were far outweighed by his successes (a renovated curriculum, a new School of Diplomacy, a beautified campus, a deepened sense of Catholic mission). He admitted to disappointments: that Seton Hall was not more firmly anchored in Tier II of *US News and World Report* universities; that there was too rapid a turnover in the provost's office; that some department chairs were weak; that there were discontinuities of leadership within the executive cabinet.[3] But these were small matters. Seton Hall was much stronger for the leadership of its talented millennial president.

Sheeran's connections with the Hall spanned a lifetime. As a teenager he had turned down offers from Georgetown and Fordham to come to South Orange in 1963 as a "divvy," a student in the college seminary. "Like any freshman I was excited, uncertain of what lay ahead, and soon I felt absolutely at home."[4] Later he studied for the priesthood at Immaculate Conception Seminary, Darlington, and at the Pontifical North

American College in Rome, completing a master's degree at the Princeton Theological Seminary and a doctorate at the Angelicum. Rome revealed that his academic preparation at Seton Hall had been "superb." After a stint as a parish priest in Cranford, New Jersey, and on the faculty of the North American College, in 1980 he returned to New Jersey to become rector of the College Seminary, beginning a thirty-year career at Seton Hall as rector, assistant and associate provost, executive vice chancellor, candidate for president in 1990 and, finally, president in late 1995.

Blessed with a sharp mind and a gift for personal relations, Sheeran moved steadily through the administration until he won the top job, McCarrick encouraging him to believe in his capacity to lead a major university and cultivate its many constituencies. As Petillo's tenure ended and potential rivals fell by the wayside, Sheeran was left as the next leader but one. At forty-five he was probably too young for the presidency when he lost out to Peterson in 1990. In September 1993, he became executive vice chancellor, a position created for him by Peterson, enabling him to serve on committees, take on special projects, and get involved in fundraising, a "new and pretty exciting job" which he enjoyed "immensely."[5] But it took another disappointment—runner-up in 1991 for the presidency of the University of Saint Thomas in Saint Paul, Minnesota—that made him feel at home in South Orange as nowhere else.[6] Addressing the university a few days after his appointment, domestic notions were in his mind, praising Bishop Bayley for seeing Seton Hall as "a home for the mind, the heart and the spirit: A home for the mind—although we pursue knowledge and teach in very different ways today. A home for the heart—although building community now requires new strategies and initiative. And a home for the soul—although the times demand that the faith be inculcated in creative and even more effective ways."[7]

Sheeran brought intellect, passion, and excitement to the task of moving Seton Hall "to the top tiers of Catholic colleges and universities in the world." "I believe with every fiber of my being," he said, "that the fabric of a transformed Seton Hall will be woven—one strand at a time—from an unvarying focus on quality—higher and more recognized quality in pursuit of our academic and Catholic mission."[8] Even at the end of his presidency, he still felt affection for the men and women who followed the path he had chosen forty years before. "He can be firm without being abrasive," Peterson wrote, "gentle and kind without being weak. He is pleasant. He is talented. He inspires confidence."[9] Bernhard Scholz admired his "great personal integrity," his enthusiasm for young people, his broad culture, his fairness. "My initial impression is terrific," said a nursing professor Leona Kleinman. "The faculty were smiling," echoed biologist Marian Glenn.[10] What Scholz called Sheeran's "sophisticated sense of the world[11] allowed him to break down barriers among administration, faculty, and students, and between the university and the community. "I leave you with an Irish wish from my late friend, M.J. Molloy" wrote Professor James McGlone. "May your roof never fall in and those under it never fall out."[12] Of hundreds of letters of congratulation, the most engaging came from Vito Daidone, who felt as close to the university as he did "when they could not pay me in the very beginning when Rt. Rev. James F. Kelley was first president."[13]

A Challenge to Change

Sheeran inherited from Peterson a project of which he himself was coauthor. Peterson's task forces and advisory panels between 1994 and 1996 produced *A Challenge to Change: Strategies for the Future of Seton Hall University*, which provided the agenda of the early years of the Sheeran presidency.[14] Its assumptions were that eighteen-year-olds, as a population segment, would shrink as a percentage of the whole but increase in absolute terms until 2009; that Latinos would become the largest minority by the turn of the century; that computers and globalization would transform the workplace; that traditional four-year full-time students would decline as a proportion of the university population with numbers made up by adult learners; that community colleges would increase in market share; that distance learning would grow; and that strategic alliances with corporations would be key to future success. Based on these ideas, Sheeran set himself six goals. The first was to achieve "measurable excellence in undergraduate education" by increasing SAT scores, raising standards of teaching and research, developing cross-disciplinary programs, and challenging faculty to create a new university core curriculum and more doctoral programs in nursing, a new MBA curriculum for business, an improved core curriculum for arts and sciences, and distance learning for the College of Education. The second was to create a Center for Academic Technology, set university-wide standards of computer proficiency, and establish the university library as a "gateway" to the internet. The third was to distinguish Seton Hall as a Catholic institution through a "concerted effort" to involve "everyone in a life beyond the classroom." The fourth was to "re-engineer" the university for "total quality and excellence" by making management systems more collaborative and giving employees greater ownership of their work. (It also entailed cost-cutting by eliminating duplication, which did not really work).[15] The fifth was to "respond to the needs of the graduate and nontraditional student" by flexible program-building and by evaluating graduate work more systematically. The sixth was to continue fund-raising to ensure "competitive standing with institutions of comparable size, scope, and mission." The key lay in persuading donors that the university "had a clear and compelling idea" of how to transform itself to meet the challenges facing higher education in the 1990s. That meant having something good to sell.

At the heart of the plans, was Sheeran himself. "I call it our 'Oregon Trail' experience," he said of cultural transformation, thinking himself a pioneer. It would be "slow, without many guideposts, constantly challenged by the perils of crossing unfamiliar and sometimes hostile terrain."[16] (He would have used a more politically adept metaphor in later years.) "Nothing is more important for Seton Hall and nothing is more difficult, than forming genuine communities, based on respect, trust, and a willingness to listen to one another."[17] Changing the culture without injuring the community would be difficult.

Indeed, as Sheeran talked of Seton Hall as a world-class Catholic university, some freshmen were unhappy. Students accepted by Seton Hall and by Rutgers, Villanova, Trenton State (now the College of New Jersey), Syracuse, Northeastern, or Fordham frequently preferred the other places. Over half of them rated Seton Hall as "worst" in physical appearance and "surroundings," insufficiently "challenging," "prestigious," "intellectual," or "exciting."[18] The "real problem," Sheeran told a business professor, was that although the number of high school graduates in New Jersey would increase substantially, most of them would come from the "urban, poor, and socio-economically disadvantaged" class—"the very students who [would] find tuition at private institutions difficult to meet."[19] Seton Hall, although private and expensive, was never a school for the wealthy. Approximately 90 percent of students received financial aid through the Federal Work-Study Program, Perkins Loans, or Pell Grants, and nearly 50 percent worked while enrolled (including work-study positions). Over 40 percent of financial aid students had loans.[20] These were the real challenges to change.

Academics

"Ours is an academic purpose first," Sheeran said at the beginning of his tenure. "Teaching is our first business." The words were penned by Scholz but they became Sheeran's vision for his presidency.[21] He wanted to break barriers between faculty and administration, encouraging the latter to return to the classroom and the former to take seriously the responsibilities of shared governance. The relationship suffered the strains of any long-distance marriage but he succeeded in promoting a sense of joint enterprise, securing better salaries and generously recognizing faculty publication. Most problems were not solved merely by money, but it helped.

As provost, Scholz prodded the faculty to greater success, knowing that not all of them enjoyed his laconic assessment of their efforts. Seton Hall boasted fine teacher-scholars. Petra Chu published a "marvelous" 726 page edition of the *Letters of Gustave Courbet* (1992).[22] Father Frank Podgorski maintained Seton Hall's distinguished tradition of Chinese and Japanese scholarship, founding *The Journal of Dharma*, devoted to world spirituality. In 1996, Angela Weisl published *Conquering the Reign of Femeny* (1995), an investigation of female tropes in Chaucer, later authoring *The Persistence of Medievalism: Narrative Adventures in Contemporary Culture* (2003). David Rogers produced an outstanding collection of lyric poetry, *The Return* (1996). Martha Carpentier produced *The Major Novels of Susan Gaspell* in 2003. Reverend John Ranieri of philosophy published *Eric Voegelin and the Good Society* (1995). Judith Stark, also of philosophy, published *Love and Saint Augustine* (1998), an edition of Hannah Arendt's doctoral dissertation. Robert Herrera, another philosopher, authored *Donoso Cortes: Cassandra of His Age* (1995). David Abalos of religious studies and sociology penned *Strategies of Transformation: Towards a Multicultural Society* (1996). Robert Augustine of Chemistry completed *Heterogeneous Catalysts for the Synthetic Chemist* (1995)straddling the boundary between chemistry and chemical engineering.[23] Father Eugene Cotter of classical studies created an online etymological dictionary for his course on the roots of English. (Richard Hughes, another classics professor, set crossword puzzles for the *New York Times*.[24] Frank Korn, another classicist, was author of eight books and many popular articles on Rome.[25]) Lonnie Athens was the subject of Richard Rhodes's Pulitzer Prize-winning book, *Why They Kill: The Discoveries of a Maverick Criminologist* (2000). William Connell, Joseph M. and Geraldine La Motta Chair in Italian studies, was a scholar of Florentine Tuscany and an internationally recognized expert on Machiavelli. Thomas Rondinella of the department of communication produced several award-winning films, notably *Charming Billy*, Best Picture in the Boston Film Festival of 2000.[26] Jeffrey Togman, a political scientist, won major awards for his documentary *Home*, a study of working-class home ownership in Newark.[27]

Ralph Walz brought a refined Catholic sensibility to teaching European history. James McGlone directed theater enthusiastically, claiming of students always, and of colleagues sometimes, that to be in their presence was a little piece of heaven on earth. Herbert Kraft was "an exceptional archaeologist and a gifted historian."[28] Joseph Mahoney taught history with high intelligence and dry wit. John Sweeney in English was "that perfect balance of genius and eccentricity that makes a three-hour morning class insightful and engaging."[29] "It's the students who keep you young," said John Saccoman, a mathematician teaching at the university since 1961, the year after he graduated from it.[30] John Deehan taught business for over forty years, twenty-four of them as chair of accounting.[31] Paul Forbes, also in the School of Business, devoted his free time to charity.[32]

Under Barbara Beeker and Phyllis Hansell, the College of Nursing showed improvement. With a doctorate from Columbia and wide experience as a teacher and researcher, Hansell won prestigious grants, including one for $775,000 to study the effects of social support in easing stress in HIV/AIDS caregivers. She established new masters programs in nursing administration and in nursing and business administration. In 2006, fulfilling a twenty-year ambition, she introduced a competitive doctoral degree funded by a grant from the Department of Health and Human Services. No other Catholic institution in the region offered such a course. These were good years

for the College of Nursing as Baby Boomers retired (needing nurses), as starting salaries rose, and as more men entered the profession.[33]

Institutional Renewal:
The ACE Initiative and the Bayley Project

The most significant of Sheeran's initiatives to transform teaching was an effort to
improve learning over the first three semesters. The American Council on Education
(ACE) sponsored an examination of institutional change at Seton Hall that lasted two
years and touched almost every aspect of university life. Much of the work fell to
Scholz and his interim successor as provost, Peter Ahr, also to Vice Chancellor for
Student Affairs Laura Wankel, who cochaired with Ahr the committee that ran the
experiment. Students had a lot of growing up to do, as, in a sense, had Seton Hall itself.
(According to a survey of 1996, over 63 percent of students had experimented with
drugs in high school and 12 percent of them had tried them *before* high school.)[34] What
Sheeran wanted, ACE could provide: the implementation of an information technology plan; the expansion of honors programs; the creation of degree programs making
greater demands on incoming students; radical rethinking of assessment mechanisms;
enhancement of the status of faculty; improvement in research culture; the reevalua-
tion of business systems. As Seton Hall was "rethinking its direction," Scholz wrote, so
ACE "could serve as a vehicle for helping make it a different university."

The ACE project, whose hoped-for outcome was institutional transformation, was
itself institutionally transformative, conducted in such a way as to make a reality of
the collaborative methods it espoused. Beginning in 1995 with roundtables made up
of faculty, students, and administrators, it continued in early 1996 with Sheeran's appointment of Peter Ahr and Laura Wankel to coordinate the work. From a conference
in fall 1996 emerged the decision to concentrate on improving students' writing skills,
the department of English encouraged to reduce the size of first-year writing courses
from twenty-five to fifteen and its remedial writing courses from fifteen to twelve. In
biology, chemistry, mathematics, history, philosophy, art history, and religion, writing
skills as well as mastery of course content became a priority.

One benefit was to encourage Seton Hall to look at undergraduate offerings as a
whole and to reexamine core requirements for a gaining a degree. Without giving
much thought to particular content, the idea was generally agreed that *some* common
intellectual experience was necessary at college and university level. The School of
Business wanted students to acquire five distinct competencies (communication, critical thinking, teamwork, using technology, managing change) while also mastering
discrete bodies of knowledge. The College of Arts and Sciences emphasized the need
for basic ability in humanities and sciences and some understanding of conceptual

links between them. ACE gave shape and a sense of possibility to these curricular conservations. Later, when the creation of a new university core curriculum became a passion, it was clear that the lessons of ACE had been learned.

Formal conversation about pedagogy was largely absent from the campus. Partners-in-Learning brought together teachers from different disciplines to share their experiences. The University Teaching Fellows program was a serious effort to capture Seton Hall's good teachers and make them better, bringing together junior professors for monthly seminars with emphasis on the use of information technology. These teaching fellows served as reminders that the classroom was the heart of Seton Hall's mission.

"Mobile computing" was a related initiative, the most significant technical innovation of the Sheeran years. After a two-year pilot scheme in the School of Business, a third of the entering freshmen in 1997 were issued with laptop computers. By 1998, every undergraduate and full-time faculty member had one. Curricula were designed and classes taught in which computers played a key part. Technology, sold as an answer to all sorts of problems, was rarely thought of as bringing problems of its own. Laptops, said Scholz, would "enable students and faculty to communicate more readily with each other, make possible a more participatory style of learning, extend discussions beyond class time and make classes more interactive, [and] enable students to spend more time on task . . ."[35] They also encouraged frivolity (and not only in students). Still, once introduced, there was no going back. From desktops to laptops to cellphones to Instagram was the future that no-one foresaw in 1992.

To encourage this collaborative learning, an Academic Exposition was held in April 1997, with presentations by over 200 students from almost every college on campus. Organized by a young professor of chemistry, Matthew Petersheim, who died in 1998 aged forty-four and in whose honor the event was subsequently named, the exposition gave students an opportunity to showcase projects in which they and their instructors took pride. It showed Seton Hall as academically serious, socially committed, morally probing, and politically aware: like Petersheim himself.

Sheeran's commitment to institutional renewal extended beyond "reengineering." He also insisted on moral self-examination. To that end, the Bayley Project (1997) headed by Professor Mary Ruzicka of education and human services, brought together many constituencies to discuss the experiences of working at Seton Hall. The idea was to "take the ethical pulse of the university" and to see how well Seton Hall made good on its commitment to Catholic social teaching in the workplace. "The whole idea is to make us a better university," she said.[36]

One finding was that the university seemed "divided into separate, isolated communities based on race" and that, administratively, it was slow to address racial and gender inequality. By a large margin, students thought their professors respectful of them and well prepared. Of the groups who participated, faculty (at 46 percent) were most involved, staff (30 percent) less so, and students (12 percent) least. That, perhaps, was the most revealing fact of all.

Ruzicka and her colleagues found the ethical pulse to be strong, if given to the occasional flutter. The project was a lengthy collaboration about the value of collaboration, a typical late-1990s exercise in introspective communitarianism. (Much premillennial ink was spilled worrying about loss of social capital, gated communities, and lonely men "bowling alone.") Sheeran thought Ruzicka did "a wonderful job with a complex process."[37] On the other hand, the project addressed problems that previous generations would have been happy to have. Years before, when faculty shared an office, a phone, a typewriter, a secretary, and sandwiches for lunch, some professors longed for precisely the kind of social isolation (calling it privacy) their successors now deplored.

At the beginning of his presidency Sheeran thus encouraged, and was himself part of, a major effort at academic and institutional renewal. The Board of Regents made large sums available to fund some of the initiatives, knowing that capital projects (intellectual and physical) required capital investment. While not perfect, the ACE project had value as a way of defining challenges and meeting them. Not a panacea, the Bayley Project was sensible and humane. Seton Hall looked to be in good shape as the millennium approached.

Provosts and Administrators Abounding

Stepping down as provost in June 1997, Scholz had served under two presidents, Peterson and Sheeran, and was a transformational leader, overseeing accreditations and reaccreditations, the establishment of the Center for College Teaching, the creation of the New Jersey Institute for College Teaching and Learning, expansion of graduate and undergraduate programs, and the launch of a nationally admired information technology initiative. When Executive Vice Chancellor James Allison also retired in 1997, Sheeran lamented the departure of "a great friend."[38] Allison had been at Seton Hall since 1985, overseeing (while never running a deficit) the construction of almost a dozen buildings totaling over a million square feet, running a tight ship like the ex-Marine he was. Allison and Scholz had a difficult final year complicated by budgetary problems, but while Scholz's dealings with the faculty were fraught,[39] he remained a towering figure.

Allison's successor was Kimberley Cline, who was not a success. Cline's successor was Mary Meehan, who was. A gifted administrator and close confidante of Sheeran, Meehan was a central if shadowy figure of his presidency, an all-purpose fixer and problem-solver on whom Sheeran instinctively relied. Between 1996 and 2003, when she left the university to become president of Alverno College in Milwaukee, Meehan

oversaw enrollment services, finance and technology, student affairs, university counsel, human resources, and university advancement, a formidable roster of responsibilities, showing her to be, Sheeran said, "one of the best managers and leaders" he had
ever met.[40] His term would not have been the success it was without her.

These arrivals and departures marked a period of unusual instability. Scholz's acer-
bity was invigorating but not to every taste. Seeking a successor, Sheeran was torn between an insider (safe and reliable) or an outsider (a more likely agent for change).[41] In
the end, he split the difference, picking five provosts, of whom two came from within
the ranks and three from outside. Peter Ahr, an all-purpose administrator for many
years, became interim provost, his main achievement a buy-out package for retiring
faculty and the ushering in of a new School of Diplomacy and International Relations.
The latter will be treated elsewhere.

After a long search, Mark Rocha from Humboldt State University, California, took
charge in July 1998. "We have placed our hopes and dreams for academic leadership in
Dr. Rocha," Sheeran told the university in September 1998, "and I am certain we will
not be disappointed."[42] Rocha arrived as Sheeran was becoming more confident, telling the faculty that the endowment stood at $120 million, "not enough to accomplish
what we plan to do but up over $40 million since I last spoke with you." Two years
before, he said, "I told you that my dream was to increase that to $250 million . . . I
was wrong . . . I hope to have an endowment of $400 million by our 150th anniver-
sary." Rocha seemed to make a difference, his most important initiative the creation
of a University Budget Committee and his most popular achievement to persuade the
Board of Regents to approve a substantial raise for the faculty.[43] Rocha hoped that the
university would be "more than a set of discreet [sic] departments" and that shared
governance would flourish.[44] He increased funding for the Faculty Senate and introduced transparency to the academic budget, creating "an open place" where information would be shared and priorities debated. He reformed the Academic Council,
making it no longer a deans' talking-shop but a monthly business meeting devoted to
policy issues, its minutes broadcast to the university as a whole.[45] Rocha was a booster
and, almost to the point of ventriloquism, a speaker of Sheeran's words. Among
achievements "pending" were the creation of a university core curriculum, the restructuring of the College of Arts and Sciences (to include a School of the Fine Arts, a
School of Journalism and Broadcasting, and an Honors College[46]), and the pruning of
inadequate departments.[47]

Rocha was well regarded by fellow managers but could be petulant when criticized.
"You've got to use today's news, not last year's news," he told critics who thought him
too slow to reform. "I'm this year's provost. [You're] having a problem taking yes for an
answer."[48] "This year's provost" was precisely what he turned out to be. In March 2000,
he resigned, apparently to return to his aging parents in California.

Mel Shay of the College of Education and Human Services was named provost in May 2001, "seasoned and soothing,"[49] a leader who stood up for academic affairs amidst the competing claims of athletics, student affairs, admissions, and financial aid. His relations with Sheeran were cordial although, being more laconic than Rocha, he was also less of a booster. "We're still reaching for 2006 to become a second-tier school," he said, "but it's not do or die." [50] This was not a rallying cry for the ages. But his ambitions were sensible: to improve academic programs, to evaluate placement tests, to provide better support services for graduate students, and to ensure that Seton Hall engaged in proper strategic planning.[51]

Shay retired in August 2004 and was succeeded by Thomas Lindsay, a political philosopher from the University of Chicago and provost of the University of Dallas. Lindsay, committed to academic excellence, a strong believer in a core curriculum, an enthusiast for the Western intellectual tradition, saw Seton Hall as "already a respected institution" that needed now "to be nationally recognized."[52] He had a quietly insistent way of speaking his mind but talents that did not transfer to the financial and administrative aspects of the office. His misfortune was to come to Seton Hall as two major initiatives, a core curriculum and flat-rate tuition, were coming on stream. Finding the retail aspects of the job difficult, working the room, offering the flattering word, he resigned in December 2005.

Lindsay's departure brought another outsider to the job. A Fordham-trained historian and Carter-era federal bureaucrat, Fred Travis was an interim provost at the tail end of his career. Sheeran sought him to push through the reforms that had brought Lindsay to grief, in particular the completion of the core curriculum and the implementation of the strategic plan. These matters are dealt with elsewhere. With a Southern courtliness that belied a sharp tongue, Travis was beholden to no-one except the president who appointed him.

Of all provosts, Gabriel Esteban of the University of Central Arkansas was the one in whom Sheeran had greatest confidence.[53] A native of the Philippines, a mathematician, an immigrant to the United States as a graduate student, a professor of marketing, Esteban arrived with a life story that matched the promise of the university. He combined the merits, while lacking the faults, of his predecessors, being firm but not inflexible, visionary but not vague, in command of broad outlines but also of specific details. Sheeran's regret was that he had not come to the university sooner. Later, in a turn of events beyond the range of the current history, Esteban was himself to succeed Sheeran as Seton Hall's president in 2011.[54]

This turbulence requires explanation. In part, the turnover seemed rapid by way of contrast with the stability that preceded it, also suggesting the turmoil of an institution undergoing rapid change. On the other hand, some of it was personal. Rocha's departure was sudden and, on the face of it, implausible. Lindsay was effectively fired.

The interim provosts were, by definition, transitional. Sheeran insisted on being surrounded by team players and by his own admission could be impatient of contradiction.[55] Some change was necessary but some was too quick for comfort.

The School of Diplomacy and International Relations

Seton Hall's School of Diplomacy and International Relations (SODIR), approved by the Faculty Senate and the Board of Regents in June 1997, was the most significant academic accomplishment of Sheeran's tenure as president. Established as the result of an alliance with the United Nations Association of the United States of America, SODIR attracted bright students from across the globe, enriching Seton Hall's diversity and depth. By the time the university celebrated its sesquicentennial in 2006, the School of Diplomacy and International Relations was firmly part of the landscape, establishing the university as a serious participant in a series of global conversations. Yet its success was never inevitable. The Board of Regents had qualms about its cost[56] and some faculty baulked at the top-down way it was announced. SODIR was initially minuscule, with one acting dean, one secretary, no faculty, no students, no curriculum, and no physical plant. Its creation was a tribute to Sheeran's persistence and to those who argued for it in the face of institutional skepticism.

The foundations were laid in the spring of 1997 by Jack Shannon, a member of Sheeran's executive cabinet, who made the initial approach to the United Nations Association. The university and the Association signed a memorandum of understanding in January 1997, after which the work was done by a cross-campus steering committee led by Terence Blackburn of the School of Law who created a school *de novo*. The initial arrangement was for Seton Hall to establish college called the United Nations Association School of Diplomacy, to be known by the unpromising acronym of UNASOD, with a dean employed by the university and with Boards of Advisers Trustees made up of representatives of the university and the Association and responsible for conducting the UNASOD Foundation as a 501(c)(3) nonprofit corporation. All funds raised would be for the benefit of the School of Diplomacy, the university, and the United Nations Association, with 50 percent of proceeds (after expenses) to a maximum of $1 million going respectively to the University and the UNA, the remaining balance going to UNASOD's endowment. The university agreed to fund the first-year budgets of UNASOD and the Foundation to the tune of $1,457,195, all start-up expenses to be reimbursed at the end of the fiscal year by the Foundation.[57]

These protocols in place, the steering committee set to work developing a curriculum and persuading the Faculty Senate to approve it. Drawing from the Fletcher School of Law and Diplomacy at Tufts, the Edmund A. Walsh School of Foreign Service at Georgetown, the Woodrow Wilson School of Public and International Affairs at Princeton, and the Graduate Institute of International Studies at the University of Geneva, they produced an program combining global studies, history, international management, internships, regional study trips, and four years of language training, all glued together by certain cultural, linguistic, and analytical competencies. The undergraduate degree was approved by the Faculty Senate in June 1997 and a Master of Arts in Diplomacy in April 1998.

Terence Blackburn was the obvious choice as acting dean in June 1997. The first student was registered in July 1997. A year later, there were sixteen students: eight freshmen and eight sophomores. Nearly half of the first graduate class of twenty was born outside the United States, including a former aide to the president of the Philippines, an award-winning journalist from Argentina, two attorneys, and a real estate executive. By the end of 1998, SODIR students came from at least thirteen countries, speaking eighteen languages, taught by a staff drawn from current faculty and adjuncts. (Full-time diplomacy faculty came later). McQuaid Hall, home of the College of Education and Human Services, was requisitioned to provide offices, meeting rooms, and a sense of institutional identity. "Everyone has their own offices which are joy-filled," said Vice President for Planning Monsignor William Harms, oddly.[58]

SODIR was popular. In its first year nearly ninety applicants from across the country yielded a class of almost forty. Gerry Adams, president of Sinn Fein and a controversial figure in Irish politics, was first of three speakers in its Distinguished Lecture Series, addressing an audience of 2,000 in Walsh Gymnasium. (Other speakers were Robert Gallucci, dean of Georgetown School of Foreign Service, and Ren Xiao Ping, vice president of the Foreign Affairs College in Beijing.) In 1997 a weekly International Affairs Symposium brought scholars and policy analysts to campus, proving popular with the public. SODIR established a Diplomacy Camp for high school students, combining briefings at the UN and participation in the model United Nations.

Proximity to New York was crucial. In 1998, the university library became the first U.S. library in twenty years to be designated a depository for United Nations materials. Students toured the UN and worked as interns during the summer. United Nations Secretary-General Kofi Annan described SODIR as "an important initiative that will foster development and cooperation between academia and various components of the United Nations system."[59] SODIR cohosted a major conference on the alleviation of Third World debt in 1998 and collaborated with Columbia University in 1999 to host Irish political leaders as they considered *The Equality Agenda: Northern Ireland in 2000*. Most high-profile events at Seton Hall in 1998 and 1999 originated from a school that had not existed two years before.

Blackburn had claim to be made permanent dean of the school as "an exceptional faculty member" who had done "a superb job."[60] Instead, in May 1999 the post went to Ambassador Clay Constaninou, a Cypriot immigrant to the United States with

graduate degrees from Seton Hall Law School and New York University. Constaninou worked on Bill Clinton's presidential campaign and was appointed United States
Ambassador to Luxembourg in 1994, serving until January 1999. International links
helped him bring President Glafcos Clerides of Cyprus to campus in 1999, the first head
of state hosted by SODIR.[61] Crown Princess Maria Teresa of Luxembourg was given
an honorary doctorate in 1999 to acknowledge her work in promoting microloans in
developing nations.[62] Kofi Annan visited (in a snowstorm) in 2000 as part of the School
of Diplomacy's Dialogue of Civilizations series. Gil Carlos Rodriguez Iglesias, president of the Court of Justice of the European Union, was honored in October 2001,[63] the
Irish Nobel laureate John Hume in March 2004, and another Nobel laureate, the former prime minister of Israel, Shimon Peres, in September 2004. In April 2005, a third
Nobel laureate, Mikhail Gorbachev, former president of the Soviet Union, addressed
the university. "Whenever there is a problem, what we need is not missiles, cannons,
and guns, but diplomacy," he said, eliding much of the history of the country he once
led.[64] Lech Walesa, former leader of Solidarity and president of Poland, spoke to the
university in December 2005. He had been awarded his honorary degree already—in
1982—but had been unable to leave Poland to receive it. "I want students to know that
this is what you can do with a Seton Hall degree," said Father Paul Holmes, introducing him. "Go on to win the Nobel Prize a year later."[65]

The most notable visit was that of President Mohammad Khatami of Iran, who addressed the university amid tight security in November 2001, only weeks after the 9/11
terrorist attacks. "The eyes of so many in the world are on President Khatami these
days," said Sheeran. "He is the president of a great nation, proud in faith, strong in its
traditions, with a remarkable history . . . That he should choose to come to Seton Hall
and speak to our students is a testament to his commitment to the Dialogue among
Civilizations and to Seton Hall." Khatami called for dialogue to "replace the discourse
of violence and hostility with a discourse of mutual understanding and reason," insisting that the "privileges of democracy" should be "augmented with spirituality."[66] Following the visit, Sheeran traveled to Iran in August 2002, where the Seton Hall party
was the first official American group to visit the country since President George W.
Bush had spoken of it as part of an "axis of evil" in the modern world.

In December 2002, the school was named the John C. Whitehead School of Diplomacy and International Relations at a dinner at the Waldorf Astoria in New York
attended by Senator Hillary Clinton and Dr. Henry Kissinger, past and future secretaries of state. Crucial in arranging the strategic alliance with the United Nations Association, Whitehead had had a career as deputy secretary of state and as a business
and civic leader. Whitehead was not the only benefactor. Shortly after the dinner, Josh
Weston of Automatic Data Processing, Roseland, New Jersey, made a gift of $100,000,
as did David Rockefeller.[67]

Constaninou's connections counted. "You have lifted the school to remarkable levels of visibility in a very short time," Sheeran told him, "and it has brought great distinction to Seton Hall University."[68] By 2003, in addition to boasting the best SAT scores in the university, the incoming class spoke thirty languages. SODIR's graduates were landing top positions at the State Department, the Defense Intelligence Agency, and the United Nations.[69] "The record speaks for itself," said Constaninou in 2005, when he stepped down from the deanship. "The School of Diplomacy has transformed Seton Hall into an international arena."[70]

Internationalism

SODIR was only one of several initiatives aimed at making Seton Hall more cosmopolitan.[71] Internationalism was crucial to Sheeran's understanding of the university as Catholic, an institution drawing on the common intellectual and cultural tradition of many such universities throughout the world. Airports were his natural habitat and he was especially interested in China, visiting several times to sign agreements with local universities. Building on this, the Office of International Programs promoted study opportunities in Ireland, Poland, Italy, France, Mexico, El Salvador, China, Japan, Jordan, and Russia. Since the early 1980s, Seton Hall professors had taught at Wuhan University in China, welcoming Wuhan professors in return. The School of Business had ties with the International University of Business in Beijing and schools in Poland and Russia. The university library had links with the Chinese Academy of Science. The Law School had connections with the Universities of Parma and Milan. The department of Asian Studies, still flourishing as it neared its fiftieth birthday, was complemented by China House, just off campus, which provided a home for visiting Chinese scholars and students.[72]

Sheeran urged the university to think creatively about globalism, hoping to "deparochialize" Seton Hall but not in such a way as to jeopardize its historic commitment to local community people of modest means.[73] Juergen Heinrichs of Art and Music coordinated the international outreach. To be a "world" university meant more than bringing the world to Seton Hall (or Seton Hall to the world). There also had to be a "joined up" approach to overseas activities, from study abroad to faculty exchange to curricular development. More and more, students demanded an overseas component to their degrees and with the faculty increasingly drawn from beyond the United States, it made sense to maximize areas of cooperation.

For Heinrichs as for Sheeran, internationalism was one piece of the larger institutional renewal that included mobile computing, the new core curriculum, the founding of SODIR, and initiatives to promote the Catholic mission. "Be it his hosting of a 1998 conference about ethical dimensions of poverty," he remarked, "or his decision to join Law School faculty on their 2008 journey to Zanzibar to probe modern day slavery and human trafficking, Monsignor Sheeran's view of internationalization consistently registers the world's deepest needs while never losing sight of suffering in the world . . . Seton Hall as a Catholic university does well in drawing from its long tradition of approaching the task in a caring, human-centered way that transcends any given institutional, economic or national preoccupations of the day."[74]

The Unanue Institute

Reaching out to a changing world changed Seton Hall. As more students and faculty traveled overseas, so they returned to a campus increasingly diverse, polyglot, and multiracial. (One illustration of the diversity: weekly Friday morning Muslim prayer took place in Duffy Hall.) Complaints that the faculty was less diverse than the student body had merit but failed to consider the complex factors involved in hiring (while also overstating student diversity). There was more to diversity than head-counting. Intellectual variety also mattered.

In the last years of the twentieth century, no demographic fact was more impressive than growth in the Latino population. In 2004, Latinos comprised 13 percent of total U.S. population, a figure (and percentage) set to increase dramatically by the middle of the twenty-first century. In business, in arts, the corporate world, and in law, Latinos and Latinas were making unprecedented strides, and it was time for Seton Hall to catch up.

From earliest days Seton Hall had had links with Central and South America, with many Spanish-speaking students coming from Cuba and elsewhere in the 1860s and 1870s to brave New Jersey's winters. The memory of those shivering boys was renewed almost 150 years later with the establishment in 2005 of the Unanue Latino Institute, designed to explore the Hispanic contribution to U.S. and world culture. Made possible by a major gift from Dr. Joseph and Carmen Ana Unanue, the Institute positioned Seton Hall as a national leader in exploring the Latino effect on American culture, politics, and society.[75] With plans for scholars and writers in residence, with affiliations to other cultural bodies such as the Instituto Cervantes, with an annual Unanue Lecture open to the growing Latino population of northern New Jersey, with endowed scholarships, with travel grants for faculty and students, with "servant leadership" student trips to Latin America (already promoted by Campus Ministry and the Division of Volunteer Efforts), with an academic major in Latino studies to promote, the Institute was a creative response to a challenging moment. Sheeran, and Seton Hall, had reason to be grateful for the "faith, optimism, and great sense of humor" of Joseph Unanue, who died in 2013.[76]

A Technological Revolution

Of the many revolutions of the Sheeran era, the most profound was the discovery of the personal computer as a way of learning, thinking, and being. Along with the rest of the world, Seton Hall discovered the brilliant versatility of personal computers in the early 1990s. In June 1995, the university's Information Technology Long Range Plan spoke of a "student-centered, network-centered, mobile computing environment" where much of Seton Hall's academic and social life would be conducted. The environment had several features: "ubiquitous" access to computers; greater attention to communication and writing skills; emphasis on "active, self-directed modes of learning"; greater institutional productivity; enhanced student expectations; and reputational improvement. Creating this world was "vital to the future of the university and once launched it "[could not] be allowed to fail."[77]

It succeeded beyond expectations. At the top was Sheeran, who sold the plan with his usual persuasiveness. Senior administrators Dennis Garbini and Stephen Landry, a former math professor, worked on the technical, financial, and strategic side, producing vast amounts of paper to show that paper would give way to gigabytes. Professors sat in workshops talking about computers and learning to use them, the talk often more confident than the use. Home pages were composed, displayed, then unvisited. Email was discovered as novelty, then pleasure, then burden, then curse. The "inter-office memo" went the way of the dodo. "Techies," mostly men but some women, were able to achieve with ease what teachers achieved, if at all, with difficulty. Physical Plant ripped up skirting boards, removed ceilings, replastered walls, installed projectors, and chained up promixa machines to make Seton Hall was the most "wired" Catholic university in the country, shortly before it went wireless.[78]

Leasing computers, "upgrading the campus backbone," training faculty, creating mobile-ready classrooms: this was expensive. Mobile computing cost over $2 million in its first year (FY 1997), $3 million in its second year, nearly $1.5 million in its third year, falling to $200,000 in FY 2000. Beginning with the class of 2001, all full-time students would pay a flat-rate program fee of $2,200 per year to cover the cost of a laptop, maintenance, insurance, and related services, the fee intended to produce $1.11 million per year in revenue. In the first three years, financial aid and marketing costs for mobile computing were estimated at $2.5 million. The entire plan, Garbini and Landry thought, would take $6,670,000.

Sheeran signed a strategic partnership with IBM in February 1997, the university committing $15 million over five years to make the alliance work, the corporation putting its weight behind the university's technology infrastructure. "We are thinking through the many sides of information technology," he said, "even its downsides . . . Five years ago I did not know what email was. Now, half a million pieces of email cross campus and beyond each week."[79] The points of connection between Seton Hall and IBM were academic, administrative, technical, and organizational: academic, in that IBM would provide laptops, establish an "electronic learning environment," create a "digital library," and start a Center for Academic Technology; administrative, in that it would assist with "reengineering"; technical, in that it would train staff and maintain the network; and organizational, in that it would put Seton Hall in touch with other educational institutions. For Seton Hall, the intellectual resources of a leading corporation would be available and competitively priced, giving a "one-of-a-kind alliance [impacting] the way we teach and the way we learn, the way we interact across campus and the world."[80] Thanks to it, Seton Hall was still rated twelfth most "connected" university in the nation in 2003.[81] Even campus ministry went online with a Catholic chat-room.[82] What did they chat about? In the 1960s, students protested the Vietnam War. In 2001, they protested their laptop "refresh."[83]

Not everything worked. In 1998, the university started Seton World Wide to offer online degrees. It lost over $1.6 million in 2003, $600,000 in 2004, and was discontinued, doomed by insufficient research, failure to recognize the strength of competition from already established programs, and unrealistic expectations about the attractiveness of the Seton Hall offerings.

Father Tom Peterson, still chancellor as Sheeran was president, signed the IBM alliance and spoke as if himself programmed by a computer when describing this new world: "Group problem-solving techniques have become part of the everyday life of large corporations . . . Seton Hall has begun a serious attempt to prepare itself for these twenty-first century challenges with new models for learner-centered/student-centered education."[84]

Even technophobes found things to enjoy about being "wired"—getting newspapers online, listening to free music, playing YouTube clips. Hardware became smaller, its pretensions larger. Armed with the latest gadget, students could correct professors at a glance or find on a screen answers that should have been in their heads. Old dogs—the faculty—taught themselves new tricks. Young dogs—students—taught themselves newer ones. Such were the pleasures of being wired, wireless, or weird.

Academic Renewal: A New Core Curriculum

Apart from founding SODIR and overseeing the technological revolution, Sheeran's chief project, the most delicate and disruptive of his undertakings, was to recreate the university core curriculum. This was easier said than done. To require students to know some things in common was to pose questions about the nature of the common life and the shared moral commitments that made it possible. It was also to challenge the faculty to think about the same questions and about the nature of the university. It was, finally, to force the administration to find time and resources to transform the classroom.

Each undergraduate school retained a core curriculum and, within it, different departmental and programmatic requirements. For the College of Arts and Sciences, encouraging critical intelligence and providing some understanding of the methods of the sciences and humanities had become for all practical purposes a set of distribution requirements, with most departments having a share of the pie and none eager to give it up. This core needed reform because Arts and Sciences as the largest undergraduate college was *de facto* provider of what was, in effect, a university core in all but name. At least, though, the Arts and Sciences core had some rationale. No coherent principle could be seen in the requirements of other colleges.

"What is probably desirable for Seton Hall at this point," Scholz had once written, "is a small university core curriculum of no more than 24 credits to which the individual schools might add a college core requirement of about twelve credits." With a grant of $75,000 from the New Jersey Department of Higher Education, he thought that Seton Hall might have a new core by the fall of 1988.[85] It never happened. In 1992, when the Faculty Senate was created, its brief included the "establishment and review of a core curriculum for the university"[86] That never happened either: it was still pending in 1999 when Mark Rocha promised the Board of Regents that a new core was next item on his agenda.[87] In 2000, there was still no new core. But in the fall of 2001, Sheeran invited the Faculty Senate to create a core to represent "a signature Seton Hall experience," something to "embody" Seton Hall's place among universities.

Educational theorist Susan Awbrey, describing the challenge of institutional change, argued that organizational restructuring mattered less than "interpersonal relationships, norms, trust, risk-taking, values, emotions, and need."[88] This proved an accurate prediction of the Seton Hall experience. Encouraged by Sheeran, the senate elected a university core curriculum committee, which soon realized that the old curricular questions with their assumptions of canonicity and epistemological privilege no longer applied in a world in which the "contents" of a course were only one aspect of a broader classroom experience. Where once a core represented those areas of intellectual endeavor that every educated person was expected to master, now it was conceived as a set of outcomes and a process of personal transformation. "What must they know?" gave way to "What do we want our students to become?" To answer those questions, the second especially, the committee proposed a campus-wide conversation which began in July 2002 with a series of faculty "town hall meetings." From these a consensus emerged that a Seton Hall education should produce graduates who were "thinking, caring, communicative, ethically responsible leaders with a service orientation." The "distinctive Seton Hall experience" was to extend beyond the classroom to include "information literacy" and research skills; competence in technology; a sense of inquiry and wonder; ethical decision-making; service to others; working in groups; living in community; and an awareness of, and commitment to, the values important to a Catholic worldview. Ideally, teaching should take place in small classes, be multi-disciplinary, and incorporate pedagogical "best practices."

Skeptics in the natural sciences and the professional schools worried that a new core, with its inevitable reallocation of credit hours, could eviscerate their programs. To win them over, more meetings took place in smaller groups and what emerged (from literally thousands of hours of workshops and training sessions) was a curriculum in which all students would take certain "signature" courses and demonstrate mastery of certain "core proficiencies." The new requirements would amount to twenty-one credits. Signature courses, focusing on key texts (with optional texts for flexibility), aimed to bring students on a "journey of transformation," introducing them to the central questions of the Catholic and other intellectual traditions. Core proficiencies included critical and ethical thinking, literacy and numeracy, informational fluency, and oral and artistic aptitude. Courses "infused" with these proficiencies would satisfy core requirements. The new core thus combined specific skills and substantial content, an inventive solution to the problem Sheeran had posed in 2001. Some faculty wished for more Catholicism in the core, some for less, but balance was achieved by recognizing that different traditions, precisely because different, demanded respect. Moreover, the journey of discovery, even of transformation, was not confined to students. Some faculty, reading or rereading key texts of the Western and Eastern traditions, discovered wisdom they had never known or had forgotten.

Complicating the story were two parallel initiatives that, from one point of view, had little to do with the core but, from another, were vital to it. For some time, Sheeran and the executive cabinet had been thinking of reducing the number of credits needed for graduation from 130 to 120. In tandem with this, they proposed to move from a credit-based to a flat rate of tuition. At the prompting of the Core Curriculum Committee, these ideas were incorporated into the core proposal, the argument being that existing academic and financial requirements for graduation were putting Seton Hall at a competitive disadvantage over peer institutions. If core and costs could be linked, a new model of fiscal and academic life would emerge that was both commercially and academically intelligible. A flat rate of tuition would allow students and the university to plan their respective budgets rationally. Reduction of credits would make Seton Hall more attractive to potential applicants.

As provost, Thomas Lindsay strongly supported a renovated core, and in January 2005 he successfully urged the Faculty Senate to approve the proposal in principle. "Laptops are nice, but it's sort of just a faster pencil. This is something that will leave a lasting imprint."[89] But Lindsay's time in charge was brief and his replacement, Fred Travis, unconvinced of the timetable for the core and resentful of the Senate's apparent usurpation of the academic oversight of individual colleges, insisted that the three "signature" courses be approved by faculty curricular bodies at once rather than, as initially proposed, sequentially. These strictures made sense, but they had the effect of slowing down already halting progress. For his part, Sheeran understood that resources would be needed to bring about a reform that was to be as much his "signature" as Seton Hall's. At annual convocations, at Senate meetings, at meetings with faculty, he made his support for the new core so obvious that failure to implement it would have seemed a vote of no confidence in him. He also made clear that improved salaries were part of the package and it was this, in the end, that generated the goodwill that brought the train to the station.

Why did this version of a university core succeed when previous efforts had failed? Sheeran's support was crucial, as was campus "ownership" of the proposal. The key insight was that at the core of the core was Catholicism, the integrative principle that connected disparate subjects: "A major thrust of [my] administration is that the "Catholic intellectual tradition" is taught through the curriculum . . . [It] is found not only in theology and philosophy; there is a Catholic tradition in social thought, in art, in literature, in music, and so on. Our Catholic tradition is an immensely rich one, and it should be experienced throughout the curriculum."[90] Here was a subtler understanding of a core than that of Rocha, who spoke crudely of a curriculum that would "turn discrete information into usable knowledge."[91]

The publicly repeated and intellectually sophisticated support of the president was not the only reason for success. The retirement of older faculty and their replacement by younger professors less committed to the status quo also helped. So did financial incentives. The role of the Senate as a promoter and persuader was decisive, transferring the conversation to university level and so freeing it from the entangling localism of earlier efforts.[92] Workshop by workshop, the faculty willed the new core into being, acting as a sort of university-wide committee of the whole. Richard Liddy, director of the Center for Catholic Studies, recognized a minor miracle of collaboration that showed the core for the transformational experience it claimed to be: "I am proud of the things I have been part of here at Seton Hall, especially the many faculty seminars through the years—in which we have reflected on what we are doing in this place—such as the seminar on the core curriculum back in 2001 that eventually led to every student being exposed to the Scriptures, Saint Augustine, Dante, and Saint Thomas Aquinas—highlights of the Catholic intellectual tradition."[93]

Catholic Initiatives

The creation of the new curriculum was one of many efforts to revitalize Seton Hall's Catholicism. Long before he became president, serving as assistant provost in 1987,

Sheeran had an idea of what an authentically Catholic university should look like. Catholicism, he thought, needed to be translated "nitty-gritty . . . into concrete policy in all units of the university." Ethics could be "better taught and integrated into the various schools and colleges on the professional and undergraduate levels." An introductory course on Roman Catholicism ("reasonably uniform . . . with a single syllabus, similar requirements and identical examinations") should be part of a university core curriculum. There could be a concentration or a minor in Catholic Studies "taught by members of different departments, even the School of Theology." A "Christian spirit and lifestyle [could be] encouraged by residential policies and student-life programs and priorities." A university-wide hiring policy could bring people who, "regardless of their own religious affiliation, understand, appreciate, and are committed to the university's Catholic mission." Students should be brought to "a better understanding of and dedication to broader social concerns during their time at Seton Hall." These were the ideas he would pursue if he were allowed to "dream a little."[94]

Sheeran knew that Catholic higher education, to be authentic, required a deeper conversation at a moral, spiritual, and philosophical level with and among faculty, students, and administration. Only then could Seton Hall be said to have made a reality of its commitment to the wholeness of the human person. He read *Ex Corde Ecclesia*, *Fides et Ratio*, and other papal documents exploring the relationship between reason and revelation, but he wondered how they were to work in practice. Was Seton Hall interested in a "preferential option" for Catholic faculty? Did a headcount of Catholic professors amount to anything? What was the role of priests? When did pluralism bleed into relativism?

To these questions there was no shortage of answers. Sheeran's goal of "bringing the Catholic intellectual tradition into the classroom"[95] prompted advice from friends and strangers, among them Joseph Varacalli, executive director of the Society of Catholic Social Scientists: "Your student body is basically working class to lower middle class to middle and hence not as corrupted as the yuppies of Georgetown . . . The best way to get around those tenured faculty of yours who will be resisting your efforts at orthodox restoration is to build *new* programs (e.g., a Catholic Studies Department)."[96]

Justice Antonin Scalia of the United States Supreme Court delivered the Charter Day address in March 1997: "A university owned and run by Catholics no more deserves to be called a Catholic university than a supermarket owned and run by Catholics deserves to be called a Catholic supermarket . . . Catholic universities can be identified by what is taught. They are a presentation of faith. [They need to stick to a Christian way of teaching] instead of succumbing to trendy cultural agnosticism."[97] Scalia's argument, like the man, was both subtle and blunt. The story of American higher education was one of institutions established out of religious zeal which then abandoned their founding principles, he said. The story of America was of similar loss of faith. A "Christian" country in 1897 had become a "Judaeo-Christian" one in 1952 and a secular one in 1997. "Our nation thinks that the Beatitudes are a female singing group." But he offered Seton Hall as a counterexample. "I feel this institution is traveling against the traffic . . . That is to say, [in] the right direction."[98]

When Bishop John J. Myers of Peoria became Archbishop of Newark, president of the Board of Regents, and chair of the Board of Trustees in September 2001, that direction seemed to be confirmed. Myers promoted Seton Hall as a university for middle-class Catholics, a more regional school than that envisaged by Sheeran, and if this caused tension between them, it was well concealed. He was a frequent presence on campus, especially in Immaculate Conception Seminary, where he took seriously his role as spiritual father, his orthodoxy working as a sort of brand mark for Seton Hall, suggesting (not always accurately) a university reflecting his own ecclesial personality.

In 2004, Sheeran arranged for senior members of the Board of Regents to travel to Rome, where they met Archbishop J. Michael Miller, secretary to the Vatican's Congregation for Catholic Education. Miller praised Seton Hall's "reputation, quality and commitment to . . . Catholic identity" but warned that the greatest challenge to Catholic higher education was a culture fundamentally inhospitable to it.[99] The "air we breathe in the United States is not Catholic . . . We must . . . be counter-cultural . . . When we use the term Catholic to describe a university, it is not merely an adjective . . . It is a radically different reality."[100]

Sheeran had already taken steps in this direction, committing himself, for instance, to strengthening the number of priests on campus,[101] a policy that bore impressive results. Seton Hall had more priests on campus than any other university in the country and their presence, individually and collectively, was unmistakable. McCarrick wanted priests appointed to the department of religious studies to bring it "into the proper relationship with the University and the Archdiocese."[102] "I never tire of saying," Sheeran assured Myers, "though some may tire of hearing, that the priests of Seton Hall are at the very heart of our university community."[103]

Richard Liddy was named University Professor of Catholic Thought in 1997. Liddy created a Center for Catholic Studies in 1997 to run seminars, lectures, and faculty retreats and to provide focus for a campus-wide Catholic conversation that had become diffuse and unstructured over the years. Enjoying generous support from many friends of the university,[104] it was an idea with a long history. In the 1980s, Joseph Mahoney of the department of history had argued that students with an academic interest in Catholicism had to piece together courses for themselves in history, English, philosophy, religious studies, and art and music without any help from a sponsoring department. Recognizing this problem, Liddy and others established a Catholic studies major in 2002. In 2006, the Board of Regents gave its approval for an undergraduate degree in theology, the work of two very bright priests, Douglas Milewski and Joseph

Chapel, the first a patristics scholar, the second a moral theologian. The degree was housed in the School of Theology, not the College of Arts and Sciences.

No-one could have mistaken Seton Hall for anything other than a Catholic university in these years. The Institute on Work, the Bayley Project on ethics, the seminary's Institute of Spirituality, the winning in 2002 of a $2 million Lilly Foundation grant to explore the nature of vocation all showed a university committed to its founding principles. Under Father Ian Boyd, founder and editor of *The Chesterton Review*, the G.K. Chesterton Institute for Faith and Culture promoted the thought of Chesterton and his circle, sponsoring conferences in Argentina, Australia, Brazil, Chile, England, Ireland, Italy, France, Lithuania, Poland, and Spain. In February 2001, the Institute hosted a conference at Seton Hall devoted to "Religion in the 21st Century," among the speakers James Billington, librarian of Congress, and Samuel Huntington, author of *The Clash of Civilizations*. The Lilly Foundation grant, the largest in the university's history, established the Center for Vocation and Servant Leadership under David Foster, a philosophy professor in the seminary. "We have always cared about our mission, but now our mission is truly driving the institution," said Father Paul Holmes, vice president for mission and ministry. "It sends a signal to the entire campus."[105] (Some of the money went to the core curriculum and to "form servant leaders for a global society.")[106] "We do not push religion or force beliefs on anyone," said director of campus ministry, Father James Spera, "but we do realize that the power of this university's faith comes from spiritual symbols."[107]

Sheeran was sensitive to criticism from "self-appointed watchdogs of orthodoxy" that his presidency had seen a dilution of Seton Hall's Catholic mission. The "fear-mongering" and "finger-pointing" of the Cardinal Newman Society annoyed him, as did any "gratuitous attack" from the Catholic "right."[108] Behind the scenes Myers (who sat on the board of the Cardinal Newman Society) cut him slack,[109] although he complained when controversial speakers (partisan critics of Pope Pius XII, for example) were invited to campus.[110] On one matter, Sheeran was uncompromising: no-one with "publicly espoused positions contrary to the teachings of the Catholic Church, especially those concerning the sanctity of human life" would be honored by the university.[111]

Sheeran welcomed *Ex Corde Ecclesiae*, Pope John Paul II's apostolic constitution of 1990 on the role of Catholic universities in the life of the Church (which insisted on a relationship of mutual respect between the Church and church-affiliated educational institutions and on a more profound and integral Catholicism in those institutions), but he worried that its implementation would be seen as ecclesiastical interference and that its moral requirements were unenforceable. Requiring a Catholic university president to take the profession of faith and the oath of fidelity ran the risk of a "bad press" (although from which quarter he did not specify). He also thought that requiring "all professors . . . to exhibit not only academic competence but integrity of doctrine and good character" was potentially "a political and legal nightmare." Making professors who taught Catholic doctrine take the *mandatum*—an episcopal certification of doctrinal orthodoxy—could also pose problems. In principle he was in favor of the mandate, in practice against it, unable to "fathom how this could be implemented in the United States taking into account where universities are at . . . in terms of their common understanding of institutional autonomy and academic freedom."[112] This was too subtle.

In the end, Sheeran thought that the Catholicism of a Catholic university had to be measured not solely by curricular and institutional commitments to morality and doctrine but also by an active encouragement of art, beauty, history, and culture as incarnational expressions of what it means to be fully human in Christ. "I cannot think of any magic formula," he told one priest who objected to the way moral philosophy was taught by some at the university, "except to reiterate my absolute commitment to our Catholic mission . . . Often the intellectual, social and theological challenges cannot easily be resolved in our pluralistic society—even within a Catholic college—and demand extra care and sensitivity as well as extra charity to see that dialogue remains at a constructive level."[113] This was his working philosophy and, by and large, it worked.

Fire in the Night

Early on Tuesday, January 19, 2000 Seton Hall's world, and Sheeran's, changed forever. At 4:28 AM, in the middle of an intermittently snowy night, fire broke out on the third floor of Boland Hall, a freshman dormitory accommodating hundreds of students who, hours before, had been celebrating victory over St. John's University in a basketball game.[114] Fire alarms were frequent in Boland, some genuine, most not.[115] This one was different. As thick, dark smoke curled into corridors and under doors, a couch, the source of the fire, burned out of control. Students forced themselves awake and made for the exits. Panic replaced fatigue, with sights and sounds that many would never forget: black smoke mingling with the blackness of night, windows broken to allow escape, screams of terror, and cries for help. "Kids were running around like crazy," said freshman Wayne Mulano. "The flames came right up the stairs." "We tried to go down the stairs but there was cinder everywhere," said Erin Burke. "We were lucky." "I couldn't see anything," said Tim van Wir. "I had to crawl out. The flames were from the floor to the ceiling." "I was walking down the stairs," said Danny Lee, "and maybe five feet away there was a kid on fire. Two guys patted him down and I tried to get out." "All I heard were people shouting 'I'm going to die'," said Virginia Wannermaker. She climbed out of a third story window and escaped down a ladder provided, it turned out, by a neighbor from across the street. Every resident of Boland Hall had a story to tell.[116]

In a matter of minutes, three eighteen-year-old students died: Frank Caltabilota, Aaron Karol, and John Giunta. Caltabilota was an athlete, a basketball fan, a son and brother. Aaron Karol was a psychology and criminal justice major who had hoped to work for the FBI. John Giunta played in the band and thought of becoming a teacher. Over the days that followed, these young men would become "Aaron and Frank and John," forever together in a trinity of loss. "What made John unique was his ability to make you smile," said his friend Doris Jones. "He could make you forget about your problems." "You are a hero," said Thomas Caltabilota of his brother Frank. "You put everyone before yourself." "He was just a genuinely good kid," said Joseph Karol of his son Aaron, "the traveling man." "He was a wonderful, compassionate human being, and he cared a lot about friends."[117]

Soon other names surfaced: Tom Pugliese, who broke his back jumping from a third-floor window; Nick Donato, jumping to safety, who broke an ankle and wrist; Dana Christmas, risking death from smoke inhalation and burned over 58 percent of her body, who summoned others to flight; Alvaro Llanos and Ken Deshawn Simons, dreadfully burned. Sixty-two people, students and resident staff, suffered physical injury. The mental scars were just as real.

As dawn broke, shock gave way to grief, anger, relief, and remorse. Some students clutched childish things as they huddled together for comfort. Others wandered around in a daze. There was fury at the pointlessness of the loss, at the large number of false alarms over the years, at the inadequacy of the building to cope with fire, at the thought that it may have been set deliberately. "Boland Hall was not prepared," said Kim Sanders. "We had no fire plan and the RAs told us the wrong things to do," said Becky Statz. Others disagreed. "We did everything we were told and more," said Tara Butler, an RA.[118] The injuries of Dana Christmas backed up that claim.

The immediate need was for spiritual as well as physical comfort. "This is a heartbreaking tragedy for Seton Hall University," said Sheeran, "for our families, for all the Seton Hall family, for the larger family of the state." Classes were cancelled, many parents coming to campus to take their children home. Governor Christine Todd Whitman called it "a huge tragedy" and President Clinton sent condolences.[119] Students, faculty and staff gathered at Immaculate Conception Chapel for a moment of shared grief and prayer after 5 PM Mass the evening following the fire. Later, Sheeran would remember this as Seton Hall at its quiet, resilient, composed, best.[120] "I think of Michelangelo's Pieta and the wordless Mother holding her Son," he said. "Our faith calls us here tonight." "We are made for the life that lasts forever," said Archbishop McCarrick, "and no tragedy can take us away from that life with God." "Jesus Christ is always present with us through the difficulties, the sorrow, the pain," said Father William Sheridan of Campus Ministry. "I've seen a lot of support and reaching out today," said Monsignor Richard Liddy. "I hope that will continue and . . . lead to a lot more love."[121]

The comforters themselves needed comfort. Father Tom Peterson had led Providence College when it had suffered the deadliest college dorm fire in U.S. history, with ten women students killed in December 1977. Now he faced the same sorrow again. "The question in the minds of each one of us this morning is, why? Why did this happen? The only answer is 'I don't know'."[122]

Nor were there good answers to more immediate questions. Boland Hall, with no sprinkler system, was built in 1951 and opened in 1952. (Sprinklers were only required in 1984). Its internal fire hoses were disconnected. It had had so many fire alarms, nineteen since the beginning of the school year, that students routinely ignored them.[123] The last of them was the only one triggered by an actual fire. The local fire department was unprepared for catastrophe.[124] Whether these factors were decisive is hard to know. Typically, firefighters use their own hoses, so dormitory hoses may have been unnecessary unless, improbably, fleeing residents could have known how to use them. Lack of sprinklers was clearly a problem. The greatest fear was that the fire was the result of arson, and no-one, or very few, knew the answer to that. Two days after the tragedy, investigators wanted to identify and talk to three people in the Boland Hall lounge less than an hour before the fire began.[125] Reports that faulty electrics were the cause were discounted as premature. *The New York Times* spoke of "an unsettling tandem: mourning and investigation."[126]

Mourning remained the priority. The university came together in Walsh Gymnasium on Tuesday, January 25 for an impressive Service of Remembrance and Hope during which Sheeran attempted to find meaning in the event. Each of us, he said, had been touched "by the terrible darkness of that night . . . Each of us longs for a light to lead us home." We have some special bond with Frank and John and Aaron, he continued, and with each other, a bond that lasts beyond this life. "Just as we were getting to know them," he continued, "they were snatched away. We want so much to call them back, to tell them what they meant to us, to tell them how much we love them." McCarrick read a prayer of blessing and consolation from Pope John Paul II, who had assured fourteen pilgrims from Seton Hall during his general audience the previous week that he had prayed for the dead and injured and invoked the "grace and peace of our Lord Jesus Christ" upon the university." At the end of the service, the fifty-strong priest community left the stage singing the *Salve Regina*, moving some to tears. "It was perfect, what people needed," said Lawrence Pierre, a nineteen-year-old resident assistant. "It let you pay respect to the people that died and was a tool of motivation to move forward."[127]

During the service, Sheeran acknowledged that the "days and weeks to come" would be "difficult." As it turned out, days and weeks turned into months and years. To begin the healing, Sheeran moved to Boland Hall when it reopened, intending to stay "for the foreseeable future." (He had lived there for two years as a divinity student in the mid-1960s.) "They're great kids who are in the process of growing up," he said, "and my experience over the past twenty years—and certainly my experience over the past month—has been that [they] are worthy of a great deal of respect."[128] Students decorated his door when he moved in, slipping notes underneath and dropping by to talk. "To be totally honest I was a bit afraid to return to my home here at Seton Hall," wrote his new neighbor, Jennifer Costa. "But as I entered Boland I felt a sense of security. When I heard that you were living on our floor I was totally convinced you and the rest of Seton Hall really are concerned and have true love for us."[129]

The need to get back to normal competed with the need never to forget.[130] Students only indirectly connected to the fire picked up the pieces of their lives. Those directly affected found the emotional scars slow to heal. "Walking by Boland Hall is hard," said freshman Ben Chibnik. Months after, he still found himself unable to sleep, to concentrate, to focus on academic work, to cope even with the small pressures of university life.[131] "A lot of people are pretending that nothing happened," he noticed. Yet the outpouring of support, good will, and practical sympathy was enormous. Students from local schools held fundraisers and bake sales, digging onto their pockets to raise sums of money touching in their modesty.[132] The staff of Saint Michael's Medical Center donated $1,000 to a scholarship fund.[133] The Chubb Corporation donated $10,000. Individuals gave similar amounts, members of the Board of Regents very substantially.[134] Cardinal John O'Connor of New York, himself ill, wrote to Sheeran of his prayers for the victims, their families, and the university. Sheeran's reply captured the moment: "This is a very trying time in Seton Hall's life, perhaps the saddest page in our long history. But these days are also witnessing an immense outpouring of generosity and, indeed, heroism, on the campus. I am so proud of our Seton Hall community, and especially our students, for the way they have rallied together."[135] The desire to do *something* was overwhelming.

Small and unheralded gestures of support were more powerful than sincere but conventional ones. One third-grader from Dix Hills, New York wrote: "Dear Frank, John and Aaron's family: I am sorry about your kids. My religion class is going to pray. Love, Mike." And another: "Dear John's, Frank's, and Aaron's families: I feel bad about your sons. I will pray for them. God is watching them right now. From Anthony."[136] Alumni wrote of their love of the university.[137] That the fire had brought out something special about Seton Hall—that it was a community, that its compassion was sincere—struck many parents and alumni with force. "When we attended parent orientation for our son three years ago," wrote a Lutheran clergyman, "one of the qualities of Seton Hall that impressed me was the claim that Seton Hall was a family. That has certainly proven to be true during the current situation. Our son did know John Giunta from both of them being in the Pep band. I very much appreciated the university making two vans available for any pep band members to attend his wake.

It was also very commendable providing bus transportation to the funeral service . . . From this personal perspective, I can say the university has truly lived up to its billing as a family."[138] "I wanted you to know," another parent wrote to Sheeran, his son a resident of Boland Hall who escaped the fire unharmed, "that whenever my wife or I had a question and called the hotline or for that matter any office at the university we were met by compassionate supportive staff and students. It is truly a compliment to the university. It was that sense of family that attracted our son to Seton Hall for his college education."[139]

That Sheeran was a priest, and a priest among priests, made a difference. An army of professionally trained counselors descended on the university, but somehow it was clergy who helped most, offering the wisdom of a tradition that had seen death in all its guises over many centuries. Correspondents thanked Sheeran for his "superb" pastoral communications to the extended Seton Hall family. "They have been YOU— coming through as the outstanding priest and human being which you are."[140] But he was not the only priest—there were dozens of them—who helped ease suffering. One parent spoke for many:

I was sitting folding laundry last Wednesday a little before 6 AM when I heard announced on the TV news that there had been a fire at the dorms at Seton Hall. Little by little the news kept getting worse. It was a high rise dorm. It was the freshman dorm. It was Boland Hall. My son is a freshman on the 3rd floor of Boland Hall. I absolutely panicked and filled with dread. Would it be my child that was hurt? I called one of the hospitals that had been mentioned but luckily [he was not there]. A friend that lived nearby offered to go to the school to look for my son. By 6:30 I was on the road to South Orange. I never drove or ran so fast in my life. When I arrived, I met another frantic parent and we both searched for our children. He had a daughter on the 5th floor. We ended in the Rec hall and one of the priests who helped us move in (he carried a big rug up three flights of stairs) spoke to us and told us that at present the students were calling home. When I called home a few minutes later, I found out that my son was fine. The other parent also heard from his child. We hugged each other as if we had known the other forever. Needless to say, I said the first thank you prayer I was to repeat over the next week.

I ache and grieve for the parents that lost their sons and for the parents that must sit by and watch their children struggle to live. I have not stopped praying for these people. I have heard a lot of criticism over this unfortunate incident. I only have gratitude to all the people that helped the students especially the young RA who was a hero saving others. . . . A million thanks to you and all the wonderful priests at Seton Hall. I am still so glad my child is a part of your institution.[141]

Liturgies of remembrance became consuming and consoling in the years ahead. Every January on the anniversary of the fire the university came together to pray for the dead and to remember the living, and, in an instant tradition, to listen to Aaron Karol's father, Joe, speak of the event and its aftermath. "Our son loved this university and the entire college atmosphere," he said on the first anniversary of his death. "The main message our family would like to convey to all students here is to remember that this is a great institution. Remember our sons Aaron, Frank, and John, who no longer have the opportunity that is before you. For them the book is closed. For you, each exciting chapter continues."[142] Joe and his wife Candy helped Seton Hall to heal, and for that Sheeran was grateful, bonding with them perhaps more strongly than with the other families. With all of them, though, he was a priest more than a president. With the Karols he also became a friend.[143]

Aftermath

With grieving and remembrance came the need for justice and prevention. Sheeran's gesture of solidarity notwithstanding, the safety of Boland Hall, and of every building on every campus in the country, became a national concern. Within several weeks of the fire the State of New Jersey took over inspections of Boland Hall, citing violations of the fire code and the apparent failure of the South Orange Fire Department to keep adequate records of their inspections. The violations included unauthorized use of Christmas lights and extension cords and excessive trash in dorm rooms.[144] Nor was Boland singular. An initial inspection revealed some 828 violations of the state fire code throughout the university, a seemingly alarming number but most of them trivial and none (as the state acknowledged) serious enough to warrant the closure of a building.[145] Above all, Seton Hall was not alone. According to the National Fire Protection Association, 72 percent of dormitories, fraternity houses, and sorority houses that suffered fires did not have sprinkler systems. (Virtually none of the dorms in Princeton had sprinklers, the university almost contemptuous of the idea that it should install them.)[146] The argument was made, although few were persuaded by it, that although new dormitories were required by law to have sprinklers, older dormitories without them were not only legal but safe.[147] (What, then, was the point of the law?) Sprinkler retrofits, although expensive, were also effective, proven to cut by up to two-thirds the risks of death and property damage in fires. Less than two weeks after the Boland Hall fire, local lawmakers introduced legislation requiring all college dorms, regardless of age, to retrofit buildings within fifteen months of the passage of the law. Legislation introduced into the U.S. House of Representatives and Senate to provide federal funding for the retrofitting of college dormitories—the College Fire Prevention Bill—cited Seton Hall's fire, among others, as its motivation.[148] Against the arguments of skeptics who claimed that sprinklers could cope with fire but not with lethal smoke, the legislation answered the psychological as well as the practical need to something— anything—to make another tragedy less likely.[149] On July 5, 2000 Governor Whitman traveled to Seton Hall to sign into law the Dormitory Safety Trust Fund Act, requiring all public and private colleges and boarding schools in New Jersey to install sprinklers in every room within four years. To help them, the state pledged $90 million in zero-interest loans.

Balancing these positive outcomes was the worry that the blaze had been deliberately set. A small but intense fire beginning on a couch in the middle of the night was unlikely to have been the result of an accident. After several months, investigators were able to establish the key details. The fire began when an open flame ignited a piece of material beneath a bulletin board in the third-floor student lounge of the dormitory. This fire then ignited the upholstered foam cushions of a couch, these flames spreading to two other couches in the lounge. The flames burned the ceiling tiles and carpeting but remained within the west half of the lounge area. The burning couches gave off an intense, acrid smoke and produced heat in excess of 1,500 degrees. The smoke confused students who, unable to find an exit, wandered into the lounge. Frank Caltabilota and Aaron Karol died in the flames. John Giunta died of smoke inhalation in his third-floor room.[150] Although forensic tests failed to uncover any traces of accelerants such as gasoline or lighter fuel near the source of the fire, and although fire itself often destroys evidence of its own origin, investigators speculated that a prank gone wrong or a dispute between students (or nonstudents) was the likely explanation.[151] Of primary interest were three individuals asked to leave Boland Hall (by Dana Christmas) some forty-five minutes before the fire broke out. One of them (it was speculated) had failed to comply. In fact, the three were quickly eliminated from inquiries, leaving authorities frustrated at the slow progress of the investigation. "The longer it drags on, the harder it becomes for us," remarked one officer. "People start to clam up. Memories fade. We're hoping to have something soon."[152] But three months after the fire, the investigation had been reduced to a legal chess game, with detectives checked by the continuing silence of three students who seemed to know more about the events of the night than they were prepared to acknowledge and with their lawyers urging them to remain quiet.[153] One of them admitted that he had vandalized the lounge where the fire had started but denied that he had set the blaze. A year later, little had changed. The initial investigative unit, well over one hundred, had dwindled to six. After nearly 220 interviews and 150 sworn statements, Donald Campolo, Essex County prosecutor, admitted it was still unclear if investigators "would ever know what had happened."[154] Sheeran was unperturbed by the speed of the investigation ("Americans like to get things resolved quickly but I trust the prosecutor's office . . .")[155] but others were less patient. Seventeen months after the fire, the prosecutors confirmed what had long been suspected, that arson was the cause,[156] but it took until October 2001 to empanel a grand jury to consider homicide charges.

The work of the grand jury bore fruit on June 11, 2003 when two men were indicted on multiple counts of setting the fire and, along with various other individuals, of conspiring to conceal their involvement in it. Joseph Lepore and Sean Ryan, both twenty-one, were charged with conspiracy to commit arson and with arson (third-degree crimes), with causing or risking widespread injury or damage (also a third-degree crime), with fifty-three counts of aggravated assault (a second-degree crime), with three counts of manslaughter (also a second-degree crime), and with three counts of felony murder (a first-degree crime). Another individual, Santino Cataldo, had already been indicted along with Lepore and Ryan in September 2002 on charges of witness tampering and obstruction of justice. Finally, several members of the Lepore and Ryan families were charged with witness tampering, perjury, and obstruction of justice in an effort to conceal their knowledge of the events of January 19, 2000. Ryan and Cataldo were students at the university and Lepore had been a student at the time of the fire. The first two were immediately suspended. The third was no longer on campus, having transferred to the University of Delaware after the fire. "While we are saddened by the news that this wrenching tragedy may not have been accidental," said Sheeran, "we can pray that today's announcement is a step toward healing for all, and that human justice will ultimately intermingle with the divine mercy upon which we all depend." "I want to be certain that the right people are caught and that accusations aren't being loosely thrown around," said Catherine Feliz, a business marketing junior. Others were less measured. "I think they deserve it," said Angel Rivera, an education student. "I think they should get the maximum sentence if convicted because they affected the lives of many in a very negative way."[157]

All three entered not guilty pleas in State Superior Court in Newark on July 30, 2003, marking the beginning of an extremely protracted legal process that only ended, the case never going to trial, with a plea bargain and admissions of culpability by Ryan and Lepore in November 2006 and their sentencing in January 2007. Following a decision by prosecutors to abandon charges of felony murder, reckless manslaughter, and conspiracy to commit arson, the two men pleaded guilty to lesser charges of third-degree arson and witness tampering.[158] All charges against family members and against Santino Cataldo were dropped. Prosecutors dropped the more serious charges against Ryan and Lepore fearing that the complexity of the scientific evidence, and its circumstantiality, might prove problematic in front of a jury. "We can only be as good as our proofs," said Paula Dow, Essex County prosecutor. "The alternative might have been their walking away with a not guilty verdict and a smirk on their faces." The key moment, for which so many people had waited for so long, was an admission of wrongdoing. It came from Joseph Lepore. "I, along with Sean Ryan, lit a banner on fire that was draped across the couch in the third-floor lounge of Boland Hall on January 19, 2000, at approximately 4 AM. When doing so, I did not intend to injure anyone. It was a prank that got out of hand." The effect was cathartic. "We have an admission of guilt, and that was what we wanted," said Joe Karol. "It might not sound like much, but they will be in prison." The reduced charges were "closer to what really happened," said William DeMarco, Joseph Lepore's lawyer. Sean Ryan's lawyer, Michael Bubb, added that a series of "intervening causes" such as lack of sprinklers and fire-retardant furniture led to the deaths and injuries. Michael Morris, prosecuting, offered a different view. He was "disappointed and relieved" at the outcome, he said. "They could have come forward nearly seven years ago," he said, "but instead they behaved like criminals, were pursued like criminals, and now they are going to jail like criminals."[159]

On January 25, 2007, Ryan and Lepore were sentenced to five years in prison. "I want you to know that I am terribly, terribly, terribly sorry for your loss," Lepore said to the families of the dead. Offering similar words of contrition, Ryan hoped they could "move on." Then, before the men were led away in handcuffs, the families and the injured got their say. "I can't see myself ever forgiving these two kids for starting this fire," said Alvaro Llanos in a letter read out to the court. "They should have been man enough to bang on doors and save everyone's life. Instead they ran away . . ."[160] "It was no prank," said Joe Karol. "A prank is a joke." Then, in the most powerful moment of the day, he showed his dead son's picture to the court. Slowly circling it, "like a pastor elevating a Gospel, or a rabbi, a Torah,"[161] he invited those present to see what he saw—a "wondrous" young man whose brilliant future had been snatched away from him. Nothing more needed to be said.

On March 25, 2009, Sean Ryan was granted parole and was released from prison on May 6, 2009 having served two years and four months of his sentence. Joseph Lepore waived his right to seek parole.

Parallel to the forensic investigation was the question of Seton Hall's legal liability. The families of the dead and injured had grounds for filing suit and some twenty of them did so. For its part, the university had a reasonable claim of charitable immunity (as a nonprofit organization) which, had such a claim succeeded, would have capped individual damages at $250,000. This was a public relations minefield that threatened to undo the community-building that had been Sheeran's most conspicuous achievement in the aftermath of the disaster. The university handled the problem well, settling most personal injury claims out of court without resort to a claim of charitable immunity and without admission of wrongdoing. (The settlements were paid by the university's insurance carrier.) "To their credit, Seton Hall and its insurer have been very fair with the plaintiffs," admitted Raymond Gill, a lawyer for one of the injured.[162] What might have ended badly ended well. The parents of John Giunta settled their wrongful death suit against the university for $207,718 (of which over $62,000 went to lawyers). The family of Frank Caltabilota settled for an undisclosed amount. The parents of Aaron Karol did not file suit, claiming their son loved the university too much for them to take it to court.[163]

The fire decisively rearranged Sheeran's presidency. It was his greatest crisis, and Seton Hall's. Together, they came through. That he was a priest—among dozens of other priests—made an enormous difference to the pastoral sensitivity with which the university handled the tragedy. Students, parents, faculty, and staff were comforted when comfort was most needed, their questions answered honestly, their anxieties never brushed aside, their suggestions given weight. The university was not beyond criticism, but its good faith was never questioned. The fire also changed Sheeran's relationship with the Board of Regents. Until 2000, he had been, in some senses, on probation, a relatively young and untested president full of plans but not yet his own boss. Now he occupied the job more fully, exercising authority without looking over his shoulder, confident in judgment and action, convincing doubters—there had always been a few—that he could be trusted with power in the most challenging and painful of moments. "I . . . can't tell you how impressed I am by you for the great leadership you have provided the university in very difficult and trying times," wrote one alumnus. "You have provided a wonderful example of what a Catholic university is all about—something that is unique and special. You have demonstrated by word and even by more by action, compassion, love, assistance, sincerity, wisdom and faith, to students, parents, faculty and alumni. You have provided strength, courage, determination, and an enduring patience to everyone. Keep up the great work."[164]

More important than these political considerations were the personal consequences of the early morning of January 19, 2000. The fire introduced Seton Hall to people it would never forget. Joe Karol, father of Aaron, revealed a moral grandeur in the days and months after the fire, showing that those with most to forgive are often the most forgiving. Every year, he found words to comfort others as they sought to comfort him. "The individuals who started this fire have hidden for two years," he said in 2002. "But let's not be filled with hate . . . Instead of vengeance or revenge, let's pray for justice."[165] Dana Christmas denied that she had acted heroically, three times refusing to leave the building as she went from door to door waking up students. "Where did that fortitude come from?" asked one firefighter. "She kept going out there to save more students. It's just unbelievable." For weeks afterwards she was unable to speak, a respirator supplying oxygen to her smoke-damaged lungs, her body covered in burns. "I think out of the whole thing, she is number one," said Dan Nugent, her fellow resident assistant. "Hero? She is it."[166] Alvaro Llanos came close to death a month after the fire, only surviving through will power and the love of family and friends. Hani Mansour, director of the Burns Unit of Saint Barnabas Hospital, brought superb skill to the work of healing. These were the faces, seen and unseen, that revealed the real meaning of the fire.

The healing took time, as it always does. Dozens of people and hundreds of families were directly affected by the disaster. Thousands of others indirectly felt its touch. When the smoke cleared, when the investigation was done, when the lawyers all had had their say, one fact remained: Aaron Karol, Frank Caltabilota, and John Giunta had had their lives cruelly snatched away from them. For those who loved them, no gain could compensate for that loss.

Toward Fulfillment

Friends and Benefactors

As any university president must, Sheeran devoted endless hours to raising money. Naturally gregarious, he enjoyed few aspects of his job more than meeting donors, alumni, benefactors, and friends to make the case that, as he liked to say, there is "no mission without a margin." He set a target of $150 million for the Ever Forward sesquicentennial capital campaign, which was met with room to spare. With Jack Shannon borrowed from the School of Business to serve as director of development, then with Joseph Sandman, hired from Notre Dame to take charge of the sesquicentennial campaign, Sheeran placed his office and personality at the disposal of the Ring Building, the headquarters of Seton Hall's development office. Shannon, a big personality, had been a crucial behind the scenes figure over several administrations, his leadership helping to generate a "significant" increase in the endowment.[167] Sheeran also relied on Sandman for "making the ask." But Shannon and Sandman were only as good as the donors themselves and, in this, the story was extraordinary. In the generosity of its benefactors and the variety of their benefactions, Seton Hall entered a different league as its 150th birthday approached. The range of the gifts was as revealing as the gifts themselves. Almost every cause at the university had supporters, many with deep pockets. Sheeran, at the center of a complex choreography of giving and receiving, relished the dance.

The largest gifts captured most attention. Robert and Jean Baldini gave $2.3 million to endow the Center for Catholic Studies. George and Dorothy Ring gave $1 million for the Science and Technology Center (the impressively renovated McNulty Hall). Frank and Mimi Walsh gave $11.5 million for a variety of purposes, notably an athletic endowment in honor of Richie and Sue Regan. Sheeran thought highly of Walsh, who joined the Board of Regents in 1983, becoming chairman of the finance and investment committees in 1993 and the Board itself in 1995. He stepped down from that position in

January 2003 but remained a co-chair of the Ever Forward Capital Campaign.[168] Robert Wussler gave $1 million to name the Hall of Fame and to support the Richie and Sue Regan Athletic Endowment. Kurt and Betsy Borowsky (along with the Pick Foundation) gave $750,000 to establish an endowed scholarship fund for undergraduate students. The Lilly Foundation gave $2 million for the Center for Vocation and Servant Leadership, the largest single corporate grant in the university's history. Charlie and Joan Alberto created the Alberto endowment for Italian Studies and Scholarships with a gift of $1 million. Lawrence Bathgate gave $1 million to endow a scholarship/loan fund for needy undergraduate students. Bruce and Carol Tomason gave $500,000 to support the Tomason Endowed International Scholars. Gerald Buccino gave $1.5 million to fund the Buccino Endowed Scholarships for undergraduate students. Philip and Mary Shannon gave $3 million for the Shannon Speaker Series and for the Shannon Endowed Scholarships for undergraduate students from Southern states.[169] Tom Sharkey, whose chairmanship of the Sesquicentennial Capital Campaign magnificently repaid the debt he felt towards the university,[170] gave $3.6 million for the Sharkey Professorship in the Humanities to direct and support the Honors Program, the Sharkey Visiting Scholar-Diplomat in Diplomacy, the Sharkey Sports Polling Center, the Academic Resource Center (ARC) in the College of Arts and Sciences, and the Richie and Sue Regan Athletic Endowment. "Seton Hall changed my life," he said when joining the Board of Regents in 1995, graduating with a degree in philosophy in 1954, going on to play in the Detroit Tigers organization for between 1955–1958, serving for another two as a private in the U.S. army, gaining professional qualifications as an insurance underwriter, and finally establishing the Meeker Sharkey Financial Group, the third largest privately held financial group in the New York area. "I was raised in an Irish ghetto in Elizabeth. I didn't know very much. They gave me a reason for our faith."[171] With his wife Ruth, he was one of its greatest benefactors.

And so, added to gifts from previous capital campaigns[172] and to the steady stream of federal and state support that came to the university year-on-year, these sesquicentennial sums amounted to major down payments from many people on Seton Hall's next 150 years.

The Ever Forward campaign raised more than $153 million, but that figure tells only a partial story. Of nearly 800 private universities in the country, Seton Hall was second (behind Drexel) in the increased percentage of gift giving between 1997 and 2007. (The figure for Seton Hall was 326 percent.) For every dollar spent in fund-raising, Seton Hall received five dollars in return. (The figures were even stronger for government fund-raising.) More alumni donated to the university, and more generously, than before. Frank Walsh, Kurt Borowsky, Thomas Sharkey, George Ring, Robert Baldini, Patrick Murray,[173] and Jim O'Brien of the Board of Regents provided leadership, but others were equally supportive behind the scenes. Forty-three donors gave separate

gifts of over $1 million each for a total of over $79 million. Sixteen donors gave between $500,000 and $999,999 for a total of nearly $11 million. Over 25,000 people gave
gifts up to a value of $4,999 for a total of over $12.5 million. Sheeran was "the face of
the campaign" and, in the words of Joseph Sandman, "the ideal development president,"[174] but if there is no mission without a margin, so there are no donations without
donors. Sheeran could have done nothing without them.

Finance

The context for the capital campaign was the financial state of the university, and here
the story was complicated. Seton Hall was better off at the end of the 1990s than at the
beginning of the decade and, with a bump or two, it continued its good run into the following century. But there were reasons for caution. Good management and the surging
stock market of the late twentieth and early twenty-first centuries lifted the endowment
and with it the university's willingness to spend. That expenditure included capital
projects such as Walsh Library, Jubilee Hall, and McNulty Hall, and human projects
such as a better paid faculty. Jubilee Hall was built at a cost of $19.5 million. Almost
the same sum, $19,650,000, was realized by selling an office building in Roseland, New
Jersey in 1997. Proceeds from that sale went into the endowment with the exception
of not more than $1.625 million annual income, which was used to offset Law School
debt service. For most of Sheeran's presidency, thanks to external and internal factors,
finances were fairly robust. "Our investment policy is diverse, moderately conservative, and mission driven," said Dennis Garbini, vice president of finance and technology. "It has many different things in it. And we have many checks and balances to
make sure nothing goes wrong." "We have a university that is primarily tuition driven
each year," said economics professor Kristin Kucsma. "Based on that I would not really
suggest a small university like Seton Hall invest too heavily in stocks."[175]

That was wise advice. The university faced a budget crunch in early 2002, with a
shortfall in tuition revenue of $1.7 million as well as the loss of $1 million from the State
of New Jersey. Contributing to the difficulties were increased employee health insurance costs and building a new parking deck. Financial aid was also expensive, up from
$10.6 million in 1997 to $23.5 million in 2002 with no end in sight. As provost, Mel Shay
had spoken of "difficult choices" and "a hard look at all faculty, staff and administrative
positions" to deal with the problem.[176] Toward the end of Sheeran's tenure (beyond the
scope of this volume), the world financial crisis of 2008 shrank endowments on every
campus across the country, in Seton Hall's case wiping more than $100 million from
the university's capital assets. This loss, gradually replenished, was smaller in relative
terms than losses suffered by larger institutions, but it was real money. Conservatively
invested, the endowment yielded an annual income of between 4 and 5 percent. A

diminished principal meant a diminished income for hiring, financial aid, academic scholarships. It also meant that donors, themselves struggling, were less willing to give precisely when gifts would be most welcome. It was providential that the sesquicentennial fell in 2006, not 2008. Then the story might have been different.

Sheeran was able to avoid job losses until his last weeks as president. The foundations were strong. The building was intact. The financial management of a major university with a multimillion-dollar annual budget requires skill, prudence, good nerves, and luck. Mostly, Sheeran enjoyed good fortune, a tribute to the robustness of a university designed to withstand storms not of its own making.

A Campus Renewed

Petillo and Peterson transformed the appearance of Seton Hall, the former not receiving enough credit for it, but Sheeran insisted, even more than they, that the look of the campus was vital to the university's spiritual well-being. He softened the landscape, finding unexpected places for gardens, trees, benches, and shrubs, all of which invited people to sit down, read a book, or simply look around—to enjoy beauty as an expression of the divine. Money thus spent was money well spent, making Seton Hall more attractive and humane. For Sheeran, trees were metaphors for permanence and stability. He was much taken with Thomas Friedman's book *The Lexis and the Olive Tree*, which saw the modern world as both rooted and rootless, caught between tradition and change. Perhaps this explains why, at Seton Hall, trees tended to disappear as quickly as they came, never seeming as rooted as they ought. Still, thanks to the uncomplaining ground staff, the university was groomed as never before, to stunning effect.

Work on Jubilee Hall, originally Kozlowski Hall, began in 1996 and was completed in time for an opening dedication in Fall 1997. Designed by Vladimir Arsene of Westfourth Associates and built on the site of McLaughlin Library, it housed the School of Business, the College of Education and Human Services, and the Center for Public Service, with the graduate department of public administration and the undergraduate department of psychology.[177] Dramatically concave in appearance, it promised to be, thought Bernhard Scholz, "the pre-eminent academic building in the country."[178] The six-story structure provided classrooms and seminar rooms on its first and second floors, a 350-seat auditorium two floors deep for concerts and conferences, a stunning atrium on the fourth floor leading to a loggia overlooking the campus. Other state-of-the art facilities included a real-time Stock Exchange room on the fifth floor. "The generosity and the dedication of Dennis Kozlowski made this building possible," said Father Tom Peterson, acknowledging his $3 million gift. "It will bear his family name and so for many decades, perhaps for centuries to come, his dedication will be known."[179] This was an unfortunate prophecy.[180] The building was renamed Jubilee Hall in August 2005.

With Presidents Hall, Jubilee Hall dominated the center of the campus, adding to the university's classroom space. To the left of the main entrance was a Bell Tower, silver-colored with three gold-colored bells, topped by a crucifix. Dedicated to the victims of the Boland Hall fire, it was donated in honor of her parents by Vice President Mary Meehan. In those bells, Seton Hall's past and present tolled together. The largest of them, the Bayley Bell, bought in 1909, stood for many years between Presidents Hall (then called the Seminary Building) and Alumni Hall. The second, the Wigger Bell, was purchased from the church of St. Venatius in Orange during the episcopate of Bishop Winand Wigger and was housed at Darlington between 1927 and 1984. The third and smallest was the Boland Hall Jubilee Bell.[181]

The W. Paul Stillman School of Business moved to the new building. Its former building, renamed Arts and Sciences Hall, was refurbished for the use of some departments formerly housed in Fahy Hall. In the freed-up space of Fahy Hall, the remaining departments expanded to give faculty separate offices. The removal of the College of Education and Human Services and the department of psychology from McQuaid Hall made room for SODIR and the growing School of Graduate Medical Education. (That McQuaid Hall should have been housed in the School of Diplomacy was an irony not lost on the spirit of Bernard McQuaid, the least diplomatic man to have been president of Seton Hall.) McQuaid and Mooney Halls had periodic brushes with the wrecking ball but were always saved by a guardian angel, generally in the form of anguished alumni.[182] Mooney Hall, a jumble of offices, classrooms, and living quarters for priests, was more attractive to look at than work in. The priests moved out after tougher fire regulations decreed in 2001, but the rest of the building stayed largely untouched. That may not always be the case. Like the man for whom it was named, it was vigorous to begin with, tired and lethargic towards the end.

Built in the 1950s and also beginning to look its age, McNulty Hall was retrofitted in 2007 as a state-of-the-art center for science and mathematics. The cost was defrayed with support from state and federal grants, support from local pharmaceutical companies, and by large gifts, in particular from Board member Robert Baldini.

Finally and most importantly, came Immaculate Conception chapel, Seton Hall's most beloved heritage building.[183] The chapel's history runs in tandem with Seton Hall's. For the College's seventy-fifth anniversary in 1931, the wooden altars were replaced with marble ones. In 1945, it was modernized with the installation of electric lights. In 1963, its hundredth anniversary, the sacristy was renovated and the ceiling beautified. In 1972, the sanctuary was redesigned to meet the needs of contemporary liturgical practice. It was always changing, always staying the same. Some changes, indeed, were simply to keep it the same: it was intermittently closed between 2006 and 2008 for repointing of much weathered stonework, a restoration which saw the replacement of 40 percent of the stone. But it was the interior renovation that was most striking. Reopened in October 2008, the chapel was immediately recognized as Sheeran's most impressive achievement in stone, a metaphor for the rooted but revitalized Catholicism of his presidency. The interior work, taking a gothic revival gem and regothicizing it, was capped by a magnificently finialed altarpiece (designed by Granda of Spain) set off against a restored painting of Our Lady of the Immaculate Conception and a ceiling repainted to suggest the stars of the vault of heaven. Other features included a new organ loft and organ and a sympathetically restored Mother Seton chapel. The altar was the gift of Monsignor Edward Fleming, the tabernacle of Father Peter Lennon. A donation of $1 million from Mrs. Lucia Palestroni was encouraged by Monsignor John Gilchrist.

A Purpose Renewed

And so, as it celebrated its sesquicentennial and looked to another president to build on the efforts of his many predecessors, Seton Hall was larger, better equipped, and more welcoming to students and faculty than any time in its history. Having lasted 150 years, it hoped to last 150 more. Bayley would have struggled to recognize his college of 1856, but the college and the people it served had changed only outwardly in the years between. In its moral and intellectual vision, in its social and economic purpose, in its openness to the Word and the world, it was still, in essence, the place he founded in Madison many lifetimes before.

Seton Hall Sport

A "continuous round of class work" unbroken by the diversion of athletics soon becomes "dull and unprofitable toil."[1] So claimed the Seton Hall yearbook in 1925, echoing a thousand commentators before and since. Plato believed that sport builds character. Milton thought a school should have "an hour and a half . . . for exercise and due rest afterwards."[2] Rousseau held that "if you wish to develop the mind of a pupil . . . exercise his body."[3] Henry Lynch (not quite in the same league as Rousseau: he was a student speaker at the 1907 Seton Hall) commencement) claimed that "courage, patience, self-restraint, [and] serenity"[4] were the virtuous consequences of athletics. Helping students to study or to forget about studying; helping them become better men[5] or better citizens;[6] helping them fill an hour, a day, a life: these were the reasons (along with money, marketing, and morale) that sport has been a central feature of Seton Hall life almost from the beginning. Monsignor John Stafford worried in 1905 that nine out of ten parents were "largely influenced" by the strength and weakness of the athletics department.[7] He could have saved his breath. He was not the first to complain,[8] nor the last, that sport, no matter how good in itself, can distort the values of a school (or a nation). Nothing about sport is simple, not even the score-line. The tidy clarity of victory or defeat conceals a hundred complexities.

Plato, Lynch, and Stafford thought that sport builds character, but they also knew that it reveals it—and frequently the character revealed is institutional. The following chapter is not a comprehensive account of sport at Seton Hall—that would take a book in itself—but an effort, rather, to suggest how some of the school's identity is revealed by its athletic history. For basketball, readers are referred to the excellent work of Professor Alan Delozier, who has made it his special study over many years.[9] For less-known sports, readers may follow the trail provided by the footnotes. For overlooked sports, a general apology for reasons of space is offered.

Early Days

The most obvious fact about sport is that it supposed to be enjoyable. Pleasure comes first:

The Unknowns of Harlem vs. Alerts of Seton Hall College

On Thursday, the 9th of November [1865], the Unknowns visited the Alerts, of South Orange, for the purpose of playing them a friendly game. At the close of the game, which was called on the seventh innings, on account of darkness, all hands marched into the dining-room of the college to partake of an elegant dinner.[10]

So reported *Turf, Field, and Farm* in 1865, one of the first accounts of a sporting event linked to the college. (Baseball was the first intercollegiate sport: Seton Hall defeated Fordham on October 22, 1863 in an away fixture, probably in the Bronx.)[11] "Most American colleges scorned sports," writes S.W. Pope of the post-Civil War era, "but tolerated them since they were run by students and were only unofficially connected to the institutions."[12] Not so Seton Hall, where extracurricular physical activity was regulated (outdoor rambles, for instance) and where away games did not happen without permission. The Alerts were the public face of the school: the authorities were alert to them.

In the nation at large, Harvard, Princeton, and Yale were the schools to watch.[13] By the 1870s, football matches between them drew crowds in the tens of thousands, turning a pastime into a business.[14] Other teams had fans—"the Rose Hills of St. John's College at Fordham, the Jaspers of Manhattan College, and the Alerts, of Seton Hall College, South Orange"[15]—but none of them were in the same league. Seton Hall's results were reported in the New York papers, admittedly in small print, providing easy publicity. One way of becoming well known was to have a winning team. Seton Hall learned that lesson early.

Football

When the American Intercollegiate Football Association (1876) standardized the rules of a game that had been the preserve of a few Eastern universities, it quickly spread beyond the confines of the elite.[16] Seton Hall's first "football" game was rugby, in the form of a loss to Fordham in 1882, a sport that does not seem to have caught on in South Orange except perhaps informally. Instead Seton Hall featured among "minor colleges" of college football in 1886, a category that included the University of Pennsylvania, Swarthmore, Haverford, Amherst, Williams, and the Massachusetts Institute of Technology.[17] Seton Hall beat a team from Montclair 65-0 in November 1886,[18] making up for a one-sided loss (60-0) to Stevens Institute in Hoboken in 1883.[19] Football was important in college life before World War I, the Alerts playing teams whose names have a kind of golden age poetry: the Princeton Freshmen, the Oritani Field Club, the Prospect Athletics, the Palma Club, the Passaic Wheelmen, the Newark Mystics, the Iron Cross of Jersey City. Against Hoboken High School, Seton Hall played football at St. George's Cricket Ground.[20] In the 1880s the Alerts played about three games a season, many more the following decade (thirteen in 1897), often winning by large margins. By 1900, many Americans "acted as if the purpose of a college was to have a football team."[21] By that standard, Seton Hall was such a school.

Reintroduced in 1926, football aimed to restore prewar glory: "Who can tell maybe in a few years Seton Hall will be the Notre Dame of the East . . . Years ago, when football was football, Seton Hall had a team worthy of any in the United States today. The name of Seton Hall instilled fear . . ."[22] These hopes proved fleeting. While Notre Dame took on all comers, Seton Hall grappled with the likes of McChesney Business College (easily beaten in 1899). Football was too expensive for a small school to mount at varsity level. The 1926 season was cancelled for lack of money. In 1927, Tom "Inky" Kearney asked James Carey to manage a side. (This was the future Father Jim Carey, a legendary booster of Seton Hall sport for many years.) Carey's "live wire tactics brought much of the success to the ensuing season." The team[23] "pranced out proudly in their new togs with flaming red jerseys" and beat Newark Academy and St. John's Brooklyn, drew with St. Peter's, Jersey City, lost to Fordham, and were crushed by New York Military Academy.[24] The 1928 season was a flop, with four games and one victory,[25] and 1929 a nonstarter. In 1930, football was "embryonic"[26] at Seton Hall, a varsity squad, the first in twenty-five years, losing 21-0 to Manhattan College in October.[27] Bryan "Bud" Conlon captained the side between 1930 and 1933,[28] after which it was dropped. Efforts to resuscitate it in 1949 came to nothing.[29]

Football returned to Seton Hall as an intervarsity sport in 1973 when the Pirates played in Division III. Bleeding money (the program lost $75,000 a year), the university dropped football in June 1977, reinstating it after protests but finally dropping it in 1982 due to "inadequate facilities, decreased attention, and lack of support."[30] Seton Hall's small, crowded campus, with little room to park, let alone to play, was, literally, not in the same league as Notre Dame or Army and Navy.

Baseball I

Baseball, not football, was Seton Hall's sport. "So long as it remains our national game, America will abide no monarchy, and anarchy will be slow," wrote a journalist in 1907.[31] Bringing these republican virtues to Seton Hall was "Jack" Fish, who captained and coached the "all-conquering" baseball team of 1915–1916, which included the Shannon twins, Joe Peploski, Billy Gilmore, and George English. Ten of the squad went on to play in the major leagues.[32] Earlier Seton Hall stars included Billy Burke, who played for the Boston Red Sox (1910–1911) and John "Cy" Ferry for the Pittsburgh Pirates (1910–1913).[33] Fish was a star on and off the field, his wartime service in France including managing the American Expeditionary Forces baseball club and representing the

U.S. Army in the inter-ally game in Paris.[34] He also played for Connie Mack's Phila-delphia Athletics.[35] Fish was appointed Seton Hall's athletics director in 1925, making an impact. "Recently I visited Seton Hall College in search of a 1915 classmate, Jack Fish," wrote George Henderson, an alumnus. "I was amazed when I saw the athletics activities. Quoits and tennis tournaments were in progress; track men were training; baseball and football candidates were out in uniform. It is evident that in the coming year big strides will be made."[36]

Baseball was "probably the most important sport" on campus,[37] building college spirit in all the usual ways. "Come on out fellows and get your teams lined up," urged *The Setonian* in 1924.[38] In 1925 Father John McClary organized a competition to iden-tify players good enough to compete at varsity level, and from these games, stars emerged.[39] Mostly, the idea was to have fun.

The memory of the "all-conquering side" of 1915–1916 lingered well into the 1920s, when the stars were Neal Nolan (a "clever back stop [and] good hitter"), Mike Hornak, Les Fries (also a basketball player), Jack Outwater, and Milt Fellers. The squad totaled twenty men, including four pitchers, three catchers, eight infielders, and five outfield-ers. Fellers, good enough to be scouted by the National League, captained the side in 1925.[40] Outwater was one of the best college pitchers in the East.[41] The manager was Bill Buckley.[42] Joe Kaiser, a fine pitcher and "demon third baseman," also batted, *The Setonian* acclaiming him "a second Babe Ruth."[43]

The 1928 team saw the debut of receiver Eddie Madjeski, who went on to play major league baseball between 1932 and 1937, starting for the Philadelphia Athletics, the Chicago White Sox, and the New York Giants. Madjeski was also a good basket-baller, possessed of an "uncanny faculty of sensing and intercepting or breaking up enemy passes." [44] With National League star Al Mamaux appointed coach in 1937, base-ball program continued to attract fine players. Coaching the Pirates from 1937 until 1942, Mamaux was inducted into the International League Hall of Fame in 1951.

Basketball I

Basketball was the brainchild of James Naismith of Springfield, Massachusetts, a lead-ing figure in the Muscular Christianity movement, who invented the game in 1891 as a way of keeping summer athletes fit during the off-season. "Basketball strikes a happy medium," said *The Crimson* (the yearbook of Transylvania University in Ken-tucky). "There is no game in which one can display more science and at the same time be in such need of his head and muscles."[45] Popular thanks to the YMCA, it was the cheap, versatile, playable-almost-anywhere sport of urban middle classes. Progressives especially liked it because it was a useful way of Americanizing immigrants through extracurricular activities.[46] The first college to play basketball was Vanderbilt, who beat Nashville YMCA 9-6 in 1893.

Seton Hall took to it early. The first outing was on December 9, 1903, when the college tied the Mohawks of Newark 15-15. On December 19, 1903, a team beat Brooklyn High School 28-18. Seton Hall then disappeared as a basketball force until 1908 when it began a stretch of ten straight winning seasons. The program was discontinued in 1918–1919 but by the early 1920s the college was making a name for itself: "Seton Hall always starts the basketball season with high hopes and splendid morale, for they know that they have, in Frank Hill, one of the best, if not the best, basketball coach in the East . . . He is intensely devoted to Seton Hall and all Setonians have confidence in him."[47]

Helping Hill was manager Tom Reilly, and together they made Seton Hall a regional force. That said, basketball was always more occasional pleasure than organized obsession.[48] The games were friendly, if edgy. Half of the pleasure came from listening to Hill's barked instructions from the bench. ("You big string-bean, you ought to be able to make that basket easier than any other member of the team.")[49]

Athletes were, literally, big men on campus, with nicknames worthy of an Edwin O'Connor novel: "Stretch" Meehan (also known as "Daddy-Long-Legs");[50] 6' 4" "Sticks" Henaby;[51] "Captain Jack" Outwater (who was actually rather stocky); "Ace" Murphy; "Bucky" Donnelly; "Bags" Griffin;[52] "Mussy" Heron; "Steamer" Flanagan; "Bip" O'Connor;[53] "Red" Clarkin and "Inky" Kearney (baseball players);[54] and Red Reilly (a footballer).[55] Outwater, capable of "sensational" shooting,[56] was the star of a basketball team that included "Big Pat" Reynolds (who displayed "brilliant floor work"), Joe Colrick, an effective blocker; Willie Hornak; and Jim Phelan,[57] a clever center.[58] Exponents of Hill's go-give-take system,[59] the team had run of victories in the 1924–1925 season, defeating Lafayette, the New York Aggies, and New York State Teachers College. Outwater, one of Seton Hall's greatest athletes,[60] became a priest. Killed in a car accident in 1936 aged thirty-two, he was elected to the Seton Hall Athletic Hall of Fame in 1976.

Basketball was a proxy for other pleasures, not least the joy of beating socially elite schools. "Setonian Terrier Routs the Yale Bulldog," ran a headline of 1926. "Consistent good playing intermingled with shots by Jack Outwater gave the Yale quintet the heebie-jeebies . . ."[61] The game was broadcast on WBPI New York radio. "Be a Catholic gentleman in all places and under all circumstances," Hill told the team in 1927. "Win if you can; but to reflect the teaching of your Alma Mater is your duty."[62] Dominated by Outwater and Hornack, the 1927 squad showed speed, swift passing, and accurate shooting.[63] The 1928 team under Raymond Nelligan played thirteen, won nine, and lost four.[64] Under Sal Basile in 1928, they played twenty-two games and won twelve.[65]

It was not until John "Honey" Russell entered the scene in 1936 that Seton Hall and basketball became interchangeable. A graduate of the Savage School of Health Education in New York, Russell enjoyed a professional career that lasted from 1919 to 1945, lining up for the New York Celtics, the Cleveland Rosenblums, the Chicago Bruins, the Rochester Centrals, and the New York Jewels, also playing football for the Chicago Bears and the Cardinals.[66] "Russell was the most honest man I ever met," said Monsignor James Kelley. "He never yelled at a referee and was respected by everyone."[67] In terms of wins, he was the most successful basketball coach in Seton Hall history.

At Seton Hall, Russell had outstanding local talent to draw upon.[68] In 1939–1940 he coached the college to its first unbeaten basketball season (19-0), leaving the best to last when, against the University of Scranton, Bernie Coyle, Pete Finnerty, and Harry Purcell played a game which "for devastating beauty" was "the nearest thing to perfection imaginable."[69]

The leading player of the 1938–1939 season (22-15) was Ed Sadowski, the "Akron Rubber Man," named in 1939 the East's outstanding center by leading sportswriters and officials of the metropolitan area.[70] Against strong opposition in 1942[71] the team registered sixteen wins in a nineteen-game season, "[dazzling] the crowds with their spectacular brand of basketball."[72]

Seton Hall gained its Pirate nickname under Russell. In 1931 a local sportswriter noted that the baseball team, aggressively stealing bases, had played like a gang of pirates against the "crusaders" of Holy Cross College, Worcester, Massachusetts. The moniker stuck.[73] *The White and Blue* yearbook became *The Galleon* in 1939.[74] Russell was the "commander" under whom "the swash-buckling sailors from South Orange sailed forth." Winning nights saw "fierce hand-to-hand engagement." Losing nights were "rough water." Sadowski, on a "campaign of pillage and plunder" was "the boldest Buccaneer of all." St. Peter's College in Jersey City, "our meek little cousins," were made to "walk the plank" when they lost.[75] The only thing missing (although not for long) were eye-patches.

Track and Field

Other than a strong running squad in the first decade of the twentieth century, track and field was unimportant at Seton Hall. However, under Jack Fish and Coach Harry Coates, a member of the relay team of 1906, the program took off. Coates's philosophy was "make haste slowly," not the most promising motto for an athlete.[76] Among standout recruits were Mel Dalton, a fine distance runner, and Addison Clohosey, a good miler.[77] In Dalton, Coates found a brilliant captain and a runner good enough to represent his country in cross-country track in the Olympic Games of 1928. Coming second in the fastest heat to Finnish champion Ville Ritola and only just missing a medal in the final, Dalton was one of the best track athletes Seton Hall ever produced.[78]

In 1940, the indoor track team won the New Jersey AAU championships against strong opposition, clocking record timings in the one-, two-, and half-mile relays. Carmen Bova and Leroy Schwartzkopf ran the mile, with Frank Fletcher and Chet Lipski running the 1,000 meters. Frank Ward, Bob Duffy, Joe Fries, and Jim Hartner won the relay. Joe Matyunas and Lou Collado were strong at 600 yards.[79]

Under Coates, Seton Hall track and field was powerful, but under Johnny Gibson, his postwar successor, the sport entered an era of greatness.[80] A 1927 Fordham graduate and a member of the 1928 U.S. Olympic team, Gibson was a former world record holder in the 400-meter hurdles. Seton Hall's finest track and field stars, athletes of the caliber of Andy Stanfield, Frank Fox, Phil Thigpen, Harry Bright, Bob Carter, and George and Herb Gehrmann, got their start under him. In Stanfield, Seton Hall could boast (and often did) of having "the world's fastest human."[81] Gibson himself was lively and lovable. At various times, he trained army special coaches in Germany, sold life and auto insurance and Japanese silk, and kept track of material for the Manhattan Project. He also lived to the age of 101.[82]

The 1947–1948 season saw victories over Villanova, Fordham, Rutgers, and Princeton and success in Boston with an intercollegiate record in the mile relay. Phil Thigpen, one of the best runners in the country,[83] declined offers from Yale and UCLA to stay at Seton Hall.[84] He won the 1,000 yard national championship in 1949 and 1950, the second when Seton Hall defeated Yale, Army, and Manhattan in the Intercollegiate Amateur Athletic Association of America (IC4A) Championships, finishing one point behind eventual victors Michigan State. The "crack quartet" of Slade, Turner, Bright, and Carter[85] won the mile relay national championship in 1950.[86] Before graduating, Thigpen brought four intercollegiate and national AAU titles to the university.[87]

Stanfield's record was unparalleled, totaling six Amateur Athletic Union titles and nine IC4A awards. (He was also Irish one hundred-yard champion in 1949,[88] and Norwegian champion at 200 meters.[89]) Already world record holder at 200 meters, he won two Olympic gold medals in the Helsinki games of 1952, one in the 200 meters and another in the 4x100 meters relay. In the 200 meters, he equaled Jesse Owens's Olympic record of 0:20:7. Stanfield went on to win Olympic silver in the 200 meters at the 1956 Melbourne games. Seton Hall's greatest track and field athlete, he was inducted into the Hall of Fame in 1973. In later life he enjoyed a distinguished career in public service.[90]

Stanfield was not the only Seton Hall star to compete in the 1952 Olympics. His academically gifted teammate Morris Curotta was also "up there with the best,"[91] running in the 100 meters, the 400 meters, and the 4x100 meters (as he had in the same events in London four years before). Curotta, a native of Sydney, ran for Australia.

Although not among the medals, he was "the fastest white man in the world" in 1948 when he ran against Arthur Wint, Herb McKenley, and Malvin Whitfield in front of 100,000 people at Wembley Stadium.

In 1946, Seton Hall joined the National College Athletic Association, the Intercollegiate Association of Amateur Athletics of America (the IC4A), and the Metropolitan Intercollegiate Athletic Association. The college now ranked with Rutgers and Princeton as one of only three New Jersey schools in the NCAA.[92] The IC4A, founded in Saratoga in 1876, declined in significance as the NCAA grew, but for many years it was the leading force in college sport, especially in the northeast. Its annual March meeting at Madison Square Garden was a season highlight.

Track and Field in the Modern Era

Stanfield and Curotta set standards that few in world, let alone college athletics, could match. The talented teams of the later 1950s were strong but never in the same league. In 1956, Seton Hall won the New Jersey AAU championships against a powerful field,[93] repeating the feat in 1957 with solid performances from Bob Carter, Jack Kushner, Bob Kasko, and Bill Zylka.[94] Ken Brown was the fastest college runner over sixty yards in the metropolitan area. The team ended the 1958 season by competing against twenty-five squads in the IC4A championships in New York, finishing third from last with a point total of 517.[95] Against regional competition they did better, in 1960 defeating the University of Pennsylvania, Princeton, Georgetown, Holy Cross, and Boston College, losing only to New York University.[96] In 1963, a Seton Hall squad consisting of Kevin Hennessey, Ed Wyrich, Tom Tushington, and George Germann won the two-mile relay at the American National Championships, clocking a record time of 7:3.[97] (Two weeks later, the same squad trounced Fordham, Georgetown, Manhattan College, and Villanova at the IC4A championships at Madison Square Garden.)[98] Germann represented the United States against the Soviet Union at a meet in Kiev in 1965, where he pulled off a surprise victory in the 800 meters final. His winning time of 1:46:8 was a career best, the second fastest time in the world that year.[99]

Now coached by John Moon, the track team won gold in the Millrose Games at Madison Square Garden in 1971, besting strong opposition to win the one-mile relay.[100] Ron Zapoticzny, John Weiss, Rich Rosa, and Al Hampton were solid performers in an otherwise disappointing season. In 1975, the "Moonmen" won the one-mile relay, setting a new Millrose record, defeating Manhattan College to take the Metropolitan championships.[101] They repeated the feat in 1977.[102] Lack of facilities made 1978 a disastrous recruiting year,[103] but 1979 was stronger,[104] the mile relay team continuing to be a major force.[105] The year 1980–1981 was another record-breaker,[106] with disappointment in the Millrose Games[107] followed by triumph as Big East champions two weeks later.[108]

Seton Hall came fourth out of 105 schools in the IC4A championships in March.[109] The season was capped when the one-mile relayers became NCAA champions in Detroit, Michigan[110] and Moon was named Big East Coach of the Year.[111]

Despite injuries, the "Moonmen" came second in the Big East championship in 1982, losing to Connecticut by two points (122-120).[112] They had a disappointing season in 1983[113] and an outstanding one in 1984, with Moses Ugbisie, Patrick Nwanguzo, Andrew Valmon, and Tracy Baskin breaking the freshman world indoor mile relay record at the Bud Light Invitational in Boston in February.[114] A week later, the squad won the Big East Indoor Track and Field Championships at Syracuse, edging long-time rivals Villanova by 106-104. Coming fifth the following season, they were comprehensively dethroned[115] but win, lose, or draw, Moon was an enthusiast. "We were last," he said, after one disappointing showing, "but we were a comparative last."[116] Indeed.

In fact, under Moon Seton Hall's runners were frequently first, even carrying off the 4x880 meters world record in December 1984.[117] Track and field was a consistent nursery of international stars. Alfred Daley had sprinted for Jamaica in 1972 and 1976. Calvin Dill and Charles Joseph ran in the 4x100 meters relay in Montreal in 1976 for Bermuda and Trinidad and Tobago respectively. Tommie Nnakwe represented Nigeria in Los Angeles in 1984. Michael Paul represented Trinidad and Tobago, also in 1984. Washington Njiri ran in the 1988 Olympics for Uganda. Benn Fields would have represented the United States in the high jump at the 1980 Moscow Olympics had it not been for the boycott of the games. Moses Ugbisie was a two-time Olympian, representing Nigeria in the Los Angeles games in 1984 and in Seoul in 1988. Andrew Valmon was also a double Olympian, representing the United States in 1988 and 1992 (winning gold in the 4x400 meters relay) and was head coach for the U.S. track and field squad in London in 2012. Tracy Baskin ran in the men's 800 meters in 1988.

Into the 1990s, the "Moonmen"—and "Moonwomen"—continued to thrive. In 1992, the cross-country five milers won the Metropolitan championships in the Bronx for the first time in twenty-five years.[118] At home, track and field men and women were even stronger.[119] (Among the women, Flirtisha Harris, Shana Williams, Julia Sandiford, and Natasha Reynolds were especially strong.[120]) In 1993, the team captured the Big East Conference title 119-118, besting Georgetown in the final race of the meet.[121] Seton Hall's women won both the Big East title and the East Coast Athletic Conference (ECAC) outdoor championships in May[122] (and retained the title the following year when they also won the ECAC championship and came third at the NCAA championships in Indiana).[123] The men also performed strongly in 1994.[124] According to Georgetown coach Bob Gagliano in 1995, Seton Hall's track and field team were the "greatest competitors" he had seen in thirty-five years.[125] In 1998, the women won the New York Metropolitan title.[126]

Soccer

Soccer started at Seton Hall in 1928 under conditions of extreme scarcity: in 1929 the only equipment the team had was the ball.[127] In 1938 a game against Panzer College (a physical education school) was abandoned when Seton Hall refused to play overtime. (A "termination of relationships in soccer" with Panzer followed.)[128] In 1940–1941, the squad never won a match but "at no time were they defeated by large scores."[129] Next year, also a losing season, they were "never overwhelmed."

Understanding soccer is simple (with the exception of the baffling offside rule), but most Americans struggled to enjoy a sport in which a scoreless draw can be hailed as "artistry."[130] After the war, though, thanks mainly to Bill Sheppell, Seton Hall soccer took off. In 1949, Sheppell became Seton Hall's first All-American soccer player, joined the following year by Jim Hanna. Sheppell played for the United States between 1949 and 1954, starting for the team that qualified for the FIFA World Cup in 1950. Under him, the Pirates were unbeaten in twelve outings in 1951.[131] Under Hanna in 1952, they played five, winning four.[132]

In 1955, Seton Hall was reduced to starting with two men, Rudy Katzenberger and Mike Sheppard, who had never played the game before. Under Coach Bill Garry, Katzenberger and Sheppard mastered the basics but the team posted a 0-9-1 record,[133] the poorest season ever recorded by a Seton Hall side.[134] In 1957 the team won eight, drew one, and lost one,[135] but the following season was dismal, with coach Nick Menza leading a squad that lost seven, drew one, and won one.[136] The 1959 season (4-6) was mediocre, Rider College and Fairleigh Dickinson providing the stiffest competition.[137] It took the rest of the world to show Seton Hall how to play the world's game. Zachary Yamba came from Ghana in the early 1960s to score a record twenty-three goals in a season (1964). He was enrolled in the Hall of Fame in 1980.[138] After graduating, Yamba could have returned to a political career in Ghana but opted to remain in the United States as a college president, finally serving on Seton Hall's Board of Regents.

Menza's twenty-seven-year run as coach had more downs than ups. "Most opposition that confronted the Pirates probably marked a 'W' on their record before the match even began."[139] Irishman Ed Kelly took over in 1985. A professional in the North American league, Kelly imported Brian Hammond and Ally Smith from Ireland to add depth to the squad,[140] Dubliner Patrick Hughes another recruit.[141] In 1986 the Pirates defeated Syracuse University 3-2 to win the Big East tournament for the first time.[142] In the middle 1980s, men's soccer "could barely field a team."[143] With the help of imported Irish talent, it was among the top ten teams of the NCAA. In the end, there was no mystery to soccer. As coach Manny Schellscheidt reminded players, the ball was round and their job was to keep it rolling.[144] They rolled it all the way to the Big East title in 1990.[145] In 1992, the team was ranked fifteenth in the nation.[146]

Fencing

Few sports brought Seton Hall greater renown in the middle of the twentieth century than fencing. Before the opening of the new gymnasium in 1940, the appointment as coach of Dr. Gerald Cetrulo was a boost to a sport in which Seton Hall excelled.[147] (If any side merited the "pirate" nickname, it was this one.) Cetrulo captained the Dartmouth University team, was winner of the national championship in 1930, and was a member of three Olympic squads. His brother Diaz "Dean" Cetrulo, Olympic bronze winner in 1948, was the finest swordsman Seton Hall ever produced.[148] With an almost unbeaten record as coach at high school level,[149] Gerald Cetrulo coached a Seton Hall team able to take on all comers.[150] Away from the gym, he was a surgeon.

Under Cetrulo, the "Setonia Stabbers" won the Eastern Collegiate championship in foil, saber, and epée three years in a row and were East-West titleholders in 1939. In 1940 they compiled a perfect record of forty-six consecutive wins, with Dean Cetrulo recording 110 wins and one loss.[151] Seton Hall regularly defeated Brown, North Carolina, Syracuse, Lafayette, Dartmouth, and Harvard, the standouts being Dean Cetrulo, Paul Riccardi, Larry Hedges, Ed Lansing, Paul Brienza, Pete Milone, and Ed Girardot.[152] The team was undefeated in 1942, taking fifty-three out of fifty-four points in the Eastern Collegiate Championships.[153]

World War II ended fencing at Seton Hall and the sport only revived when Harry Boutsikaris, a member of the championship teams of the early 1940s, took charge in 1960.[154] The first season was disappointing (two wins, nine losses)[155] but in 1963 a squad of Jack Felice, Don Bowie, and Ted Heller won nine and lost two.[156] A few quiet seasons were followed in 1969 by an impressive 9-3 record, Ron Skopak (25-3) on epée leading the way. The 1971 saw a 7-3 record against strong opposition, Jacob Hayward, Larry Brown, and Frank Stefanelli the top performers,[157] with only Hayward having fenced before coming to Seton Hall.[158] Captained by Dave Kelly and Allen Adler, the swordsmen had an undefeated 10-0 season in 1972, the first Seton Hall team in thirty years to record that feat, carrying off the North Atlantic Intercollegiate Fencing Championship at Pace University.[159] Seton Hall ended the 1972 season ranked eighteenth in the nation.[160]

A second North Atlantic championship came in 1973,[161] and the streak of twenty-two straight victories continued until January 1974, when the team finally lost to Rutgers.[162] Seton Hall won the North Atlantic championship in 1974, mustering a total of forty-four points to edge out Johns Hopkins by two.[163] In 1976, it took a very strong Rutgers team to end a twenty-seven-match winning streak.[164]

Victory[165] and disappointment[166] continued for another decade. Fencing lost its luster not for lack of fencers but for lack of interest. In 1983, the local powerhouses were Rutgers and William Paterson College, Seton Hall only able to mount a team if one or two students showed curiosity.[167] In 1984, *The Setonian* called fencing "an obscure, non-publicized sport around the country, especially at Seton Hall,"[168] unaware of its illustrious history at the university. Derrick Hoff, Seton Hall's outstanding fencer of the 1980s compiling a 109-10 record over four years, complained that fencing was "definitely unnoticed and underrated." In 1985, the team came eighth out of ten in the North Atlantic championships at Penn State.[169] (The women fencers, despite high morale, lost every outing in 1985.)[170] Although fencing made a strong recovery in 1988,[171] the glory days of the Cetrulos were a memory, perhaps not even that.

Golf

For years, golf was a minority interest at Seton Hall. A foursome in 1939 consisting of Jim Liddy, George Harhen, Phil Madden, and Dick Hildbrand recorded one victory and six defeats, a decent effort given that coach Jack Reitemeier struggled to find practice courses for them.[172] Bud Geohegan became coach after the war and turned Seton Hall into one of the best teams in the East, running up a string of twenty-four victories between 1948 and 1950,[173] a streak not matched until 1968 when the university beat Rider, Villanova, and Fordham and compiled an overall 7-1 record.[174] Under Nick Menza, the team posted a respectable 6-4 season in 1973, with strong showings by John Scranton, Kevin McGrain, Roger Race, and Mike Clifford.[175] In 1975, diminished by illness, the team had a 6-5 season. But success tended to be defined as degrees of failure. Not until 1992 did Seton Hall win the Big East in golf.[176] In 1996, Mike Costigan won the Big East individual title.[177]

Swimming

The appointment in 1940 of Bill Feriden as swimming coach showed that Seton Hall, with its new pool, intended to take the sport seriously.[178] Ferinden's best swimmers were Jim Sullivan and Vic Peccarelli in freestyle, Al Gallo in diving, and Joe Dougherty in backstroke.[179] The outstanding swimmer of 1941 was Robert "Red" Donnelly.[180] In 1942, the team could defeat stronger squads,[181] but swimming was dropped in 1943, a casualty of war, returning in 1946. In 1950, the "tankmen" won the Eastern Collegiate championship, closing a season in which they outswam Rutgers, Princeton, Penn State, and Catholic University, losing only to La Salle.[182] Top performers were George Carr, Aaron Kurtzman, and Charles Hammell.

Swimming again disappeared for five years, returning in 1955 under Harry McGarrigle. The team lost to Villanova, Adelphi, and LIU, but pulled off a victory against St. Peter's, Jersey City.[183] The 1959–1960 season was a "mild success," a generous way of describing eight outings and one victory. "Is it not better to have swum and lost than never to have swum at all?"[184] *The Galleon* yearbook asked, to which the answer was, "probably not."

Tennis

"If Setonia has a tennis team it will be a good one for there is a galaxy of stars who only wait the word to bring new glory to Alma Mater."[185] This optimistic assessment came in 1926. Boosted by the construction of two new courts and the repair of old ones in 1925, the college produced decent players (the 1925 champion was Harold Brown with a "cannonball service").[186] But tennis proved unappealing to most students as players or spectators well into the 1930s. The best players were Matty O'Brien, Ray Miles, and Denny Buttimore, but "with track, basketball, and baseball successively holding the sportlight [sic] . . . recognition [for tennis] was almost nil."[187] The new gymnasium gave tennis a boost. Coached by Hank Quinn, the team won four matches in 1942, losing two. The highlight of the season was a set of exhibition matches featuring Don Budge, Bobby Riggs, Frank Kovacs, and Fred Perry.[188]

Baseball II

As we have seen, Albert Mamaux took charge of baseball in 1937, coaching the squad to nineteen victories and thirteen narrow losses in his first two seasons. Under Frank Spatuzzi, a three-year veteran of the squad, the 1940 team was one of the strongest of the era.[189] Mamaux saw his role in careerist terms: "The opportunities in baseball are greater today than ever before in this field of business . . . A young man of college breed or ability can command a salary of $10,000 or more in a year or two after graduation . . . Let me emphasize that you receive your degree first that you may have something to rely on after your baseball days . . ."[190] He was right both in confidence and caution. He was also right to professionalize Seton Hall baseball in other ways, introducing helmets in 1941, for instance, to make the game better and safer.[191]

After Mamaux, Owen Carroll was appointed coach in 1948 to replace Bob Davies. Carroll dominated postwar Seton Hall baseball, coaching the Pirates until 1972 and compiling a winning record in twenty-one of those twenty-five years, his low-key manner endearing him to generations of players and administrators. After his death Monsignor Tom Fahy—a shrewd judge—remembered him as the greatest gentleman he ever met in athletics.[192]

The other great figure of Seton Hall baseball was Mike Sheppard ("Shep"), coach from 1973 until his retirement in 2003 just two victories shy of a career total of 1,000 wins. (The final tally was 998-540-11.) Between 1973 and 1979, he led the squad to six NCAA tournaments and two College World Series (in 1974 and 1975). The Pirates made it to the NCAA tournament three times in the 1980s (1982, 1984, and 1987), losing to Maine in the 1984 Northeast regional final. Joining the Big East conference in 1985, the baseball squad won the South Division five times in its first six years, also winning the Big East tournament in 1987. Although the Pirates did not qualify for the NCAA in the 1990s, they won the conference championship in 1990. Their best year came when they compiled a 38-16 record in 1995. In 2000, they went 40-18; in 2002, 25-28; in 2003, Shep's last year, 23-24.

Sheppard's program produced outstanding players. Rick Cerone went on to play for the New York Yankees after smashing almost every Seton Hall record: most RBIs in a season (sixty-four), most home runs in a season (fifteen), highest slugging percentage (.765).[193] Sheppard considered Cerone "the biggest thing we ever had here at Seton Hall."[194] Cerone himself was modest. "It still doesn't dawn on me that I'm a Yankee," he said. "I still see myself as a Seton Hall Pirate."[195] Other greats included Charlie Puleo, who played for the New York Mets, the Cincinnati Reds, and the Atlanta Braves. "If you play hard at Seton Hall, the coaches will like you," Puleo said of Sheppard. "They were hard players and they want you to play hard to win."[196] Puleo's pitching record at Seton Hall was 21-7, 8-1 in his final year.[197]

Standout players of the 1980s included Mo Vaughn (named Big East Athlete of the Decade in 1989),[198] who went on to play for the Boston Red Sox, the Anaheim Angels, and the New York Mets; Dan Morogiello, who started for the Baltimore Orioles in 1983; Craig Biggio, who played for the Houston Astros from 1988 to 2003 and was inducted into the Baseball Hall of Fame in 2015; John Morris, who played for the St. Louis Cardinals (1986–1990) and the Philadelphia Phillies (1990–1992); and John Valentin, who played for the Boston Red Sox and the New York Mets. In addition, Phil Cundari represented Italy in exhibition baseball in the 1984 Los Angeles Olympics.[199] The 1990s stars included Jason Grilli, who once struck out eighteen batters in a game, a Big East record, and who went on to play for the Florida Marlins, the Chicago White Sox, and the Detroit Tigers; Mike Moriarty, who played for the Baltimore Orioles; and Matt Morris, who pitched for the St. Louis Cardinals, the San Francisco Giants, and the Pittsburgh Pirates.

Citing reasons of health, Sheppard stepped down in 2003 following criticism of his coaching style from some former players.[200] The manner of his departure caused ill feeling, but a decade later, Sheppard was "still a man who makes grown men stop in their tracks and willingly bow in his presence."[201]

Women and Sport

The arrival of women on the South Orange campus in 1968 transformed the culture of the university. Four years later, when Title IX of the United States Education Amendment Act (1972) outlawed discrimination "on the basis of sex" in "any education or program or activity receiving federal financial assistance," the culture of universities, including sport, across the nation was also transformed. To begin with, "girls" were restricted to use of the gym for two hours a week, confining themselves to archery, badminton, softball, "slimnastics [sic] and golf."[202] Ten percent of women wanted to participate in some kind of sport[203] and 125 of them petitioned the administration to that effect.[204] A "Girls Athletics Program" was announced in October 1969 consisting of basketball, swimming, fencing, and tennis ("if the courts are available"), with the possibility of karate and softball.

Fencing was the first varsity-level female sport at Seton Hall.[205] Managed by Mary Scusi and led by Diane Cree, the women competed (not very successfully) against the best teams in the east. By the mid-1970s they had parried their way to respectability[206] and by 1978 their competitiveness was plain.[207] By the early 1980s they outperformed the male fencers[208] (who remained strong).[209]

If Pirates were Buccaneers or "Bucs," so women were "Bucettes." (Female fencers were "Swashbucettes.")[210] Coached by Laura Menza, the basketball team debuted in February 1972 against Caldwell College, losing 42-21 in a dismal opener.[211] Defeats against St. Peter's and Newark State continued the poor run, but victories against Ramapo, Georgian Court, Upsala, and Drew closed out the season 4-3. Maureen Keenan was the speedy play-maker captain, Eileen O'Rourke, at 5-9, the most daunting physical presence, and other players included Dawn Cooper, Rhoda Champ, and Liz Fahy.

Women's basketball was granted varsity status in 1973, with Sue Dilley coming from a winning program at the University of Wisconsin Madison to take charge. Helped by center Kathy Keating, Dilley coached the side to a 5-2 record for the season.

Tennis debuted as a varsity sport for women in 1974, with Robin Cunningham and Eileen Lam giving depth to the squad.[212] (Cunningham was also an outstanding basketball player, the first to win score 1,000 points in a college career, which she did in the last game of her senior year.)[213] Women tennis players ended the 1980 season with twelve victories and four defeats, their eighth successive winning season.[214] In 1982, they won the state championship with Peggy Pauli and Peggy Savage the outstanding performers.[215] They also made it to the Big East championships, placing seventh against strong competition.[216] In 1982, the women enjoyed an undefeated season,[217] much of the success due to coach Sue Patton who, in eight seasons to 1983, compiled a 80-21 record.[218] In 1992–1993, they enjoyed an eighteen-month, twenty-five-match unbroken streak, placing second in the Big East.[219]

In basketball, an improving defense and the "consistent, aggressive thrusts" of Robin Cunningham and Kathy Pund allowed the Bucettes to record one-sided victories over modest opposition in 1975.[220] Against stronger sides they struggled, coming seventh in the AIAW Small College tournament in Colorado in March 1975.[221] In 1976, they enjoyed an 11-5 season and made it to the second round of the AIAW championships, defeating Texas Wesleyan before falling to eventual champions, South Carolina State.[222] In 1979, they posted a 26-8 record.[223] The squad's sharpest player was Leslie Chavies, who joined the New Jersey Gems after leaving Seton Hall.[224] In 1980–1981, Dilley coached the squad to a 25-5 season. In 1984 she chalked up her 200th win in the same game that Leslie Fairbanks scored her 1,000th point.[225] In 1985, the team compiled a poor 4-25 record (the worst in its history) but made it to the second round of the Big East postseason tournament.[226] In 1986, they went 5-25 and were knocked out in the first round of the postseason competition.[227] In 1989, coached by Phyllis Mangina, the squad traveled to Amsterdam for its first international tournament, taking on teams from Holland, Czechoslovakia, and Poland.[228] In 1990, they placed third in the Big East.[229]

In November 1976, Dilley became assistant athletics director, coordinating intramural sport for women.[230] She expanded the program in 1978, adding swimming and volleyball.[231] By 1986, the swimmers were performing well against strong opposition.[232]

Track was added in 1979,[233] the program not a large as Rutgers' or Princeton's but comparable to most state schools.[234] In 1981, the women's volleyball team became Division II state champions.[235] By the late 1980s and early 1990s the squad was posting impressive performances at eastern collegiate level,[236] enjoying a spectacular season (31-4) in 1994.[237] Yet for a long time, facilities had been rudimentary.[238] Women did well at Seton Hall, sometimes despite, not because of, the university.

Twenty years after Title IX, the NCAA released a gender equity report showing that severe disparities still existed nationally between men's and women's sports, with men making up nearly 70 percent of the athletes who played top-level college sport and women receiving less than a third of all collegiate sports scholarships. Other disparities included budget allocations made by universities to their male and female athletics programs and salaries paid to coaches, the gap in the latter startling. The findings prompted a similar survey at Seton Hall, which found certain disparities in programs that, in the case of men, had had a hundred-year head start on women. It also found goodwill and a relatively modest gap to be made up before the university would be in full compliance with NCAA and federal regulations. Sue Regan (formerly Dilley) pointed to "tremendous strides" already made, acknowledging university chancellor Father Tom Peterson's "great support" for the women's athletics.[239] "You can't expect things to happen overnight," she said. Complete parity, in any case, was not required. (The NCAA allowed 5 percent leeway on either side.) By 1996, 54 percent of Seton Hall's athletics budget went to male programs.[240]

Basketball II

A casualty of war, basketball returned in 1945–1946 to a campus overflowing with ex-servicemen. Coach Bob Davies had played as a student in the early 1940s and, at twenty-six, was one of the youngest coaches in the country. "Lil Abner" (as he was nicknamed) had been a scintillating performer as a student ("he shot, passed, and dribbled with extraordinary speed and accuracy")[241] and his prewar teammates were also sharp. Bob Fisher was also very fast and Ken "Porky" Pine was "the hub" around which the rest of the team revolved.[242] The Pirates enjoyed an unbeaten season in 1942, completing a twenty-three game winning streak with a close end-of-season victory over Fordham.[243] Then came war.

"Honey" Russell was a hard act to follow, but Davies coached the Pirates to twenty-four victories and only three defeats in the 1946–1947 season. In March 1947 he was named "Coach of the Year" by Metropolitan Basketball Writers Association.[244] In 1948, Harry Reitemeir took over, coaching the Pirates to a 18-3 season, the stars Frank "Pep" Saul (with his "sparkling floor game and set shooting") and John "Whitey" Macknowski.[245] In 1949, Honey Russell returned to coach Bobby Hurt, John Ligos, Dave Latimer, Dave Putnam, and Tom Gibbons to an 11-15 season.

In 1951, the Pirates won twenty-two and lost five, helped by 6' 8" Walter Dukes, one of the greatest players to start for the university. Dukes was the leading point-scorer in a season that saw Seton Hall play in the National Invitation Tournament (NIT) for the first time since 1941, losing in the consolation game to St. John's University 70-68 in double overtime.[246] In 1952, the Pirates recorded twenty-five wins and two losses in the regular season, with a postseason elimination by ultimately victorious La Salle in the opening game of the NIT. Two players surpassed the 1,000 points mark: Richie "Cat" Regan with 1,182 and Walter Dukes with 1,121.[247]

In 1953 Seton Hall defeated St. John's 58-46 in Madison Square Garden to win the NIT championship in front of a crowd of 18,496. It remains (with one exception) Seton Hall basketball's finest hour. The game was anticlimactically one-sided, with Seton Hall easy favorites, but after years in the doldrums no-one minded a comfortable win. In addition to Dukes (MVP) and Richie Regan, the squad consisted of Arnie Ring, Harry Brooks, Ronnie Nathanic, Mickey Hannon, and Hank Cooper. Of the winning game, *The Setonian* caught the flavor: "Seton Hall turned in as masterful a defensive exhibition as the NIT has ever witnessed in its long 16-year history . . . Dukes, closing out one of the very best collegiate careers anyone ever had . . . scored 21 points and picked off 20 rebounds. Regan, also ending an amazing collegiate career, notched 13 points and whipped seven scoring passes."[248]

When Dukes and Regan graduated, Dukes to play for the Harlem Globetrotters and the New York Knicks, Regan to join the Marines and the NBA, the team noticed the difference. Winning thirteen and losing ten, the 1954 season was a disappointment.[249] The following year, after posting a 17-9 season, the Pirates accepted an invitation to compete in the NIT but lost in the opening round 89-78 to eventual winners St. Francis of Loreto.[250]

The Pirates,[251] 20-5 in the 1955–1956 season, appeared in the NIT, defeating Marquette in the first round (96-78) before falling to St. Joseph's. Russell's problem was to find a fifth starter from a bench that was thinner than previous years.[252] The following season, the team began with high expectations but ended only 17-9.[253] Dick Gaines was the star, completing a record 1,000 points in college basketball against Scranton in January 1957 and bettering Walter Dukes's record of twenty-four points in a half, racking up twenty-six against Albright.[254] The Pirates made it to the NIT in 1957, their seventh appearance in eleven seasons, losing to Xavier University 85-79 in the opener.[255] The next year was memorable for the wrong reasons, the first losing season since 1949–1950, the Pirates conceding their last nine games.[256] In 1959–1960, his last season as coach, Honey Russell notched his 300th victory in college basketball with the squad posting sixteen wins and seven losses but failing to secure a place in the NIT.[257]

In March 1960, Richie Regan succeeded Honey Russell as coach. Regan was respected by the squad, but in 1961 he was at the helm when the program suffered a point-shaving scandal that plunged the squad, and the university, into crisis. Point-shaving was nothing new, but when two Seton Hall players were shown to be involved in a scheme with thirty-seven players from twenty-one schools, it represented a humiliating low for the program. The players in question, Art Hicks and Henry Gunter, alleged to have accepted $1,000 each to shave points, were dismissed from the university following an internal investigation.[258] The Board of Trustees imposed a number of penalties, barring the program from participating in in-season tournaments for five years and from accepting postseason invitations for the next ten. Only games against in the mid-Atlantic region and New England region were scheduled. Seton Hall basketball suffered a ten year setback from which it took another five years to recover.

The ban deprived talented players of a national stage. Nick "the Quick" Werkman, the finest pirate of his generation, played between 1962 and 1964, the last season as co-captain alongside Al Senavitis, famed for an unusual one-handed jump shot. Averaging thirty-two points a game, Werkman was leading scorer in three consecutive seasons, the third most prolific scorer in the nation in 1962, the second in 1964, the first in 1963. He was the first of only three Seton Hall basketball players to score more than 2,000 points in a three-year career, and this before the introduction of the three-point shot.[259] Werkman was in the same league as Walter Dukes,[260] an athlete good enough to be drafted for the Boston Celtics (although he never played). Also starting from 1959 to 1962 (and averaging seventeen points a game for the 1961–1962 season) was Al Senavitis, a perfect foil to Werkman,[261] "fast in every phase of the game."[262] The Pirates ended the 1961–1962 season with a 15-9 record, posting a record-breaking average of 88.1 points per game.

Regan resigned in January 1970 after five seasons in which the Pirates had failed to post a winning record, this not reversed until 1972–1973.[263] Overall, Regan compiled a

108-124 record, but most of his victories came early. Still, the era had its stars, of whom Regan himself was chief. (The field house inside Walsh Gymnasium was named in his and his wife Sue's honor. The Recreation Center was also named for him.) John Suminski played between 1966 and 1969, scoring 846 points and earning a spot in the Hall of Fame in 1982; Charles Mitchel (the "Columbus Comet") scored 944 points between 1963 and 1966 and was inducted in 1991.[264] Gerry ("the Hawk") Mackey played sixty-three games between 1965 and 1968, scoring 673 points at an average of 10.6. The outstanding player was "Marvelous Mel" Knight (1968–1971),[265] whose appearances (only fifty) were curtailed by injury but whose record was a superb 774 points at an average of 24.7.

Under Regan's successor Bill Raftery, the Pirates landed a berth in the NIT in 1974 after a seventeen-year gap. Raftery began the season confidently but not expecting an NIT bid. In the event, although the Pirates fell to Memphis State 73-72 in the first round, making the postseason ended a decade of defeat and decline.[266] Raftery restored vitality to the program, a renaissance that may be traced in the careers of John Ramsey, Nick Gallis, Greg Tynes, Danny ("Mr. Clutch") Callandrillo, and Glenn Mosley, all drafted to the NBA.

Of these, Mosley (1973–1977) had difficulty, failing to maintain a 2.0 GPA in his freshman year and thus ruled technically ineligible to remain on the team. Allegations that Regan, Raftery, and assistant coach Hoddy Mahon had misreported his academic performance to allow him to continue to play prompted an internal investigation that declared Mosley ineligible under NCAA rules. Regan, Raftery, and Mahon were also held in material breach of their responsibilities to the university and the NCAA. They denied this, claiming the rules open to conflicting interpretation, a view for which Fahy as president had sympathy. Regan was fined $500 and suspended for three weeks, Raftery $650 and suspended for a week, Mahon $100 and suspended for two weeks. Arguing that he was unaware of his ineligibility and that others had put him in a false position, Mosley decided to stay at Seton Hall rather than transfer to another college, prompting Fahy to praise him as "a remarkable young man."[267] The NCAA required him to sit out twenty-one games and handed the program a two-year suspension from postseason tournaments.[268] When Mosley returned to the line-up in the middle of his junior year he led the Pirates to an 18-9 season. Mosley returned to the university in 1979 to see his number retired.[269] "The man had a dedication to the truth," he said of Fahy, "and I will always appreciate what he did for me."[270]

Meantime, Seton Hall moved, literally, into a different league. The Big East Conference was inaugurated in May 1979, with Seton Hall one of its founding members, the other northeast schools being Boston College, Georgetown, Providence, St. John's, and the University of Connecticut, later joined by Villanova and Pittsburgh. The Big East represented glamor, prestige, money and, not least, television. Seton Hall won its first Big East encounter against Providence in January 1980.

Raftery resigned in 1981 to begin a career as a television commentator, having coached the Pirates to seven consecutive winning seasons (the best 1975–1976, when they ended 18-9 and won the Madison Square Garden classic). Hoddy Mahon stood in until April 1982, when the coaching job went to thirty-three-year-old Peter J. ("PJ") Carlesimo of Scranton, Pennsylvania. Carlesimo had had an outstanding career at Wagner College, Fordham, and as athletics director of New Hampshire College, but he did not apply for the Seton Hall position (thinking it would go to Mahon). When approached, he accepted instantly.[271] Witty and personable, with a sharp tactical mind, PJ was a marketer's dream, the face of Seton Hall basketball for over a decade. He led the program to its greatest triumph.

All the same, his first season was inauspicious, with six wins and twenty-one losses,[272] and the second only marginally better at 9-19. By the middle of the decade, he began to find his stride, the Pirates compiling a 10-18 record in 1985 and narrowly falling to Providence in the opening round of the postseason Big East.[273] Carlesimo was named Big East Coach of the year in 1988, again in 1989, and National Coach of the Year in 1989. He had some stellar players at his disposal, including Andre McCloud, a sixth-round pick for the Philadelphia 76s in the 1985 draft; Mark Bryant, a first-round pick for the Portland Trailblazers in 1988; John Morton, a first-round pick for the Cleveland Cavaliers in 1989; and Antony Avent, a first-round pick for the Atlanta Hawks in 1991. Ramon Ramos, Big East Scholar-Athlete of the year in 1989, played for the Pirates between 1985 and 1989 (and for his native Puerto Rico in the 1988 Seoul Olympics). Ramos had a brilliant future ahead of him (playing for the Portland Blazers for a season after graduation) when, in December 1989, he was grievously injured in a car accident. In his honor, the university annually bestows the Ramon Ramos Medal of Courage to the student who shows "extraordinary courage" in conquering physical challenges.

In 1988 the Pirates made it to the NCAA for the first time and in 1989 Carlesimo led them to the Final Four. Upsetting second-seeded Indiana 78-65 and besting Duke by 17, the Pirates faced the Michigan Wolverines in the championship game. They lost 80-79 in overtime, an unforgotten defeat that still has the power to sting. The Pirates were leading 79-78 with three seconds of overtime remaining when referee John Clougherty called a blocking foul on Seton Hall point guard Gerald Greene, allowing Rumeal Robinson for the Wolverines to make two free throws to win the game. Players, fans, and officials have been debating the decision ever since. "I've had to answer for that call for twenty-five years," said Clougherty in 2014. Carlesimo and his squad handled the disappointment superbly. Carlesimo never criticized Clougherty (possibly saving his career) and the team acted so graciously that they were remembered almost as much as winners. "We thought it was important not to detract from Michigan winning the national championship," Carlesimo said. "There was nothing to be gained. It was over. I thought our guys handled it extremely well."[274]

This was the moment—April 1989—when town and gown went crazy for a day. In some ways, the madness went on longer than that. Under pressure to stay competitive, the university doubled the athletic budget, linking increased expenditure to the new Recreation Center. Carlesimo secured the services of brilliant New York high school athletes (and some from farther afield including, controversially, Andrew Gaze from Australia),[275] promising them immediate playing time and the chance of an NBA contract. Making the Final Four seemed to cap not only the Carlesimo but the Petillo years, rounding out a decade in which the university went from near-bankruptcy to national acclaim. The success of the Pirates made for a compelling metaphor, allowing Seton Hall a moment of collective exhilaration.

It is hard not to see subsequent years as anticlimax. After Carlesimo brought Seton Hall to the heights, fans wondered why those realms later proved elusive. In reality, the program did well enough, clocking up performances earlier squads would happily envied. The 1991–1992 team (23-9 overall) made it to the NCAA Sweet Sixteen, eventually falling to powerhouse Duke. The 1992–1993 team beat Syracuse 103-70 to win the Big East Conference title in 1993. (Among members of that squad was Terry Dehere, all-time highest scorer for the Pirates with a career total of 2,394 points.)[276] Arturas Karnishovas, who played for the Pirates between 1990 and 1994, won an Olympic bronze medal representing Lithuania in the 1992 games.

After Carlesimo's departure to become head coach of the Portland Trailblazers, George Blaney coached the squad between 1994 and 1997, amassing a 38-38 record. Blaney's replacement was Tommy Amaker from Duke, one of the youngest basketball coaches in Pirate history, who managed the team from 1997 to 2000, putting together a 68-55 record. His resignation to become head coach at Michigan, after protestations of loyalty to Seton Hall, left a sour taste.

Rounding out a remarkable basketball and sporting history, Amaker's successor was Louis Orr, who had played for Syracuse and later in the NBA. "A strong athletic program generates energy and excitement," said Robert Sheeran, introducing him. "It's good for our students—and good for the University. Our pride in the Pirates and our pride in the University draws us together. It's a great feeling."[277] With one or two disappointments along the way, that was the story in a nutshell.

Seton Hall Priests, 1856–2013

John A. Abbo

Michael Acocella

Stanley Adamczyk

+George Ahr

Angelus Almarcequi

John Annese

James Annicchiarico

John Ansbro

Robert Antczak

Richard Asakiewicz

William Baird

George Baker

John Ballweg

Edward Barrett

Renato Bautista

+James Bayley

Henry Beck

Edward Begley

Hubert Behr

Christopher Belber
    O.R.S.A.

Willibald Berger

Duverney Bermudez

Thomas Berry C.P.

Antonio I. Bico

Francis Bischoff

Stafford Blake

Donald Blumenfeld

Paul Bocchichio

+Thomas Boland

Theodore Bonelli

Flavian Bonifazi S.A.C.

+Paul Bootkoski

Diego Borgatello S.D.B.

Alan Borsuk

David Bossman O.F.M.

Ian Boyd C.S.B.

Peter Boyle

Cornelius Boyle

W. Jerome Bracken C.P.

William Bradley

Edward Bradley

Joseph Brady

Harry Brann

+Vincent Breen

William Brennan

Robert Brennan

George Brown

John Buchman

Gerald Buonopane

Thomas Burke

Francis Byrne

William Caffrey

James Cafone

James Cahalan

John Cain

Daniel Callahan

Thomas Callery

John Campbell

Thomas Canty

Gerald Caprio

James Carey

Thomas Carey

James Carroll

Lawrence Carroll

Eugene Carroll

+Lawrence Casey

John Cassells

Frank Cassidy

Alfred Celiano

John Chadwick

Joseph Chapel

+James F.Checchio

Joseph Chmely

Hong-Ray Cho

James Choma

Joseph Christopher

Christopher Ciccarino

Edward Ciuba

Herbert Clancy S.J.

John Clark

George Clausing

Cornelius Clifford

James Cloherty

Patrick Cody

Dennis Cohan

Robert Coleman

Paul Collins

Anthony Connell

James Connollen

James Connolly

John Connolly

Joseph Connor

Cornelius Corcoran

George Corrigan

James Corrigan

+Michael Corrigan

Gabriel Costa

Eugene Cotter

Timothy Coughlin

Charles Covert

Phillip Coyne

George Crone

John Cryan

John Culliney

Declan Cunniff O.S.B.

Thomas Cunningham

Thomas Curry

+Walter Curtis

Andrew Cusack

William Daly

James Daly

+Celestine Damiano

Jerome Dawson O.F.M.

Harold Darcy

John Dauenhauer

John Davis

P. Michael DeAngelis

Walter Debold

Januarius De Concilio

Francis DeDomenico

Daniel Degnan S.J.

John Delaney

John Dennehy

Arnold De Rosa

Harold Dilger

John Dillon

+Nicholas DiMarzio

George Doane

Peter Doherty

+Thomas Donato

Michael Donnelly

William Donnelly

Patrick Donohue

Joseph Dooling

John Doran

+John Dougherty

John Dowd

John Downes

Joseph Doyle

William Driscoll

+Michael Dudick

Mark Duffy

Stephen Duffy

William Duffy

+John Duffy

Francis Duffy

Thomas Duffy

Andrew Egan

Edward Ellard

Sylvester Elwood

A. Eudine O.S.B.

Thomas Fahy

Francis Fallon

Leo Farley

Edward Farrell

Stephen Feehan

John Feeley

William Feeney

Michael Feketie

Robert Fennell

William Field

Anthony Figueiredo

Nicholas Figurelli

Francis Finn

John Finnerty

James Finnerty

John Finnerty

Donald Fisher

Harold Fitzpatrick

Joseph Fitzpatrick

Robert Fitzpatrick

Thomas Fitzpatrick

James Flanagan

John Flanagan

Edward Flannery

Edward Fleming

+John Flesey

Joseph Flusk

Martin Foran

Thomas Frain

Hugh Friel

Lawrence Frizzell

Michael Fronczak

Robert Fuhrmann

Hubert Funk

William Furlong

John Furman

Pablo Gadenz

Eugene Gallagher

Owen Garrigan

Francis Gavin

Prudentius Gehin

Nicholas Gengaro

+Peter Gerety

JosephMarie Gervais

William Gibbons

William Giblin

Robert Gibney

John Gilchrist

Thomas Gilhooly

James Glotzbach

Ralph Glover

Thomas Glover

Edward Glynn S.J.
Stanley Gomes
Paul Goni O.R.S.A.
Walter Gorski
Stanley Grabowski
Robert Grady
Gaudence Gregory O.F.M.
+William Griffin
Arthur Griffith
Ugo Groppi
Thomas Guarino
Kevin Gugliotta
+George Guilfoyle
Charles Gusmer
Paul Guterl
Peter Guterl
John Hagan
Robert Haggerty
Albert Hakim
Warren Hall
William Halliwell
James Hamilton
Albert Hammenstede
 O.S.B.
Kevin Hanbury
Robert Harahan
William Harms
John Haughey S.J.
Paul Hayes
Clarence Heavey
+Bernard A. Hebda
Samuel Hedges
Walter Hennesey
Arthur Henry
Eugene Herbster
Joseph Hewetson
Edward Hickey
William Hickey
Edward Higgins

Walter Hill
Edward F. Hillock
Carl Hinrichsen
James Hobson
Lawrence Hoey
William Hogan
William Holland
Paul Holmes
John Holton
John Horgan
Francis Hourigan
John Hourihan
Benedict Howe
David Hubba
+Edward Hughes
James Hughes
Robert Hunt
Christopher Hynes
Simon Ignacio
Bruce Janiga
Stanley Jaki
Joseph Jaremczuk
Walter Jarvais
John Kakalewski
Cornelius Kane
John Karolewski
George Keating
William Keller
James Kelley
Charles Kelly
Michael Kelly
Thomas Kelly
Ignatius Kemelis
Edward Kern
John Kiernan
Stephen Kilcarr
John Kiley
William King
John Kinney

James Kirchner
Edward Kirk
Dennis Klein
Eugene (Mariusz) Koch
 C.F.R.
+Stephen Kocisko
Ekhard Koehle O.S.B.
John Koenig
Joseph Kukura
Anthony Kulig
Raymond Kupke
Peter Kurz
Jean Baptiste Kyabuta
William Landers
Stephen Landherr C.SS.R.
Paul Lang
Joseph Laracy
Edward Larkin
William Lawlor
S. David Lee
Aime Legendre S.S.S.
Peter Lennon
Richard Liddy
Charles Lillis
Ronald Little
Sylvester Livolsi
Joseph LoCigno
Walter Lucey
Henry Lynch
Stephen Lynch
Charles Mackel
John Mackin
Michael Madden
Dennis Mahon
John Mahon
Patrick Mahoney
Adrian Maine
Francis Maione
John Makowski

Patrick Maloney

Paul Manning

John Mannion

Baldimero Marcilla

Albert Marino

Francis Mariones O.R.S.A.

Joseph A. Marjanczyk

William Marshall

Leo Martin

Thomas Martin

John Maxwell

J. Martin

Joseph Masiello

Gerard McCarren

+Theodore Cardinal
  McCarrick

Pierce McCarthy

+Justin McCarthy

Denis McCartie

John McClary

Donald McConnell

Thomas McDade

James McDonald

John McDonald

Joseph McDonald

William McDonald

+Charles McDonnell

John McGeary

Michael McGlue

Gerard McGlynn O.F.M.

Michael McGuiness

Paul McGuire

Francis McHugh

+James McHugh

Lalor McLaughlin

Robert McLaughlin

+Thomas McLaughlin

James McManus

James McMenemie

Frank McNulty

+James McNulty

John McNulty

William McNulty

+Bernard McQuaid

Charles McTague

LeRoy McWilliams

Michael Mechler

Daniel Meehan

Carl Merzena

+Sebastian Messmer

Francis Mestice

Charles Meyer

Robert Meyer

Douglas Milewski

Frederick Miller

Chester Miros

Richard Molnar

+Francis Monaghan

Vincent Monella

James Mooney

Bernard Moore

Patrick Moran

John Morley

Philip Morris

Boleslaus Moscinski

David Mulcahy

John Mulvey

Charles Murphy

Edward Murphy

John Murphy

Joseph Murphy

Daniel Murphy

Lawrence Murphy M.M.

Harrold Murray

James Murray

Brian Muzas

+John Myers

Richard Nardone

+James Navagh

Frank Nead

Brian Needles

Henry Nelson

Robert Nestor

John Nolan

John Nuberg

Thomas Nydegger

John E. O'Brien

John F. O'Brien

Richard O'Brien

Martin O'Brien

+John O'Connor

Joseph O'Connor

Maurice O'Connor

Peter O'Connor

Thomas O'Donnell

Gerald O'Leary

Thomas O'Leary

T. Kenneth O'Leary

Mark O'Malley

Felix O'Neill

George O'Neill

Paul O'Neill

Gerald O'Sullivan

Joseph O'Sullivan

Edward O'Toole

Clement Ockay

Caesar Orrico

Eldred Olajos O.S.B.

Roberto Ortiz

Stanley Ortyl

John Osterreicher

John Outwater

James Owens

William Pardow S.J.

+Andrew Pataki

David Pathe

Raymond Pavlick

Thomas Peterson O.P.

John Petillo

Edward Phalon

Henry Phelan

James Pindar

James Platania

Francis Podgorski

Lawrence Porter

Thomas Powers

Vicent Prestera

Walter Pruschowicz

Joseph Przezdziecki

Walter Purcell

Michael Quinlan O.F.M.

John Radano

Boniface Ramsey O.P.

John Ranieri

Thomas Reardon

James Reid

Francis M. Reilly

George Reilly

Joseph Reilly

+John Reiss

Louis Remmele

+Frank Rodimer

Andrew Romanak

Philip Rotunno

Ronald Rozniak

David Rubino

Leo von Rudloff O.S.B.

Russell Ruffino

Peter Rush

John Russell O.Carm.

Joseph Russell

Michael Russo

Stephen Rutkowski

John Ryan

William Salt

Richard Scaine

John Schandel

Donald Scherer

Sebastian Schmidt

Louis Schneider

Gregory Schramm O.S.B.

Henry Schreitmueller

Edward Scully

George Senderak

+Arthur Serratelli

+Robert Seton

Francis Seymour

John Shanley

James Sharp

George Shea

Joseph Shea

James Sheehan

Robert Sheeran

John Sheerin

John Sheppard

Joseph Sherer

Henry Sheridan

William Sheridan

Joseph Simonatis

Joseph Slinger

+John Smith

George Smith

Neil Smith

Donald Smith

Patrick Smyth

Alexander Sokolich

James Spera

Maurice Spillane

J. Felix Spilman

Vincent Sprouls

John Stafford

Virgil Stallbaumer O.S.B.

Kenneth St. Amand

John Starkus

Aloysius Stauble

Charles Stengel

Joseph Stewart

George Strack

Richard Strelecki

Emil R. Suchon

+Dennis J.Sullivan

Edwin Sullivan

James Sullivan

John Sullivan

Robert Suszko

Robert Svec

Vincent Svirnelis

Leo Sweeney

Edward Synan

Joseph Synnott

Leo Thebaud

Charles Tichler

John Tierney

James Tierney

Alfred Tobey

+Joseph Cardinal Tobin
  C.Ss.R

Thomas Toomey

Anthony Tralka

Thomas Trapasso

Mark Tsai

Joseph Tuite

Joseph Tuohy

Thomas Tuohy

James Turro

Henry Unkraut

John Vaccaro

John Vasallo

Bernard Vogt O.F.M.

Leonard Volenski

Joseph Vopelak

T. A. Wallace

+Thomas Walsh

John Walsh

Henry Watterson
James F. Weisbecker
John A. Weisbrod
Robert Wells
Aloysius Welsh
Paul Wenzel
John Westman
John Weyland
Michael Whalen

Isaac Whelan
+Winand Wigger
Damasus Winzen O.S.B.
W. Wiseman
Robert Wister
Carl Wolsin
John Woods
Stephen Woodstock
Joseph Wortmann

Joseph Wozniak
Alfred Young
Henry Zaraton O.R.S.A.
Anthony Ziccardi
Donald Zimmerman
Henry Zolzer
Theodore Zubek

Acknowledgments

I am happy to acknowledge the many people who have contributed in large and small ways to the publication of this book.

Of these debts, the first is unquestionably to Monsignor Robert Sheeran, former president of Seton Hall University, who asked me to write it, who gave me unfettered access to archival materials in order to do so, who encouraged me to tell the story honestly, and who waited for it, year after year, with miraculous patience and restraint. I am also grateful to Interim President Mary Meehan whose financial support helped to defray the costs of publication.

For a long time, the archives of Seton Hall University became a second home to me where I found exceptional colleagues and friends. Alan Delozier, Kate Dodds, Anthony Lee, and Howard McGinn deserve unstinting praise for their skill and professionalism. Monsignor Robert Wister offered many insights over the years. Dr. Delozier and Monsignor Wister read the manuscript in its entirety, correcting mistakes. I regret that Monsignor Francis Seymour, a prodigiously knowledgeable and kindly priest, did not live to see the appearance of the book.

The list of those, some now deceased, who shared their knowledge of Seton Hall is lengthy. I have much enjoyed conversations with David Abalos, Richard Adinaro, Peter Ahr, Michael Ambrosio, Mary Balkun, Bill Barto, George Browne, Monsignor James Cafone, Father Al Celiano, Petra Chu, Monsignor Robert Coleman, Father Eugene Cotter, John Coverdale, Robin Cunningham, Gordon Dippel, Father William Driscoll, John and Tom Duff, Monsignor William Noé Field, Father Nick Figurelli, Father Larry Frizzell, Denis Garbini, Jeff Grey, Chrys Grieco, Albert Hakim, Tom Hughes, Ron Infante, Catherine Kiernan, Dan Leab, Father Peter Lennon, Monsignor Richard Liddy, Monsignor Dennis Mahon, Michael McMahon, Father Dan Murphy, Francis McQuade, Roseanne Mirabella, Peter Mitchell, Father Richard Nardone, Nick Tomasicchio, Bill Radkte, Angela Raimo, Michael Risinger, David Rogers, John T. Saccoman, Bernhard Scholz, Jack Shannon, Bill Smith, Judith Stark, John Sweeney, John Wefing, and Father Joseph Wortmann. I am also grateful to David Foster, Monsignor Anthony Ziccardi, and members of their Mission and Ministry seminar for valuable commentary on a later chapter of the book.

Supreme among Setonian conversationalists have been my coffee or pasta consuming companions of many years: Father Ian Boyd, James McGlone, Father Douglas Milewski, Father John Ranieri, Ralph Walz, and the late Joe Mahoney and John J. Saccoman.

My departmental colleagues offered invariably intelligent insights: William Connell, Larry Greene, Anne Giblin Gedacht, Golbarg Rekabtelaiei, Sean Harvey, Williamjames Hoffer, Maxine Lurie, Maxim Matusevich, Vanessa May, Mark Molesky, Tom Rzeznik, Kirsten Schultz, and Laura Wangerin.

Kristine Foley provided photographic services and Gregory Burton, as associate provost, paid for them.

At Rutgers University Press, Peter Mickulas was an excellent editor. I thank also Terry Golway, at one point the anonymous reader of the manuscript, for his very helpful commentary on it. Thanks are due, finally, to the painstaking copyeditor who knocked it into shape.

Brian and Katharine Quinn endured many conversations over many years about "Corrigan and McQuaid," men who became synecdoches for the larger history they helped to inaugurate. I suspect they are now sick of the sound of them.

Mistakes are inevitable in a work of this scope. I am responsible for all of them.

Notes

Chapter 1. Foundations

1. M. Hildegarde Yeager, *The Life of James Roosevelt Bayley 1814–1877 first Bishop of Newark and Eighth Archbishop of Baltimore* (Washington, DC, 1947), 123.

2. James Roosevelt Bayley, Diary, January 23, 1845. SHU Archives.

3. Yeager, *Life*, 232.

4. Some uncertainty surrounds the year of Richard Bayley's birth, with several sources giving it as 1745. See Annabelle M. Melville, *Elizabeth Bayley Seton 1744–1821* (New York, 1976), 2, 301 n.3, 4, for reasons to prefer 1744.

5. Yeager, *Life*, 3.

6. Trusted by the British authorities, Seton held important positions in the port of New York, becoming effectively superintendent in 1782. See Melville, *Elizabeth Bayley Seton*, 17.

7. His grave now forms the centerpiece in the grounds of the Church of Saint Elizabeth Ann Seton in Livorno. Led by Reverend Douglas Milewski and the author, a group of students from Seton Hall prayed there in 2006, the sesquicentennial year of the university's foundation.

8. Helen DeBarberey, *Elizabeth Seton*, (New York: Macmillan Co. 1927) 106.

9. Edward F. Kennelly, *A Historical Study of Seton Hall College* (EdD dissertation, New York University, 1944), 17, 18.

10. Judith Metz, S.C., "The Founding Circle of Elizabeth Ann Seton's Sisters of Charity," *U.S. Catholic Historian*, 14, no. 1 (Winter 1996), 24.

11. Kennelly, *A Historical* Study, 24.

12. *The Catholic Telegraph*, August 27, 1842, 35.

13. James R. Bayley, European Diary, January 3 and 12, 1842. SHU Archives.

14. James R. Bayley, European Diary, August 4, 1842. SHU Archives.

15. James R. Bayley, European Diary, March 22, 1842. SHU Archives.

16. James R. Bayley, European Diary, April 28, 1842. SHU Archives.

17. James R. Bayley, European Diary, April 28, 1842. SHU Archives.

18. Daniel Robinson to Bayley, December 18, 1842, in Yeager, *Life*, 60.

19. Yeager, *Life*, 69.

20. The American Catholic hierarchy was established in 1789 with the appointment of John Carroll as first Bishop of Baltimore. In 1808, Carroll became an archbishop with suffragan sees set up in Boston, New York, Philadelphia, and Bardstown, Kentucky. In 1815 Louis William Dubourg, the priest who had persuaded Elizabeth Ann Bayley Seton to open her school in Baltimore, became bishop of New Orleans, erected as a diocese in 1793. Charleston and Richmond became dioceses in 1820. The creation of Newark was part of the first great wave of diocese building in the American church, an institutional response to the needs of an immigrant church. The personalities and politics of the new bishops are nicely explored in Gerald P. Fogarty, "The American Hierarchy: A Retrospect of Two Hundred Years," *U.S. Catholic Historian*, 8, no. 4 (Fall 1989), 37sqq.

21. American anti-Catholicism is too big a subject for brief treatment but acknowledgment must be made of it if Seton Hall's founding and history are to be understood. According to the 1850 census, the Catholic Church was the largest single denomination in the United States, making up more than 12 percent of the population. As most of this population lived in the North, that was where most anti-Catholicism manifested itself, spectacularly so in Philadelphia in 1844 (with the burning of several churches) but also in Massachusetts and elsewhere. New York was spared because Archbishop John Hughes armed his parishioners to defend their churches. The story is well summarized by Gerald P. Fogarty: "Most of the northern problem centered on the Protestant character of the public schools. Hughes and Bishop Francis Kenrick of Philadelphia sought to remove reading material offensive to Catholic students from the curricula, gain a share of the common fund for Catholics and have Catholic teachers appointed in areas where Catholics were numerous. Failing in these objectives, they embarked on the ambitious project of creating a vast parochial school system that spread throughout the north east, Midwest and Ohio. Out of self-defense, they created a Catholic ghetto." Gerald P. Fogarty, "Reflections on Contemporary American Anti-Catholicism," *U.S. Catholic Historian*, 21, no. 4 (Fall 2003), 38. Seton Hall was a diocesan college rather than parochial school but Fogarty's broader analysis still holds good for it.

22. A social conservative, Bayley's career as Archbishop of Baltimore was marked by hostility to labor unions and secret societies, in part because he did not wish to arouse the sleeping spirit of Know-Nothingism. See James Edmund Roohan, *American Catholics and the Social Question, 1865–1900* (New York: Arno Press, 1976).

23. James Roosevelt Bayley, Notes 1842 and 1853 Bayley Papers, ADN 0002-001 Monsignor Field Special Collections and Archives Box 1, Folder 2

24. William J. Shea, review of Yeager, *Life*, in *The Catholic Historical Review*, 34, no. 4 (January 1949), 461.

Chapter 2. A College Begins

1. See Dermot Quinn, *The Irish in New Jersey: Four Hundred Years of American Life* (New Brunswick, NJ: Rutgers University Press, 2004).

2. Walter Cox, *Advice to Emigrants, or Observations made during a Nine Months Residence in the Middle States of the American Union* (Dublin, 1802).

3. Nearly 490,000 people lived in New Jersey in 1850, an increase of 31 percent over 1840. Of the 56,000 foreign-born residents in 1850, 31,092 were from Ireland, the number from Germany about a third of that. By 1870, the population had almost doubled to 906,096, of whom 188,943 had been born outside the country. Of that latter figure, nearly 87,000 were from Ireland, 54,000 from Germany.

4. Yeager, *Life*, 116.

5. John J. O'Connor, Pastoral Letter, November 1, 1902. ADN 0002.004, O'Connor Papers, Box 2, Folder 5.

6. Yeager, *Life*, 116.

7. Yeager, *Life*, 118.

8. E.V. Sullivan, An annotated copy of the diary of James Roosevelt Bayley, first bishop of Newark, New Jersey 1853–1872, March 30, 1855. Monsignor Field Special Collections and Archives.

9. Yeager, *Life*, 121.

10. Yeager, *Life*, 116.

11. Yeager, *Life*, 66.

12. Quoted in Frederick J. Zwierlein, *The Life and Letters of Bishop McQuaid*, (Rome: 1925) 1: 317.

NOTES TO PAGES 10–20

13. Zwierlein, *Bishop McQuaid*, 1: 319.

14. Sister Mary Agnes Sharkey, *Mother Mary Xavier Mehegan and the New Jersey Sisters of Charity* (New York, 1933), 6.

15. Joseph M. Flynn, *The Catholic Church in New Jersey* (Morristown, NJ, 1904), 598.

16. Zwierlein, *Bishop McQuaid*, 1: 319.

17. Zwierlein, *Bishop McQuaid*, 1: 320.

18. Flynn, *Catholic Church*, 275–77.

19. Yeager, *Life*, 155n.11.

20. Zwierlein, *Bishop McQuaid*, 1: 319.

21. Bayley to Hughes, April 1, 1856, quoted in Yeager, *Life*, 156n12.

22. Bayley to Hughes, April 1, 1856, quoted in Yeager, *Life*, 156n12.

23. Bayley to Hughes, April 1, 1856, quoted in Yeager, *Life*, 156n12.

24. Bayley to Hughes, April 1, 1856, quoted in Yeager, *Life*, 156n12.

25. Bayley Letter Book, ADN, 1.31, May 30, 1856.

26. Bayley Letter Book, ADN, 1.31, June 4, 1856.

27. This staff list from the *Catholic Almanac* (1857) is the first of which we have evidence.

28. *The State Gazette* (Trenton), November 11, 1856, quoted in *The Setonian: A Quarterly* 9, no. 3 (Christmas 1931). Joseph H. Brady Papers, ADN 0004.005, Series II, Folder 61.

29. J. Monroe to Bernard McQuaid, April 24, 1855. Office of the President and Chancellor, Bernard McQuaid Papers, 0003.001, Box 1, Folder 1.

30. RG 1 1.84, James Roosevelt Bayley Papers, Bills, Folder 1 of 2.

31. *Freeman's Journal*, October 15, 1856, 3.

32. *The Catholic Almanac* (Baltimore: F. Lucas, 1857),

33. See Patrick B. Miller, "Athletes in Academe: College Sports and American Culture, 1850–1920" (PhD dissertation, University of California, Berkeley, 1987), 15.

34. Bayley, Diocesan Diary, October 30, 1855.

35. Bayley, Diocesan Diary, April 28, 1869.

36. Bayley, Diocesan Diary, June 24, 1858.

37. Bayley, Diocesan Diary, June 24, 1859.

38. Bayley, Diocesan Diary, May 6, 1859.

39. W.E. Robinson to Bayley. ADN 2.1, Bayley Papers 1836–1872, Box 9, Folder 15.

40. "Our Catholic Education Institutions," in *The Record* (June 1859), Bayley Scrapbook. ADN 2.1, Bayley Papers 1836–1872, Box 24.

41. Bayley, Diocesan Diary, July 16, 1859.

42. Bayley Letter Book, October 29, 1857. ADN, 1.31.

43. Bayley Letter Book, March 5, 1859. ADN, 1.31.

44. Bayley circular, May 16, 1860. ADN 2.1, Bayley Papers 1836–1872, Box 1, Folder 23.

45. Bayley to Robert Seton, January 15, 1865, quoted in Yeager, *Life*, 203n163.

46. William F. Marshall, *Seton Hall College Catalogue, 1895*, 2, quoted in Robert J. Wister, *Stewards of the Mysteries of God: Immaculate Conception Seminary, 1860–2010* (South Orange, NJ: Immaculate Conception Seminary, 2010), 24.

47. Bayley, Diocesan Diary, April 2, 1860

48. McQuaid to Archbishop Williams, April 13, 1886. Letter Book, Diocese of Rochester, 188.

49. Catalogue of the officers and students of Seton Hall College, 1861-1862, 5

50. Bayley, Diocesan Diary, May 15, 1860

51. Bayley, Diocesan Diary, September 10, 1860

52. Seton Hall College Catalogue, 1865–1866, 22.

53. Catalogue of the officers and students of Seton Hall College, 1861-1862, 7.

54. Zwierlein, *Bishop McQuaid*, 1: 327.

55. Charles Herberman, *Historical Records and Sources II* (New York, 1901.)

56. Henry Brann, "Seton Hall from 1862–1864." Typescript in Carl Hinrichsen Papers, ADN 0004-012, Monsignor Field Special Collections and Archives, Seton Hall University.

57. Ibid.

58. Robert Seton to Bayley, September 24, 1862. ADN 2.1, Bayley Papers 1836–1872, Box 1, Folder 7.

59. Bayley circular, May 1862. ADN 2.1, Bayley Papers 1836–1872

60. Bayley circular, May 1, 1863. ADN 2.1, Bayley Papers 1836–1872, Box 1, Folder 23.

61. Ibid

62. Yeager, *Life*, 471.

63. Brann, "Seton Hall"

64. Brann, "Seton Hall."

65. The Independent—Devoted to the Consideration of Politics, Social and Economic tendencies, August 30, 1883, 9 (New York: 1883).

66. Anthony Rieff to Michael Corrigan, September 1871. SHU 0003.003, Michael A. Corrigan Papers, Box 1, Folder 8.

67. For all references in this paragraph, Student Punishment Book, Seton Hall College Ledger Collection, Monsignor Field Special Collections and Archives

68. Miller, "Athletes in Academe," 143.

69. RG 10, Student Affairs, Roosevelt Debating Society 1860–1866 (Seminarians). Minutes, January 26, 1865.

70. RG 10, Minutes, June 14, 1866.

71. Henry Patterson to McQuaid, November 8, 1864. Office of the President and Chancellor, Bernard McQuaid Papers, 0003.001, Box 1, Folder 1.

72. John Darby to McQuaid, February 16, 1865. Office of the President and Chancellor, Bernard McQuaid Papers, 0003.001, Box 1, Folder 1.

73. Charles Clarmont to McQuaid, December 15, 1865. Office of the President and Chancellor, Bernard McQuaid Papers, 0003.001, Box 1, Folder 1.

74. John Binsse to McQuaid, August 20, 1866. Office of the President and Chancellor, Bernard McQuaid Papers, 0003.001, Box 1, Folder 1.

75. J.C. Droneux to McQuaid, July 27, 1866. Office of the President and Chancellor, Bernard McQuaid Papers, 0003.001, Box 1, Folder 1.

76. Annie Febiger to McQuaid, March 11, 1866. Office of the President and Chancellor, Bernard McQuaid Papers, 0003.001, Box 1, Folder 1.

77. Henry Fullerton to McQuaid, April 18, 1866. Office of the President and Chancellor, Bernard McQuaid Papers, 0003.001, Box 1, Folder 1.

78. H.D. Kernan to McQuaid, October 5, 1865. Office of the President and Chancellor, Bernard McQuaid Papers, 0003.001, Box 1, Folder 1.

79. Mrs. Charles Tillman to McQuaid, March 3, 1866. Office of the President and Chancellor, Bernard McQuaid Papers, 0003.001, Box 1, Folder 1.

80. Henry Patterson to McQuaid, November 8, 1864. Office of the President and Chancellor, Bernard McQuaid Papers, 0003.001, Box 1, Folder 1.

81. Aug. Edwards to McQuaid, September 11, 1865. Office of the President and Chancellor, Bernard McQuaid Papers, 0003.001, Box 1, Folder 1.

82. I. Inligi to McQuaid, n.d. Office of the President and Chancellor, Bernard McQuaid Papers, 0003.001, Box 1, Folder 1.

83. Alfonse Bossier to McQuaid, August 18, 1865. Office of the President and Chancellor, Bernard McQuaid Papers, 0003.001, Box 1, Folder 1.

84. William J. Tiers to McQuaid, n.d. Office of the President and Chancellor, Bernard McQuaid Papers, 0003.001, Box 1, Folder 1.

85. Sarah Peter to McQuaid, December 5, 1866. Office of the President and Chancellor, Bernard McQuaid Papers, 0003.001, Box 1, Folder 1.

86. I. Inligi to McQuaid, n.d. Office of the President and Chancellor, Bernard McQuaid Papers, 0003.001, Box 1, Folder 1.

87. Thomas Addis Emmet to McQuaid, August 28, 1865. Office of the President and Chancellor, Bernard McQuaid Papers, 0003.001, Box 1, Folder 1.

88. Edwin V. Sullivan, *An annotated copy of the diary of James Roosevelt Bayley, first Bishop of Newark 1853–1872*, Monsignor Field Special Collections and Archives, SHU January 28, 1866.

89. *Newark Advertiser*, January 29, 1866.

90. https://www.shu.edu/theology/history/hazard-zet-forward.cfm

91. Annie Febiger to McQuaid, January 30, 1866. McQuaid Papers, 0003.001, Box 1, Folder 1.

92. L.J. O'Connor to McQuaid, February 1, 1866. McQuaid Papers, 0003.001, Box 1, Folder 1.

93. William Righter to McQuaid, February 14, 1866. McQuaid Papers, 0003.001, Box 1, Folder 1.

94. Seton Hall College Catalogue, 1862–1866, 23–24.

95. Edward Robins to McQuaid February 5, 1866, McQuaid Papers, 0003.001, Box 1, Folder 1.

96. John Butler, Joseph Butler's son, died on September 14, 1865, at the age of 14. A memorial to him may be seen in the Seton Hall chapel.

97. Seton Hall College Catalogue 1895, 29.

98. M.A. Madden to McQuaid, n.d., McQuaid Papers, 0003.001, Box 1, Folder 1.

99. Brann to McQuaid, February 6, 1866. McQuaid Papers, 0003.001, Box 1, Folder 1.

100. Minutes of the Board of Trustees, 1867, Board of Trustees minutes 1861-1936, Monsignor James Kelly papers, Folder 1 of 3.

101. Brann to McQuaid, February 6, 1866. McQuaid Papers, 0003.001, Box 1, Folder 1.

102. Zwierlein, *Bishop McQuaid*, 1: 331.

103. Yeager, *Life*, 235.

104. Yeager, *Life*, 476.

105. Zwierlein, *Bishop McQuaid*, 1: 326.

Chapter 3. The Michael Corrigan Years

1. Yeager, *Life*, 451.

2. *The Outlook*, May 17, 1902, 153.

3. Robert Seton to Bayley, September 24, 1862. ADN 2.1, Bayley Papers 1836–1872, Box 1, Folder 7.

4. Charles Warren Stoddart to Hudson Covington, Kentucky, April 7, 1888. AUND Hudson Papers.

5. *The Outlook*, May 17, 1902, 143.

6. Joseph F. Mahoney and Peter Wosh (eds.), *The Diocesan Journal of Michael Augustine Corrigan, Bishop of Newark, 1872–1880* (South Orange, NJ: SHU Special Collections, 1987), 79.

7. Joseph Flynn, *The Catholic Church in New Jersey* (Morristown, NJ: 1904), 293.

8. Some historians have been critical of his "flaws of character" and "abuse of power" (R. Emmett Curran, *Michael Augustine Corrigan and the Shaping of Conservative Catholicism in America, 1878–1902* [New York: Arno Press, 1978]), 1–2.

9. *Freeman's Journal*, October 9, 1880.

10. See R. Emmett Curran, "Confronting 'The Social Question': American Catholic Thought and the Socio-Economic Order in the Nineteenth Century," *U.S. Catholic Historian* 5, no. 2 (1986), 165–193

11. Edwin V. Sullivan, *An annotated copy of the diary of Bishop James Roosevelt Bayley, first Bishop of Newark 1853-1872*, Monsignor Field Special Collections and Archives Seton Hall University, September 5, 1864.

12. McQuaid to Bayley, September 1862, quoted in Zwierlein, *Bishop McQuaid*, 328.

13. Bayley to Brann, June 2, 1865, November 2, 1866, Bayley letter book, ADN RG 1.31.

14. William McCloskey to Bayley, November 27, 1863. ADN 2.1, Bayley Papers 1836–1872, Box 9, Folder 27.

15. Bayley to McCloskey, Rome, July 18, 1864. Bayley Letter Book, ADN, RG 1, 1.31.

16. Corrigan to McQuaid, September 18, 1868, quoted in Zwierlein, *Bishop McQuaid*, 1.

17. *A Memorial to Archbishop Corrigan* (New York: Catholic Library Association 1902), 70.

18. McQuaid to Corrigan, July 18, 1868, AANY C-3.

19. Zwierlein, *Bishop McQuaid*, 3: 367.

20. See E. F. Kennelly, "A Historical Study of Seton Hall College" (EdD dissertation, New York University, 1944), 81ff.

21. McQuaid to Archbishop Williams, April 13, 1886, Diocese of Rochester Letter Book, 188.

22. William McNulty to McQuaid, April 26, 1871, Archives of the Diocese of Rochester.

23. Corrigan to Orestes Brownson, April 21, 1871, Brownson Papers. University of Notre Dame Microfilm, Roll 7.

24. McNulty to McQuaid, April 29, 1871, Archives of the Diocese of Rochester (in Carl Hinrichsen's research materials/ADN 0004-012).

25. James Corrigan to Winand Wigger, May 15, 1882. Wigger Papers, ADN RG 3, 3.36, Clerical and General Correspondence.

26. James Corrigan to Bayley, October 23, 1870. Bayley Papers, ADN RG1, 1.433, Folder 3 of 3.

27. Miller, "Athletes in Academe," 144.

28. Yeager, *Life*, 212.

29. "Eminent Teachers and Educators Deceased in 1870," *The American Educational Monthly* (March 1871), 121.

30. Corrigan to Brownson, September 25, 1871. Brownson Papers, University of Notre Dame Microfilm, Roll 7.

31. Before turning Catholic, he was a Universalist, free thinker, and Unitarian.

32. Brownson to Mrs Goddard, December 20, 1863, Archbishop John Ireland Papers, Minnesota Historical Society Microfilms, Reel 2.

33. Richard Shaw, *Dagger John: The Unquiet Life and Times of Archbishop Hughes of New York* (New York: Paulist Press, 1977), 261.

34. William Seton to Orestes Brownson, February 28, 1872, Orestes Brownson Papers, University of Notre Dame Microfilm, Roll 7.

35. *The Catholic World: A Monthly Magazine of General Literature and Science* (October 1883), 211.

36. *The Morning Star and Catholic Messenger* (New Orleans, Louisiana), August 17, 1873.

37. *Newark Daily Journal*, June 1869.

38. J. & R. Lamb to Corrigan, January 23, 1871. Corrigan Letters, L, Monsignor Wm. Noé Field Special Collections and Archives, SHU. In the references that follow, letters indicated as "Corrigan Letters, A/B/C, Monsignor Field Special Collections and Archives, SHU" are unprocessed copies of originals.

39. Wm. Bailey & Co. to Corrigan, January 31, 1871. Corrigan Letters, B, Monsignor Field Special Collections and Archives SHU.

40. William Chambers to Corrigan, February 1, 1871. Corrigan Letters, C, Monsignor Field Special Collections and Archives, SHU.

41. McQuaid to Corrigan, December 10, 1871. Corrigan Letters, M, Monsignor Field Special Collections and Archives, SHU.

42. Thomas O'Connell to Corrigan, February 10, 1871. Corrigan Letters, O, Monsignor Field Special Collections and Archives, SHU.

43. W. Reand to Corrigan, February 1, 1871. Corrigan Letters, R, Monsignor Field Special Collections and Archives, SHU.

44. Fred. Coudert to Corrigan, March 30, 1871. Corrigan Letters, C, Monsignor Field Special Collections and Archives, SHU.

45. John Russell to Corrigan, April 12, 1871. Corrigan Letters, R, Monsignor Field Special Collections and Archives, SHU.

46. Mrs. B. Quinlan to Corrigan, February 19, 1872. SHU 0003.003 Michael A. Corrigan Papers, Box 1, Folder 19.

47. Rev. Pierce McCarthy to Corrigan, July 17, 1871. Corrigan Letters, M, Monsignor Wm. Noé Field Special Collections and Archives, SHU.

48. J.A. Fuller to Corrigan, February 7, 1871. Corrigan Letters, F, Monsignor Field Special Collections and Archives, SHU.

49. *Brownson's Quarterly Review* 2, no. 4 (October 1874), 565.

50. *The Sun* (New York), March 7, 1895. http://chroniclingamerica.loc.gov/lccn/sn83030272/1895-03-07/ed-1/seq-5.pdf.

51. F. Bloomer to Corrigan, July, 21, 1871. Corrigan Letters, B, Monsignor Field Special Collections and Archives, SHU.

52. David Bisset to Corrigan, May 24, 1871. Corrigan Letters, B, Monsignor Field Special Collections and Archives, SHU.

53. Richard Corrigan to Corrigan, February 9, 1872. SHU 0003.003, Michael A. Corrigan Papers, Box 1, Folder 23.

54. P.F. Burke to Corrigan, March 9, 1871. Corrigan Letters, B, Monsignor Wm. Noé Field Special Collections and Archives, SHU.

55. Corrigan to McQuaid, August 28, 1868, quoted in Frederick J. Zwierlein, *The Life and Letters of Bishop McQuaid, prefaced with the history of Catholic Rochester,* (Rochester, NY: 1909), 1.

56. Martin O'Brennan to Corrigan, January 16, 1873. SHU 0003.003, Michael A. Corrigan Papers, Box 1, Folder 23.

57. C.J. Beleke to Corrigan, December 17, 1871. SHU 0003.003, Michael A. Corrigan Papers, Box 1, Folder 23.

58. John McGuire to Corrigan, January 8, 1872. SHU 0003.003, Michael A. Corrigan Papers, Box 1, Folder 16.

59. Seton Hall College Catalogue, 1872.

60. N.J. O'Connell Ffrench to Corrigan, June 23, 1872. SHU 0003.003, Michael A. Corrigan Papers, Box 1, Folder 8.

61. A.S. Arkman to Corrigan, n.d., Corrigan Letters, A, Monsignor Field Special Collections and Archives, SHU.

62. Bernard Costello to Corrigan, February 3, 1871. SHU 0003.003, Michael A. Corrigan Papers, Box 1, Folder 10.

63. R. Prendiville to Corrigan, September 8, 1871. Corrigan Letters, P, Monsignor Field Special Collections and Archives, SHU.

64. S.O. Haldeman to Corrigan, January 16, 1872. RG 2 2.13, Michael Corrigan Correspondence, Folder 8.

65. John Nenninger to Corrigan, November 24, 1871. SHU 0003.003, Michael A. Corrigan Papers, Box 1, Folder 20.

66. R. Bachen to Corrigan, April 19, 1871. Corrigan Letters, B, Monsignor Field Special Collections and Archives, SHU.

67. Bernard Costello to Corrigan, March 7, 1871. Corrigan Letters, C, Monsignor Field Special Collections and Archives, SHU.

68. William Preston to Corrigan, January 23, 1872. Corrigan Letters, P, Monsignor Field Special Collections and Archives, SHU.

69. C.J. Caruana to Corrigan, February 7, 1871. Corrigan Letters, C, Monsignor Field Special Collections and Archives, SHU.

70. F.M Byrnes to Corrigan, February 4, 1871. Corrigan Letters, B, Monsignor Field Special Collections and Archives, SHU.

71. Frank Clark to Corrigan, May 24, 1871 Corrigan Letters, C, Monsignor Field Special Collections and Archives, SHU.

72. Edward Malley to Corrigan, December 31, 1872. SHU 0003.003, Michael A. Corrigan Papers, Box 1, Folder 16.

73. S.O. Haldeman to Corrigan, January 16, 1872. SHU 0003.003, Michael A. Corrigan Papers, Box 1, Folder 14.

74. John Foley to Corrigan, 1872. Corrigan Letters, F, Monsignor Field Special Collections and Archives, SHU.

75. S. Haldeman to Corrigan, August 19, 1871. SHU 0003.003, Michael A. Corrigan Papers, Box 1, Folder 14.

76. Dr. J.H. McDonnell to Corrigan, January 6, 1872. Corrigan Letters, M, Monsignor Field Special Collections and Archives, SHU.

77. John Foley to Corrigan, January 22, 1872. Corrigan Letters, F, Monsignor Field Special Collections and Archives, SHU.

78. E.L. Watson to Corrigan, March 23, 1871. Corrigan Letters, W, Monsignor Field Special Collections and Archives, SHU.

Chapter 4. Another Corrigan, Another Fire

1. *New York Daily Tribune*, January 6, 1910.

2. Bayley to Corrigan, May 22, 1872. ADN 2.1, Bayley Papers 1836–1872, Box 1, Folder 24.

3. Bernard Sheridan to Corrigan, September 1, 1871. SHU 0003.003, Michael A. Corrigan Papers, Box 1, Folder 3.

4. *New Ulm Weekly Review*, May 15, 1878.

5. Mahoney and Wosh, *Diocesan Journal*, 12.

6. *American Catholic Quarterly Review* 6 (October 1881), 24.

7. Mahoney and Wosh, *Diocesan Journal*, 8.

8. *American Catholic Quarterly Review* 6 (October 1881), 24.

9. F.W. Clarke, "Catholic Colleges," *The Independent—Devoted to the Consideration of Politics, Social and Economic Tendencies* 5, no. 18 (1876), 4.

10. Clarke, "Catholic Colleges," 4.

11. *The Catholic World* (September 1878), 855.

12. Kennelly, "Historical Study," 83.

13. Mahoney and Wosh, *Diocesan Journal*, 34.

14. Mahoney and Wosh, *Diocesan Journal*, 267.

15. *The National Republican* (Washington, DC), December 25, 1875.

16. Corrigan to Gibbons, February 5, 1884. Archdiocese of Baltimore Archives, AAB 205, 78 A5.

17. Wigger to Seton, May 21, 1888. Wigger Papers 0002-003, Correspondence Book, Volume 1, f. 348.

18. Seton to Wigger, May 24, 1888. Wigger Papers, ADN, RG 3, Box 7, 3.36.

19. *The Minneapolis Journal*, July 13, 1901.

20. Steven M. Avella, "Sebastian G. Messmer and the Americanization of Milwaukee's Catholicism." *U.S. Catholic Historian* 12, no. 3 (Summer 1994) 87–107.

21. John Keane to Archbishop John Ireland, April 11, 1889. Archbishop John Ireland Papers, Minnesota Historical Society Microfilms, Reel 4.

22. Avella, "Messmer."

23. Seton Hall College Catalogue 1895, 35.

24. Seton Hall College Catalogue 1895, 40.

25. Corrigan to William McCloskey, April 28, 1876. Hinrichsen Papers, Monsignor William Noe Field Special Collections and Archives, Seton Hall University.

26. Corrigan to Offult, July 13, 1876 SHU 0003.003, Michael A. Corrigan Papers, Box 1, Folder 3.

27. Kennelly, "Historical Study," 84–85.

28. Owen Harris to Corrigan, July 8, 1871. SHU 0003.003, Michael A. Corrigan Papers, Box 1, Folder 26.

29. Harold Tiers to Corrigan, June 6, 1871. SHU 0003.003, Michael A. Corrigan Papers, Box 1, Folder 23.

30. Kennelly, "Historical Study," 93.

31. Seton Hall College Catalogue 1895, 62.

32. Seton Hall College Catalogue 1895, 62.

33. Kennelly, "Historical Study," 95.

34. S.J. Ahern to Corrigan, September 17, 1877. ADN 2.2, Michael A. Corrigan Papers, Box 3, File 3.

35. Seton Hall College Catalogue 1878, 29.

36. James Corrigan to Wigger, May 14, 1882. Wigger Correspondence, ADN RG3, 3.36 Clerical and General Correspondence, 1880–1884.

37. Zwierlein, *Bishop McQuaid*, 21.

38. Zwierlein, *Bishop McQuaid*, 21.

39. Zwierlein, *Bishop McQuaid*, 21.

40. Zwierlein, *Bishop McQuaid*, 30.

41. Corrigan to McQuaid, January 18, 1881, quoted in Zwierlein, *Bishop McQuaid*, 30.

42. Corrigan to Archbishop McCloskey, April 28, 1876, Archdiocese of New York Archives, A30A, 184.

43. Corrigan to Wigger, May 14, 1882. Wigger Correspondence, ADN RG3, 3.36 Clerical and General Correspondence, 1880–1884.

44. Corrigan to Wigger, May 14, 1882. Wigger Correspondence, ADN RG3, 3.36 Clerical and General Correspondence, 1880–1884.

45. Corrigan to Wigger, May 14, 1882. Wigger Correspondence, ADN RG3, 3.36 Clerical and General Correspondence, 1880–1884.

46. Corrigan to Wigger, May 14, 1882. Wigger Correspondence, ADN RG3, 3.36 Clerical and General Correspondence, 1880–1884.

47. Corrigan to Wigger, May 14, 1882. Wigger Correspondence, ADN RG3, 3.36 Clerical and General Correspondence, 1880–1884.

48. Corrigan to McQuaid, November 22, 1882. Diocese of Rochester Archives (Hinrichsen Papers, SHU).

49. Boniface Wimmer to Alexius Edelbrock, November 27, 1882, in Jerome Oetgen (ed.), "Draft 2000," *The Letters of Boniface Wimmer*, 3: 390

50. Corrigan to McQuaid, November 20, 1882. Diocese of Rochester Archives (Hinrichsen Papers, Monsignor Field Special Collections and Archives SHU).

51. Jerome Oetgen, *Mission to America: A History of Saint Vincent Archabbey, the First Benedictine Monastery in the United States* (Washington, DC: CUA Press, 2000), 144–146.

52. Boniface Wimmer to Alexius Edelbrock, November 27, 1882, in Jerome Oetgen (ed.), "Draft 2000," *The Letters of Boniface Wimmer*, 3: 390.

53. McQuaid to Wigger, September 12, 1881. RG 3.37, Wigger Papers, Bishops, Archbishops.

54. McQuaid to Archbishop Williams, April 13, 1886. Hinrichsen Papers, Monsignor William Noe Field Special Collections, SHU.

55. John Tracy Ellis, *The Life of James Cardinal Gibbons, Archbishop of Baltimore 1834–1921* (Milwaukee, WI: Bruce Publishing Company: 1952), 1: 390.

56. Ellis, *Cardinal Gibbons*, 393.

57. Ellis, *Cardinal Gibbons*, 394.

58. "Be kind enough to write down for me the cost of chapel, college, etc. On the other page I have written down as well as I could remember the cost of the different buildings. Will you kindly correct any mistakes that may have been made? . . . Please make all necessary changes in the list, and return it, and I will then write a letter stating what I expect to get for Seton Hall." Wigger to Corrigan, January 15, 1885. Hinrichsen Papers, Field Collections, SHU.

59. See Wigger to Corrigan, May 14, 1888, Hinrichsen Papers, thanking him for $10,000.

60. McQuaid to Archbishop Williams, April 13, 1886, Hinrichsen Papers. "The property cost for ground and buildings about $300,000. The value of the land has greatly appreciated since I bought it in 1860. The buying price was about $500 per acre, with the Marble building thrown in. The land today, about 68 acres, should be worth from two to three thousand dollars per acre. The neighborhood today is one of New York suburban residences, and in the future will have still more of them."

61. Spalding to Gibbons, April 21, 1885. AAB, Hinrichsen Papers.

62. James Corrigan to Wigger, May 14, 1882. Wigger Correspondence, ADN RG3, 3.36 Clerical and General 1880–1884.

63. Wigger to James Corrigan, July 27, 1886. Wigger Papers, ADN, 0002-003, Correspondence Book, Vol. 1, f.97.

64. Wigger to J.F. Duffy, March 23, 1886. Wigger Papers ADN, 0002-00,3 Correspondence Book Correspondence Book, Vol. 1.

65. Wigger to J.F. Duffy, August 20, 1887. Correspondence Book, Vol. 2, f.241.

66. William Marshall to Wigger, August 11, 1892. RG3, Box 11, 3.36, Clerical and General Correspondence.

67. *New York Times*, May 28, 1910, 2.

68. RG 10, Student Affairs, Setonia Literary Society, Constitution and Minutes, 1886–1888, October 6, 1886.

69. Student Affairs, Setonia Literary Society, October 20, 1886.

70. Student Affairs, Setonia Literary Society, January 26, 1887.

71. Corrigan to McQuaid September 5, 1881. Diocese of Rochester Archives.

72. *New York Times*, March 10, 1886, 8.

73. Board of Trustees minutes, 1861-1936 James F. Kelley papers, Box 1 Folder 1, Monsignor Field Special Collection and Archives, SHU

74. Thomas Weston to Wigger, September 7, 1888 and January 9, 1889(?). RG 3, 3.36, Box 8, General and Clerical Correspondence.

75. J.A. McCreery to Wigger, March 7, 1886. RG 3, 3.36, Box 5, Clerical and General Correspondence.

76. *New York Times*, June 18, 1891, 6.

77. Edwin Simon to Wigger, March 10, 1887. RG 3, 3.36, Box 6, Clerical and General Correspondence.

78. James Corrigan to Wigger, February 14, 1882. RG 3, 3.36, Clerical and General Correspondence 1880–1884.

79. "There are 89 parochial schools in the Diocese, the attendance being 28,496. This is a large number of children, as the Catholic population is only about 220,000." Wigger to Michael Corrigan, August 13, 1895, Hinrichsen Papers.

80. *The Summit of a Century: The Centennial Story of Seton Hall University 1856–1956* (South Orange, NJ: 1956), 31.

81. Wigger to John F. Salaun, January 18, 1895. Correspondence Book, Vol. 2, f.193.

82. Eugene Kinkead, "A Reminiscence." *The Setonian* (May 1932), 34.

83. Leo Thebaud to Winand Wigger, January 21, 1889. RG 3, 3.36, Box 8, General and Clerical Correspondence.

84. Thomas T. McAvoy, "Manuscript Collection Among American Catholics." *The Catholic Historical Review* 37, no. 3 (October 1951), 288.

85. James Durkin to Kelley, September 26, 1946. SHU 3.11, Monsignor James F. Kelley Papers, Personal, SHU and SHU Student Records, Box 46, Folder 14.

86. *Newark Star-Ledger*, November 30, 1947.

87. Lionel Barrymore, *We Barrymores* (New York: Appleton-Century-Crofts, 1951), 23.

88. Barrymore, *We Barrymores*, 24–25.

89. *Philadelphia Inquirer*, April 22, 1897, 5.

90. "As I Remember Seton Hall," *The Setonian*, October 15, 1934, 3.

91. Office of the President and Chancellor: William F. Marshall records 0003-002, Monsignor Field Special Collection and Archives

92. *New York Times*, June 20, 1894, 9.

93. *The Setonian*, April 27, 1950, 1.

94. Board of Trustees, Minutes, June 21, 1899. RG 2.1, Board of Trustees Minutes 1864–1936, Box 1 of 1.

95. Wigger to William F. Marshall, February 5, 1895. Correspondence Book, Vol. 2, f.216.

96. Wigger to Michael J. Lenihan, May 2, 1896. Correspondence Book, Vol. 2, f. 400.

97. Wigger to F.G. Effray, August 23, 1895. Correspondence Book, Vol. 2, f. 301.

98. *New York Times*, December 8, 1894, 8.

99. *New York Times*, August 7, 1890, 5.

100. *New York Tribune*, May 22, 1897, 1.

101. Otto Zardette DD to Wigger, July 23, 1884. RG3, Box 4, 3.36, Clerical and General Correspondence.

102. O'Connor to Corrigan, October 10, 1877. ADN 2.2, Michael A. Corrigan Papers, Box 3, File 8.

103. *New York Times*, November 20, 1892, 10.

104. "A Voice from Seton Hall," *The Catholic Ledger*, September 23, 1893. *The Evening World*, (New York), September 15, 1893.

105. *New York Times*, August 3, 1890, 12.

106. William Marshall to Wigger, 1892 RG 3 3.36, Clerical and General Correspondence

107. *The Setonian*, October 1931, 27. Marshall, bedridden for seventeen years, died in Los Angeles in 1935 at the age of eighty-six. *New York Times*, October 17, 19 35, 23.

108. Board of Trustees, Minutes, June 16, 1897. RG 2.1, Board of Trustees Minutes 1864–1936, Box 1 of 1.

109. Felix O'Neill to Wigger, May 7, 1899. RG 3 3.36, Clerical and General Correspondence.

110. Board of Trustees, Minutes, March 4, 1897. RG 2.1, Board of Trustees, Minutes 1864–1936, Box 1 of 1.

111. Board of Trustees, Minutes, June 16, 1897. RG 2.1, Board of Trustees Minutes 1864–1936, Box 1 of 1.

112. The will was declared invalid but the executor offered a payment of $2,000, later reduced to $1,000. Board of Trustees, Minutes, June 15, 1898. RG 2.1, Board of Trustees, Minutes 1864–1936, Box 1 of 1.

113. Board of Trustees, Minutes, June 16, 1897. RG 2.1, Board of Trustees Minutes 1864–1936, Box 1 of 1.

114. Brian Regan, *Gothic Pride: The Story of Building a Great Cathedral in Newark* (New Brunswick, NJ: Rivergate Books, Rutgers University Press, 2012), 25.

115. *The New York Daily Tribune*, December 21, 1894.

116. *The New York Tribune*, April 12, 1899.

117. *The Independent—Devoted to the Consideration of Politics, Social and Economic Tendencies*, April 20, 1899.

118. Wigger to John O'Connor, March 26, 1899. ADN 0002-003.

Chapter 5. A New Century

1. *The Xavier* 13, no. 2 (February 1901), 144.

2. Zardetti to Wigger, July 23, 1884. RG 3, Box 4, Clerical and General Correspondence.

3. Minutes of the Board of Trustees, June 12, 1901. RG 2.1, 1864–1936, Box 1 of 1.

4. *The Xavier*, 13, no. 2 (February 1901), 64.

5. J.A. Mooney, *Memorial of Most Reverend Michael Augustine Corrigan, Archbishop of New York* (New York: Cathedral Library Association 1902).

6. Minutes, Board of Trustees, June 9, 1909. RG 2.1, 1864–1936, Box 1 of 1.

7. Edward J. Power, *A History of Catholic Higher Education in the United States* (Milwaukee, WI: Bruce Publishers, 1958), 154.

8. Power, *Catholic Higher Education*, 154.

9. John J. O'Connor, Pastoral Letter, November 1, 1902. O'Connor papers, and 0002.004, Box 2, 2.4, Folder 5.

10. Mary Agnes Sharkey, *The New Jersey Sisters of Charity* (New York: Longmans, 1933), 234–236.

11. Thomas Kelly to O'Connor, June 15, 1901. John J. O'Connor Papers, ADN 0002.004, Box 2.4, Folder 11.

12. *New York Times*, May 21, 1927, 19.

13. *New York Daily Tribune*, December 31, 1902, 3.

14. *New York Daily Tribune*, March 21, 1898.

15. Seton Hall College Catalogue, 1911–1912, 84.

16. John Talbot Smith, *Our Seminaries: An Essay on Clerical Training* (New York: W.H. Young, 1896), 99.

17. Seton Hall College Catalogue, 1911–1912, 84–85.

18. John J. O'Connor, Pastoral Letter, August 22, 1905. ADN 0002.004, O'Connor, Box 22.4, Folder 5.

19. John J. O'Connor, Pastoral Letter, August 22, 1905. ADN 0002.004, O'Connor, Box 22.4, Folder 5.

20. All quotations in this section from J. A. Stafford to O'Connor, January 13, 1905. O'Connor Papers, ADN, RG4, 4.42, Institutions and Agencies/Seton Hall College.

21. Geo. Meyer to Thomas Wallace, June 1903, ADN, R.G. 4, 4.76.2, General Correspondence, ME-R.

22. *New York Times*, September 28, 1903, 3.

23. *New York Times*, August 6, 1908, 5.

24. *New York Times*, November 10, 1910, 10.

25. *New York Times*, July 15, 1910, 3. *The Sun* (New York), April 30, 1909.

26. Seton Hall College Catalogue, 1908–1909, 22.

27. *The Setonian*, 1856–1931 Diamond Jubilee Number, June 4, 1931, 27.

28. *The Setonian*, 1856–1931 Diamond Jubilee Number, June 4, 1931, 27.

29. Seton Hall College Catalogue, 1907–1908, 116.

30. Seton Hall College Catalogue, 1922–1930.

31. Seton Hall College Catalogue, 1922–1930, 15.

32. Charles Mackel to Mulligan, January 24, 1904. ADN R.G. 8, Priests' Papers, Michael Mulligan.

33. Mackel to John Sheppard, December 8, 1904. ADN R.G. 4, O'Connor Papers, 4.36, Vicar-General John Sheppard Papers.

34. *New York Times*, August 3, 1904, 3.

35. LeRoy McWilliams (with Jim Bishop), *Parish Priest* (New York: McGraw Hill, 1953), 49.

36. Will and Ariel Durant, *A Dual Autobiography* (New York: Simon and Shuster, 1977), 30.

37. *The Setonian*, March 24, 1928, 8.

38. *The Setonian*, March 24, 1928, 8.

39. *The Newark Evening News*, March 28, 1909, 4.

40. *The Washington Times*, March 28, 1909.

41. *The Alliance Herald* (Box Butte, Nebraska), April 1, 1909.

42. *Alliance Herald*, April 1, 1909.

43. Vicar General John Sheppard Papers, Minute Book, April 6, 1909, ADN, R.G. 4.36.

44. Vicar General John Sheppard Papers, Minute Book, April 6, 1909, ADN, R.G. 4.36.

45. Minutes, Board of Trustees, April 5, 1909. RG 2.1, 1864–1936, Box 1 of 1.

46. The builders went into receivership, leaving Mooney, using tradesmen and suppliers under the original contract, to finish the work. A complicated set of claims for payment then ensued.

47. Mooney to Pastors of the Diocese of Newark, August 31, 1910. SHU 0003.8, Folder 41.

48. Will Durant, *Transition: A Mental Autobiography* (New York: Simon and Shuster, 1927), 134.

49. John J. O'Connor to Pastors of the Diocese of Newark, July 13, 1911. RG #4, 5, 6, ADN. Accession 14-89 Walsh. Series 1: Form Letters 1911–1941.

50. John J. O'Connor to Pastors of the Diocese of Newark, July 13, 1911. RG #4, 5, 6, ADN. Accession 14-89 Walsh. Series 1: Form Letters 1911–1941.

51. Seton Hall College Catalogue, June 1905, 11.

52. Treasurer's Report, June 1914. RG 2.1, 1864–1936, Box 1 of 1.

53. Seton Hall College Catalogue, 1922–1930, 13.

54. *The Setonian*, 1856–1931 Diamond Jubilee Number, June 4, 1931, 62.

55. *The Setonian*, 1856–1931 Diamond Jubilee Number, June 4, 1931, 62,

56. The details of what follows may be found in New Jersey Supreme Court, State of the Case, Seton Hall College, a corporation, prosecutor, v. Village of South Orange, Joseph Arnold, Assessor and Collector of Taxes in the Village of South Orange, defendants. SHU 0003.8, James F. Mooney Papers, Folder 42. See also John Griffin, attorney at law-James F. Mooney, September 11, 1911, same folder.

57. New Jersey Laws of 1903, p. 394, section 3, sub. div. 4.

58. Also sub. div. 4.

59. The stipulated facts of the case are worth recording as a record of Seton Hall's legal personality:

(1) Seton Hall College was incorporated under an act of the legislature of the state of New Jersey entitled, "An Act to Incorporate Seton Hall College," chapter 86, pages 198 and 199, approved March 8th, 1861.

(2) A supplement to said act was passed, being chapter 267 of the laws of 1870, pages 199 and 199, entitled, 'Supplement to an Act to Incorporate Seton Hall College,' approved March 8th, 1861, which supplement was approved March 16th, 1870.

(3) The act incorporating Drew Theological Seminary of the Methodist Episcopal Church, referred to in the supplement above mentioned, was approved February 12th, 1868 (Laws of 1868, chapter 2, p.4)

(4) That Seton Hall College accepted its charter contained in the Laws of 1861 aforesaid, and thereafter purchased real and personal property from time to time, erected college buildings thereon, and continuously since has been and is still actively engaged in carrying out the purchases of its creation and fulfilling its obligations imposed by said charter, and has been and is exercising all the powers granted by said charter.

(5) After the supplement to its charter was passed in 1870, Seton Hall College accepted the same, and purchased further lands and erected further buildings, and has continued ever since to live up to the terms of both acts and carry out the purposes of its creation, and has been and is exercising all the powers granted thereby.

(6) That the lands in question, with other lands, were acquired by the college by a conveyance dated 17th day of October 1864, and recorded in the office of the register of the county of Essex on the 21st day of February, 1865, in book M-12 of deeds for said county, on p.343.

(7) That no assessment or tax has been levied or imposed upon the property, real or personal, of Seton Hall College from the date of its original charter in 1861, down to the year 1911; and the tax in question, imposed in the year 1911, is the first tax imposed or attempted to be imposed upon the property of said Seton Hall college, real or personal.

60. United States Supreme Court: Seton Hall College v. Village of South Orange (1916). http://caselaw.findlaw.com/us-supreme-court/242/100.html.

61. Kelley to John Petillo, March 3, 1984. R.G. 2, 4-89, Petillo, Box 3 of 3.

62. McWilliams, op. cit., 42.

63. McWilliams, *Parish Priest*, 45

64. William Egan to O'Connor, September 30, 1924. John J. O'Connor papers ADN 2.4 Box 2 Folder 2.6 Correspondence A–Z, 1922–1926.

65. McWilliams, *Parish Priest*, 50.

66. *The Setonian*, May 1933, 16.

67. McWilliams, *Parish Priest*, 40.

68. *New York Times*, January 12, 1937, 26.

69. Seton Hall College Catalogue, 1911–1912, 18.

70. McWilliams, *Parish Priest*, 45.

71. McWilliams, *Parish Priest*, 46–47.

72. Seton Hall University Ninth Annual Athletic Hall of Fame Dinner, April 4, 1981. RG 2, SHU, 2.18.1, Conley, Fahy, D'Alessio, A–B 1980–1984.

73. *The University Missourian*, January 12, 1911, 2.

74. *Forum*, March 1910, 217.

75. "*Transition* [is] a mass of self-praise and a disparagement of everything we regard as sacred." Thomas McLaughlin to James O'Toole, March 7, 1931, Immaculate Conception Seminary, Rectors Correspondence, D.

76. Durant, *Transition*, 111.

77. Durant and Durant, *Dual Autobiography*, 35.

78. John Tibbuts, *Thought*, September 1928, 349.

79. *The Saturday Review of Literature*, August 28, 1928, 78.

80. William Noe Field to Thomas Peterson, July 24, 1997. R.G. 2.21, Office of the Chancellor, Peterson, 24 of 48.

81. Walter McDonald, *Reminiscences of a Maynooth Professor* (Dublin: Mercier Press, 1967), 17.

82. *Transition*, 115–116.

83. Una M. Cadegan, *All Good Books Are Catholic Books: Print Culture, Censorship, and Modernity in Twentieth-Century America* (Ithaca, NY: Cornell University Press, 2013), 194.

84. Seton Hall College Catalogue, 1911–1912, 23.

85. Seton Hall College Catalogue, 1911–1912, 47–48.

86. In 1921, Edward Cahill from East Orange, was sentenced to five years imprisonment in Ireland for participation in that country's war of independence. Cahill seems to have been Seton Hall's first freedom fighter, as Macy King, in Cuba, was its first foreign legionary. *New York Times*, July 30, 1921, 4.

87. *New York Times*, April 20, 1917, 5.

88. Seton Hall College Catalogue, 1911–1912, 95–100. New Jersey accounted for 169, New York 39, Connecticut, Massachusetts, and Pennsylvania combined came to 12.

89. Kennelly, "Historical Study," 139.

90. *New York Times*, November 29, 1918, 9.

91. J. F. Mooney Papers, RG 2, 2.8.1.

92. Minutes, Board of Trustees, June 9, 1920. RG 2.1, 1864–1936, Box 1 of 1.

93. Minutes, Board of Trustees , June 15, 1921. RG 2.1, 1864–1936, Box 1 of 1.

94. James Kelley to Thomas Fahy, October 15, 1970. RG 2 2.15.5.1, Fahy, Box 21 of 24.

Chapter 6. McLaughlin at the Helm

1. John Francis Neylan to McLaughlin, February 19, 1926. RG 2.9.1.3, Office of the President, McLaughlin.

2. John Francis Neylan to McLaughlin, February 19, 1926. RG 2.9.1.3, Office of the President, McLaughlin.

3. John Francis Neylan to McLaughlin, February 19, 1926. RG 2.9.1.3, Office of the President, McLaughlin.

4. After Seton Hall, he moved to California. In April 1935, he appeared on the cover of *Time* magazine as representative of the Hearst newspaper group.

5. John O'Connor to McLaughlin, July 4, 1923. ADN 0002.004, O'Connor, Box 2, Folder 19.

6. Durant, *Transition*, 126.

7. Such was the memory of Father Leo Martin as told to Francis Seymour. *Fratres in Unum*, (Quarterly newsletter of the priests of the Archdiocese of Newark), ADN 0057, Monsignor Field Special Collections and Archive, SHU Fall 1992.

8. Maura Rossi, "Bishop McLaughlin Remembered," *The Beacon* (Paterson), March 13, 1997, 10.

9. *The Setonian*, April 10, 1986.

10. Such was the memory of Father Leo Martin as told to Francis Seymour. *Fratres in Unum*, (Quarterly newsletter of the priests of the Archdiocese of Newark), ADN 0057, Monsignor Field Special Collections and Archive, SHU Fall 1992.

11. McLaughlin, Appointment Book, 1924, f.47. RG 2.9.13.

12. McLaughlin Papers, Appointment Books 1927–1928, RG 2.9.1.3.

13. McLaughlin to Rev. Daniel O'Connell, S.J. July 20, 1927. RG 2 2.9.2.3, McLaughlin, Correspondence, 1927–1929.

14. McLaughlin to Rev. Daniel O'Connell, S.J. July 20, 1927. RG 2 2.9.2.3, McLaughlin, Correspondence, 1927–1929.

15. McLaughlin to Rev. Daniel O'Connell, S.J. July 20, 1927. RG 2 2.9.2.3, McLaughlin, Correspondence, 1927–1929.

16. McLaughlin to Rev. Daniel O'Connell, S.J. July 20, 1927. RG 2 2.9.2.3, McLaughlin, Correspondence, 1927–1929.

17. McLaughlin to Rev. Daniel O'Connell, S.J. July 20, 1927. RG 2 2.9.2.3, McLaughlin, Correspondence, 1927–1929.

18. McLaughlin to Priests of the Diocese of Newark, 1923. RG 4, O'Connor, 4.23, Folder 3.

19. Kennelly, "Historical Sources," 144.

20. Kennelly, "Historical Sources," 151.

21. Kennelly, "Historical Sources," 145.

22. Henry G.J. Beck, *Immaculate Conception Seminary Centennial* (Mahwah, NJ: Darlington, 1962), 38.

23. McLaughlin, Appointment Book, 1924,

24. W.W. Husband to McLaughlin, February 14, 1925. RG 2, Thomas McLaughlin/, 2.1.9 Foreign Students Correspondence 1924–1925.

25. Charles Cobb to J.J. Synott, August 30, 1898. RG 2, Synott, 2.6.1 Correspondence.

26. James Sullivan to McLaughlin, October 1, 1924. RG 2, McLaughlin, 2.9.3.7 Correspondence 1923–1925.

27. McLaughlin to O'Connor, June 28, 1924. RG 2, McLaughlin, 2.9.2.2 Correspondence 1923–September 1925.

28. Philip Gleason, *Contending With Modernity: Catholic Higher Education in the Twentieth Century* (New York: Oxford University Press, 1995), 48–56.

29. McLaughlin to O'Connor, June 28, 1924. RG 2, McLaughlin, 2.9.2.2 Correspondence 1923–September 1925.

30. Allen O. Pfinster, "Regional Accrediting Agencies at the Crossroads," *Journal of Higher Education* 42, no. 7, 1971, 561.

31. McLaughlin to O'Connor, June 28, 1924. RG 2, McLaughlin, 2.9.2.2 Correspondence 1923–September 1925.

32. McLaughlin to O'Connor, June 28, 1924. RG 2, McLaughlin, 2.9.2.2 Correspondence 1923–September 1925.

33. McLaughlin to Augustus Downing, August 14, 1924. RG 2, McLaughlin, 2.9.2.2 Correspondence 1923–September 1925.

34. George McClelland to McLaughlin, October 13, 1922. RG 3, Accreditation Documentation, 3.2, Membership Approval, November 1932, Library and Laboratory.

35. McLaughlin to E.D. Grizzell, December 31, 1927. RG 3, Accreditation Documentation 3.1, Middle States Inspection and Accreditation, Reports and Correspondence.

36. RG 4. 4.3, Office of the Registrar, Folder 1, Middle States Accreditation 1927.

37. By now, the seminary had relocated to Darlington.

38. RG 4. 4.3, Office of the Registrar, Folder 1, Middle States Accreditation 1927.

39. Seton Hall College Catalogue, 1926, 24–25.

40. Minutes, Board of Trustees, May 27, 1932. James F. Kelley papers, Monsignor Field Special Collections, SHU Box 1 Folder 3.

41. Record: The Aquinas House of Studies, SHU 3.22, 14, President's Hall documents.

42. There were eight "outside" heads of department in 1933–1934: John Savage, PhD (Harvard), head of classical languages; James Lackey, PhD (Columbia), head of natural science; Allen Woodall, PhD (Pittsburgh), head of English; Milton Proctor, PhD (New York University), head of the department of education; Lawrence McGrath, PhD (Stanford), head of social science; Ernest Howald, PhD (Minnesota), head of modern languages; Lawrence Loveridge, PhD (California), head of mathematics; George Brooks, LLB (Fordham), head of public speaking.

43. Seton Hall College Catalogue, June 1933, 33.

44. Seton Hall College Catalogue, June 1933, 34.

45. Seton Hall College Catalogue, June 1933, 38–39.

46. Sigmund J. Sluszka, "Polish Language Teaching in America," *Polish American Studies* 8, nos.1–2 (January–June 1951), 31.

47. Seton Hall College Catalogue, June 1933, 11.

48. RG 2 2.9.5, McLaughlin, Presidents Report 1933.

49. Seton Hall College Catalogue, June 1933, 49.

50. "As I Remember *The Setonian*," *The Setonian*, March 1934.

51. *The Setonian*, March 15, 1924, 1.

52. *The Setonian*, March 20, 1925, 9.

53. *The Setonian*, March 20, 1925, 2.

54. *The Setonian*, May 29, 1925.

55. *The Setonian*, December 16, 1925.

56. *The Setonian*, May 29, 1925.

57. *The Setonian*, March 20, 1926.

58. *The Setonian*, Christmas 1931, 16.

59. *The Setonian*, February 27, 1929.

60. Canons 1352 through 1383 dealt with seminaries.

61. Robert James Wister, *Stewards of the Mysteries of God: Immaculate Conception Seminary 1860–2010* (South Orange NJ: Immaculate Conception Seminary, 2010), 120.

62. The closing price was $478,488.41. Beck, *Immaculate Conception*, 39.

63. Wister, *Stewards*, 122.

64. Beck, *Immaculate Conception*, 41.

65. *Newark Call*, March 11, 1928.

66. George L.A. Reilly, "Thomas J. Walsh," in *The Bishops of Newark* (South Orange, NJ: Seton Hall University Press, 1978), 98.

67. Reilly, "Walsh," 99.

68. *New York Times*, March 30, 1928, 30.

69. "75th Year fete Being Planned for Seton Hall," *Newark Call*, February 8, 1931.

70. Francis R. Seymour, "Bishop Thomas Henry McLaughlin, 1881–1947," in *Fratres in Unum*, (Quarterly newsletter of the priests of the Archdiocese of Newark), ADN 0057, Monsignor Field Special Collections and Archive, SHU Fall 1992.

71. *The Sunday Call* (Newark), March 15, 1931.

72. *The Newark Evening News*, June 4, 1931.

73. *The Setonian*, October 1931, 3.

74. *The Setonian*, October 1931, 14.

75. In private conversation. Minutes, Board of Trustees, May 31, 1931, 78. James F. Kelley papers, Monsignor Field Special Collections, SHU Box 1 Folder 3.

76. *The South Orange Record*, June 4, 1931, 4.

77. *New York Times*, September 20, 1925, E7.

78. *New York Times*, April 27, 1927, 5.

79. *New York Times*, November 7, 1928, 25.

80. *New York Times*, January 23, 1933, 13.

81. *New York Times*, November 29, 1933, 19.

82. *New York Times*, January 21, 1934, X4.

Chapter 7. From McLaughlin to Monaghan to Kelley

1. Born in Pennsylvania in 1873, Walsh served in Buffalo, New York before becoming Bishop of Trenton in 1918 and of Newark in 1928.

2. A spittoon in Sacred Heart Cathedral testified to his tobacco-chewing habit.

3. Minutes of the Board of Trustees, May 27, 1932, 95–96.

4. McLaughlin to Walsh, December 10, 1932. and, 9a, Seton Hall.

5. Thomas A. Boland to William A Griffin, January 10, 1939. I.C.S. 3.2.4, Rector's Correspondence, Bishop of Newark.

6. Walsh to James F. Kelley, September 7, 1935; Walsh to Guterl, September 7, 1935. and, 9a, Seton Hall.

7. Walsh to Monaghan, January 8, 1936. and, 9a, Seton Hall.

8. *New York Times*, June 6, 1925, 4.

9. *Newark Evening News*, January 4, 1932.

10. McLaughlin to Albert Meredith, January 5, 1932. R.G. 2, 2.1.9, McLaughlin, New Jersey Board of Regents, 1932.

11. McLaughlin to Albert Meredith, January 5, 1932. R.G. 2, 2.1.9, McLaughlin, New Jersey Board of Regents, 1932.

12. *New York Times*, June 6, 1925, 4.

13. Raymond J. Kupke, *Living Stones: A History of the Catholic Church in the Diocese of Paterson* (Marceline, M): Walworth Publishing, 1987), 223–224.

14. Francis Seymour, "Serious Msgr. Lawlor Had a Funny Ending." *The Catholic Advocate* (Newark, NJ), December 4, 1991, 6.

15. *The Setonian*, October 14, 1933, 1.

16. Walsh to Monaghan, May 21, 1933. Minutes of the Board of Trustees, May 25, 1933.

17. R.G. 2, 2.1.10, Monaghan, Sacred Congregations of Seminaries, Reports 1932–33.

18. Pastoral Letters, January 14, 1936, January 12, 1937, January 11, 1938. RG 5 5.21, Box 13, P: Pastorals, Circulars, Letters 1928–1950, Folders 1936, 1937, 1938.

19. *The Setonian*, December 19, 1924.

20. Minutes of the Board of Trustees, June 4, 1942, 112.

21. R.J. Bretnall, Millburn High School to John J. Carlin, May 6, 1935. and, 9a, Seton Hall.

22. Monaghan to McClary, July 23, 1934. McClary to Monaghan, July 24, 1934. ADN, 9a, Seton Hall.

23. Minutes of the Board of Trustees, May 17, 1934, 167–168.

24. Board of Trustees minutes of meeting, 1934 James F. Kelley papers, Box 1 Folder 3, Monsignor Field Special Collections and Archives, SHU

25. Conversation with the author, October 7, 2004.

26. RG 2 2.9.3.7, McLaughlin, 1928.

27. This was a trait of Seton Hall's chemist-priests. In a later era, Father Alfred Celiano was also an organist.

28. *The White and Blue* (Seton Hall yearbook 1925), 48.

29. Brady's best-known book was *Confusion Twice Confounded* (South Orange, NJ: Seton Hall University Press, 1955), an account of the Establishment Clause of the U.S. Constitution.

30. Bishop Walter Curtis, *Eulogy*, Joseph H. Brady Papers, ADN 0004.005, Series VII, Folder 200.

31. *The Setonian*, October 15, 1937.

32. William E. Luithle to Robert Sheeran, April 12, 2003. Uncatalogued letter in author's possession.

33. *The White and Blue* (1926), 50.

34. *New York Times*, December 8, 1935, N4.

35. *The Setonian*, September 26, 1963, 3.

Chapter 8. Resurgence

1. Neylan to Kelley, September 3, 1946. RG 2, 2.1.11, Kelley, Neylan Correspondence 1937–1946.

2. Hoover to Kelley, RG 2, 2.1.11, Kelley, Speeches, Convocations, Correspondence.

3. George [Strack?] to Joseph Brady, January 3, 1935. ADN 0004.005, Series VII, Folder 142, Letters to Brady 10/26–6/36.

4. James Kelley, *Memoirs of Msgr. ("Doc") J.F. Kelley* (privately printed, 1987), 82.

5. Kelley, *Memoirs*, 85.

6. Kelley, *Memoirs*, 87.

7. *New York Times*, August 30, 1936, SM 22.

8. "Head of Seton Hall Hails Small Schools," *Newark Star-Eagle*, August 19, 1936.

9. Ibid

10. Meador Wright, "The Many-Sided Dr. Kelley," July 1945, unidentified periodical, RG2, 2.11.4, James F. Kelley Papers.

11. *The Setonian*, October 16, 1936, 1.

12. *The Setonian*, October 29, 1937, 1.

13. Kennelly, "Historical Study," 190.

14. *The Setonian*, February 25, 1937, 1.

15. *The Setonian*, December 10, 1937, 1.

16. *Seton Hall College Bulletin*, 1939, 27.

17. *The Setonian*, January 21, 1938, 2.

18. "Education," in Maxine Lurie and Marc Mappen (eds.) *The Encyclopedia of New Jersey* (New Brunswick: Rutgers University Press, 2004), 242.

19. Neylan to Kelley, May 3, 1944. RG 2, 2.11, Kelley, Americanism.

20. Quoted in Philip Gleason, *Contending With Modernity: Catholic Higher Education in the Twentieth Century* (New York: Oxford University Press, 1995), 77.

21. Neylan to Kelley, May 3, 1944. RG 2, 2.11, Kelley, Americanism.

22. Minutes of the Board of Trustees, Seton Hall College, June 5, 1941, 348.

23. Nathaniel Baum to Kelley, November 14, 1938. RG 2. 2.11/Kelley/Americanism.

24. Fanny Mae Warren to Kelley, October 21, 1937. RG 2. 2.11/Kelley/Americanism.

25. H.H. Fisher to Kelley, October 7, 1938. RG 2. 2.11/Kelley/Americanism.

26. *The Setonian*, May 6, 1938, 2.

27. *The Setonian*, May 20, 1938, p. 2. See Matthew J. O'Brien, "Wartime Revisions of Irish American Catholicism: Stars, Stripes and Shamrocks," *U.S. Catholic Historian* 21, no. 4 (Fall 2004), 77.

28. Lawrence McCaffrey, "Ireland and Irish America: Connections and Disconnections," *U.S. Catholic Historian* 22, no. 3 (Summer 2004), 12.

29. SHU 3.11, Monsignor James F. Kelley Papers, Box 11, Folder 34, Student Information, Undated.

30. SHU 3.11, Monsignor James F. Kelley Papers, Box 11, Folder 34, Student Information, Undated.

31. *The Setonian*, November 5, 1937, 1.

32. *The Setonian*, November 5, 1937, 1.

33. *The Setonian*, November 19, 1937, 2.

34. Kelley, *Memoirs*, 117.

35. Meador Wright, "Many-Sided Dr. Kelley."

36. Kelley, *Memoirs*, 125.

37. Gleason, *Contending with Modernity*, 168.

38. Gleason, *Contending with Modernity*, 168.

39. *The Setonian*, January 25, 1937, 2.

40. *The Setonian*, October 29, 1937, 4.

41. *The Setonian*, October 29, 1937, 1.

42. *The Setonian*, October 29, 1937, 1.

43. *Irish Press*, August 4, 1938, 4.

44. Kennelly, "Historical Sources," 188.

45. Kelley, *Memoirs*, 125.

46. *Seton Hall College Bulletin: Extension Division* 1937–1940, 9, 10, 14.

47. *The Setonian*, October 29, 1937, 1.

48. *The Setonian*, February 8, 1937, 3.

49. RG 2.2.1.11, Kelley, John C. McClary Correspondence, 1937–1942.

50. RG 3 SHU, Accreditation Documentation, 3/3/1940–1942.

51. RG 3 SHU, Accreditation Documentation, 3/3/1940–1942.

52. RG 3 SHU, Accreditation Documentation, 3/3/1940–1942.

53. RG 3 SHU, Accreditation Documentation, 3/3/1940–1942.

54. Guterl to Kelley, March 17, 1942. RG 3 SHU, Accreditation Documentation, 3/3/1940–1942

55. Charles B. Murphy to Kelley, April 4, 1940, R.G. 2, John L. McNulty, 2.12.7, Folder 122, Report on the Library, 1938–1939.

56. *New York Times*, April 4, 1937, 52.

57. RG 2, 2.11, Kelley, Bayley Seton League Historical Sketch.

58. It served as an auditorium, refectory and classroom building until, derelict, it was demolished in 2013. Its replacement, Muscarelle Hall, in honor of Joseph and Sharon Muscarelle for their generosity to the university, is a classroom building which opened in 2014.

59. *New York Times*, April 27, 1937 April 27, 1937.

60. *New York Times* February 28, 1935.

61. *Newark Evening News* October 1, 1939, 2.

Chapter 9. Seton Hall at War

1. Meador Wright, "Many-Sided Dr. Kelley."

2. *The Setonian*, September 19, 1996, 4.

3. *The Setonian*, October 18, 1940, 1.

4. Peter Guilday to Joseph Brady, March 1, 1938. ADN 0004.005, Series VII, Folder 155.

5. ADN 0004.005, Joseph H. Brady, Box 5, Folder 217.

6. Kelley to Brady, February 17, 1941. ADN 0004.005, Series VII, Folder 156.

7. ADN 0004.005, Series II, Folder 59, August 9, 1939.

8. Faculty meeting, November 28, 1938. Brady, ADN 0004.005, Series II, Folder 53.

9. Kelley to Bedell, March 5, 1941. Brady, ADN 0004.005, Series VII, Folder 149.

10. Kelley to Brady, December 18, 1940. Joseph H. Brady Papers, ADN 0004.005, Series VII, Folder 149.

11. Memorandum on Admissions, March 5, 1940. Brady, ADN 0004.005, Series II, Folder 53.

12. Brady to Kelley, December 18, 1939. Joseph H. Brady Papers, ADN 0004.005, Series II, Folder 53.

13. Brady to Kelley, December 18, 1939. Joseph H. Brady Papers, ADN 0004.005, Series II, Folder 53.

14. Brady to Kelley, December 18, 1939. Brady, ADN 0004.005, Series II, Folder 53.

15. Meeting of the Executive Advisory Committee, December 18, 1939. Brady to Kelley, December 18, 1939. ADN 0004.005, Series II, Folder 53.

16. Meeting of the Executive Advisory Committee, December 18, 1939. Brady, ADN 0004.005, Series II, Folder 53.

17. Boniface Reger to James Kelley, November 8, 1940. RG 2 2.11.4, Kelley, Newark-St. Benedict's Prep Correspondence 1940–1943.

18. *Hudson Dispatch*, August 14, 1939.

19. SHU 3.11, Kelley, Box 15, Folder 48, Meeting Minutes Faculty, November 15, 1939.

20. SHU 3.11, Kelley, Box 15, Folder 48, Meeting Minutes Faculty, November 21, 1939.

21. Brady Papers, ADN 0004.005, Series II, Folder 54.

22. Kelley to James Hamilton *et. al*, May 19, 1941. Brady, ADN papers, Series VII, Folder 155.

23. Minutes of the Board of Trustees, June 5, 1941, 356.

24. Minutes of the Board of Trustees, June 4, 1942, 220.

25. Minutes of the Board of Trustees, June 5, 1941, 351.

26. Minutes of the Board of Trustees, June 5, 1941, 356.

27. Minutes of the Board of Trustees, June 4, 1942, 230.

28. SHU 3.11, Kelley, Box 15, Folder 50, Minutes of Administration meeting, December 7, 1942.

29. Kelley to James Hughes, March 17, 1942. and, 9a, Seton Hall.

30. Kennelly, "Historical Sources," 204.

31. Kennelly, "Historical Sources," 206.

32. Kelley to McClary, May 4, 1942. RG 2, 2.11, Kelley, McClary 1937–1943.

33. Stella Jasina to McClary, September 21, 1942. ADN, 9a, Seton Hall.

34. Kelley to McClary, June 16, 1943. ADN, 9a, Seton Hall.

35. Kelley to McClary, June 16, 1943. ADN, 9a, Seton Hall.

36. Minutes of the Board of Trustees, May 11, 1944.

37. Minutes of the Board of Trustees, May 21, 1943. Financial Report, 8.

38. Minutes of the Board of Trustees, Seton Hall College, June 4, 1942, 223.

39. Total enrollments for Seton Hall College (that is to say, the South Orange campus) were as follows: 1935–1936, 271; 1936–1937, 290; 1937–1938, 425; 1938–1939, 481; 1939–1940, 581; 1940–1941, 676; 1941–1942, 704; 1942–1943, 563; 1943–1944, 165; 1944–1945, 157. Total enrollments at the Urban Division were: 1938–1939, 1,025; 1939–1940, 1,336; 1940–1941, 1,365; 1941–1942, 1,545; 1942–1943, 1,132; 1943–1944, 808; 1944–1945, 1,460. SHU 3.11, Kelley, Box 11, Folder 21, Student Enrollment Totals, 1938–1948.

40. In fall 1942, total enrollment was 1,132, of whom 318 were men, 578 lay women, and 236 nuns. In spring 1944, total enrollment was 1,025, of whom 138 were men, 698 lay women, and 207 nuns. Guterl to Thomas Walsh, October 14, 1943. SHU 3.11, Kelley, Box 15, folder 26, Correspondence on Urban Division 1943–1944.

41. Kelley, SHU 3.11, Kelley, Box 11, Folder 22.

42. Guterl to Walsh, March 3, 1944. SHU 3.11, Kelley, Box 11, Folder 22.

43. Guterl to Walsh, August 30, 1944. SHU 3.11, Kelley, Box 11, Folder 22.

44. *The Alumni: Seton Hall University's Alumni Magazine*, Winter 1990, 16.

45. *Newark Star-Ledger*, May 8, 1942.

46. *Newark Star-Ledger*, May 31, 1942.

47. Kelley to Lillis, August 24, 1942. SHU 3.11, Kelley, Student SHU Records, Box 46, Folder 9.

48. *Newark Star-Ledger*, May 31, 1942, 34.

49. RG 7, Accession 6-86, Office of the Provost, Box 5 of 9, Physical Education, Open Letter to All Majors.

50. RG 7, Accession 6-86, Office of the Provost, Box 5 of 9, Physical Education, Open Letter to All Majors.

51. Kennelly, "Historical Sources," 210.

52. Kelley, *Memoirs* p. 116.

53. *Newark Evening News*, November 9, 1942.

54. SHU RG8, Office of Alumni 8.2.2, Box 12, File 2 of 2, Seton Hall Alumni Bulletin, November 30, 1944.

55. Daniel McCormick, "A Report on Seton Hall Alumni in Service," *Action*, 1944, ADN, 9a, Seton Hall.

56. United States Army Transport.

57. *The Jersey Journal*, January 29, 2004, 18.

58. RG 2.18.1, D'Alessio, Edward D'Alessio to Suzette Jones, April 12, 1982.

59. SHU RG8, Office of Alumni 8.2.2, Box 12, File 9 of 9, Alumni Association Correspondence Censorship, March 2, 1943.

60. *The Star-Ledger*, May 13, 2010.

61. SHU RG8, Office of Alumni, 8.2.2 Miscellaneous Documents, Box 12, File 5 of 9, Alumni Association Correspondence with World War II Servicemen.

62. SHU RG8, Office of Alumni, 8.2.2 Miscellaneous Documents, Box 12, File 5 of 9, Alumni Association Correspondence with World War II Servicemen.

63. SHU RG8, Office of Alumni, 8.2.2 Miscellaneous Documents, Box 12, File 5 of 9, Alumni Association Correspondence with World War II Servicemen.

64. SHU RG8, Office of Alumni, 8.2.2 Miscellaneous Documents, Box 12, File 5 of 9, Alumni Association Correspondence with World War II Servicemen.

65. SHU RG8, Office of Alumni, 8.2.2 Miscellaneous Documents, Box 12, File 5 of 9, Alumni Association Correspondence with World War II Servicemen.

66. SHU RG8, Office of Alumni, 8.2.2 Miscellaneous Documents, Box 12, File 5 of 9, Alumni Association Correspondence with World War II Servicemen.

67. SHU RG8, Office of Alumni, 8.2.2 Miscellaneous Documents, Box 12, File 5 of 9, Alumni Association Correspondence with World War II Servicemen.

Chapter 10. A New Beginning

1. Census Enumeration District Descriptions, New Jersey, Essex County, ED 7-358, ED 7-359, Ed 7-360, ED 7-361.

2. *Inside Seton Hall*, (in-house magazine) October 1984. Monsignor Field Special Collections and Archives.

3. In March 1945, Kelley welcomed the fact that veterans were "free to select their own school, not only with federal monies under the GI Bill of Rights but also with any New Jersey funds that might be appropriated for them." That was hard to reconcile with his distaste for "all efforts to federalize the traditional American educational system." (SHU 3.11, Monsignor James F. Kelley papers, Box 11, Folder 14, Intolerance in Education and Bill 69.) Kelley wanted the benefits of the GI Bill without realizing that *it* had federalized Seton Hall.

4. *The Setonian*, November 16, 1945, 2.

5. *The Setonian*, November 16, 1945, 2.

6. "The Challenge Was Met," Department of Public Relations, Seton Hall University, July 1947.

7. Paul G.E. Clemens, *Rutgers Since 1945: A History of the State University of New Jersey* (New Brunswick, NJ: Rutgers University Press: 2015), 1.

8. Clemens, *Rutgers*, 2.

9. Clemens, *Rutgers*, 2.

10. Neylan to Kelley, September 3, 1946. RG 2, 2.1.11, Kelley Papers, J.F. Neylan Correspondence, 1937–1944.

11. Neylan to Kelley, November 22, 1946. RG 2, 2.1.11, Kelley Papers, J.F. Neylan Correspondence, 1937–1944.

12. *Newark Star-Ledger*, April 28, 1946.

13. *The Setonian*, November 13, 1946, 5.

14. *The Setonian*, May 23, 1946, 5.

15. *The Setonian*, November 16, 1945, 2.

16. "The Challenge Was Met."

17. Philip Gleason, "A Half-Century of Change in Catholic Higher Education," *U.S Catholic Historian* 19, no. 1 (Winter 2001), 1–2.

18. SHU 3.11, Kelley papers, SHU records, Box 24, President's Report to the Board of Trustees, 20 May 1948, f. 321.

19. SHU 3.11, Kelley Papers, Box 15, Folder 18, Correspondence and Information with Rutgers 1946–1948.

20. Joseph Varacalli, *The Catholic Experience in America* (Westport, CT: Greenwood Press, 2006), 34.

21. Minutes of the Board of Trustees, May 21, 1943, 171.

22. SHU 2.1, Board Affairs, Board of Trustee Minutes 1937–1957, Box 1 of 4, Minutes of the Board of Trustees, May 9, 1947, President's Report, f.97.

23. *The Setonian*, March 3, 1946, 1.

24. *The Galleon*, 1947, 102.

25. *The Setonian*, October 21, 1946, 3.

26. *The Setonian*, December 17, 1949, 2.

27. *The Setonian*, May 23, 1946, 5.

28. "The Challenge Was Met."

29. Kelley, *Memoirs*, 283.

30. *The Setonian: Urban News. News and Views of the Students of the Urban Division of Seton Hall*, March 30, 1950, 1.

31. *The Setonian*, January 12, 1950, 2.

32. *The Setonian*, October 21, 1946, 4.

33. *The Setonian*, October 21, 1946, 4.

34. *The Setonian*, December 12, 1946, 2.

35. *The Setonian*, November 18, 1947, 1.

36. *The Setonian*, November 26, 1946, 4.

37. *The Setonian*, May 22, 1947, 7.

38. *The Setonian*, January 18, 1946, 2.

39. *The Setonian*, January 18, 1946, 2.

40. *The Setonian*, September 21, 1949, 2.

41. *The Setonian*, March 9, 1949, 2.

42. *The Setonian*, April 12, 1949, 2.

43. *The Setonian*, September 21, 1949, 3.

44. *The Setonian*, November 2, 1950, 1.

45. *The Setonian*, October 21, 1946, 3.

46. *The Setonian*, October 21, 1946, 3.

47. *The Setonian*, February 23, 1984, 11.

48. *The Setonian*, March 9, 1949, 2.

49. *The Setonian*, November 2, 1951, 3.

50. *The Setonian*, March 18, 1947, 4.

51. *The Setonian*, March 18, 1947, 4.

52. President's Report, Minutes of the Board of Trustees, May 19, 1949.

53. *The Setonian*, November 13, 1946, 2.

54. President's Report, Minutes of the Board of Trustees, May 19, 1949.

55. *The Setonian*, November 17, 1994, 1.

56. William Field to Edward D'Alessio, March 25, 1983 RG 2.18.1, D'Alessio, Hig-End of H].

57. President's Report, Minutes of the Board of Trustees, May 19, 1949.

58. *The Setonian*, February 15, 1952, 2.

59. *The Setonian*, April 8, 1953, 2.

60. Richard Gid Powers, "American Catholics and Catholic Americans: The Rise and Fall of Catholic Anti-Communism," *U.S. Catholic Historian* 22, no. 4 (Fall 2004), 17-35.

61. *The Setonian*, November 13, 1946, 1.

62. *The Setonian*, October 21, 1946, 5.

63. *Newark Star-Ledger*, November 29, 1947.

64. President's Report, Minutes of the Board of Trustees, May 19, 1949.

65. Robert Conley to John J. Dougherty, March 1, 1964. RG 2. 2.13.6.130.

66. *The Setonian: Urbannews: News and Views of the Students of the Urban Division of Seton Hall*, March 30, 1950, 1.

67. SHU 3.11, Kelley papers, SHU records, Box 24, f. 261.

68. Daniel Young to William Furlong, June 7, 1949. ADN, 9a, Seton Hall.

69. SHU 3.22, Presidents Hall Documents, 15, Army Surplus Folder.

70. Conlin to John McClary, June 16, 1949. ADN, 9a, Seton Hall.

71. Kelley, *Memoirs*, 304.

72. Kelley to Mother Joseph, August 4, 1949. SHU 3.11, Kelley Papers, Box 2, Folder 10.

73. *The Setonian*, March 9, 1949, 1.

74. *The Setonian*, March 9, 1949, 1.

75. RG 2, Kelley Papers, 2.1.11, Correspondence with John McNulty 1944–53.

Chapter 11. A New University

1. Frank Bowles to William Furlong, May 9, 1949. RG 3. 3.3, Accreditation and Documentation, Middle States Association Correspondence, 1949–1950.

2. Irving Saypol to Fred Gassert, April 2, 1951. RG 6, Boland papers, ADN 2-89, 3 of 8, Correspondence 1971–1979.

3. *The Galleon*, 1960, 12.

4. *The Setonian*, September 21, 1949, 1.

5. Rocco DePaolo to McNulty, March 19, 1957. RG 2, John L. McNulty, 2.12.4, Folder 3.

6. This was in 1951. By 1955, the book value of all endowment assets was $1,095,254. Almost everything was on the rise except faculty salaries. In 1955 the Ford Foundation gave Seton Hall a grant of $50,000 to improve them. RG 2, 2.12.7, Folder 108.

7. 4,556 men and 767 women in 1950–1951, up from 3,826 and 590 in 1946–1947.

8. 116 in 1946, 140 in 1950.

9. RG 3 3.3, SHU Accreditation Documentation, Middle States Report 1952; RG 7, SHU Accession 6-86, Box 8 of 9, Orientation Manual for Instructors of the School of Nursing, 1952; RG 2.18.1, D'Alessio, Nur-end of N, O-P-Per, Summary History of the College of Nursing, 1983.

10. Middle States Report 1952.

11. SHU 2.1, Board Affairs, Board of Trustee Minutes 1937–1957, Box 1 of 4, Minutes May 19, 1948, President's Report, f.201.

12. SHU 2.1, Board Affairs, Board of Trustee Minutes 1937–1957, Box 1 of 4, Minutes September 2, 1949, Remarks Made by the President of Seton Hall College on University Status.

13. Bowles to Kelley, October 19, 1948. RG 3, SHU, Accreditation Documents, 3.3, Middle States Association Inspection and Accreditation, Correspondence January 1947–December 1948.

14. RG 4.2, University Governance, University Council, Minutes of Meetings 1950–1963, Box 1 of 3, June 29, 1951.

15. Bowles to McNulty, May 21, 1952. RG 3 3.3, Accreditation Documentation, Middle States Association Inspection, Box 2.

16. SHU 4.1, Board Affairs, Board of Trustees Minutes 1937–1957, May 19, 1949, President's Report.

17. SHU 2.1, Board Affairs, Board of Trustee Minutes 1937–1957, Box 1 of 4, Minutes September 2, 1949, Remarks Made by the President of Seton Hall College on University Status.

18. The library went from 28,000 volumes to more than 110,000, making it, McNulty told the Board, "outstanding . . . for its size and proportion." (As soon as the inspectors left, some of the books went back to their original owners.) SHU 2.1, Board Affairs, Board of Trustee Minutes 1937–1957, Box 1 of 4, May 11, 1950, Committee on Correlation of Library Facilities with Instruction.

19. SHU 2.1, Board Affairs, Board of Trustee Minutes 1937–1957, Box 1 of 4, May 11, 1950, Committee on Improvement of Instruction.

20. A "Committee on Pensions, Tenure and Retirement" under Francis Hammond proposed that Seton Hall participate in the college retirement program of the Teachers Insurance Annuity Association (TIAA) of New York City. The first batch of eligible faculty members—eighteen in all—was enrolled on February 1, 1950. SHU 2.1, Board Affairs, Board of Trustee Minutes 1937–1957, Box 1 of 4, May 11, 1950, Committee on Pensions, Tenure and Retirement.

21. RG 2, SHU Office of the President, John L. McNulty Papers, 2.12.7, University Reorganization Files, Folder 188.

22. RG 2, SHU Office of the President, John L. McNulty Papers, 2.12.7, University Reorganization Files, Folder 188.

23. W.H. Conley, Recommendations Concerning Various Factors of Organization, Administration, and Faculty of Seton Hall University (August 17, 1950). RG 2, SHU, McNulty Papers, 2.12.7, University Reorganization Files, Folder 189.

24. *Newark Evening News*, June 5, 1950, 1–5.

25. In 1953–1954, total enrollment stood at 6,000. Ten years before the number of students in South Orange was scarcely in three figures. *The Setonian*, October 28, 1953, 2.

26. Much of the success of the School of Business Administration was due to its founding dean, Austin Murphy, and many of its difficulties to his tense relations with McNulty. Faculty salaries were inadequate, as was the library.

27. Caroline Di Donato, later Schwartz, resigned as dean of Nursing in 1951 and was replaced by Margaret Haley. By then, the School had five full-time faculty and twenty-two adjuncts.

28. Bowles to McNulty, November 26, 1952. RG 3 3.3, Accreditation Documentation, Middle States Association (1950–52), Box 2.

29. Edmund Cuneo to McNulty, March 15, 1952. RG 3 3.3, Accreditation Documentation, Middle States Association (1950–52), Box 2.

30. Roy Deferrari to McNulty, March 13, 1952. RG 3 3.3, Accreditation Documentation, Middle States Association (1950–52), Box 2.

31. Robert Morrison to McNulty, March 12, 1952. RG 3 3.3, Accreditation Documentation, Middle States Association (1950–52), Box 2.

32. Austin Murphy to McNulty, June 6, 1955. RG 7 Accession 6-86, Office of the Provost, 4 of 9.

33. Board of Trustee Minutes 1937–1957, Box 1 of 4, May 15, 1952.

34. For the section below, see Board of Trustees Minutes 1937–1957, Box 1 of 4, and Seton Hall University, *The General Bulletin*, 1951–1952, Publications Catalogs 1.1.2 University Undergraduate Bulletins 1950–1956.

35. Board of Trustees Minutes 1937–1957, Box 1 of 4, May 7, 1951, Report on Department of Student Personnel Services.

36. Board of Trustees Minutes 1937–1957, Box 1 of 4, May 7, 1951, Report on Department of Student Personnel Services.

37. *The Setonian*, November 17, 1955, 17.

38. *The Setonian*, February 18, 1952, 1.

39. Seton Hall University, *The General Bulletin*, 1951–1952, The School of Education, 29. Publications Catalogs 1.1.2 University Undergraduate Bulletins 1950–1956.

40. *The Setonian*, September 21, 1951, 1.

41. *The Setonian*, October 27, 1955, 1

42. *The Setonian*, November 18, 1947, 7.

43. *The Setonian*, April 19, 1956, 5.

44. *The Setonian*, February 3, 2000, 9.

45. *The Setonian*, October 14, 1953, 3.

46. Cunningham to McNulty, October 18, 1955. RG 2, SHU. 2.17.7, Folder 176.

47. *The Setonian*, December 16, 1953, 1.

48. *The Setonian*, February 3, 2000, 9.

49. *The Setonian*, March 3, 1960, 2.

50. *The Setonian*, November 9, 1950, 2.

51. *The Setonian*, November 2, 1951.

52. *The Setonian*, December 2, 1951, 2.

53. *The Setonian*, March 19, 1959, 6.

54. *The Setonian*, April 27, 1950, 1.

55. *The Galleon*, 1951, 314.

56. Joe Donegan, *The Boys from Company K: A P/R from the 50s Recollects*. http://captainslogblog
.typepad.com/companyk8/2006/12/index.html

57. Vince Byrnes, *The Boys from Company K: Back in the Day, 2, 23, 2016*. http://captainslogblog
.typepad.com/companyk8/2016/02/back-in-the-day.html

58. W.H. Conley, Recommendations Concerning Various Factors of Organization, Administration, and Faculty of Seton Hall University (August 17, 1950). RG 2, SHU, McNulty Papers,
2.12.7, University Reorganization Files, Folder 189.

59. *The Setonian*, October 5, 1951, 1.

60. *The Setonian*, April 22, 1953, 3.

61. *The Setonian*, December 16, 1953, 1.

62. Timothy B. Noone, "In Memoriam: Edward A. Synan (1918-1997)," *Review of Metaphysics*
51, no. 2 (December 1997), 491–493.

63. *The Setonian*, May 25, 1955, 2.

64. *The Setonian*, February 17, 1954, 1.

65. RG 7, Accession 6-86, Office of the Provost, 3 of 9, English, February 16, 1955, February
25, 1955.

66. Bowles to McNulty, November 26, 1952. RG 3 3.3, Accreditation Documentation, Middle
States Association (1950–52), Box 2.

67. Cunningham to McNulty, April 23, 1956. RG 2, SHU. 2.17.7, McNulty Papers, Folder 177.

68. Francis Caminiti to Cunningham, April 1, 1960. RG 9 9.1, Vice President for Academic Affairs, Faculty Contracts, Arts and Sciences, 1952–1966.

69. William Dunham to Cunningham, June 5, 1959. RG 9 9.1, Vice President for Academic
Affairs, Faculty Contracts, Arts and Sciences, 1952–1966.

70. Cunningham to McNulty, June 3, 1955, June 20, 1955. RG 2, SHU. 2.17.7, McNulty, Folder
175.

71. Ellis Brown to Cunningham, May 16, 1957. RG 2, 2.12.7, McNulty, Folder 105.

72. Alfred Donovan to McNulty, October 10, 1957. RG 2, SHU. 2.12.7, McNulty, Folder 107.

73. *The Setonian*, December 3, 1953, 3.

74. RG 9 9.1, Vice President for Academic Affairs, Vice President for Instruction, Faculty Contract, School of Business.

75. *The Setonian*, September 10, 1951, 2.

76. Cunningham to Maurice O'Sullivan, January 14, 1955. RG 7, Office of the Provost, 5 of 9,
General Correspondence.

77. Cunningham to Clement Ockay, February 9, 1955. RG 7, Accession 6-86, Office of the Provost, 3 of 9, Mathematics.

78. *The Setonian* January 19, 1956, 7.

79. RG 7, Accession 6-86, Office of the Provost, 3 of 9, Modern Languages, October 24, 1952.

80. RG 7, Accession 6-86, Office of the Provost, 3 of 9, Modern Languages, September 19, 1951

81. *The Setonian*, March 19, 1954, 15.

82. *Irish Press*, August 19, 1954, 6.

83. *The Setonian*, March 17, 1960, 1.

84. *The Setonian*, April 27, 1950, 1.

85. *The Setonian*, December 10, 1952, 4.

86. *The Setonian*, December 10, 1952, 4.

87. *The Setonian*, October 4, 1956, 8.

88. *The Setonian*, October 4, 1956, 8.

89. *The Setonian*, October 4, 1956, 16.

90. McNulty to Ewald Nyquist, March 1, 1954. RG 3 3.3, SHU Accreditation Documentation, MS I + A/2, Correspondence 1950–1952.

91. *Twenty-Fifth Anniversary: Diocese of Paterson, 1938–1963* (Paterson, NJ: 1963), 5–8.

92. McNulty to Justin McCarthy, August 30, 1957. RG 2. 2.12.2, Folder 5.

93. Cunningham to McNulty, February 8, 1954. RG 2, 2.12.3, Folder 7, Legal Papers.

94. Cunningham to McNulty, March 25, 1954. RG 2, 2.12.3, Folder 7, Legal Papers.

95. Cunningham to McNulty, March 25, 1954. RG 2, 2.12.3, Folder 7, Legal Papers.

96. Seton Hall University Bulletin, University College 1955–1956, Schedule of Spring Classes, 1955, Paterson, 1.

97. Richard Adinaro, conversation with the author, January 26, 2005.

98. *The Setonian*, November 17, 1955, 6.

99. *Paterson Morning News*, May 27, 1961.

100. *The Record*, October 29, 1964.

101. RG 4 4.7, University Governance, University Wide Committees, Minutes, Reports, Correspondence, Box 4 of 5, October 25, 1971.

102. RG 3 3.4, Accreditation Documentation, Self Evaluation Commission 1958–1961, Folder 11, University Self Evaluation Commission, Memorandum 32.

103. *The Setonian*, November 2, 1951, 1; March 19, 1954, 15.

104. SHU 4.1, Board of Trustees Minutes 1937–1957, Box 1 of 4, May 5, 1956, f.11.

105. RG 2, 2.12.7, ff.112sqq, McNulty, Institute of Far Eastern Studies.

106. RG 2, Office of the President, John L. McNulty Papers, 2.12.7, Folder 11, Institute of Far Eastern Studies, McNulty to President Ngo Dinh-Diem, July 16, 1956.

107. *The Setonian*, May 29, 1957, 2.

108. The Institute, originally in Newark, transferred to South Orange in the late 1950s. In February 1961 it yielded responsibility for instruction to the newly established department of Asian studies in the College of Arts and Sciences, remaining in existence to conduct research.

109. SHU 2.1, Board Affairs, Board of Trustee Minutes 1937–1957, Box 1 of 4, May 13, 1953.

110. John Connelly, *From Enemy to Brother: The Revolution in Catholic Teaching on the Jews 1933–1965* (Cambridge, MA: Harvard University Press, 2012), 2.

111. Connelly, *From Enemy to Brother*, 4.

112. Connelly, *From Enemy to Brother*, 116.

113. Connelly, *From Enemy to Brother*, 64.

114. Connelly, *From Enemy to Brother*, 117.

115. Connelly, *From Enemy to Brother*, 125.

116. Connelly, *From Enemy to Brother*, 163.

117. Connelly, *From Enemy to Brother*, 161.

118. Connelly, *From Enemy to Brother*, 151.

119. Albert Hakim, conversation with the author, October 1999.

120. Connelly, *From Enemy to Brother*, 189.

121. SHU 4.1 Board Affairs, Board of Trustee Minutes 1937–1957, Box 1 of 4, May 9, 1956, f.51.

122. Connelly, *From Enemy to Brother*, 180.

123. Connelly, *From Enemy to Brother*, 189.

124. RG 2, John L. McNulty, Box 4, 2.12.7.8.8.

125. *Newark Sunday News*, December 11, 1955, 36.

126. RG 2, John L. McNulty, Box 4, 2.12.7.8.8.

127. RG 2, John L. McNulty, Box 4, 2.12.7.8.8.

128. Edward Flynn to McNulty, January 9, 1956. RG 2, John L. McNulty, Box 4, 2.12.7.8.8.

129. McNulty to Brennan, November 5, 1956. RG 2, John L. McNulty, Box 4, 2.12.7.8.8.

130. Charles Murphy to Daniel J. Brady, April 21, 1953. SHU 3.22, Presidents Hall Documents, Box 15.

131. Gleason, "A Half-Century of Change," 289.

132. See Richard Hofstadter, *Anti-Intellectualism in American Life* (New York: Knopf, 1963).

133. Gleason, "A Half-Century of Change," 289.

134. Dolores Liptak and Timothy Walch, "American Catholics and the Intellectual life: An Interview with Monsignor John Tracy Ellis," *U.S. Catholic Historian* 4, no. 2 1985, 190.

135. Roy J. Deferrari (ed.), *Theology, Philosophy, and History as Integrating Disciplines in the Catholic College of Liberal Arts*, (Washington, DC: CUA Press, 1953).

136. Deferrari, *Theology*, 333.

137. *The Setonian*, October 4, 1956, 4.

138. Eugene D. McCarraher, "The Saint in the Gray Flannel Suit: The Professional-Managerial Class, 'The Layman,' and American Catholic Religious Culture, 1945–1965," *U.S. Catholic Historian* 15, no. 3 (Summer 1997), 104.

139. *The Setonian*, October 6, 1994, 8.

140. Thomas F. O'Dea, *American Catholic Dilemma: An Inquiry into the Intellectual Life* (New York: New American Library, 1958), 71.

141. O'Dea, *American Catholic Dilemma*, 72.

142. O'Dea, *American Catholic Dilemma*, 82.

143. O'Dea, *American Catholic Dilemma*, 92.

144. Seymour Warkov and Andrew M. Greeley, "Parochial School Origins and Educational Achievement," *American Sociological Review* 31, no. 3 (June 1966), 406ff; Andrew Greeley, "The Ethnic and Religious Origins of Young American Scientists and Engineers: A Research Note," *International Migration Review* 6, no. 3 (Autumn 1972), 286.

145. O'Dea, *American Catholic Dilemma*, 97.

146. O'Dea quoted in Gleason, "A Half-Century of Change," 292.

147. John D. Donovan, *The Academic Man in the Catholic College* (New York: Sheed and Ward, 1964), vii.

148. Donovan, *The Academic Man*, 190–193.

149. McCarraher, "The Saint in the Gray Flannel Suit," 113.

150. McCarraher, "The Saint in the Gray Flannel Suit," 114.

151. RG 7, Accession 6-86, Office of the Provost, Box 8 of 9.

152. RG 7, Accession 6-86, Office of the Provost, Box 1 of 9, School of Business, Graduate School.

153. RG 7, Accession 6-86, Office of the Provost, 3 of 9, English.

154. *The Setonian*, March 13, 1958, 1.

155. Clemens, *Rutgers*, 111.

156. Seton Hall University, The General Bulletin, 1951–1952, 107, 108, 113. Publications Catalogs 1.1.2, University Undergraduate Bulletins 1950–1956.

157. Seton Hall University, The General Bulletin, 1951–1952, The School of Business Administration, 72. Publications Catalogs 1.1.2, University Undergraduate Bulletins 1950–1956.

158. RG 2, Office of the President, John L. McNulty Papers, 2.12.6, folder 5.

159. *The Setonian*, October 5, 1951, 2.

Chapter 12. A Law School for the City

1. Lori Ruckstuhl, *With Honor and Dignity: A History of the Legal Profession in Essex County* (Dallas, TX: Taylor Publishing, 1998).

2. Robert Stevens, *Law School: Legal Education in America from the 1850s to the 1980s* (Chapel Hill: University of North Carolina Press, 1983), 8.

3. Edward J. Power, *A History of Catholic Higher Education in the United States* (Wilwaukee, WI: Bruce Publishing, 1958), 248.

4. Stevens, *Law School*, 25.

5. Stevens, *Law School*, 52.

6. Power, *Catholic Higher Education*, 253.

7. *The Sun*, June 6, 1901. http://chroniclingamerica.loc.gov/lccn/sn83030272/1901-06-03/ed-1/seq-3.pdf.

8. Power, *Catholic Higher Education*, 252.

9. Stevens, *Law School*, 76.

10. Stevens, *Law School*, 77; 577.

11. Stevens, *Law School*, 575.

12. Jerold S. Auerbach, *Unequal Justice: Lawyers and Social Change in Modern America* (New York: Oxford University Press, 1976), 94.

13. Stevens, *Law School*, 101.

14. Auerbach, *Unequal Justice*, 94.

15. Auerbach, *Unequal Justice*, 107.

16. Stevens, *Law School*, 207.

17. Stevens, *Law School*, 207.

18. RG 18, Seton Hall University School of Law Publications, John Marshall College: College, School of Business, School of Law, Graduate School of Law, 7.

19. RG 18, Seton Hall University School of Law Publications, John Marshall College: College, School of Business, School of Law, Graduate School of Law, 28.

20. John Matthews to McNulty, April 11, 1950. RG 2, McNulty, 2.12.7, folder 139.

21. McNulty to Ewald B. Nyquist, June 24, 1950. RG 2, McNulty. 2.12.7, folder 139.

22. McNulty to Ewald B. Nyquist, June 24, 1950. RG 2, McNulty. 2.12.7, folder 139.

23. RG 7, Peter Mitchell, Colleges and Institutes Files, I-Law, December 21, 1950.

24. Rooney to John J. Dougherty, September 23, 1963. RG 18.1.2, Acc 11-18, Law, Irving, Box 9 of 9.

25. Miriam Rooney, review of Leo Strauss, Natural Right and History, *The Catholic Historical Review* 40, no. 2 (July 1954), 219.

26. Henry Janzen, review of Lawlessness, Law, and Sanction, *The American Political Science Review* 31, no. 6 (December 1937), 1146.

27. Edward A. Purcell, Jr. "American Jurisprudence between the Wars: Legal Realism and the Crisis of Democratic Theory," *American Historical Review* 75, no. 2 (December 1969), 446.

28. Sheila Smith Noonan, "The Law School at 50: Perspectives Past and Present," *Seton Hall University Magazine* (Summer 2004), 18.

29. Noonan, "The Law School at 50," 18.

30. *The Setonian*, January 17, 1952, 1.

31. Seton Hall University General Bulletin, 1952–1953, 234.

32. RG 7, Peter Mitchell, Colleges and Institutes Files, I-Law, December 21, 1950.

33. *The Setonian*, January 18, 1951, 1.

34. Rooney to John J. Dougherty, September 23, 1963. RG 18.1.2, Acc 11-18, Law, Irving, Box 9 of 9.

35. Sander Griffioen, Proximity and Distance: China and the Christian West in Jerald Gort et al. (eds.), *Crossroads Discourses between Christianity and Culture* (Amsterdam: Brill, 2010), 484.

36. Karl Schmude, "John Wu: A Chinese Chesterton with a Seton Hall Connection," *The Chesterton Review* 33, nos. 1–2 (Spring-Summer 2007), 412.

37. John C.H. Wu, *Beyond East and West* (New York: Sheed and Ward, 1951), viii.

38. Lloyd Haft, "Perspectives on John C.H. Wu's Translation of the New Testament," in Chloe Starr (ed.), *Reading Christian Scripture in China* (London: T. and T. Clark, 2008), 189, 190.

39. Li Xiuquin, "John C.H. Wu at the University of Michigan School of Law," *Journal of Legal Education* 58, no. 4 (December 2008), 545.

40. Paul K.T. Sih, *From Confucius to Christ* (New York: Sheed and Ward, 1952), 129.

41. Schmude, "John Wu," 412.

42. Li Xiuquin, "John C.H. Wu," 560.

43. Li Xiuquin, "John C.H. Wu," 552.

44. *The Setonian*, February 18, 1953, 5.

45. Seton Hall Law School faculty meeting minutes, July 1951. Seton Hall University, School of Law, RG 18.1.8, Monsignor William Noe Field Archives and Special Collection Center.

46. Seton Hall Law School faculty meeting minutes, July 1951. Seton Hall University, School of Law, RG 18.1.8, Monsignor William Noe Field Archives and Special Collection Center.

47. *Precis: News for Alumni and friends of the Seton Hall University School of Law* 4, no. 1 (Winter 1995), 5. RG 18 School of Law Publications 18.1.6.

48. Seton Hall Law School Faculty meeting minutes, April 25, 1953.

49. *Precis: News for Alumni and friends of the Seton Hall University School of Law* 4, no. 1 (Winter 1995), 5. RG 18 School of Law Publications 18.1.6.

50. *Precis: News for Alumni and friends of the Seton Hall University School of Law* 4, no. 1 (Winter 1995), 5. RG 18 School of Law Publications 18.1.6.

51. *Precis: News for Alumni and friends of the Seton Hall University School of Law* 4, no. 1 (Winter 1995), 5. RG 18 School of Law Publications 18.1.6.

52. Seton Hall Law School Faculty meeting minutes, September 8, 1955.

53. Seton Hall Law School Faculty meeting minutes, June 3, 1952.

54. Seton Hall Law School Faculty meeting minutes, May 20, 1955.

55. Seton Hall Law School Faculty meeting minutes, February 15, 1956.

56. Seton Hall Law School Faculty meeting minutes, August 5, 1953.

57. Seton Hall Law School Faculty meeting minutes, March 16, 1956.

58. Seton Hall Law School Faculty meeting minutes, March 16, 1956.

59. Seton Hall Law School Faculty meeting minutes, September 8, 1955.

60. Seton Hall Law School Faculty meeting minutes, March 22, 1957.

61. Seton Hall Law School Faculty meeting minutes, September 8, 1955.

62. Seton Hall Law School Faculty meeting minutes, April 22, 1955.

63. Seton Hall Law School Faculty meeting minutes, April 22, 1955.

64. Seton Hall Law School Faculty meeting minutes, April 25, 1953.

65. Rooney to McNulty, May 4, 1954. RG 18.1.21, Accession 11-36, Box 1 of 12, Law School, Annual Reports to the President 1952–61, Folder 2 of 7.

66. Seton Hall Law School Faculty meeting minutes, February 17, 1956.

67. Seton Hall Law School Faculty meeting minutes, January 11, 1957.

68. Seton Hall Law School Faculty meeting minutes, June 17, 1953.

69. Ibid.

70. Seton Hall Law School Faculty meeting minutes, July 1951.

71. Seton Hall Law School Faculty meeting minutes, April 22, 1955.

72. Seton Hall Law School Faculty meeting minutes, April 22, 1955.

73. Seton Hall Law School Faculty meeting minutes, April 25, 1953.

74. Seton Hall Law School Faculty meeting minutes, October 14, 1953.

75. Seton Hall Law School Faculty meeting minutes, April 25, 1953.

76. Ibid

77. Rooney to McNulty, May 4, 1954. RG 18.1.21, Accession 11-36, Box 1 of 12, Law School, Annual Reports to the President 1952–61

78. Wu, *Fountain of Justice*, 8.

79. E. Garth Moore, review of *Fountain of Justice, Cambridge Law Journal* 17, no. 2 (1959), 258.

80. James A. Pike, review of *Fountain of Justice, The Christian Scholar* 40, no. 3 (September 1957), 247.

81. Wu, *Fountain*, 276.

82. John Connelly, *From Enemy to Brother: The Revolution in Catholic Teaching on the Jews 1933–1965* (Cambridge, MA: Harvard University Press, 2012), 8, 179.

83. Wu, *Fountains*, 279.

84. Thomas E. Grieff, "The Principle of Human Rights in Nationalist China: John C.H. Wu and the Ideological Origins of the 1946 Constitution," *The China Quarterly* 103 (September 1985), 456.

85. John C.H. Wu, *Fountain*, 10.

86. John C.H. Wu, *Beyond East and West* (New York: Sheed and Ward, 1951), 254.

87. Sih, *From Confucius to Christ*, 229.

88. *The Setonian*, April 12, 1962, 5.

89. Ralph Walz, letter to the author, June 6, 2016.

90. Rooney to John Hervey (ABA), February 6, 1955. RG 18.1.1, SHU, Box 1 of 12, Law, Loftus, ABA Approval, Folder 3-07.

91. Sih, *From Confucius to Christ*, 229.

92. The collection exceeded 23,000 accessioned volumes in 1956. RG 2, SHU 2.12.7, folder 145.

93. Seton Hall Law School Faculty meeting minutes, December 9, 1960.

94. Seton Hall Law School Faculty meeting minutes, June 10, 1959.

95. Seton Hall Law School Faculty meeting minutes, September 10, 1959.

96. Seton Hall Law School Faculty meeting minutes, March 22, 1957.

97. Seton Hall Law School Faculty meeting minutes, March 22, 1957.

98. Seton Hall Law School Faculty meeting minutes, March 22, 1957.

99. RG 7 Accession 6-86, Box 7 of 9, Rooney-Cunningham-Miriam Rooney, November 16, 1960.

100. Bulletin of Seton Hall University School of Law, 1958–1960, 15–16.

Chapter 13. A Revolution under Dougherty

1. *The Galleon* (Seton Hall yearbook) 1960, 12.

2. Leonard Dreyfuss to Boland, May 20, 1960. RG 6, Boland, ADN Series 1, Clerical and General, 1953–1963, Box 1 of 6.

3. *The Setonian*, February 7, 1963, 6.

4. He removed the ivy on Presidents Hall, realizing that it was ruining the building.

5. John J. Dougherty, "Three Years at Seton Hall: Account of a Stewardship." RG 2, 2.13.3.5, f4.

6. *The Setonian*, May 12, 1960, 4.

7. RG 2, 2.13.3.5, Folder 3, "Catholic Higher Education."

8. Dougherty, a Prelate of Honor in 1954, became auxiliary bishop of Newark in 1962 and was consecrated in 1963.

9. Philip Gleason, "A Half-Century of Change in American Catholic Higher Education," *U.S. Catholic Historian* 19, no. 1 (Winter 2001), 9.

10. Louis Gallo to Dougherty, December 13, 1966. RG. 2, 2.13.6, folder 4.

11. *North County Catholic*, January 19, 1969, 4.

12. David O'Brien, *"The Renewal of American Catholicism*: A Retrospective," *U.S. Catholic Historian* 23, no. 4 (Fall 2005), 87.

13. *The Setonian*, November 3, 1960, 1.

14. Andrew Greeley to John J. Dougherty, March 6, 1966. RG 9, 9.1, Vice President for Academic Affairs, Correspondence with President.

15. Gleason, *Contending With Modernity*, 295.

16. John Botti to Edward Fleming, June 23, 1961. RG 2, 2.13.6.124.1.

17. RG 3 3.4, Accreditation Documentation, Self-Evaluation Commission, 1958–1961, Self-Study Committee No. 2.

18. RG 3 3.4, Accreditation Documentation, Self-Evaluation Commission, 1958–1961, Self-Study Committee No. 2.

19. RG 3 3.4, Accreditation Documentation, Self-Evaluation Commission, 1958–1961, Self-Study Committee No. 2.

20. The average faculty salary rose from $6,472 in 1962–1963 (giving Seton Hall an AAUP rating of E-E) to $11,512 in 1969–1970 (giving an AAUP rating of B-B). RG 4, University Governance 4.6, Board of Trustees, 13 of 13.

21. The full-time lay faculty remained constant (262 in 1966; 267 in 1968) despite an increase of nearly 19 percent in student enrollment since 1966. RG 4, University Governance 4.6, Board of Trustees, 13 of 13.

22. RG 9, 9.1, Vice President for Instruction, Faculty Contracts, Arts and Sciences.

23. RG 4, University Governance, 4.4, Faculty Senate, Minutes and Reports, 1961–1968, 1 of 2, Faculty Senate Meeting, Report June 3, 24, 1964.

24. Charles Murphy to John J. Dougherty, July 18, 1961. RG 9, Vice President for Academic Affairs, Faculty Contracts, 1952–1966.

25. School of Business Administration, Survey of Student Preferences for classes at South Orange-Newark-Paterson March 22, 1961, RG 2, 2.14, Executive Vice President, Edward Fleming, Box VII.

26. Edward Fleming to James Keegan, March 9, 1961. RG 2, 2.14, Box VII.

27. RG 2, SHU 2.14, Box Va, Office of the Executive Vice President, Fleming, Minutes of November 15, 1962 meeting.

28. RG 3, 3.4, Accreditation Documentation, Self-Evaluation Commission 1959–1961, Minutes and Memoranda, Central Coordinating Committee.

29. Lawrence A. Nespoli, *Community Colleges: A New Jersey Success Story* (Trenton, NJ: New Jersey Council of County Colleges, 2010.), 1.

30. Nespoli, *Community Colleges*, 1.

31. Office of the President, John J. Dougherty Papers. RG 2.13.6.49.17, Edward Fleming to John J. Dougherty, February 26, 1964.

32. University Statutes, Supplement to Chapter 1, Article 5. Faculty Senate. RG 4, University Governance, 4.4, Faculty Senate, Minutes and Reports 1961–1968, 1 of 2.

33. University Statutes, Supplement to Chapter 1, Article 5. Faculty Senate. RG 4, University Governance, 4.4, Faculty Senate, Minutes and Reports 1961–1968, 1 of 2.

34. The senate was to consist of two university-wide representatives and two alternates appointed by the president and to serve at his pleasure; of one senator and one alternate to be

elected, according to rules of their own devising, from the Library; one senator and one alternate from personnel services; four senators and four alternates from the College of Arts and Sciences; two senators and two alternatives from the School of Business Administration; one senator and one alternate from the School of Nursing; one senator and one alternate from the School of Law.

35. RG 2, SHU 2.14, Box Va, Fleming, Minutes, November 15, 1962.

36. Robert Hassenger, *The Structure of Catholic Higher Education*, in Philip Gleason (ed.), *Contemporary Catholicism in the United States* (South Bend, IN: University of Notre Dame Press, 1969), 296.

37. Hassenger, *The Structure of Catholic Higher Education*, 296.

38. Hassenger, *The Structure of Catholic Higher Education*, 297.

39. *The Setonian*, October 3, 1963, 7.

40. *The Setonian*, September 15, 1965, 1

41. Hassenger, *The Structure of Catholic Higher Education*, 298.

42. Hassenger, *The Structure of Catholic Higher Education*, 310.

43. Hassenger, *The Structure of Catholic Higher Education*, 298.

44. Hassenger, *The Structure of Catholic Higher Education*, 301.

45. Hassenger, *The Structure of Catholic Higher Education*, 303, n.19.

46. Cunningham to Hart, May 15, 1957. RG 7, 6-86, Provost, 2 of 9.

47. Hakim to Fahy, March 30, 1973. RG 7, Mitchell, 1972–1978 (Fac-Fac).

48. Murphy to Sheeran, February 5, 2003. SHU 3.22, Sheeran, Chronological Files, November 2002–April 2003.

49. *The Setonian*, March 1, 1962, 5.

50. Fleming to E.J. McGrath, September 25, 1961. RG 2, 2.14, Box II.

51. RG 7, Accession 6-86, Provost, 3 of 9, English.

52. College of Arts and Sciences, Preliminary Budget Proposal, December 23, 1963, RG 2, 2.14 Fleming, Box III.

53. *The Setonian*, March 3, 1960, 3.

54. *The Setonian*, May 27, 1960, 9.

55. *The Setonian*, February 5, 1969, 7.

56. Roy Nichols to Dougherty, July 14, 1965. VP for Academic Affairs, Graduate Studies, 1978 and prior.

57. Tsu to Fleming, November 8, 1960. RG 4.4.2, University Governance, University Council, 1 of 3.

58. RG 9, 9.2, Provost, Annual Reports, 1963–1972, Asian Studies and Non-Western Civilization.

59. Mitchell to Conley, August 17, 1978. RG 7, Provost, Mitchell, 1972–1978, Bud-end of B.

60. Hakim to Tsu, May 28, 1969. RG 2, 2.14, Fleming, Dean's Correspondence 1966–1969, Box 1.

61. See John De Francis Memorial Page, http://johndefrancis.wordpress.com, accessed March 26, 2012.

62. Janis Aldridge, in conversation with the author, February 28, 2013.

63. After President Nixon's visit to China in 1972, the Asian studies department's Taiwanese complexion was the subject of confidential State Department telegrams. When a delegation of linguists from the PRC threatened to cancel an invitation to visit Seton Hall in 1973, the State Department knew why: "Seton Hall program has large numbers of Chinese from Hong Kong and Taiwan, and school is reputed to be a bastion of pro-Republic of China sentiment." Confidential State 226243: US-PRC Weekly Activities Report about Cultural Exchanges 73/45, November 14–20, 1973. (Declassified June 2005). https://www.archives.gov/research/foreign-policy/state-dept/rg-59-central-files/1973-1979.

64. The social studies department became the social studies and political science department in July 1963, following the creation of a separate department of sociology. In turn, the former

department was divided in two—the department of history and the department of government—in September 1968. Father Edwin V. Sullivan was founding chair of the department of sociology. The department of government became the department of political science in September 1976. *The Setonian*, April 2, 1976, 8.

65. RG 2. 2.14, Fleming, History and Political Science File, 1966–1967, Box 1.

66. *The Setonian*, April 30, 1964, 2.

67. Stock arrived at Seton Hall in 1965, a pioneer in a very male terrain.

68. *The Setonian*, November 25, 1964, 2.

69. RG 2. 2.14, Fleming, History and Political Science, 1968–1970, Box 1.

70. John Tracey Ellis to Joseph Brady, January 10, 1956. ADN 0004. 005, Series VIII, Folder 235.

71. *The Setonian*, September 29, 1960, 1.

72. Peter Mitchell, letter to the author, May 2017.

73. Middle States Association April 1964, 17. RG 4, Accession 10-88, University Governance, University Wide Committees, Box 1 of 1.

74. Klose taught mass communication, mass communication law, and cinematography. He restored the theater program by hiring Gil Rathbun and James McGlone in 1959 and 1965. Klose to Fahy, May 7, 1974. RG 2. 2.15, Fahy, College of Arts and Science General Correspondence 1973–1976, 15 of 24.

75. *The Setonian*, May 27, 1960, 9.

76. *The Setonian*, September 27, 1968, 2.

77. Albert Hakim, in conversation with the author, February 10, 2005.

78. *The Setonian*, October 13, 1961, 2.

79. *The Setonian*, April 4, 1963, 1.

80. Fleming to Dougherty, June 4, 1964. RG 2, Dougherty, 2.13.6.49.19.

81. *The Setonian*, October 16, 1968, 5.

82. *The Setonian*, April 18, 1975, 3.

83. Hakim, College of Arts and Sciences Five Year Report 1960–1965, March 15, 1965.

84. Frank Paparello to Dougherty, November 8, 1961. RG 7, Duff, Faculty Resigned Deceased, Arts and Sciences O–Z.

85. Eugene Petrik to Fleming, January 10, 1962. RG2, Fleming, 2.14, Box 1.

86. The requirements for the major were increased from thirty-six to forty-nine credits. *The Setonian*, February 22, 1962, 3.

87. There were two PhDs in a department of six in 1960.

88. The MS degree was introduced in 1963, the BS degree for research-oriented undergraduates in 1964.

89. Joseph Brady, PhD Columbia, preceded him by a few years.

90. Chemistry Department Minutes, June 26, 1963. RG 2. 2.14, Fleming, Box 1, Chemistry.

91. Hakim to Celiano, June 12, 1969. RG 2, 2.14, Fleming, Dean's Correspondence 1966–1969, Box 1.

92. In 1962, it received grants totaling $48,000 from the National Science Foundation, putting it a different league from the rest of the College. *The Setonian*, September 26, 1962, 6.

93. *The Setonian*, February 5, 1969, 2.

94. RG 9, 9.2, Duff, Annual Reports 1968–1972.

95. Minutes, Sociology, September 29, 1968. RG 2. 2.14, Fleming, Sociology, Box 1.

96. *The Setonian*, September 29, 1960, 2.

97. Middle States Association April 1964, 17. RG 4, Accession 10-88, University Governance, University Wide Committees, Box 1 of 1.

98. Modern Languages Minutes, February 2, 1967. RG 2, 2.14, Fleming, Modern Languages 1961–1964, Box 1.

99. Modern Languages Minutes, April 29, 1966. RG 2, 2.14, Fleming, Modern Languages 1961–1964, Box 1.

100. Middle States Association April 1964, 17. RG 4, Accession 10-88, University Governance, University Wide Committees, Box 1 of 1.

101. Gleason, *Contending With Modernity*, 258.

102. Gleason, *Contending With Modernity*, 258.

103. Dean's Committee on Educational Goals, November 29, 1965. [Copy in the possession of Dr. Albert Hakim.]

104. Proposals to be presented to the University Council, October 25, 1960. RG 2.2.14, Fleming, Philosophy, Box 1. In December 2006, the Faculty Senate approved a new undergraduate degree in theology to be offered through Immaculate Conception Seminary, School of Theology.

105. Philosophy minutes, April 11; 1962. RG 2.2.14, Fleming, Philosophy File, Box 1.

106. *The Setonian*, October 6, 1960, 7.

107. *The Setonian*, October 24, 1963, 4.

108. Quoted in Philip Gleason, "Neo-Scholasticism as Preconciliar Ideology," *U.S. Catholic Historian* 7, no. 4 (Fall 1988), 403.

109. Mary Rose Barral, "The Varieties of Psychedelic Experience," *International Philosophical Quarterly* 7 (1967), 680.

110. As reported to the author by James McGlone, who taught in the classroom afterwards.

111. William Smith to Fleming, April 3, 1970. RG 9, 9.2, Duff, Faculty Active-Inactive Files, Reports 1963–1972.

112. Most sections were taught by priests drafted for the purpose.

113. Hakim, interview with author, January 27, 2005.

114. Hakim, interview with author, January 27, 2005.

115. *The Setonian*, February 27, 1964, 4.

116. John Coulson et al., *Theology and The University* (Baltimore: Helicon Press, 1964), 1.

117. *College of Arts and Sciences Five Year Report, 1960–1965*, March 15, 1965. RG 9, 9.2, Duff, Annual Reports 1960–1972.

118. "A Proposal for an Undergraduate Major in Religious Studies," Department of Theology, April 1969. RG 2, 2.14, Executive Vice President, Edward Fleming Papers, Religious Studies Proposal, Box 1.

119. "A Proposal for an Undergraduate Major in Religious Studies," Department of Theology, April 1969. RG 2, 2.14, Executive Vice President, Edward Fleming Papers, Religious Studies Proposal, Box 1.

120. "Minority Report," "A Proposal for an Undergraduate Major in Religious Studies," Department of Theology, April 1969. RG 2, 2.14, Executive Vice President, Edward Fleming Papers, Religious Studies Proposal, Box 1.

121. Fleming to Dougherty, April 18, 1969. RG 2, Dougherty, 2.13.6.49.49.

122. Albert Hakim, interview with the author, January 27, 2005.

123. Peter Mitchell, *The Coup at Catholic University: The 1968 Revolution in American Catholic Education* (San Francisco, CA: Ignatius Press, 2015).

124. RG 4, Accession 4.6.1, University Governance, Box 3 of 13, Board of Trustees Minutes, October 2, 1968.

125. Thomas Melady to Terence Cardinal Cooke, October 11, 1969. RG 7, Accession 6-86, Office of the Provost, 4 of 9, Convocations.

126. Philip Gleason, *Keeping the Faith: American Catholicism Past and Present* (South Bend, IN: University of Notre Dame Press, 1989), 174.

127. Annual Report of the President to the Board of Trustees, May 7, 1969; Office of the University Chaplain, James P. McMenemie. RG 4. 4.6, Board of Trustees, 13 of 13.

128. *The Setonian*, March 15, 1962, 3.

129. RG 2, 2.14, Box 1, Fleming, Honors Program 1964.

130. Ibid.

131. *The Setonian*, March 15, 1962, 1.

132. *The Setonian*, March 8, 1962, 1.

133. Gleason, *Contending with Modernity*, 295.

134. Keller, Harrington to Hakim, June 13, 1967. RG 7, Accession 6-86, Provost, Box 6 of 9.

135. *The Setonian*, May 3, 1963, 1.

136. The second iteration of the Honors Program in 1978 formalized the curriculum into four colloquia taken in the freshman and sophomore years—Ancient Civilizations, Christianity and Medieval Culture, Renaissance and Reformation Thought, and the Enlightenment. *The Setonian*, April 26, 1984, 11.

137. RG 7, Accession 6-86, Provost, 4 of 9, Deans' Meetings Minutes.

138. Raymond Schroth, *Fordham: A History and Memoir* (New York: Fordham University Press, 2008), 152.

139. Dean's Committee on Educational Goals College of Arts and Sciences, May 18, 1965, Robert Pollock. [Document in possession of Dr. Albert Hakim.]

140. Dean's Committee on Educational Goals College of Arts and Sciences, May 18, 1965, Robert Pollock.

141. Francis Caminiti to Frank Katz, November 15, 1971. RG 9. 9.2, Duff, Faculty Personnel Files, 1969–1976, M–Z.

142. *The Setonian*, February 27, 1967, 5.

143. *The Setonian*, January 26, 1995, 1.

144. "Building Humanistic Education," RG 7, Mitchell, Department Files, cla–end of c.

145. *The Setonian*, December 12, 1968, 3.

146. College of Arts and Sciences, Committee on Core Curriculum, November 22, 1968. RG 4, 4.2, University Council, Minutes, 1964–1968, Box 2 of 3.

147. RG 4, 10-88, University Governance, University Wide Committees, Box 1 of 1.

148. Harold Petipas, *The Setonian*, November 19, 1969, 4.

149. Minutes, Physics, March 12, 1968. RG 7, Accession 6-89, Provost, 3 of 9, Physics.

150. "The Free University," RG 7, 6-86, Provost, 5 of 9.

151. *The Setonian*, April 17, 1978, 5.

152. "The Free University," RG 7, 6-86, Provost, 5 of 9.

153. *The Setonian*, November 10, 1972, 3; October 21, 1982, 3.

154. Minutes, History, November 6, 1969. RG 7, 6-89, Provost, 3 of 9, History.

155. *The Setonian*, December 8, 1994, 5.

156. Middle States Association April 1964, 17. RG 4, Accession 10-88, University Governance, University Wide Committees, Box 1 of 1.

157. *The Setonian*, March 17, 1967, 7.

158. RG 3, 3.5, Accreditation, University Self-Study 1960–1965, Committee XVI, School of Nursing.

159. Applicants were required to submit a dental report.

160. Middle States Association April 1964, 17. RG 4, Accession 10-88, University Governance, University Wide Committees, Box 1 of 1.

161. *The Setonian*, May 10, 1967, 5.

162. *The Setonian*, November 9, 1962, 3

163. *The Setonian*, February 21, 1968, 5

164. *The Setonian*, March 17, 1967, 7.

165. *The Setonian*, March 17, 1967, 7.

166. RG 4, 4.2, University Governance, University Council, Minutes of Meetings, 1964–1968, Box 2 of 3.

167. Gordon Dippel, interview with the author, February 1999.

168. Report to the President of Seton Hall University by the Special Committee of the Business School Advisory Council, July 1964, Gordon Dippel loan to the author.

169. RG 4, Accession 10-88, University Governance, University Wide Committees, Box 1 of 1.

170. William Noe Field to Thomas Fahy, November 25, 1968. RG 7, Accession 4-86, Provost, Box 7 of 9.

171. Field to Alfred Celiano, October 29, 1968. RG 7, Accession 4-86, Provost, Box 7 of 9.

172. Field to Fahy, July 14, 1969. RG 7, Accession 4-86, Provost, Box 7 of 9.

173. William Noe Field to John Cole, February 21, 1969. RG 7, Accession 4-86, Office of the Provost, Box 7 of 9.

174. William Noe Field to Stanley L. Jaki, September 21, 1965. RG 7, Accession 4-86, Office of the Provost, Box 7 of 9.

175. RG 2, 2.12.6.43, Office of the President, John J. Dougherty, Executive Memorandum No. 7, 1962 series, November 2, 1962.

176. A Ten-Year Plan for Institutional Advancement, March 15, 1963. RG 2, 2.13.6.49.8.

177. Board of Trustees, Minutes, February 9, 1966. RG 4.6.1.

178. Paul G.E. Clemens, *Rutgers since 1945: A History of the State University of New Jersey* (New Brunswick, NJ: Rutgers University Press, 2015), 17, 19.

179. Meeting of the Board of Trustees, Minutes, November 6, 1966. RG 4.6.1.

180. Seton Hall's expansion owed much to Congressman Joseph Minish (D.-NJ) who represented New Jersey's 11th Congressional District (which included South Orange) between 1963 and 1984.

181. Dougherty to Mrs. Malcolm Rogers, October 29, 1962. RG 2 2.13.6.55.2.

182. *The Setonian*, January 19, 1961, 1.

183. *The Setonian*, December 7, 1961, 1.

184. *The Setonian*, October 3, 1963, 1.

185. Rathbun taught at Notre Dame for four years before coming to Seton Hall in 1960 as Director of Drama.

186. *The Setonian*, October 17, 1963, 1.

187. John J. Dougherty, letter for the 1982 Theater-in-the-Round Summer Program, in the possession of Mark Roger, Class of 1982, and reproduced with permission.

188. *The Setonian*, October 12, 1966, 1.

189. *The Setonian*, October 30, 1968, 1. The Humanities Building cost $2,084,300, of which $650,000 came from grants received under the Higher Education Facility Act (1964), the rest financed by the University. Meeting of the Board of Trustees, Minutes, February 9, 1966. RG 4.6.1.

190. Robert Senkier to Dougherty, February 5, 1968. RG 2, 2.15, Fahy, 15 of 24, School of Business.

191. Enrollment in 1968 in the Business School was 900 full-time undergraduates, 450 MBA students, and 300 evening students.

192. Senkier to Fahy, September 11, 1974. RG 7, Mitchell, Fac-Fac, 1972–1978.

193. In 1983, Sister Agnes established the Wema Catholic Mission of the Garissa Diocese, East Africa. In July 1989, while at evening prayer, she was murdered by bandits during an attempted armed robbery. *The Setonian*, September 7, 1989, 1.

194. *The Setonian*, February 20, 1964, 2.

195. De Value to Dougherty, April 21, 1964. RG 2, 2.13.6.26.2.

196. De Value to Dougherty, May 1, 1964. RG 2, 2.13.6.26.2.

197. The fact that the archdiocese was "one of the largest contributors to the [Catholic University of America] was "stressed and deplored" at a meeting of university vice presidents in 1961. RG 2.2.14, Box IV, Vice Presidents Meetings 1961–1963.

198. De Value to Dougherty, May 1, 1964. RG 2, 2.13.6.26.2

199. DeValue to Dougherty, April 22, 1964. RG 2 2.13.6.26.2.

200. Arthur Young and Company to DeValue, October 18, 1966. RG 2 2.13.6.26.2.

201. Arthur Young and Company to DeValue, October 18, 1966. RG 2 2.13.6.26.2.

202. Middle States Association April 1964, 17. RG 4, Accession 10-88, University Governance, University Wide Committees, Box 1 of 1.

203. Fahy to Dougherty, May 1, 1967. RG 4, 4.6.2, University Governance, Trustees, Correspondence 1967–1977.

204. Board of Trustees Meeting, October 18, 1967. RG 4. 4.6.1, University Governance, Minutes of Meeting, 1962–1968.

205. Board of Trustees Meeting, October 18, 1967. RG 4. 4.6.1, University Governance, Minutes of Meeting, 1962–1968.

206. "Power without Government," in *The Setonian*, October 23, 1970, 7.

207. Board of Trustees Meeting, October 18, 1967. RG 4. 4.6.1, University Governance, Minutes of Meeting, 1962–1968.

208. Leslie Miller to Bernal and Susan Poulson (eds.), *Going Coed: Women's Experiences in Formerly Men's Colleges and Universities, 1950–2000* (Nashville, TN: Vanderbilt University Press, 2004), ix.

209. Miller to Bernal and Poulson, *Going Coed*, 222.

210. Fleming to Dougherty, February 26, 1963. RG 4, Board of Trustees, 4.6.2, Correspondence (1962–1966) Box 7 of 13.

211. Miller to Bernal and Poulson, *Going Coed*, 222.

212. J.R. Kennedy to Dougherty, December 22, 1964. RG 4, Board of Trustees, 4.6.2, Correspondence (1962–1966) Box 7 of 13.

213. Minutes of Vice Presidents Meeting, November 19, 1964. RG 9, 9.1, Vice President for Instruction, Correspondence File with President 1959–1965.

214. *The Setonian*, October 11, 1962, 1.

215. Minutes of Vice Presidents Meeting, November 19, 1964. RG 9, 9.1, Vice President for Instruction, Correspondence File with President 1959–1965.

216. *The Setonian*, March 14, 1963, 5.

217. Miller to Bernal and Poulson, *Going Coed*, 221.

218. Miller to Bernal and Poulson, *Going Coed*, 225.

219. RG 3.3.5 Accreditation Documentation, University Self Study 1960–1965, Report of Committee IX Committee.

220. Miller to Bernal and Poulson, *Going Coed*, 224.

221. Miller to Bernal and Poulson, *Going Coed*, 23.

222. Fleming to Dougherty, February 26, 1963. RG 4, Board of Trustees, 4.6.2, Correspondence (1962–1966) Box 7 of 13

223. Board of Trustees Meeting, October 18, 1967. RG 4. 4.6.1, University Governance, Minutes of Meeting, 1962–1968

224. *The Setonian*, February 7, 1968, 1.

225. *The Setonian*, May 14, 1969, 8.

226. Ed. Hendrikson, interview with the author, May 2003

227. *The Setonian*, February 28, 1968, 5.

228. RG 4. 4.6.3. Annual Report of the President to the Board of Trustees, May 8, 1968.

229. *The Setonian*, February 7, 1968, 1.

230. *The Setonian*, February 28, 1968, 5.

231. Victoria Quinn, *Simply Beautiful* December 12, 2006. http://captainslogblog.typepad.com/companyk8/2006/12/index.html accessed November 18, 2017.

232. *The Setonian*, March 13, 1968, 6.

233. *The Setonian*, March 13, 1968, 3.

234. *The Setonian*, April 10, 1968, 6.

235. According to Professor Ron Infante, in conversation with the author, June 6, 2019.

236. RG 2 2.13.6.130, Dougherty, "A Dormitory for Women."

237. Fleming to Dougherty, n.d. RG 2, 2.13.6.49.46.

238. RG 2.2.14, Box IV, Fleming, Vice Presidents Meetings 1961–1963.

239. Minutes of Vice Presidents Meeting, November 19, 1964. RG 9, 9.1, Vice President for Instruction, Correspondence File with President 1959–1965.

240. De Value to Dougherty, May 1, 1964. RG 2 2.13.6.26.2.

241. *The Setonian*, March 17, 1967, 1.

242. *The Setonian*, March 17, 1967, 1.

243. Board of Trustees Minutes, October 18, 1967. RG 4.4.6.1, Board of Trustees, Minutes of Meetings.

244. *The Setonian*, October 4, 1967, 1.

245. *The Setonian*, March 17, 1967, 2.

246. *The Setonian*, March 17, 1967, 1.

247. De Value to Dougherty, August 11, 1967. RG 4.4.6.1, Board of Trustees, Minutes of Meetings.

248. Board of Trustees Minutes, October 18, 1967. RG 4.4.6.1, Board of Trustees, Minutes of Meetings.

249. In 1962, fees were increased to $23 per credit for undergraduate courses (except for nursing courses, which cost $25 per credit); $25 per credit for graduate courses. *The Setonian*, May 17, 1962, 1.

250. Board of Trustees Minutes, February 7, 1968. RG 4.4.6.1.

251. RG 7, Accession 6-86, Provost, Box 2 of 9.

252. *National Review,* July 29, 1961, 38.

253. *The Setonian*, September 28, 1961, 2.

254. Russell Kirk to Thomas Gassert, July 1, 1963. RG 2.13.6.70, Office of the President, Dougherty.

255. *The Setonian*, September 26, 1963, 5.

256. RG 7, Accession 6-86, Provost, 4 of 9, Dean of Students, June 1963 and November 1963.

257. *The Setonian*, October 11, 1962, 4.

258. *The Setonian*, May 5, 1965, 3

259. *The Setonian*, September 23, 1965, 1

260. Lynch to Dougherty, March 7, 1965. RG 2, 2.13.6.41.1.

261. *Newark Evening News,* February 28, 1964, 5.

262. *The Setonian*, February 20, 1964, 5.

263. RG 2.13.6.116.24, Statement to the Staff of *The Setonian*, February 27, 1964.

264. RG 4, 4.2, University Council, Minutes of Meetings, 1964–1968, Box 2 of 3, March 24, 1964.

265. James Zuccarelli to Dougherty, February 28, 1964. RG 2.13.6.116.24.

266. Fahy to Dougherty, March 3, 1964. RG 2.13.6.116.24.

267. *The Setonian*, November 15, 1984, 9.

268. *The Setonian*, September 28, 1966, 1

269. *The Setonian*, October 4, 1967, 1.

270. *The Setonian*, November 14, 1963, 4.

271. RG 4, 4.2, University Council, Minutes, 1964–1968, Box 2 of 3.

272. John M. Carlson, Class of 1966, *The Boys from Company K: Back in the Day* http://captain-slogblog.typepad.com/companyk8/2016/02/back-in-the-day.html.

273. *The Setonian*, May 25, 1961, 1.

274. Major Charles Watters calls for special mention. Watters attended Seton Hall Prep and Seton Hall University before being ordained a priest in 1953 and a U.S. Army chaplain in 1964. In November 1967 he was with the 2nd Battalion, 503d Infantry during fierce fighting for Hill 875 around Dak To and was posthumously awarded the Medal of Honor on November 4, 1969 "for his conspicuous gallantry, unyielding perseverance and selfless devotion to his comrades" during the battle. The first Army chaplain to receive the Medal of Honor (America's highest military decoration) since the Civil War, he is one of only five army chaplains so honored. https://army history.org/chaplain-maj-charles-j-watters/

275. RG 2, 2.14, Fleming, College and University Environment Scales, A Report on Student Responses (1965).

276. RG 2.13.6.116.9, Edward Fleming Announcement to Students, December 12, 1966.

277. *The Setonian*, February 14, 1968, 5.

278. "First SHU Blacks, Latinos Revisit School," *The Setonian*, February 28, 2002, 9.

279. "First SHU Blacks, Latinos Revisit School," *The Setonian*, February 28, 2002, 9.

280. *The Setonian*, January 16, 1964, 1.

281. *The Setonian*, March 17, 1965, 1.

282. *The Setonian*, March 17, 1965, 4.

283. *The Setonian*, March 25, 1965, 7.

284. *The Setonian*, March 10, 1968, 1.

285. Edwin Sullivan, May 24, 1968. RG 2. 2.13.6.61.1, Office of the President, Dougherty.

286. Donovan to Dougherty, June 10, 1968. RG 2. 2.13.6.61.1.

287. Joseph Spiegel to Dougherty, June 10, 1968. RG 2. 2.13.6.61.1.

288. RG 7, Accession 6-86, Office of Provost, 4 of 9, Deans' Meetings, August 4, 1970.

289. Donovan to Dougherty, December 11, 1968. RG 2. 2.13.6.61.1.

290. Fleming to Dougherty December 13, 1968. RG 2. 2.13.6.61.1.

291. Thomas Melady to John Tsu, February 16, 1970. RG 2. 2.14, Fleming, Box 1, Asian Studies File 1970.

292. *The Setonian*, February 21, 1963, 2.

293. Fahy to William Valentine, November 11, 1969. RG 2 2.15, Fahy, 4 of 24.

294. *The Setonian*, February 5, 1969, 1.

295. Fahy to Fred Crossland, January 28, 1974. RG 2.2.15, Fahy, Box 8 of 24.

296. *The Setonian*, March 15, 1974, 10.

297. RG 2, 2.13.6.116.7, Statement from the President, March 17, 1969.

298. Fahy to Dougherty, March 13, 1969. RG 2 2.13.6.116.7.

299. Library Faculty Minutes, 1970. RG 2.2.14 Fleming, Box VII.

300. *The Setonian*, February 8, 1974, 11.

301. Juanita Allen to Edward D'Alessio, November 16, 1981. RG 2.18.1, D'Alessio, Petillo Asian Bilingual Curriculum.

302. John Duff, Aide-Memoire, November 15, 1973. RG 3, 3.4, Accreditation Documentation, Self-Evaluation Commission, 1958–1961.

303. *The Setonian*, September 17, 1969, 4.

304. *The Setonian*, September 24, 1969, 7.

305. SHU, 3.22, Presidents Hall Documents, Box 18, Speeches and Correspondence, Box 2.

306. After serving as pastor of Saint Rose of Lima, Short Hills, NJ, Dougherty returned to Seton Hall as a scholar-in-residence between 1977 and 1986. He died in 1986.

307. Albert Hakim, interview with the author, January 27, 2005.

Chapter 14. Noble Dream

1. *The Setonian*, November 20, 1956, 1.

2. *In their hands*, promotional material, Seton Hall University School of Medicine and Dentistry, RG 24.5.

3. *In their hands*, promotional material, Seton Hall University School of Medicine and Dentistry, RG 24.5.

4. Seton Hall Presents its Medical and Dental College, RG 24.5.

5. John McNulty to Ewald Nyquist, July 29, 1954. RG 3, SHU Accreditation Documentation, 2, Middle States Association, Correspondence 1950–1954.

6. The relationship between the American Medical Association and the Association of Medical Colleges was managed by the Liaison Committee on Medical Education (1942), which allowed the AMA the AAMC to avoid duplicate inspections and double standards.

7. "Memorandum of meeting . . . October 1, 1954," RG 24.5.

8. Smiley and Wiggins to Fronczak, October 7, 1954. RG 24.5.

9. Naomi Rogers, *An Alternative Path: The Making and Remaking of Hahnemann Medical College and Hospital of Philadelphia* (New Brunswick, NJ: Rutgers University Press, 1998), 178.

10. Michael Nevins, *Still More Meanderings in Medical History* (Bloomington, IN: iUniverse LLC, 2013), 132.

11. Survey of the Seton Hall College of Medicine and Dentistry, November 1956. RG 24.5.

12. John J. Sheerin to McNulty, September 13, 1956. RG 24.5.

13. Survey of the Seton Hall College of Medicine and Dentistry, November 1956. RG 24.5.

14. Student Handbook Seton Hall College of Medicine, RG 24.5.

15. Survey of the Seton Hall College of Medicine and Dentistry, November 1956. RG 24.5.

16. Survey of the Seton Hall College of Medicine and Dentistry, November 1956. RG 24.5.

17. *The Setonian*, November 1, 1956, 1.

18. McNulty to Bernard Berry, December 9, 1958. RG 24.5.

19. William Kellow to Hugh Grady, May 11, 1960. RG 24.5.

20. William Kellow to Hugh Grady, May 11, 1960. RG 24.5.

21. Liaison Committee, Survey Report, December 1959. RG 24.5.

22. One in ten New Jersey applications was successful (47 out of 469 in 1964). The figure was less than 4 percent (35 out of 1,078 in 1964) for out-of-state applications.

23. Kellow to Grady, May 11, 1960. RG 24.5.

24. Liaison Committee, Survey Report, December 1959. RG 24.5.

25. Kellow to Grady, May 11, 1960. RG 24.5.

26. James McCormack to Thomas Boland, February 2, 1962. RG 24.5.

27. Excerpts from Liaison Committee report, October 25, 1962. RG 24.5. The quotations that follow in this paragraph are taken from this document.

28. Excerpts from Liaison Committee report, October 25, 1962. RG 24.5.

29. Excerpts from Liaison Committee report, October 25, 1962. RG 24.5.

30. Report of the Liaison Committee, January 11, 1963. RG 24.5.

31. Summary of AAMC report, March 22, 1962. RG24.5.

32. Dougherty to Walter Wiggins, Ward Darley, December 10, 1962. RG24.5.

33. John O'Connor to Dougherty, February 2, 1962. RG 24.5.

34. Glen Leymaster to Council on Medical Education and Hospitals, January 11, 1963. RG 24.5.

35. Draft Memo for File, Liaison Committee on Medical Education, April 26, 1963.

36. "State May Rescue Med School," *Medical World News*, May 8, 1964. RG 24.5.

37. Report of the Seton Hall Fact-Finding Committee, July 1964, 4, 19–22, upon which this paragraph is based.

38. "State May Rescue Med School," *Medical World News,* May 8, 1964. RG 24.5.

39. Report of the Seton Hall Fact-Finding Committee, July 1964, 4, 19–22.

40. SH 3.22, 14, Presidents Hall Documents, Seton Hall College of Medicine and Dentistry Folder. College of Medicine and Dentistry Board of Trustees, Special Meeting, December 21, 1964.

41. Excluding this last agreement, there were four affiliation agreements between Jersey City and the Seton Hall College of Medicine and Dentistry: December 10, 1954; November 28, 1955; July 17, 1958; July, 17/1963.

42. SH 3.22, 14, Presidents Hall Documents, Seton Hall College of Medicine and Dentistry Folder. College of Medicine and Dentistry Board of Trustees, Special Meeting, December 21, 1964.

Chapter 15. Dangerous Decade

1. Michael Valente in *The Setonian,* September 17, 1969, 7.

2. *The Setonian,* September 17, 1969, 8.

3. Gerard Kelly to Seton Hall Alumni Fund, April 3, 1970. RG 2.13.6.43.

4. *The Setonian,* September 24, 1969, 6.

5. Letters to the Editor, *The Setonian,* November 19, 1969, 5.

6. RG 4 4.6.3.1, University Governance, Board of Trustees Minutes, May 21, 1970.

7. Rev. James McMenemie, report to the Board of Trustees, RG 4 4.6.3.1, University Governance, Board of Trustees Minutes, May 21, 1970.

8. Minutes, Special Meeting of the Faculty Senate, May 8, 1970. RG 4, 4.4, University Governance Faculty Senate, 1968–1971, Box 2 of 2.

9. Robert L Beisner, "On Student Reaction to the Indochina Crisis," *The North American Review* 255, no. 3 (Fall 1970), 55–58.

10. RG 4, 4.7, Deans' Meetings: Minutes, Reports, Correspondence (1970–1980), Box 1 of 5, July 1, 1970.

11. RG 4, 4.7, President's Cabinet, Minutes, Reports, Correspondence (1970–1978), Box 4 of 5 July 7, 1970.

12. Frederick J. Garrity to Fahy, January 21, 1971. RG 2, 2.15.2, Fahy, Nursing-General 1970–1973, Box 17 of 24.

13. "The radicals marched on me, but I held to the principles upon which the university was founded." *The Setonian,* March 26, 1987, 10.

14. "At Seton Hall, A New Image," *The New York Times,* March 7, 1976, NJ4.

15. RG 4, 4.7, University Wide Committees, Box 4 of 5, Meeting of Vice-Presidents and Presidential Assistants, October 2, 1972, 5.

16. "At Seton Hall, A New Image."

17. Peter Mitchell in conversation with the author, April 2017.

18. Professor Larry Greene in conversation with the author, April 3, 2008.

19. "Seton Hall's New President," *The Monitor,* June 4, 1970, 7.

20. RG 2.2.15.5.1, Office of the President, Fahy, 21 of 24, Inauguration.

21. Peter Mitchell in conversation with the author, April 2017.

22. Kelley to Fahy, October 15, 1970. RG 2, 2.15.1, Fahy, Box 21 of 24.

23. RG 7, Accession 6-86, Provost, Box 4 of 9.

24. *The Setonian,* October 24, 1975, 1.

25. RG2, 2.13.6.130, Dougherty, Women's Dormitory Committee 1969.

26. RG2, 2.13.6.130, Dougherty, Women's Dormitory Committee 1969.

27. Aquinas Hall is now a freshman dormitory.

28. RG 4, 4.7, Minutes, Presidential Advisers' Meeting, Box 4 of 5, November 21, 1973.

29. John Duff, Aide-Memoire, November 15, 1973. RG 3, 3.4, Accreditation, Self-Evaluation Commission, 1958–1961.

30. Middle States Association Report, 1973. 5 RG 3, 3.4, Accreditation Documentation, Self-Evaluation Commission, 1958–1961.

31. Middle States Association Report, 1973, 7. 5 RG 3, 3.4, Accreditation Documentation, Self-Evaluation Commission, 1958–1961.

32. Senate Document #76, 74, 75. RG 4.3, University Senate, Documents, Reports, Correspondence, 1973–1976, Box 2 of 4.

33. *The Setonian*, September 7, 1989, 1.

34. *The Setonian*, February 13, 1978, 10.

35. *The Setonian*, October 8, 1981, 1.

36. *The Setonian*, February 13, 1978, 10.

37. *The Setonian*, February 13, 1978, 10.

38. Robert Senkier to Business Faculty, September 10, 1974. RG 2.2.15, Fahy, School of Business General Correspondence 1970–1976.

39. *The Setonian*, November 22, 1976, 6.

40. *The Setonian*, October November 1979, 3.

41. Senkier to Peter Mitchell, July 9, 1974. RG 2.2.15, Fahy, School of Business General Correspondence 1970–1976, 6.

42. Peter Mitchell, letter to the author, May 2017.

43. In 1957, teachers were paid $20 to supervise students in the classroom, an amount unchanged in 1977. *The Setonian*, January 28, 1977, 11.

44. *The Setonian*, January 28, 1977, 11.

45. Robert Hassenger, "The Structure of Catholic Higher Education," in Philip Gleason (ed.), *Contemporary Catholicism in the United States* (South Bend, IN: University of Notre Dame Press, 1969), 304–306.

46. Hassenger, "Structure," 306–307.

47. Middle States Association Report, 1973, 7. 5 RG 3, 3.4, Accreditation Documentation, Self-Evaluation Commission, 1958–1961.

48. *The Setonian*, September 12, 2002, 6.

49. RG 2, 2.15.1, Office of the President, Thomas Fahy, Budget Committee, 1970–1977, Box 2 of 24.

50. RG 2, 2.15, Fahy, Box 2 of 24, Announcement to the University Community, November 20, 1976.

51. Fahy, Cabinet Minutes, October 11, 1976. RG 2, 2.15, Fahy, Box 2 of 24.

52. *The Setonian*, April 18, 1975, 1.

53. RG 4.3, University Senate, Documents, Reports, Correspondence, 1973–1976 , February 13, 1976.

54. *The Setonian*, February 20, 1976, 1.

55. *The Setonian*, September 24, 1976, 1.

56. *The Setonian*, October 26, 1976, 4.

57. *The Setonian*, October 26, 1976, 1.

58. *The Setonian*, January 26, 1973, 1.

59. *The Setonian*, April 28, 1972, 1; February 17, 1976, 1.

60. Bernhard Scholz to Stephen Lang, April 8, 1991. RG 7, Provost, Scholz, Bu-S, 1991–1992.

61. The others were Tom, a Shakespeare scholar, and Peter, briefly a teacher in the history department.

62. Minutes, Presidential Advisers' Meeting, February 5, 1973. 7 RG 4, 4.7, University Governance, University Wide Committees, Box 4 of 5.

63. RG 7 Provost, Duff, cos–end of c, d–dev, Minutes of Cabinet, March 4, 1974.

64. Andreas Pogany to William Field, October 16, 1972. RG 7, Provost, Mitchell, Colleges and Institutes, Lib–end of L

65. RG 7, Provost, Duff, Cos–end of c, d–deve, March 4, 1974, May 7, 1973.

66. RG 7, Provost, Duff, Office Files, Far–Fin, 1969–1976, University Financial Aid.

67. *The Setonian*, February 4, 1972, 5.

68. *The Setonian*, February 4, 1972, 6.

69. RG 4, 4.7, President's Cabinet, Minutes, Reports, Correspondence (1970–1978), 4 of 5, October 25, 1971.

70. *The Setonian*, February 4, 1972, 1.

71. To Peter Mitchell, Paterson was for "cast-off faculty members, someone the department wants to get rid of." RG 4, 4.7, President's Cabinet, Minutes, Reports, Correspondence (1970–1978), 4 of 5.

72. *The Setonian*, April 30, 1973, 11.

73. Elizabeth Baumgartner to Mitchell, August 9, 1977. RG 7, Provost, Mitchell, Colleges and Institutes, Nur–end of Nur.

74. *The Setonian*, May 3, 1974, 47.

75. Vice Presidents' Meeting, July 25, 1961. RG 2.2.14, Box IV, Fleming, Vice Presidents Meetings 1961–1963.

76. "The tenure policy of the university is hereby amended to include the following: 'a fully-affiliated faculty member who holds an ordinary appointment at least in the rank of instructor and who has served the University fulltime for at least seven consecutive years has tenure.'" Minutes of Board of Trustees, March 3, 1978.

77. RG 2, 18.1.2, Accession 11-86, Law School, Irving, Box 4 of 12, January 16, 1973.

78. RG 4.3, University Senate, Documents, Reports, Correspondence, 1973–1976, Box 2 of 4. Senate Document #29, December 7, 1974.

79. Deans' Meeting, September 7, 1971. RG 7, Accession 18-86, Provost, Series 1, University Files, Box 5.

80. Deans' Meeting, September 7, 1971. RG 7, Accession 18-86, Provost, Series 1, University Files, Box 5.

81. Lawrence Whipple to Leonard Zemeckis, RG 2.20, Petillo, 1984–1989, Box 5.

82. Deans' Meetings, November 27, 1979. RG 7, Accession 18-86, Provost, Series 1, University Files, Box 5.

83. Thomas Fahy Statement, August 20, 1971. RG 4.3, University Senate, Box 1 of 4.

84. Mostly from Essex, Union, Bergen, and Hudson Counties.

85. *The Profile of Entering Freshmen at Seton Hall University*, January 1972.RG 7, Accession 6-86, Office of the Provost, Box 6 of 9.

86. Nicholas de Prospo to D'Alessio, June 27, 1983. RG 2.18.1, D'Alessio, Elem–Facu.

87. *The Evening News* (Newark, NJ), September 30, 1970, 1, 6.

88. *The Setonian*, November 15, 1974, 1.

89. Philip Kayal to John Duff, November 4, 1970. RG 7, Accession 6-89, Provost, Box 4 of 9.

90. This was in 1978, two years after Fahy's death. *The Setonian*, April 28, 1978, 1.

91. *The Setonian*, September 28, 1973, 3.

92. *The Setonian*, March 6, 1980, 5.

93. *The Setonian*, April 30, 1969, 5.

94. *The Setonian*, October 30, 1970, 1.

95. RG 5.2, Accession 11-87, Series 4: John Cole, Box 9 of 12, ABA report 1975.

96. RG 4, 4.7, President's cabinet, Assistants Meeting, April 17, 1972, 2.

97. *The Setonian*, February 28, 1975, 9.

98. George Devine to Fahy, May 27, 1971. RG 7, Accession 4-88, Series 14, Bossman, 13a.

99. RG 2.118.1, MAC-MID[PRE], Middle States Period Review Report, 1978, 2.

100. RG 2.18.1, D'Alessio, Petillo, Business-China [1982].

101. D'Alessio to Linda Steiner, February 18, 1981. RG 2.18.1, D'Alessio, Elm–Fac.

102. Robert Antczak to Dougherty, December 4, 1975. RG 7, Provost, Mitchell, Office Files, Pay–Prie, 1972–1978.

103. Antczak to Robert Conley, May 31, 1978. January 25, 1979. RG 2, 3-89, Petillo, 5 of 6.

104. James McGlone, "Catholic University—A Definition," *Journal of the First Campus Ministry Symposium*, Seton Hall University, April 1977, 13.

105. *The Setonian*, April 15, 1970, 4.

106. Jerry Izenberg, "No Sad Songs," *The Star-Ledger*, October 28, 1976.

107. *The Setonian*, November 1, 1976, 3.

108. He joined the faculty in 1959 as assistant professor of marketing.

109. RG 2.2.16, Acting President John Cole, April 25, 1977.

110. *The Setonian*, October 22, 1976, 1.

111. *The Setonian*, June 17, 1977, 7.

112. *The Setonian*, February 11, 1977, 4.

113. Peter Mitchell, letter to the author, May 2017.

114. Albert Hakim in conversation with the author, February 1998. In effect, Murphy's candidacy was vetoed by Dougherty.

115. *The Setonian*, June 17, 1977, 1.

116. *The Setonian*, September 19, 1977, 1.

117. RG 4.6.1, Board of Trustees, Minutes of Meetings, October 10, 1979, Box 4 of 13.

118. Peter Ahr to Conley, June 23, 1977. RG 2.18.1, D'Alessio, IBM–INS.

119. *The Setonian*, April 21, 1978, 8.

120. The debt of $52,000 was written off in 1983. RG 2, Accession 1-87, Petillo, 2 of 3.

121. *The Setonian* , April 17, 1978, 10.

122. *The Setonian*, April 17, 1978, 10.

123. *The Setonian*, October 27, 1978, 1.

124. RG 7.2.4.1, Gerety, Box 99, Folder 6, Seton Hall University.

125. Peter Mitchell, letter to the author, May 2017.

126. Robert Conley to Finance Committee, Board of Trustees, December 8, 1978. RG 7.2.4.1, Gerety, Box 100, Folder 1, Seton Hall University, Main Folder.

127. *The Setonian*, February 13, 1978, 3.

128. *The Setonian*, February 13, 1978, 3; also September 22, 1978, 4.

129. *The Setonian*, October 7, 1977, 1.

130. *The Setonian*, April 7, 1978, 1.

131. *The Setonian*, September 15, 1978, 10.

132. Peter Ahr, in conversation with the author, May 22, 2009.

133. *The Setonian*, September 22, 1978, 1.

134. *The Setonian*, June 11, 1979, 9.

135. John J. Petillo, Faculty Convocation Address. RG 2, 3-89 Office of the Chancellor, Petillo, 2 of 6.

136. Albert Hakim, in conversation with the author, February 17, 2006.

137. *The Setonian*, October 25, 1979, 1.

138. Peter Ahr, in conversation with the author, October 5, 2003.

139. Report of the University Budget Committee on the proposed 1980–1981 budget. RG 2, Accession 7-86, Murphy, Series 1: Finance, Box 1 of 2.

140. *The Setonian*, September 29, 1979, 17.

141. *The Setonian*, September 29, 1979, 19.

142. Peter Ahr in conversation with the author, May 22, 2009.

143. *The Setonian*, September 20, 1979, 19.

144. *The Setonian*, September 20, 1979, 11.

145. Coopers and Lybrand Report1984. RG 2, 3-89, Petillo, 4 of 6.

146. Professor John Shannon quoted in *The Setonian* October 11, 1979, 1.

147. Alfred Celiano-Budget Managers, November 12, 1979. RG 5.2, Accession 11-87, Controller, Series 5, Box 12 of 12.

148. Alfred Celiano, Richard Connors to Faculty January 18, 1980. RG 7, Accession 16-87, Connors, Series 2 and 3, Box 4 of 7.

149. *The Setonian*, October 25, 1979, 1.

150. The university's telephone bill for 1979 came to nearly a third of a million dollars, with "enormous" numbers of calls made to Iran, West Germany, Italy, and Switzerland. *The Setonian*, October 30, 1980, 3.

151. *The Setonian*, November 15, 1979, 5.

152. *The Setonian*, April 24, 1980, 10.

153. Reverend Al Celiano in conversation with the author, October 2008.

154. *The Setonian*, September 5, 1980, 1.

155. *The Setonian*, September 5, 1980, 5.

156. RG 5, Accession 11-87, Controller, Executive Vice Chancellor, series 5, Box 12 of 12, Presidential Staff meeting, 8, 25, 1980.

157. RG 5, Accession 11-87, Controller, Executive Vice Chancellor, series 5, Box 12 of 12, Presidential Staff meeting, 8, 25, 1980.

158. *The Setonian*, Spring 2006 Special Edition, 8.

159. *The Setonian* September 5, 1980, 3.

160. Scholz to D'Alessio, August 28, 1980. RG 2, Box 1 of 1, SHU Finance Committee.

161. *The Setonian*, October 23, 1980, 1.

162. *The Setonian*, September 10, 1981, 1.

163. *The Setonian*, Orientation 1981, 1.

164. *The Setonian*, January 28, 1982, 3.

165. *The Setonian*, February 11, 1982, 1.

166. *The Setonian*, March 25, 1982, 1.

167. *The Setonian*, April 1, 1981, 1.

168. *The Setonian*, May 6, 1981, 1.

169. *The Setonian*, September 23, 1981, 1.

170. *The Setonian*, September 23, 1981, 1.

171. *The Setonian*, September 9, 1982, 1.

172. John Oesterreicher to D'Alessio, January 5, 1983. RG 2.18.1, D'Alessio, End of I–Jud.

173. Petillo to Francis LoBianco, October 14, 1987. RG 2, 4-89, Petillo, 4 of 53.

174. RG 6, SHU, 14-86, Vice Chancellor for University Affairs, Box 2 of 4, Middle States Report 1983, 5.

175. *The Setonian*, February 11, 1982, 1.

176. *The Setonian*, April 14, 1983, 1.

Chapter 16. The Seton Hall Renaissance

1. Bernhard Scholz, College of Arts and Sciences Annual Report 1982–1983, 12.

2. Preliminary Self-Evaluation Report June 7, 1982. RG 7, Accession 18-86, Provost, Series 1, University Files, Box 10.

3. Preliminary Self-Evaluation Report June 7, 1982. RG 7, Accession 18-86, Provost, Series 1, University Files, Box 10.

4. James O'Connor to John Petillo, June 14, 1983. RG 2.18.1, Petillo, Box 1 of 3, A–C 1981–1988.

5. Jerry Hirsch to Petillo, June 6, 1983. RG 2.18.1, Petillo, Box 1 of 3, A–C 1981–1988, 8.

6. Albert Reiners to Petillo August 20, 1983. RG 2.18.1, Petillo, Box 1 of 3, A-C 1981-1988.

7. Nicholas DeProspo to Board of Regents September 15, 1980. RG 4.8, Board of Regents, Minutes of Meeting, 1980–1984.

8. *The Setonian*, April 24, 1980, 12.

9. Gleason, *Keeping the Faith*, 92.

10. Nicholas DeProspo to Board of Regents September 15, 1980. RG 4.8, Board of Regents, Minutes of Meeting, 1980–1984.

11. Nicholas DeProspo to Board of Regents September 15, 1980. RG 4.8, Board of Regents, Minutes of Meeting, 1980–1984.

12. Minutes of the Board of Regents, June 9, 1983, 18.

13. RG 6, SHU 14-86, Vice Chancellor for University Affairs, Box 2 of 4, Middle States Report 1983, 6.

14. DeProspo to Robert Sheeran, December 8, 1995. SHU 3.22, Correspondence Welcoming President Sheeran, Box 24.

15. Minutes of the Board of Regents, June 7, 1984, 10.

16. *The Setonian*, September 22, 1983, 3.

17. *The Setonian*, September 22, 1983, 4.

18. Bernhard Scholz, Introduction to *Partners in Learning*, 1993.

19. RG 7, Accession 4-88, Office of the Provost, Series 2, Administrative Offices, Box 1 of 13.

20. RG 7, Accession 4-88, Office of the Provost, Series 2, Administrative Offices, Box 1 of 13.

21. *The Setonian*, October 15, 1985, 10.

22. RG 7, Accession 4-88, Office of the Provost, Series 2, Administrative Offices, Box 1 of 13.

23. Petillo, Faculty Convocation 1983. RG 2, 3-89, Petillo, 2 of 6.

24. RG 2, 15-88, Petillo, 2 of 2.

25. RG 2, 4-89, Petillo, 1 of 3, Convocation Remarks 1987.

26. Robert J. Wister, *Stewards of the Mysteries of God: Immaculate Conception Seminary, 1860–2010* (South Orange, NJ: Immaculate Conception Seminary 2010), 296.

27. *Seton Hall University Catalogue*, 1965, 82.

28. Wister, *Stewards*, 290.

29. Minutes of the Board of Trustees, Immaculate Conception Seminary, March 6, 1978. RG 7.2.4.1, Gerety Papers, Box 99, Folder 2, Seminary Board of Trustees.

30. Minutes of the Board of Trustees, Immaculate Conception Seminary, March 6, 1978. RG 7.2.4.1, Gerety Papers, Box 99, Folder 2, Seminary Board of Trustees.

31. Wister, *Stewards*, 292.

32. Minutes of the Board of Trustees, Immaculate Conception Seminary, 1972. RG 7.2.4.1, Gerety Papers, Box 99, Folder 2, Seminary Board of Trustees.

33. Minutes of the Board of Trustees, Immaculate Conception Seminary, 1977. RG 7.2.4.1, Gerety Papers, Box 99, Folder 2, Seminary Board of Trustees.

34. Wister, *Stewards*, 310.

35. Wister, *Stewards*, 330.

36. Wister, *Stewards*, 336.

37. Wister, *Stewards*, 340.

38. *The Setonian*, March 4, 1982, 1

39. *The Setonian* February 2, 1984, 1.

40. Wister, *Stewards*, 355.

41. The withholding of tenure should not be seen as a way of keeping priests under episcopal control but a way, rather, of *protecting* seminary faculty from the possibility of being denied

tenure, and thus employment, by members of the University Rank and Tenure Committee not well disposed to the seminary.

42. Affiliation Agreement between Seton Hall University and Immaculate Conception Seminary (1982, renewed 1993), RG 2.21, Office of the Chancellor, Peterson, 28 of 48.

43. John Mitchell to Scholz, July 20, 1987. RG 7, 6-86, Provost, Scholz, 5 of 9.

44. Peter Ahr to Scholz October 15, 1985. ADN, 9a, Seton Hall.

45. *The Setonian*, April 18, 1985, 4.

46. Wister, *Stewards*, 370.

47. Wister, *Stewards*, 372.

48. Wister, *Stewards*, 373.

49. Wister, *Stewards*, 374.

50. George Ring to James Allison, September 29, 87 RG 2.21. Chancellor, Peterson, 26 of 48.

51. George Ring to James Allison, September 29, 87 RG 2.21. Chancellor, Peterson, 26 of 48.

52. Minutes of the Board of Regents, September 20, 1984.

53. Minutes of the Board of Regents, March 26, 1985.

54. The Board of Regents authorized a total of $28.5 million to be spent on both buildings although, by June 1986, the cost was nearer $29 million (Minutes of the Board of Regents, June 5, 1986). A gift of $1 million from Robert Brennan, member of Board of Regents, helped defray the expense (Minutes of the Board of Regents, March 21, 1986).

55. *The Setonian*, March 21, 1985, 1.

56. *The Setonian*, February 16, 1988, 6.

57. RG 7, Accession 4-88, Provost, Series 1, University Governance, Box 1 of 13.

58. *The Setonian*, September 24, 1987, 1.

59. In January 1988, two workers, Ernest Taylor and Luiz Alfonso, were killed and two others seriously injured when a crane collapsed during the building of Serra Hall. *The Setonian*, January 10, 1988, 1, 4.

60. *The Setonian*, October 1, 1987, 8.

61. Donated by Frank Farinella, a Seton Hall alumnus who joined the Board of Regents in October 1987. *The Setonian*, October 29, 1987, 4.

62. *The Setonian*, September 17, 1987, 1.

63. *The Setonian*, February 16, 1988, 7.

64. *The Setonian*, February 16, 1988, 11.

65. *The Setonian*, September 9, 1988, 2.

66. Minutes of the Board of Regents, December 10, 1984.

67. *The Setonian*, December 13, 1984, 1.

68. *The Setonian*, December 13, 1984, 5.

69. *The Setonian*, December 13, 1984, 5.

70. Joseph Stetar to Charles Dees, August 20, 1984. RG 7 Accession 4-88, Provost, Series 2: Administrative Offices, Box 2 of 13.

71. Richard Connors to Frank Morales, September 27, 1984. RG 7, Accession 16-87, Provost, Series 4, Special Academic Programs, Box 7 of 7.

72. Joseph Stetar to Charles Dees, August 20, 1984. RG 7 Accession 4-88, Provost, Series 2: Administrative Offices, Box 2 of 13.

73. Joseph Stetar to South Orange Deans and Faculty, May 2, 1986. RG 7 Accession 4-88, Provost, Series 2: Administrative Offices, Box 2 of 13.

74. Scholz to Kathleen Rice, October 10, 1984. RG 6, Accession 14-86, Vice Chancellor for University Affairs, Box 2 of 4.

75. Scholz to Connors, January 25, 1983. RG 7, SHU 18-86, Provost, Series 2, College Files, Box 13, College of Arts and Sciences.

76. Scholz to Deans, December 17, 1986. RG 7, Accession 28-88, Provost, Series 1, Box 2 of 8.

77. Scholz to Petillo, December 16, 1986. RG 7, Accession 28-88, Provost, Series 1, Box 2 of 8.

78. *The Setonian*, May 1, 1986, 5.

79. RG 2, Accession 4-89, Petillo, 1 of 3, Convocation Remarks 1987.

80. *The Setonian*, March 27, 1987, 3.

81. *The Setonian*, November 5, 1987, 3.

82. *The Setonian*, March 27, 1987, 3.

83. Art Shriberg to D'Alessio, December 1, 1982. RG 5.2, Accession 11-87, Controller, Series 5, Box 12 of 12.

84. Proposal for a Freshman College, November 21, 1986, 2. RG 6, 91:11, Executive Vice Chancellor, Allison, Box 2 of 2.

85. RG 2, 4-89, Petillo, 1 of 3, Convocation Remarks 1987.

86. Almost 90 percent attended between one and four church services per month.

87. Freshman Survey 1986–1987. RG 2.20, Petillo, February 1, 1993, Archbishop McCarrick-NJ Department of Higher Education.

88. Scholz to Ray Grillo, February 17, 1987. RG 7, SHU 28-88, Provost, Series 1, Box 2 of 8.

89. Evaluation of the Department of Chemistry, March 1987. RG 7, SHU 28-88, Provost, Series 1, Box 5 of 5.

90. Evaluation of the Department of Chemistry, March 1987. RG 7, SHU 28-88, Provost, Series 1, Box 5 of 5, 15.

91. *The Setonian*, January 21, 1988, 4.

92. *The Setonian*, November 19, 1987, 1.

93. This was the fourth Fulbright in the Department of History in seven years.

94. *The Setonian*, December 10, 1987, 1.

95. *The Setonian*, December 10, 1987, 1.

96. RG 7, Accession 4-88, Provost, Series 10, Faculty Files, Box 10 of 13.

97. *The Setonian*, March 12, 1987, 1.

98. Paul Barnas to Bossman, August 26, 1985. RG 7, Accession 4-88, Provost, Series 7, Box 6 of 13.

99. College of Nursing, Middle States Association Self-Evaluation Report, 1983. RG 4, Accession 10-88, University Wide Committees, 1 of 1.

100. *The Setonian*, January 11, 1985, 4.

101. *The Setonian*, June 1985, 1.

102. *The Setonian*, September 22, 1988, 3.

103. *The Setonian*, October 17, 1985, 1.

104. *The Setonian*, October 17, 1985, 1.

105. RG 6, SHU 14-86, Vice Chancellor for University Affairs, Box 2 of 4, Middle States Report 1983, 17.

106. *The Setonian*, September 22, 1988, 3.

107. W. Paul Stillman College of Business, Middle States Association Self-Evaluation Report, 1983. RG 4, Accession 10-88, University Wide Committees, 1 of 1.

108. W. Paul Stillman College of Business, Middle States Association Self-Evaluation Report, 1983. RG 4, Accession 10-88, University Wide Committees, 1 of 1.

109. Seton Hall University, Academic Affairs Annual Report, 1991, 2, 24–25.

110. *The Setonian*, November 14, 1985, 13.

111. RG 6, SHU 14-86, Vice Chancellor for University Affairs, Box 2 of 4, Middle States Report 1983, 18.

112. Seton Hall University, Academic Affairs Annual Report, 1990–1991, 33.

113. *The Setonian*, January 24, 1985, 12.

114. *The Setonian*, January 24, 1985, 1, 5.

115. *The Setonian*, November 14, 1985, 13.

116. Scholz to Peterson, April 1, 1992; Peterson to Scholz, April 14, 1992. RG 2, 2.21, Peterson, Provost Correspondence, Box 5 of 48.

117. McCarrick served as Archbishop of Newark from 1986 until 2000 and as Archbishop of Washington from 2001 to 2006. He became a cardinal in 2001. In June 2018, following "credible and substantiated" allegations of historical sexual misconduct against a New York altar boy, he was removed from public ministry. In July 2018, following further allegations of misconduct towards adults and seminarians, he resigned as a cardinal. In February 16, 2019, the Holy See Press Office announced that McCarrick had been laicized.

118. Minutes of the Board of Regents, March 26, 1987, 19.

119. John Patterson to Peterson May 18, 1992. RG 2.21, Peterson, Box 5 of 48.

120. National Labor Relations Board v. Yeshiva University, 444 U.S. 672.

121. See RG 2, 3-89, Petillo, 3 of 6, Yeshiva Decision.

122. In October 1982, by a vote of 176–123 on a turnout of 82 percent, the faculty voted to af-filiate with AFT. *The Setonian*, October 21, 1982, 3.

123. Joseph Stetar to Petillo, July 29, 1986. RG 2, 3-89, Petillo, 2 of 6.

124. *The Setonian*, October 7, 1982, 9.

125. *The Setonian*, November 4, 1982, 9.

126. Scholz to John Hampton, September 30, 1986. RG 7, Accession 28-88, Provost, Series 1, Box 2 of 8.

127. *The Setonian*, December 10, 1981, 9.

128. *The Setonian*, October 28, 1986, 3.

129. *The Setonian*, February 19, 1982, 6.

130. *The Setonian*, November 1, 1984, 6.

131. *The Setonian*, September 20, 1984, 6.

132. *The Setonian*, September 20, 1984, 16.

133. *The Setonian*, October November 1984, 5. Professor of marketing from 1963 until his re-tirement in 1985, with graduate degrees from Columbia and NYU, Stukas was the long-time host of "Memories of Lithuania" on WSOU. *The Setonian*, May 5, 1994, 6.

134. Task Force on Catholicity, RG 2.8, McCarrick, Series 1, Topical Files, Box 8 of 75.

135. Task Force on Catholicity, RG 2.8, McCarrick, Series 1, Topical Files, Box 8 of 75.

136. Task Force on Catholicity, RG 2.8, McCarrick, Series 1, Topical Files, Box 8 of 75.

137. Joseph Mahoney to Task Force on Catholicity, RG 2.8, McCarrick, Series 1, Topical Files, Box 8 of 75.

138. Joseph Maloy to Dennis Mahon et. al., November 5, 1987. RG 2.8, McCarrick, Series 1, Topical Files, Box 8 of 75.

139. Dennis Mahon to Members of the Task Force on Catholicity, September 24, 1987. RG 2.8, McCarrick, Series 1, Topical Files, Box 8 of 75.

140. RG 2, 4-89, Petillo, 1 of 3, Convocation Remarks 1987.

141. RG 2, 4-89, Petillo, 1 of 3, Convocation Remarks 1987.

142. Philip Gleason, *Contending With Modernity*, 250ff.

143. Ahr to Scholz, October 15, 1985. RG 7, SHU 4-88, Provost, 7, College, Box 5 of 13.

144. John Ballweg to Petillo, October 7, 1986. RG 2, 3-89, Petillo, 2 of 6.

145. *The Setonian*, February 19, 1987, 1, 3.

146. Volenski "resigned" as a priest of the Archdiocese of Newark in a June 1984 letter to Ge-rety but was never laicized. Toward the end of his life, he expressed a wish to return to active ministry and may even have done so, a position somewhat at odds with the fact that when he died in 2001 he was also engaged to be married.

147. RG 7, Accession 18-66, Office of the Provost, University Files.

148. See William Berlinghoff and Rodger Allen, *Academic Freedom and Tenure: Seton Hall University* (March 1985), from which the paragraphs above are drawn. RG 7, Accession 18-66, Office of the Provost, University Files.

149. John Morley to Priest Community, February 20, 1985. RG 2.21, Peterson, Box 44 of 48.

150. Dennis Mahon to Peterson, May 28, 1992. RG 2.21, Peterson, Box 44 of 48.

151. Scholz to College Rank and Tenure Board, November 28, 1983. RG 7, Accession 4-88, Provost, 9, University Rank and Tenure Board, Box 8 of 13.

152. Scholz to College Rank and Tenure Board, November 28, 1983. RG 7, Accession 4-88, Provost, 9, University Rank and Tenure Board, Box 9 of 13.

153. *The Setonian*, January 24, 1985, 1, 5.

154. Dennis Notari to D'Alessio, November 9, 1982. RG 2.18.1, D'Alessio, NJ Coll-Not.

155. Ahr to DeProspo, February 7, 1979. RG 7, SHU 18-86, Provost, 2, College Files, Box 20, College of Arts and Sciences.

156. *The Setonian*, October 15, 1976, 5.

157. *The Setonian*, December 11, 1989, 10.

Chapter 17. Toward the New Millennium

1. *The Setonian*, Spring 2006 Special Edition, Seton Hall Through the Years, 8.

2. Keyes Martin, Public Relations Outline, 2. RG 2, SHU 3-89, Petillo, 4 of 6.

3. Keyes Martin, Public Relations Outline, 2. RG 2, SHU 3-89, Petillo, 4 of 6.

4. *The Star-Ledger*, December 12, 1989, 43.

5. Richard Liddy, in conversation with the author, October 20, 2017.

6. Richard Liddy, in conversation with the author, October 20, 2017.

7. *Providence Journal*, October 26, 2000, B4.

8. *The Setonian*, September 15, 1994, 8.

9. *The Setonian*, September 6, 1990, 2.

10. Peterson to Edward Glynn, May 15, 1996. RG 2.2.21, Peterson, 29 of 48.

11. William Dettling to Peterson, June 27, 1990. RG 2.21, Peterson, 13 of 48.

12. Laurence Murphy to Peterson, June 21, 1990. RG 2.21, Peterson, 13 of 48.

13. Jim Plunkett to Peterson, June 1990. RG 2.21, Peterson, 13 of 48.

14. Peter Gerety to Peterson, June 15, 1990. RG 2.21, Peterson, 13 of 48.

15. *The Setonian*, October 18, 1990, 1.

16. *Current Issues in Catholic Higher Education, Presidential Visions*, 50. https://files.eric.ed.gov /fulltext/ED342314.pdf.

17. Seton Hall University Financial Health Assessment (1995), 2. RG 2.21, Peterson, 40 of 48.

18. Seton Hall University Financial Health Assessment (1995), 2. RG 2.21, Peterson, 40 of 48.

19. In 1991, an internal and federal investigation discovered that $1 million had been stolen from the university by director of finance Richard Maragni. The university was fully insured for the loss. *The Setonian*, May 25, 1995, 1.

20. Minutes, Board of Regents Meeting, December 19, 1991. RG 2.21, Peterson, 9 of 48.

21. *The Setonian*, December 5, 1990, 3.

22. Seton Hall University Financial Health Assessment (1995), 2. RG 2.21, Peterson, 40 of 48.

23. Seton Hall University Financial Health Assessment (1995), 2. RG 2.21, Peterson, 40 of 48.

24. Seton Hall University Financial Health Assessment (1995), 2. RG 2.21, Peterson, 40 of 48.

25. Seton Hall University Action Plan, Business and Finance Division, 1995.RG 2.21Peterson, 41 of 48.

26. Seton Hall University Financial Health Assessment (1995), 2. RG 2.21, Peterson, 40 of 48.

27. Matt Dowling, an honors program student, proposed that "we should gather up all the faulty software systems and broken hardware on campus, tie them to a very large package of plastic explosives, and use it to demolish the old McLaughlin Library." *The Setonian*, March 30, 1995, 13.

28. The average SAT score was 877 in 1981, 964 in 1991.

29. Scholz to J. Hirsch et al., October 3, 1991. Records Transfer Memo 3, RG7 Office of the Provost, Scholz.

30. *The Setonian*, November 1, 1990, 6.

31. In 1990 in the College of Arts and Sciences, 26 percent of full-time faculty were female; between 1985 and 1990, fifteen women were hired and seventeen men; of twenty academic departments, five were headed by women. *The Setonian*, November 1, 1990, 6.

32. *The Setonian*, December 5, 1990, 12.

33. *The Setonian*, October 7, 1993, 1, 7.

34. *The Setonian*, January 27, 1994, 6.

35. *The Setonian*, March 24, 1994, 7.

36. *The Setonian*, April 14, 1994, 9.

37. Scholz to J. Hirsch et al., October 3, 1991. Records Transfer Memo 3, RG7 Office of the Provost, Scholz.

38. *The Setonian*, May 23, 1996, 2.

39. Minutes of the Board of Regents, June 18, 1991. RG 2, 21, Peterson, 9 of 48.

40. Robert Sheeran to Alfred Guillaeme, January 30, 1995. SHU 3.22, Presidents Hall Documents, 18.

41. *The Setonian*, September 28, 1990, 1.

42. *The Setonian*, February 28, 1991, 1.

43. *The Setonian*, February 28, 1991, 1.

44. *The Setonian*, February 28, 1991, 1.

45. David Lehrer, Anti-Defamation League of B'nai B'rith, February 3, 1992. RG 2, 2.1, Peterson, 6 of 48.

46. *The Setonian*, February 6, 1992, 11.

47. *The Setonian*, February 6, 1992, 1.

48. *The Setonian*, February 6, 1992, 11.

49. *The Setonian*, February 6, 1992, 1.

50. Peterson to Fabio Fernandez, March 12, 1992. RG 2.2.1, Peterson, 6 of 48.

51. Peterson to University Community, February 23, 1992. RG 2.2.1, Peterson, 6 of 48.

52. McCarrick to Peterson, February 27, 1992. RG 2.2.1, Peterson, 6 of 48.

53. *The Setonian*, February 16, 1995, 1.

54. Minutes of Priest Community meeting, November 5, 1992. RG 2.2.21, Peterson, 4 of 48.

55. *The Setonian*, February 11, 1993, 3.

56. Joseph Varacalli, "Homophobia at Seton Hall University: Sociology in Defense of the Faith," in *Faith and Reason* (Front Royal, Virginia: Christendom College, 1995), 286–287, an excellent summary of the episode.

57. *The Setonian*, January 28, 1993, 10.

58. *The Setonian*, November 11, 1993, 8.

59. *The Setonian*, February 18, 1993, 8.

60. The issue recurred in 2003–2004 when another homosexual group—TRUTH—sought and was denied official recognition by the university. *The Setonian*, January 22, 2004, 5.

61. *The Setonian*, January 19, 1995, 1.

62. Executive Committee, Faculty Senate to Peterson, January 22, 1995; Peterson to University Community, January 23, 1995. RG 2.21, Peterson, 23 of 48.

63. *New York Post*, January 24, 1995.

64. Peterson to Robert Coleman, April 20, 1995. RG 2. 21, Peterson, 29 of 48.

65. Middle States Report 1994, 9. RG 2.21, Peterson, 16 of 48.

66. Seton Hall University: A Self-Evaluation, January 28, 1994, 1. RG 2.21, Peterson, 16 of 48.

67. Peterson to Howard Simmons, May 10, 1994, 2. RG 2.21, Peterson, Box 16 of 48.

68. *The Setonian*, October 12, 1995, 5.

69. *The Setonian*, March 10, 1994, 1.

70. *The Setonian*, February 3, 1994, 1.

71. Tom Landy to Albert Hakim, February 22, 1995. [email]

72. Angela Raimo to Peterson, October 31, 1990. RG 2.20, Petillo, 1984-9, Box 5.

73. Angela Raimo to Peterson, October 31, 1990. RG 2.20, Petillo, 1984-9, Box 5.

74. RG 2.21, Peterson, 46 of 48.

75. McCarrick to Peterson, November 11, 1994. RG 2.21, Peterson, 21 of 48.

76. McCarrick to Peterson, June 24, 1996; Peterson to McCarrick, July 10, 1996. RG 2.21, Peterson, 46 of 48.

77. In House Forum on Catholicity, Minutes, March 20, 1995; Continuing Dialogue, *Ex Corde Ecclesiae*, January 18, 1995. RG 2.21, Peterson, Box 43 of 48.

78. Continuing Dialogue, *Ex Corde Ecclesiae*, January 18, 1995. RG 2.21, Peterson, Box 43 of 48.

79. Continuing Dialogue, *Ex Corde Ecclesiae*, January 18, 1995. RG 2.21, Peterson, Box 43 of 48.

80. Scholz to John Russell et al., May 14, 1993. RG 7, Provost, Scholz Correspondence 1993. Many of the details of the following paragraphs come from Scholz's summary.

81. *The Setonian*, April 22, 1993, 1, 6.

82. Paul Cardinal Poupard to Andrew Cusack, April 8, 1992. RG 2.21, Peterson, 27 of 48.

83. *The Setonian*, May 25, 1995, 5.

84. Scholz to John Russell et al., May 14, 1993. RG 7, Provost, Scholz Correspondence 1993.

85. Academic Affairs Report 1994. RG 2.2.21, Office of the Chancellor, Peterson, 36 of 48.

86. Scholz to Peterson, November 20, 1990. RG 2.21, Peterson, Provost Correspondence, 5 of 48.

87. Scholz to Jane Norton, April 23, 1993. RG 2.22, Sheeran, Box 11, 1992–1996.

88. RG 7, James O. Allison, Middle States 9, Study Group 7, Petra Chu.

89. Scholz to Wendy Budin, August 14, 1992. Record transfer memo RG 7, Provost, 7.

90. *The Setonian*, September 3, 1992, 1.

91. As explained to Peterson by Kelly, March 1994. RG 2.21, Office of the Chancellor, Peterson, Box 21 of 48.

92. *The Setonian*, October 18, 1990, 1.

93. RG 7, Accession 18-86, Provost, 15, Series 2, College of Arts and Sciences, David Kaser report January 1980.

94. RG 7, Accession 18-86, Provost, 15, Series 2, College of Arts and Sciences, David Kaser report January 1980.

95. RG 2. 21, Peterson, Board of Regents Meeting, October 7, 1991.

96. RG 2. 21, Peterson, Board of Regents Meeting, April 18, 1991.

97. RG 2. 21, Peterson, Board of Regents Meeting, April 18, 1991.

98. *The Setonian*, October 11, 1990, 1.

99. *The Setonian*, April 23, 1992, 3.

100. The capsule was opened by Monsignor William Noé Field, who had been present when the foundation stone had been laid.

101. *The Setonian*, May 25, 1995, 1.

102. Chairman of the Board of Regents in 1995.

103. Seton Hall University Financial Health Assessment (1995), 2. RG 2.21, Peterson, 40 of 48.

104. *The Setonian*, September 2, 1993, 7.

105. Peterson to Raymond Chambers, June 8, 1992. RG 2.21, Peterson, 8 of 48.

106. *The Setonian*, October 6, 1994, 1.

107. *The Setonian*, September 1, 1994, 1.

108. *The Setonian*, September 18, 1994, 1.

109. Challenge of Excellence Task Force, December 15, 1994. RG 2.21, Peterson, 40 of 48.

110. Long Range Planning Task Force, Minutes, March 22, 1994. RG 2.21 Peterson, 41 of 48.

111. Chancellor's Advisory Council, Minutes, January 13, 1996. RG 2.21 Peterson, 40 of 48.

112. Challenge of Excellence Task Force, December 15, 1994. RG 2.21 Peterson, 40 of 48.

113. Chancellor's Advisory Council, Minutes, November 15, 1996. RG 2.21 Peterson, 40 of 48.

114. Chancellor's Advisory Council, Minutes, November 15, 1996. RG 2.21 Peterson, 40 of 48.

115. Beyond the scope the present volume, Meehan was named Seton Hall's Interim President in March 2017.

116. Mary Meehan to John Schimpf, February 10, 1996. RG 2.21, Peterson, Chancellor's Advisory Council, Box 40 of 48.

117. *The Setonian*, January 21, 1993, 1.

118. *The Setonian*, October 14, 1993, 10.

119. Scholz, Remarks to General Faculty Meeting, November 11, 1994. RG 2.22, Sheeran, 11, 1992–1996.

120. *The Setonian*, December 8, 1995, 1.

121. Scholz to Sheeran, December 8, 1995. RG 2.2.22, Sheeran, 2, 1993–1998.

122. *The Setonian*, December 8, 1995, 1.

123. Scholz to Sheeran, December 8, 1995. RG 2.2.22, Sheeran, 2, 1993–1998.

124. *The Setonian*, December 8, 1995, 1.

Chapter 18. A Law School for the City

1. Law School Faculty minutes, January 26, 1963. SHU School of Law, RG Special Collections and Archives, 18.1.8.

2. The freshman class of 1962 was drawn from 104 different colleges and universities. Law School Faculty minutes, December 14, 1962. SHU School of Law, RG Special Collections and Archives, 18.1.8.

3. Thomas Cunningham to Miriam Rooney, October 9, 1952. RG 7, Accession 6-86, Provost, Box 7 of 9.

4. Law School Faculty minutes, January 26, 1963. SHU School of Law, RG Special Collections and Archives, 18.1.8.

5. Law School Faculty minutes, March 6, 1961. SHU School of Law, RG Special Collections and Archives, 18.1.8.

6. Law School Faculty minutes, April 22, 1960. SHU School of Law, RG Special Collections and Archives, 18.1.8.

7. Law School Faculty minutes, December 14, 1962. SHU School of Law, RG Special Collections and Archives, 18.1.8.

8. Law School Faculty minutes, September 7, 1961. SHU School of Law, RG Special Collections and Archives, 18.1.8.

9. Student Bar Association Faculty Evaluations, August 15, 1972. RG 18.1.2, SHU Accession 11-86, Seton Hall School of Law, Irving, Box 2 of 12.

10. Professor D. Michael Risinger, in conversation with the author, June 10, 2010.

11. Law School Faculty minutes, May 13, 1969. SHU School of Law, RG Special Collections and Archives, 18.1.8.

12. Law School Faculty minutes, May 13, 1969. SHU School of Law, RG Special Collections and Archives, 18.1.8.

13. For New Jersey's suburbanization, see Maxine Lurie (ed.), *A New Jersey Anthology* (New Brunswick, NJ: Rutgers University Press, 2010), 24.

14. Jeffrey Paige, "Political Orientation and Riot Participation," *American Sociological Review* 36 (October 1971): 810–820.

15. Daniel Matlin, "Lift Up Yr' Self! Reinterpreting Amiri Baraka (Le Roi Jones), Black Power and the Uplift Tradition," *Journal of American History* 93, no. 1 (June 2006), 90–110.

16. Allan Mazur, "The Causes of Black Riots," *American Sociological Review* 37, no. 4 (August 1972), 490–493.

17. Kenneth O'Reilly, "The FBI and the Politics of the Riot, 1964–1968," *Journal of American History* 75, no. 1 (June 1988), 91–114.

18. Matlin, "Lift Up Yr' Self!," 103.

19. School of Law Faculty Minutes, August 20, 1971. RG 18.1.2, Irving, Box 12 of 12.

20. RG 18.1.2, Irving, Box 2 of 12.

21. Law School Faculty minutes, September 14, 1970. SHU School of Law, RG Special Collections and Archives, 18.1.8.

22. Reginald Stanton to Edward Fleming, May 12, 1970. Law School Faculty meeting, May 11, 1970. SHU School of Law, RG Special Collections and Archives, 18.1.8.

23. Seton Hall Law Orientation, 1973, 4. RG 18.1.2, Irving, Orientation, Box 12 of 12.

24. John Morgan to Thomas Fahy, October 11, 1973. RG 18.1.2, Irving, Box 6 of 12, Financial Aid. Edward Hendricksen to Irving, October 11, 1973. RG 18.1.2, Irving, Box 6 of 12, Financial Aid.

25. RG 4, Accession 10-88, University Governance, University Wide Committees, Box 1 of 1, Seton Hall University School of Law, Middle States Self-Evaluation Report 1983.

26. *Res Ipsa Loquitur*, September 1977, 4.

27. RG 7, Accession 6-86, Provost, 4 of 9, Deans' Meetings, December 14, 1971, 5.

28. RG 4, 4.7, President's Cabinet: Minutes, Reports, Correspondence 1970–1978, Box 4 of 5, Meeting of Vice Presidents, October 25, 1971.

29. RG 4, 4.7, President's Cabinet: Minutes, Reports, Correspondence 1970–1978, Box 4 of 5, Meeting of Vice Presidents, October 25, 1971.

30. Law School Faculty minutes, August 20, 1971. SHU School of Law, RG Special Collections and Archives, 18.1.8.

31. "The twig was bent long ago." RG 18.1.2, Irving, Box 5 of 12.

32. RG 18.1.2, Irving, Box 2 of 12. More electives were allowed.

33. RG 2.2.15.2, Fahy, Box 17 of 24, Law School Self-Evaluation 1975.

34. Noel Schablik to John Irving, June 1, 1973. RG 18.1.2, Irving, Box 7 of 12.

35. Irving to Duff, December 3, 1973, Recommendations for rank and tenure. RG 18.1.2, Irving, Box 5 of 12.

36. See his "Trust, Cynicism and Machiavellianism Among entering First Year Law Students" in *Journal of Urban Law*, (University of Detroit), Vol. 53, 3, 1976, 1–15.

37. RG 18.1.2, Irving, Box 7 of 12.

38. *Res Ipsa Loquitur*, September 1977, 4.

39. RG 18.1.2, Irving, Box 7 of 12, Speeches.

40. Law Day 1975: Statement by John F.X. Irving. RG 18.1.2, Irving, Box 7 of 12, Speeches.

41. The national median salary for a law professor in 1975 was $23,350. The figure for Seton Hall was $23,900, which did not go far in the New York area. RG 2.2.15.2, Fahy Box 17 of 24, Law School Self-Evaluation 1975.

42. "The Law School Then and Now: An Interview with Professor Bob Diab," *Precis* 1, no. 2 (1991–1992), 8–9.

43. *Res Ipsa Loquitur*, September 1977, 5.

44. *Res Ipsa Loquitur*, September 1977, 6.

45. *Res Ipsa Loquitur*, February 23, 1976, 7.

46. RG 4, 4.7, President's Cabinet: meeting, Box 4 of 5, November 21, 1973.

47. Richard Cushing to Fahy, February 29, 1972. RG 2.15.2, Fahy, 17 of 24, Law School 1971–1972.

48. *Dicta: An Occasional Newsletter of Seton Hall University School of Law* 1, no. 3 (Spring 1975), 1.

49. Fahy to Irving, December 17, 1975. RG 9, 9.2, Provost, Duff, Faculty Personnel Files.

50. *Res Ipsa Loquitur*, September 1977, 4.

51. The School of Law Alumni Association was committed to raising over $500,000 for the Law Center (its total cost was expected to be $4.5 million). By the beginning of 1975, it had raised $2,000. *Dicta* 1, no. 3 (Spring 1975), 1. Over $100,000 was raised by the end of 1975. *Dicta* 2, no. 1 (Winter 1975), 1. Failure to recognize graduates of the John Marshall School of Law as Seton Hall alumni cost goodwill and dollars among senior lawyers in the state. RG 4, 4.7, President's Cabinet: Minutes, Reports, Correspondence 1970–1978, Box 4 of 5, Meeting of Vice Presidents, October 25, 1971.

52. *Res Ipsa Loquitur*, September 1977, 4.

53. I am grateful to Professor D. Michael Risinger for these details.

54. "The Law School Then and Now: An Interview with Professor Bob Diab," *Precis* 1, no. 2 (1991–1992), 2.

55. *Res Ipsa Loquitur*, September 1977, 3.

56. *Res Ipsa Loquitur*, September 1977, 6.

57. *Res Ipsa Loquitur*, November 1976, 6.

58. RG 7.2.4.1. Peter Leo Gerety Papers Box 100, Folder 1, Seton Hall University, Main Folder.

59. Daniel Degnan to Gerety, September 18, 1978. Peter Leo Gerety Papers Box 100, Folder 1, Seton Hall University, Main Folder.

60. Mark Denbeaux to Richard Connors, January 24, 1983. RG 7, Accession 4-88, Provost, 9, Rank and Tenure, Box 7 of 13.

61. Edward D'Alessio, Daniel Degnan to James P. White, October 23, 1981. ADN RG 2, Series 1, Box 8 of 75, Seton Hall Law School, Self-Study.

62. *The Setonian*, December 2, 1982, 1.

63. Jerrold Glassman to Petillo, November 18, 1983. RG 2, 3-89, Petillo, 4 of 6.

64. Scholz to Petillo, January 20, 1987. RG 2, 4-89, Petillo, 1 of 3, Law School.

65. Joseph Lynch to Rev. Michael Sharkey, November 10, 1987. RG 2.20, Petillo, 1984–1989, Box 1.

66. In 1984, six faculty members held a news conference at the school to celebrate their legal representation of a woman notorious for living by immoral earnings, Sydney Biddle Barrows. This "Mayflower Madam" case later appeared as an examination question cast in terms patently offensive to Jews, Catholics, Protestants, and the Archbishop of Newark. Defeis, objecting, was reproved by the question-setter for her infringement of his academic freedom. Joseph Lynch to Theodore McCarrick, November 5, 1987. RG 2, 4-89, Petillo, 1 of 3, Law School.

67. Joseph Lynch to Theodore McCarrick, November 5, 1987. RG 2, 4-89, Petillo, 1 of 3, Law School.

68. Scholz to Riccio, April 2, 1993. Records Transfer Memo, Box 6, RG 7-Provost.

69. Michael Zimmer to Anthony Santoro, September 29, 1987, RG 7, Accession 15-89, Provost, COE-SUL, Box 9 of 9.

70. RG 2.2.20, Petillo, February 1, 1993, Box 1, ABA Report 1987.

71. Ronald Riccio to Finance Committee, Board of Regents, May 2, 1992, RG 2.2.22, Sheeran, Box 1, 1993–1998.

72. Judson Jennings, Planning Committee Report to the Faculty, April 15, 1986: Separate Report RG 2, 4-89, Petillo, Law School.

73. *The Dean's Letter*, Fall 1986, 2. RG 2.21, Peterson, Box 28 of 48.

74. Herb Jaffe, "There's Life in Government after Law School," *The Star-Ledger*, April 1, 1986.

75. Petillo to Defeis, January 26, 1988. RG 2, 4-89, Petillo, 1 of 3.

76. RG 2, 4-89, Petillo, 1 of 3, Minutes of the Board of Trustees, October 9, 1987.

77. McCarrick to William Cardinal Baum, January 15, 1988. RG 2.20, Petillo, 1984–1989, Box 1.

78. McCarrick to Petillo, October 26, 1987. RG 2, 4-89, Petillo, 2 of 3.

79. McCarrick to Baum, January 15, 1988. RG 2.20, Petillo, 1984–1989, Box 1.

80. Mark Denbeaux to Bernhard Scholz, phone message, September 24, 1987. RG 7, Accession 5-89, Provost, Appointment Books, Box 1 of 1.

81. *New Jersey Law Journal*, July 5, 1990, 1.

82. *New Jersey Law Journal*, July 5, 1990, 1.

83. Petillo to James White, September 26, 1988. RG 2.30, Petillo, 1984–1989, Box 3.

84. RG 7, 15-89, Provost, COE-SOL, Box 9 of 9.

85. RG 7, Provost, Accession 92-12, Box 5.

86. After negotiations with the ABA in 1993–1994, it was agreed that the contribution to the overall budget of the university should be no higher than 20 percent.

87. Riccio thought the pro-Catholic group at the school was a "very small [and] extremely disruptive" minority of an otherwise "productive, harmonious and peaceful faculty," a formulation which made their case for them. Claiming a lively Catholic "presence" at the school suggested that it was not substantially Catholic at all. Ronald Riccio to Academic Committee of the Board of Regents, April 12, 1989. RG 2.21, Office of the Chancellor, Peterson, 28 of 48.

88. The property, consisting of four acres and two buildings totaling 65,000 square feet, was valued at approximately $8 million.

89. Technically the abatements were payable to Bellmead, but the corporation passed them on to the university.

90. *The Star-Ledger*, November 28, 1990, 38.

91. Frank Lautenberg to Louis Azzato, December 12, 1990. RG 2.21, Peterson, Box 28 of 48, Seton Hall Law School, Center for Social Justice, $5.3 Federal Appropriation.

92. Charles Dees to Thomas Peterson, November 29, 1990. RG 2.21, Peterson, Box 28 of 48, Seton Hall Law School, Center for Social Justice, $5.3 Federal Appropriation.

93. For the preceding paragraphs, see "Seton Hall Shows Reach in Aid Push," *New Jersey Law Journal*, November 9, 1989, 1, 15.

94. *The Sunday Star-Ledger*, March 1, 1992, 23.

95. Steven Frankino to McCarrick, November 10, 1993. RG 2.21, Peterson, Box 46 of 48.

96. *The Star-Ledger*, December 11, 1993, 12.

97. James Boskey to Robert Brennan, January 14, 1988. RG 2.20, Petillo, 1984–1989, Box 3.

98. *The Dean's Letter*, Winter 1990, 2. RG 2.21, Peterson, Box 28 of 48.

99. Professor John Coverdale, in conversation with the author, October 2010.

100. Riccio to Sheeran, November 17, 1998. RG 2.21, Box 28 of 48, Dean of Law School.

101. Ronald Riccio to Law School community, November 17, 1998. RG 2.21, Box 28 of 48, Dean of Law School.

102. Mark Rocha to University Community, RG 2.21, Box 28 of 48.

103. *The Setonian*, May 6, 1999, 1, 3.

104. *The Setonian*, April 22, 2004, 10.

105. RG 18, 18.1.13, Information Brochures and Magazines.

106. RG 2.2.21, Office of the Chancellor, Peterson, 46 of 48.

Chapter 19. The Sheeran Years

1. *The Setonian*, December 8, 2005, 1.

2. There were bereavements. Sohayla Massachi, an Honors Program student, was murdered in May 2000, days after her graduation. In August 2000, Dr. William Jordan of the School of Business, was killed in a helicopter accident in Hawaii. *The Setonian*, September 7, 2000, 9. Fourteen alumni died at the World Trade Center on September 11, 2001: Anthony Infante Jr., James Romito, Fred Morrone (all three also adjunct instructors), John Bocchi, Dean Eberling, Craig Lilore, William Martin, Daniel McGinley, James Nelson, Alfonse Niedermeyer, Angel Pena, James Pocher, Kenneth Tarantino, and Mark Whitford.

3. Robert Sheeran, in conversation with the author, March 2010.

4. *Seton Hall Magazine: A home for the mind, the heart and the spirit* (Winter, Spring 2010), 2.

5. Sheeran to Russell Viehmann, October 28, 1993. SHU 3.22, Sheeran Correspondence 1993–1996, 21.

6. Sheeran declined to be considered for the presidencies of Catholic University of America (SHU 3.22, Sheeran Correspondence 1997–1998, Box 22, 2 of 4) and Georgetown University (SHU 3.22, Sheeran Correspondence 1999–2001, Box 23).

7. Records Management Center, Provost, Box 6, Board of Regents, 1995–96.

8. State of the University Address, September 9, 1998. RG 2.21, Peterson, 25 of 48.

9. RG 2.21, Peterson, 28 of 48.

10. *The Star-Ledger*, December 8, 1995, 9.

11. Scholz to Archbishop John Roach, January 11, 1991. Record Transfer Memo, 4, RG7, Provost, Bu-S, 1991–92.

12. James McGlone to Sheeran, January 23, 1996. SHU 3.22, Box 24.

13. Vito Daidone to Sheeran December 8, 1995. SHU 3.22, Box 24.

14. A Challenge to Change: Strategies for the Future of Seton Hall University (1995), RG 2.21, Peterson, 41 of 48.

15. Combining the office of bursar, admissions, financial aid, and registration into a super department failed. *The Setonian*, January 28, 1999.

16. RG 2.21, Peterson, 28 of 48.

17. RG 2.21, Peterson, 28 of 48.

18. Such was the finding of a survey into credit shortfall in Fall 1994.

19. Sheeran to Amar Amar, September 27, 1993. SHU 3.22, Sheeran Correspondence 1993–1996, 21.

20. Sheeran to Senator Frank T. Lautenberg, September 16, 1996. SHU 3.22, Sheeran Correspondence 1993–1996, 21.

21. SHU 3.22, Sheeran Correspondence 1993–1996, 21.

22. *New York Times*, March 29, 1992.

23. *The Setonian*, April 25, 1996, 8.

24. *The Setonian*, February 10, 2000, 7.

25. *The Setonian*, November 21, 2002, 9.

26. *The Setonian*, October 12, 2000, 9.

27. *The Setonian*, September 26, 2006, 13.

28. *The Setonian*, November 9, 2000, 5.

29. *The Setonian*, November 11, 2004 15.

30. *The Setonian*, February 24, 2005, 5–7.

31. *The Setonian*, September 9, 2004, 5.

32. *The Setonian*, May 2, 1996, 8.

33. *The Setonian*, September 28, 2006, 18.

34. *The Setonian*, April 11, 1996, 1.

35. "Transforming the First Three Semesters," December 1997. RG 2.21, Peterson, 41 of 48.

36. *The Setonian*, February 12, 1998, 4.

37. Sheeran to Robert Allen, July 1, 1999. SHU 3.22, Sheeran Correspondence, 1999–2001, 23.

38. *The Setonian*, November 14, 1996, 1.

39. Sheeran to Maxine Lurie, May 6, 1996. SHU 3.22, Sheeran Correspondence 1993–1996, Box 21.

40. Sheeran to Archbishop Timothy Dolan, August 18, 2003. SHU 3.22, Sheeran, Chronological Files, April–September 2003.

41. Robert Sheeran, in conversation with the author, February 16, 2010.

42. RG 2.21, Peterson, 28 of 48.

43. The idea was to establish floors for all academic ranks, with assistant professors to earn no less than $42,000, associate professors $50,000, and professors $60,000. *The Setonian*, September 9, 1999, 1.

44. Mark Rocha to Robert Kaffer February 10, 1998. RG 2.22, Sheeran, 2, 1993–1998.

45. Provost's Report to Faculty, August 31, 1998. RG 2.21, Peterson, 37 of 48.

46. Still pending.

47. Rocha to Board of Regents, September 28, 1999. RG 2.21, Peterson, 35 of 48.

48. *The Setonian*, October 15, 1998, 1.

49. RG 2.21, Peterson, 28 of 48.

50. *The Setonian*, September 20, 2001, 1.

51. *The Setonian*, September 14, 2000, 1.

52. *The Setonian*, April 22, 2004, 6.

53. RG 2.21, Peterson, 28 of 48.

54. Sheeran retired in June 2010. Esteban, appointed acting president in July 2010, was inaugurated as president in October 2011.

55. RG 2.21, Peterson, 28 of 48.

56. RG 2.21, Peterson, 28 of 48.

57. Sheeran to Alvin Adams, January 21, 1997. RG 5.6, Provost, 1996–1997, 3.

58. *The Setonian*, December 11, 1997, 3.

59. "Seton Hall University's School of Diplomacy and International Relations Announces New Graduate Degree Program," April 7, 1998. RG 2.21, Peterson, 19 of 48.

60. Sheeran to Blackburn, April 30, 1999. SHU 3.22, Sheeran Correspondence, 1999–2001, Box 23.

61. *The Setonian*, September 23, 1999, 1.

62. *The Setonian*, October 14, 1999, 1.

63. *The Setonian*, November 1, 2001, 1.

64. *The Setonian*, April 21, 2005, 1.

65. *The Setonian*, December 1, 2005, 1. Holmes was interim dean of SODIR in 2005.

66. *The Setonian*, November 15, 2001, 4.

67. Sheeran to John C. Whitehead, January 23, 2003. SHU 3.22 Sheeran, Chronological Files, November 2002–April 2003.

68. Sheeran to Clay Constaninou, September 15, 2003. SHU 3.22, Sheeran, Chronological File, April–September 2003.

69. Sheeran to Whitehead, October 8, 2003. SHU 3.22, Sheeran, Chronological File, October 2003–November 2004.

70. *The Setonian*, March 25, 2004, 6; April 28, 2005, 7.

71. In July 2013, at his request, the university removed Whitehead's name from the School of Diplomacy and International Relations.

72. China House, a gift to the university from the Maryknoll Fathers in 1994, was sold in 2002.

73. RG 2.21, Peterson, 28 of 48.

74. *Seton Hall Magazine* (Winter, Spring 2010), 19.

75. SHU 3.22, Sheeran, Chronological Files, June 2004–September 2004.

76. Sheeran to Joseph and Carmen Unanue, September 3, 2004. SHU 3.22, Sheeran, Chronological Files, June 2004–September 2004.

77. "Transforming Seton Hall University," November 4, 1996. RG 5.6, Provost, 1996–1997, Box 2.

78. *The Setonian*, September 27, 2001, 1.

79. *The Setonian*, February 27, 1997, 1.

80. *The Setonian*, February 27, 1997, 1.

81. *The Setonian*, October 9, 2003, 3.

82. *The Setonian*, February 12, 1998, 6.

83. *The Setonian*, April 26, 2001, 1.

84. RG 2.21, Peterson, 20 of 48.

85. RG 7, SHU 4-88, Series 4, 5, 6, Box 4 of 13, Academic Affairs, Annual Report 1986–1987.

86. *Faculty Guide*, revised April 2006. https://blogs.shu.edu/senate/files/2012/01/Faculty -Guide.pdf

87. Rocha to Board of Regents September 28, 1999 RG 2.21 Peterson, 35 of 48

88. Susan Mawbrey, "General Education Reform as Organizational Change," *Journal of General Education* 65, no. 1, 5.

89. *The Setonian*, September 8, 2005, 1.

90. Sheeran to Lawrence Long, September 21, 1999. SHU 3.22, Sheeran Correspondence, 1999–2001, 23.

91. *The Setonian*, September 23, 1999, 5.

92. Mary Balkun and Roseanne Mirabella, "Developing a Four-Year Integrated Core Curriculum: Advice for Avoiding the Pitfalls and Building Consensus for Change," 18. I am indebted to Drs. Balkun and Mirabella for sharing their unpublished paper with me, many of whose ideas are incorporated in the preceding paragraphs.

93. Richard Liddy, homily preached in Immaculate Conception Chapel, Seton Hall University, December 18, 2013.

94. Sheeran to Dennis Mahon, November 3, 1987, Recommendations to the Task Force on Catholicity; Theodore McCarrick to Sheeran, December 23, 1987. ADN RG 2.8, McCarrick Series 1, 8 of 75, Seton Hall University Board of Trustees.

95. *The Catholic Advocate*, April 17, 1996.

96. Joseph Varacalli to Sheeran, April 19, 1996. SHU 3.22, Correspondence welcoming President Sheeran, Box 24.

97. *The Setonian*, March 6, 1997, 1.

98. *The Setonian*, March 6, 1997, 1.

99. Dr. Joseph Sandman, summarizing in conversation with the author comments made by Archbishop J. Michael Miller to Board of Regents, October 23, 2004.

100. Dr. Joseph Sandman, summarizing in conversation with the author comments made by Archbishop J. Michael Miller to Board of Regents, October 23, 2004.

101. Seton Hall University Affirmative Action Policy Regarding Priests of the Archdiocese of Newark. SHU 3.22, 16, Executive Cabinet Agenda, June 27, 1997.

102. McCarrick to Sheeran, January 8, 1999. SHU 3.22, Box 17, Presidents Hall Documents, McCarrick.

103. Sheeran to John J. Myers, January 15, 2002. SHU 3.22, Presidents Hall Documents, 19, Myers folder, Speeches and Correspondence, Box 3.

104. Robert Baldini, a member of the Board of Regents, gave $2.3 million. SHU.3.22, Robert Sheeran, Chronological Files, October 2003–January 2004, Sheeran to Baldini, October 22, 2003. Therese Liddy donated $100,000.

105. *The Setonian*, December 5, 2002, 1.

106. *The Setonian*, January 31, 2002, 1, 4.

107. *The Setonian*, January 3, 2003, 1, 4.

108. Sheeran to Myers, November 12, 2001. SHU 3.22, Box 17, Presidents Hall Documents

109. Myers to Sheeran, November 20, 2001 SHU 3.22, Box 17, Presidents Hall Documents.

110. Myers to Sheeran, November 27, 2001; Sheeran to Myers December 10, 2001. SHU 3.22, Box 17, Presidents Hall Documents.

111. Sheeran to Patrick Hobbs, May 13, 2004. SHU 3.22, Robert Sheeran, Chronological Files, February 2004–May 2004. To Sheeran's "deep disappointment," the law school's student organization, with the support of the administration, continued to award its Sandra Day O'Connor medal to pro-choice figures. Sheeran to Myers, May 6, 2004. SHU 3.22, Box 17, Presidents Hall Documents.

112. Sheeran to Bishop Paul Bootkoski, November 10, 1998. SHU 3.22, Sheeran Correspondence 1996-1997-1998, Box 22, 2 of 4.

113. Sheeran to Rev. William A. Ferruzzi, SDB, June 25, 1997. SHU 3.22, Sheeran Correspondence 1997–1998, Box 22, 2 of 4.

114. Boland Hall, a 350-room, six-story residence hall, housed approximately 600 students. It had fifty-five fire extinguishers, all in working order as of their last inspection, November 23, 1999. The smoke alarms were also fully functional.

115. The Department of Public Safety had responded to all eighteen alarms in Boland Hall since September 1999.

116. *The Setonian*, January 20, 2000, 1.

117. *The Setonian*, January 27, 2000, 3.

118. *The Setonian*, January 20, 2000, 1, 7.

119. SHU 3.22, Box 25, President's Office, Boland Fire documents.

120. RG 2.21, Peterson, 28 of 48.

121. *The Setonian*, January 20, 2000, 2.

122. *Herald News*, January 20, 2000, 1. Peterson died, aged seventy-one, on October 22, 2000 at Providence College, Rhode Island where he had returned to teach philosophy.

123. As happened at other schools as well. *New York Times*, February 1, 2000, 9.

124. "S. Orange Chief Voiced Fears on Covering Seton," *Star-Ledger*, January 29, 2000, 1.

125. *New York Times*, January 21, 2000, B5.

126. *New York Times*, January 23, 2000, A11.

127. *Star-Ledger*, January 28, 2000, 1.

128. *The Record*, February 24, 2000, 2.

129. Jennifer Costa to Sheeran, n.d. SHU 3.22, Box 25, President's Office, Boland Fire.

130. "Seton Hall's Emotional Quandary," *Star-Ledger*, March 22, 2000, 11.

131. *Star-Ledger*, March 26, 2000, 19.

132. Sheeran to Judith Mautone, April 25, 2000; Sheeran to Eileen Cassels, April 4, 2000; Sheeran to Allana Attamante, April 4, 2000. SHU 3.22, Sheeran Correspondence 1999–2000, Box 23, 4 of 4.

133. Sheeran to Nicholas Barnetsky, April 25, 2000. SHU 3.22, Sheeran Correspondence 1999–2000, Box 23, 4 of 4.

134. Sheeran to Philip and Mary Shannon, February 15, 2000. SHU 3.22, Sheeran Correspondence 1999–2000, Box 23, 4 of 4.

135. Sheeran to John Cardinal O'Connor, February 8, 2000. SHU 3.22, Sheeran Correspondence 1999–2000, Box 23, 4 of 4.

136. A. Kamen et al. to Sheeran, February 4, 2000. SHU 3.22, Presidents Hall, Boland Fire, Box 25.

137. Jennifer Browne to Sheeran, February 4, 2000. SHU 3.22, Presidents Hall, Boland Fire, Box 25.

138. Rev. Donald Brand to Sheeran, January 28, 2000. SHU 3.22, Presidents Hall, Boland Fire, Box 25.

139. Joseph Lagana to Sheeran, January 30, 2000. SHU 3.22, Presidents Hall, Boland Fire, Box 25.

140. Joseph Lagana to Sheeran, January 30, 2000. SHU 3.22, Presidents Hall, Boland Fire, Box 25.

141. Diane Gerardi to Sheeran, January 25, 2000. Joseph Lagana to Sheeran, January 30, 2000. SHU 3.22, Presidents Hall, Boland Fire, Box 25.

142. *The Setonian*, January 25, 2001, 1, 4.

143. Sheeran to Joe and Candy Karol, February 5, 2002. SHU 3.22, Sheeran Correspondence 1993–1996; 2002, Box 21.

144. *Star-Ledger*, February 17, 2000, 1.

145. *New York Times*, March 2, 2000, B7. In a separate matter, the university paid $12,600 in federal (OSHA) fines for failing to have a plan in place to protect employees during the fire and for failing to assess what kind of protective gear employees they might have needed. *Star-Ledger*, August 30, 2000, 18.

146. *Trenton Times*, January 20, 2000, 1.

147. *USA Today*, January 26, 2000, 16A.

148. The bill never became law.

149. *Star-Ledger*, March 21, 2000, 11.

150. *Star-Ledger*, January 4, 2001, 6.

151. *Star-Ledger*, February 2, 2000, 1.

152. *Star-Ledger*, February 20, 2000, 11.

153. *Star-Ledger*, April 19, 2000, 1, 19.

154. *Trenton Times*, January 14, 2001, A10.

155. *Star-Ledger*, December 7, 2000, 33.

156. *Star-Ledger*, June 13, 2001, 1.

157. *The Setonian*, June 12, 2003, 1.

158. Lepore and Ryan admitted that the day after the fire they had met with other students who were in the lounge that night, urging them to lie to investigators about what they saw.

159. *New York Times*, November 16, 2006, A1, B6.

160. *New York Times*, January 27, 2007, B1.

161. Robert Braun, *The Star-Ledger*, January 29, 2007, 13.

162. *The Star-Ledger*, January 25, 2001, 13.

163. *The Star-Ledger*, June 2, 2001, 13.

164. Dick Kleissler to Sheeran, June 23, 2000. SHU 3.22, Sheeran Correspondence 1999–2001, Box 23.

165. *Star-Ledger*, January 22, 2002, 7.

166. *Star-Ledger*, August 28, 2000, 1.

167. Sheeran to Board of Regents, July 10, 2001. SHU 3.22, Presidents Hall Documents, Box 19, Speeches and Correspondence 1996-1997, Box3.

168. To Sheeran, Walsh exhibited "Board leadership at its best," understanding the distinction between policy-making and management issues. Sheeran to Association of Governing Boards of Universities and Colleges, September 30, 1997. SHU 3.22, Sheeran Correspondence 1997–1998, Box 22. When Walsh faced legal difficulties in 2004 because of an undisclosed $20

million "finder's fee" he received for setting up a meeting that enabled Dennis Kozlowski's Tyco International to acquire CIT Group, Sheeran defended the "totality" of his life as more important than one mistake for which he had paid a price. *The Setonian*, March 25, 2004.

169. Sheeran to Suzanne M. Spero, October 18, 2004. SHU 3.22, Sheeran, Chronological Files.

170. *The Setonian*, April 14, 1994, 10.

171. *The Courier-News* (Bridgewater, NJ), October 12, 1995, 7.

172. Robert Brennan contributed over $10 million to the capital campaign in 1991. Some years later, Dennis Kozlowski, a graduate of the School of Business, contributed to the new academic building that bore his name before it was renamed Jubilee Hall.

173. Murray, a double graduate of Seton Hall's School of Business (BS 1964, MBA 1972) retired in 2007 as president and CEO of Dresser, Inc. and went on to serve as chairman of the Board of Regents following Sheeran's retirement in 2010.

174. Dr. Joseph Sandman, in conversation with the author, December 9, 2009.

175. *The Setonian*, January 31, 2002, 1, 4.

176. *The Setonian*, March 1, 2001, 1.

177. *The Setonian*, September 4, 1997, 1.

178. Academic Affairs Annual Report 1994–1995, iv. RG 2. 21, Peterson, Box 37 of 48.

179. *The Setonian*, October 9, 1997, 3.

180. Kozlowski, CEO of Tyco International, was convicted for financial crimes in 2005, serving a prison sentence until 2014. Some lawyers thought the conviction flawed and the prosecutorial tactics extreme. See Dan Ackman, "Tyco Trial II: Verdict First, Law Second" (https://www.forbes.com/consent/?toURL=https://www.forbes.com/2005/06/17/kozlowski-tyco-verdict-cx_da_0617tycoverdict.html), June 17, 2005) and Catherine S. Neal, *Taking Down the Lion: The Triumphant Rise and Tragic Fall of Tyco's Dennis Kozlowski* (London: Palgrave Macmillan, 2014).

181. *The Setonian*, April 27, 2000, 1.

182. Board of Regents, Building and Grounds Committee Minutes, September 18, 1997. RG 2.21, Peterson, 32 of 48.

183. *The Setonian*, October 6, 1988, 11.

Appendix A. Seton Hall Sport

1. *The White and Blue* (1925), 94.

2. George H. Sabine (ed.), *Areopagitica and Of Education*: (Arlington Heights: Harlan Davidson, 1952), 69.

3. Patrick B. Miller, "Athletes in Academe: College Sports and American Culture, 1850–1920" (University of California, Berkeley, PhD diss., 1987, UMI), 23.

4. Seton Hall College Catalogue 1907–1908, 110.

5. Axel Bundgaard, *Muscle and Manliness: The Rise of Sport in the American Boarding School* (Syracuse, NY: Syracuse University Press, 2005).

6. S.W. Pope, *Patriotic Games: Sporting Traditions in the American Imagination 1876–1926* (New York: Oxford University Press, 1997), 5.

7. J.A. Stafford to J. O'Connor, January 13, 1905. RG4 4.42 John O'Connor, Institutions and Agencies, Seton Hall College.

8. Miller, "Athletes in Academe," 455.

9. Alan Delozier, *Seton Hall Pirates: A Basketball History* (Charleston, SC: Arcadia Press, 2002). My thanks are due to Professor Delozier for sharing with me his expertise on this and many other related sporting matters.

10. *Turf, Field, and Farm* November 18, 1865.

11. Athletics Department Collection, SHU 31, Box 4, Baseball Results 1862–1983.

12. Pope, *Patriotic Games*, 22.

13. Pope, *Patriotic Games*, 7.

14. Miller, "Athletes in Academe," 235.

15. Henry Chadwick, "Baseball: The Amateur Arena of the Metropolitan District in 1889," *Outing, an Illustrated Monthly of Recreation*, August 1889, 392.

16. Pope, *Patriotic Games*, 6.

17. *Outing*, December 1886, 280.

18. "Football," *Turf, Field and Farm*, November 12, 1886, 20, 428.

19. "Football," *Turf, Field and Farm*, November 30, 1883: 37

20. See http://www.luckyshow.org/football/sh.htm for a complete listing of football fixtures featuring Seton Hall from 1882.

21. Marvin Washington and Marc Ventresca, "Institutional Contradictions and Struggles in the Formation of U.S. Collegiate Basketball 1880–1938," *Journal of Sport Management*, 22 (January 2008), 41.

22. *The Setonian*, March 20, 1926.

23. It was a freshman squad, not a varsity team.

24. *The White and Blue*, 1927, 115.

25. *The White and Blue*, 1928, 115.

26. *The White and Blue*, 1930, 155.

27. *The White and Blue*, 1931, 135. A few weeks later, Seton Hall defeated Brooklyn College 84-0. *The White and Blue*, 1931, 139.

28. *The Setonian*, November 2, 1948.

29. *The Setonian*, June 17, 1977.

30. *The Setonian*, March 4, 1982.

31. Mitchell Nathanson, *A People's History of Baseball* (Champaign: University of Illinois Press, 2012), 3.

32. *The White and Blue*, 1926, 107. http://www.shupirates.com/ot/seha-pirates-in-pros.html

33. *The White and Blue*, 1926, 107.

34. *The Setonian*, October 16, 1925.

35. *The Setonian*, October 18, 1935.

36. George Henderson to John Duffy September 26, 1925. RG 4 O'Connor papers, 4.42, Seton Hall.

37. *The White and Blue*, 1925, 97.

38. *The Setonian*, April 15, 1924.

39. *The Setonian*, January 16, 1925.

40. *The Setonian*, April 19, 1925.

41. *The White and Blue*, 1926, 108.

42. Managers were seniors or recent graduates.

43. *The Setonian*, May 29, 1925.

44. *The White and Blue*, 1929, 137.

45. Miller, "Athletes in Academe," 349–350.

46. Washington and Ventresca, "Institutional Contradictions," 41.

47. *The Setonian*, November 14, 1924.

48. *The Setonian*, 42.

49. Delozier, *Seton Hall Pirates*, 19.

50. Delozier, *Seton Hall Pirates*, 14.

51. *The Setonian*, December 18, 1925

52. *The Setonian*, February 19, 1926.

53. Delozier, *Seton Hall Pirates*, 10.

54. *The Setonian*, April 16, 1926.

55. *The Setonian*, November 19, 1926.

56. *The Setonian*, January 16, 1925.

57. *The White and Blue* 1925, 101.

58. *The Setonian*, January 16, 1925.

59. *The Setonian*, February 18, 1927.

60. *The White and Blue* 1928, 105.

61. *The Setonian*, January 15, 1926.

62. *The White and Blue*, 1927, 105.

63. *The White and Blue*, 1927, 105.

64. *The White and Blue*, 1928, 107.

65. *The White and Blue*, 1930, 157. In 1932–1933, they played twelve and won eight. *The White and Blue*, 1933, 98.

66. *The Setonian*, October 22, 1937. Russell coached at Seton Hall between 1936 and 1942, and between 1950 and 1961. *The Reading Eagle*, November 16, 1973.

67. Delozier, *Seton Hall Pirates*, 25.

68. *The Setonian*, October 15, 1937.

69. *The Galleon*, 1940, 90. So said the *Scranton Times*.

70. *The Galleon*, 1939, 98. *The Setonian*, January 14, 1938.

71. Tulane, Dartmouth, Holy Cross, LIU, Holy Cross, De Paul.

72. *The White and Blue*, 1942, 118.

73. Professor Alan Delozier pieced together this information.

74. It reverted to *The White and Blue* in 1941.

75. *The Galleon*, 1939, 100.

76. *The White and Blue*, 1927, 113.

77. *The White and Blue*, 1926, 115.

78. *The White and Blue*, 1927, 111; 1929, 149.

79. *The Setonian*, December 17, 1959, 8.

80. *The Galleon*, 1950, 436.

81. *The Galleon*, 439.

82. *The New York Times*, January 1, 2007.

83. *The Galleon*, 1948, 180–181.

84. *The Setonian*, March 18, 1948, 7.

85. *The New York Times* January 7, 1951, 133.

86. *The Galleon*, 1950, 438.

87. *The Galleon*, 1951, 338.

88. *The New York Times*, September 4, 1949, 82.

89. *The Galleon*, 1951, 340.

90. *The New York Times*, May 21, 1973, 71.

91. Ivan Curotta, *Up There With the Best: The Story of Morris Curotta, Dual Olympian 1948–1952* (Ivan Curotta: Matraville, N.S.W., Australia 1996)

92. *The Setonian*, November 13, 1946.

93. *The Setonian*, March 1, 1956, 8.

94. *The Setonian*, March 13, 1957, 11.

95. *The Galleon*, 1959, 321.

96. *The Setonian*, February 18, 1960, 9.

97. *The Setonian*, February 23, 1963, 1.

98. *The Setonian*, March 14, 1963, 8.

99. *The Setonian*, September 29, 1965, 10.

100. *The Setonian*, February 5, 1971, 9.

101. *The Setonian*, February 21, 1975, 16.

102. *The Setonian*, January 28, 1977, 18.

103. *The Setonian*, March 10, 1978 17.

104. *The Setonian*, February 2, 1979, 16.

105. *The Setonian*, February 9, 1979, 14.

106. *The Setonian*, January 22, 1981, 15.

107. *The Setonian*, February 12, 1981, 18.

108. *The Setonian*, February 26, 1981, 16.

109. *The Setonian*, March 12, 1981, 17.

110. *The Setonian*, March 19, 1981, 11.

111. *The Setonian*, October 29, 1981, 16.

112. *The Setonian*, May 6, 1982, 20.

113. *The Setonian*, February 24, 1983, 15.

114. *The Setonian*, February 16, 1984, 19.

115. *The Setonian*, February 21, 1985, 15.

116. *The Setonian*, November 14, 1985, 17.

117. *The Setonian*, January 23, 1986, 15.

118. *The Setonian*, October 15, 1992, 16.

119. *The Setonian*, December 10, 1992, 14.

120. *The Setonian*, March 25, 1993, 11; May 6, 1993, 13.

121. *The Setonian*, February 25, 1993, 11.

122. *The Setonian*, May 6, 1993, 13; May 27, 1993, 15.

123. *The Setonian*, March 10, 1994, 17; March 17, 1994, 16.

124. *The Setonian*, February 7, 1994, 13; February 24, 1994, 11.

125. *The Setonian*, March 9, 1995, 18.

126. *The Setonian*, February 12, 1998, 11.

127. *The White and Blue*, 1930, 171.

128. *The Setonian*, October 21, 1938, 8.

129. *The White and Blue*, 1941, 184.

130. *The Setonian*, November 9, 1950, 8.

131. *The Galleon*, 1951, 380–381.

132. *The Galleon*, 1952, 380.

133. *The Galleon*, 1956, 386.

134. *The Galleon*, 1956, 386.

135. *The Galleon*, 1958, 290.

136. *The Galleon*, 1959, 318.

137. *The Galleon*, 1960, 340.

138. *The Setonian*, March 31, 1980, 11.

139. *The Setonian*, September 19, 1985, 18.

140. *The Setonian*, September 12, 1985, 14.

141. *The Setonian*, February 5, 1987, 16.

142. *The Setonian*, November 13, 1986, 16.

143. *The Setonian*, November 13, 1986, 16.

144. *The Setonian*, November 2, 1989, 17.

145. *The Setonian*, October 4, 1990, 11.

146. *The Setonian*, September 3, 1992, 9.

147. *The Galleon*, 1939, 105

148. His ninety-six consecutive victories represented "arguably the greatest achievement in the history of collegiate fencing." *The Star-Ledger*, May 13, 2010.

149. *The Setonian*, February 25, 1937, 8.
150. *The Setonian*, January 21, 1938, 9.
151. *The Galleon*, 1940, 94.
152. *The Galleon*, 1939, 105.
153. *The White and Blue*, 1942, 112.
154. *The Setonian*, October 27, 1960, 10.
155. *The Setonian*, April 5, 1962, 12.
156. *The Galleon*, 1963, 319.
157. *The Setonian*, January 29, 1971, 16.
158. *The Setonian*, February 26, 1971, 18.
159. *The Setonian*, March 24, 1972, 12.
160. *The Setonian*, April 28, 1972, 12.
161. *The Setonian*, March 16, 1973, 12.
162. *The Setonian*, January 25, 1974, 14.
163. *The Setonian*, March 15, 1974, 12.
164. *The Setonian*, February 20, 1976, 18.
165. *The Setonian*, February 3, 1978, 3.
166. *The Setonian*, March 20, 1978, 5.
167. *The Setonian*, February 24, 1983, 14.
168. *The Setonian*, March 29, 1984, 23.
169. *The Setonian*, March 7, 1985, 22.
170. *The Setonian*, March 7, 1985, 24.
171. *The Setonian*, February 18, 1988, 18.
172. *The Galleon*, 1940, 99.
173. *The Galleon*, 1950, 442.
174. *The Setonian*, May 1, 1968, 12.
175. *The Setonian*, May 4, 1973, 17.
176. *The Setonian*, October 1, 1992, 19.
177. *The Setonian*, October 3, 1996, 14.
178. *The Setonian*, October 21, 1946, 18.
179. *The Galleon*, 1940, 98.
180. *The White and Blue*, 1941, 186.
181. *The White and Blue*, 1942, 113.
182. *The Setonian*, March 30, 1950, 4.
183. *The Galleon*, 1956, 391.
184. *The Galleon*, 1960, 363.
185. *The Setonian*, February 19, 1926, 2
186. *The Setonian*, March 20, 1925, 9.
187. *The Setonian*, May 11, 1935, 5.
188. *The White and Blue*, 1942, 117.
189. *The Galleon*, 1939, 104.
190. *The Setonian*, March 9, 1937, 9.
191. *The White and Blue*, 1941, 180.
192. *The New York Times*, June 10, 1975, 41.
193. *The Setonian*, April 24, 1980, 20.
194. *The Setonian*, October 23, 1980, 11.
195. *The Setonian*, October 23, 1980, 11.
196. *The Setonian*, October 15, 1981, 12.
197. *The Setonian*, September 24, 1981, 14.
198. *The Setonian*, November 16, 1989, 9.

199. *The Setonian*, October 13, 1983, 20.

200. *The Star-Ledger*, March 16, 2003.

201. http://www.nj.com/hssports/blog/baseball/index.ssf/2012/04/mike_sheppard_jrs_600th_and_father_and_son_affair.html.

202. *The Setonian*, December 4, 1968, 4.

203. *The Setonian*, May 14, 1969, 2.

204. *The Setonian*, October 29, 1969, 3.

205. *The Setonian*, November 6, 1970, 12.

206. *The Setonian*, February 7, 1975, 14; January 30, 1976, 18.

207. *The Setonian*, February 3, 1978, 3.

208. *The Setonian*, February 5, 1981, 18.

209. *The Setonian*, February 12, 1981, 19.

210. *The Setonian*, February 7, 1975, 14.

211. *The Setonian*, February 4, 1972, 12.

212. *The Setonian*, September 27, 1974, 14.

213. *The Setonian*, December 13, 1979, 23.

214. *The Setonian*, November 7, 1980, 11.

215. *The Setonian*, October 21, 1982, 20.

216. *The Setonian*, November 4, 1982, 20.

217. *The Setonian*, September 22, 1983, 18.

218. *The Setonian*, October 27, 1983, 20.

219. *The Setonian*, October 7, 1993, 18.

220. *The Setonian*, February 21, 1975, 14.

221. *The Setonian*, March 26, 1975, 21.

222. *The Setonian*, March 12, 1976, 16.

223. *The Setonian*, March 29, 1979, 16.

224. *The Setonian*, December 13, 1979, 23.

225. *The Setonian*, January 19, 1984, 15.

226. *The Setonian*, March 7, 1985, 24.

227. *The Setonian*, March 20, 1986, 18.

228. *The Setonian*, September 7, 1989, 19.

229. *The Setonian*, March 1, 1990, 12.

230. *The Setonian*, November 30, 1976, 18.

231. *The Setonian*, September 15, 1978, 20.

232. *The Setonian*, March 13, 1986, 19.

233. *The Setonian*, June 11, 1979, 27.

234. *The Setonian*, June 11, 1979, 28.

235. *The Setonian*, November 5, 1981, 20.

236. *The Setonian*, March 3, 1988, 1; February 6, 1992, 18.

237. *The Setonian*, December 1, 1994, 17.

238. *The Setonian*, January 27, 1983, 15.

239. *The Setonian*, January 27, 1994, 12.

240. *The Setonian*, October 31, 1996, 1.

241. *The Setonian*, November 26, 1946, 7.

242. *The White and Blue*, 1941, 173.

243. *The White and Blue*, 1942, 122.

244. *The Galleon*, 1947, 92. Race was a factor in college sport. The Pirates were all-White and one of their most emphatic victories was a 66-33 defeat of "Lincoln University's all-negro five." *The Galleon*, 1947, 91.

245. *The Galleon*, 1948, 176.

246. *The Galleon*, 1951, 375.

247. *The Galleon*, 1952, 375–376.

248. *The Setonian*, March 16, 1953, 1.

249. *The Galleon*, 1954, 292.

250. *The Galleon*, 1955, 317–318.

251. The Pirates and Seton Hall are synonymous, but "Pirates" were not the only team to play for the university. With the opening of the Paterson campus, the "Silk Mill Setonians" also took to the court beginning in 1954, competing in Division III against local sides and coached by Jim Comerford. Seton Hall Paterson's best-known face was Dick Vitale, '62, a TV talker of almost freakish fluency.

252. *The Galleon*, 1956, 376.

253. *The Galleon*, 1957, 234.

254. *The Setonian*, January 17, 1957, 9.

255. *The Galleon*, 1957, 238.

256. *The Galleon*, 1958, 274.

257. *The Galleon*, 1960, 345.

258. *The Setonian*, March 23, 1961, 1.

259. Delozier, *Seton Hall Pirates*, 84.

260. *The Setonian*, February 13, 1964, 8.

261. *The Setonian*, March 15, 1962, 6.

262. *The Setonian*, November 9, 1961, 8.

263. Delozier, *Seton Hall Pirates*, 158–9.

264. Delozier, *Seton Hall Pirates*, 87. Mitchel later served as professor of education at the university.

265. *The Setonian*, January 21, 1970, 10.

266. *The Setonian*, March 22, 1974, 11.

267. *The Setonian*, February 14, 1975, 11.

268. *The Setonian*, January 31, 1975, 1.

269. *The Setonian*, December 13, 1979, 22.

270. *The Setonian*, November 1, 1976, 11.

271. *The Setonian*, April 6, 1982, 1.

272. Delozier, *Seton Hall Pirates*, 109.

273. *The Setonian*, March 7, 1985, 21.

274. Mark Cannizzaro, "25 Years Later," *New York Post*, April 5, 2014.

275. Gaze never concealed his quasiprofessional arrangement with the university. On the other hand, he was another of Seton Hall's Olympians, representing Australia in the 1988 games (playing against his Seton Hall teammate Ramon Ramos in the opening encounter).

276. Delozier, *Seton Hall Pirates*, 121.

277. Delozier, *Seton Hall Pirates*, 127.

Index

About the Author

Dermot Quinn is a professor of history at Seton Hall University in South Orange, New Jersey. Educated at Trinity College, Dublin, and New College, Oxford, his books include *Understanding Northern Ireland*; *Patronage and Piety: English Roman Catholics and Politics 1850–1900*; and *The Irish in New Jersey: Four Centuries of American Life*.